D1369532

LEADERSHIP EXPLORED

Lessons in Leadership from Great Works of Literature

LEADERSHIP EXPLORED

Lessons in Leadership from Great Works of Literature

Edited by Joseph J. Thomas

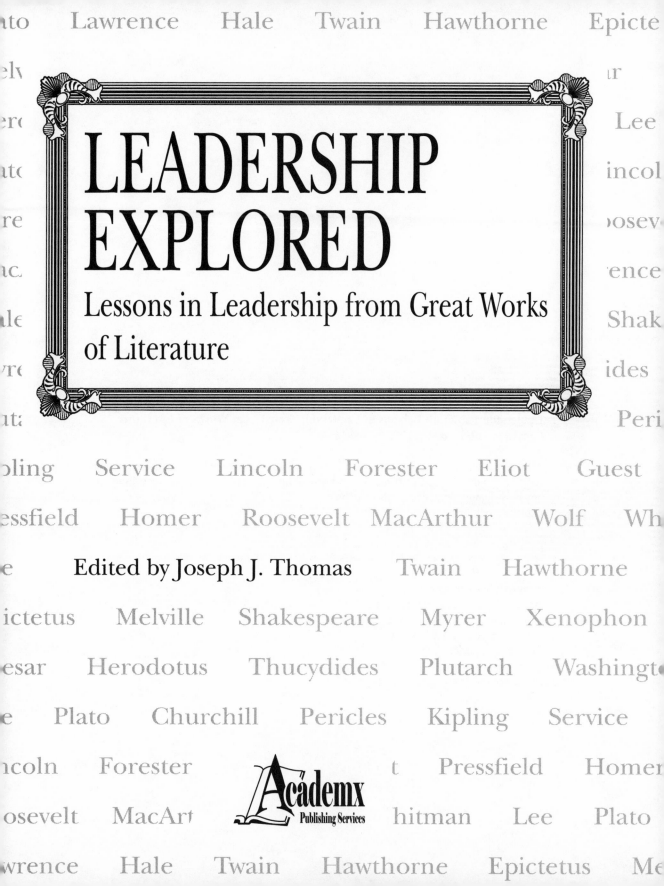

Academx
Publishing Services

Requests for permission to make copies of any part of the work should be mailed to:

Permissions Department
Academx Publishing Services, Inc.
P.O. Box 56527
Virginia Beach, VA 23456
http://www.academx.com

Printed in the United States of America

ISBN: 1-60036-006-8

To those whose names appear on the Scroll of Honor in Memorial Hall.
It is through their sacrifice that we are able to read, learn, and grow.

Contents

Contents

Foreword

The Naval Academy remains strongly focused on developing leadership and character in our nation's future combat leaders. Our goal is to imbue in you the highest ethical character and the leadership skills you will need to succeed as ensigns and second lieutenants.

Many of your former upperclass (and their upperclass before them) are forward deployed and leading Sailors and Marines in the War on Terror. You too will soon join them, serving on the front lines as division officers and platoon commanders, leading troops into battle, shooting missiles, dropping bombs, and making battlefield decisions where lives hang in the balance. The naval service needs officers who understand how important character and ethics are to leadership.

Accordingly, we seek to develop leaders who:
- Exhibit the highest standards of professionalism and integrity
- Understand themselves and the traditions of the Naval Service
- Take the initiative, foster teamwork, and display a relentless pursuit of mission success
- Have a passion for knowledge
- Lead their Sailors and Marines selflessly, courageously, and creatively, in peace and in war.

It is leadership development and especially character development that sets the U.S. Naval Academy apart from mainstream colleges and universities. Character is the essence of personal integrity, the ability to stand up for what is right, to forcefully lead others, even in the face of combat and catastrophe, and to motivate other people to excel. We focus on character and we focus specifically on developing leaders. Other universities conduct education in character or leadership, but it is our primary focus, our reason for being. Our approach is to not just teach leadership and character in every aspect of Academy life, we endeavor to explore what makes a good leader.

Learning about leadership and character development doesn't end with graduation. The Naval Academy provides but one step along a path of lifelong learning. In order to be successful in the Fleet, continue to learn and grow throughout your career, whether it involves advanced training in your warfare community, graduate programs at the Naval Postgraduate School, the Naval War College, or a civilian institution.

Stay current in your professional reading and develop a professional library of leadership biographies. Keep your intellectual edge honed with the latest tactics and technical developments of our warfare systems. But also continue to improve your knowledge of our profession and what it means to be a naval officer.

Vice Admiral Rodney P. Rempt
43rd Superintendent of the United States Naval Academy

Introduction

Much of leadership is about *inspiration*. Leaders inspire others to accomplish missions. Effective leaders inspire their fellows to attain greatness. But from where do great leaders draw their inspiration? For many it is through trial and error. There is certainly no substitute for the seasoned leader during times of crisis and challenge. For the developing leaders, I submit, it is through both observation and *study* that inspiration is drawn. Young leaders must incorporate experiential learning, observation of (preferably mentoring by) proper role models, and rigorous study of the tenets and principles of successful leadership.

A large part of this rigorous study should be a portal into effective words, effectively communicated. This book is designed to assist the reader in exploring such forceful language.

Included in this book is a letter from Abraham Lincoln, poems by Rudyard Kipling, a play by William Shakespeare, the fiction of Homer, and speeches by some of the towering leaders in the history of Western Civilization such as Pericles, Washington and Churchill. Even so, there are also many entries from non-classical sources such as Lou Gehrig and Judge William Young. This book is not exhaustive on the subject of inspirational literary sources for leaders—no thousand volumes could ever be—but it does provide a starting point, a reference when searching for words, *searching for inspiration*, in the quest to be a more effective leader. Appendices were added to provide further resources for inspiration. The broad variety of selections is an attempt to provide universal interest.

History and Literature as Vehicles for Leadership Development

I am of the somewhat heretical viewpoint that it is just as effective to "learn" leadership through a reading of Pressfield's *Gates of Fire*, Homer's *Odyssey* or Ambrose's *Undaunted Courage* as it is to study psychological or sociological theory. This attitude is driven by my own interests and biases, but in the context of military leadership development I am perhaps more traditionalist than heretic. It really has been merely four decades that management theory, psychology, and sociology have eclipsed history and literature as the primary vehicles for teaching leadership. And for the most part, these developments have been overwhelmingly positive. While the majority of the developments in leadership studies are cause for great optimism, I am saddened to observe the near loss of valuable tools in the quest to develop well-rounded, well-informed leaders. The general, if unspoken, view that great leaders are born rather than made has given way to a more egalitarian view—and for sound reason. The art of leadership has given way to the science of leadership.

Wharton, the Jepsen School at the University of Richmond, and Harvard Business School all produce outstanding leaders. Almost without exception, those leaders will go on to lead in the corporate environment. Leadership in that context is predominantly management: the quest for greater efficiencies through organization, coordination, communication, and best practice. Government leadership development programs as taught at the Federal Executive Institute or USDA Graduate School of

Management also focus on education and skills development centered on management excellence. Leadership is frequently spoken of but just as frequently mislabeled. Management should be the focus of the vast majority of curricula in those settings.

The service academies have a decidedly different target audience. In the military context, management is also of critical importance. However, leadership is the specified mission. Effectiveness rather than efficiency is the final measure. *Inspiration, character, morality, ethos, sacrifice, honor* are terms that permeate the curriculum and culture. The very nature of the military profession demands no less. So how can these fundamental differences in audience be used differences in methods for leader development? Simply put, there is a need to blend contemporary leadership (read management) development methodology with more traditional leadership preparation approaches.

Leadership Explored promises to do just that. The stories collected here are designed to inspire junior and future officers in their duties. The use of historical or literary example is an attempt to inspire the reader as well as it is to inform. Use this text to inspire yourself, your subordinates, in fact, anyone who could benefit from the timeless lessons contained herein.

Acknowledgements

The debts owed to those who made this work possible are great; the generous contribution of Debbie and Larry Brady, USNA Class of 1965, and family through The Brady Fund, which is held and managed by the United States Naval Academy Foundation, Inc., and by the unrestricted contributions of alumni, parents, friends and organizations to the Naval Academy Annual Fund; the administration of the US Naval Academy supported an "outside the box" approach to the teaching of leadership; most of all, those who contributed their time and expertise in offering important readings. Ensigns Ben Pittard and Chris Pisani were instrumental in scanning, selecting pictures, and collating this document. Both Ben and Chris dedicated countless hours to this effort as "graduate assistants" before heading off to SEAL and Surface Warrior careers respectively. It was an honor to work with two such fine young officers.

Professor Bob Madison was not only a major contributor to this book, he and his wife Karen were immensely helpful in bringing it into a form worthy of publication. Their hours of detailed editing, soliciting copyright permissions, and working with the publisher were the critical elements in pulling this project together. Joann Manos, Managing Editor of Academx Publishing Services showed great patience and understanding while we worked to prepare the manuscript for publication. Having such valuable teammates in this effort was a blessing—without them, *Leadership Explored* would have remained another "good idea."

As with *Leadership Embodied*, our hope is that midshipmen, officers, Marines and Sailors will gain by reading this book. The mosaic painted on these pages is rich with the wisdom of the ages. From the famous to the obscure, each chapter is unique in its message to the reader. While not exhaustive, these offerings represent a considerable start on developing a "two thousand year old mind"—at least in regard to leadership.

Preface

The works excerpted or reproduced in full contained in this volume offer the reader a broad variety of insights into the phenomenon of leadership. There are nineteen works of classic non-fiction, seventeen speeches, thirteen works of fiction, eight poems, and appendices for quotes and recommendations for further reading. The only thread binding these diverse musings is their potential to inspire leadership and the desire to read further. Each was chosen to assist the leader or aspiring leader in selecting material for his or her own professional library. From the works of classic Greek philosophers to contemporary authors, each chapter of *Leadership Explored* provides a window into the murky topics of personal and group values, virtue, character, ethics, personal challenge, or leadership technique. There is an obvious bias toward military virtue and leadership, but leadership (and this book) is by no means exclusive to the military. Great deeds and thoughts can be universally applied. Timeless lessons should be embraced by anyone seeking to enhance themselves personally and professionally.

There are several compendiums of inspirational material that were consulted in the creation of this book. Principal among them are William Safire's *Lend Me Your Ears: Great Speeches in History* (New York: W.W. Norton & Co., 1992), William J. Bennett's *The Book of Virtues: A Treasury of Great Moral Stories* (New York: Simon & Schuster, 1993), and Peter G. Tsouras' *Warriors' Words: A Dictionary of Military Quotations* (London: Arms and Armour Press, 1994).

1

Outwitting the Foe: Homer's The Odyssey

Dr. Joseph J. Thomas

If the telling of great stories is the key to inspiring leaders, then the blind bard Homer's *Illiad* and *Odyssey* are the template for such inspiration. It is said that Alexander the Great slept with a copy of *The Illiad* under his pillow even into adulthood. *The Odyssey* is some 2700 years old and is purported to be the most commonly told epic in the history of the Western World. It was standard reading in the development of young Athenians, Romans, Prussians, Russians, English, and Americans. The tale of the homeward journey of Odysseus and his men inspires initiative, judgment, and adaptability—timeless traits for leaders of any genration.

The protagonist, Odysseus (or Ulysses to the Romans) departs for his beloved home island of Ithaca at the conclusion of the Trojan War. During his struggle to return to his wife Penelope and his son Telemachos he is blown off course by capricious gods. He uses his wits and leadership to face the obstacles thrown in his path, the following excerpt matches the wily Odysseus against the power of the great Cyclops Polyphemos.

from Book IX
Translated by Samuel Butler

"When the child of morning, rosy-fingered Dawn, appeared, we admired the island and wandered all over it, while the nymphs Jove's daughters roused the wild goats that we might get some meat for our dinner. On this we fetched our spears and bows and arrows from the ships, and dividing ourselves into three bands began to shoot the goats. Heaven sent us excellent sport; I had twelve ships with me, and each ship got nine goats, while my own ship had ten; thus through the livelong day to the going down of the sun we ate and drank our fill,- and we had plenty of wine left, for each one of us had taken many jars full when we sacked the city of the Cicons, and this had not yet run out. While we were feasting we kept turning our eyes towards the land of the Cyclopes, which was hard by, and saw the smoke of their stubble fires. We could almost fancy we heard their voices and the bleating of their sheep and goats, but when the sun went down and it came on dark, we camped down upon the beach, and next morning I called a council.

" 'Stay here, my brave fellows,' said I, 'all the rest of you, while I go with my ship and exploit these people myself: I want to see if they are uncivilized savages, or a hospitable and humane race.'

"I went on board, bidding my men to do so also and loose the hawsers; so they took their places and smote the grey sea with their oars. When we got to the land, which was not far, there, on the face of a cliff near the sea, we saw a great cave overhung with laurels. It was a station for a great many sheep and goats, and outside there was a large yard, with a high wall round it made of stones built into the ground and of trees both pine and oak. This was the abode of a huge monster who was then away from home shepherding his flocks. He would have nothing to do with other people, but led the life of an outlaw. He was a horrid creature, not like a human being at all, but resembling rather some crag that stands out boldly against the sky on the top of a high mountain.

"I told my men to draw the ship ashore, and stay where they were, all but the twelve best among them, who were to go along with myself. I also took a goatskin of sweet black wine which had been given me by Maron, Apollo son of Euanthes, who was priest of Apollo the patron god of Ismarus, and lived within the wooded precincts of the temple. When we were sacking the city we respected him, and spared his life, as also his wife and child; so he made me some presents of great value- seven talents of fine gold, and a bowl of silver, with twelve jars of sweet wine, unblended, and of the most exquisite flavour. Not a man nor maid in the house knew about it, but only himself, his wife, and one housekeeper: when he drank it he mixed twenty

parts of water to one of wine, and yet the fragrance from the mixing-bowl was so exquisite that it was impossible to refrain from drinking. I filled a large skin with this wine, and took a wallet full of provisions with me, for my mind misgave me that I might have to deal with some savage who would be of great strength, and would respect neither right nor law.

"We soon reached his cave, but he was out shepherding, so we went inside and took stock of all that we could see. His cheese-racks were loaded with cheeses, and he had more lambs and kids than his pens could hold. They were kept in separate flocks; first there were the hoggets, then the oldest of the younger lambs and lastly the very young ones all kept apart from one another; as for his dairy, all the vessels, bowls, and milk pails into which he milked, were swimming with whey. When they saw all this, my men begged me to let them first steal some cheeses, and make off with them to the ship; they would then return, drive down the lambs and kids, put them on board and sail away with them. It would have been indeed better if we had done so but I would not listen to them, for I wanted to see the owner himself, in the hope that he might give me a present. When, however, we saw him my poor men found him ill to deal with.

"We lit a fire, offered some of the cheeses in sacrifice, ate others of them, and then sat waiting till the Cyclops should come in with his sheep. When he came, he brought in with him a huge load of dry firewood to light the fire for his supper, and this he flung with such a noise on to the floor of his cave that we hid ourselves for fear at the far end of the cavern. Meanwhile he drove all the ewes inside, as well as the she-goats that he was going to milk, leaving the males, both rams and he-goats, outside in the yards. Then he rolled a huge stone to the mouth of the cave- so huge that two and twenty strong four-wheeled waggons would not be enough to draw it from its place against the doorway. When he had so done he sat down and milked his ewes and goats, all in due course, and then let each of them have her own young. He curdled half the milk and set it aside in wicker strainers, but the other half he poured into bowls that he might drink it for his supper. When he had got through with all his work, he lit the fire, and then caught sight of us, whereon he said:

" 'Strangers, who are you? Where do sail from? Are you traders, or do you sail the as rovers, with your hands against every man, and every man's hand against you?'

"We were frightened out of our senses by his loud voice and monstrous form, but I managed to say, 'We are Achaeans on our way home from Troy, but by the will of Jove, and stress of weather, we have been driven far out of our course. We are the people of Agamemnon, son of Atreus, who has won infinite renown throughout the whole world, by sacking so great a city and killing so many people. We therefore humbly pray you to show us some hospitality, and otherwise make us such presents as visitors may reasonably expect. May your excellency fear the wrath of heaven, for we are your suppliants, and Jove takes all respectable travellers under his protection, for he is the avenger of all suppliants and foreigners in distress.'

"To this he gave me but a pitiless answer, 'Stranger,' said he, 'you are a fool, or else you know nothing of this country. Talk to me, indeed, about fearing the gods or shunning their anger? We Cyclopes do not care about Jove or any of your blessed gods, for we are ever so much stronger than they. I shall not spare either yourself or your companions out of any regard for Jove, unless I am in the humour for doing so. And now tell me where you made your ship fast when you came on shore. Was it round the point, or is she lying straight off the land?'

"He said this to draw me out, but I was too cunning to be caught in that way, so I answered with a lie; 'Neptune,' said I, 'sent my ship on to the rocks at the far end of your country, and wrecked it. We were driven on to them from the open sea, but I and those who are with me escaped the jaws of death.'

"The cruel wretch vouchsafed me not one word of answer, but with a sudden clutch he gripped up two of my men at once and dashed them down upon the ground as though they had been puppies. Their brains were shed upon the ground, and the earth was wet with their blood. Then he tore them limb from limb and supped upon them. He gobbled them up like a lion in the wilderness, flesh, bones, marrow, and entrails, without leaving anything uneaten. As for us, we wept and lifted up our hands to heaven on seeing such a horrid sight, for we did not know what else to do; but when the Cyclops had filled his huge paunch, and had washed down his meal of human flesh with a drink of neat milk, he stretched himself full length upon the ground among his sheep, and went to sleep. I was at first inclined to seize my sword, draw it, and drive it into his vitals, but I reflected that if I did we should all certainly be lost, for we should never be able to shift the stone which the monster had put in front of the door. So we stayed sobbing and sighing where we were till morning came.

"When the child of morning, rosy-fingered Dawn, appeared, he again lit his fire, milked his goats and ewes, all quite rightly, and then let each have her own young one; as soon as he had got through with all his work, he clutched up two more of my men, and began eating them for his morning's meal. Presently, with the utmost ease, he rolled the stone away from the door and drove out his sheep, but he at once put it back again- as easily as though he were merely clapping the lid on to a quiver full of arrows. As soon as he had done so he shouted, and cried 'Shoo, shoo,' after his sheep to drive them on to the mountain; so I was left to scheme some way of taking my revenge and covering myself with glory.

"In the end I deemed it would be the best plan to do as follows. The Cyclops had a great club which was lying near one of the sheep pens; it was of green olive wood, and he had cut it intending to use it for a staff as soon as it should be dry. It was so huge that we could only compare it to the mast of a twenty-oared merchant vessel of large burden, and able to venture out into open sea. I went up to this club and cut off about six feet of it; I then gave this piece to the men and told them to fine it evenly off at one end, which they proceeded to do, and lastly I brought it to a point myself, charring the end in the fire to make it harder. When I had done this I hid it under dung, which was lying about all over the cave, and told the men to cast lots which of them should venture along with myself to lift it and bore it into the monster's eye while he was asleep. The lot fell upon the very four whom I should have chosen, and I myself made five. In the evening the wretch came back from shepherding, and drove his flocks into the cave- this time driving them all inside, and not leaving any in the yards; I suppose some fancy must have taken him, or a god must have prompted him to do so. As soon as he had put the stone back to its place against the door, he sat down, milked his ewes and his goats all quite rightly, and then let each have her own young one; when he had got through with all this work, he gripped up two more of my men, and made his supper off them. So I went up to him with an ivy-wood bowl of black wine in my hands:

" 'Look here, Cyclops,' said I, you have been eating a great deal of man's flesh, so take this and drink some wine, that you may see what kind of liquor we had on board my ship. I was bringing it to you as a drink-offering, in the hope that you would take compassion upon me and further me on my way home, whereas all you do is to go on ramping and raving most intolerably. You ought to be ashamed yourself; how can you expect people to come see you any more if you treat them in this way?'

"He then took the cup and drank. He was so delighted with the taste of the wine that he begged me for another bowl full. 'Be so kind,' he said, 'as to give me some more, and tell me your name at once. I want to make you a present that you will be glad to have. We have wine even in this country, for our soil grows grapes and the sun ripens them, but this drinks like nectar and ambrosia all in one.'

"I then gave him some more; three times did I fill the bowl for him, and three times did he

drain it without thought or heed; then, when I saw that the wine had got into his head, I said to him as plausibly as I could: 'Cyclops, you ask my name and I will tell it you; give me, therefore, the present you promised me; my name is Noman; this is what my father and mother and my friends have always called me.'

"But the cruel wretch said, 'Then I will eat all Noman's comrades before Noman himself, and will keep Noman for the last. This is the present that I will make him.'

As he spoke he reeled, and fell sprawling face upwards on the ground. His great neck hung heavily backwards and a deep sleep took hold upon him. Presently he turned sick, and threw up both wine and the gobbets of human flesh on which he had been gorging, for he was very drunk. Then I thrust the beam of wood far into the embers to heat it, and encouraged my men lest any of them should turn faint-hearted. When the wood, green though it was, was about to blaze, I drew it out of the fire glowing with heat, and my men gathered round me, for heaven had filled their hearts with courage. We drove the sharp end of the beam into the monster's eye, and bearing upon it with all my weight I kept turning it round and round as though I were boring a hole in a ship's plank with an auger, which two men with a wheel and strap can keep on turning as long as they choose. Even thus did we bore the red hot beam into his eye, till the boiling blood bubbled all over it as we worked it round and round, so that the steam from the burning eyeball scalded his eyelids and eyebrows, and the roots of the eye sputtered in the fire. As a blacksmith plunges an axe or hatchet into cold water to temper it- for it is this that gives strength to the iron- and it makes a great hiss as he does so, even thus did the Cyclops' eye hiss round the beam of olive wood, and his hideous yells made the cave ring again. We ran away in a fright, but he plucked the beam all besmirched with gore from his eye, and hurled it from him in a frenzy of rage and pain, shouting as he did so to the other Cyclopes who lived on the bleak headlands near him; so they gathered from all quarters round his cave when they heard him crying, and asked what was the matter with him.

" 'What ails you, Polyphemus,' said they, 'that you make such a noise, breaking the stillness of the night, and preventing us from being able to sleep? Surely no man is carrying off your sheep? Surely no man is trying to kill you either by fraud or by force?

"But Polyphemus shouted to them from inside the cave, 'Noman is killing me by fraud! Noman is killing me by force!'

" 'Then,' said they, 'if no man is attacking you, you must be ill; when Jove makes people ill, there is no help for it, and you had better pray to your father Neptune.'

"Then they went away, and I laughed inwardly at the success of my clever stratagem, but the Cyclops, groaning and in an agony of pain, felt about with his hands till he found the stone and took it from the door; then he sat in the doorway and stretched his hands in front of it to catch anyone going out with the sheep, for he thought I might be foolish enough to attempt this.

"As for myself I kept on puzzling to think how I could best save my own life and those of my companions; I schemed and schemed, as one who knows that his life depends upon it, for the danger was very great. In the end I deemed that this plan would be the best. The male sheep were well grown, and carried a heavy black fleece, so I bound them noiselessly in threes together, with some of the withies on which the wicked monster used to sleep. There was to be a man under the middle sheep, and the two on either side were to cover him, so that there were three sheep to each man. As for myself there was a ram finer than any of the others, so I caught hold of him by the back, esconced myself in the thick wool under his belly, and flung on patiently to his fleece, face upwards, keeping a firm hold on it all the time.

"Thus, then, did we wait in great fear of mind till morning came, but when the child of morning, rosy-fingered Dawn, appeared, the male sheep hurried out to feed, while the ewes remained bleating about the pens waiting to be milked, for their udders were full to bursting; but their master in spite of all his pain felt the backs of all the sheep as they stood upright, without being sharp enough to find out that the men were underneath their bellies. As the ram was going out, last of all, heavy with its fleece and with the weight of my crafty self; Polyphemus laid hold of it and said:

" 'My good ram, what is it that makes you the last to leave my cave this morning? You are not wont to let the ewes go before you, but lead the mob with a run whether to flowery mead or bubbling fountain, and are the first to come home again at night; but now you lag last of all. Is it because you know your master has lost his eye, and are sorry because that wicked Noman and his horrid crew have got him down in his drink and blinded him? But I will have his life yet. If you could understand and talk, you would tell me where the wretch is hiding, and I would dash his brains upon the ground till they flew all over the cave. I should thus have some satisfaction for the harm a this no-good Noman has done me.'

"As spoke he drove the ram outside, but when we were a little way out from the cave and yards, I first got from under the ram's belly, and then freed my comrades; as for the sheep, which were very fat, by constantly heading them in the right direction we managed to drive them down to the ship. The crew rejoiced greatly at seeing those of us who had escaped death, but wept for the others whom the Cyclops had killed. However, I made signs to them by nodding and frowning that they were to hush their crying, and told them to get all the sheep on board at once and put out to sea; so they went aboard, took their places, and smote the grey sea with their oars. Then, when I had got as far out as my voice would reach, I began to jeer at the Cyclops.

" 'Cyclops,' said I, 'you should have taken better measure of your man before eating up his comrades in your cave. You wretch, eat up your visitors in your own house? You might have known that your sin would find you out, and now Jove and the other gods have punished you.'

"He got more and more furious as he heard me, so he tore the top from off a high mountain, and flung it just in front of my ship so that it was within a little of hitting the end of the rudder. The sea quaked as the rock fell into it, and the wash of the wave it raised carried us back towards the mainland, and forced us towards the shore. But I snatched up a long pole and kept the ship off, making signs to my men by nodding my head, that they must row for their lives, whereon they laid out with a will.

Suggested Readings

Aurbach, Erich. *Mimesis: The Representation of Reality in Western Literature*. Translated by Willard R. Trask. Princeton: Princeton University Press, 1953.

Camps, W. A. *An Introduction to Homer*. Oxford: Clarendon Press, 1980.

Homer. *The Odyssey of Homer*. Translated by Richmond Lattimore. New York: Harper & Row, 1975.

Lord, Albert B. *The Singer of Tales*. Cambridge: Harvard University Press, 1960.

About the Author

Dr. Joseph J. Thomas, LtCol USMC (Ret.) currently serves as the Class of 1971 Distinguished Military Professor of Leadership at the U.S. Naval Academy. He is the editor of *Leadership Embodied: The Secrets to Success of the Most Effective Navy and Marine Corps Leaders* (Naval Institute Press and Naval Historical Center, 2005).

2

Go Tell the Spartans: Herodotus' The Persian War

Dr. Joseph J. Thomas

In *The Persian Wars*, Herodotus is far more similar in style and method to the bard Homer than one would expect from the recognized "father" of the discipline of history. However, the story of King Leonidas and his Three Hundred Spartans is so compelling that it could only be read like an epic tragedy. This timeless excerpt has been the inspiration for countless books (see Shannon French's chapter on Pressfield's *Gates of Fire*) and continues to inspire the courage and steadfast devotion of warriors.

The battle took place in 480 BC and pitted a small Greek blocking force against the massive Persian army of Xerxes I. This famous "last stand" took place at Thermopylae (Hot Gates) in a narrow mountain pass. The Greek delaying action cost the Persians several days and an estimated 35,000 were killed in the attempt to clear the defenders from the pass. Although Xerxes would eventually break through and sack Athens, the delay enabled the Greek fleet to prepare for the battle of Salamis, the sea action that saw the destruction of the Persian fleet and the end of the threat to Greece.

* * *

And here I feel constrained to deliver an opinion which most men, I know, will mislike, but which, as it seems to me to be true, I am determined not to withhold. Had the Athenians, from fear of the approaching danger, quitted their country, or had they without quitting it submitted to the power of Xerxes, there would certainly have been no attempt to resist the Persians by sea; in which case, the course of events by land would have been the following.

Though the peloponnesians might have carried ever so many breastworks acrosS the Isthmus, yet their allies would have fallen off from the Lacedaemonians, not by voluntary desertion, but be cause town after town must have been taken by the fleet of the barbarians; and so the Lacedaemonians would at last have stood alone, and, standing alone, would have displayed prodigies of valor, and died nobly. Either they would have done thus, or else, before it came to that extremity, seeing one Greek state after another embrace the cause of the Medes, they would have come to terms with King Xerxes; and thus, either way Greece would have been brought under Persia. For I cannot understand of what possible use the walls across the' Isthmus could have been, if the King had had the mastery of the sea. If then a man should noW say that the Athenians were the saviors of Greece, he would not exceed the trUth. For they truly held the scales; and whichever side And here I feel constrained to deliver an opinion which most men, I know, will mislike, but which, as it seems to me to be true, I am determined not to withhold. Had the Athenians, from fear of the approaching danger, quitted their country, or had they without quitting it submitted to the power of Xerxes, there would certainly have been no attempt to resist the Persians by sea; in which case,. the course of events by land would have been the following. Though the peloponnesians might have carried ever so many breastworks acrosS the Isthmus, yet their allies would have fallen off from the Lacedaemonians, not by voluntary desertion, but be cause town after town must have been taken by the fleet of the barbarians; and so the Lacedaemonians would at last have stood alone, and, standing alone, would have displayed prodigies of valor, and died nobly. Either they would have done thus, or else, before it came to that extremity, seeing one Greek state after another embrace the cause of the Medes, they would have come to terms with King Xerxes; and thus, either way Greece would have been brought under Persia. For I cannot understand of what possible use the walls across the' Isthmus could have been, if the King had had the mastery of the sea. If then a man should noW say that the Athenians were the saviors of Greece, he would not exceed the trUth. For they truly held the scales; and whichever side And here I feel constrained to deliver an opinion which most men, I

know, will mislike, but which, as it seems to me to be true, I am determined not to withhold. Had the Athenians, from fear of the approaching danger, quitted their country, or had they without quitting it submitted to the power of Xerxes, there would certainly have been no attempt to resist the Persians by sea; in which case, the course of events by land would have been the following. Though the Peloponnesians might have carried ever so many breastworks across the Isthmus, yet their allies would have fallen off from the Lacedaemonians, not by voluntary desertion, but be cause town after town must have been taken by the fleet of the barbarians; and so the Lacedaemonians would at last have stood alone, and, standing alone, would have displayed prodigies of valor, and died nobly. Either they would have done thus, or else, before it came to that extremity, seeing one Greek state after another embrace the cause of the Medes, they would have come to terms with King Xerxes; and thus, either way Greece would have been brought under Persia. For I cannot understand of what possible use the walls across the Isthmus could have been, if the King had had the mastery of the sea. If then a man should now say that the Athenians were the saviors of Greece, he would not exceed the truth. For they truly held the scales; and whichever side they espoused must have carried the day. They too it was who, when they had determined to maintain the freedom of Greece, roused up that portion of the Greek nation which had not gone over to the Medes; and so, next to the gods, *they* repulsed the invader. Even the terrible oracles which reached them from Delphi, and struck fear into their hearts, failed to persuade them to fly from Greece. They had the courage to remain faithful to their land, and await the coming of the foe. *(VII, 139)*

King Xerxes pitched his camp in the region of Malis called Trachinia, while on their side the Greeks occupied the straits. These straits the Greeks in general call Thermopylae (the Hot Gates); but the natives, and those who dwell in the neighborhood, call them Pylae (the Gates).

Here then the two armies took their stand; the one master of all the region lying north of Trachis the other of the country extending southward of that place to the verge of the continent.

The Greeks who at this spot awaited the coming of Xerxes were the following:-From Sparta, three hundred men-at-arms: from Arcadia, a thousand T egeans and Mantineans, five hundred of each people; a hundred and twenty Orchomenians, from the Arcadian Orchomenus; and a thousand from other cities: from Corinth, four hundred men: from Phlius, two hundred: and from Mycenae eighty. Such was the number from the Peloponnese. There were also present, from Boeotia, seven hundred Thespians and four hundred Thebans.

Besides these troops, the Locrians of Opus and the Phocians had obeyed the call of their countrymen, and sent, the former all the force they had, the latter a thousand men. For envoys had gone from the Greeks at Thermopylae among the Locrians and Phocians, to call on them for assistance, and to say-They were themselves but the vanguard of the host, sent to precede the main body, which might every day be expected to follow them. The sea was in good keeping, watched by the Athenians, the Eginetans, and the rest of the fleet. There was no cause why they should fear; for 'after all the invader was not a god but a man; and there never had been, and never would be, a man who was not liable to misfortunes from the very day of his birth, and those misfortunes greater in proportion to his own greatness. The assailant therefore, being only a mortal, must needs fall from his glory." Thus urged, the Locrians and the Phocians had come with their troops to T rachis.

The various nations had each captains of their own under whom they served; but the one to whom all especially looked up, and who had the command of the entire force, was the Lacedaemonian, Leonidas. . . .

He had now come to Thermopylae, accompanied by the three hundred men which the law assigned him, whom he has himself chosen from among the citizens, and who were all of them fathers with sons living. On his way he had taken the troops from Thebes, whose number I have already mentioned, and who were under the command of Leontiades, the son of Eurymachus. The reason why he made a point of taking troops from Thebes, and Thebes only, was, that the Thebans .were strongly suspected of being well inclined to the Medes. Leonidas therefore called on them to come with him to the war, wishing to see whether they would comply with his demand, or openly refuse, and disclaim the Greek alliance. They, however, though their wishes leant the other way, nevertheless sent the men.

The force with Leonidas was sent forward by the Spartans in advance of their main body, that the sight of them might encourage the allies to fight, and hinder them from going over to the Medes, as it was likely they might have done had they seen that Sparta was backward. They intended presently, when they had celebrated the Carneian festival, which was what now kept them at home, to leave a garrison in Sparta, and hasten in full force to join the army. The rest of the allies also intended to act similarly; for it happened that the Olympic festival fell exactly at this same period. None of them looked to see the contest at Thermopylae decided so speedily; wherefore they were content to send forward a mere advance guard. Such accordingly were the intentions of the allies.

The Greek forces at Thermopylae, when the Persian army drew near to the entrance of the pass, were seized with fear; and a council was held to consider about a retreat. It was the wish of the Peloponnesians generally that the army should fall back upon the Peloponnese, and there guard the Isthmus. But Leonidas, who saw with what indignation the Phocians and Locrians heard of this plan, gave his voice for remaining where they were while they sent envoys to the several cities to ask for help, since they were too few to make a stand against an army like that I the Medes.

While this debate was going on, Xerxes sent a mounted spy to observe the Greeks, and note how many they were, and see what they were doing. He had heard, before he came out of Thessaly, that a few men were assembled at this place, and that their head were certain Lacedaemonians, under Leonidas, descendant of Heracles. The horseman rode up to the camp, and looked about him, but did not, see the whole army; for such were on the further side of the wall (which had been rebuilt and was now carefully guarded) it was not possible for him behold; but he observed those on the outside, who were encamped in front of the rampart. It chanced that at this time the Lacedamonians held the outer guard, and were seen by the spy, son of them engaged in gymnastic exercises, others combing the long hair. At this the spy greatly marveled, but he counted the number, and when he had taken accurate note of everything, he rode back quietly; for no one pursued after him, nor paid any heed to his visit. So he returned, and told Xerxes all that he had seen.

Upon this, Xerxes, who had no means of surmising the truth -namely, that the Spartans were preparing to do or die manful -but thought it laughable that they should be engaged in sue employments, sent and called to his presence Demaratus the sc of Ariston, who still remained with the army. When he appeared Xerxes told him all that he had heard, and questioned him concerning the news, since he was anxious to understand the meaning of such behavior on the part of the Spartans. Then Demaratus said:

"I spake to thee, O King! concerning these men long since, when we had but just begun our march upon Greece; thou, however, didst only laugh at my words, when I told thee of all this, which I saw would come to pass. Earnestly do I struggle at all times to speak truth to thee, sire; and now listen to it once more. These men have come to dispute the pass with us; and it is for this that they are now making ready. 'Tis their custom, when they are about to hazard their lives, to adorn their heads with care. Be assured, however, that if thou canst subdue the men who are

here and the Lacedaemonians who remain in Sparta, there is no other nation in all the world which will venture to lift a hand in their defense. Thou hast now to deal with the first kingdom and town in Greece, and with the bravest men."

Then Xerxes, to whom what Demaratus said seemed altogether to surpass belief, asked further, "how it was possible for so small an army to contend with his?"

"O King!" Demaratus answered, "let me be treated as a liar, if matters fall not out as I say."

But Xerxes was not persuaded any the more. Four whole days he suffered to go by, expecting that the Greeks would run away. When, however, he found on the fifth that they were not gone, thinking that their firm stand was mere impudence and recklessness, he grew wroth, and sent against them the Medes and Cissians, with orders to take them alive and bring them into his presence. Then the Medes rushed forward and charged the Greeks, but fell in vast numbers: others however took the places of the slain, and would not be beaten off, though they suffered terrible losses. In this way it became clear to all, and especially to the King, that though he had plenty of combatants, he had but very few warriors. The struggle, however, continued during the whole day.

Then the Medes, having met so rough a reception, withdrew from the fight; and their place was taken by the band of Persians under Hydarnes, whom the King called his "Immortals": they, it was thought, would soon finish the business. But when they joined battle with the Greeks, 'twas with no better success than the Median detachment-things went much as before-the two armies fighting in a narrow space, and the barbarians using shorter spears than the Greeks, and' having no advantage from their numbers. The Lacedaemonians fought in a way worthy of note, and showed themselves far more skillful in fight than their adversaries, often turning their backs; and making as though they were all flying away, on which the barbarians would rush after them with much noise and shouting, when the Spartans at their approach would wheel round and face their pursuers, in this way destroying vast numbers of the enemy. Some Spartans like wise fell in these encounters, but only a very few. At last the Persians, finding that all their efforts to gain the pass availed nothing, and that, whether they attacked by divisions or in any other way, it was to no purpose, withdrew to their own quarters.

During these assaults, it is said that Xerxes, who was watching the battle, thrice leaped from the throne on which he sat, in terror for his army.

Next day the combat was renewed, but with no better success on the part of the barbarians. The Greeks were so few that the barbarians hoped to find them disabled, by reason of their wounds, from offering any further resistance; and so they once more attacked them. But the Greeks were drawn up in detachments according to their cities, and bore the brunt of the battle in turns,-all except the Phocians, who had been stationed on the mountain to guard the pathway. So, when the Persians found no difference between that day and the preceding, they again retired to their quarters.

Now, as the King was in a great strait, and knew not how he should deal with the emergency, Ephialtes, the son of Eurydemus, a man of Malis, came to him and was admitted to a conference. Stirred by the hope of receiving a rich reward at the King's hands, he had come to tell him of the pathway which led across the mountain to Thermopylae; by which disclosure he brought destruction on the band of Greeks who had there withstood the barbarians. (VII, 201-213)

Great was the joy of Xerxes on this occasion; and as "he approved highly of the enterprise which Ephialtes undertook to accomplish, he forthwith sent upon the errand Hydames, and the Persians under him. The troops left the camp about the time of the lighting of the lamps. The pathway along which they went was first discovered by the Malians of these parts, who soon afterward led the Thessalians by it to attack the Phocians, at the time when the Phocians for-

tified the pass with a wall, and so put themselves under covert from danger. And ever since, the path has always been put to an ill use by the Malians. (VII, 215)

The Persians took this path, and, crossing the Asopus, continued their march through the whole of the night, having the mountains of Oeta on their right hand,' and on their left those of Trachis. At dawn of day they found themselves close to the summit. Now the hill was guarded, as I have already said, by a thousand Phocian men-at-arms, who were placed there to defend the pathway, and at the same time to secure their own country. They had been given the guard of the mountain path, while the other Greeks defended the pass below, because they had volunteered for the service, and had pledged themselves to Leonidas to maintain the post.

The ascent of the Persians became known to the Phocians in the following manner:-During all the time that they were making their way up, the Greeks remained unconscious of it, inasmuch as the whole mountain was covered with groves-of oak; but it happened that the air was very still, and the leaves which the Persians stirred with their feet made, as it was likely they would, a loud rustling, whereupon the Phocians jumped up and flew to seize their arms. In a moment the barbarians came in sight, and, perceiving men arming themselves, were greatly amazed; for they had fallen in with an enemy when they expected no opposition. Hydames, alarmed at the sight and fearing lest the Phocians might be Lacedaemonians, inquired of Ephialtes to what nation those troops belonged. Ephialtes told him the exact truth, whereupon he arrayed his Persians for battle. The Phoclans, galled by the showers of arrows to which they were exposed, and imagining themselves the special object of the Persian attack, fled hastily to the crest of the mountain, and there made ready to meet death; but while their mistake continued, the Persians, with Ephialtes and Hydarnes, not thinking it worth their while to delay on account of Phocians, passed on and descended the mountain with all possible speed.

The Greeks at Thermopylae received the first warning of the destruction which the dawn would bring on them from the seer Megistias, who read their fate in the victims as he was sacrificing. After this deserters came in, and brought the news that the Persians were marching round by the hills: it was still night when these men arrived. Last of all, the scouts came running down from the heights, and brought in the same accounts, when the day was just beginning to break. Then the Greeks held a council to consider what they should do, and here opinions were divided: some were strong against quitting their post, while others contended to the contrary. So when the council had broken up, part of the troops departed and went their ways homeward to their several states; part however resolved to remain, and to stand by Leonidas to the last.

It is said that Leonidas himself sent away the troops who departed, because he tendered their safety, but thought it unseemly that either he or his Spartans should quit the post which they had been especially sent to guard. For my own part, I incline to think that Leonidas gave the order, because he perceived the allies to be out of heart and unwilling to encounter the danger, to which his own mind was made up. He therefore commanded them to retreat, but said that he himself could not draw back with honor; knowing that, if he stayed, glory awaited him, and that Sparta in that case would not lose her prosperity. For when the Spartans, at the very beginning of the war, sent to consult the oracle concerning it, the answer which they received from the Pythoness was, "that either- Sparta must be overthrown by the barbarians, or one of her kings must perish." The prophecy was delivered in hexameter verse, and ran thus:

"O ye men who dwell in the streets of broad
    Lacedaemon!
Either your glorious town shall be sacked by
    the children of Perseus

Or, in exchange, must all through the whole
    Laconian country
Mourn for the loss of a king descendant of
    great Heracles.
He cannot be withstood by the courage of
    bulls nor of lions,
Strive as they may; he is mighty Zeus; there
    is nought that shall
stay him,
Till he have got for his prey your king, or
    your glorious city."

The remembrance of this answer, I think; and the wish to secure the whole glory for the Spartans, caused Leonidas to send the allies away. This is more likely than that they quarreled with him and took their departure in such unruly fashion.

To me it seems no small argument in favor of this view, that the seer also accompanied the army, Megistias, the Acarnanian, said to have been of the blood of Melampus, and the same who was led by the appearance of the victims to warn the Greeks of the danger which threatened them, received orders to retire (as it is certain he did) from Leonidas, that he might escape the coming destruction. Megistias, however, though bidden to depart, refused, and stayed with the army; but he had an only son present with the expedition, whom he now sent away.

So the allies, when Leonidas ordered them to retire, obeyed him and forthwith departed. Only the Thebans and the Thespians remained with the Spartans; and of these the Thebans were kept back by Leonidas as hostages, very much against their will. The Thespians, on the contrary, stayed entirely of their own accord, refusing to retreat, and declaring that they would not forsake Leonidas and his followers. So they abode with the Spartans, and died with them. Their leader was Demophilus, the son of Diadromes.

At sunrise Xerxes made libations, after which he waited until the time when the forum is wont to fill, and then began his advance. Ephialtes had instructed him thus, as the descent of the mountain is much quicker, and the distance much shorter than the way round the hills, and the ascent. So the barbarians under Xerxes began to draw nigh; and the Greeks under Leonidas, as they now went forth determined to die, advanced much further than on previous days, until they reached the more open portion of the pass. Hitherto they had held their station within the wall, and from this had gone forth to fight at the point where the pass was the narrowest. Now they joined battle beyond the defile, and carried slaughter among the barbarians, who fell in heaps. Behind them the captains of the squadrons, armed with whips, urged their men forward with continual blows. Many were thrust into the sea, and there perished; a still greater number were trampled to death by their own soldiers; no one heeded the dying. For the Greeks, reckless of their own safety and desperate, since they knew that, as the mountain had been crossed, their destruction was nigh at hand, exerted themselves with the most furious valor against the barbarians.

By this time the spears of the greater number were all shivered, and with their swords they hewed down the ranks of the Persians; and here, as they strove, Leonidas fell fighting bravely, together with many other famous Spartans, whose names I have taken care to learn on account of their great worthiness, as indeed I have those of all the three hundred. There fell too at the same time very many famous Persians: among them, two sons of Darius, Abrocomes and Hyperanthes, his children by Phratagune, the daughter of Artanes. Artanes was brother of King Darius, being a son of Hystaspes, the son of Arsames; and when he gave his daughter to the King, he made him heir likewise of all his substance; for she was his only child.

Thus two brothers of Xerxes here fought and fell. And now there arose a fierce struggle between the Persians and the Lacedaemonians over the body of Leonidas, in which the Greeks four times drove back the enemy, and at last by their great bravery succeeded in bearing off the body. This combat was scarcely ended when the Persians with Ephialtes approached; and the Greeks, informed that they drew nigh, made a change in the manner of their fighting. Drawing back into the narrowest part of the pass, and retreating even behind the cross wall, they posted themselves upon a hillock, where they stood all drawn up together in one close body, except only the Thebans. The hillock whereof I speak is at the entrance of the straits, where the stone lion stands which was set up in honor of Leonidas. Here they defended themselves to the last, such as still had swords using them, and the others resisting with their hands and teeth; till the barbarians, who in part had pulled down the wall and attacked them in front, in part had gone round and now encircled them upon every side, overwhelmed and buried the remnant which was left beneath showers of missile weapons.

Thus nobly' did the whole body of Lacedaemonians and Thespians behave; but nevertheless one man is said to have distinguished himself above all the rest, to wit, Dieneces the Spartan. A speech which he made before the Greeks engaged the Medes, remains on record. One of the Trachinians told him, "Such was the number of the barbarians, that when they shot forth their arrows the sun would be darkened by their multitude." Dieneces, not at all frightened at these words, but making light of the Median numbers, answered, "Our Trachinian friend brings us excellent tidings. If the Medes darken the sun, we shall have our fight in the shade." Other sayings too of a like nature are reported to have been left on record by this same person.

Next to him two brothers, Lacedaemonians, are reputed to have made themselves conspicuous: they were named Alpheus and Maro, and were the sons of Orsiphantus. There was also a Thespian who gained greater glory than any of his countrymen:

he was a man called Dithyrambus, the son of Harmatidas.

The slain were buried where they fell; and in

their honor, nor less in honor of those who died before Leonidas sent the allies away, an inscription was set up, which said,

> "Here did four thousand men from Pelops'
>   land
> Against three hundred myriads bravely
>   stand."

This was in honor of all. Another was for the Spartans alone:

> "Go, stranger, and to Lacedaemon tell, that
>   here, obeying her behests, we fell."

This was for the Lacedaemonians. The seer had the following:

> "The great Megistias' tomb you here may
>   view,
> Whom slew the Medes, fresh from
>   Spercheius' fords.
> Well the wise seer the coming death
>   foreknew,
> Yet scorned he to forsake his Spartan lords."

These inscriptions, and the pillars likewise, were all set up by the Amphictyons, except that in honor of Megistias, which was inscribed to him (on account of their sworn friendship) by Simonides, the son of Leoprepes.

> O xein', angellein Lakedaimoniois hoti têde
> keimetha tois keinon rhémasi peithomenoi.

The poetic translation of the monument to the fallen is: "Go tell the Spartans, stranger passing by, that here, obedient to their laws, we lie."

Suggested Readings

Arrian. *Anabasis Alexandria: Books I-IV.* Cambridge: Harvard University Press, 1976.

Herodotus. *The Histories.* Oxford: Oxford University Press, 1998.

Herodotus. *The Persian Wars.* New York: Modern Library, 1942.

Thucydides. *History of the Peloponnesian War.* New York: W.W. Norton & Co., 1998.

Xenophon, *The Persian Expedition.* New York: Penguin Classics (Rex Warner translation), 1972.

3

The Indispensable Leadership Quality: The Book of Daniel

LCDR Thomas B. Webber, USN, Chaplain Corps

Daniel is not one of the most discussed leaders in the Bible. However, his inner strength and character just may be the most consistent of all. The book of Daniel references Daniel as the writer (9:2, 10:2) and Jesus speaks of Daniel the prophet (Matthew 24:15) and even quotes from the book of Daniel. Daniel's volume is divided into two sections: first (chapter 1–6) is historical narrative, and second (chapter 7–12) is apocalyptic (revelatory) in nature. The first six chapters are where I will focus my discussion. In these chapters, Daniel walks the reader through each stage of leadership as he reveals his circumstances and context.

I.

In Daniel chapter one, we are immediately thrust into a historical moment in antiquity. It is the third year of Jehoikim's reign as the king of Judah in the city of Jerusalem. The year is 605 B.C., the same year that King Nebuchadnezzar, King of Babylon, captured Jerusalem, clearing out the precious articles of Solomon's Temple, and deporting exiles to his capital city of Babylon. Three times Nebuchadnezzar deported people from Jerusalem: first in 605 B.C. Daniel and his three friends, second in 597 B.C. Ezekiel, and third in 586 B.C. when Jerusalem finally fell and Jeremiah lamented the disgrace of the people of Israel. Nebuchadnezzar took the best and the brightest of the youth from Jerusalem to be trained by the best and the brightest of his newly formed empire. Nebuchadnezzar's practice was to secure the best of all cultures and incorporate it into his, creating a better and stronger kingdom from all his conquered kingdoms.

A youth of this time was somewhere between the ages of fourteen and seventeen years old. They were old enough to have mastery of their own language and culture as well as having the intellect to reason and debate with others. The primary tutor of these youths had to choose them based upon looks, intellect, aptitude, and attitude. Daniel is a teenager of noble birth (1:3), who exemplifies these qualities.

Daniel had three special friends: Hananiah (Shadrach), Mishael (Meshach) and Azariah (Abednego). The Babylonians, for some very specific reasons changed the names of Daniel and his three friends. The first reason is to show authority over their lives; second, to remove the influences of the past culture from their present and future; and third, the names they received spoke to the different deities in the Babylonian culture. The Babylonian Empire systematically sought to remove all cultural ties of these youths. Changing their names was the first step in total immersion into the Babylonian culture—the first violation, if you would, of their personal autonomy.

The second violation of personal autonomy was what these youths put into their bodies. Nebuchadnezzar's training plan for these youths was to completely understand all cultures, but to become dependent upon and loyal to his benevolence. Therefore, he made sure they had the best of everything. The food and drink served to them everyday was from the king's own table. But this was the first thing Daniel and his three friends objected to. The dietary laws of the Jews were far stricter than all cultures around them. Therefore, if a Jewish person did not follow the dietary restriction of the Law of Moses, they defiled themselves and did not receive God's blessing. Daniel and his friends determined not to defile themselves with the King's meat (1:8). The word *defile* means to pollute or violate. These youths were unwilling to pollute or violate their bodies with the things society accepted. These teens were already leaders of convictions.

However, once Daniel and his friends made this decision, they had to get approval from the chief official in charge of their training. It is clear that the official had grown to know the type of character these four Hebrew youths possessed. Their character must have demonstrated integrity, because when Daniel offered a sugges-

tion on how they could eat vegetables and drink water for the next ten days rather than defile themselves through the king's food, the official was willing to take that risk. The official knew that if anything that the king did not like happened to these youths, he would have the official killed (1:10).

At the end of the ten days, these four young men looked healthier than everyone else who had been eating the royal food (1:15), so they received vegetables and water for the rest of their training. When their training was complete all the youths from all conquered kingdoms were brought to Nebuchadnezzar for a time of testing in the area of wisdom and knowledge. It was clear that these Hebrew boys, Daniel and his three friends, were head and shoulders above their peers and even their instructors (1:19-20).

Let's take a closer look at how Daniel and his three friends were dedicated to possessing integrity. They were leaders with conviction. For them, the issue was wrong even if the society they lived in said it was just fine. Next they choose the battles carefully. They learned the language of another nation. They studied the stars. But when it came to polluting their bodies, they drew the line. Lastly, they provided a test plan to see if their choice was possible. The test was short enough not to get the chief official in trouble, but long enough to provide results.

II.

The second year of Nebuchadnezzar's reign as the first Emperor of Babylon, was 604 B.C. It was during this year that Nebuchadnezzar had a dream that did not allow him to rest. He called upon the wise men of the land to calm his mind by providing an interpretation of his dream. This was the accepted practice of the day. The dream was told to the wise men, at which point the interpretation was forthcoming.

However, Nebuchadnezzar, who has been testing these men and their students, has come to know that there are specific clues in interpretation. Therefore, he is going to test the reliability of these wise men. He is going to request that they tell him the dream first and then he will accept their interpretation (2:5). It is clear that Nebuchadnezzar is not playing a game ("he had firmly decided"), but he has changed the rules of interpreting dreams. The wise men ask for more time, but the king believes that they are simply using a stall technique. When the king refuses to give them extra time, the wise men declare that no king has done this before and that Nebuchadnezzar does not have the authority to do this. This makes the king so angry that he decides to kill all the wise men and not wait for the dream or its interpretation.

News of this latest declaration reaches the ears of Daniel and his three friends. Daniel approaches Nebuchadnezzar and asks for a little more time. What is amazing at this point is that the king grants Daniel's request. Daniel must have already proven himself as a wise man, because the first emperor of the world would listen to a fifteen to eighteen year old boy, rather than the 'more learned' elders. Place yourself in Daniel's shoes (sandals), and imagine having enough courage and confidence to tell the king, 'I will get you an answer; please do not kill your wise men.'

Daniel is given insight by God to tell Nebuchadnezzar his dream and the interpretation of the dream. Nebuchadnezzar trusted Daniel's interpretation because he declared the dream prior to the interpretation. There is something else that is important to notice. Daniel's character was trusted over the senior wise men of the empire.

III.

Warning: when your personal integrity exceeded your peers and even some seniors, you will become a target. Few people have the grace to defer to their juniors.

The interpretation of Nebuchadnezzar's dream leads to the construction of a golden image and to everyone bowing in worship and tribute to this image. Everyone bows down as was commanded, except for Daniel's three friends. Daniel is not mentioned here in this context. It is likely that he has been promoted faster than his three friends (2:48) and is now doing some business for the king in another part of the empire.

The law said, "As soon as you hear the sound of . . . music, you must fall down and worship the image of gold that King Nebuchadnezzar has set up. Whoever does not fall down and worship will immediately be thrown into a blazing furnace," (3:5,6). There was a group of wise men (astrologers) that denounced the Jews (3:8), which came forward and told the king that these three Hebrew boys did not bow down when the music played. How did they know that? Were they truly worshipping? I think not. I have a feeling that they were just going through the motions, waiting for their opportunity to make other leaders look bad so that they could get their positions. Remember, Daniel and his three friends have been promoted over all their peers and some of their seniors. Daniel is on the royal court and his three friends are the administrators of Babylon. We have some prejudice happening in the ranks of the wise men.

Nebuchadnezzar is furious with rage (3:13) and calls these three leaders before him and asks if the report is true. But before they answer, the king is willing to violate his law for their well being. Instead of throwing them into the blazing furnace *immediately* he is willing to give them another chance. It is apparent that the king considers these men some of his best leaders. Not wanting them to be falsely accused, he asks for their side of the story and offers them another chance to comply with the law.

Their response to the king is one of the greatest statements of courage I have ever read: "O Nebuchadnezzar, we do not need to defend ourselves before you in this matter. If we are thrown into the blazing furnace, the God who we serve is able to save us from it, and he will rescue us from your hand, O king. But even if he does not, we want you to know O king, that we will not serve your gods or worship the image of gold you have set up," (3:16-18). These three men were defenseless, non-vindicating, and unapologetic, while being brave, secure and uncompromising. These leaders were composed under fire!

You can guess how Nebuchadnezzar responded to this kind of conviction—"His attitude toward them changed. He ordered the furnace to be heated seven times hotter than usual...tie up [the three Hebrews boys] and throw them into the blazing furnace, (3:19–20).

The king and the accusers thought that was going to be the end, but it was not. The king looked and said that he saw four men walking around in the furnace, but he knew that he only threw in three. He called to the three Hebrews boys to come out. When they came out of the furnace there was no evidence that they had been close to a fire. The fire had not harmed their bodies; their hair was not singed, nor was their clothes scorched (3:27).

IV.

In Daniel chapter four, Nebuchadnezzar is nearing the end of his reign as the King of Babylon. The Babylon Museum in Al Hillah, Iraq declares the end of Nebuchadnezzar's reign as 562 B.C. Therefore, when King Nebuchadenzzar dies, Daniel is approximately 57—60 years old. It would be fair to say that Daniel and Nebuchadnezzar have grown to understand one another and even to develop a friendship, even though Daniel remains a servant to the king.

Sometime prior to 562 B.C., Nebuchadnezzar has another dream and Daniel is summoned to interpret it's meaning. During these forty plus years that Daniel has been the king's adviser, there has been a trust built up between them. Their trust is evident as Nebuchadnezzar tells the dream to Daniel, unlike in chapter two.

Daniel is perplexed (4:19) and the king knows it. Daniel knows what the dream is saying about Nebuchadnezzar and his life for the next seven seasons. However, the king tells Daniel not to

worry about the interpretation and tell him what he knows. Daniel is desirous that the meaning refers to one of the king's enemies (4:19).

The dream, the interpretation, and the experiences of Nebuchadnezzar are not the focus of our present study. The relationship of these two men is what is most important. When the king was distressed by this vision, he called his trusted advisor. This trusted advisor has a track record of being truthful, trustworthy, honest, and filled with conviction. As a young man, he did not allow the king's declarations to sway him from maintaining personal integrity. Therefore, Daniel's indisputable integrity makes him the only man to call. This is why the king says do not let the interpretation trouble you. Good news or bad news, the king knew the words of Daniel come from a man of unquestionable integrity.

Plato said, "When men speak ill of you, live so that nobody will believe them." There was no longer anyone or group who was speaking ill of Daniel. For over forty years, he has maintained and created an indisputable integrity in his character.

V.

King Belshazzar, also known as Nabonidus (555–539 B.C.), was throwing a great party for all royalty and nobility of the empire in chapter five of Daniel. He was toasting the many gods that they worshipped in the kingdom, from the gold and silver utensils from Solomon's Temple. While this party was going on, a hand appeared and wrote an inscription on the wall (5:5). You can imagine the fear it put into everyone, especially King Nabonidus. He was so scared that his face turned pale, his knees knocked together and they gave way (5:6)—he fainted!

The king called for the wise men to come and interpret the inscription, but no one could. At which point the king fainted again. Finally, the queen said that Nebuchadnezzar had a wise counselor who was appointed the chief of the wise men. The king remembered and called for Daniel (5:10-12). At this time (539 B.C.), Daniel is 80-83 years old. His wisdom, consistency, and integrity are legendary in the Babylonian Empire.

Daniel was not called when all the wise men were called. I am not really sure, but it may be the same when there is turnover in any administration. Sometimes when there is a leadership turnover, those who remain have to prove their worth. Daniel is most likely much older than the king and the wise men he is keeping by his side. The king may have thought, 'Daniel was good in his day, but this is a new world. The ways of that older person just do not fit in our world, or the society I am trying to create.'

The king told Daniel that if he could tell him the interpretation of the inscription, he would give him possessions and a position of status in the kingdom (5:16, third highest ruler). Daniel told him to keep his things and then he proceeded to interpret the inscription. The reality was that the king lacked the quality of leadership that Nebuchadnezzar possessed and that the kingdom was going to be lost under his control. During that very night, the Empire of the Medes and Persians killed Nabonidus and took control of Babylon.

VI.

In the sixth chapter of Daniel, Darius the Mede is placed in control of the Babylon area, while Cyrus, the Persian, gains control over the rest of the Babylonian Empire. Darius places 120 leaders through the empire, while three individuals watched over the 120. Daniel is one of these three chief leaders. Under the Medes and Persians we have a change to leadership. There are teams of leaders working under one leader, who answers to the king. These three administrators are responsible to the king so that everything and everyone was accounted for.

Daniel and the two other administrators were providing the king his needed information, but Daniel was distinguishing himself over the other two and Darius was planning to make Daniel the chief over all administrators (6:3). When these others leaders received word of the king's plan they sought to discredit Daniel anyway they could. First, they tried to discredit his ability to lead. They looked through all his dealings and the dealings of his managers and found no corruption (6:4). Wow! You have got to be kidding me! Here is a public official appointed by the head of state and no one can find any "dirt" on him! Not only is there no "dirt" on Daniel, there is no "dirt" that is found on managers under his responsibility and authority. It is clear that Darius knew exactly what he was doing and why. It seems to me that human nature seeks to bring others down to a level of duplicity if our inferiority is threatened.

It became clear to these other leaders of the empire that the only way to get Daniel out of the picture was by forcing him to violate either the law of the state or the law of his God (6:5). A test of integrity was created, so that Daniel would forfeit his personal integrity though disobeying the king. A law was drafted and signed by the king; the only object of prayer for the next thirty days was King Darius (6:6-9). These unscrupulous leaders knew Daniel's prayer pattern and knew that he could not obey this law. Therefore, after finding him praying they immediately told the king. When Darius heard of this has was greatly distressed (6:14). He sought to rescue Daniel, determining to find a loophole in the law; however, he found none. Daniel, in his early to mid 80s, is thrown literally into the lions' den.

Daniel survived the night with the lions to the overwhelming joy of King Darius (6:19-23). The king found out that these other leaders had falsely accused Daniel (6:24) and ordered that they and their families be thrown to into the lions' den. Look closely at this account; those who maintain their integrity will be exonerated; and the leaders who lacked integrity, and their associates were removed from leadership. Each of us must be cautious about the company we keep, because the corrosion of other's character might leave on residue on us.

The life of Daniel, from age 15 to 85, tells us how we need to become leaders with the indispensable quality of integrity.

Suggested Reading

Armerding, Hudson T. *The Heart of Godly Leadership*. Crossway Books, 1992.

Arterburn, Stephen, Kenny Luck, and Todd Wendorff. *Being God's Man in the Search for Success*. WaterBrook Press, 2003.

Baker, Mike. *Counsel Fit for a King: Leadership Lessons from the Old Testament Kings*. College Press Publishing Company, Incorporated, 2003.

Baron, David and Lynette Padwa. *Moses on Management: 50 Leadership Lessons from the Greatest Manager of All Time*. Simon & Schuster Adult Publishing Group, 2000.

Bennett, William J. *Virtues Of Leadership*. Thomas Nelson, 2004.

Blackaby, Henry and Tom Blackaby. *The Man God Uses*. Broadman & Holman Publishers, 1999.

Blackaby, Henry and Richard Blackaby. *Called to Be God's Leader: How God Prepares His Servants for Spiritual Leadership*. Thomas Nelson, 2004.

Borek, John M., Elmer L. Towns and Danny Lovett. *The Good Book on Leadership: Case Studies from the Bible*. Broadman & Holman Publishers, 2005.

Bramble, R. L. *Leadership Lessons from the Bible*. Xulon Press, 2005.

Dale, Robert D. *Leading Edge: Leadership Strategies from the New Testament*. Abingdon Press, 1996.

Farrar, Steve. *Finishing Strong*. Multnomah Books, 1995.

Ford, Leighton. *Transforming Leadership*. Inter-Varsity Press, 1991.

Hansen, Mark Victor and Joe Batten. *The Master Motivator: Secrets of Inspiring Leadership*. Barnes & Noble Books, 2005.

Harris, James Henry. *Courage to Lead*. Rowman & Littlefield Publishers, Inc., 2002.

Hian, Chua Wee. *The Making of A Leader*. Inter-Varsity Press, 1987.

Hughes, R. Kent. *Disciplines of a Godly Man*. Crossway Books, 1991.

Jones, Laurie Beth. *Jesus, CEO*. Hyperion Books, 1993.

MacArthur, John. *The Book on Leadership*. Thomas Nelson, 2004.

Meyer, Joyce. *Leader in the Making*. Harrison House, Incorporated, 2001.

Maxwell, John. *Maxwell Leadership Bible: Lessons in Leadership from the Word of God*. Nelson Bibles, 2003.

———. *Running with the Giants: What Old Testament Heroes Want You to Know about Life and Leadership*. Warner Books, Incorporated, 2002.

———. *The 21 Irrefutable Laws of Leadership*. Thomas Nelson Publishers, 1998.

Miller, Keith. *Habitation of Dragons: Meditations for Men*. Fleming H. Revell Co., 1992.

Peterson, Eugene H. *Working the Angles: The Shape of Personal Integrity*. Eerdmans Publishing Co., 1987.

Phillips, Richard D. *Heart of an Executive: Lessons on Leadership from the Life of King David*. Doubleday Publishing, 1999.

Porter, Jeanne L. *Leading Ladies: Transformative Biblical Images for Women's Leadership*. Innisfree Press, Inc., 2004.

———. *Leading Lessons: Insights on Leadership from Women of the Bible*. Augsburg Fortress, Publishers, 2005.

Rima, Samuel D. *Leading from the Inside Out*. Baker Book House, 2000.

Sanders, J. Oswald. *Spiritual Leadership*. Moody Press, 1967.

Schierbaum, Al. *Kings and Coaches: Discovering Biblical Leadership through the Lives of Israel's Kings*. Cross Training Publishing, 2002.

Stott, John. *Basic Christian Leadership*. InterVarsity Press, 2002.

Woolfe, Lorin. *Bible on Leadership: From Moses to Matthew: Management Lessons for Contemporary Leaders*. AMACOM, 2002.

About the Author

Chaplain Webber has been married to the former Ms Karen Millard for 26 years and has two children Hannah and Micah. Tom enjoys most sports, but especially golfing, hunting and fishing. His interests also include martial arts. As a second-degree black belt in Tae Kwon Do he started a school in Virginia Beach and later turned it over to his business partners. He is currently a third-degree black belt in Tae Kwon Do and holds a world record for breaking 491 boards in 60 seconds. Educationally, LCDR Webber earned a Bachelors of Arts (Cornerstone University), Master of Divinity (Grand Rapids Theological School), Master of Theology (Emory University), and a Doctor of Ministry (Faith Evangelical Lutheran Seminary). Currently he is a research fellow at The Center for the Study of Professional Military Ethics at USNA. Prior to coming on active duty, Chaplain Webber was a civilian pastor for 14 years, mainly in the Midwest and western United States.

4

Victory at Sea: Thucydides' The Peloponnesian War

Dr. Joseph J. Thomas

Thucydides' history of the Peloponnesian War is written from the perspective of a battlefield commander. His insights cover the causes and beginning of war in 431 BC and continue through the twenty-seven year conflict. Thucydides' style is direct and he avoids speculation and fantasy concerning the involvement of the gods in the affairs of man. *The Peloponnesian War* is a continuation of Herodotus' *The Persian War*, and Xenophon's *Hellenica* in turn picks up where Thucydides leaves off. This three part narrative of ancient Greek politics and warfare provides readers with a comprehensive view of an entire age.

The following excerpt chronicles the sea battle at Syracuse (Sicily) in 413 BC. Nearly 50,000 Athenians were wiped out in the action and resulting overland withdrawl. The Delian League (of which Athens was the primary power) would eventually surrender and bow to the superior might and will of the Peloponnesian League (of which Sparta and Corinth were the dominant powers).

* * *

When Gylippus and the other Syracusan generals had, like Nicias, encouraged their troops, perceiving the Athenians to be manning their ships they presently did the same. Nicias, overwhelmed by the situation, and seeing how great and how near the peril was, (for the ships were on the very point of rowing out), feeling too, as men do on the eve of a great struggle, that all which he had done was nothing, and that he had not said half enough, again addressed the trierarchs, and calling each of them by his father's name, and his own name, and the name of his tribe, he entreated those who had made any reputation for themselves not to be false to it and those whose ancestors were eminent not to tarnish their hereditary fame. He reminded them that they were the inhabitants of the freest country in the world, and how in Athens there was no interference with the daily life of any man. He spoke to them of their wives and children and their fathers' Gods, as men will at such a time; for then they do not care whether their common- place phrases seem to be out of date or not, but loudly reiterate the old appeals, believing that they may be of some service at the awful moment. When he thought that he had exhorted them, not enough, but as much as the scanty time allowed, he retired, and led the land-forces to tlle shore, extending the line as far as he could, so that they might be of the greatest use in encouraging the combatants on board ship. Demosthenes, Menander, and Euthydemus, who had gone on board the Athenian fleet to take the command, now quitted their own station, and proceeded straight to the closed mouth of the harbor, intending to force their way to the open sea where a passage was still left.

The Syracusans and their allies had already put out with nearly the same number of ships as before. A detachment of them guarded the entrance of the harbor; the remainder were disposed all round it in such a manner that they might fall on the Athenians from every side at once, and that their land-forces might at the same time be able to co-operate wherever the ships retreated to the shore. Sicanus and Agatharchus commanded the Syracusan fleet, each of them a wing; Pythen and the Corinthians occupied the center. When the Athenians approached the closed mouth of the harbor the violence of their onset overpowered the ships which, were stationed there; they then attempted to loosen the fastenings. Whereupon from all sides the Syracusans and their allies came bearing down upon them, and the conflict was no longer confined to the entrance, but extended throughout the harbor. No previous engagement had been so fierce and obstinate.

Great was the eagerness with which the rowers on both sides rushed upon their enemies whenever the word of command was given; and keen was the contest between the pilots as they maneuvered one against another. The marines too were full of anxiety that, when ship struck ship, the service on deck should not fall short of the rest; every one in the place assigned to him was eager to be foremost among his fellows. Many vessels meeting-and never did so many fight in so small a space, for the two fleets together amounted to nearly two hundred-they were seldom able to strike in the regular manner, because they had no opportunity of first retiring or breaking the line; they generally fouled one another as ship dashed against ship in the hurry of flight or pursuit. All the time that another vessel was bearing down, the men on deck poured showers of javelins and arrows add stones upon the enemy; and when the two closed, the marines fought hand to hand, and endeavored to board. In many places, owing to the want of room, they who had struck another found that they were struck themselves; often two or even more vessels were unavoidably entangled about one, and the pilots had to make plans of attack and defense, not against one adversary only, but against several coming from different sides. The crash of so many ships dashing against one another took away the wits of the crews, and made it impossible to hear the boatswains, whose voices in both fleets rose high, as they gave directions to the rowers, or cheered them on in the excitement of the struggle. On the Athenian side they were shouting to their men that they must force a passage and seize the opportunity now or never of returning in safety to their native land.

To the Syracusans and their allies was represented the glory of preventing the escape of their enemies, and of a victory by which every man would exalt the honor of his own city. The commanders too, when they saw any ship backing without necessity, would call the captain by his name, and ask, of the Athenians, whether they were retreating because they expected to be more at home upon the land of their bitterest foes than upon that sea which had been their own so long; on the Syracusan side, whether, when they knew perfectly well that the Athenians were only eager to find some means of Bight, they would themselves fly from the fugitives.

While the naval engagement hung in the balance the two armies on shore had great trial and conflict of soul. The Sicilian soldier was animated by the hope of increasing the glory which he had already won, while the invader was tormented by the fear that his fortunes might sink lower still. The last chance of the Athenians lay in their ships, and their anxiety was dreadful.

The fortune of the battle varied; and it was not possible that the spectators on the shore should all receive the same impression of it. Being quite close and having different points of view, they would some of them see their own ships victorious; their courage would then revive, and .they would earnestly call upon the Gods not to take from them their hope of deliverance. But others, who saw their ships worsted, cried and shrieked aloud, and were by the sight alone more utterly unnerved than the defeated combatants themselves. Others again, who had fixed their gaze on some part of the struggle which was undecided, were in a state of excitement still more terrible; they kept swaying their bodies to and fro in an agony of hope and fear as the stubborn conflict went on and on; for at every instant they were all but saved or all but lost. And while the strife hung in the balance you might hear in the Athenian army at once lamentation, shouting, cries of victory or defeat, and all the various sounds which are wrung from a great host in extremity of danger. Not less agonizing were the feelings of those on board. At length the Syracusans and their allies, after a protracted struggle, put the Athenians to flight, and triumphantly bearing down upon them, and encouraging one another with loud cries and exhortations, drove them to land. Then that part of the navy which had not been taken in the deep water fell back in confusion to the shore, and the crews rushed out of the ships into the camp. And the land-forces, no longer now divided in feeling, but uttering one universal groan of intolerable anguish, ran, some of them to save the ships, others to defend what remained of the wall; but the greater number began to look to themselves and to their own safety. Never had there been a greater panic in an Athenian army than at that moment. They now suffered what, they had done to others at

Pylos. For at Pylos the Lacedaemonians, when they saw their ships destroyed, knew that their friends who had crossed over into the island of Sphacteria were lost with them. And so now the Athenians, after the rout of their fleet, knew that they had no hope of saving themselves by land unless events took some extraordinary turn.

Thus, after a fierce battle and a great destruction of ships and men on both sides, the Syracusans and their allies gained the victory. They gathered up the wrecks and bodies of the dead, and sailing back to the city, erected a trophy. The Athenians, overwhelmed by their misery, never so much as thought of recovering their wrecks or of asking leave to collect their dead. Their intention was to retreat that very night. Demosthenes came to Nicias and proposed that they should once more man their remaining vessels and endeavor to force the passage at daybreak, saying that they had more ships fit for service than the enemy. For the Athenian fleet still numbered sixty, but the enemy had less than fifty. Nicias approved of his proposal, and they would have manned the ships, but the sailors refused to embark; for they were paralyzed by their defeat, and had no longer any hope of succeeding. So the Athenians all made up their minds to escape by land.

Hermocrates the Syracusan suspected their intention, and dreading what might happen if their vast army, retreating by land and settling somewhere in Sicily, should choose to renew the war, he went to the authorities, and represented to them that they ought not to allow the Athenians to withdraw by night (mentioning his own suspicion of their intentions), but that all the Syracusans and their allies should go out in advance, wall up the roads, and occupy the passes with a guard. They thought very much as he did, and wanted to carry out his plan, but doubted whether their men, who were too glad to repose after a great battle, and in time of festival-for there happened on that very day to be a sacrifice to Heracles-could be induced to obey. Most of them, in the exultation of victory, were drinking and keeping holiday, and at such a time how could they ever be expected to take up arms and go forth at the order of the generals? On these grounds the authorities decided that the thing was impossible. Whereupon Hermocrates himself, fearing lest the Athenians should gain a start and quietly pass the most difficult places in the night, contrived the following plan: when it was growing dark he sent certain of his own acquaintance, accompanied by a few horsemen, to the Athenian camp. They rode up within earshot, and pretending to be friends (there were known to be men in the city who gave information to Nicias of what went on) called to some of the soldiers, and bade them tell him not to withdraw his army during the night, for the Syracusans were guarding the roads; he should make preparation at leisure and retire by day. Having delivered their message they departed, and those who had heard them informed the Athenian generals.

On receiving this message, which they supposed to he genuine, they remained during the night. And having once given up the intention of starting immediately, they decided to remain during the next day, that the soldiers might, as well as they could, put together their baggage in the most convenient form, and depart, taking with them the bare necessaries of life, but nothing else.

Meanwhile the Syracusans and Gylippus, going forth before them with their land-forces, blocked the roads in the country by which the Athenians were likely to pass, guarded the fords of the rivers and streams, and posted themselves at the best points for receiving and stopping them. Their sailors rowed up to the beach and dragged away the Athenian ships. The Athenians themselves had burnt a few of them, as they had intended, but the rest the Syracusans towed away, unmolested and at their leisure, from the places where they had severally run aground, and conveyed them to the city.

On the third day after the sea-fight, when Nicias and Demosthenes thought that their preparations were complete, the army began to move. They were in a dreadful condition; not only was there the great fact that they had lost their whole fleet, and instead of their expected triumph had brought the utmost peril upon Athens as well as upon themselves, but also the sights which presented themselves as they quitted the camp were painful to every eye and mind. The dead were unburied, and when anyone saw the body of a friend lying on the ground he was smitten with sorrow and dread, while the sick or wounded who still survived but had to he left were even a greater trial to the living, and more to he pitied than those who were gone.

Their prayers and lamentations drove their companions to distraction; they would beg that they might he taken with them, and call by name any friend or relation whom they saw passing; they would hang upon their departing comrades and follow as far as they could, and, when their limbs and strength failed them, and they dropped behind, many were the imprecations and cries which they uttered. So that the whole army was in tears, and such was their despair that they could hardly make up their minds to stir, although they were leaving an enemy's country, having suffered calamities too great for tears already, and dreading miseries yet greater in the unknown future. There was also a general feeling of shame and self-reproach, indeed they seemed, not like an army, but like the fugitive population of a city captured after a siege; and of a great city too. For the whole multitude who were marching together numbered not less than forty thousand. Each of them took with him anything he could carry which was likely to be of use. Even the heavy-armed and cavalry, contrary to their practice when under arms, conveyed about their persons their own food, some because they had no attendants, others because they could not trust them; for they had long been deserting, and most of them had gone off all at once. Nor was the food which they carried sufficient; for the supplies of the camp had failed. Their disgrace and the universality of the misery, although there might be some consolation in the very community of suffering, were nevertheless at that moment hard to bear, especially when they remembered from what pride and splendor they had fallen into their present low estate. Never had a Hellenic army experienced such a reverse. They had come intending to enslave others, and they were going away in fear that they would be themselves enslaved. Instead of the prayers and hymns with which they had put to sea, they were now departing amid appeals to heaven of another sort. They were no longer sailors but landsmen, depending, not upon their fleet, but upon their infantry. Yet in face of the great danger which still threatened them all these things appeared endurable.

Nicias, seeing the army disheartened at their terrible fall, went along the ranks and encouraged and consoled them as well as he could. In his fervor he raised his voice as he passed from one to another and spoke louder and louder, desiring that the benefit of his words might reach as far as possible.

"Even now, Athenians and allies, we must hope: men have been delivered out of worse straits than these, and I would not have you judge yourselves too severely on account either of the reverses which you have sustained or of your present undeserved miseries. I too am as weak as any of you; for I am quite prostrated by my disease, as you see. And although there was a time when I might have been thought equal to the best of you in the happiness of my private and public life, I am now in as great danger, and as much at the mercy of fortune, as the meanest. Yet my days have been passed in the performance of many a religious duty, and of many a just and blameless action. Therefore my hope of the future is still courageous, and our calamities do not appall me as they might. Who knows that they may not be lightened? For our enemies have had their full share of success, and if we were under the jealousy of any God when our fleet started, by this time we have been punished enough. Others ere now have attacked their neighbors; they have done as men will do, and suffered what men can bear. We may therefore begin to hope that the Gods will be more merciful to us; for we now invite their pity rather than their jealousy. And look at your own well-armed

ranks; see how many brave soldiers you are, marching in solid array, and do not be dismayed; bear in mind that wherever you plant yourselves you are a city already, and that no city in Sicily will find it easy to resist your attack, or can dislodge you if you choose to settle. Provide for the safety and good order of your own march, and remember every one of you that on whatever spot a man is compelled to fight, there if he conquer he may find a native land and a fortress. We must press forward day and night, for our supplies are but scanty .The Sicels through fear of the Syracusans still adhere to us, and if we can only reach any part of their territory we shall be among friends, and you may consider yourselves secure. We have sent to them, and they have been told to meet us and bring food. In a word, soldiers let me tell you that you must be brave; there is no place near to which a coward can fly. And if you now escape your enemies, those of you who are not Athenians will see once more the home for which they long, while you Athenians will again rear aloft the fallen greatness of Athens. For men, and not walls or ships in which are no men, constitute a state."

Thus exhorting his troops Nicias passed through the army, and wherever he saw gaps in the ranks or the men dropping out of line, he brought them back to their proper place. Demosthenes did the same for the troops under his command, and gave them similar exhortations. The army marched disposed in a hollow oblong: the division of Nicias leading, and that of Demosthenes following; the hoplites enclosed within their ranks the baggage-bearers and the rest of the host. When they arrived at the ford of the river Anapus they found a force of the Syracusans and of their allies drawn up to meet them; these they put to flight, and getting command of the ford, proceeded on their march. The Syracusans continually harassed them, the cavalry riding alongside, and the light-armed troops hurling darts at them. On this day the Athenians proceeded about four and a half miles and encamped at a hill. On the next day they started early, and, having advanced more than two miles, descended into a level plain, and encamped.

The country was inhabited, and they were desirous of obtaining food from the houses, and also water which they might carry with them, as there was little to be had for many miles in the country which lay before them. Meanwhile the Syracusans had gone forward, and at a point where the road ascends a steep hill called the Acraean height, and there is a precipitous ravine on either side, were blocking up the pass by a wall. On the next day the Athenians advanced, although again impeded by the numbers of the enemy's cavalry who rode alongside, and of their javelin-men who threw darts at them. For a long time the Athenians maintained the struggle, but at last retired to their own encampment. Their supplies were now cut off, because the horsemen circumscribed their movements.

In the morning they started early and resumed their march. They pressed onward to the hill where the way was barred, and found in front of them the Syracusan infantry drawn up to defend the wall, in deep array, for the pass was narrow. Whereupon the

Athenians advanced and assaulted the barrier, but the enemy, who were numerous and had the advantage of position, threw missiles upon them from the hill, which was steep, and so, not being able to force their way, they again retired and rested. During the conflict, as is often the case in the fall of the year, there came on a storm of rain and thunder, whereby the Athenians were yet more disheartened, for they thought that everything was conspiring to their destruction. While they were resting, Gylippus and the Syracusans dispatched a division of their army to raise a wall behind them across the road by which they had come; but the Athenians sent some of their own troops and frustrated their intention. They then retired with their whole army in the direction of the plain and passed the night. On the following day they again advanced. The Syracusans now surrounded and attacked them on every side, and wounded many of them. If the Athenians advanced they retreated, but charged them when

they retired, falling especially upon the hindermost of them, in the hope that, if they could put to flight a few at a time, they might strike a panic into the whole army. In this fashion the Athenians struggled on for a long time, and having advanced about three-quarters of a mile rested in the plain. The Syracusans then left them and returned to their own encampment.

The army was now in a miserable plight, being in want of every necessary; and by the continual assaults of the enemy great numbers of the soldiers had been wounded. Nicias and Demosthenes, perceiving their condition, resolved during the night to light as many watch-fires as possible and to lead off their forces. They intended to take another route and march toward the sea in the direction opposite to that from which the Syracusans were watching them. Now their whole line of march lay, not toward Catana, but toward the other side of Sicily, in the direction of Camarina and Gela, and the cities, Hellenic or Barbarian, of that region. So they lighted numerous fires and departed in the night. And then, as constantly happens in armies, especially in very great ones, and as might be expected when they were marching by night in an enemy's country, and with the enemy from whom they were flying not far off, there arose a panic among them, and they fell into confusion. The army of Nicias, which was leading the way, kept together, and got on considerably in advance, but that of Demosthenes, which was the larger half, was severed from the other division, and marched in worse order. At daybreak, however, they succeeded in reaching the sea, and striking into the Helorine road marched along it, intending as soon as they arrived at the Cacyparis to follow up the course of the river through the interior of the island. They were expecting that the Sicels for whom they had sent would meet them on this road. When they had reached the river they found there also a guard of the Syracusans cutting off the passage by a wall and palisade. They forced their way through and, crossing the river, passed on toward another river which is called the Erineus, this being the direction in which their guides led them.

When daylight broke and the Syracusans and their allies saw that the Athenians had departed, most of them thought that Gylippus had let them go on purpose, and were very angry with him. They easily found the line of their retreat, and quickly following, came up with them about the time of the midday meal. The troops of Demosthenes were last; they were marching slowly and in disorder, not having recovered from the panic of the previous night, when they were overtaken by the Syracusans, who immediately fell upon them and fought. Separated as they were from the others, they were easily hemmed in by the Syracusan cavalry and driven into a narrow space. The division of Nicias was now as much as six miles in advance, for he marched faster, thinking that their safety depended at such a time, not in remaining and fighting, if they could avoid it, but in retreating as quickly as they could, and resisting only when they were positively compelled. Demosthenes, on the other hand, who had been more incessantly harassed throughout the retreat, because marching last he was first attacked by the enemy, now, when he saw the Syracusans pursuing him, instead of pressing onward, ranged his army in order of battle. Thus lingering he was surrounded, and he and the Athenians under his command were in the greatest confusion. For they were crushed into a walled enclosure, having a road on both sides and planted thickly with olive-trees, and missiles were hurled at them from all points. The Syracusans naturally preferred this mode of attack to a regular engagement; For to risk themselves against desperate men would have been only playing into the hands of the Athenians. Moreover, every one was sparing of his life; their good fortune was already assured, and they did not want to fall if the hour of victory. Even by this irregular mode of fighting they thought that they could overpower and capture the Athenians.

And so when they had gone on all day assailing them with missiles from every quarter, and

saw that they were quite worn out with their wounds and all their other sufferings, Gylippus and the Syracusans made a proclamation, first of all to the islanders, that any of them who pleased might come over to them and have their freedom. But only a few cities accepted the offer. At length an agreement was made for the entire force under Demosthenes. Their arms were to be surrendered, but no one was to suffer death, either from violence or from imprisonment, or from want of the bare means of life. So they all surrendered, being in number six thousand, and gave up what money they. had. This they threw into the hollows of shields and filled four. The captives were at once taken to the city. On the same day Nicias and his division reached the river Erineus, which he crossed, and halted his army on a rising ground.

On the following day he was overtaken by the Syracusans, who told him that Demosthenes had surrendered, and bade him do the same. He, not believing them, procured a truce while he sent a horseman to go and see. Upon the return of the horseman bringing assurance of the fact, he sent a herald to Gylippus and the Syracusans, saying that he would agree, on behalf of the Athenian state, to pay the expenses which the Syracusans had incurred in the war, on condition that they should let his army go; until the money was paid he would give Athenian citizens as hostages, a man for a talent. Gylippus and the Syracusans would not accept these proposals, but attacked and surrounded this division of the army as they had the other, and hurled missiles at them from every side until the evening. They too were grievously in want of food and necessaries. Nevertheless they meant to wait for the dead of the night and then to proceed. They were just resuming their arms, when the Syracusans discovered them and raised the Paean. The Athenians, perceiving that they were detected, laid down their arms again, with the exception of about three hundred men who broke through the enemy's guard, and made their escape in the darkness as best they could.

When the day dawned Nicias led forward his

army, and the Syracusans and the allies again assailed them on every side, hurling javelins and
other missiles at them. The Athenians hurried
on to the river Assinarus. They hoped to gain a
little relief if they forded the river, for the mass
of horsemen and other troops overwhelmed and
crushed them; and they were worn out by fatigue
and thirst. But no sooner did they reach the
water than they lost all order and rushed in;
every man was trying to cross first, and, the
enemy pressing upon them at the same time, the
passage of the river became hopeless. Being
compelled to keep close together they fell one
upon another, and trampled each other under
foot: some at once perished, pierced by their
own spears; others got entangled in the baggage
and were carried down the stream. The Syracusans stood upon the further bank of the rivet,
which was steep, and hurled missiles from above
on the Athenians, who were huddled together in
the deep bed of the stream and for the most part
were drinking greedily. The Peloponnesians
came down the bank and slaughtered them,
falling chiefly upon those who were in the river.
Whereupon the water at once be- came foul, but
was drunk all the same, although muddy and
dyed with blood, and the crowd fought for it.

At last, when the dead bodies were lying in
heaps upon one another in the water and the
army was utterly undone, some perishing in the
river, and any who escaped being cut off by the
cavalry, Nicias surrendered to Gylippus, in
whom he had more confidence than in the Syracusans. He entreated him and the Lacedaemonians to do what they pleased with himself, but not
to go on killing the men. So Gylippus gave the
word to make prisoners. Thereupon the survivors, not including however a large number
whom the soldiers concealed, were brought in
alive. As for the three hundred who had broken
through the guard in the night, the Syracusans
sent in pursuit and seized them. The total of the
public prisoners when collected was not great;
for many were appropriated by the soldiers, and
the whole of Sicily was full of them, they not
having capitulated like the troops under Demos-

thenes. A large number also perished; the
slaughter at the river being very great, quite as
great as any which took place in the Sicilian war;
and not a few had fallen in the frequent attacks
which were made upon the Athenians during
their march. Still many escaped, some at the
time, others ran away after an interval of slavery,
and all these found refuge at Catana.

The Syracusans and their allies collected their
forces and returned with the spoil, and as many
prisoners as they could take with them, into the
city. The captive Athenians and allies they deposited in the quarries, which they thought
would be the safest place of confinement. Nicias
and Demosthenes they put to the sword, although against the will of Gylippus. For Gylippus thought that to carry home with him to
Lacedaemon the generals of the enemy, over and
above all his other successes, would be a brilliant
triumph. One of them, Demosthenes, happened
to be the greatest foe, and the other the greatest
friend of the Lacedaemonians, both in the same
matter of Pylos and Sphacteria. For Nicias had
taken up their cause, and had persuaded the
Athenians to make the peace which set at liberty
the prisoners taken in the island. The Lacedaemonians were grateful to him: for the service,
and this was the main reason why he trusted
Gylippus and surrendered himself to him. But
certain Syracusans, who had been in communication with him, were afraid (such was the report) that on some suspicion of their guilt he
might be put to the torture and bring trouble on
them in the hour of their prosperity. Others, and
especially the Corinthians, feared that, being
rich, he might by bribery escape and do them
further mischief. So the Syracusans gained the
consent of the allies and had him executed. For
these or the like reasons he suffered death. No
one of the Hellenes in my time was less deserving of so miserable an end; for he lived in the
practice of every virtue.

Those who were imprisoned in the quarries
were at the beginning of their captivity harshly
treated by the Syracusans. There were great
numbers of them, and they were crowded in a

deep and narrow place. At first the sun by day was still scorching and suffocating, for they had no roof over their heads, while the autumn nights were cold, and the extremes of temperature engendered violent disorders. Being cramped for room they had to do everything on the same spot. The corpses of those who died from their wounds, exposure to heat and cold, and the like, lay heaped one upon another. The smells were intolerable; and they were at the same time afflicted by hunger and thirst. During eight months they were allowed only about half a pint of water and a pint of food a day. Every kind of misery which could befall man in such a place befell them. This was the condition of all the captives for about ten weeks. At length the Syracusans sold them, with the exception of the Athenians and of any Sicilian or Italian Greeks who had sided with them in the war. The whole number of the public prisoners is not accurately known, but they were not less than seven thousand.

Of all the Hellenic actions which took place in this war, or indeed, as I think, of all Hellenic actions which are on record, this was the greatest-the most glorious to the victors, the most ru-inous to the vanquished; for they were utterly and at all points defeated, and their sufferings were prodigious. Fleet and army perished from the face of the earth; nothing was saved, and of the many who went forth few returned home.

Thus ended the Sicilian expedition.

Suggested Readings

Goldhill, Simon. *Aeschylus, the Oresteia*. Cambridge: Cambridge University Press, 1992.

Grene, David, ed. *The Complete Greek Tragedies: Sophocles I (Vol 1)*. Chicago: University of Chicago Press, 1959.

Murray, A.T., ed. *The Iliad of Homer*. Cambridge: Harvard University Press, 1999.

Plato. *The Republic*. Trans. G.M.A. Grube, rev. C.D.C. Reeve. Indianapolis: Hackett Publishing

Company, Inc., 1992.

Plutarch. *The Rise and Fall of Athens: Nine Greek Lives*. Harmondsworth: Penguin Books, 1960.

Thucydides. *History of the Peloponnesian War*. New York: W.W. Norton & Co., 1998.

5

Acrobatics of the Mind: Plato's Parmenides and Communication

LT Michael C. Zito, USNR

For Paul Duff

Parmenides is a difficult and complicated dialogue—even more so than *Republic*, for example—but it is particularly relevant to the students of the United States Naval Academy and future military officers, because it is one of the only extant accounts of the youth of Socrates. Just as the students of the Naval Academy are developing their leadership styles in preparation for their work in the fleet or in the field, Socrates, who earlier in his life fought as a foot-soldier in the Peloponnesian War, lived and learned in an environment that was conducive to building up his mental fitness and rhetorical strength.

The following tract from *Parmenides* covers young Socrates questioning Zeno on the meaning of Parmenides' philosophical poem on nature—which now only exists in fragments—and moves into the beginning of the dialogue in which Parmenides and Aristotle (not the philosopher) discuss the hypothesis "One *is*," a topic found in Parmenides' poem. In this text, although young Socrates is admonished for the zeal in his manner of speech and generating ideas, he also is applauded and encouraged to spend more time in a *gymnastic*.

A gymnastic, at the time of the philosophical patriarchs, was a place in which people investigated the mysteries of life or conducted mathematical deduction and reasoning—as a collective. In *Republic*, or what can be considered Plato's perfect world, leaders would be philosophers and philosophers would be leaders. The work of the gymnastic, the first academy, was to challenge and train young men to think critically, analytically, and methodically—to craft their ability to make decisions with logic.

Like many of the dialectics that took place in the gymnastic, the important part of *Parmenides* is not the conclusion or whether or not hypotheses can be proved. Rather, it is what happens and what is said in the course of the dialogue from which the most brilliant gems of wisdom can be garnered.

This said, we started walking and came upon Antiphon at home, handling a bridle-bit or something to a smith to fit. Once he'd freed himself of that fellow and the brothers began to tell him why we were there, he recognized me from my previous stay and greeted me warmly. We then asked him to go through the speeches. At first, he balked—for he said it was a lot of work—but at last he led us through them in full. And so Antiphon said that Pythodorus used to say that both Zeno and Parmenides once came to the Great Panathea.

Now, Parmenides was already quite old—his hair all white—but the vision of a gentleman. He was sixty-five at most. Zeno was then nearly forty, tall and pleasing to look at. (He was said to have been Parmenides' young beloved.) They were staying, he said, with Pythodorus outside the city-wall in the Potter's Quarter.

So Socrates and many others with him were there, since they desired to hear Zeno's writings—after all, that was the first time they had brought them there. Socrates was then very young. Zeno himself read to them, but Parmenides chanced to be out. And there was, all-in-all, only a short part of the speeches left to be read, Pythodorus said, when he and Parmenides with him came from outside—and Aristotle too (who became one of the Thirty). So they heard only a little of the writings. However, Pythodorus, in fact, had heard them before on his own from Zeno.

After listening, Socrates asked him to re-read the first hypothesis of the first speech. Once it was read he said, "Zeno, how do you mean that? If the things that *are*, are many, then, according to you, they must be both like and unlike. But this is clearly impossible, since the unlike cannot be like nor the like unlike. Isn't that what you mean?"

"That's so," replied Zeno.

"And so if it is impossible for the unlike to be like and the like unlike, it's also impossible for

there to be many things? For if there should be many, they would suffer these impossibilities. Is this, then, what your speeches seek—nothing else than to battle against everything that is commonly said by maintaining that there *is* no many? And do you think that each of your speeches is a proof of this very thing—so that the supposed proofs that 'There *is* no many' are as many speeches you have written? Is that what you mean, or don't I understand you right?"

"No," said Zeno, "on the contrary, you have beautifully grasped the whole of what my writing seeks."

"I'm coming to understand, Parmenides," Socrates said, "that Zeno here seeks to be your partner not only in friendship but in writing! For he has written, in a certain way, the very same thing as you, but by changing it around he tries to trick us into thinking that he is saying some other thing. You in your poems say that All is one, and you do a both beautiful and good job of proving that; but this fellow, in turn, says that it's not many, and he offers proofs that are very many and very great. One says 'The One' and one says 'Not Many,' and so each speaks so as to seem to say nothing the same, while you are saying nearly the same thing. That's why what you say appears to be over the heads of the rest of us."

"Yes, Socrates," said Zeno. "But you have perceived the entire truth of the writing. To be sure, you both chase and hunt down what I said like a Laconian hound! But this much has escaped you from the first: that in no way whatsoever is my writing so pretentious as to have been written for the reason you offer, namely, to conceal from men that it's furthering some great plot. What you mentioned is just an accidental result. The truth is that it's sort of aid to Parmenides' speech against those who attack him by joking that if one *is*, then he and his speech suffer many laughable and contradictory results. So this writing refutes the asserters of the Many and pays back the same and more. It seeks to make this point clear: that if sufficiently prosecuted, their hypothesis—'If many is'—would suffer even more laughable results than that of the

One's *being*. I wrote it, in fact, when I was young, because I loved to fight. But someone stole a copy, so I couldn't decide whether it should be brought to light or not. That's what escapes you, Socrates: you don't think it was written because of a youth's love for fighting, but because of an older man's love of honor. Though, as I said, your description is not a bad likeness."

"I accept that," replied Socrates, "and I believe it is as you say. But tell me this: don't you think that there exists, in itself, some form of Likeness, to which is opposed a different one, which is unlike, and that both you and I and the different things which we do in fact call 'many' come to partake of these two things which *are*? And that the things that come to partake of Likeness become like in both the manner and extent that they partake, but those of Unlikeness unlike, and those of both, both? And even if all things come to partake of both these opposing things and are, by partaking in both, both like and unlike in themselves—why wonder? For if someone were to show that the like things themselves become unlike or the unlike like, I'd think that a marvel. But if he shows that whatever partakes of both of these has experienced both, then, Zeno, it doesn't seem at all out of place to me. No, not even if he were to show that all things are many, in turn, by partaking in Multitude! But if he demonstrates that whatever one is, this very thing, is many and that the Many, in turn, are one—of course I'll wonder at that. Likewise for all the different things: if he should reveal that both the kinds and forms themselves experience these opposite experiences in themselves, it's right to wonder. But if someone demonstrates that I am one and many, why wonder? For when he seeks to show that I am many, he just mentions that my right is one thing and my left another, my front's one thing and my back's another, and likewise for upper and lower—for I do, I believe, partake of the Multitude. But when he wants to show that I am one, he'll say that out of the seven of us who are here, I myself am one man and partake of the One. So he can show that both are true."

"If, then, someone shall try to show for things such as stones and wood and the like, the same things are many and one, then we will say that he's demonstrated that something is many and one, not that the One is many or the Many's one. He's not even said anything wondrous, but only what in fact all of us should readily agree upon. But if someone, as I just said, shall first distinguish the forms as separate in themselves, such as Likeness and Unlikeness and Multitude and the One and Rest and Motion and all the like, and then will show that in themselves these things can be mixed together and separated, I'd admire that with wonder, Zeno!" he said. "Now I do believe that you've worked over these things quite bravely; but, as I've said, I would admire this much more: if someone could demonstrate that even in the forms themselves—in the things grasped by reasoning—there is everywhere tangled up that same impasse which you proved is present in the things we see."

While Socrates was speaking, Pythodorus said, he himself thought at each word both Parmenides and Zeno were going to get angry. But they kept their mind on Socrates and, with frequent glances to one another, they smiled as if admiring him. Which is, in fact, what Parmenides told him, once he was done.

"Socrates," he said, "you ought to be admired for your zeal for speeches! And tell me, did you, on your own, come up with this division that you speak of between these forms, separate unto themselves, and, separated from them, the things that partake of them?

And does it seem to you that Likeness itself is separate from the likeness that we possess? And so on with one and many and everything that you heard of just now from Zeno?"

"It certainly does," answered Socrates.

"Well how about these sorts of things," said Parmenides," such as a form of Justice in itself and of Beauty and of Good and so on?"

"Yes," he said.

"But what about this: a form of Man separate from us and all those like us—some very form of Man, or of Fire or Water?"

"I've hit a dead end many times, Parmenides," he replied, "over these, over whether it's necessary to speak much the same about them or differently."

"Well then, Socrates, what about those things that would seem to be laughable, such as Hair and Mud and Dirt or any different thing that's very worthless and lowly? Are you at an impasse over whether it is or is not necessary to say that there is a separate form of each of these, something different than what we can lay our hands on?"

"No, not at all!" answered Socrates. "For these things are as we see them right here, and it would be grossly out of place to think that there is some form of them. To be sure, it has troubled me that the same case does not apply to all, but whenever I come to this, I run off, fearing to fall and perish in some abyss of foolishness. In the end, then, I return to these things that just now we were saying are forms and I spend my time working over them."

"Well, you are still young, Socrates," said Parmenides, "and philosophy has not yet grabbed you as it will, in my opinion. Then you will dishonor none of these things; but as for now, you still look to the opinions of men, because of your age. But tell me this, then: does it seem to you that, as you say, there are these forms from which the different things here, by partaking in them, get their names? For example, the things that partake in Likeness become like, but those in Greatness great, and those in Beauty and Justice both just and beautiful?"

"Of course," replied Socrates.

"And so each thing that partakes comes to partake either of the whole form or of a part? Or could there be some way of partaking separate from these?"

"How could there be?" he said.

"Then does it seem to you that the whole form is in each of the many things, while still being one, or how?"

"What prevents it, Parmenides," said Socrates, "from being one?"

"Although one and the same, then, its whole will be in many separate beings at the same time, and so it would be separated from itself."

"Not if it is like a day," he said, "which, although one and the same, is many places at once and is not at all separate from itself. In this way each of the forms could be one, the same and in all things at once."

"Socrates," he replied, "how nicely you make one and the same thing many places at once! It is as if after covering many men with a sail you would say that it is one whole over many. Or is that not what you mean to say?"

"That's fair," he answered.

"Well then would the whole sail be over each man, or a different part of it over each different man?"

"A part."

"Then, Socrates," he said, "the forms themselves can be partitioned and the things that partake of them would partake of a part. The whole would no longer be in each, but each would possess a part."

"So it appears."

"Well then Socrates, are you willing to say that one form can, in truth, be partitioned by us and still be one?"

"No way," he replied.

"Try to see then," he said, "if you will partition Greatness itself, then each of the many great things will be great by means of a part that's smaller than Greatness itself—doesn't that appear illogical?"

"Of course," he answered.

"But what? If something possesses an individual small part of the Equal, will it possess something that, though less than the Equal itself, will make its possessor equal to anything else?"

"Impossible!"

"Then let one of us possess a part of the Small. Since it's just a part, the Small will be greater than it. Get it?—the Small itself will be greater! But whatever that subtracted piece is added to will be smaller, not greater, than before!"

"Well that certainly can't be," he said.

"Is there, then, some other way, Socrates," he

asked, "that the different things will partake of your forms, since they're able to partake neither as parts nor as wholes?"

"No by Zeus!" he exclaimed. "It doesn't seem to me to be at all easy to determine that!"

"But what then? How do you feel about this—"

"What's that?"

"—I think that you think that each form is one because of this: whenever many things seem to you to be great, it seems probable to you, as you look over them all, that there *is* some one and the same idea. From this you conclude that the Great is one."

"That's the truth," he replied.

"But what about the Great itself and the different great things—if, in the same way, you look over them all with your soul, will there not appear, in turn, some great thing that makes all of them, by necessity, appear great?"

"It looks that way."

"A different form of Greatness, then, will be revealed, in addition to what was Greatness itself and the things that partake of it. And above all of these, in turn, another, that makes them all great. And so each of your forms will no longer be one, but will be boundless in multitude."

"But Parmenides," Socrates said, "couldn't it be that each of these forms is a thought and property comes to *be* nowhere but in souls? Then each could in fact be one and would not still suffer the things you just mentioned."

"What then?" he asked. "Each is one of our thoughts—but are there thoughts of nothing?"

"Impossible," he replied.

"So of something?"

"Yes."

"Of something that is or is not?"

"That is."

"So of one thing—which thing in fact the thought thinks is present in all cases as some one idea?"

"Yes."

"Then won't a form be this thing that is thought to be one, since it's always the same in all cases?"

"It appears necessary."

"But what now?" asked Parmenides. "For doesn't it seem to you that, since it is necessary, you say, for other things to partake of forms, either each thing consists of thoughts and everything thinks or, although thoughts, they're thought-less?"

"Well that too," he replied, "makes no sense. However Parmenides, here's how it really appears to me to be: these forms stand in nature like patterns. The different things resemble them and are likenesses, and so the different things' participation in the forms turns out to be nothing else than to be made in their likeness!"

"If then," he asked, "something looks like a form, can the form not be its likeness, insofar as that thing's been made like it? Or is there some trick that can make the like be like what's not like it?"

"No, there isn't."

"But doesn't a great necessity force the like, along with the thing like it, to partake of one and the same form?"

"Necessarily."

"But whatever the like things are like by participating in—isn't that the form itself?"

"Entirely so."

"Nothing, then, can be like the form nor can the form be like anything else. Otherwise there will always appear a different form beyond the form; and if that is like anything, another still. And there will never be an end to the genesis of new forms as long as the form becomes like the thing that partakes of it."

"That's most true."

"It's not by likeness, then, that the different things come to partake of forms. Instead it's necessary to seek a different way of partaking."

"It looks that way."

"Do you see then, Socrates," he asked, "how great an impasse lies before anyone who tries to determine that there are forms in themselves?"

"Very much so!"

"And so know well," he said, "that you have, so to speak, not even touched upon how great an impasse there is if you try to posit each form as one, somehow distinguishing them from the be-ings."

"How's that?" he replied.

"There are many different reasons," he an-swered, "but here's the greatest. If someone should argue that the forms themselves—should they be as we say they must be—cannot, prop-erly speaking, be known, no one could prove to whomever argues this that he's mistaken, unless the one arguing chanced to be experienced in many things and not naturally dull. This person would have to be willing to follow the fellow working over the proof through many cases, and over a long distance, otherwise he who forces them to be unknowable would be persuasive."

"Why's that Parmenides?" asked Socrates.

"Because, Socrates, I think that both you and anyone else who posits that there's a certain be-inghood in itself for each thing would first agree that none of them *are* among us."

"How could it still be 'in itself' then?" replied Socrates

"Beautiful," he said. "And so all those ideas are what they are relative to one another have their beinghood relative to themselves and not in relation to the things among us—whether likenesses or, however one posits them, what we partake of and from which, then, we are called by certain names. The things among us, then, these things which take the forms' names, are themselves related only to themselves and not to whatever things are named the same."

"How do you mean that?" asked Socrates.

"Here's an example," said Parmenides. " If one of us is a master or a slave of someone, he is not, of course, as slave to what Master itself is, nor is the master a master of what Slave itself is. Instead, since he's a man, he's both of these to another man. For Mastership itself is what it is of Slavery itself, and likewise Slavery itself is slavery to Mastership itself. The things among us have no power in relation to those things, nor they to us; instead, like I said, those things among us to themselves. Or do you not under-stand what I mean?"

"Oh, I understand well," replied Socrates.

"And so also knowledge. Would what Knowl-edge itself is," he asked, "be knowledge of what Truth itself is?"

"Of course."

"But then what each branch of knowledge is would be knowledge of what each of the beings is, or no?"

"Yes."

"But wouldn't the knowledge among us be of the truth among us; and, in turn, each branch of knowledge among us would have to be knowl-edge of each of the beings among us?"

"Necessarily."

"And yet the forms themselves, as you agree—neither do we possess them nor could they *be* among us."

"No, they couldn't."

"But surely what each of the kinds themselves is, is known by that very form of Knowledge?"

"Yes."

"Which we certainly don't possess."

"No, we don't."

"None of the forms, then, is known by us, since we don't partake of Knowledge itself."

"It doesn't look that way."

"Then what the Beautiful itself is and the Good and all the things that we do suppose to be ideas are known to us."

"I'm afraid so."

"See then something still more terrible than this!"

"What's that?"

"You would probably say that if there *is* in fact a certain kind itself of Knowledge, it is far more precise than the knowledge among us, and the same for Beauty and all the rest."

"Yes."

"And so if anything else does partake of Knowledge itself, wouldn't you say that god, more than anyone else, possesses this most pre-cise knowledge?"

"Necessarily."

"Then will the god, in turn, be able to know the things among us, since he possesses Knowl-edge itself?"

"Why not?"

"Because," said Parmenides, "we agreed, Socrates, that whatever power they do have, those forms have no power relative to the things among us, nor the things among us relative to them. Instead, each group relates only to themselves."

"Yes, this was agreed."

"And so if the god possesses this most precise Mastership and this most precise Knowledge, then their mastership could never master us, nor could their knowledge know us or anything else of the things among us. Likewise, we do not rule over them by the authority among us, nor by our knowledge, do we know anything of the divine. According to this speech, in turn, they are not our masters nor do they know anything of human affairs—since they are gods!"

"But what an altogether wondrous speech, if it strips the god of knowing!"

"Nevertheless, Socrates," said Parmenides, "the forms must, by necessity, have these problems and many more still, if there are these ideas of the beings and if one distinguishes each form on its own. The result is that whoever hears this hits a dead end and argues that these things *are* not; and if, at most, they should *be*, well, then, great necessity keeps them unknown to human nature. And while he says these things this fellow will even seem to be talking sense and, as we said before, he will be wondrously hard to convince. Only a naturally gifted man could learn that there is a certain kind and beinghood, in itself, for each thing; and only a still more wondrous person will discover all these things and be able to teach someone else to judge them clearly and sufficiently for himself."

"I agree with you, Parmenides," Socrates said. "To my mind, you speak well."

"And yet," said Parmenides, "if someone, in turn, Socrates, after focusing on all these problems and others still, shall deny that there are forms of the beings and will not distinguish a certain form of each single thing, wherever he turns he'll understand nothing, since he does not allow that there is an ever-same idea for each of the beings. And so he will entirely destroy the power of dialogue. But you seem to me only too aware of this."

"That's the truth," he replied.

"What then will you do about philosophy? Where will you turn if all this is unknown?"

"At present, at least, I can't seem to see."

"It's because, Socrates," he said, "you are trying too soon, before being trained, to define some Beautiful and Just and Good and each one of the forms I noticed this even the day before yesterday when I overheard your conversation with this fellow Aristotle. Know well: that zeal which drives you towards speeches is beautiful and divine. But you must draw yourself back and train more, while you're still young, in a gymnastic that seems useless and which many call 'idle talk.' If you don't, the truth will escape you."

"What's the manner, Parmenides," he asked, "of this gymnastic?"

"It is what you heard just now from Zeno," he replied. "Except for this, in fact, I really admired you when you were speaking to him, because you wouldn't investigate this perplexity among the visible things nor even in reference to them, but only in reference to what most of all one should grasp by speech and consider forms."

"That's because," he replied," this way, there seems to me no difficulty in showing what beings are like and unlike and experience anything else."

"Beautiful," he said, "But, in addition, you must do this: do not only investigate the results of a hypothesis if each hypothesized thing *is*, but also hypothesize that this same thing *is* not. Do that, if you want to get more gymnastic training."

"What do you mean?" he asked.

"Take, if you like," he said, "this hypothesis that Zeno hypothesized: 'If many *is*, what must result both for the Many themselves in relation to themselves and in relation to the One and for the One both in relation to itself and in relation to the Many?' Then, in turn, if many *is* not, you must inquire what will result both for the One and the Many both in relation to themselves and in relation to each other. And yet again, if you'll hypothesize, 'If Likeness *is*' or *is* not, what in the case of each hypothesis will be the result both for the very things hypothesized and for the different things both in relation to themselves and in relation to each other? And it's the same speech for Unlikeness and Motion and Rest and Generation and Corruption and even *being* itself and *not-being*. In a word, whatever you hypothesize about, whether it *is* or *is* not and whatever other experience it suffers, you must always investigate the results in relation to itself and in relation to each one of the different things, whichever you choose—in relation both to many and to all of them, likewise. And, in turn, whether you hypothesize that what you have hypothesized *is* or *is* not, you must investigate these different things both in relation to themselves and in relation to whatever else you choose, if you intend, after being completely trained, to attain a lordly view of the True."

"It's quite an impossible task, Parmenides, that you're talking about, and I really don't understand it. But why don't you hypothesize something and go through it for me, so that I can understand better?"

"Why, that's a lot of work, Socrates," he replied, "to demand from a man my age!"

"Well then you," said Socrates, "Zeno—why don't you go through it for us?"

And Zeno, he said, said laughing, "Socrates, let's ask Parmenides himself, since it's not, as he says, a trivial thing. Or don't you see how much work you're demanding? If there were more of us, it wouldn't be right to ask. For it's unseemly, especially for someone of his age, to speak such things before the many, since the many do not know that without this digressing and wandering through all things it is impossible to possess a mind that's hit upon the True. And so Parmenides, I join Socrates in asking, that I may also listen after all this time."

Now once Zeno said that, Antiphon said that Pythodorus said that he and Aristotle and the others asked Parmenides to do nothing else than demonstrate what he meant. Then Parmenides

said, "Necessary it is to obey. And yet I seem to be suffering something like that Ibyceian horse, which, as a prizewinner but old, is about to take part in a chariot race and, being experienced, trembles at what is about to happen. Ibycus says that he resembles the horse since, although he is so old and unwilling, Necessity forces him to fall in love. And so I seem quite fearful, since I remember what sort of and how great a multitude of speeches I must swim through at my age. Nevertheless, I must show you this favor, especially since, as Zeno says, we are by ourselves."

"So where will we start and what will we hypothesize first? Or, since now it seems I must play at this worklike game, shall I begin with myself and my hypothesis, that is, hypothesizing about the One itself, whether one *is* or *is* not, what must result?"

"Of course," said Zeno.

"Who then," he asked, "will answer me? How about the youngest? He would be the least trouble and would say exactly what he thinks. And, at the same time, his answers would give me some time to relax."

"I'm ready for you, Parmenides," said Aristotle. "For you mean me if you mean the youngest. Just ask and I'll answer."

So be it, he said. If there's one, then the One could in no way be the many?

How could it?

So it must neither have a part nor be a whole?

Why's that?

Surely the part is a part of the whole —

Yes.

—But what is the whole? Wouldn't a whole be whatever lacks no part?

Of course.

So in both cases the One would consist of parts—if it were a whole or if it had parts.

Necessarily.

Then in both cases, likewise, the One would be many and not one.

True.

But surely it must be one, not many.

It must.

Therefore it will neither be a whole nor have parts—if the One will be one.

It won't.

And so, if the One has no part, it would neither have beginning nor end nor middle. For such things would be its parts.

Right.

And yet beginning and end are certainly a limit to each thing.

How not?

Then the one is limitless, if it has neither beginning nor end.

Limitless.

And without shape, therefore: for it partakes of neither round nor straight.

How's that?

Well round, of course, is that whose extremities on every side hold off equally from the center.

Yes.

And straight, then, is whose middle is in front of both extremities.

That's so.

And so the One would have parts and would be many, if it should partake of either a straight or round shape.

Of course.

Therefore it's neither straight nor round, since, in fact, it has no parts.

Right.

The translation of *Parmenides* (127a–138a) that I have used comes from Albert Keith Whitaker for Focus Publishing. In my suggestions for further reading, I offer some alternative translations to other works by Plato. *This Side of Paradise*, by F. Scott Fitzgerald, and a couple of books of the Bible are also included in order to provide more literary and historical-critical, perhaps spiritual, steerage in the study and gaining of wisdom, as well as principles for conduct and leadership.

Suggested Reading

"Ecclesiastes." *The Bible*. New Revised Standard Version. New York: HarperCollins, 1993.

Fitzgerald, F. Scott. *This Side of Paradise*. New York: Scribner, 1920.

Joyce, James. *A Portrait of the Artist as a Young Man*. London: Penguin, 1993.

Plato. *Meno*. Trans. George Anastaplo and Laurence Berns. Newburyport: Focus Publishing, 2004.

Plato. *Meno*. Trans. G.M.A. Grube. *Plato: Complete Works*. Indianapolis: Hackett Publishing Company, Inc, 1997.

Plato. *Meno*. Trans. W.R.M. Lamb. Cambridge: Harvard University Press, 1999.

Plato. *Parmenides*. Trans. Harold North Fowler. Cambridge: Harvard University Press, 2002.

Plato. *Parmenides* Trans. Mary Louise Gill and Paul Ryan. *Plato: Complete Works*. Indianapolis: Hackett Publishing Company, Inc., 1997.

Plato. *Parmenides*. Trans. Albert Keith Whitaker. Newburyport: Focus Publishing, 1996.

Plato. *Republic*. Trans. G.M.A. Grube, rev. C.D.C. Reeve. Indianapolis: Hackett Publishing Company, Inc., 1992.

"The Letter of James." *The Bible*. New Revised Standard Version. New York: HarperCollins, 1993.

Thucydides. *The Peloponnesian War*. Trans. Steven Lattimore. Indianapolis: Hackett Publishing Company, Inc., 1998.

About the Author

LT Zito has a Bachelor of Arts degree in Religion from The George Washington University, Washington, DC and a Master of Arts degree in Liberal Arts from St. John's College in Annapolis, Maryland. He is a Surface Warfare Officer who has deployed to the Arabian Gulf onboard USS TRENTON (LPD-14) and USS GEORGE WASHINGTON (CVN-73) and is currently Instructor of English at the United States Naval Academy.

6

Honor in Death: Pericles' Address to the Council of Five Hundred

Dr. Joseph J. Thomas

The Athenian general Pericles (495–429 BC) was a son of privilege, an accomplished builder, and patron of Greek theater. Amazingly, his legacy is one of ensuring that power was kept firmly in the hands of the citizens of Athens. He despised tyranny and worked tirelessly to ensure his country was secure and democratic. Greek civilization, in many ways, reached its pinnacle during the Periclean Age. The Athenian Assembly served as a legislative branch of government while the elected Council of Five Hundred served as the executive branch. Jurors were chosen and paid. All citizens, regardless of wealth or family status, had the opportunity to participate in the affairs of government.

Pericles' ability to articulate the delicate balance of rights and responsibilities still stands as a primer for representative democracies. As a warrior, he understood particularly well the responsibility of defending the state from threats. His eulogy for the fallen soldiers of Athens has inspired countless generations of orators tasked with similar patriotic speeches. His concepts are reflected in American history from the language of the Declaration of Independence, to the Gettysburg Address, to the inscription on the tablet held by the Statue of Liberty.

Many of those who have spoken before me on these occasions have commended the author of that law which we now are obeying for having instituted an oration to the honor of those who sacrifice their lives in fighting for their country. For my part, I think it sufficient for men who have proved their virtue in action, by action to be honored for it-by such as you see the public gratitude now performing about this funeral; and that the virtues of many ought not to be endangered by the management of anyone person when their credit must precariously depend on his oration, which may be good and may be bad. . . .

We are happy in a form of government which

cannot envy the laws of our neighbors-for it hath served as a model to others, but is original at Athens. And this our form, as committed not to the few but to the whole body of the people, is called a democracy. How different soever in a private capacity, we all enjoy the same general equality our laws are fitted to preserve; and superior honors just as we excel. The public administration is not confined to a particular family but is attainable only by merit. Poverty is not a hindrance, since whoever is able to serve his country meets with no obstacle to preferment from his first obscurity. The offices of the state we go through without obstructions from one another, and live together in the mutual endearments of private life without suspicions, not angry with a neighbor for following the bent of his own humor, nor putting on that countenance of discontent which pains though it cannot punish—so that in private life we converse without diffidence or damage, while we dare not on any account offend against the public, through the reverence we bear to the magistrates and the laws, chiefly to those enacted for redress of the injured, and to those unwritten, a breach of which is thought a disgrace.

Our laws have further provided for the mind most frequent intermissions of care by the appointment of public recreations and sacrifices throughout the year, elegantly performed with a peculiar pomp, the daily delight of which is a charm that puts melancholy to flight. The grandeur of this our Athens causeth the produce of the whole earth to be imported here, by which we reap a familiar enjoyment, not more of the delicacies of our own growth than of those of other nations.

In the affairs of war we excel those of our enemies, who adhere to methods opposite to our own. For we lay open Athens to general resort, nor ever drive any stranger from us whom either improvement or curiosity hath brought amongst us, let any enemy should hurt us by seeing what is never concealed. We place not so great a confidence in the preparatives and artifices of war as in the native warmth of our souls impelling us to action. In point of education the youth of some peoples are inured, by a course laborious exercise, to support toil and exercise like men, but we, notwithstanding our easy and elegant way of life, face all the dangers of war as intrepidly as they . . .

In our manner of living we show an elegance tempered with frugality, and we cultivate philosophy without enervating the mind. We display our wealth in the season of beneficence, and not in the vanity of discourse. A confession of poverty is disgrace to no man; no effort to avoid it is disgrace indeed. There is visible in the same persons an attention to their own private concerns and those of the public; and in others engaged in the labors of life there is a competent skill in the affairs of government. For we are the only people who think him that does not meddle in state affairs not indolent but good for nothing. And yet we pass the soundest judgments and are quick at catching the right apprehensions of things, not thinking that words are prejudicial to actions, but rather the not being duly prepared by previous debate before we are obliged to proceed to execution. Herein consists our distinguishing excellence, that in the hour of action we show the greatest courage, and yet debate beforehand the expediency of our measures. The courage of others is the result of ignorance; deliberation makes them cowards. And those undoubtedly must be owned to have the greatest souls, who, most acutely sensible of the miseries of war and the sweets of peace, are not hence in the least deterred from facing danger.

In acts of beneficence, further, we differ from the many. We preserve friends not by receiving, but by conferring, obligations. For he who does a kindness hath the advantage over him who, by the law of gratitude, becomes a debtor to his benefactor. The person obliged is compelled to act the more insipid part, conscious that a return of kindness is merely a payment and not an obligation. And we alone are splendidly beneficent to others, not so much from interested motives as for the credit of pure liberality. I shall sum up what yet remains by only adding that our

Athens in general is the school of Greece, and that every single Athenian amongst us is excellently formed, by his personal qualification, for all the various scenes of active life, acting with a most graceful demeanor and a most ready habit of dispatch. That I have not on this occasion made use of a pomp of words, but the truth of facts, that height to which by such a conduct this state hath risen, is an undeniable proof. For we are now the only people of the world who are found by experience to be greater than in report. . . .

In the just defense of such a state, these victims of their own valor, scorning the ruin threatened to it, have valiantly fought and bravely died. And every one of those who survive is ready, I am persuaded, to sacrifice life in such a cause. And for this reason have I enlarged so much on national points, to give the clearest proof that in the present war we have more at stake than men whose public advantages are not so valuable, and to illustrate, by actual evidence, how great a commendation is due to them who are now my subject, and the greatest part of which they have already received. For the encomiums with which I have celebrated the state have been earned for it by the bravery of these and of men like these. And such compliments might be thought too high and exaggerated if passed on any Greeks but them alone.

The fatal period to which these gallant souls are now reduced is the surest evidence of their merit-an evidence begun in their lives and completed in their deaths. For it is a debt of justice to pay superior honors to men who have devoted their lives in fighting for their country, though inferior to others in every virtue but that of valor. Their last service effaceth all former demerits-it extends to the public; their private demeanors reached only to a few. Yet not one of these was at all induced to shrink from danger, through fondness of those delights which the peaceful affluent life bestows-not one was the less lavish of his life, through that flattering hope attendance upon want, that poverty at length might be exchanged for affluence. One passion

there was in their minds much stronger than these-the desire of vengeance on their enemies. Regarding this as the most honorable prize of dangers, they boldly rushed towards the mark to glut revenge and then to satisfy those secondary passions. The uncertain event they had already secured in hope; what their eyes showed plainly must be done they trusted their own valor to accomplish, thinking it more glorious to defend themselves and die in the attempt than to yield and live. From the reproach of cowardice, indeed, they fled, but presented their bodies to the shock of battle; when, insensible of fear, but triumphing in hope, in the doubtful charge they instantly dropped-and thus discharged the duty which brave men owed to their country.

As for you, who now survive them, it is your business to pray for a better fate, but to think it your duty also to preserve the same spirit and warmth of courage against your enemies; not judging of the expediency of this from a mere harangue-where any man indulging a flow of words may tell you what you yourselves know as well as he, how many advantages there are in fighting valiantly against your enemies-but, rather, making the daily-increasing grandeur of this community the object of your thoughts and growing quite enamored of it. And when it really appears great to your apprehensions, think again that this grandeur was acquired by brave and valiant men, by men who knew their duty, and in the moments of action were sensible of shame-who, whenever their attempts were unsuccessful thought it no dishonor for their country to stand in need of anything their valor could do for it, and so made it the most glorious present. Bestowing thus their lives on the public, they have every one received a praise that will never decay, a sepulcher that will always be most illustrious-not that in which their bones lie moldering, but that in which their fame is preserved, to be on every occasion, when honor is the employ of either word or act, eternally remembered.

For the whole earth is the sepulcher of illustrious men; nor is it the inscription on the columns in their native land alone that shows their merit, but the memorial of them, better than all inscriptions in every foreign nation, reposited more durably in universal remembrance than on their own tombs. From this very moment, emulating these noble patterns, placing your happiness in liberty, and liberty in valor, be prepared to encounter all the dangers of war. For to be lavish of life is not so noble in those whom misfortunes have reduced to misery and despair, as in men who hazard the loss of a comfortable subsistence and the enjoyment of all the blessings this world affords by an unsuccessful enterprise. Adversity, after a series of ease and affluence, sinks deeper into the heart of a man of spirit than the stroke of death insensibly received in the vigor of life and public hope.

For this reason, the parents of those who are now gone, whoever of them may be attending here, I do not bewail-I shall rather comfort. . . . I know it in truth a difficult task to fix comfort in those breasts which will have frequent remembrances, in seeing the happiness of others, of what they once themselves enjoyed. And sorrow flows not from the absence of those good things we have never yet experienced but from the loss of those to which we have been accustomed. . . . But you, whose age is already far advanced, compute the greater share of happiness your longer time hath afforded for so much gain, persuaded in yourselves the remainder will be but short, and enlighten that space by the glory gained by these. It is greatness of soul alone that never grows old, nor is it wealth that delights in the latter stage of life, as some give out, so much as honor. To you, the sons and brothers of the deceased, whatever number of you are here, a field of hardy contention is opened. For him who no longer is, everyone is ready to commend, so that to whatever height you push your deserts, you will scarce ever be thought to equal but to be somewhat inferior to these. Envy will exert itself against a competitor while life remains; but when death stops the competition, affection will applaud without restraint.

If after this it be expected from me to say anything to you who are now reduced to a state of widowhood, about female virtue, I shall express it all in one short admonition: it is your greatest glory not to be deficient in the virtue peculiar to your sex, and to give men as little handle as possible to talk of your behavior, whether well or ill.

I have now discharged the province allotted me by the laws, and said what I thought most pertinent to this assembly. Our departed friends have by facts been already honored. Their children from this day till they arrive at manhood shall be educated at the public expense of the state which hath appointed so beneficial a meed for these and all future relics of the public contests. For wherever the greatest rewards are proposed for virtue, there the best of patriots are ever to be found. Now let everyone respectively indulge in becoming grief for his departed friends, and then retire.

Suggested Readings

Hopkinson, Leslie W. *Greek Leaders*. Boston, New York: Houghton Mifflin Company, 1918.

Plutarch. *Lives*. Cambridge: Harvard University Press, 1959.

7

Expeditionary Leadership: Xenophon's The Persian Expedition

Dr. Joseph J. Thomas

To generations of students of military leadership, the Greek title of *The Persian Expedition*, the *Anabasis* (literally "the journey up"), calls to mind ten thousand sturdy Greek soldiers, ably led by Xenophon, tackling and conquering countless challenges in their journey to "The Sea! The Sea!" Unfortunately, classical literature as a vehicle for teaching leadership has become increasingly eclipsed by managerial and personal effectiveness theory. *The Persian Expedition* today is read almost exclusively by students of classical history and not by students of leadership.

The Persian Expedition serves as an instructive primer on hardships faced and hardships conquered, of loyalty, initiative, adaptability, and leadership by example. The expedition takes place between 401 BC and March 399 BC, but its lessons are timeless. The Greeks encounter conventional war, insurgencies, terrorism, unforgiving weather, unfriendly local populations, and an unappreciative home front on their journey back to their beloved home—themes that may sound familiar to veterans of Vietnam or Operation Iraqi Freedom. The more we read Xenophon the more we realize the face of battle and the political realities of war remain virtually unchanged.

Xenophon, among the first in a line of distinguished warrior-authors, chronicles the hardships of campaigning with unflinching detail. In classic Greek fashion, he describes how reason and personal courage command the respect of soldiers far more than positional authority or seniority. The Ten Thousand Greeks behave in many ways like a modern division of American Marines or soldiers fighting on principle rather than at the behest of a sovereign. The Greeks themselves were but mercenaries, employed by Cyrus the Younger in his quest to unseat his brother Artaxerxes II from the throne of Persia. After Cyrus is killed at the battle of Cunaxa, the very reason for Greek participation is lost and the Ten Thousand find themselves deep in enemy territory. When the Spartan Clearchus and other generals are killed, it falls to Xenophon (among a few others) to lead his countrymen "up" to the Black Sea for safe passage back to Greece.

The Persian Expedition has inspired generations of historians chronicling of the exploits of determined, well-led soldiers facing down great odds to accomplish their mission. The fighting withdrawal of the 1st Marine Division from the "Frozen Chosin" Resevoir in Northern Korea has been compared to Xenophon's Anabasis. More recently, Bing West and MajGen Ray Smith's *The March Up: Taking Baghdad with the 1st Marine Division* drew its primary inspiration from Xenophon's classic work. *The Persian Expedition* will doubtlessly continue as the standard account of soldierly perseverance and military leadership. No officer's preparation is complete without an introduction to this important book.

* * *

Next day they decided that they ought to get away as fast as they could before the native army could reassemble and occupy the pass. They packed their belongings at once and, taking a number of guides with them, set off through the deep snow. From here a march of forty-five miles through desert country brought them to the river Euphrates, which they crossed without getting wet beyond their navel. The source of the river was said to be not far from here.

The third day's march was a hard one, with a north wind blowing into their faces, cutting into absolutely everything like a knife and freezing people stiff. One of the soothsayers then proposed making a sacrifice to the wind and his suggestion was carried out. It was agreed by all that there was then a distinct falling off in the violence of the wind. The snow was six feet deep and many of the animals and slaves perished in it., as did about thirty of the soldiers. They kept their fires going all night, as there was plenty of wood in the place where they camped, though those who came up late got no wood. The ones who had arrived before and had lit the fires would not let the late-comers approach their fire

unless they gave them a share of their corn or any other foodstuff they had. So each shared with the other party what he had. When the fires were made, great pits were formed reaching down to the ground as the snow melted. This gave one a chance of measuring the depth of the snow.

Soldiers who had lost the use of their eyes through snow blindness or whose toes had dropped off from frostbite were left behind. It was a relief to the eyes against snow blindness if one held something black in front of the eyes while marching; and it was a help to the feet if one kept on the move and never stopped still, and took off one's shoes at night. If one slept with one's shoes on, the straps sank into the flesh and the soles of the shoes froze to the feet. This was the more likely to happen since, when their old shoes were worn out, they had made themselves shoes of undressed leather from the skins of oxen that had just been flayed…

It seemed safe for the troops to take up their quarters in the villages. Christophus stayed where he was, and the other officers drew lots for the villages which were in sight, and each went with his men to the one he got. On this occasion Polycrates, an Athenian captain, asked to leave to go on independently and, taking with him the men who were quickest on their feet, ran to the village which had been allotted to Xenophon and surprised all the villagers, with their headman, inside the walls, together with seventeen colts which were kept there for tribute to the king, and the headman's daughter, who had been married only nine days ago. Her husband had gone out to hunt hares and was not captured in the village.

The houses were built underground; the entrances were like wells, but they broadened out lower down. There were tunnels dug in the ground for animals, while the men went down by ladder. Inside the houses there were goats, sheep, cows and poultry with their young. All these animals were fed on food that was kept inside the houses. There was also wheat, barley, beans and barley wine in great bowls. The actual grains of barley floated on top of the bowls, level with the brim, and in the bowls there were reeds of various sizes and without joints in them. When one was thirsty, one was meant to take a reed and suck the wine into one's mouth. It was a very strong wine, unless one mixed it with water, and, when one got used to it, it was a very pleasant drink.

Xenophon invited the chief of the village to have supper with him, and told him to be of good heart, as he was not going to be deprived of his children, and that if he showed himself capable of doing the army a good turn until they reached another tribe, they would restock his house with provisions when they went away. He promised to co-operate and, to show his good intentions, told them of where some wine was buried. So for that night all the soldiers were quartered in the villages and slept there with all sorts of food around them, sitting a guard over the headman of the village and keeping a watchful eye on his children too.

On the next day Xenophon visited Chirisophus and took the headman with him. Whenever he went past a village he turned into it to see those who were quartered there. Everywhere he found them feasting and merry-making, and they would invariably refuse to let him go before they had given him something for breakfast. In every single case they would have on the table lamb, kid, pork, veal, and chicken, and a number of loaves, both wheat and barley. When anyone wanted, as a gesture of friendship, to drink to a friend's health, he would drag him to a huge bowl, over which he would have to lean, sucking up the drink like an ox. They invited the headman too to take what he liked, but he refused their invitations, only, if he caught sight of any of his relatives, he would take them along with him.

When they came to Chirisophus, they found his men also feasting, with wreaths of hay round their heads, and with Armenian boys in native dress waiting on them. They showed the boys what to do by signs, as though they were deaf mutes. After greeting each other, Chirisophus and Xenophon together interrogated the headman through the interpreter who spoke Persian, and asked him what country this was. He replied that it was Armenia. Then they asked him for whom the horses were being kept, and he said that they were a tribute paid to the King. The next country, he said, was the land of the Chalybes, and he told them the way there.

Xenophon then went away and took the headman back to his own people. He gave him back the horse (rather an old one) which he had taken, and told him to fatten it up and sacrifice it. This was because he had heard it was sacred to the Sun and he was afraid that it might die, as the journey had done it no good. He took some of the colts himself, and gave one colt each to the generals and captains. The horses in this part of the world were smaller than the Persian horses, but much more finely bred. The headman told the Greeks to tie small bags round the feet of the horses and baggage animals whenever they made them go through snow, as, without these bags, they sank in up to their bellies . . .

Then came a seven days' march of a hundred and fifty miles through the country of the Chalybes. These were the most warlike of all the tribes on their way, and they fought with the Greeks at close quarters. They had body armour of linen, reaching down to the groin, and instead of skirts to their armor they wore thick twisted cords. They also wore greaves and helmets, and carried on their belts a knife of about the size of a Spartan dagger. With these knives they cut the throats of those they managed to overpower, and then cut off their heads and carry them as they marched, singing and dancing whenever their enemies were likely to see them. They also carried a spear with one point, about twenty feet long. They used to stay inside their settlements, and then, when the Greeks had gone past, they would follow behind and were always re4ady for a fight. They had their houses in fortified positions, and brought all their provisions inside the fortifications. Consequently, the Greeks could take nothing from them, but lived on the supplies which they had seized from the Taochi.

The Greeks arrived next at the river Harpasus

which was four hundred feet across. Then they marched through the territory of the Scytheni, a four days' march of sixty miles over level ground until they came to some villages, where they stayed for three days and renewed their stocks and provisions. Then a march of sixty miles brought them to a large, prosperous and inhabited city, which was called Gymnias. The governor of the country sent the Greeks a guide from this city, with the idea that he should lead them through country which was at war with his own people. When the guide arrived, he said that in five days he would lead them to a place from which they could see the sea; and he said he was ready to be put to death f he failed to do so. So he led the way, and, when they had crossed the border into his enemies' country, he urged them to burn and lay waste to the land, thus making it clear that it was for this purpose that he had come to them, and not because of any goodwill to the Greeks.

They came to the mountain on the fifth day, the name of the mountain being Thekes. When the men in front reached the summit and caught sight of the sea there was great shouting. Xenophon and the rearguard heard it and thought that there were some more enemies attacking in the front, since there were natives of the country they had ravaged following them up behind, and the rearguard had killed some of them and made prisoners of others in an ambush, and captured about twenty raw ox hide shields, with the hair on. However, when the shouting got louder and drew nearer, and those who were constantly going forward started running towards the men in front who kept on shouting, and the more there were of them the more shouting there was, it looked then like it was something of considerable importance. So Xenophon mounted his horse and, taking lycus

and the cavalry with him, rode forward to give support, and quite soon, the soldiers shouting out, 'The sea! The sea!' and passing the word down the column. Then certainly they all began to run, the rearguard and all, and drove on the baggage anumals and the horses at full speed; and when they had all got to the top, the soldiers, with tears in their eyes, embraced each other and their generals and captains. In a moment, at somebody or other's suggestion, they collected stones and made a great pile of them. On top they put a lot of raw ox-hides and staves and shields which they had captured. The guide himself cut the shields into pieces and urged the others to do so too. Afterwards the Greeks sent the guide back and gave him as presents from the common store a horse, and a silver cup and a Persian robe and ten darics. What he particularly wanted was the rings which the soldiers had and he got a number of these from them. He pointed out to them a village where they could camp, and showed them the road by which they had to go to the country of the Macrones. It was then evening and he went away, traveling by night.

Suggested Reading

Arrian. *Anabasis Alexandria: Books I-IV.* Cambridge: Harvard University Press, 1976.

Herodotus. *The Histories.* Oxford: Oxford University Press, 1998.

Plutarch. *The Rise and Fall of Athens: Nine Greek Lives.* Harmondsworth: Penguin Books, 1960.

Thucydides. *History of the Peloponnesian War.* New York: W.W. Norton & Co., 1998.

Xenophon, *The Persian Expedition.* New York: Penguin Classics (Rex Warner translation), 1972.

8

Death Stands Close Upon Us Now: Steven Pressfield's Gates of Fire

Shannon E. French, Ph.D.

The centerpiece of this book discussion is not the usual scholarly volume or collection of essays, but rather a compelling work of historical fiction that raises timeless issues concerning military leadership, training, and values. The novel *Gates of Fire*, by Steven Pressfield, depicts the heroic, desperate stand of three hundred Spartans and their allies against an overwhelming force of Persians at the narrow pass of Thermopylae in 480 B.C. The Spartans fought to the last man in a crucial delaying action that allowed the rest of the Greeks to pull together and defeat the invading Persians decisively at the battles of Salamis and Plataea. Against the backdrop of the Spartans' unflinching sacrifice, Pressfield explores matters of lasting significance for those who serve in the military, such as: the need for warriors to find a way to hold on to their humanity and successfully transition out of their warfighting roles, the true definition of courage, the importance of the bonds among comrades-in-arms, appreciation for the strength of the spouses and families of warriors and for their vital contributions, and the obligations of political leaders to understand the military and deploy troops responsibly.

Facing the horrors of war puts at risk the precious humanity of the men and women we ask to do our fighting for us. They must both witness and cause unspeakable carnage. In order to survive, they often have to suppress normal human emotions, blocking impulses of fear, pity, and disgust until their enemy surrenders and the rules suddenly change. Then they must somehow reach inside themselves and reconnect with their ability to recognize their now disarmed opponents as individuals with rights who should be treated with dignity and respect (and even given aid if they are injured).

Many modern military missions blend traditional combat objectives with humanitarian goals, so that our warriors must not only snap out of their aggressive mode when a particular firefight concludes, but must transition continually between warfighting and peacekeeping, between taking lives and trying to improve them. And should they survive the conflict, our warriors must make yet another transition: from the chaos of combat to the steady grind of civilian life. They must remember how to be husbands and wives, how to be gentle with their children, and how to manage frustration, boredom, and stress without erupting into fits of rage or violence.

In *Gates of Fire*, Pressfield has his Spartan warriors perform a ritual before they go into battle. Each man carves his name twice on a wooden "ticket," and then breaks the ticket in half so that both halves bear his name. One half is kept in safety while the warrior wears the other half into battle, tied to his wrist like an ancient version of a G.I.'s 'dog tags'. Pressfield has his Leonidas, the Spartan king, explain the significance of the ritual, beyond its practical purpose of aiding identification of the fallen:

> When a man seats before his eyes the bronze face of his helmet and steps off from the line of departure, he divides himself, as he divides his 'ticket', in two parts. One part he leaves behind. That part which takes delight in his children, which lifts his voice in the chorus, which clasps his wife to him in the sweet darkness of their bed. That half of him, the best part, a man sets aside and leaves behind. . . . When a man joins the two pieces of his ticket [after surviving a battle] and sees them weld together, he feels that part of him, the part that knows love and mercy and compassion, come flooding back over him. (pp. 131–132)

Today, we need our warriors to be able to keep both halves of their 'tickets' close, so they are never too far removed from the better part of themselves. We want them to retain their humanity even as they accomplish their missions, and then be able to return to their homes as whole people, still capable of enjoying what they have labored to defend.

In order for warriors to survive combat morally, mentally, and physically, they must possess the virtue of courage in all its forms, from the courage needed to stand fast when the enemy attacks to the courage it takes to remain true to a code of conduct under the harshest duress. Pressfield's Spartan warriors and their allies certainly recognize the importance of courage. Pressfield weaves through the novel a continuing debate about the meaning and source of courage. The characters try to agree on a definition of courage, and they settle for a time on "the opposite of fear." (p. 264) This does not satisfy the warrior-philosopher Dienekes, however, and he presses them to flesh out what the opposite of fear really is:

> To call it *aphobia*, fearlessness, is without meaning. This is just a name, thesis expressed as antithesis. . . . How does one conquer fear of death, that most primordial of terrors, which resides in our very blood, as in all life, beasts as well as men? (p. 265)

Finally, a slave named Suicide who fights with the Spartans strikes upon the answer that Dienekes sought:

> What can be more noble than to slay oneself? Not literally. Not with a blade in the guts. But to extinguish the selfish self within, that part which looks only to its own preservation, to save its own skin. . . . When a warrior fights not for himself, but for his brothers, when his most passionately sought goal is neither glory nor his own life's preservation, but to spend his substance for them, his comrades, not to abandon them, not to prove unworthy of them, then his heart truly has achieved contempt for death, and with that he transcends himself and his actions touch the sublime. (pp. 378–379)

After hearing Suicide's description of the bonds of absolute trust that form among warriors, giving them the strength to overcome their basic instincts of self-preservation, "The opposite of fear," Dienekes said, "is love." (p. 380).

The conclusion to which Pressfield brings his fictional Spartans is the same that has been reached by innumerable real-life warriors throughout history: the warrior's courage comes from the love he feels for his fellow warriors. It is this truth that makes sense of the persisting practice of retrieving the corpses of fallen comrades, even when doing so puts more lives as risk. To leave men behind is to break faith with them or with their memories, and that faith in each other is in fact essential to the warriors' survival.

Another enduring form of courage Pressfield examines in *Gates of Fire* is the courage of those who stay behind and send their loved ones off to war. In a wrenching description of the warriors' departure from Sparta, Pressfield has his King Leonidas pay tribute to the courage of the women who must remain in the city, aware that they are not likely to see their loved ones ever again:

> "Death stands close upon us now," the king spoke. "Can you feel him, brothers? I do. I am human and I fear him. My eyes cast about for a sight to fortify the heart for that moment when I come to look him in the face. . . . Shall I tell you where I find this strength, friends? . . . My heart finds courage from these, our women, who watch in tearless silence as we go. . . . Men's pain is lightly borne and swiftly over. Our wounds are of the flesh, which is nothing; women's is of the heart—sorrow unending, far more bitter to bear." (pp. 240–241)

Pressfield returns to this theme of the valor of the warriors' loved ones near the end of the book, when he has his King Leonidas speak to one Spartan woman whose husband and son have both been selected to be among the doomed three hundred who will defend the Thermopylae pass. Leonidas explains to her why he chose these particular three hundred warriors from all the men in Sparta:

> I chose them not for their own valor, lady, but for that of their women. . . . When the battle is over, when the Three Hundred have gone down to death, then will all Greece look to the Spartans, to see how they bear it. But who, lady, who will the Spartans look to? To you. To you and the other wives and mothers, sisters and daughters of the fallen. If they behold your hearts riven and broken with grief, they, too, will break. And Greece will break with them. . . . Why have I nominated you, lady, to bear up beneath this most terrible of trials, you and your sisters of the Three Hundred? Because you can. (pp. 426–427)

Today, both men and women serve in the militaries of many nations, on lengthy and dangerous deployments all over the world, leaving behind husbands and fathers as well as wives, mothers, and children. Although we hope these service members are not being sent to certain death like the Three Hundred, the risks are nevertheless great and some we know will be asked to make the ultimate sacrifice. Modern leaders must attempt, like Pressfield's Leonidas, to gage the courage and commitment not only of their troops but also of their families. How much separation can military families bear, and how much loss can the homefront endure before a nation's will to remain in any given conflict is eroded to such an extent that all support for the leadership and its policies dissolves into nothing? That is the practical, political question. The moral question is: How much does any nation have a right to ask of its military families and what must be at stake before leaders should be willing to risk pushing the limits of those families' endurance?

Pressfield raises a further issue about leadership in times of war that is unquestionably relevant in today's world. He asks what obligation leaders have to understand the military—who its members are, how they feel, how they train and what they do. Can a commander who is too distanced from his forces ever deploy them responsibly?

Pressfield's Spartans have nothing but disdain for the Persian king, Xerxes—not because he is the leader of their enemies, but because he is not a warrior himself. At Thermopylae, Xerxes sets himself up to view to view the battle from a cushioned throne on top of a tall platform, like a wealthy spectator at a sporting event, in some ancient equivalent of 'luxury sky box' in a stadium:

> High above the armies, a man of between thirty and forty years could be descried plainly, in robes of purple fringed with gold, mounting the platform and assuming his station upon the throne. The distance was perhaps eight hundred feet, up and back, but even at that range it was impossible to mistake the Persian monarch's surpassing handsomeness and nobility of stature. Nor could the supreme self-assurance of his carriage be misread even at this distance. He looked like a man come to watch an entertainment. A pleasantly diverting show, one whose outcome was foreordained and yet which promised a certain level of amusement. He took his seat. A sunshade was adjusted by his servants. We could see a table of refreshments placed at his side and, upon his left, several writing desks set into place, each manned by a secretary. (p. 282)

In contrast, the Spartan king Leonidas fights and dies with his men, down in the dirt alongside them. He inspires this defiant description of what it is to be a king:

> "A king does not abide within his tent while his men bleed and die upon the field.

A king does not dine while his men go hungry, nor sleep when they stand at watch up on the wall. A king does not command his men's loyalty through fear nor purchase it with gold; he earns their love by the sweat of his own back and the pains he endures for their sake. That which comprises the harshest burden, a king lifts first and sets down last. A king does not require service of those he leads but provides it to them. He serves them, not they him. . . . A king does not expend his substance to enslave men, but by his conduct and example makes them free." (p. 412–413)

Most nations no longer expect their political leaders literally to lead their troops into battle. Yet there is an ongoing debate concerning whether it is appropriate for a man or woman with no combat experience at all to serve as Commander-in-Chief and order others into combat. In the United States, this matter became a heated campaign issue for the 2004 presidential elections, where decorated combat veterans such as John Kerry and Wesley Clark wished to unseat incumbent George W. Bush, whose record of service with the National Guard had been called into question. Others raise a broader concern that there is within many powerful nations a growing divide between military and civilian subcultures, so that warriors and those whose interests they are charged to defend no longer understand or appreciate one another. The Spartan model depicted by Pressfield in which every citizen is also a soldier represents the opposite extreme, with its own advantages and serious perils. As such, it provides a valuable counterpoint for those seeking an ideal balance in civil-military relations.

Pressfield's *Gates of Fire* closes with the famous inscription on an ancient memorial to the Spartan heroes at Thermopylae: "Go tell the Spartans, stranger passing by, that here obedient to their laws we lie." (p.440) These words provoke an unanswerable question: how might the history of Western civilization have been different if the Three Hundred had not held their ground that day at the 'hot gates'? In his historical note before the first chapter, Pressfield asserts that if the Spartan force had failed it is unlikely the Greeks would have been able to "preserve the beginnings of Western democracy and freedom from perishing in the cradle." Thus Pressfield's novel serves as a powerful reminder of the fragility of the systems and values on which so many now depend.

Suggested Readings

Bellamy, Alex. *Just Wars*. Cambridge: Polity Press, 2006.

Cook, Martin L. *The Moral Warrior: Ethics and Service in the U.S. Military*. Albany, New York: State University of New York Press, 2004.

French, Shannon E. *The Code of the Warrior: Exploring Warrior Values, Past and Present*. New York: Rowman and Littlefield Publishers, 2003.

Grossman, Lt.Col. Dave. *On Killing: The Psychological Cost of Learning to Kill in War and Society*. New York: Little, Brown, and Company, 1996.

Osiel, Mark. *Obeying Orders: Atrocity, Military Discipline, and the Law of War*. New Brunswick and London: Transaction Publishers, 1999.

Shay, Jonathan. *Achilles in Vietnam: Combat Trauma and the Undoing of Character*. New York: Simon and Schuster, 1994.

About the Author

Associate Professor Shannon E. French earned her Ph.D. in philosophy from Brown University in 1997 and currently teaches in the department of Leadership, Ethics, and Law at the United States Naval Academy. She is the author of *The Code of the Warrior: Exploring Warrior Values, Past and Present* (Rowman and Littlefield Publishers, 2003), and numerous other works in military ethics.

9

Leadership from the Front: Plutarch's Lives ("Alexander")

Dr. Joseph J. Thomas

Plutarch's *Lives* contains one of few extant "primary" histories of the life of Alexander. As such, it is considered to be among the most reliable and valuable resources on the greatest military leader in the ancient world. Plutarch himself was educated in the classical (Platonic) style at Athens and chronicled the lives of prominent Greek and Roman statesmen, warriors, and nobles. The following excerpt provides a window into the very point at which Alexander achieved his greatest conquest, his climactic victory over his Persian nemesis Darius. The passage also provides insight on Alexander's personal leadership style and method for success.

* * *

On this occasion Alexander gave a long address to the Thessalians and the rest of the Greeks. They acclaimed by shouting for him to lead them against the barbarians, and at this he shifted his lance into his left hand, so Callisthenes tells us, and raising his right he called upon the gods and prayed that if he were really the son of Zeus they should protect and encourage the Greeks. Then Aristander the diviner, who was wearing a white robe and a crown of gold, rode along the ranks and pointed out to the men an eagle which hovered for a while over Alexander's head and then flew straight towards the enemy. The sight acted as an immediate inspiration to the watching troops, and with shouts of encouragement to one another the cavalry charged the enemy at full speed and the phalanx rolled forward like a flood. Before the leading ranks could engage, the barbarians began to fall back, hotly pursued by Alexander, who drove the retreating enemy towards the centre, where Darius was stationed.

Alexander had sighted his adversary through the ranks of the royal squadron of cavalry, as they waited drawn up in deep formation in front of him. Darius was a tall and handsome man and he towered conspicuously above this large and superbly equipped body of horsemen, who were closely massed to guard the lofty chariot in which he stood. But the horseguards were seized with panic at the terrible sight of Alexander bearing down upon them and driving the fugitives before him against those who still held their ground, and the greater number of them broke and scattered. The bravest and most highly born, however, stood fast and were slaughtered in front of their king: they fell upon one another in heaps, and in their dying struggles they clung to the legs of horses and riders, entwining themselves about them so as to hinder the pursuit. As for Darius, all the horrors of the battle were now before his eyes. The forces which had been stationed in the centre for his protection had now been driven back upon him: it had become difficult to turn his chariot round and drive it away, since the wheels were encumbered and entangled with heaps of bodies, and the horses which were surrounded and almost covered by the dead began to rear and plunge so that the charioteer could not control them. In this extremity the king abandoned his chariot and his armour, mounted a mare which, so the story goes, had recently foaled, and rode away. It is believed that he would not have escaped at that moment, had not Parmenio sent another party of horsemen begging Alexander to come to his rescue, because he was engaged with a strong enemy force which still held together and would not give way.

In this battle Parmenio is generally accused of having been sluggish and lacking in spirit, either because old age had dulled his courage, or because he had become envious of the authority and pomp, to use Callisthenes' words, which Alexander now displayed. Alexander was vexed by this appeal for help, but at the time he did not reveal to his men the fact that it had been made. Instead he ordered the recall to be sounded on the ground that it was growing dark and that he wished to bring the slaughter to an end. Then as he rode back to the part of the field where Par-

menio's troops were supposedly threatened, he learned on his way that the enemy had been utterly defeated and put to flight.

After the battle had ended in this way, the authority of the Persian empire was regarded as having been completely overthrown. Alexander was proclaimed king of Asia and after offering splendid sacrifices to the gods, he proceeded to reward his friends with riches, estates and governorships. As he wished to increase his prestige in the Greek world, he wrote to the states saying that all tyrannies were now abolished and that henceforth they might live under their own laws: to the Plataeans in particular he wrote that he would rebuild their city because their ancestors had allowed the Greeks to make their territory the seat of war in the struggle for their common freedom. He also sent a share of the spoils to the people of Croton in Italy in honour of the spirit and valour shown by their athlete Phayllus: this man, when the rest of the Greeks in Italy had refused to give any help to their compatriots in the Persian wars, had fitted out a ship at his own expense and sailed with it to Salamis to share in the common danger. Such was Alexander's desire to pay tribute to any manifestation of courage and to prove himself the friend and guardian of noble actions.

Suggested Readings

Goldhill, Simon. *Aeschylus, the Oresteia*. Cambridge: Cambridge University Press, 1992.

Livy. *The Early History of Rome (Books I–V)*. Harmondsworth: Penguin, 1971.

Plutarch. *Lives*. Cambridge: Harvard University Press, 1959.

Plutarch. *The Rise and Fall of Athens: Nine Greek Lives*. Harmondsworth: Penguin Books, 1960.

Suetonius. *Lives of the Twelve Caesars*. New York: Welcome Rain, 2001.

10

Maxims of War: Instruction from Alexander the Great in Steven Pressfield's Virtues of War

CDR Mary Kelly, USN

Alexander the Great assumed the Macedonian throne from his father, Philip II, at the age of twenty, but he had already proven himself in battle at Chaerona. Known to the Greeks as Alexander Poliorcetes, the "Sacker of Cities" he fought his greatest battles and conquered the Persian Empire before he was twenty-five. When he died at thirty-two, he had never known defeat in battle. Alexander the Great (356–323 BC) was known as a fearless wartime commander, and a passionate leader. He relentlessly pursued enemies and seized their territory. Yet his quest for more land, power and glory ultimately led to the failure of his health and the loss of countless lives. The vast and diverse territory proved difficult to rule, and after his death, the region fragmented. But there is no denying that Alexander the Great, as the Romans called him, was a charismatic leader who knew how to mobilize forces and vanquish enemies.

The historic novel *Virtues of War*, authored by Steven Pressfield, is the story of Alexander the Great from an autobiographical perspective. Readers feel as though they are reading the private diary and sharing the personal thoughts and adventures of Alexander the Great. Pressfield's meticulous research on life in Macedonia and battles brings this period of history to life, and makes *Virtues of War* an exciting recounting of leadership almost 2500 years ago.

This section is Alexander the Great allowing a page access to his correspondence with his generals and leaders, instructing them on tactics, strategy, ideology and philosophy. There is strident force, empathetic compassion, and humor.

Nineteen

MAXIMS OF WAR

You have spent nine months now, Itanes, as a Page in my service. Time to emerge from the womb, don't you think?

Yes, you shall have your commission. You shall soon lead men in battle. Don't grin broadly! For my eye will be on you, as on every cadet who graduates from the academy of war that is my tent.

It has been your privilege, these months since your acceptance into the corps in Afghanistan, to attend upon commanders of such genius as warfare has seldom seen. The officers whose meat you carve and wine you pour-Hephaestion and Craterus, Perdiccas, Ptolemy, Seleucus, Coenus, Polyperchon, Lysimachus, not to say Parmenio, Philotas, and Nicanor, Antigonus One-Eye, and Antipater, whom you have not had the fortune of knowing-each stands in his own right with the great captains of history. Now I require of you the same fidelity I demand of them. You must incorporate the conventions and principles by which this army fights. Why? Because once battle is joined, I shall be where I can control nothing beyond the division immediately under my hand, and, in the inevitable chaos, will barely be able to direct even that. You must command on your own, my young lieutenant, but how you do so cannot be random or idiosyncratic; it must follow my thought and my will. This why we talk here nightlong, my generals and I, and why you and the other Pages attend and listen. That is why we rehearse fundamentals over and over, until they become second nature to us all.

I have asked Eumenes, my Counsel of War, to make correspondence of mine available to you. Study these letters as if they were lessons in school, but hold this foremost in mind: The pupil may differ with his tutor, the cadet never. What I set in your hands this night is law. Follow it and no force can stand against you. Defy it and I will not need to settle with you, for the foe will already have done so.

On Philosophy of War

TO PTOLEMY, AT EPHESUS:

Always attack. Even in defense, attack. The attacking arm possesses the initiative and this commands the action. To attacks makes men brave; to defend makes them timorous. If I learn that an office of mine has assumed a defensive posture in the field, that office will never hold command under me again.

TO PTOLEMY, IN EGYPT:

When deliberating, think in campaigns and not battles; in wars and no campaigns; in ultimate conquest and not wars.

TO PEDICCAS, FROM TYRE:

Seek the decisive battle. What good does it do us to win ten scraps of no consequence if we lose the one that counts? I want to fight battles that decide the fate of empires.

TO SELEUCUS, IN EGYPT:

It is important to win morally as to win militarily. By which I mean out victories must break the foe's heart and tear from him all hope of contesting us again. I do not wish to fight war upon war, but by war to produce such a peace as will admit of no insurrection.

On Strategy and Campaign

TO COENUS, IN PALESTINE:

The object of campaign is to bring about a battle that will prove decisive. We feint; we maneuver; we provoke to one end: to compel the foe to face us in the field.

What I want is a battle, one great pitched clash in which Darius comes out to us in the flower of his might. Remember, our object is to break the will to resist, not only of the king's soldiers, but of his peoples.

The subjects of the empire are the real audience of these events. They must be made to believe by the scale and decisiveness of our triumphs that no force on earth, however numerous or well generaled, can prevail against us.

TO PERDICCAS, AT GAZA

The object of pursuit after victory is not only to prevent the enemy from reforming in the instance (this goes without saying), but to burn such fear into his vitals that he will never think of reforming again. Therefore, pursue by all means and don't relent until hell or darkness compels you. The foe who has been a fugitive once will never be the same fighter again.

I would rather lose five hundred horses in pursuit, if it prevents the enemy from re-forming, than to spare those horses, only to lose them-and five hundred more-in a second fight.

TO SELEUCUS, IN SYRIA:

As commander, we must save our supreme ruthlessness for ourselves. Before we make and move in the face of the enemy, we must ask ourselves, free of vanity and self-deception, how the foe will counter. Unearth every stroke and have an answer for it. Even when you think you have though of everything, there will be more work to do. Be merciless with yourself, for every careless act is paid in out own blood and the blood of our countrymen.

On Generosity
TO PARMENIO, AFTER ISSUS:

Cyrus the Great sought to detach from his enemy disaffected elements of the latter's forces, or others serving under compulsion. To this end he showed the Armenians and Hyrcanians honor and spared no measure to make their condition happier under his rule than under the Assyrian's. In Cyrus's view the purpose of victory was to prove more generous in gifts than the enemy. He felt it the greatest shame to lack the means to requite the munificence of others; he always wished to give more than he received, and he amasses treasure with the understanding that he held it in trust, not for himself, but for his friends to call upon in need.

TO HEPHAESTON, ALSO AFTER ISSUS:

Make generosity our first option. If an enemy shows the least sign of accommodation, match him twice over.

Let us conduct ourselves in such a fashion that all nations wish to be our friends and all fear to be our enemies.

On Tactics, Battles, and Soldiers

No advantage in war is greater than speed. To appear suddenly in strength where the enemy least expects you overawes him and throws him into consternation.

Great multitudes are not necessary. The optimal size of a fighting corps is that number that can march from one camp to another and arrive in one day. Any more are superfluous and only slow you down.

All tactics in conventional warfare seek to produce this single result: a breakthrough in the enemy line. This is as true of naval warfare as it is of war on land.

A static defensive line is always vulnerable. Once penetrated in force at any point, every other post on the line becomes moot. Its men cannon bring their arms to bear and, in fact, can do nothing except to wait in impotence to be overrun by the own comrades fleeing in panic as our penetrating force rolls them up from the flank.

Be conservative until the crucial moment. Then strike with all the violence you possess.

Remember: We need win at only one point on the field, so long as that point is decisive.

Every battle is constitutes of a number of sub-battles of differing degrees of consequence. I don't care if we lose every sub-battle, so long as we win the one that counts.

We fight with a holding wing and an attacking win. The purpose of the former is to paralyze in place, by its advance and its posture of threat, the enemy wing opposed to it. The purpose of the latter is to strike and penetrate.

We concentrate our force and hurl it with the utmost violence upon one point in the enemy line.

I want to feel as if I hold a lightning bolt. By which I mean that blow, poised beneath my command, which when hurled against the enemy will break his line. As the boxer waits with patience for the moment to throw his knockout punch, the general holds his decisive strike poised, careful not to loose it too early or too late.

Don't punch: counterpunch. The purpose of an initial evolution-a feint or draw-is to provoke the enemy into committing himself prematurely. Once he moves, we countermove.

We seek to create a breach in the enemy's line, into which cavalry can charge.

The line soldier need remember only two things: Keep in ranks and never abandon his colors.

An officer must lead from the front. How can we ask our soldiers to risk death if we ourselves shrink from hazard?

War is academic only on mapboard. In the field it is all emotion.

Leverage of position means the occupation of that site which compels the enemy to move. When we face an enemy marshaled in a defensive posture, our first though must be: What post can we seize that will make him withdraw?

The officer's charge is to control the emotion of the men under his command, neither letting them yield to fear, which will render them cowards, nor allowing them to give themselves over to rage, which will make them brutes.

Entering any territory, capture the wine stocks and breweries first. An Army without spirits is prey to disgruntlement and insurrection.

Use forced marches to cross waterless territory. This minimizes suffering for the men and animals. For a march of two days, I have found it an excellent method to rest till nightfall before setting out, march all night, rest through the heat of the next day, then march again all night. By this scheme we compress two days' marching into a day and a half, and, if we find ourselves still shy of our goal with the second day's sun, it is easier for the men and horses to push on in daylight, knowing water and rest are near.

On Cavalry

The strength of the cavalry is speed and shock. A static line of cavalry is no cavalry at all.

A horse must be a bit mad to be a good cavalry mount, and its rider must be completely so.

Cohesion of ranks, paramount with infantry, is even more crucial with cavalry. An enemy on foot may stand his ground against scattered horses of any number but never against mounted squadrons attacking boot-to-boot.

Cavalry need not work execution in the assault. Just break through. We can kill the enemy at leisure once we put him to flight.

It takes five years to train a trooper and ten to train his horse.

Green cavalry is worthless.

What I want in a cavalry mount is "push," or, as the riding masters call it, "impulsion."

The skills of mounted warfare require constant practice. Even a brief furlough can put a horse and rider "off their stuff," until they regain their sharpness by a return to training.

A cavalryman's horse should be smarter than he is. But the horse must never be allowed to know this.

About the Author

CDR Mary Kelly teaches history at the Naval Academy. Her current research focus includes globalization and economic trends in Asia.

11

The Unchanging Nature of Amphibious Operations: Julius Caesar's Gallic Wars

Dr. Joseph J. Thomas

Julius Caesar's *Commentaries* on the the Gallic Wars or *De Bello Gallico* are a chronicle of the first century BCE campaigns between Rome and the inhabitants of Gaul (France). The campaigns are typically divided into three phases, the war against the Gauls themselves, punitive expeditions against Gallic allies, and a counter-insurgency against rebelling Gallic tribes. During the phase in which Rome sought to punish supporters of Gaul, Caesar assembled an amphibious force made up of two legions aboard eighty transport ships and set out on a reconnaissance-in-force of Britain. In support of the landing force were many war ships designed to protect the transports underway as well as cover any opposed landings. An additional eighteen transports were dedicated to landing Caesar's cavalry.

The Roman fleet was detected by the British defenders and infantry, cavalry, and charioteers shadowed the movement of the legions for miles as Caesar sought a suitable place to land his force. When a suitable beach was finally found, the large Roman ships were unable to maneuver into shallow water. The Romans were forced to disembark in deep water, under hail of projectiles from the defenders. Caesar's experience parallels the experiences of amphibious forces in the 20th Century and reveals the timeless hazards of opposed amphibious landings.

* * *

The Romans were faced with very grave difficulties. The size of the ships made it impossible to run them aground except in fairly deep water; and the soldiers, unfamiliar with the ground, with their hands full, and weighed down by the heavy burden of their arms, had at the same time to jump down from the ships, get a footing in the waves, and fight the enemy, who, standing on dry land or advancing only a short way into the water, fought with all their limbs unencumbered and on perfectly familiar ground, boldly hurling javelins and galloping their horses, which were trained to this kind of work. These perils frightened our soldiers, who were quite unaccustomed to battles of this kind, with the result that they did not show the same alacrity and enthusiasm as they usually did in battles on dry land.

Seeing this, Caesar ordered the warships - which were swifter and easier to handle than the transports, and likely to impress the natives more by their unfamiliar appearance -to be removed a short distance from the others, and then to be rowed hard and run ashore on the enemy's right flank, from which position slings, bows, and artillery could be used by men on deck to drive them back. This maneuver was highly successful. Scared by the strange shape of the warships, the motion of the oars, and the unfamiliar machines, the natives halted and then retreated a little. But as the Romans still hesitated, chiefly on account of the depth of the water, the man who carried the eagle of the tenth legion, after praying to the gods that his action might bring good luck to the legion, cried in a loud voice, 'Jump down, comrades, unless you want to surrender our eagle to the enemy; I, at any rate, mean to do my duty to my country and my general.' With these words he leapt out of the ship and advanced towards the enemy with the eagle in his hands. At this the soldiers, exhorting each other not to submit to such a disgrace,

jumped with one accord from the ship, and the men from the next ships, when they saw them, followed them and advanced against the enemy.

The Romans were able, through sheer will of the landing force, to drive off the British defenders. But as the cavalry was delayed in coming ashore, the Romans were unable to exploit their immediate gains. Caesar's stay in Briton proved brief and he was forced to return to Gaul to assemble reinforcements. While back in Gaul Caesar had a new fleet built to better negotiate beach landings. The following year, 54 BCE, the Romans returned to the shores of Britain to consolidate their holdings and besiege Britain's warlike tribes. Domestic political disturbances in Rome forced Caesar to abandon Britain, but not before diplomatic and trading alliances were forged with tribal chieftans.

Suggested Readings

Catherine, Gilliver, *Caesar's Gallic Wars*. Osceola: Osprey, 2002.

Caesar, Julius. *The Conquest of Gaul*. Harmondsworth: Penguin, 1982.

Polybius. *The Rise of the Roman Empire*. New York: Penguin, 1979.

12

Handbook of Honor: Epictetus' Enchiridion

Dr. Robert D. Madison

Most of us know about Epictetus (A.D. 55?–135) from the essay by Vice Admiral James B. Stockdale entitled "The World of Epictetus." It was Epictetus, after all, who helped Stockdale survive eight years as a prisoner of war in North Vietnam.

In the basement of Nimitz Library a tattered copy of *The Works of Epictetus* sits on a shelf with other philosophy books. It's a translation by Thomas Wentworth Higginson, published in 1866. It is tattered because a generation of midshipmen has turned immediately and somewhat roughly to the "Enchiridion, or Manual," leaving most of the rest of the book unskimmed. And Higginson's summary of Epictetus in the Preface has been entirely read to pieces by perhaps even more readers who hadn't the patience to read the "Enchiridion" for themselves.

The "Enchiridion" presents the principles of the philosophy of Epictetus; the rest of his discourses elaborate on them and so might understandably be set aside for more systematic study. Epictetus was a slave, and perhaps he himself had to live his life before he examined it. Even without the apparatus of the discourses, nevertheless, we may find ourselves forced to wonder how trained leaders can adopt an ethic that appears to forswear leadership: "We are not to lead events, but to to follow them," Epictetus writes in a dictum that must surely seem strange to military officers.

When Higginson began his translation—a reworking of a much earlier English version by Elizabeth Carter—he had just been sent home on furlough from the Civil War. Until he had been grazed by a cannonball on an expedition up the Edisto, he had led the First Regiment of South Carolina Volunteers—the first regiment to be made up of escaped slaves. He himself was suffering quite literally from shell-shock, and he would never return to war. He found it almost impossible psychologically to write of his combat experienc, and turned instead to Epictetus, which he finished in a year of concentrated activity. It would be nearly five years before his classic war book, *Army Life in a Black Regiment*, was ready for the public.

In war and peace, Epictetus has been a stoic voice of survival.

THE ENCHIRIDION.

I.

There are things which are within our power, and there are things which are beyond our power. Within our power are opinion, aim, desire, aversion, and, in one word, whatever affairs are our own. Beyond our power are body, property, reputation, office, and, in one word, whatever are not properly our own affairs.

Now the things within our power are by nature free, unrestricted, unhindered; but those beyond our power are weak, dependent, restricted, alien. Remember then, that, if you attribute freedom to things by nature dependent, and take what belongs to others for your own; you will be hindered, you will lament, you will be disturbed, you will find fault both with Gods and men. But if you take for your own only that which is your own, and view what belongs to others just as it really is, then no one will ever compel you, no one will restrict you, you will find fault with no one, you will accuse no one, you will do nothing against your will; no one will hurt you, you will not have an enemy, nor will you suffer any harm.

Aiming therefore at such great things, remember that you must not allow yourself any inclination, however slight, towards the attainment of the others; but that you must entirely quit some of them, and for the present postpone the rest. But if you would have these, and possess power and wealth likewise, you may miss the latter in seeking the former; and you will certainly fail of that, by which alone happiness and freedom are procured.

Seek at once, therefore, to be able to say to every unpleasing semblance, "You are but a semblance and by no means the real thing." And then examine it by those rules which you have; and first and chiefly, by this: whether it concerns the things which are within our own power, or those which are not; and if it concerns anything beyond our power, be prepared to say that it is nothing to you.

II.

Remember that desire demands the attainment of that of which you are desirous; and aversion demands the avoidance of that to which you are averse; that he who fails of the object of his desires, is disappointed; and he who incurs the object of his aversion, is wretched. If, then, you shun only those undesirable things which you can control, you will never incur anything which you shun. But if you shun sickness, or death, or poverty, you will run the risk of wretchedness. Remove aversion, then, from all things that are not within our power, and transfer it to things undesirable, which are within our power. But for the present altogether restrain desire; for if you desire any of the things not within our own power, you must necessarily be disappointed; and you are not yet secure of those which are within our power, and so are legitimate objects of desire. Where it is practically necessary for you to pursue or avoid anything, do even this with discretion, and gentleness, and moderation.

III.

With regard to whatever objects either delight the mind, or contribute to use, or are tenderly beloved, remind yourself of what nature they are, beginning with the merest trifles: if you have a favorite cup, that it is a cup of which you are fond; for thus, if it is broken, you can bear it: if you embrace your child, or your wife, that you embrace a mortal; and thus, if either of them dies, you can bear it.

IV.

When you set about any action, remind your-self of what nature the action is. If you are going to bathe, represent to yourself the incidents usual in the bath; some persons pouring out, others pushing in, others scolding, others pilfer-ing. And thus you will more safely go about this action, if you say to yourself, "I will now go to bathe, and keep my own will in harmony with nature." And so with regard to every other ac-tion. For thus, if any impediment arises in bathing, you will be able to say, "It was not only to bathe that I desired, but to keep my will in harmony with nature; and I shall not keep it thus, if I am out of humor at things that hap-pen."

V.

Men are disturbed not by things, but by the views which they take of things. Thus death is nothing terrible, else it would have appeared so to Socrates. But the terror consists in our notion of death, that it is terrible. When, therefore, we are hindered, or disturbed, or grieved, let us never impute it to others, but to ourselves; that is, to our own views. It is the action of an unin-structed person to reproach others for his own misfortunes; of one entering upon instruction, to reproach himself; and of one perfectly in-structed, to reproach neither others nor himself.

VI.

Be not elated at any excellence not your own. If a horse should be elated, and say, "I am hand-some," it might be endurable. But when you are elated, and say, "I have a handsome horse," know that you are elated only on the merit of the horse. What, then, is your own? The use of the phenomena of existence. So that when you are in harmony with nature in this respect, you will be elated with some reason; for you will be elated at some good of your own.

VII.

As in a voyage, when the ship is at anchor, if you go on shore to get water, you may amuse yourself with picking up a shell-fish or a truffle in your way; but your thoughts ought to be bent towards the ship, and perpetually attentive, lest the captain should call; and then you must leave all these things, that you may not have to be car-ried on board the vessel, bound like a sheep. Thus likewise in life, if, instead of a truffle or shell-fish, such a thing as a wife or a child be granted you, there is no objection; but if the cap-tain calls, run to the ship, leave all these things, and never look behind. But if you are old, never go far from the ship, lest you should be missing when called for.

VIII.

Demand not that events should happen as you wish; but wish them to happen as they do happen, and you will go on well.

IX.

Sickness is an impediment to the body, but not to the will, unless itself pleases. Lameness is an impediment to the leg, but not to the will; and say this to yourself with regard to everything that happens. For you will find it to be an imped-iment to something else, but not truly to your-self.

X.

Upon every accident, remember to turn to-wards yourself and inquire what faculty you have for its use. If you encounter a handsome person, you will find continence the faculty needed; if pain, then fortitude; if reviling, then patience. And when thus habituated, the phenomena of existence will not overwhelm you.

XI.

Never say of anything, "I have lost it"; but, "I have restored it." Has your child died? It is restored. Has your wife died? She is restored. Has your estate been taken away? That likewise is restored. "But it was a bad man who took it." What is it to you, by whose hands He who gave it hath demanded it again? While He permits you to possess it, hold it as something not your own; as do travellers at an inn.

XII.

If you would improve, lay aside such reasonings as these: "If I neglect my affairs, I shall not have a maintenance; if I do not punish my servant, he will be good for nothing." For it were better to die of hunger, exempt from grief and fear, than to live in affluence with perturbation; and it is better that your servant should be bad than you unhappy.

Begin therefore with little things. Is a little oil spilt or a little wine stolen? Say to yourself, "This is the price paid for peace and tranquillity; and nothing is to be had for nothing." And when you call your servant, consider that it is possible he may not come at your call; or, if he does, that he may not do what you wish. But it is not at all desirable for him, and very undesirable for you, that it should be in his power to cause you any disturbance.

XIII.

If you would improve, be content to be thought foolish and dull with regard to externals. Do not desire to be thought to know anything; and though you should appear to others to be somebody, distrust yourself. For be assured, it is not easy at once to keep your will in harmony with nature, and to secure externals; but while you are absorbed in the one, you must of necessity neglect the other.

XIV.

If you wish your children, and your wife, and your friends, to live forever, you are foolish; for you wish things to be in your power which are not so; and what belongs to others, to be your own. So likewise, if you wish your servant to be without fault, you are foolish; for you wish vice not to be vice, but something else. But if you wish not to be disappointed in your desires, that is in your own power. Exercise, therefore, what is in your power. A man's master is he who is able to confer or remove whatever that man seeks or shuns. Whoever then would be free, let him wish nothing, let him decline nothing, which depends on others; else he must necessarily be a slave.

XV.

Remember that you must behave as at a banquet. Is anything brought round to you? Put out your hand, and take a moderate share. Does it pass by you? Do not stop it. Is it not yet come? Do not yearn in desire towards it, but wait till it reaches you. So with regard to children, wife, office, riches; and you will some time or other be worthy to feast with the Gods. And if you do not so much as take the things which are set before you, but are able even to forego them, then you will not only be worthy to feast with the Gods, but to rule with them also. For, by thus doing, Diogenes and Heraclitus, and others like them, deservedly became divine, and were so recognized.

XVI.

When you see any one weeping for grief, either that his son has gone abroad, or that he has suffered in his affairs; take care not to be overcome by the apparent evil. But discriminate, and be ready to say, "What hurts this man is not this occurrence itself, for another man might not be hurt by it;—but the view he chooses to take of it." As far as conversation goes, however, do not disdain to accommodate yourself to him, and if need be, to groan with him. Take heed, however, not to groan inwardly too.

XVII.

Remember that you are an actor in a drama of such sort as the author chooses. If short, then in a short one; if long, then in a long one. If it be his pleasure that you should act a poor man, see that you act it well; or a cripple, or a ruler, or a private citizen. For this is your business, to act well the given part; but to choose it, belongs to another.

XVIII.

When a raven happens to croak unluckily, be not overcome by appearances, but discriminate, and say, "Nothing is portended to *me;* but either to my paltry body, or property, or reputation, or children, or wife. But to *me* all portents are lucky, if I will. For whatsoever happens, it belongs to me to derive advantage therefrom."

XIX.

You can be unconquerable, if you enter into no combat, in which it is not in your own power to conquer. When, therefore, you see any one eminent in honors or power, or in high esteem on any other account, take heed not to be bewildered by appearances and to pronounce him happy; for if the essence of good consists in things within our own power, there will be no room for envy or emulation. But, for your part, do not desire to be a general, or a senator, or a consul, but to be free; and the only way to this is, a disregard of things which lie not within our own power.

XX.

Remember that it is not he who gives abuse or blows who affronts; but the view we take of these things as insulting. When, therefore, any one provokes you, be assured that it is your own opinion which provokes you. Try, therefore, in the first place, not to be bewildered by appearances. For if you once gain time and respite, you will more easily command yourself.

XXI.

Let death and exile, and all other things which appear terrible, be daily before your eyes, but death chiefly; and you will never entertain any abject thought, nor too eagerly covet anything.

XXII.

If you have an earnest desire towards philosophy, prepare yourself from the very first to have the multitude laugh and sneer, and say, "He is returned to us a philosopher all at once"; and "Whence this supercilious look?" Now for your part, do not have a supercilious look indeed; but keep steadily to those things which appear best to you, as one appointed by God to this particular station. For remember that, if you are persistent, those very persons who at first ridiculed, will afterwards admire you. But if you are conquered by them, you will incur a double ridicule.

XXIII.

If you ever happen to turn your attention to externals, for the pleasure of any one, be assured that you have ruined your scheme of life. Be contented, then, in everything, with being a philosopher; and, if you wish to seem so likewise to any one, appear so to yourself, and it will suffice you.

XXIV.

Let not such considerations as these distress you: "I shall live in discredit, and be nobody anywhere." For if discredit be an evil, you can no more be involved in evil through another, than in baseness. Is it any business of yours, then, to get power, or to be admitted to an entertainment? By no means. How then, after all, is this discredit? And how is it true that you will be nobody anywhere; when you ought to be somebody in those things only which are within your own power, in which you may be of the greatest consequence? "But my friends will be unassisted." What do you mean by unassisted? They will not have money from you; nor will you make them Roman citizens. Who told you, then, that these are among the things within our own power; and not rather the affairs of others? And who can give to another the things which he himself has not? "Well, but get them, then, that we too may have a share." If I can get them with the preservation of my own honor, and fidelity, and self-respect, show me the way, and I will get them; but if you require me to lose my own proper good, that you may gain what is no good, consider how unreasonable and foolish you are. Besides, which would you rather have, a sum of money, or a faithful and honorable friend? Rather assist me, then, to gain this character, than require me to do those things by which I may lose it. Well, but my country, say you, as far as depends upon me, will be unassisted. Here again, what assistance is this you mean? It will not have porticos nor baths of your providing? And what signifies that? Why, neither does a smith provide it with shoes, nor a shoemaker with arms. It is enough if every one fully performs his own proper business. And were you to supply it with another faithful and honorable citizen, would not he be of use to it? Yes. Therefore neither are you yourself useless to it. "What place then," say you, "shall I hold in the state?" Whatever you can hold with the preservation of your fidelity and honor. But if, by desiring to be useful to that, you lose these, how can you serve your country, when you have become faithless and shameless?

XXV.

Is any one preferred before you at an entertainment, or in courtesies, or in confidential intercourse? If these things are good, you ought to rejoice that he has them; and if they are evil, do not be grieved that you have them not. And remember that you cannot be permitted to rival others in externals, without using the same means to obtain them. For how can he, who will not haunt the door of any man, will not attend him, will not praise him, have an equal share with him who does these things? You are unjust, then, and unreasonable, if you are unwilling to pay the price for which these things are sold, and would have them for nothing. For how much are lettuces sold? An obolus, for instance. If another, then, paying an obolus takes the lettuces, and you, not paying it, go without them, do not imagine that he has gained any advantage over you. For as he has the lettuces, so you have the obolus which you did not give. So, in the present case, you have not been invited to such a person's entertainment; because you have not paid him the price for which a supper is sold. It is sold for praise; it is sold for attendance. Give him, then, the value, if it be for your advantage. But if you would at the same time not pay the one, and yet receive the other, you are unreasonable and foolish. Have you nothing, then, in place of the supper? Yes, indeed you have; not to praise him whom you do not like to praise; not to bear the insolence of his lackeys.

XXVI.

The will of Nature may be learned from things upon which we are all agreed. As, when our neighbor's boy has broken a cup, or the like, we are ready at once to say, "These are casualties that will happen." Be assured, then, that when your own cup is likewise broken, you ought to be affected just as when another's cup was broken. Now apply this to greater things. Is the child or wife of another dead? There is no one who would not say, "This is au accident of mortality." But if any one's own child happens to die, it is immediately, "Alas! how wretched am I!" It should be always remembered how we are affected on hearing the same thing concerning others.

XXVII.

As a mark is not set up for the sake of missing the aim, so neither does the nature of evil exist in the world.

XXVIII.

If a person had delivered up your body to some passer-by, you would certainly be angry. And do you feel no shame in delivering up your own mind to any reviler, to be disconcerted and confounded?

XXIX.

In every affair consider what precedes and follows, and then undertake it. Otherwise you will begin with spirit indeed, careless of the consequences, and when these are developed, you will shamefully desist. "I would conquer at the Olympic Games." But consider what precedes and follows, and, then, if it be for your advantage, engage in the affair. You must conform to rules, submit to a diet, refrain from dainties; exercise your body, whether you choose it or not, at a stated hour, in heat and cold; you must drink no cold water, and sometimes no wine. In a word, you must give yourself up to your trainer as to a physician. Then, in the combat, you may be thrown into a ditch, dislocate your arm, turn your ankle, swallow abundance of dust, receive stripes [for negligence]; and after all, lose the victory. When you have reckoned up all this, if your inclination still holds, set about the combat. Otherwise, take notice, you will behave like children who sometimes play wrestlers, sometimes gladiators; sometimes blow a trumpet, and sometimes act a tragedy, when they happen to have seen and admired these shows. Thus you too will be at one time a wrestler, at another a gladiator; now a philosopher, now an orator; but

nothing in earnest. Like an ape you mimic all you see, and one thing after another is sure to please you; but is out of favor as soon as it becomes familiar. For you have never entered upon anything considerately, nor after having surveyed and tested the whole matter; but carelessly, and with a half-way zeal. Thus some, when they have seen a philosopher, and heard a man speaking like Euphrates,— though indeed who can speak like him?—have a mind to be philosophers too. Consider first, man, what the matter is, and what your own nature is able to bear. If you would be a wrestler, consider your shoulders, your back, your thighs; for different persons are made for different things. Do you think that you can act as you do and be a philosopher? That you can eat, drink, be angry, be discontented, as you are now? You must watch, you must labor, you must get the better of certain appetites; must quit your acquaintances, be despised by your servant, be laughed at by those you meet; come off worse than others in everything, in offices, in honors, before tribunals. When you have fully considered all these things, approach, if you please; if, by parting with them, you have a mind to purchase serenity, freedom, and tranquillity. If not, do not come hither; do not, like children, be now a philosopher, then a publican, then an orator, and then one of Cæsar's officers. These things are not consistent. You must be one man either good or bad. You must cultivate either your own Reason or else externals; apply yourself either to things within or without you; that is, be either a philosopher, or one of the mob.

XXX.

Duties are universally measured by relations. Is a certain man your father? In this are implied, taking care of him; submitting to him in all things; patiently receiving his reproaches, his correction. But he is a bad father. Is your natural tie, then, to a *good* father? No, but to a father. Is a brother unjust? Well, preserve your own just relation towards him. Consider not what *he* does; but what *you* are to do, to keep your own will in a state conformable to nature. For another cannot hurt you, unless you please. You will then be hurt when you consent to be hurt. In this manner, therefore, if you accustom yourself to contemplate the relations of neighbor, citizen, commander, you can deduce from each the corresponding duties.

XXXI.

Be assured that the essence of piety towards the Gods lies in this, to form right opinions concerning them, as existing, and as governing the universe justly and well. And fix yourself in this resolution, to obey them, and yield to them, and willingly follow them amidst all events, as being ruled by the most perfect wisdom. For thus you will never find fault with the Gods, nor accuse them of neglecting you. And it is not possible for this to be effected in any other way, than by withdrawing yourself from things which are not within our own power, and by making good or evil to consist only in those which are. For if you suppose any other things to be either good or evil, it is inevitable that, when you are disappointed of what you wish, or incur what you would avoid, you should reproach and blame their authors. For every creature is naturally formed to flee and abhor things that appear hurtful, and that which causes them; and to pursue and admire those which appear beneficial, and that which causes them. It is impracticable, then, that one who supposes himself to be hurt, should rejoice in the person who, as he thinks, hurts him; just as it is impossible to rejoice in the hurt itself. Hence, also, a father is reviled by his son, when he does not impart the things which seem to be good; and this made Polynices and Eteocles mutually enemies, that empire seemed good to both. On this account the husbandman reviles the Gods;— the sailor, the merchant, or those who have lost wife or child. For where our interest is, there too is piety directed. So that

whoever is careful to regulate his desires and aversions as he ought, is thus made careful of piety likewise. But it also becomes incumbent on every one to offer libations, and sacrifices, and first-fruits, according to the customs of his country, purely, and not heedlessly nor negligently; not avariciously, nor yet extravagantly.

XXXII.

When you have recourse to divination, remember that you know not what the event will be, and you come to learn it of the diviner; but of what nature it is you knew before coming; at least, if you are of philosophic mind. For if it is among the things not within our own power, it can by no means be either good or evil. Do not, therefore, bring with you to the diviner either desire or aversion,—else you will approach him trembling,—but first clearly understand, that every event is indifferent, and nothing to *you*, of whatever sort it may be; for it will be in your power to make a right use of it, and this no one can hinder. Then come with confidence to the Gods as your counsellors; and afterwards, when any counsel is given you, remember what counsellors you have assumed, and whose advice you will neglect, if you disobey. Come to divination, as Socrates prescribed, in cases of which the whole consideration relates to the event, and in which no opportunities are afforded by reason, or any other art, to discover the matter in view. When, therefore, it is our duty to share the danger of a friend or of our country, we ought not to consult the oracle as to whether we shall share it with them or not. For though the diviner should forewarn you that the auspices are unfavorable, this means no more than that either death or mutilation or exile is portended. But we have reason within us; and it directs us, even with these hazards, to stand by our friend and our country. Attend, therefore, to the greater diviner, the Pythian God, who once cast out of the temple him who neglected to save his friend.

XXXIII.

Begin by prescribing to yourself some character and demeanor, such as you may preserve both alone and in company.

Be mostly silent; or speak merely what is needful, and in few words. We may, however, enter sparingly into discourse sometimes, when occasion calls for it; but let it not run on any of the common subjects, as gladiators, or horse-races, or athletic champions, or food, or drink,— the vulgar topics of conversation; and especially not on men, so as either to blame, or praise, or make comparisons. If you are able, then, by your own conversation, bring over that of your company to proper subjects; but if you happen to find yourself among strangers, be silent.

Let not your laughter be loud, frequent, or abundant.

Avoid taking oaths, if possible, altogether; at any rate, so far as you are able.

Avoid public and vulgar entertainments; but if ever an occasion calls you to them; keep your attention upon the stretch, that you may not imperceptibly slide into vulgarity. For be assured that if a person be ever so pure himself, yet, if his companion be corrupted, he who converses with him will be corrupted likewise.

Provide things relating to the body no farther than absolute need requires; as meat, drink, clothing, house, retinue. But cut off everything that looks towards show and luxury.

Before marriage, guard yourself with all your ability from unlawful intercourse with women; yet be not uncharitable or severe to those who are led into this, nor frequently boast that you yourself do otherwise.

If any one tells you that such a person speaks ill of you, do not make excuses about what is said of you, but answer: "He was ignorant of my other faults, else he would not have mentioned these alone."

It is not necessary for you to appear often at public spectacles; but if ever there is a proper occasion for you to be there, do not appear more solicitous for any other, than for yourself; that is, wish things to be only just as they are, and only

the best man to win; for thus nothing will go against you. But abstain entirely from acclamations, and derision, and violent emotions. And when you come away, do not discourse a great deal on what has passed, and what contributes nothing to your own amendment. For it would appear by such discourse that you were dazzled by the show.

Be not prompt or ready to attend private recitations; but if you do attend, preserve your gravity and dignity, and yet avoid making yourself disagreeable.

When you are going to confer with any one, and especially with one who seems your superior, represent to yourself how Socrates or Zeno would behave in such a case, and you will not be at a loss to meet properly whatever may occur.

When you are going before any one in power, fancy to yourself that you may not find him at home, that you may be shut out, that the doors may not be opened to you, that he may not notice you. If, with all this, it be your duty to go, bear what happens, and never say to yourself, "It was not worth so much." For this is vulgar, and like a man bewildered by externals.

In society, avoid a frequent and excessive mention of your own actions and dangers. For however agreeable it may be to yourself to allude to the risks you have run, it is not equally agreeable to others to hear your adventures. Avoid likewise an endeavor to excite laughter. For this may readily slide you into vulgarity, and, besides, may be apt to lower you in the esteem of your acquaintance. Approaches to indecent discourse are likewise dangerous. Therefore when anything of this sort happens, use the first fit opportunity to rebuke him who makes advances that way; or, at least, by silence, and blushing, and a serious look, show yourself to be displeased by such talk.

XXXIV.

If you are dazzled by the semblance of any promised pleasure, guard yourself against being bewildered by it; but let the affair wait your leisure, and procure yourself some delay. Then bring to your mind both points of time; that in which you shall enjoy the pleasure, and that in which you will repent and reproach yourself, after you have enjoyed it; and set before you, in opposition to these, how you will rejoice and applaud yourself, if you abstain. And even though it should appear to you a seasonable gratification, take heed that its enticements and allurements and seductions may not subdue you; but set in opposition to this, how much better it is to be conscious of having gained so great a victory.

XXXV.

When you do anything from a clear judgment that it ought to be done, never shrink from being seen to do it, even though the world should misunderstand it; for if you are not acting rightly, shun the action itself; if you are, why fear those who wrongly censure you?

XXXVI.

As the proposition, *either it is day, or it is night*, has much force in a disjunctive argument, but none at all in a conjunctive one; so, at a feast, to choose the largest share, is very suitable to the bodily appetite, but utterly inconsistent with the social spirit of the entertainment. Remember, then, when you eat with another, not only the value to the body of those things which are set before you, but also the value of proper courtesy towards your host.

XXXVII.

If you have assumed any character beyond your strength, you have both demeaned yourself ill in that, and quitted one which you might have supported.

XXXVIII.

As in walking you take care not to tread upon a nail, or turn your foot, so likewise take care not to hurt the ruling faculty of your mind. And if we were to guard against this in every action, we should enter upon action more safely.

XXXIX.

The body is to every one the proper measure of its possessions, as the foot is of the shoe. If, therefore, you stop at this, you will keep the measure; but if you move beyond it, you must necessarily be carried forward, as down a precipice; as in the case of a shoe, if you go beyond its fitness to the foot, it comes first to be gilded, then purple, and then studded with jewels. For to that which once exceeds the fit measure there is no bound.

XL.

Women from fourteen years old are flattered by men with the title of mistresses. Therefore, perceiving that they are regarded only as qualified to give men pleasure, they begin to adorn themselves, and in that to place all their hopes. It is worth while, therefore, to try that they may perceive themselves honored only so far as they appear beautiful in their demeanor, and modestly virtuous.

XLL.

It is a mark of want of intellect, to spend much time in things relating to the body; as to be immoderate in exercises, in eating and drinking, and in the discharge of other animal functions. These things should be done incidentally and our main strength be applied to our reason.

XLII.

When any person does ill by you, or speaks ill of you, remember that he acts or speaks from an impression that it is right for him to do so. Now, it is not possible that he should follow what appears right to you, but only what appears so to himself. Therefore, if he judges from false appearances, he is the person hurt; since he too is the person deceived. For if any one takes a true proposition to be false, the proposition is not hurt, but only the man is deceived. Setting out, then, from these principles, you will meekly bear with a person who reviles you; for you will say upon every occasion, "It seemed so to him."

XLIII.

Everything has two handles: one by which it may be borne; another by which it cannot. If your brother acts unjustly, do not lay hold on the affair by the handle of his injustice; for by that it cannot be borne: but rather by the opposite, that he is your brother, that he was brought up with you; and thus you will lay hold on it as it is to be borne.

XLIV.

These reasonings have no logical connection: "I am richer than you; therefore I am your superior": "I am more eloquent than you; therefore I am your superior." The true logical connection is rather this: "I am richer than you; therefore my possessions must exceed yours": "I am more eloquent than you; therefore my style must surpass yours." But you, after all, consist neither in property nor in style.

XLV.

Does any one bathe hastily? Do not say, that he does it ill, but hastily. Does any one drink much wine? Do not say that he does ill, but that he drinks a great deal. For unless you perfectly understand his motives, how should you know if he acts ill? Thus you will not risk yielding to any appearances but such as you fully comprehend.

XLVI.

Never proclaim yourself a philosopher; nor make much talk among the ignorant about your principles, but show them by actions. Thus, at an entertainment, do not discourse how people ought to eat; but eat as you ought. For remember that thus Socrates also universally avoided all ostentation. And when persons came to him, and desired to be introduced by him to philosophers, he took them and introduced them; so well did he bear being overlooked. So if ever there should be among the ignorant any discussion of principles, be for the most part silent. For there is great danger in hastily throwing out what is undigested. And if any one tells you that you know nothing, and you are not nettled at it, then you may be sure that you have really entered on your work. For sheep do not hastily throw up the grass, to show the shepherds how much they have eaten; but, inwardly digesting their food, they produce it outwardly in wool and milk. Thus, therefore, do you not make an exhibition before the ignorant of your principles; but of the actions to which their digestion gives rise.

XLVII.

When you have learned to nourish your body frugally, do not pique yourself upon it; nor, if you drink water, be saying upon every occasion, "I drink water." But first consider how much more frugal are the poor than we, and how much more patient of hardship. But if at any time you would inure yourself by exercise to labor and privation, for your own sake and not for the public, do not attempt great feats; but when you are violently thirsty, just rinse your mouth with water, and tell nobody.

XLVIII.

The condition and characteristic of a vulgar person is, that he never looks for either help or harm from himself, but only from externals. The condition and characteristic of a philosopher is, that he looks to himself for all help or harm. The marks of a proficient are, that he censures no one, praises no one, blames no one, accuses no one; says nothing concerning himself as being anybody, or knowing anything; when he is in any instance hindered or restrained, he accuses himself; and if he is praised, he smiles to himself at the person who praises him; and if he is censured, he makes no defence. But he goes about with the caution of a convalescent, careful of interference with anything that is doing well, but not yet quite secure. He restrains desire; he transfers his aversion to those things only which thwart the proper use of our own will; he employs his energies moderately in all directions; if he appears stupid or ignorant, he does not care; and, in a word, he keeps watch over himself as over an enemy and one in ambush.

XLIX.

When any one shows himself vain, on being able to understand and interpret the works of Chrysippus, say to yourself: "Unless Chrysippus had written obscurely, this person would have had nothing to be vain of. But what do I desire? To understand Nature, and follow her. I ask, then, who interprets her; and hearing that Chrysippus does, I have recourse to him. I do not understand his writings. I seek, therefore, one to interpret *them*." So far there is nothing to value myself upon. And when I find an interpreter, what remains is, to make use of his instructions. This alone is the valuable thing. But if I admire merely the interpretation, what do I become more than a grammarian, instead of a philosopher? Except, indeed, that instead of Homer I interpret Chrysippus. When any one, therefore, desires me to read Chrysippus to him, I rather blush, when I cannot exhibit actions that are harmonious and consonant with his discourse.

L.

Whatever rules you have adopted, abide by them as laws, and as if you would be impious to transgress them; and do not regard what any one says of you, for this, after all, is no concern of yours. How long, then, will you delay to demand of yourself the noblest improvements, and in no

instance to transgress the judgments of reason? You have received the philosophic principles with which you ought to be conversant; and you have been conversant with them. For what other master, then, do you wait as an excuse for this delay in self-reformation? You are no longer a boy, but a grown man. If, therefore, you will be negligent and slothful, and always add procrastination to procrastination, purpose to purpose, and fix day after day in which you will attend to yourself, you will insensibly continue to accomplish nothing, and, living and dying, remain of vulgar mind. This instant, then, think yourself worthy of living as a man grown up and a proficient. Let whatever appears to be the best, be to you an inviolable law. And if any instance of pain or pleasure, glory or disgrace, be set before you, remember that now is the combat, now the Olympiad comes on, nor can it be put off; and that by one failure and defeat honor may be lost—or won. Thus Socrates became perfect, improving himself by everything; following reason alone. And though you are not yet a Socrates, you ought, however, to live as one seeking to be a Socrates.

LI.

The first and most necessary topic in philosophy is the practical application of principles; as, *We ought not to lie:* the second is that of demonstrations; as, *Why it is that we ought not to lie:* the third, that which gives strength and logical connection to the other two; as, *Why this is a demonstration.* For what is demonstration? What is a consequence? What a contradiction? What truth? What falsehood? The third point is then necessary on account of the second; and the second on account of the first. But the most necessary, and that whereon we ought to rest, is the first. But we do just the contrary. For we spend all our time on the third point, and employ all our diligence about that, and entirely neglect the first. Therefore, at the same time that we lie, we are very ready to show how it is demonstrated that lying is wrong.

Upon all occasions we ought to have these maxims ready at hand:—
Conduct me, Zeus, and thou, O Destiny,
Wherever your decrees have fixed my lot.
I follow cheerfully; and, did I not,
Wicked and wretched, I must follow still.
Whoe'er yields properly to Fate is deemed
Wise among men, and knows the laws of
Heaven.†
And this third:—

Suggested Readings

Aurelius, Marcus. *Meditations*. Buffalo: Prometheus Books, 1991.

Epictetus. *The Art of Living: the Classic Manual on Virtue, Happiness, and Effectiveness*. San Francisco: Harper San Francisco, 1995.

Epictetus. *The Enchiridion*. Indianapolis: Bobbs-Merrill, 1955.

Seneca, Lucius A. *The Stoic Philosophy of Seneca: Essays and Letters of Seneca*. New York: Norton, 1968.

Stockdale, James B. *Thoughts of a Philosophical Fighter Pilot*. Stanford: Hoover Institution Press, 1995.

Biography

Bob Madison is Professor of English at the U.S. Naval Academy. He has edited several volumes of military and maritime history, including *The Bounty Mutiny* (Penguin, 2001), Jack London's *Cruise of the Snark* (Penguin, 2004), and William Clark Russell's *Pictures from the Life of Nelson* (Naval Institute Press, 2005).

13

The Impression of Iron: Notker the Stammerer's Charlemagne

Dr. Joseph J. Thomas

Notker the Stammerer, often referred to as The Monk of Saint Gall, produced *Charlemagne* as a biography and book of leadership anecdotes for the Great King's great-grandson "Charles the Fat." Charlemagne, oldest son of Pepin the Short, was Emperor of the Carolingian Dynasty from 768-810. His reign was characterized by an almost unbroken series of battles and campaigns against the Saxons and other tribes of Europe. His personal leadership, development of martial effectiveness, and vision for a united Europe are still revered on the continent. The extant primary histories of Charlemagne are a blend of adoring legends and actual accomplishment and serve as a window into military leadership of the medieval period.

Once the unconquerable Pepin was dead, the Longobards began again to harass Rome. Chailemagne who, like his father, was never beaten in battle, was fully occupied to the north of the Alps, but he marched swiftly into Italy. After a bloodless campaign, the Longobards were sufficiently humbled to surrender of their own free will and Charlemagne received them into subjection. For security's sake and to stop them ever again seceding from Frankish rule or doing harm to the territories of Saint Peter, Charlemagne married the daughter of Desiderius, King of the Longobards.IZ9 Some short time afterwards, since she was bedridden and unable to bear a child, she was, by the advice of his devout clergy, put on one side as if already dead. Her father was furious. He bound his neighbors to him by oath, shut himself up within the walls of Pavia and prepared to do battle with the invincible Charlemagne. As soon as he had made sure that this was true, Charlemagne hurried with all speed to Pavia.

Now it had happened some years earlier that one of Charlemagne's principal nobles, Otker by name, had incurred the wrath of the formidable

Emperor and had therefore fled to this same Desiderius. When they heard that the dreaded Charlemagne was coming near, these too went up into a high tower from which they could see anyone approaching from far and wide. As soon as the baggage trains came into sight; moving even more quickly than those of Darius or Julius Caesar, Desiderius said to Otker: 'Is Charles in the midst of that vast array?' 'Not yet, not yet,' answered Otker. When he perceived the army itself, collected together from all the nations of Charlemagne's vast Empire, Desiderius said sharply to Otker: 'Now Charles is advancing proudly in the midst of his troops.' 'Not yet, not yet;' answered Otker. Desiderius than flew into a panic and said: 'If even more soldiers come into battle with him, what can we possibly do?' 'When he comes,' said Otker, 'you will see what he is like. I don't know what will happen to us.' As they spoke together, the sovereign's escort appeared, tireless as ever. When he saw them Desiderius was stupefied. 'This time it really is Charles,' he said 'Not yet, not yet: said Otker once more. After this the bishops came into sight, and the abbots and the clergy of Charlemagne's chapel, with their attendants. When he saw them Desiderius longed for death and began to hate the light of day. With a sob in his voice he stammered:

'Let us go down and hide ourselves in the earth, in the face of the fury of an enemy so terrible.' Otker, too, was terrified, for in happier days he had been in close contact with the strategy and the military equipment of the peerless Charlemagne, and he knew all about them. 'When you see the fields bristle as with ears of iron com,' he said, 'when you see the Po and the Ticino break over the walls of your city in great waves which gleam black with the glint of iron, then indeed you can be sure that Charlemagne is at hand.' He had not yet finished his words when from the west a mighty gale and with it the wind of the true north began to blow up like some great pall of cloud, which turned the bright daylight into frightful gloom. As the Emperor rode

on and ever on, from the gleam of his weapons dawned as it were another day, more dark than any night for the beleaguered force.

Then came the sight of that man of iron, Charlemagne, topped with his iron helm, his fists in iron gloves, his iron chest and his Platonic shoulders, clad in an iron cuirass. An iron spear raised high against the sky he gripped in his left hand, while in his right he held his still unconquered sword. For greater ease of riding other men keep their thighs bare of armour; Charlemagne's were bound in plates of iron. As for his greaves, like those of all his army, they too, were made of iron. His shield was all of iron. His horse gleamed iron-coloured andits very mettle was as if of iron. All those who rode before him, those who kept him company on either flank, those who followed after, wore the same armour and their gear was as close a copy of his own as it is possible to imagine. Iron filled the fields and all the open spaces. The rays of the sun were thrown back by this battle-line of iron. This race of men harder than iron did homage to me very hardness of iron. The pallid face of the man fu the condemned cell grew paler at the bright gleam of iron. 'Oh! The iron! Alas for the iron!' Such was the confused clamour of the citizens of Pavia. The strong walls shook at the touch of iron. The resolution of the young grew feeble before the iron of these older men. When therefore Otker, who had foreseen the truth, with one swift glance observed all this, which I, a toothless man with stammering speech, have tried to describe, not as I ought, but slowly and with labyrinthine phrase, he said to Desiderius: 'That is Charlemagne, whom you have sought so long.' As he spoke he fell half conscious to the ground.

The inhabitants of the city, either through madness or because they had some hope of resisting, refused to let Charlemagne enter on that day. The ingenious Emperor therefore said to his men: 'Let us today construct something memorable, so that we may not be accused of passing the day in idleness. Let us make haste to build a little house of prayer, in which, if they do not soon throw open the gates to us, we may devote ourselves to the service of God.' As soon as he had said this, his men hurried off to collect lime and stones, with wood and paint, and brought them to the workmen who always accompanied him. Between the fourth hour of the day and the twelfth, with the help of the leaders and the common soldiery, they had built such a cathedral, with walls and roofs, Paneled ceilings and painted frescoes that no one watching would have believed that it could have been achieved in a whole year. How, on the following day, some of the citizens wanted to open the gates to him, others wished to resist him, hopeless as it seemed, and yet others chose to shut themselves up, and how Charlemagne, with great ease, without any shedding of blood, but simply by his military skill, conquered and captured the city, all this I leave for others to tell, for those who follow your Highness not for love but in the hope of gain.

Suggested Readings

Einhard and Notker the Stammerer, *The Two Lives of Charlemagne*, (Lewis Thorpe trans.) New York: Penguin Classics, 1969.

14

Happy Few: The Five Leadership Lessons of Shakespeare's Henry V

LCDR Tyrus Lemerande, USNR

Leadership is an art. Like music, literature, dance, performance, or any of the visual mediums, leadership requires exhaustive study, diligent preparation, and constant practice. And like these other art forms, leadership also depends a great deal upon insight and inspiration. For those with the courage to pursue them, that insight and inspiration can be found anywhere, especially in the works of William Shakespeare. However, finding leadership lessons in a knotty and often difficult text can be frustrating. After all, Shakespeare wrote plays—not instruction manuals. But with constancy and effort, a wealth of wisdom about the price, and purpose, of leadership can be found in the pages of his play titled *King Henry V*.

I have taught this play to midshipman on several different occasions and at the end of each week find myself pleading for additional time. The discussions that are generated by a classroom filled with military men and women never cease to engage and intrigue me. And although I have colleagues who continually remind me "civilians like this play too," I cannot ignore the fact that this play connects with a military audience in unique and resounding ways. It certainly spoke to me while I was at Annapolis. I was first exposed to *Henry V* in Dr. David White's Shakespeare Seminar during my youngster year at the Academy. The play, and more specifically, the character of the Henry himself, made a lasting impression upon me. So much so that when I was asked more than ten years later to create a one-man show for my master's thesis, I immediately thought of Shakespeare's young, warrior king.

Harry of Monmouth has fascinated me from the first moment I met him in that Sampson Hall classroom. From his rambunctious youth as the mad-cap Prince of Wales to the shedding and shunning of his former self with his ascent to the throne of England, here is a man driven to atone for the sins of his father. Harry needs to be a good king so that he might quell the rebellion that has tormented his land and unite his people against a common foe. That drive, that need, is fueled by a great love of country and an even greater sense of responsibility. Henry was an ordinary man thrust into extraordinary circumstances. And he prevailed, sustained by honor, duty and an unwavering faith in God—values he and I have shared ever since I raised my right hand and swore to defend my country as a member of the U.S. Navy.

For the past five years, I have lived with King Harry. I have studied him, questioned him, admired him. And every so often I have had the great privilege of *becoming* him on stage. As an actor, I am able to live his journey—a journey I call, "the constitution of a king." The five aspects of leadership discussed below are waypoints on that journey. These values of sacrifice, justice, courage, responsibility and faith are more than simply concepts to be studied. They are, in fact, beliefs that define a way of life. Leadership, true leadership, is born of *sacrifice*, forged with *justice*, defined by *courage*, fed by *responsibility* and sustained by *faith*.

SACRIFICE

Harry is one of only a handful of Shakespearean characters who are allowed to mature over a series of plays. We first meet the man who will become King Henry V in the pair of plays named for his father, *Henry IV, Parts 1 & 2*. Hal, as he is known, is far from a model citizen. In fact, in the eyes of his father, the prince is a disgrace and an embarrassment, as he repeatedly gets drunk and revels in the streets of Eastcheap with that "old white-bearded Satan," Falstaff. Best described as an "abominable misleader of youth," Falstaff is young Hal's confidant, drinking companion and, in many ways, surrogate father.

But the fat knight will unwittingly serve a higher purpose. At King Harry's coronation, which occurs in the very last pages of *Henry IV, Part 2*, Falstaff is exposed, berated and ridiculed

as the personification of what the prince has been and will never be again. Before the assembled masses, Harry insults his old friend without mercy but not without purpose. By verbally, and very publicly, abusing his so-called "mentor," Harry completely and utterly admonishes his checkered past and, in so doing, grandly pronounces the gravity and severity with which he accepts the crown.

If leadership begins with sacrifice, here then is the painful beginning of Harry's journey. In this single moment, the king must decide which is more important: friendship or country. For a man of Harry's character, the choice is simple, yet extremely difficult to execute. Sacrifice is never easy, especially when one is asked to give up one's dear friend. However, the safety and stability of England is wholly dependant upon the king's ability to maintain good order and discipline. And thus, the raucous, carefree behavior, which defined a young man, simply cannot be allowed to taint the image of this new monarch.

When done well, the "rejection of Falstaff," as this scene is known, is one of the most heart wrenching you will ever see on stage. The heir-apparent has been called home to court, as his father has taken deathly ill. Falstaff and his fellows are left behind in an Eastcheap pub, dreaming of the riches and the glory that will now befall them as "friends" of the newly crowned king. But the Hal who leaves is not the Harry who returns. When the king's coronation parade passes by, Falstaff haughtily and self-assuredly calls to his friend, who responds with one of the most scalding rebukes in all of Shakespeare.

I know thee not, old man. Fall to thy prayers.
How ill white hairs becomes a fool and jester.
I have long dreamt of such a kind of man,
So surfeit-swelled, so old, and so profane,
But being awaked I do despise my dream.
Make less thy body hence, and more thy
    grace;
Leave gormandizing. Know the grave doth
    gape
For thee thrice wider than for other men.

Reply not to me with some fool born jest.
Presume not that I am the thing I was,
For God doth know, so shall the world
    perceive,
That I have turned away my former self;
So will I those that kept me company.
When thou dost hear I am as I have been,
Approach me, and thou shalt be as thou wast,
The tutor and the feeder of my riots.
Till then, I banish thee, on pain of death,
As I have done the rest of my misleaders,
Not to come near our person by ten mile.

To all those watching, Hal has transformed seemingly overnight into the vision of kingliness. But that change, which to the outside eye seems instantaneous, continues to gnaw at the king for the rest of his life. People do not change so quickly, not in their hearts. Outward appearances may be altered, but that which burns at our core cannot be so easily transfigured. One does not simply give up a friend like Falstaff and feel no ill effects. And that is what makes this moment in the king's life so momentous. Given the abject pain he must be feeling as he speaks these words, he speaks them all the same, without hesitation or remorse.

Henry has been thrust into the public eye. He has been asked to become something greater than himself. Henry is no longer just a man, but a symbol of his country. When he accepts the reins of command, he also accepts the sacrifices he must make for the sake of his office. When he puts on the crown, he ceases to be Hal and becomes King Henry V. Henry acknowledges, understands and respects the weight of that charge.

The Naval Academy is filled with young Hals. Some, unfortunately, discover too late the "requirements of office." Every year, invariably, a handful of rebellious souls will go out drinking on a Saturday night, do something stupid and end up on the front page of Sunday's *Washington Post*. And, invariably, the headline plastered across the paper in big, bold letters will begin, "Naval Academy Midshipman…" The names of those involved become insignificant when compared to the symbol, the school, the service, they represent.

That loss of identity, that sacrifice of self, is something "students" at the Naval Academy will continue to resist for as long as her gates remain open. But the transformation cannot be denied. When a young man or woman puts on the uniform, they are no longer simply responsible for themselves. They are responsible for the history, tradition and respect of the entire naval service. They become more than what they are alone. Like Henry, they become symbols. And when they bring shame, or glory, upon themselves, they bring the same upon all those who have ever worn, or will ever wear, the uniform.

To accept such responsibility requires a great sacrifice. Some, like Harry, will answer the call. Others, sadly, will not. But the paradigm, as it has done for thousands of years, will remain the same. The public's expectation of those in power will not change. In medieval England, the people looked to the king for inspiration, for guidance, for wisdom, for strength. More than a man, the king was God's minister on Earth. To become that symbol, Harry must give up whole parts of himself. He understands the needs of his country and that they are far more important than his own. He has been called to sacrifice so that he might become more than what he was before. Only then will he be able to lead his country to new and greater glory.

JUSTICE

If leadership is born of sacrifice, authority is born of justice. And a leader cannot function without authority. An officer of the naval service is called upon to deliver judgment. That officer's authority—that is, his or her ability to command respect—will be directly proportional to his or her perceived ability to be fair and just. But although justice has something to do with the severity of the punishment, it has everything to do with the consistency with which that punishment is handed down.

Authority is only truly respected when it is delivered with consistency. Maintaining that consistency is not always easy. Delivering punishment is hard. In fact, it may be one of the hardest charges bestowed upon a naval officer. An officer's judgments will be met with consternation and appeal, to be sure. Delivering punishment may be hard, but accepting punishment is even harder. And in today's litigious society, it seems even the wisdom of Solomon could be tempered by extenuating circumstances. However, an officer's judgment will always be met with respect, as long as it is delivered with equality and uniformity.

As God's minister on Earth, the king must be forged of integrity and ruled by justice. King Harry's resolve is tested in Act II, when he is faced with "dangerous treason." Three of his most trusted nobles have conspired with the enemy to sabotage the expedition into France. They have been paid in gold to assassinate the king before he sails from Southampton on England's southern shore.

The king, upon learning of the plot, stages a public display of authority in which his "friends" unknowingly seal their own fate. Devoid of mercy, these "corrupted men" will be shown none in return. But first, the king must deal with the betrayal of his childhood friend and most trusted advisor, Henry, Lord Scroop of Masham. Henry's speech to Scroop contains some of the most solemn and heart-felt lines in the play, as if a small piece of the king himself is snuffed out as he acknowledges the level of his friend's deception. In the speech's ultimate image, Harry likens this betrayal to the original fall from grace in the Garden of Eden, so sharp is the pain that stings the young king's heart.

> What shall I say to thee, Lord Scroop, thou
> cruel,
> Ingrateful, savage and inhuman creature?
> Thou that didst bear the key of all my coun-
> sels,
> That knew'st the very bottom of my soul,

> That almost mightst have coined me into
> gold,
> Wouldst thou have practiced on me for thy
> use:
> May it be possible that foreign hire
> Could out of thee extract one spark of evil
> That might annoy my finger? 'Tis so strange
> That though the truth of it stands off as
> gross
> As black and white, my eye will scarcely see
> it.
> Such and so finely bolted didst thou seem.
> And thus thy fall hath left a kind of blot
> To mark the full-fraught man and best en-
> dued
> With some suspicion. I will weep for thee;
> For this revolt of thine, methinks, is like
> Another fall of man.

The challenge of bringing King Henry to life on stage has always been and, at least for me, will always be finding his humanity, which lies somewhere between knowing what must be done and actually doing it. That is the struggle that defines the young king and that, in truth, defines each and every one of us. We call this struggle integrity: doing what is right, not what is easy. Justice simply cannot exist without impeccable integrity.

I discussed earlier the sacrifices that Henry must make for the sake of his office. Here again we see yet another piece that must be cut away for the good of the whole. Henry's integrity is being tested and, as is so often the case, in front of everyone. Leniency is not an option. Because in this case leniency would translate to favoritism and favoritism would lead to a breakdown in authority. Henry cannot allow that to happen. He has but one option, execution.

As the ultimate public figure, the king's every act, every move is scrutinized, analyzed, and interpreted. Henry knows that his authority depends upon his ability to deliver justice. He understands that the fate of these three men will impact the life of every man who sails with him for the shores of France. So he does what he must. Forced by circumstance to ignore their cries for mercy, the king sentences the three men to death. It is not easy, but it is right. And in that unshakeable integrity, King Harry finds the authority to command.

COURAGE

Once more unto the breach, dear friends,
    once more,
Or close the wall up with our English dead.
In peace there's nothing so becomes a man
As modest stillness, and humility.
But when the blast of war blows in our ears,
Then imitate the action of the tiger:
Stiffen the sinews, conjure up the blood,
Disguise fair nature with hard-favored rage.
Then lend the eye a terrible aspect:
Let it pry through the portage of the head
Like the brass cannon; let the brow
    o'rewhelm it
As fearfully as doth a gallèd rock
O'rehang and jutty his confounded base,
Swilled with the wild and wasteful ocean.
Now set the teeth and stretch the nostril
    wide,
Hold hard the breath, and bend up every
    spirit
To his full height. On, on, you noblest
    English,
Whose blood is fet from Fathers of
    war-proof,
Fathers that, like so many Alexanders,
Have in these parts from morn till even
    fought,
And sheathed their swords for lack of
    argument.
Dishonor not your mothers; now attest
That those whom you called fathers did
    beget you.
Be copy now to men of grosser blood,
And teach them how to war. And you, good
    yeomen,
Whose limbs were made in England, show us
    here
The mettle of your pasture. Let us swear,

That you are worth your breeding, which I
    doubt not,
For there is none of you so mean and base
That hath not noble luster in your eyes.
I see you stand like greyhounds in the slips,
Straining upon the start. The game's afoot.
Follow your spirit, and upon this charge
Cry, "God for Harry! England, and Saint
    George!"

If justice relies upon integrity, then inspiration is built upon courage. In the previous section you witnessed what is known as moral courage. In this section, I want discuss what I call "essential courage"—courage that is born of fear, yet ruled by purpose. Courage, the type of courage so often displayed on the field of battle, is not characterized by the absence of fear, but the suppression of fear. The speech printed above is one of the most famous examples of battlefield inspiration in all of literature. But, believe it or not, these words are born of desperation.

A few years ago, I had the opportunity to bring my one-man adaptation of *Henry V* to the Edinburgh Fringe Festival in Scotland. It just so happened that Edinburgh Castle was on the walk between my flat and the space where I performed every day for three weeks. In the morning, and again at night, I would trudge past the massive walls of the castle. Often I would stop to gaze up at the imposing stone structure and wonder: how did anyone ever capture a castle? With Henry's words ringing in my ears, I would try to imagine the courage such an assault would require.

But in the age of medieval warfare, such a siege would take not only courage but a great deal of stamina as well. Castles did not fall in a day, or even in a week. Battles like this one, before the gates of Harfleur, would take months, during which time the men outside the castle would be at a distinct disadvantage. Exposed to the elements, sleeping in the mud and the muck, more men would be lost to sickness and disease than to actual battle. In fact, famine was one of the many "weapons" used to attack a castle; cut off their supply lines and hope they starve before you do.

Even if your cannons were powerful enough to blow a hole into the side of such a fortress, that opening would need to be charged by men before those on the inside could shore up the gap in their defenses. You can imagine who would hold the advantage in such a situation: the wolves within the castle would wait for the lambs to come pouring through. Then they would mow them down and pile them up.

And yet, this is what the king is asking of his men. And therein lies the challenge of this speech, and of this moment. Henry must inspire his men to action even in the face of grave danger. Here then is a defining time in the evolution of a young leader. He pushes down his own fear and through that act of suppression finds the courage to inspire a sickly band of battle-weary soldiers to charge one more time into the breech.

This moment dramatizes one of the most essential elements of leadership—inspiration. Leadership is more than just being in charge. Leadership is *taking* charge. As I stated in the beginning, leadership is an art. To achieve greatness requires practice, practice and more practice. But, as with any art form, true greatness begins and ends with talent. In the world of leadership, we call it charisma—that innate ability to persuade: to make people listen, to make people hear. Some have this gift and some don't. King Henry had it in bunches. The strength of his personality united a country. When Harry assumed the throne, not only did he seem to change overnight, but the civil wars that had plagued his land for more than a decade stopped in an instant. The people of England beheld this new king and simply knew without a doubt that he was the true heir to the throne.

At the siege of Harfleur, Henry is tasked with channeling that charisma—that energy—into the limbs and hearts of his charges. He does this by looking into their eyes and speaking to their souls. An essential part of our humanity is grounded in our sense of worth. We need to feel as if we belong, as if we are part of something greater than ourselves. A child who is scolded by his parent is not equal to the parent, nor is a subordinate who is reprimanded by his superior officer. But soldiers who are motivated by the glory of a higher cause, soldiers who are invited to share in the spoils of victory, soldiers who are bound together by honor and by friendship, those soldiers will fight, scratch and claw until the day is won.

When Henry rallies his men at Harfleur, he does what all great leaders hope to do—he leads. Henry is right there with his men amongst the fire and the fear, the dirt and the danger. He is not asking his men to do anything that he is not willing to do himself. That kind of courage, that kind of leadership, can inspire men to greatness.

RESPONSIBILITY

Perhaps my favorite act in all of *Henry V* is Act IV—what I call the "responsibility and accountability" act. Borrowing a cloak from one of his knights on the eve of Agincourt, the disguised king encounters a group of soldiers by a fireside where they proceed to discuss the responsibilities of leadership. The men have no idea they are addressing their master and commander when they seek to put the blame of every man's impending death upon the king's head. Henry tries to disabuse this notion, saying "every subject's duty is the king's, but every subject's soul's his own," but the debate is brought to an abrupt halt when one of the soldiers, overwrought by their impending doom, assaults the disguised king. The men scatter into the darkness and the king is left alone to ponder the merits of their argument. What results is one of the most honestly revealing speeches in the play.

Upon the King. Let us our lives, our souls,
Our debts, our careful wives,
Our children, and our sins, lay on the King.
We must bear all. O hard condition,

Twin-born with greatness, subject to the
    breath
Of every fool, whose sense no more can feel
But his own wringing. What infinite heart-
    sease
Must kings neglect that private men enjoy?
And what have kings that privates have not
    too,
Save Ceremony, save general Ceremony?
And what art thou, thou idol Ceremony?
What kind of god art thou, that suffer'st
    more
Of mortal griefs then do thy worshippers?
What are thy rents? What are thy comings-
    in?
O Ceremony, show me but thy worth.
What is thy soul of adoration?
Art thou aught else but place, degree, and
    form,
Creating awe and fear in other men?
Wherein thou art less happy, being feared,
Then they in fearing.
What drink'st thou oft, instead of homage
    sweet,
But poisoned flattery? O, be sick, great
    greatness,
And bid thy Ceremony give thee cure.
With titles blown from adulation?
Will it give place to flexure and low bending?
Canst thou, when thou command'st the
    beggar's knee,
Command the health of it? No, thou proud
    dream,
That play'st so subtly with a king's repose.
I am a king that find thee, and I know,
'Tis not the balm, the scepter, and the ball,
The sword, the mace, the crown imperial,
The intertissued robe of gold and pearl,
The farcèd title running 'fore the king,
The throne he sits on, nor the tide of pomp
That beats upon the high shore of this
    world—
No, not all these, thrice-gorgeous
    Ceremony,
Not all these, laid in bed majestical,

Can sleep so soundly as the wretched slave
Who, with a body filled and vacant mind,
Gets him to rest, crammed with distressful
    bread
Never sees horrid night, the child of hell,
But like a lackey from the rise to set
Sweats in the eye of Phoebus, and all night
Sleeps in Elysium; next day after dawn
Doth rise and help Hyperion to his horse,
And follows so the ever-running year
With profitable labor to his grave.
And but for Ceremony, such a wretch,
Winding up days with toil and nights with
    sleep,
Had the forehand and vantage of a king.

In this speech the king rails against "Ceremony" as if it were a devil sent to tempt and tor-
ment him. And finally, in the silence of the night,
we get to see the king as he sees himself: as a
man, just a man. A man haunted by fear, yet
ruled by fate. Henry knows he is no more immortal than anyone else, a sword will penetrate
his flesh just as soon as the next man's. Yet his
position makes him different, makes him more.
He is the king, after all. As such, he is a beacon
of hope. He can inspire with a look, bind with a
smile. Still, "Ceremony" cannot truly define
him. And, in many ways, he must not allow it to
define him. For only in acknowledging his weaknesses does he eventually find his strength.

Here we see the king wishing for a simpler
time. We are allowed to witness the extreme
weight of the burden he carries. And in the despair that fills these lines we find the human
being beneath the crown. Leaders are not free
from doubt and fear. Henry is unsure and he is
undoubtedly afraid. He needs only to look across
the rain-soaked field to see ample reason for
worry: an army five times as large as his own,
filled with competent French troops eager to
slice a few English throats.

He must fear deep in his heart that he and his
army will be slaughtered tomorrow on this field
of France. And that fear is compounded by the

fact that he is responsible for the lives and those men whom he will lead into battle with the dawn. As a leader he, of course, takes full responsibility. After all, he has brought them here. He has brought them to the very edge of damnation. But, at this moment, alone in the silence of the night, unencumbered by "Ceremony," the weight of that responsibility seems too much even for the king to bear.

Leaders are not superhuman. Nor are they always right. But they must be prepared to accept responsibility for their decisions. Responsibility is devoid of blame or accusation. Responsibility simply is. As a leader one makes decisions and stands by them regardless of the consequences. The sincerity of that simplicity is wholly freeing and utterly dangerous. Responsibility is not something to be toyed with, nor is it to be taken lightly. Responsibility is what feeds us as leaders. The more responsibility we accept, the greater we become. When we shy away from responsibility, ignore it or abuse it, we weaken and eventually disappear.

FAITH

And finally, we come to the most famous speech in the play and perhaps in all of Shakespeare—at least for a military audience—the "band of brothers" or "Crispin's Day" speech. In this speech we find a totally different Harry than the one we just watched wrestle with uncertainty. Unlike the solemn, contemplative king we witnessed among the campfires, the Harry that appears at dawn is brimming with confidence and filled with excitement. And, of course, we know why this must be so: he has returned to the public eye. He cannot allow any trace of his private fear or doubt to "dishearten his army." For many of his men, that image of strength and confidence is all they have left to hang on to.

His men are tired, hungry and sick. They have been marching across the French countryside on foot for weeks, trying unsuccessfully to find a quiet way back to the port town of Calais and the ships that will bring them home to England. A superior French army, outnumbering the English five to one, stands in their way, just beyond the River Somme. The French force is well rested, better equipped and, unlike Harry's force, eager for battle. As the sun rises on October 25th, Harry's army looks across the narrow field and finds death staring back at them. An eerie silence grips the English camp as an atmosphere of desperation seems to choke the air. No one believes they can win. Even the knights find the odds overwhelming. And in a moment of weakness, the king's own cousin, Westmorland, finds himself wishing aloud for but a few more men. The king's response is pointed and direct.

What's he that wishes so?
My cousin Westmorland? No, my fair
    cousin.
If we are marked to die, we are enough
To do our country loss; and if to live,
The fewer men, the greater share of honor.
God's will, I pray thee, wish not one man
    more.
By Jove, I am not covetous for gold,
Nor care I who doth feed upon my cost;
It yearns me not if men my garments wear;
Such outward things dwell not in my desires.
But if it be a sin to covet honor
I am the most offending soul alive.
No, faith, my coz, wish not a man from
    England.
God's peace, I would not lose so great an
    honor
As one man more, methinks, would share
    from me
For the best hope I have. O, do not wish one
    more.
Rather proclaim it, Westmorland, through
    my host
That he which hath no stomach to this fight,
Let him depart; his passport shall be made
And crowns for convoy put into his purse.
We would not die in that man's company
That fears his fellowship to die with us.

This day is called the Feast of Crispian.
He that outlives this day and comes safe
　　home
Will stand a-tiptoe when this day is named
And rouse him at the name of Crispian.
He that shall see this day and live old age
Will yearly on the vigil feast his neighbors
And say, "Tomorrow is Saint Crispian."
Then will he strip his sleeve and show his
　　scars,
And say, "These wounds I had on Crispin's
　　Day."
Old men forget; yet all shall be forgot
But he'll remember with advantages
What feats he did that day. Then shall our
　　names,
Familiar in his mouth as household words—
Harry the King, Bedford and Exeter,
Warwick and Talbot, Salisbury and
　　Gloucester—
Be in their flowing cups freshly rememberèd.
This story shall the good man teach his son;
And Crispin Crispian shall ne'er go by,
From this day to the ending of the world,
But we in it shall be rememberèd—
We few, we happy few, we band of brothers.
For he today that sheds his blood with me
Shall be my brother; be he ne'er so vile,
This day shall gentle his condition.
And gentlemen in England now abed
Shall think themselves accurst they were not
　　here,
And hold their manhoods cheap whiles any
　　speaks
That fought with us upon Saint Crispin's
　　Day.

By the time King Harry finishes this speech, his men are ready to follow him to the ends of the Earth and beyond. Because in the course of this speech, Harry makes them believe. He rekindles their faith in him and in each other. And in the face of overwhelming odds, that faith is what, in the end, wins the day. Henry binds his men together with passion and with honor. The English soldiers who defeat the French at Agin-court are not fighting for God or for country, they are fighting for each other.

Faith is by far the most powerful weapon any leader can possess. An army who doesn't believe it can win has already lost. But an army filled with hope and bound together by brotherhood can snatch victory even from the jaws of death.

At the Naval Academy there is a saying that every plebe must commit to memory: we are only as strong as our weakest link. Henry undoubtedly would have subscribed to that axiom. For in this one speech he successfully pinpoints and eradicates his most dangerous enemy: individual fear and doubt. In this one moment, Harry transforms a rag-tag band of ruined men into a cohesive brotherhood of warriors, engaged and focused on a single purpose. But the true genius of this speech lies in the desperation that inspires it and the total lack of desperation found in the delivery. Harry conquers his personal demons and finds a way to gather and steel himself. For this speech is about hope. And Harry finds his hope in the faces of the men staring back at him.

For those of us in the military, we know a bond of service that extends beyond class and distinction. That bond is forged by a common belief in the values I have discussed above—sacrifice, justice, courage, responsibility and faith. These words have weight and merit and a significance that goes far beyond simple definition. They have become symbols that define a way of life. That is the type of brotherhood Harry offers his men on the eve of Agincourt. He offers them immortality. The immortality that can only be achieved by being part of something greater than themselves, by being part of something that will never be forgotten.

Shakespeare may have written this play more than four hundred years ago, but the leadership lessons that can be pulled from its pages are indeed timeless. The quotations and excerpts included above are, of course, a limited sampling of the riches this play has to offer. There is so much more to be found. Keep looking. Leadership is a delicate and dangerous art that must be studied and practiced with great care and consideration. It is also a journey—a journey of exploration and discovery, fueled by inspiration and marked by wisdom.

Suggested Reading

Bolt, Robert. *A Man for All Seasons*. Westminster: Vintage International, 1990.

Heaney, Seamus. *The Burial at Thebes: A Version of Sophocles' Antigone.* New York: Farrar, Straus and Giroux, 2004.

Shakespeare, William. *Coriolanus*. London: Arden, 2005.

Shaw, George Bernard. *Arms and the Man*. London: Penguin, 1988.

Shaw, George Bernard. *Saint Joan*. London: Penguin, 1946.

Barnet, Sylvan. "The English History Plays." *A Short Guide to Shakespeare*, pp. 113–37. San Diego: Harcourt Brace & Company, 1972.

Battenhouse, Roy W. "*Henry V* as Heroic Comedy." *Essays on Shakespeare and Elizabethan Drama*, pp. 163–82. Columbia: University of Missouri.

Shakespeare, William. *Henry V*. New York: Penguin, 1968.

About the Author

LCDR Lemerande graduated with a B.S. in English from the Naval Academy in 1994. He left active duty in 1999 to pursue a graduate degree in acting at Penn State University, where he received his M.F.A. in 2002. As a member of the Naval Reserve, he is currently assigned to the Naval War College in Newport, RI. He is the co-founder and Artistic Director of Knighthorse Theatre Company, which is dedicated to bringing innovative, imaginative and inspiring theatre to schools, colleges and universities across the country and around the world.

15

Unanticipated Courage: The Story of Hannah Dustan

Dr. Robert D. Madison

For nearly three hundred years, the story of Hannah Dustan has thrilled students of American consciousness. And yet each new teller of the tale tells a different story. To Cotton Mather (1663–1728), Hannah's trial is simply an illustration of the workings of God among his faithful. "Salvages," Quakers, Papists—all alike are worthy of extermination to Mather, and Hannah is the agent of God's just revenge on diabolical interference with His plan.

Writing a hundred years later, Timothy Dwight (1752–1817), president of Yale College, briefly explores the moral logic of Hannah's action and even wonders what she must feel. But he does not imagine answers to his own questions and shifts his concern to the unquestionably (to him) honorable behavior of her husband.

The American Quaker poet John Greenleaf Whittier (1807–1892) contrasts conventional feminine virtues with Hannah's "dark and terrible passions." He develops, or invents, the mindset of the savages and especially Hannah at the moment her newborn child is slain. Whittier's graphic detail heightens the moral impact of Hannah's decision to spare the last Indian child. Whittier's "simple" but not "unvarnished" tale concludes by echoing Dwight's call for antiquarian curiosity.

Nathaniel Hawthorne (1804–1864) wraps Hannah's revenge in a setting more Gothic than graphic. It is apprehension rather than experience that creates the horror for both Hannah and her husband, but even more remarkably it is the Ishmaelic Indians who receive Hawthorne's ultimate sympathy. Mather is a bigot and Hannah a "raging tigress" who takes her place with Hawthorne's other crones and witches.

Henry David Thoreau (1817–1862) focused on Hannah's "nervous energy" to develop a parallel between Hannah's escape and John and Henry Thoreau's own boat trip down the Merrimack. Indian lore replaces horror; scalping is an afterthought. Despite the imagery Thoreau lavishes on the riverine setting, Hannah's act has separated her from Nature as she paddles through a "drear and howling wilderness." The apple tree emphasizes the loss of Eden, a theme that is reinforced in Thoreau's conclusion and immediate recollection that all this took place since "Milton wrote his Paradise Lost."

"A Notable Exploit; wherein, Dux Faemina Facti"

Cotton Mather

On *March* 15, 1697, the *Salvages* made a Descent upon the Skirts of *Haverhil*, Murdering and Captiving about Thirty-nine Persons, and Burning about half a Dozen Houses. In this Broil, one *Hannah Dustan* having lain-in about a Week, attended with her Nurse, *Mary Ness,* a Widow, a body of terrible *Indians* drew near unto the House where the lay, with Designs to carry on their Bloody Devastations. Her Husband hastened from his Employments abroad unto the relief of his Distressed Family; and first bidding *Seven* of his *Eight* Children (which were from *Two* to *Seventeen* Years of Age) to get away as fastt as they could unto some Garrison in the Town, he went in to inform his Wife of the horrible Distress come upon them. E'er she could get up, the fierce *Indians* were got so near, that utterly despairing to do her any Service, he ran out after his Children; resolving that on the Horse which he had with him, he would Ride away with *That* which he should in this Extremity find his Affections to pitch most upon, and leave the rest unto the Care of the Divine Providence. He overtook his Children about Forty Rod from his Door; but then such was the *Agony* of his Parental Affections, that she found it impossible for him to distinguish any one of them from the rest; wherefore he took up a Courageous Resolution to Live and Die with them all. A Party of *Indians* came up with him; and now though they Fired at him, and he Fired at them, yet he Manfully kept at the Rear of his *Little Army* of Unarmed Children, while they Marched off with the Pace of a Child of Five

Years Old; until, by the Singular Providence of God, he arrived safe with them all unto a Place of Safety about a Mile or two from his House. But his House must in the mean time have more dismal *Tragedies* acted at it. The *Nurse* trying to escape with the New-born Infant, fell into the Hands of the Formidable *Salvages*; and those furious Tawnies coming into the House, bid poor *Dustan* to rise immediately. Full of Astonishment she did so; and sitting down in the Chimney with an Heart full of most fearful *Expectation*, she saw the raging Dragons rifle all that they could carry away, and set the House on Fire. About Nineteen or Twenty *Indians* now led these away, with about half a Score other *English Captives*; but e'er they had gone many Steps, they dash'd out the Brains of the *Infant* against a Tree; and several of the other *Captives*, as they began to Tire in their sad *Journey*, were soon sent unto their *Long Home*; the *Salvages* would presently Bury their Hatchets in their Brains, and leave their Carcases on the Ground for Birds and Beasts to Feed upon. However, *Dustan* (with her Nurse) notwithstanding her present Condition, Travelled that Night about a Dozen Miles, and then kept up with their New Masters in a long Travel of an Hundred and Fifty Miles, more or less, within a few Days Ensuing, without any sensible Damage in their Health, from the Hardships of their *Travel*, their *Lodging*, their *Diet*, and their many other Difficulties. These Two poor Women were now in the Hands of those whose *Tender Mercies are Cruelties*; but the good God, who hath all *Hearts in his own Hands*, heard the Sighs of these *Prisoners*, and gave them to find unexpected Favour from the *Master* who laid claim unto them. That *Indian Family* consisted of Twelve Persons; Two Stout Men, Three Women, and Seven Children; and for the Shame of many an *English Family*, that has the Character of *Prayerless* upon it, I must now Publish what these poor Women assure me: 'Tis this, in Obedience to the Instructions which the *French* have given them, they would have *Prayers* in their Family no less than Thrice every Day, in the *Morning*, at *Noon*, and in the *Evening*; nor would they ordinarily let their Children *Eat or Sleep* without first saying their *Prayers*. Indeed these *Idolaters* were like the rest of their whiter Brethren *Persecutors*, and would not endure that these poor Women should retire to their *English Prayers*, if they could hinder them. Nevertheless, the poor Women had nothing but Fervent Prayers to make their Lives Comfortable or Tolerable; and by being daily sent out upon Business, they had Opportunities together and asunder to do like another *Hannah*, in *Pouring out their Souls before the Lord:* Nor did their praying Friends among our selves forbear to *Pour out* Supplications for them. Now they could not observe it without some Wonder, that their *Indian* Master sometimes when he saw them dejected would say unto them, *What need you Trouble your self? If your God will have you delivered, you shall be so!* And it seems our God would have it so to be. This *Indian Family* was now Travelling with these Two Captive Women, (and an *English* Youth taken from *Worcester* a Year and half before,) unto a Rendezvouz of *Salvages*, which they call a *Town* somewhere beyond *Penacook*, and they still told these poor Women, that when they came to this Town they must be Stript, and Scourg'd, and Run the *Gantlet* through the whole Army of *Indians*. They said this was the *Fashion* when the Captives first came to a Town; and they derided some of the Faint-hearted *English*, which they said, fainted and swoon'd away under the *Torments* of this Discipline. But on *April* 30, while they were yet, it may be, about an Hundred and Fifty Miles from the *Indian* Town, a little before break of Day, when the whole Crew was in a *Dead Sleep*, (Reader, see if it prove not so!) one of these Women took up a Resolution to intimate the Action of *Jael* upon *Sisera*; and being where she had not her own *Life* secured by any *Law* unto her, she thought she was not forbidden by any *Law* to take away the *Life* of the *Murderers*, by whom her *Child* had been Butchered. She heartened the *Nurse* and the *Youth* to assist her in this Enterprize; and all furnishing themselves with *Hatchets* for the purpose, they struck such home Blows upon the

Heads of their *Sleeping Oppressors*, that e'er they could any of them struggle into any effectual resistance, *at the Feet* of those poor Prisoners, *they bow'd, they fell, they lay down; at their Feet they bowed, they fell; where they bowed, there they fell down Dead.* Only one *Squaw* escaped sorely Wounded from them in the Dark; and one *Boy*, whom they reserved asleep, intending to bring him away with them, suddenly wak'd and Scuttled away from this Desolation. But cutting off the *Scalps* of the *Ten Wretches*, they came off, and received *Fifty Pounds* from the General Assembly of the Province, as a Recompence of their Action; besides which, they received many *Presents of Congratulation* from their more private Friends; but none gave 'em a greater Taste of Bounty than Colonel *Nicholson*, the Governor of *Maryland*, who hearing of their Action, sent 'em a very generous Token of his Favour.

from *Travels in New England and New York* (1821)

Timothy Dwight

Haverhill was settled in the year 1637, and incorporated in 1645. During the first seventy-five years from its settlement it suffered often, and greatly, by savage depredations. The story of these depredations is, however, imperfectly known at the present time. Even the facts which are still known are so dispersed in the possession of different persons as to render it very difficult to obtain them correctly. This kind of knowledge is daily becoming less, and will soon be lost. It is much to be wished that inquisitive men throughout this country would glean and preserve the little which is left. It is a serious and unfortunate error of men in general to suppose that events familiarized to themselves by fireside repetition will be uninteresting to others, and that efforts to preserve them will be considered as either trifling or arrogant. In no country, probably, are the inhabitants more inquisitive than in New England. But their inquiries terminate, or have until lately terminated chiefly in things remote in time or place, and have been very little occupied by subjects pertaining to their own country. It is perhaps natural to man to feel that his own concerns, or any concerns which are familiar to him, will be little regarded by those who come after him. Few parents are solicitous to have their own portraits taken; yet, after their decease, scarcely any legacy is thought more valuable by their children.

In the year 1697, on the 5th day of March, a body of Indians attacked this town, burnt a small number of houses, and killed and captivated about forty of the inhabitants. A party of them, arrayed in all the terrors of the Indian war dress, and carrying with them the multiplied horrors of a savage invasion, approached near to the house of a Mr. Dustin. This man was abroad at his usual labor. Upon the first alarm, he flew to the house, with a hope of hurrying to a place of safety his family, consisting of his wife, who had been confined a week only in childbed; her nurse a Mrs. Mary Neff, a widow from the neighborhood; and eight children. Seven of his children he ordered to flee with the utmost expedition in the course opposite to that in which the danger was approaching, and went himself to assist his wife. Before she could leave her bed, the savages were upon them. Her husband, despairing of rendering her any service, flew to the door, mounted his horse, and determined to snatch up the child with which he was unable to part when he should overtake the little flock. When he came up to them, about two hundred yards from his house, he was unable to make a choice, or to leave any one of the number. He therefore determined to take his lot with them and to defend them from their murderers, or die by their side. A body of the Indians pursued and came up with him, and from near distances fired at him and his little company. He returned the fire and retreated, alternately. For more than a mile he kept so resolute a face to his enemy, retiring in the rear of his charge, returned the fire of the savages so often and with so good success, and sheltered so effectually his terrified companions that he finally lodged them all, safe from the pursuing butchers, in a distant house. When it is remembered how numerous his assailants were,

how bold when an overmatch for their enemies, how active, and what excellent marksmen, a devout mind will consider the hand of Providence as unusually visible in the preservation of this family.

Another party of the Indians entered the house immediately after Mr. Dustin had quitted it, and found Mrs. Dustin and her nurse, who was attempting to fly with the infant in her arms. Mrs. Dustin they ordered to rise instantly; and, before she could completely dress herself, obliged her and her companion to quit the house after they had plundered it and set it on fire. In company with several other captives, they began their march into the wilderness; she, feeble, sick, terrified beyond measure, partially clad, one of her feet bare, and the season utterly unfit for comfortable traveling. The air was chilly and keen; and the earth covered, alternately, with snow and deep mud. Her conductors were unfeeling, insolent, and revengeful. Murder was their glory, and torture their sport. Her infant was in her nurse's arms, and infants were the customary victims of savage barbarity.

The company had proceeded but a short distance when an Indian, thinking it encumbrance, took the child out of the nurse's arms and dashed its head against a tree. What were then the feelings of the mother?

Such of the other captives as began to be weary and to lag, the Indians tomahawked. The slaughter was not an act of revenge, nor of cruelty. It was a mere convenience: an effort so familiar as not even to excite an emotion.

Feeble as Mrs. Dustin was, both she and her nurse sustained without yielding the fatigue of the journey. Their intense distress for the death of the child and of their companions, anxiety for those whom they had left behind, and unceasing terror for themselves raised these unhappy women to such a degree of vigor that, notwithstanding their fatigue, their exposure to cold, their sufferance of hunger, and their sleeping on damp ground under an inclement sky, they finished an expedition of about one hundred and fifty miles without losing their spirits or injuring their health.

The wigwam to which they were conducted, and which belonged to the savage who had claimed them as his property, was inhabited by twelve persons. In the month of April this family set out with their captives for an Indian settlement still more remote, and informed them that, when they arrived at the settlement, they must be stripped, scourged, and run the gauntlet, naked, between two files of Indians containing the whole number found in the settlement; for such, they declared, was the standing custom of their nation. This information, you will believe, made a deep impression on the minds of the captive women, and led them, irresistibly, to devise all the possible means of escape. On the 31st of the same month, very early in the morning, Mrs. Dustin, while the Indians were asleep, having awakened her nurse and a fellow prisoner (a youth taken some time before from Worcester), dispatched, with the assistance of her companions, ten of the twelve Indians. The other two escaped. With the scalps of these savages, they returned through the wilderness; and, having arrived safely at Haverhill, and afterwards at Boston, received a handsome reward for their intrepid conduct from the legislature.

Whether all their sufferings, and all the danger of suffering anew, justified this slaughter may probably be questioned by you or some other exact moralist. Precedents innumerable and of high authority may indeed be urged in behalf of these captives, but the moralist will equally question the rectitude of these. Few persons, however, agonizing as Mrs. Dustin did, under the evils which she had already suffered and in the full apprehension of those which she was destined to suffer, would have been able to act the part of nice casuists; and fewer still, perhaps, would have exercised her intrepidity. That she herself approved of the conduct which was applauded by the magistrates and divines of the day, in the cool hours of deliberation cannot be doubted. The truth is, the season of Indian invasion, burning, butchering, captivity, threatening, and torture is an unfortunate time for nice investigation and critical moralizing. A wife who had just seen her house burnt, her infant dashed against a tree, and her companions coldly murdered one by one; who supposed her husband and her remaining children to have shared the same fate; who was threatened with torture and indecency more painful than torture, and who did not entertain a doubt that the threatening would be fulfilled would probably feel no necessity, when she found it in her power to dispatch the authors of her sufferings, of asking questions concerning anything but the success of the enterprise.

But, whatever may be thought of the rectitude of *her* conduct, that of her husband is in every view honorable. A finer succession of scenes for the pencil was hardly ever presented to the eye than is furnished by the efforts of this gallant man, with their interesting appendages. The artist must be destitute indeed of talents who could not engross every heart, as well as every eye, by exhibitions of this husband and father flying to rescue his wife, her infant, and her nurse from the approaching horde of savages; attempting on his horse to select from his flying family the child which he was the least able to spare, and unable to make the selection; facing, in their rear, the horde of hell hounds; alternately and sternly retreating behind his inestimable charge, and fronting the enemy again; receiving and returning their fire; and presenting himself equally as a barrier against murderers, and a shelter to the flight of innocence and anguish. In the background of some or other of these pictures might be exhibited, with powerful impression, the kindled dwelling, the sickly mother, the terrified nurse with the newborn infant in her arms, and the furious natives, surrounding them, driving them forward, and displaying the trophies of savage victory and the insolence of savage triumph.

"The Mother's Revenge" (1831)
John Greenleaf Whittier

Woman's attributes are generally considered of a milder and purer character than those of man. The virtues of meek affection, of fervent piety, of winning sympathy and of that "charity which forgiveth often," are more peculiarly her own. Her sphere of action is generally limited to the endearments of home—the quiet communion with her friends, and the angelic exercise of the kindly charities of existence. Yet, there have been astonishing manifestations of female fortitude and power in the ruder and sterner trials of humanity; manifestations of a courage rising almost to sublimity; the revelation of all those dark and terrible passions, which madden and distract the heart of manhood.

The perils which surrounded the earliest settlers of New-England were of the most terrible character. None but such a people as were our forefathers could have successfully sustained them. In the dangers and the hardihood of that perilous period, woman herself shared largely. It was not unfrequently her task to garrison the dwelling of her absent husband, and hold at bay the fierce savages in their hunt for blood. Many have left behind them a record of their sufferings and trials in the great wilderness, when in the bondage of the heathen, which are full of wonderful and romantic incidents, related however without ostentation, plainly and simply, as if the authors felt assured that they had only performed the task which Providence had set before them, and for which they could ask no tribute of admiration.

In 1698 the Indians made an attack upon the English settlement at Haverhill—now a beautiful village on the left bank of the Merrimack. They surrounded the house of one Duston, which was a little removed from the main body of the settlement. The wife of Duston was at that time in bed with an infant child in her arms. Seven young children were around her. On the first alarm Duston bade his children fly towards the Garrison-house, and then turned to save his wife and infant. By this time the savages were pressing close upon them. The heroic woman saw the utter impossibility of her escape—and she bade her husband fly to succor his children, and leave her to her fate. It was a moment of terrible trial for the husband—he hesitated between his affection and his duty—but the entreaties of his wife fixed his determination.

He turned away, and followed his children. A part of the Indians pursued him, but he held them at a distance by the frequent discharge of his rifle. The children fled towards the gurrison, where their friends waited, with breathless anxiety, to receive them. More than once, during their flight, the savages gained upon them; but a shot from the rifle of Duston, followed, as it was, by the fall of one of their number, effectually checked their progress. The garrison was reached, and Duston and his children, exhausted with fatigue and terror, were literally dragged into its enclosure by their anxious neighbors.

Mrs. Duston, her servant girl and her infant were made prisoners by the Indians, and were compelled to proceed before them in their retreat towards their lurking-place. The charge of her infant necessarily impeded her progress; and the savages could ill brook delay when they knew the avenger of blood was following closely behind them. Finding that the wretched mother was unable to keep pace with her captors, the leader of the band approached her, and wrested the infant from her arms. The savage held it before him for a moment, contemplating, with a smile of grim fierceness the terrors of its mother, and then dashed it from him with all his powerful strength. Its head smote heavily on the trunk of an adjacent tree, and the dried leaves around were sprinkled with brains and blood.

"Go on I" said the Indian.

The wretched mother cast one look upon her dead infant, and another to Heaven, as she obeyed her suvage conductor. She has often said, that at this moment, all was darkness and horror—that her very heart seemed to cense heating, and to lie cold and dead in her bosom, and that her limbs moved only as involuntary machinery. But when she gazed around her and saw the unfeeling savages, grinning at her and mocking her, and pointing to the mangled body of her infant with fiendish exultation, a new and terrible feeling came over her. It was the thirst of revenge; and from that moment her purpose was fixed. There was a thought of death at her heart—an insatiate longing for blood. An instantaneous change had been wrought in her very nature; the angel had become a demon,—and she followed her captors, with a stern determination to embrace the earliest opportunity for a bloody retribution.

The Indians followed the course of the Merrimack, until they had reached their canoes, a distance of seventy or eighty miles. They paddled to a small island, a little above the upper falls of the river. Here they kindled a fire; and fatigued by their long marches and sleepless nights, stretched themselves around it, without dreaming of the escape of their captives.

Their sleep was deep—deeper than any which the white man knows,—a sleep from which they were never to awaken. The two captives lay silent, until the hour of midnight; but the bereaved mother did not close her eyes. There was a gnawing of revenge at her heart, which precluded slumber. There was a spirit within her which defied the weakness of the body.

She rose up and walked around the sleepers, in order to test the soundness of their slumber. They stirred not limb or muscle. Placing a hatchet in the hands of her fellow captive, and bidding her stand ready to assist her, she grasped another in her own hands, and smote its ragged edge deeply into the skull of the nearest sleeper. A slight shuddor and a feeble groan followed. The savage was dead. She passed on to the next. Blow followed blow, until ten out of twelve, the whole number of the savages, were stiffening in blood. One escaped with a dreadful wound. The last—a small boy—still slept amidst the scene of carnage. Mrs. Duston lifted her dripping hatchet above his head, but hesitated to strike the blow.

"It is a poor boy," she said, mentally, "a poor child, and perhaps he has a mother!" The thought of her own children rushed upon her mind, and she spared him. She was in the net of leaving the bloody spot, when, suddenly reflecting that the people of her settlement would not credit her story, unsupported by any proof save her own assertion, she returned and deliberately scalped her ten victims. With this fearful evidence of her prowess, she loosed one of the In-

dian canoes, and floated down the river to the falls, from which place she travelled through the wilderness to the residence of her husband.

Such is the simple and unvarnished story of a New-England woman. The curious historian, who may hereafter search among the dim records of our twilight time"—who may gather from the uncertain responses of tradition, the wonderful history of the past—will find much, of a similar character, to call forth by turns, admiration and horror. And the time is coming, when all these traditions shall be treasured up as a sacred legacy—when the tale of the Indian inroad and the perils of the hunter—of the sublime courage and the dark superstitions of our ancestors, will be listened to with an interest unknown to the present generation,—and those who are to fill our places will pause hereafter by the Indian's burial-place, and on the scite of the old battle-field, or the thrown-down garrison, with a feeling of awe and reverence, as if communing, face to face, with the spirits of that stern race, which has passed away forever.

"The Duston Family" (1836)
Nathaniel Hawthorne

Goodman Duston and his wife, somewhat less than a century and a half ago, dwelt in Haverhill, at that time a small frontier settlement in the province of Massachusetts Bay. They had already added seven children to the King's liege subjects in America; and Mrs. Duston about a week before the period of our narrative, had blessed her husband with an eighth. One day in March, 1698, when Mr. Duston had gone forth about his ordinary business, there fell out an event, which had nearly left him a childless man, and a widower besides. An Indian war party, after traversing the trackless forest all the way from Canada, broke in upon their remote and defenceless town. Goodman Duston heard the war whoop and alarm, and, being on horseback, immediately set off full speed to look after the safety of his family. As he dashed along, he beheld dark wreaths of smoke eddying from the roofs of several dwellings near the road side;

while the groans of dying men,—the shrieks of affrighted women, and the screams of children, pierced his ear, all mingled with the horrid yell of the raging savages. The poor man trembled yet spurred on so much the faster, dreading that he should find his own cottage in a blaze, his wife murdered in her bed, and his little ones tossed into the flames. But, drawing near the door, he saw his seven elder children, of all ages between two years and seventeen, issuing out together, and running down the road to meet him. The father only bade them make the best of their way to the nearest garrison, and, without a moment's pause, flung himself from his horse, and rushed into Mrs. Duston's bedchamber.

The good woman, as we have before hinted, had lately added an eighth to the seven former proofs of her conjugal affection; and she now lay with the infant in her arms, and her nurse, the widow Mary Neff, watching by her bedside. Such was Mrs. Duston's helpless state, when her pale and breathless husband burst into the chamber, bidding her instantly to rise and flee for her life. Scarcely were the words out of his mouth, when the Indian yell was heard: and staring wildly out of the window, Goodman Duston saw that the blood-thirsty foe was close at hand. At this terrible instant, it appears that the thought of his children's danger rushed so powerfully upon his heart, that he quite forgot the still more perilous situation of his wife; or, as is not improbable, he had such knowledge of the good lady's character, as afforded him a comfortable hope that she would hold her own, even in a contest with a whole tribe of Indians. However that might be, he seized his gun and rushed out of doors again, meaning to gallop after his seven children, and snatch up one of them in his flight, lest his whole race and generation should be blotted from the earth, in that fatal hour. With this idea, he rode up behind them, swift as the wind. They had, by this time, got about forty rods from the house, all pressing forward in a group; and though the younger children tripped and stumbled, yet the elder ones were not prevailed upon, by the fear of death, to take to their

heels and leave these poor little souls to perish. Hearing the tramp of hoofs in their rear, they looked round, and espying Goodman Duston, all suddenly stopped. The little ones stretched out their arms; while the elder boys and girls, as it were, resigned their charge into his hands; and all the seven children seemed to say.—'Here is our father! Now we are safe!'

But if ever a poor mortal was in trouble, and perplexity, and anguish of spirit, that man was Mr. Duston! He felt his heart yearn towards these seven poor helpless children, as if each were singly possessed of his whole affections; for not one among them all, but had some peculiar claim to their dear father's love. There was his first-born; there, too, the little one who, till within a week past, had been the baby; there was a girl with her mother's features, and a boy, the picture of himself, and another in whom the looks of both parents were mingled; there was one child, whom he loved for his mild, quiet, and holy disposition, and destined him to be a minister; and another, whom he loved not less for his rough and fearless spirit, and who, could he live to be a man, would do a man's part against these bloody Indians. Goodman Duston looked at the poor things, one by one; and with yearning fondness, he looked at them all, together; then he gazed up to Heaven for a moment, and finally waved his hand to his seven beloved ones. 'Go on, my children,' said he, calmly. 'We will live or die together!'

He reined in his horse, and caused him to walk behind the children, who, hand in hand, went onward, hushing their sobs and wailings, lest these sounds should bring the savages upon them. Nor was it long, before the fugitives had proof that the red devils had found their track. There was a curl of smoke from behind the huge trunk of a tree—a sudden and sharp report echoed through the woods—and a bullet hissed over Goodman Duston's shoulder, and passed above the children's heads. The father, turning half round on his horse, took aim and fired at the skulking foe, with such effect as to cause a momentary delay of the pursuit. Another shot—and another—whistled from the covert of the forest; but still the little band pressed on, unharmed; and the stealthy nature of the Indians forbade them to rush boldly forward, in the face of so firm an enemy as Goodman Duston. Thus he and his seven children continued their retreat, creeping along, as Cotton Mather observes, 'at the pace of a child of five years old,' till the stockades of a little frontier fortress appeared in view, and the savages gave up the chase.

We must not forget Mrs. Duston, in her distress. Scarcely had her husband fled from the house, ere the chamber was thronged with the horrible visages of the wild Indians, bedaubed with paint and besmeared with blood, brandishing their tomahawks in her face, and threatening to add her scalp to those that were already hanging at their girdles. It was, however, their interest to save her alive, if the thing might be, in order to exact a ransom. Our great-great-grandmothers, when taken captive in the old times of Indian warfare, appear, in nine cases out of ten, to have been in pretty much such a delicate situation as Mrs. Duston; notwithstanding which, they were wonderfully sustained through long, rough, and hurried marches, amid toil, weariness, and starvation, such as the Indians themselves could hardly endure. Seeing that there was no help for it, Mrs. Duston rose, and she and the widow Neff, with the infant in her arms, followed their captors out of doors. As they crossed the threshold, the poor babe set up a feeble wail; it was its death cry. In an instant, an Indian seized it by the heels, swung it in the air, dashed out its brains against the trunk of the nearest tree, and threw the little corpse at the mother's feet. Perhaps it was the remembrance of that moment, that hardened Hannah Duston's heart, when her time of vengeance came. But now, nothing could be done, but to stifle her grief and rage within her bosom, and follow the Indians into the dark gloom of the forest, hardly venturing to throw a parting glance at the blazing cottage, where she had dwelt happily with her husband, and had borne him eight children—the

seven, of whose fate she knew nothing, and the infant, whom she had just seen murdered.

The first day's march was fifteen miles; and during that, and many succeeding days, Mrs. Duston kept pace with her captors; for, had she lagged behind, a tomahawk would at once have been sunk into her brains. More than one terrible warning was given her; more than one of her fellow captives,—of whom there were many,—after tottering feebly, at length sank upon the ground; the next moment, the death groan was breathed, and the scalp was reeking at an Indian's girdle. The unburied corpse was left in the forest, till the rites of sepulture should be performed by the autumnal gales, strewing the withered leaves upon the whitened bones. When out of danger of immediate pursuit, the prisoners, according to Indian custom, were divided among different parties of the savages, each of whom were to shift for themselves. Mrs. Duston, the widow Neff, and an English lad, fell to the lot of a family, consisting of two stout warriours, three squaws, and seven children. These Indians, like most with whom the French had held intercourse, were Catholics; and Cotton Mather affirms, on Mrs. Duston's authority, that they prayed at morning, noon, and night, nor ever partook of food without a prayer; nor suffered their children to sleep, till they had prayed to the christian's God. Mather, like an old hardhearted, pedantic bigot, as he was, seems trebly to exult in the destruction of these poor wretches, on account of their Popish superstitions. Yet what can be more touching than to think of these wild Indians, in their loneliness and their wanderings, wherever they went among the dark, mysterious woods, still keeping up domestic worship, with all the regularity of a house-hold at its peaceful fireside.

They were travelling to a rendezvous of the savages, somewhere in the northeast. One night, being now above a hundred miles from Haverhill, the red men and women, and the little red children, and the three pale faces, Mrs. Duston, the widow Neff, and the English lad, made their encampment, and kindled a fire beneath the gloomy old trees, on a small island in Contocook river. The barbarians sat down to what scanty food Providence had sent them, and shared it with their prisoners, as if they had all been the children of one wigwam, and had grown up together on the margin of the same river within the shadow of the forest. Then the Indians said their prayers—the prayers that the Romish priests had taught them—and made the sign of the cross upon their dusky breasts, and composed themselves to rest. But the three prisoners prayed apart; and when their petitions were ended, they likewise lay down, with their feet to the fire. The night wore on; and the light and cautious slumbers of the red men were often broken, by the rush and ripple of the stream, or the groaning and moaning of the forest, as if nature were wailing over her wild children; and sometimes, too, the little red skins cried in sleep, and the Indian mothers awoke to hush them. But, a little before break of day, a deep, dead slumber fell upon the Indians. 'See,' cries Cotton Mather, triumphantly, 'if it prove not so!'

Uprose Mrs. Duston, holding her own breath, to listen to the long, deep breathing of her captors. Then she stirred the widow Neff, whose place was by her own, and likewise the English lad; and all three stood up, with the doubtful gleam of the decaying fire hovering upon their ghastly visages, as they stared round at the fated slumberers. The next instant, each of the three captives held a tomahawk. Hark! that low moan, as of one in a troubled dream—it told a warriour's death pang! Another!—Another!—and the third half-uttered groan was from a woman's lips. But, Oh, the children! Their skins are red; yet spare them, Hannah Duston, spare those seven little ones, for the sake of the seven that have fed at your own breast. 'Seven,' quoth Mrs. Duston to herself. 'Eight children have I borne—and where are the seven, and where is the eighth!' The thought nerved her arm; and the copper coloured babes slept the same dead sleep with their Indian mothers. Of all that fam-

ily, only one woman escaped, dreadfully wounded, and fled shrieking into the wilderness! and a boy, whom, it is said, Mrs. Duston had meant to save alive. But he did well to flee from the raging tigress! There was little safety for a red skin, when Hannah Duston's blood was up.

The work being finished, Mrs. Duston laid hold of the long black hair of the warriors, and the women, and the children, and took all their ten scalps, and left the island, which bears her name to this very day. According to our notion, it should be held accursed, for her sake. Would that the bloody old hag had been drowned in crossing Contocook river, or that she had sunk over head and ears in a swamp, and been there buried, till summoned forth to confront her victims at the Day of Judgment; or that she had gone astray and been starved to death in the forest, and nothing ever seen of her again, save her skeleton, with the ten scalps twisted round it for a girdle! But, on the contrary, she and her companions came safe home, and received the bounty on the dead Indians, besides liberal presents from private gentlemen, and fifty pounds from the Governour of Maryland. In her old age, being sunk into decayed circumstances, she claimed, and, we believe, received a pension, as a further price of blood.

This awful woman, and that tender hearted, yet valiant man, her husband, will be remembered as long as the deeds of old times are told round a New England fireside. But how different is her renown from his!

from A Week on the Concord and Merrimack Rivers (1849)
Henry D. Thoreau

On the thirty-first day of March, one hundred and forty-two years before this, probably about this time in the afternoon, there were hurriedly paddling down this part of the river, between the pine woods which then fringed these banks, two white women and a boy, who had left an island at the mouth of the Contoocook before daybreak. They were slightly clad for the season, in the English fashion, and handled their paddles unskilfully, but with nervous energy and determination, and at the bottom of their canoe lay the still bleeding scalps of ten of the aborigines. They were Hannah Dustan, and her nurse, Mary Neff, both of Haverhill, eighteen miles from the mouth of this river, and an English boy, named Samuel Lennardson, escaping from captivity among the Indians. On the 15th of March previous, Hannah Dustan had been compelled to rise from childbed, and half-dressed, with one foot bare, accompanied by her nurse, commence an uncertain march, in still inclement weather, through the snow and the wilderness. She had seen her seven elder children flee with their father, but knew not of their fate. She had seen her infant's brains dashed out against an apple-tree, and had left her own and her neighbors' dwellings in ashes. When she reached the wigwam of her captor, situated on an island in the Merrimack, more than twenty miles above where we now are, she had been told that she and her nurse were soon to be taken to a distant Indian settlement, and there made to run the gauntlet naked. The family of this Indian consisted of two men, three women, and seven children, beside an English boy, whom she found a prisoner among them. Having determined to attempt her escape, she instructed the boy to inquire of one of the men, how he should dispatch an enemy in the quickest manner, and take his scalp. "Strike 'em there," said he, placing his finger on his temple, and he also showed him how to take off the scalp. On the morning of the 31st she arose before daybreak, and awoke her nurse and the boy, and taking the Indians' tomahawks, they killed them all in their sleep, excepting one favorite boy, and one squaw who fled wounded with him to the woods. The English boy struck the Indian who had given him the information on the temple, as he had been directed. They then collected all the provision they could find, and took their master's tomahawk and gun, and scuttling all the canoes but one, commenced their flight to Haverhill, distant about sixty miles by the river. But after having proceeded a short

distance, fearing that her story would not be believed if she should escape to tell it, they returned to the silent wigwam, and taking off the scalps of the dead, put them into a bag as proofs of what they had done, and then retracing their steps to the shore in the twilight, recommenced their voyage.

Early this morning this deed was performed, and now, perchance, these tired women and this boy, their clothes stained with blood, and their minds racked with alternate resolution and fear, are making a hasty meal of parched corn and moose-meat, while their canoe glides under these pine roots whose stumps are still standing on the bank. They are thinking of the dead whom they have left behind on that solitary isle far up the stream, and of the relentless living warriors who are in pursuit. Every withered leaf which the winter has left seems to know their story, and in its rustling to repeat it and betray them. An Indian lurks behind every rock and pine, and their nerves cannot bear the tapping of a woodpecker. Or they forget their own dangers and their deeds in conjecturing the fate of their kindred, and whether, if they escape the Indians, they shall find the former still alive. They do not stop to cook their meals upon the bank, nor land, except to carry their canoe about the falls. The stolen birch forgets its master and does them good service, and the swollen current bears them swiftly along with little need of the paddle, except to steer and keep them warm by exercise. For ice is floating in the river; the spring is opening; the muskrat and the beaver are driven out of their holes by the flood; deer gaze at them from the bank; a few faint-singing forest birds, perchance, fly across the river to the northernmost shore; the fish-hawk sails and screams overhead, and geese fly over with a startling clangor; but they do not observe these things, or they speedily forget them. They do not smile or chat all day. Sometimes they pass an Indian grave surrounded by its paling on the bank, or the frame of a wigwam, with a few coals left behind, or the withered stalks still rustling in the Indian's solitary cornfield on the interval. The birch stripped of its bark, or the charred stump where a tree has been burned down to be made into a canoe, these are the only traces of man,—a fabulous wild man to us. On either side, the primeval forest stretches away uninterrupted to Canada or to the "South Sea;" to the white man a drear and howling wilderness, but to the Indian a home, adapted to his nature, and cheerful as the smile of the Great Spirit.

While we loiter here this autumn evening, looking for a spot retired enough, where we shall quietly rest to-night, they thus, in that chilly March evening, one hundred and forty-two years before us, with wind and current favoring, have already glided out of sight, not to camp, as we shall, at night, but while two sleep one will manage the canoe, and the swift stream bear them onward to the settlements, it may be, even to old John Lovewell's house on Salmon Brook to-night.

According to the historian, they escaped as by a miracle all roving bands of Indians, and reached their homes in safety, with their trophies, for which the General Court paid them fifty pounds. The family of Hannah Dustan all assembled alive once more, except the infant whose brains were dashed out against the apple-tree, and there have been many who in later times have lived to say that they had eaten of the fruit of that apple-tree.

This seems a long while ago, and yet it happened since Milton wrote his Paradise Lost.

Suggested Readings

Arvin, Newton, ed. *Hawthorne's Short Stories*. Random House, 1972.

Hawthorne, Nathaniel. "The Duston Family." *The American Magazine of Useful and Entertaining Knowledge*, May 1836, p. 397.

Whitford, Kathryn. "Hannah Dustin: The Judgement of History." *Essex Institute Historical Collections*. Vol. CVIII, No. 4, October 1972, pp. 304–325.

16

Liberty or Death: Patrick Henry's Address to the Virginia Delegates

Dr. Joseph J. Thomas

Patrick Henry's speech at St. John's Church in Richmond, Virginia, on March 23, 1775 is considered by many historians to be among the critical catalysts of the American Revolution. So impassioned, convincing, and impressive was it that it was thought to be the key factor in the largest colony's decision to support revolution. Henry did not consult notes nor did he provide a manuscript for the record. This famous address is given to history by a witness, George Tucker, and appeared in the first known biography of Patrick Henry written by William Wirt. Whether Henry spoke these words exactly matters little. Generations of Americans have been inspired by his challenge. "I know not what course others may take; but as for me, give me liberty, or give me death!" stands as axiomatic of the American spirit of liberty and independence.

* * *

Mr. President:

No man thinks more highly than I do of the patriotism, as well as abilities, of the very worthy gentlemen who have just addressed the House. But different men often see the same subject in different lights; and, therefore, I hope that it will not be thought disrespectful to those gentlemen, if, entertaining as I do opinions of a character very opposite to theirs, I shall speak forth my sentiments freely and without reserve. This is no time for ceremony. The question before the House is one of awful moment to this country. For my own part I consider it as nothing less than a question of freedom or slavery; and in proportion to the magnitude of the subject ought to be the freedom of the debate. It is, only in this way that we can hope to arrive at truth, and fulfill the great responsibility which we hold to God and our country. Should I keep back my opinions at such a time, through fear of giving offense, I should consider myself as guilty of treason towards my country, and of an act of disloyalty towards the majesty of heaven, which I revere above all earthly kings.

Mr. President, it is natural to man to indulge in the illusions of hope. We are apt to shut our eyes against a painful truth, and listen to the song of that siren, till she transforms us into beasts. Is this the part of wise men, engaged in a great and arduous struggle for liberty? Are we disposed to be of the number of those who, having eyes, see not, and having ears, hear not, the things which so nearly concern their temporal salvation? For my part, whatever anguish of spirit it may cost, I am willing to know the whole truth-to know the worst and to provide for it.

I have but one lamp by which my feet are guided; and that is the lamp of experience. I know of no way of judging of the future but by the past. And judging by the past, I wish to know what there has been in the conduct of the British ministry for the last ten years, to justify those hopes with which gentlemen have been pleased to solace themselves and the House? Is it that insidious smile with which our petition has been lately received? Trust it not, sir; it will prove a snare to your feet. Suffer not yourselves to be betrayed with a kiss.

Ask yourselves how this gracious reception of our petition comports with these warlike preparations which cover our waters and darken our land. Are fleets and armies necessary to a work of love and reconciliation? Have we shown ourselves so unwilling to be reconciled that force must be called in to win back our love? Let us not deceive ourselves, sir. These are the implements of war and subjugation-the last arguments to which kings resort. I ask gentlemen, sir, what means this martial *array*, if its purpose be not to force us to submission? Can gentlemen assign any other possible motives for it? Has Great Britain any enemy, in this quarter of the world, to call for all this accumulation of navies and armies? No, sir, she has none. They are meant for us; they can be meant for no other. They are sent over to bind and rivet upon us those chains which the British ministry have been so long forging.

And what have we to oppose to them? Shall we try argument? Sir, we have been trying that for the last ten years. Have we anything new to offer on the subject? Nothing. We have held the subject up in every light of which it is capable; but it has been all in vain. Shall we resort to entreaty and humble supplication? What terms shall we find which have not been already exhausted? Let us not. I beseech you, sir, deceive ourselves longer.

Sir, we have done everything that could be done to avert the storm which is now coming on. We have petitioned; we have remonstrated; we have supplicated; we have prostrated ourselves before the throne, and have implored its interposition to arrest the tyrannical hands of the ministry and Parliament. Our petitions have been slighted; our remonstrances have produced additional violence and insult; our supplications have been disregarded; and we have been spurned, with contempt, from the foot of the throne. In vain, after these things, may we indulge the fond hope of peace and reconciliation. There is no longer any room for hope.

If we wish to be free-if we mean to preserve inviolate those inestimable privileges for which we have been so long contending-if we mean not basely to abandon the noble struggle in which we have been so long engaged, and which we have pledged ourselves never to abandon until the glorious object of our contest shall be obtained, we must fight! I repeat it, sir, we must fight! An appeal to arms and to the God of Hosts is all that is left us!

They tell us, sir, that we are weak-unable to cope with so formidable an adversary. But when shall we be stronger? Will it be the next week, or the next year? Will it be when we are totally disarmed, and when a British guard shall be stationed in every house? Shall we gather strength by irresolution and inaction? Shall we acquire the means of effectual resistance, by lying supinely on our backs, and hugging the delusive phantom of hope, until our enemies shall have bound us hand and foot?

Sir, we are not weak, if we make a proper use of the means which the God of nature hath placed in our power. Three millions of people, armed in the holy cause of liberty, and in such a country as that which we possess, are invincible by any force which our enemy can send against us. Besides, sir, we shall not fight our battles alone. There is a just God who presides over the destinies of nations, and who will raise up friends to fight our battles for us. The battle, sir, is not to the strong alone; it is to the vigilant, the active, the brave. Besides, sir, we have no election. If we were base enough to desire it, it is now too late to retire from the contest. There is no retreat but in submission and slavery! Our chains are forged! Their clanking may be heard on the plains of Boston! The war is inevitable-and let it come! I repeat it, sir, let it come!

It is in vain, sir, to extenuate the matter. Gentlemen may cry, "Peace! Peace!" –but there is no peace. The war is actually begun! The next gale that sweeps from the north will bring to our ears the clash of resounding arms! Our brethren are already in the field! Why stand we here idle?

What is it that gentlemen wish? What would they have? Is life so dear, or peace so sweet as to be purchased at the price of chains and slavery? Forbid it. Almighty God! I know not what course others may take; but as for me, give me liberty, or give me death!

Suggested Readings

Einhorn, Lois J. "Basic Assumptions in the Virginia Ratification Debates: Patrick Henry vs. James Madison on the Nature of Man and Reason." *Southern Speech Communication Journal*, 46, 1981.

McCants, David A. "The Authenticity of James Maury's Account of Patrick Henry's Speech in the Parson's Cause." *Southern Speech Communication Journal*, 42, 1976.

Storing, Herbert J., ed. *The Complete Anti-Federalist*. 7 vols. Chicago: University of Chicago Press, 1981.

17

Leadership Defuses Insurrection: General George Washington's Speech at Newburgh

Dr. Joseph J. Thomas

During the winter of 1782–1783 the Continental Army was on the verge of insurrection. Soldiers and officers had not been paid by Congress, creditors and supportive politicians encouraged them to forcefully demand that all back-pay be provided immediately or "drastic measures" would be taken. It appeared that a military coup was in the offing. The conspirators assembled at Newburgh, NY (the town for which the conspiracy was named) and invited George Washington to address their assembly—many with the intention of offering him the position of "emperor" or even king. Washington saw the peril to the new Republic for what it was, a direct threat to the nation's newly founded liberties. He diffused the situation in typical dramatic fashion.

In the process of addressing the assembled officers and promising to appeal to Congress for all that was owed, he slowly pulled a pair of spectacles from his pocket. The room fell deadly silent, for no one knew the great general required eye glasses. Even such a simple device to aid the aging Washington was treated with disbelief. As he fumbled to adjust his glasses he stated apologetically, "Gentlemen, you will permit me to put on my spectacles, for I have not only grown gray but nearly blind in the service of my country." The Army's differences with their civilian masters were resolved immediately. Many in the room welled up with tears. A clear, important message had been sent by the nation's greatest leader—the Army was the servant protector of the people, and the people were directly represented by their elected officials. The precedent and message set by Washington assured that the country would never again come so perilously close to a military coup. American representative democracy was ensured; civilization, as we know it, was preserved.

* * *

Gentlemen:

By an anonymous summons, an attempt has been made to convene you together; how inconsistent with the rules of propriety, how unmilitary, and how subversive of all order and discipline, let the good sense of the army decide. . . .

Thus much, gentlemen, I have thought it incumbent on me to observe to you, to show upon what principles I opposed the irregular and hasty meeting which was proposed to have been held on Tuesday last: and not because I wanted a disposition to give you every opportunity consistent with your own honor, and the dignity of the army, to make known your grievances. If my conduct heretofore has not evinced to you that I have been a faithful friend to the army, my declaration of it at this time would be equally unavailing and improper. But as I was among the first who embarked in the cause of our common country. As I have never left your side one moment, but when called from you on public duty. As I have been the constant companion and witness of your distresses, and not among the last to feel and acknowledge your merits. As I have ever considered my own military reputation as inseparably connected with that of the army. As my heart has ever expanded with joy, when I have heard its praises, and my indignation has arisen, when the mouth of detraction has been opened against it, it can *scarcely be supposed*, at this late stage of the war, that I am indifferent to its interests.

But how are they to be promoted? The way is plain, says the anonymous addresser. If war continues, remove into the unsettled country, there establish yourselves, and leave an ungrateful country to defend itself. But who are they to defend? Our wives, our children, our farms, and other property which we leave behind us. Or, in this state of hostile separation, are we to take the two first (the latter cannot be removed) to perish in a wilderness, with hunger, cold, and nakedness? If peace takes place, never sheathe your swords, says he, until you have obtained full and ample justice; this dreadful alternative, of either

deserting our country in the extremist hour of her distress or turning our arms against it (which is the apparent object, unless Congress can be compelled into instant compliance), has something so shocking in it that humanity revolts at the idea.

My God! What can this writer have in view, by recommending such measures? Can he be a friend to the army? Can he be a friend to this country? Rather, is he not an insidious foe? Some emissary, perhaps, from New York, plotting the ruin of both, by sowing the seeds of discord and separation between the civil and military powers of the continent? And what a compliment does he pay to our understandings when he recommends measures in either alternative, impracticable in their nature? . . .

I cannot, in justice to my own belief, and what I have great reason to conceive is the intention of Congress, conclude this address, without giving it as my decided opinion, that that honorable body entertain exalted sentiments of the services of the army; and, from a full conviction of its merits and sufferings, will do it complete justice. That their endeavors to discover and establish funds for this purpose have been unwearied, and will not cease till they have succeeded, I have not a doubt. But, like all other large bodies, where there is a variety of different interests to reconcile, their deliberations are slow. Why, then, should we distrust them? And, in consequence of that distrust, adopt measures which may cast a shade over that glory which has been so justly acquired; and tarnish the reputation of an army which is celebrated through all Europe, for its fortitude and patriotism? And for what is this done? To bring the object we seek nearer? No! Most certainly, in my opinion, it will cast it at a greater distance.

For myself (and I take no merit in giving the assurance. being induced to it from principles of gratitude, veracity, and justice), a grateful sense of the confidence you have ever placed in me, a recollection of the cheerful assistance and prompt obedience I have experienced from you, under every vicissitude of fortune, and the sincere affection I feel for an army I have so long had the honor to command will oblige me to declare, in this public and solemn manner, that, in the attainment of complete justice for all your toils and dangers, and in the gratification of every wish, so far as may be done consistently with the great duty I owe my country and those powers we are bound to respect, you may freely command my services to the utmost of my abilities.

While I give you these assurances, and pledge myself in the most unequivocal manner to exert whatever ability I am possessed of in your favor, let me entreat you, gentlemen, on your part, not to take any measures which, viewed in the calm light of reason, will lessen the dignity and sully the glory you have hitherto maintained; let me request you to rely on the plighted faith of your country .and place a full confidence in the purity of the intentions of Congress; that, previous to your dissolution as an Army, they will cause all your accounts to be fairly liquidated, as directed in their resolutions, which were published to you two days ago, and that they will adopt the most effectual measures in their power to render ample justice to you, for your faithful and meritorious services. And let me conjure you, in the name of our common country, as you value your own sacred honor, as you respect the rights of humanity, and as you regard the military and national character of America, to express your utmost horror and detestation of the man who wishes, under any specious pretenses, to overturn the liberties of our country, and who wickedly attempts to open the floodgates of civil discord and deluge our rising empire in blood.

Suggested Reading

Alden, John R. *George Washington: A Biography*. New York: Wings Books, 1984.

Freeman, Douglas S. *George Washington*. New York: Charles Scribner and Sons, 1957.

18

More Than Mere Duty: E. E. Hale's The Man Without a Country

Dr. Robert Madison

During the Civil War, Edward Everett Hale (1822–1909) became frustrated at the ease with which many Americans accepted the dissolution of the Union. He watched with dismay as "Copperheads" like Senator Clement Vallandigham of Ohio openly supported rebels in arms against the Federal government. In the middle of the war, after the Battle of Gettysburg but still with no end to the war in sight, Hale published his patriotic tale in the *Atlantic Monthly*, the journal which had published Julia Ward Howe's "Battle Hymn of the Republic" a year before.

In the midst of war, Hale found that love of country—not self, state, or region—was more than mere duty. Hale's protagonist Philip Nolan repudiates his native country—and the country in turn grants him his wish, and "forgets" him.

By setting his story early in our nationhood, Hale sets up a much less equivocal situation than the one he was living through during the War between the States. As the youngest of nations grows to maturity, Nolan is left only to guess at its progress, even though he himself participates in some of the nation's most formative exploits. Ultimately, however, history leaves Nolan behind: he is never forgiven for his unforgivable treason.

Hale's story is not heavy-handed, although its moral is clear. For generations, Hale's story was reprinted as a moral tale for young people, complete with a patronizing introduction and notes. Stripped of these later accretions, however, the tale remains (as in the version reprinted here from the *Atlantic Monthly* of December 1863) a mature plea for an unsentimental patriotism that may often go out of fashion, but has not yet become extinct.

I suppose that very few casual readers of the "New York Herald" of August 13th observed, in an obscure corner, among the "Deaths," the announcement,

"NOLAN. DIED, on board U. S. Corvette Levant, Lat. 2° 11' S., Long. 131° W., on the 11th of May, PHILIP NOLAN."

I happened to observe it, because I was stranded at the old Mission-House in Mackinac, waiting for a Lake-Superior steamer which did not choose to come, and I was devouring, to the very stubble, all the current literature I could get hold of, even down to the deaths and marriages in the "Herald." My memory for names and people is good, and the reader will see, as he goes on, that I had reason enough to remember Philip Nolan. There are hundreds of readers who would have paused at that announcement, if the officer of the Levant who reported it had chosen to make it thus:—"Died, May 11th, THE MAN WITHOUT A COUNTRY." For it was as "The Man without a Country" that poor Philip Nolan had generally been known by the officers who had him in charge during some fifty years, as, indeed, by all the men who sailed under them. I dare say there is many a man who has taken wine with him once a fortnight, in a three years' cruise, who never knew that his name was "Nolan," or whether the poor wretch had any name at all.

There can now be no possible harm in telling this poor creature's story. Reason enough there has been till now, ever since Madison's Administration went out in 1817, for very strict secrecy, the secrecy of honor itself, among the gentlemen of the navy who have had Nolan in successive charge. And certainly it speaks well for the *esprit de corps* of the profession and the personal honor of its members, that to the press this man's story has been wholly unknown,—and, I think, to the country at large also. I have reason to think, from some investigations I made in the Naval Archives when I was attached to the Bureau of Construction, that every official report relating to him was burned when Ross burned the public buildings at Washington. One of the Tuckers, or possibly one of the Watsons, had Nolan in charge at the end of the war; and when, on returning from his cruise, he reported at Washington to one of the Crowninshields,—who was in the Navy Department when he came home,—he

found that the Department ignored the whole business. Whether they really knew nothing about it, or whether it was a "*Non mi ricordo*," determined on as a piece of policy, I do not know. But this I do know, that since 1817, and possibly before, no naval officer has mentioned Nolan in his report of a cruiso.

But, as I say, there is no need for secrecy any longer. And now the poor creature is dead, it seems to me worth while to tell a little of his story, by way of showing young Americans of to-day what it is to be

A MAN WITHOUT A COUNTRY.

Philip Nolan was as fine a young officer as there was in the "Legion of the West," as the Western division of our army was then called. When Aaron Burr made his first dashing expedition down to New Orleans in 1805, at Fort Massac, or somewhere above on the river, he met, as the Devil would have it, this gay, dashing, bright young fellow, at some dinner-party, I think. Burr marked him, talked to him, walked with him, took him a day or two's voyage in his flat-boat, and, in short, fascinated him. For the next year, barrack-life was very tame to poor Nolan. He occasionally availed of the permission the great man had given him to write to him. Long, high-worded, stilted letters the poor boy wrote and rewrote and copied. But never a line did he have in reply from the gay deceiver. The other boys in the garrison sneered at him, because he sacrificed in this unrequited affection for a politician the time which they devoted to Monongabela, sledge, and high-low-jack. Bourbon, euchre, and poker were still unknown. But one day Nolan had his revenge. This time Burr came down the river, not as an attorney seeking a place for his office, but as a disguised conqueror. He had defeated I know not how many district-attorneys; he had dined at I know not how many public dinners; he had been heralded in I know not how many Weekly Arguses; and it was rumored that he had an army behind him and an empire before him. It was a great day—his arrival—to poor Nolan. Burr had not been at the fort an hour before he sent for him. That evening he asked Nolan to take him out in his skiff, to show him a canebrake or a cotton-wood tree, as he said,—really to seduce him; and by the time the sail was over, Nolan was enlisted body and soul. From that time, though he did not yet know it, he lived as A MAN WITHOUT A COUNTRY.

What Burr meant to do I know no more than you, dear reader. It is none of our business just now. Only, when the grand catastrophe came, and Jefferson and the House of Virginia of that day undertook to break on the wheel all the possible Clarences of the then House of York, by the great treason-trial at Richmond, some of the lesser fry in that distant Mississippi Valley, which was farther from us than Puget's Sound is to-day, introduced the like novelty on their provincial stage, and, to while away the monotony of the summer at Fort Adams, got up, for *spectacles*, a string of court-martials on the officers there. One and another of the colonels and majors were tried, and, to fill out the list, little Nolan, against whom, Heaven knows, there was evidence enough,—that he was sick of the service, had been willing to be false to it, and would have obeyed any order to march any-whither with any one who would follow him, had the order only been signed, "By command of His Exe. A. Burr." The courts dragged on. The big flies escaped,— rightly for all I know. Nolan was proved guilty enough, as I say; yet you and I would never have heard of him, reader, but that, when the president of the court asked him at the close, whether he wished to say anything to show that he had always been faithful to the United States, he cried out, in a fit of frenzy,—

"D—n the United States! I wish I may never hear of the United States again!"

I suppose he did not know how the words shocked old Colonel Morgan, who was holding the court. Half the officers who sat in it had served through the Revolution, and their lives, not to say their necks, had been risked for the very idea which he so cavalierly cursed in his madness. He, on his part, had grown up in the West of those days, in the midst of "Spanish plot," "Orleans plot," and all the rest. He had

been educated on a plantation, where the finest company was a Spanish officer or a French merchant from Orleans. His education, such as it was, had been perfected in commercial expeditions to Vera Cruz, and I think he told me his father once hired an Englishman to be a private tutor for a winter on the plantation. He had spent half his youth with an older brother, hunting horses in Texas; and, in a word, to him "United States" was scarcely a reality. Yet he had been fed by "United States" for all the years since he had been in the army. He had sworn on his faith as a Christian to be true to "United States." It was "United States" which gave him the uniform he wore, and the sword by his side. Nay, my poor Nolan, it was only because "United States" had picked you out first as one of her own confidential men of honor, that "A. Burr" cared for you a straw more than for the flat-boat men who sailed his ark for him. I do not excuse Nolan; I only explain to the reader why he damned his country, and wished he might never hear her name again.

He never did hear her name but once again. From that moment, September 23, 1807, till the day he died, May 11, 1863, he never heard her name again. For that half century and more he was a man without a country.

Old Morgan, as I said, was terribly shocked. If Nolan had compared George Washington to Benedict Arnold, or had cried, "God save King George," Morgan would not have felt worse. He called the court into his private room, and returned in fifteen minutes, with a face like a sheet, to say,—

"Prisoner, hear the sentence of the Court. The Court decides, subject to the approval of the President, that you never hear the name of the United States again."

Nolan laughed. But nobody else laughed. Old Morgan was too solemn, and the whole room was hushed dead as night for a minute. Even Nolan lost his swagger in a moment. Then Morgan added,—

"Mr. Marshal, take the prisoner to Orleans in

an armed boat, and deliver him to the naval commander there."

The marshal gave his orders, and the prisoner was taken out of court.

"Mr. Marshal," continued old Morgan, "see that no one mentions the United States to the prisoner. Mr. Marshal, make my respects to Lieutenant Mitchell at Orleans, and request him to order that no one shall mention the United States to the prisoner while he is on board ship. You will receive your written orders from the officer on duty here this evening. The court is adjourned without day."

I have always supposed that Colonel Morgan himself took the proceedings of the court to Washington City, and explained them to Mr. Jefferson. Certain it is that the President approved them,—certain, that is, if I may believe the men who say they have seen his signature. Before the Nautilus got round from New Orleans to the Northern Atlantic coast with the prisoner on board, the sentence had been approved, and he was a man without a country.

The plan then adopted was substantially the same which was necessarily followed ever after. Perhaps it was suggested by the necessity of sending him by water from Fort Adams and Orleans. The Secretary of the Navy—it must have been the first Crowninshield, though he is a man I do not remember—was requested to put Nolan on board a Government vessel bound on a long cruise, and to direct that he should be only so far confined there as to make it certain that he never saw or heard of the country. We had few long cruises then, and the navy was very much out of favor; and as almost all of this story is traditional, as I have explained, I do not know certainly what his first cruise was. But the commander to whom he was intrusted—perhaps it was Tingey or Shaw, though I think it was one of the younger men,—we are all old enough now—regulated the etiquette and the precautions of the affair, and according to his scheme they were carried out, I suppose, till Nolan died.

When I was second officer of the Intrepid, some thirty years after, I saw the original paper of instructions. I have been sorry ever since that I did not copy the whole of it. It ran, however, much in this way:—

"*Washington,*" (with the date, which must have been late in 1807.)

"SIR,—You will receive from Lt. Neale the person of Philip Nolan, late a Lieutenant in the United States Army.

"This person on his trial by court-martial expressed with an oath the wish that he might 'never hear of the United States again.'

"The Court sentenced him to have his wish fulfilled.

"For the present, the execution of the order is intrusted by the President to this department.

"You will take the prisoner on board your ship, and keep him there with such precautions as shall prevent his escape.

"You will provide him with such quarters, rations, and clothing as would be proper for an officer of his late rank, if he were a passenger on your vessel on the business of his Government.

"The gentlemen on board will make any arrangements agreeable to themselves regarding his society. He is to be exposed to no indignity of any kind, nor is he ever unnecessarily to be reminded that he is a prisoner.

"But under no circumstances is he ever to hear of his country or to see any information regarding it; and you will specially caution all the officers under your command to take care, that, in the various indulgences which may be granted, this rule, in which his punishment is involved, shall not be broken.

"It is the intention of the Government that he shall never again see the country which he has disowned. Before the end of your cruise you will receive orders which will give effect to this intention.

"Resp'y yours,

"W. SOUTHARD, for the Sec'y of the Navy."

If I had only preserved the whole of this paper, there would be no break in the beginning of my sketch of this story. For Captain Shaw, if it was he, handed it to his successor in the charge, and he to his, and I suppose the commander of the Levant has it to-day as his authority for keeping this man in this mild custody.

The rule adopted on board the ships on which I have met "the man without a country" was, I think, transmitted from the beginning. No mess liked to have him permanently, because his presence cut off all talk of home or of the prospect of return, of politics or letters, of peace or of war,—cut off more than half the talk men like to have at sea. But it was always thought too hard that he should never meet the rest of us, except to touch hats, and we finally sank into one system. He was not permitted to talk with the men, unless an officer was by. With officers he had unrestrained intercourse, as far as they and he chose. But he grew shy, though he had favorites: I was one. Then the captain always asked him to dinner on Monday. Every mess in succession took up the invitation in its turn. According to the size of the ship, you had him at your mess more or less often at dinner. His breakfast he ate in his own state-room,—he always had a state-room,—which was where a sentinel, or somebody on the watch, could see the door. And whatever else he ate or drank he ate or drank alone. Sometimes, when the marines or sailors had any special jollification, they were permitted to invite "Plain-Buttons," as they called him. Then Nolan was sent with some officer, and the men were forbidden to speak of home while he was there. I believe the theory was, that the sight of his punishment did them good. They called him "Plain-Buttons," because, while he always chose to wear a regulation army-uniform, he was not permitted to wear the army-button, for the reason that it bore either the initials or the insignia of the country he had disowned.

I remember, soon after I joined the navy, I was on shore with some of the older officers from our ship and from the Brandywine, which we had met at Alexandria. We had leave to make a party and go up to Cairo and the Pyramids. As we jogged along, (you went on donkeys then,) some of the gentlemen (we boys called them "Dons," but the phrase was long since changed) fell to talking about Nolan, and some one told

the system which was adopted from the first about his books and other reading. As he was almost never permitted to go on shore, even though the vessel lay in port for months, his time, at the best, hung heavy; and everybody was permitted to lend him books, if they were not published in America and made no allusion to it. These were common enough in the old days, when people in the other hemisphere talked of the United States as little as we do of Paraguay. He had almost all the foreign papers that came into the ship, sooner or later; only somebody must go over them first, and cut out any advertisement or stray paragraph that alluded to America. This was a little cruel sometimes, when the back of what was cut out might be as innocent as Hesiod. Right in the midst of one of Napoleon's battles, or one of Canning's speeches, poor Nolan would find a great hole, because on the back of the page of that paper there had been an advertisement of a packet for New York, or a scrap from the President's message. I say this was the first time I ever heard of this plan, which afterwards I had enough, and more than enough, to do with. I remember it, because poor Phillips, who was of the party, as soon as the allusion to reading was made, told a story of something which happened at the Cape of Good Hope on Nolan's first voyage; and it is the only thing I ever knew of that voyage. They had touched at the Cape, and had done the civil thing with the English Admiral and the fleet, and then, leaving for a long cruise up the Indian Ocean. Phillips had borrowed a lot of English books from an officer, which, in those days, as indeed in these, was quite a windfall. Among them, as the Devil would order, was the "Lay of the Last Minstrel," which they had all of them heard of, but which most of them had never seen. I think it could not have been published long. Well, nobody thought there could be any risk of anything national in that, though Phillips swore old Shaw had cut out the "Tempest" from Shakspeare before he let Nolan have it, because he said "the Bermudas ought to be ours, and, by Jove, should be one day." So Nolan was permitted to join the circle one afternoon when a lot of them sat on deck smoking and reading aloud. People do not do such things so often now; but when I was young we got rid of a great deal of time so. Well, so it happened that in his turn Nolan took the book and read to the others; and he read very well, as I know. Nobody in the circle knew a line of the poem, only it was all magic and Border chivalry, and was ten thousand years ago. Poor Nolan read steadily through the fifth canto, stopped a minute and drank something, and then began, without a thought of what was coming,—

"Breathes there the man, with soul so dead,
Who never to himself hath said,"—

It seems impossible to us that anybody ever heard this for the first time; but all these fellows did then, and poor Nolan himself went on, still unconsciously or mechanically,—

"This is my own, my native land!" Then they all saw something was to pay; but he expected to get through, I suppose, turned a little pale, but plunged on,—

"Whose heart hath ne'er within him burned,
As home his footsteps he hath turned
From wandering on a foreign strand?—
If such there breathe, go, mark him well."

By this time the men were all beside themselves, wishing there was any way to make him turn over two pages; but he had not quite presence of mind for that; he gagged a little, colored crimson, and staggered on,—

"For him no minstrel raptures swell;
High though his titles, proud his name,
Boundless his wealth as wish can claim,
Despite these titles, power, and pelf,
The wretch, concentred all in self,"—

and here the poor fellow choked, could not go on, but started up, swung the book into the sea, vanished into his state-room, "and by Jove," said Phillips, "we did not see him for two months again. And I had to make up some beggarly story to that English surgeon why I did not return his Walter Scott to him."

That story shows about the time when Nolan's braggadocio must have broken down. At first, they said, he took a very high tone, considered his imprisonment a more farce, affected to enjoy the voyage, and all that; but Phillips said that after he came out of his state-room he never was the same man again. He never read aloud again, unless it was the Bible or Shakspeare, or something else he was sure of. But it was not that merely. He never entered in with the other young men exactly as a companion again. He was always shy afterwards, when I knew him,— very seldom spoke, unless he was spoken to, except to a very few friends. He lighted up occasionally,—I remember late in his life hearing him fairly eloquent on something which had been suggested to him by one of Fléchier's sermons,—but generally he had the nervous, tired look of a heart-wounded man.

When Captain Shaw was coming home,—if, as I say, it was Shaw,—rather to the surprise of everybody they made one of the Windward Islands, and lay off and on for nearly a week. The boys said the officers were sick of salt-junk, and meant to have turtle-soup before they came home. But after several days the Warren came to the same rendezvous; they exchanged signals; she sent to Phillips and these homeward-bound men letters and papers, and told them she was outward-bound, perhaps to the Mediterranean, and took poor Nolan and his traps on the boat back to try his second cruise. He looked very blank when he was told to get ready to join her. He had known enough of the signs of the sky to know that till that moment he was going "home." But this was a distinct evidence of something he had not thought of perhaps,—that there was no going home for him, even to a prison. And this was the first of some twenty such transfers, which brought him sooner or later into half our best vessels, but which kept him all his life at least some hundred miles from the country he had hoped he might never hear of again.

It may have been on that second cruise,—it was once when he was up the Mediterranean,— that Mrs. Graff, the celebrated Southern beauty of those days, danced with him. They had been lying a long time in the Bay of Naples, and the officers were very intimate in the English fleet, and there had been great festivities, and our men thought they must give a great ball on board the ship. How they ever did it on board the Warren I am sure I do not know. Perhaps it was not the Warren, or perhaps ladies did not take up so much room as they do now. They wanted to use Nolan's state-room for something, and they hated to do it without asking him to the ball; so the captain said they might ask him, if they would be responsible that he did not talk with the wrong people, "who would give him intelligence." So the dance went on, the finest party that had ever been known, I dare say; for I never heard of a man-of-war ball that was not. For ladies they had the family of the American consul, one or two travellers who had adventured so far, and a nice bevy of English girls and matrons, perhaps Lady Hamilton herself.

Well, different officers relieved each other in standing and talking with Nolan in a friendly way, so as to be sure that nobody else spoke to him. The dancing went on with spirit, and after a while even the fellows who took this honorary guard of Nolan ceased to fear any *contre-temps*. Only when some English lady—Lady Hamilton, as I said, perhaps—called for a set of "American dances," an odd thing happened. Everybody then danced contra-dances. The black band, nothing loath, conferred as to what "American dances" were, and started off with "Virginia Reel," which they followed with "Money-Musk," which, in its turn in those days, should have been followed by "The Old Thirteen." But just as Dick, the leader, tapped for his fiddles to begin, and bent forward, about to say, in true negro state, "'The Old Thirteen,' gentlemen and ladies!" as he had said, "'Virginny Reel,' if you please!" and "'Money-Musk,' if you please!" the captain's boy tapped him on the shoulder, whispered to him, and he did not announce the name of the dance; he merely bowed, began on the air, and they all fell to,—the officers teaching the English girls the figure, but not telling them why it had no name.

But that is not the story I started to tell.—As the dancing went on, Nolan and our fellows all got at case, as I said,—so much so, that it seemed quite natural for him to bow to that splendid Mrs. Graff, and say,—

"I hope you have not forgotten me, Miss Rutledge. Shall I have the honor of dancing?"

He did it so quickly, that Shubrick, who was by him, could not hinder him. She laughed, and said,—

"I am not Miss Rutledge any longer, Mr. Nolan; but I will dance all the same," just nodded to Shubrick, as if to say he must leave Mr. Nolan to her, and led him off to the place where the dance was forming.

Nolan thought he had got his chance. He had known her at Philadelphia, and at other places had met her, and this was a Godsend. You could not talk in contra-dances, as you do in cotillons, or even in the pauses of waltzing; but there were chances for tongues and sounds, as well as for eyes and blushes. He began with her travels, and Europe, and Vesuvius, and the French; and then, when they had worked down, and had that long talking-time at the bottom of the set, he said, boldly,—a little pale, she said, as she told me the story, years after,—

"And what do you hear from home, Mrs. Graff?"

And that splendid creature looked through him. Jove! how she must have looked through him!

"Home!! Mr. Nolan!!! I thought you were the man who never wanted to hear of home again!"—and she walked directly up the deck to her husband, and left poor Nolan alone, as he always was.—He did not dance again.

I cannot give any history of him in order: nobody can now: and, indeed, I am not trying to. These are the traditions, which I sort out, as I believe them, from the myths which have been told about this man for forty years. The lies that have been told about him are legion. The fellows used to say he was the "Iron Mask"; and poor George Pons went to his grave in the belief that this was the author of "Junius," who was being punished for his celebrated libel on Thomas Jefferson. Pons was not very strong in the historical line. A happier story than either of these I have told is of the War. That came along soon after. I have heard this affair told in three or four ways,—and, indeed, it may have happened more than once. But which ship it was on I cannot tell. However, in one, at least, of the great frigate-duels with the English, in which the navy was really baptized, it happened that a round shot from the enemy entered one of our ports square, and took right down the officer of the gun himself, and almost every man of the gun's crew. Now you may say what you choose about courage, but that is not a nice thing to see. But, as the men who were not killed picked themselves up, and as they and the surgeon's people were carrying off the bodies, there appeared Nolan, in his shirt-sleeves, with the rammer in his hand, and, just as if he had been the officer, told them off with authority,—who should go to the cockpit with the wounded men, who should stay with him,—perfectly cheery, and with that way which makes men feel sure all is right and is going to be right. And he finished loading the gun with his own hands, aimed it, and bade the men fire. And there he stayed, captain of that gun, keeping those fellows in spirits, till the enemy struck,—sitting on the carriage while the gun was cooling, though he was exposed all the time,—showing them easier ways to handle heavy shot,—making the raw hands laugh at their own blunders,—and when the gun cooled again, getting it loaded and fired twice as often as any other gun on the ship. The captain walked forward, by way of encouraging the men, and Nolan touched his hat and said,—

"I am showing them how we do this in the artillery, Sir."

And this is the part of the story where all the legends agree: that the Commodore said,—

"I see you do, and I thank you, Sir; and I shall never forget this day, Sir, and you never shall, Sir."

And after the whole thing was over, and he had the Englishman's sword, in the midst of the state and ceremony of the quarter-deck, he said,—

"Where is Mr. Nolan? Ask Mr. Nolan to come here."

And when Nolan came, the captain said,—

"Mr. Nolan, we are all very grateful to you to-day; you are one of us to-day; you will be named in the despatches."

And then the old man took off his own sword of ceremony, and gave it to Nolan, and made him put it on. The man told me this who saw it. Nolan cried like a baby, and well he might. He had not worn a sword since that infernal day at Fort Adams. But always afterwards, on occasions of ceremony, he wore that quaint old French sword of the Commodore's.

The captain did mention him in the despatches. It was always said he asked that he might be pardoned. He wrote a special letter to the Secretary of War. But nothing ever came of it. As I said that was about the time when they began to ignore the whole transaction at Washington, and when Nolan's imprisonment began to carry itself on because there was nobody to stop it without any new orders from home.

I have heard it said that he was with Porter when he took possession of the Nukahiwa Islands. Not this Porter, you know, but old Porter, his father, Essex Porter,—that is, the old Essex Porter, not this Essex. As an artillery officer, who had seen service in the West, Nolan knew more about fortifications, embrasures, ravelins, stockades, and all that, than any of them did; and he worked with a right good will in fixing that battery all right. I have always thought it was a pity Porter did not leave him in command there with Gamble. That would have settled all the question about his punishment. We should have kept the islands, and at this moment we should have one station in the Pacific Ocean. Our French friends, too, when they wanted this little watering-place, would have found it was preoccupied. But Madison and the Virginiaus, of course, flung all that away.

All that was near fifty years ago. If Nolan was thirty then, he must have been near eighty when he died. He looked sixty when he was forty. But he never seemed to me to change a hair afterwards. As I imagine his life, from what I have seen and heard of it, he must have been in every sea, and yet almost never on land. He must have known, in a formal way, more officers in our service than any man living knows. He told me once, with a grave smile, that no man in the world lived so methodical a life as he. "You know the boys say I am the Iron Mask, and you know how busy he was." He said it did not do for any one to try to read all the time, more than to do anything else all the time; but that he read just five hours a day. "Then," he said, "I keep up my note-books, writing in them at such and such hours from what I have been reading; and I include in these my scrap-books." These were very curious indeed. He had six or eight, of different subjects. There was one of History, one of Natural Science, one which he called "Odds and Ends." But they were not merely books of extracts from newspapers. They had bits of plants and ribbons, shells tied on, and carved scraps of bone and wood, which he had taught the men to cut for him, and they were beautifully illustrated. He drew admirably. He had some of the funniest drawings there, and some of the most pathetic, that I have ever seen in my life. I wonder who will have Nolan's scrap-books.

Well, he said his reading and his notes were his profession, and that they took five hours and two hours respectively of each day. "Then," said he, "every man should have a diversion as well as a profession. My Natural History is my diversion." That took two hours a day more. The men used to bring him birds and fish, but on a long cruise he had to satisfy himself with centipedes and cockroaches and such small game. He was the only naturalist I ever met who knew anything about the habits of the house-fly and the mosquito. All those people can tell you whether they are *Lepidoplera* or *Steptopotera;* but as for telling how you can get rid of them, or how they get away from you when you strike them,—why, Linnæus knew as little of that as John Foy the idiot did. These nine hours made

Nolan's regular daily "occupation." The rest of the time he talked or walked. Till he grew very old, he went aloft a great deal. He always kept up his exercise; and I never heard that he was ill. If any other man was ill, he was the kindest nurse in the world; and he knew more than half the surgeons do. Then if anybody was sick or died, or if the captain wanted him to on any other occasion, he was always ready to read prayers. I have remarked that he read beautifully.

My own acquaintance with Philip Nolan began six or eight years after the War, on my first voyage after I was appointed a midshipman. It was in the first days after our Slave-Trade treaty, while the Reigning House, which was still the House of Virginia, had still a sort of sentimentalism about the suppression of the horrors of the Middle Passage, and something was sometimes done that way. We were in the South Atlantic on that business. From the time I joined, I believe I thought Nolan was a sort of lay chaplain,—a chaplain with a blue coat. I never asked about him. Everything in the ship was strange to me. I knew it was green to ask questions, and I suppose I thought there was a "Plain-Buttons" on every ship. We had him to dine in our mess once a week, and the caution was given that on that day nothing was to be said about home. But if they had told us not to say anything about the planet Mars or the Book of Deuteronomy, I should not have asked why; there were a great many things which seemed to me to have as little reason. I first came to understand anything about "the man without a country" one day when we overhauled a dirty little schooner which had slaves on board. An officer was sent to take charge of her, and, after a few minutes, he sent back his boat to ask that some one might be sent him who could speak Portuguese. We were all looking over the rail when the message came, and we all wished we could interpret, when the captain asked who spoke Portuguese. But none of the officers did; and just as the captain was sending forward to ask if any of the people could, Nolan stepped out and said he should be glad to interpret, if the captain wished, as he understood the language. The captain thanked him, fitted out another boat with him, and in this boat it was my luck to go.

When we got there, it was such a scene as you seldom see, and never want to. Nastiness beyond account, and chaos run loose in the midst of the nastiness. There were not a great many of the negroes; but by way of making what there were understand that they were free, Vaughan had had their hand-cuffs and ankle-cuffs knocked off, and, for convenience' sake, was putting them upon the rascals of the schooner's crew. The negroes were, most of them, out of the hold, and swarming all round the dirty deck, with a central throng surrounding Vaughan and addressing him in every dialect and *patois* of a dialect, from the Zulu click up to the Parisian of Beledeljereed.

As we came on deck, Vaughan looked down from a hogshead, on which he had mounted in desperation, and said,—

"For God's love, is there anybody who can make these wretches understand something? The men gave them rum, and that did not quiet them. I knocked that big fellow down twice, and that did not soothe him. And then I talked Choctaw to all of them together; and I'll be hanged if they understood that as well as they understood the English."

Nolan said he could speak Portuguese, and one or two fine-looking Kroomen were dragged out, who, as it had been found already, had worked for the Portuguese on the coast at Fernando Po.

"Tell them they are free," said Vaughan; "and tell them that these rascals are to be hanged as soon as we can get rope enough."

Nolan "put that into Spanish,"*—that is, he explained it in such Portuguese as the Kroomen could understand, and they in turn to such of the negroes as could understand them. Then there was such a yell of delight, clinching of fists, leaping and dancing, kissing of Nolan's feet, and a general rush made to the hogshead by way of spontaneous worship of Vaughan, as the *deus ex machina* of the occasion.

"Tell them," said Vaughan, well pleased, "that I will take them all to Cape Palmas."

This did not answer so well. Cape Palmas was practically as far from the homes of most of them as New Orleans or Rio Janeiro was; that is, they would be eternally separated from home there. And their interpreters, as we could understand, instantly said, "*Ah, non Palmas*," and began to propose infinite other expedients in most voluble language. Vaughan was rather disappointed at this result of his liberality, and asked Nolan eagerly what they said. The drops stood on poor Nolan's white forehead, as he hushed the men down, and said,—

"He says, 'Not Palmas.' He says, 'Take us home, take us to our own country, take us to our own house, take us to our own pickaninnies and our own women.' He says he has an old father and mother, who will die, if they do not see him. And this one says he left his people all sick, and paddled down to Fernando to beg the white doctor to come and help them, and that these devils caught him in the bay just in sight of home, and that he has never seen anybody from home since then. And this one says," choked out Nolan, "that he has not heard a word from his home in six months, while he has been locked up in an infernal barracoon."

Vaughan always said he grew gray himself while Nolan struggled through this interpretation. I, who did not understand anything of the passion involved in it, saw that the very elements were melting with fervent heat, and that something was to pay somewhere. Even the negroes themselves stopped howling, as they saw Nolan's agony, and Vaughan's almost equal agony of sympathy. As quick as he could get words, he said,—

"Tell them yes, yes, yes; tell them they shall go to the Mountains of the Moon, if they will. If I sail the schooner through the Great White Desert, they shall go home!"

And after some fashion Nolan said so. And then they all fell to kissing him again, and wanted to rub his nose with theirs.

But he could not stand it long; and getting

Vaughan to say he might go back, he beckoned me down into our boat. As we lay back in the stern-sheets and the men gave way, he said to me,—"Youngster, let that show you what it is to be without a family, without a home, and without a country. And if you are over tempted to say a word or to do a thing that shall put a bar between you and your family, your home, and your country, pray God in His mercy to take you that instant home to His own heaven. Stick by your family, boy; forget you have a self, while you do everything for them. Think of your home, boy; write and send, and talk about it. Let it be nearer and nearer to your thought, the farther you have to travel from it; and rush back to it, when you are free, as that poor black slave is doing now. And for your country, boy," and the words rattled in his throat, "and for that flag," and he pointed to the ship, "never dream a dream but of serving her as she bids you, though the service carry you through a thousand hells. No matter what happens to you, no matter who flatters you or who abuses you, never look at another flag, never let a night pass but you pray God to bless that flag. Remember, boy, that behind all these men you have to do with, behind officers, and government, and people even, there is the Country Herself, your Country, and that you belong to Her as you belong to your own mother.

Stand by Her, boy, as you would stand by your mother, if those devils there had got hold of her to-day!"

I was frightened to death by his calm, hard passion; but I blundered out, that I would, by all that was holy, and that I had never thought of doing anything else. He hardly seemed to hear me; but he did, almost in a whisper, say,—"Oh, if anybody had said so to me when I was of your age!"

I think it was this half-confidence of his, which I never abused, for I never told this story till now, which afterward made us great friends. He was very kind to me. Often he sat up, or even got up, at night to walk the deck with me, when it was my watch. He explained to me a great deal of my mathematics, and I owe to him my taste

for mathematics. He lent me books, and helped me about my reading. He never alluded so directly to his story again; but from one and another officer I have learned, in thirty years, what I am telling. When we parted from him in St. Thomas harbor, at the end of our cruise, I was more sorry than I can tell. I was very glad to meet him again in 1830; and later in life, when I thought I had some influence in Washington, I moved heaven and earth to have him discharged. But it was like getting a ghost out of prison. They pretended there was no such man, and never was such a man. They will say so at the Department now! Perhaps they do not know. It will not be the first thing in the service of which the Department appears to know nothing!

There is a story that Nolan met Burronce on one of our vessels, when a party of Americans came on board in the Mediterranean. But this I believe to be a lie; or rather, it is a myth, *ben trovato*, involving a tremendous blowing-up with which he sunk Burr,—asking him how he liked to be "without a country." But it is clear, from Burr's life, that nothing of the sort could have happened; and I mention this only as an illustration of the stories which get a-going where there is the least mystery at bottom.

So poor Philip Nolan had his wish fulfilled. I know but one fate more dreadful: it is the fate reserved for those men who shall have one day to exile themselves from their country because they have attempted her ruin, and shall have at the same time to see the prosperity and honor to which she rises when she has rid herself of them and their iniquities. The wish of poor Nolan, as we all learned to call him, not because his punishment was too great, but because his repentance was so clear, was precisely the wish of every Bragg and Beau-regard who broke a soldier's oath two years ago, and of every Maury and Barron who broke a sailor's. I do not know how often they have repented. I do know that they have done all that in them lay that they might have no country,—that all the honors, associations, memories, and hopes which belong to "country" might be broken up into little shreds and distributed to the winds. I know, too, that their punishment, as they vegetate through what is left of life to them in wretched Boulognes and Leicester Squares, where they are destined to upbraid each other till they die, will have all the agony of Nolan's, with the added pang that every one who sees them will see them to despise and to execrate them. They will have their wish, like him.

For him, poor fellow, he repented of his folly, and then, like a man, submitted to the fate he had asked for. He never intentionally added to the difficulty or delicacy of the charge of those who had him in hold. Accidents would happen; but they never happened from his fault. Lieutenant Truxton told me, that, when Texas was annexed, there was a careful discussion among the officers, whether they should get hold of Nolan's handsome set of maps, and cut Texas out of it,—from the map of the world and the map of Mexico. The United States had been cut out when the atlas was bought for him. But it was voted, rightly enough, that to do this would be virtually to reveal to him what had happened, or, as Harry Cole said, to make him think Old Burr had succeeded. So it was from no fault of Nolan's that a great botch happened at my own table, when, for a short time, I was in command of the George Washington corvette, on the South-American station. We were lying in the La Plata, and some of the officers, who had been on shore, and had just joined again, were entertaining us with accounts of their misadventures in riding the half-wild horses of Buenos Ayres. Nolan was at table, and was in an unusually bright and talkative mood. Some story of a tumble reminded him of an adventure of his own; when he was catching wild horses in Texas with his brother Stephen, at a time when he must have been quite a boy. He told the story with a good deal of spirit,—so much so, that the silence which often follows a good story hung over the table for an instant, to be broken by Nolan himself. For he asked, perfectly unconsciously,—

"Pray, what has become of Texas? After the Mexicans got their independence. I thought that province of Texas would come forward very fast. It is really one of the finest regions on earth; it is the Italy of this continent. But I have not seen or heard a word of Texas for near twenty years."

There were two Texan officers at the table. The reason he had never heard of Texas was that Texas and her affairs had been painfully cut out of his newspapers since Austin began his settlements; so that, while he read of Honduras and Tamaulipas, and, till quite lately, of California, this virgin province, in which his brother had travelled so far, and, I believe, had died, had ceased to be to him. Waters and Williams, the two Texas men, looked grimly at each other, and tried not to laugh. Edward Morris had his attention attracted by the third link in the chain of the captain's chandelier. Watrous was seized with a convulsion of sneezing. Nolan himself saw that something was to pay, he did not know what. And I, as master of the feast, had to say,—

"Texas is out of the map, Mr. Nolan. Have you seen Captain Back's curious account of Sir Thomas Roe's Welcome?"

After that cruise I never saw Nolan again. I wrote to him at least twice a year, for in that voyage we became even confidentially intimate; but he never wrote to me. The other men tell me that in those fifteen years he *aged* very fast, as well he might indeed, but that he was still the same gentle, uncomplaining, silent sufferer that he ever was, bearing as best he could his self-appointed punishment,—rather less social, perhaps, with new men whom he did not know, but more anxious, apparently, than ever to serve and befriend and teach the boys, some of whom fairly seemed to worship him. And now it seems the dear old fellow is dead. He has found a home at last, and a country.

Since writing this, and while considering whether or no I would print it, as a warning to the young Nolans and Vallandighams and Tatnalls of to-day of what it is to throw away a country, I have received from Danforth, who is on board the Levant, a letter which gives an account of Nolan's last hours. It removes all my doubts about telling this story.

To understand the first words of the letter, the non-professional reader should remember that after 1817 the position of every officer who had Nolan in charge was one of the greatest delicacy. The Government had failed to renew the order of 1807 regarding him. What was a man to do? Should he let him go? What, then, if he were called to account by the Department for violating the order of 1807? Should he keep him? What, then, if Nolan should be liberated some day, and should bring an action for false imprisonment or kidnapping against every man who had had him in charge? I urged and pressed this upon Southard, and I have reason to think that other officers did the same thing. But the Secretary always said, as they so often do at Washington, that there were no special orders to give, and that we must act on our own judgment. That means, "If you succeed, you will be sustained; if you fail, you will be disavowed." Well, as Danforth says, all that is over now, though I do not know but I expose myself to a criminal prosecution on the evidence of the very revelation I am making.

Here is the letter:—

"*Levant*, 2° 2' S. @ 131° W.

"DEAR FRED,—I try to find heart and life to tell you that it is all over with dear old Nolan. I have been with him on this voyage more than I ever was, and I can understand wholly now the way in which you used to speak of the dear old fellow. I could see that he was not strong, but I had no idea the end was so near. The doctor had been watching him very carefully, and yesterday morning came to me and told me that Nolan was not so well, and had not left his state-room,—a thing I never remember before. He had let the doctor come and see him as he lay there,—the first time the doctor had been in the state-room,—and he said he should like to see me. Oh, dear! do you remember the mysteries we boys used to invent about his room, in the old Intrepid days? Well, I went in, and there, to be sure, the poor fellow lay in his berth, smiling pleasantly as he gave me his hand, but looking very frail. I could not help a glance round, which showed me what a little shrine he had made of the box he was lying in. The stars and stripes were triced up above and around a picture of Washington, and he had painted a majestic eagle, with lightings blazing from his beak and his foot just clasping the whole globe, which his wings overshadowed. The dear old boy saw my glance, and said, with a sad smile, 'Here, you see, I have a country!' And then he pointed to the foot of his bed, where I had not seen before a great map of the United States, as he had drawn it from memory, and which he had there to look upon as he lay. Quaint, queer old names were on it, in large letters: 'Indiana Territory,' 'Mississippi Territory,' and 'Louisiana Territory,' as I suppose our fathers learned such things: but the old fellow had patched in Texas, too; he had carried his western boundary all the way to the Pacific, but on that shore he had defined nothing.

"'Oh, Dauforth,' he said, 'I know I am dying. I cannot get home. Surely you will tell me something now?—Stop! stop! Do not speak till I say what I am sure you know, that there is not in this ship, that there is not in America,—God bless her!—a more loyal man than I. There cannot be a man who loves the old flag as I do, or prays for it as I do, or hopes for it as I do. There are thirty-four stars in it now, Danforth. I thank God for that, though I do not know what their names are. There has never been one taken away: I thank God for that. I know by that, that there has never been any successful Burr. Oh, Danforth, Danforth,' he sighed out, 'how like a wretched night's dream a boy's idea of personal fame or of separate sovereignty seems, when one looks back on it after such a life as mine! But tell me,—tell me something,—tell me everything, Danforth, before I die!'

"Ingham, I swear to you that I felt like a monster that I had not told him everything before. Danger or no danger, delicacy or no delicacy, who was I, that I should have been acting the tyrant all this time over this dear, sainted old man, who had years ago expiated, in his whole manhood's life, the madness of a boy's treason? 'Mr. Nolan,' said I, 'I will tell you everything you ask about. Only, where shall I begin?'

"Oh, the blessed smile that crept over his white face! and he pressed my hand and said, 'God bless you!' 'Tell me their names,' he said, and he pointed to the stars on the flag. 'The last I know is Ohio. My father lived in Kentucky. But I have guessed Michigan and Indiana and Mississippi,—that was where Fort Adams is,—they make twenty. But where are your other fourteen? You have not cut up any of the old ones, I hope?'

"Well, that was not a bad text, and I told him the names, in as good order as I could, and he bade me take down his beautiful map and draw them in as I best could with my pencil. He was wild with delight about Texas, told me how his brother died there; he had marked a gold cross where he supposed his brother's grave was; and he had guessed at Texas. Then he was delighted as he saw California and Oregon;—that, he said, he had suspected partly, because he had never been permitted to land on that shore, though the ships were there so much. 'And the men,' said he, laughing, 'brought off a good deal besides furs.' Then he went back—heavens, how far!—to ask about the Chesapeake, and what was done to Barron for surrendering her to the Leopard, and whether Burr ever tried again,—and he ground his teeth with the only passion he showed. But in a moment that was over, and he said, 'God forgive me, for I am sure I forgive him.' Then he asked about the old war,—told me the true story of his serving the gun the day we took the Java,—asked about dear old David Porter, as he called him. Then he settled down more quietly, and very happily, to hear me tell in an hour the history of fifty years.

"How I wished it had been somebody who knew something! But I did as well as I could. I told him of the English war I told him about Fulton and the steam-boat beginning. I told him about old Scott, and Jackson; told him all I could think about the Mississippi, and New Orleans,

and Texas, and his own old Kentucky. And do you think he asked who was in command of the "Legion of the West." I told him it was a very gallant officer, named Grant, and that, by our last news, he was about to establish! his headquarters at Vicksburg. Then 'Where was Vicksburg?' I worked that out on the map; it was about a hundred miles, more or less, above his old Fort Adams; and I thought Fort Adams must be a ruin now. 'It must be at old Vicks's plantation,' said he; 'well, that is a change!'

"I tell you, Ingham, it was a hard thing to condense the history of half a century into that talk with a sick man. And I do not now know what I told him,—of emigration, and the means of it,—of steamboats and railroads and telegraphs,—of inventions and books and literature,—of the colleges and West Point and the Naval School,—but with the queerest interruptions that ever you heard. You see it was Robinson Crusoe asking all the accumulated questions of fifty-six years!

"I remember he asked, all of a sudden, who was President now; and when I told him, he asked if Old Abe was General Benjamin Lincoln's son. He said he met old General Lincoln, when he was quite a boy himself, at some Indian treaty. I said no, that Old Abe was a Kentuckian like himself, but I could not tell him of what family; he had worked up from the ranks. 'Good for him!' cried Nolan; 'I am glad of that. As I have brooded and wondered, I have thought our danger was in keeping up those regular successions in the first families.' Then I got talking about my visit to Washington. I told him of meeting the Oregon Congressman, Harding; I told him about the Smithsonian and the Exploring Expedition; I told him about the Capitol,—and the statues for the pediment,—and Crawford's Liberty,—and Greenough's Washington: Ingham, I told him everything I could think of that would show the grandeur of his country and its prosperity; but I could not make up my mouth to tell him a word about this infernal Rebellion!

"And he drank it in, and enjoyed it as I cannot tell you. He grew more and more silent, yet I never thought he was tired or faint. I gave him a glass of water, but he just wet his lips, and told me not to go away. Then he asked me to bring the Presbyterian 'Book of Public Prayer,' which lay there, and said, with a smile, that it would open at the right place,—and so it did. There was his double red mark down the page; and I knelt down and read, and he repeated with me,—'For ourselves and our country, O gracious God, we thank Thee, that, notwithstanding our manifold transgressions of Thy holy laws, Thou hast continued to us Thy marvellous kindness,'—and so to the end of that thanksgiving. Then he turned to the end of the same book, and I read the words more familiar to me,—'Most heartily we beseech Thee with Thy favor to behold and bless Thy servant, the President of the United States, and all others in authority,'—and the rest of the Episcopal collect. 'Danforth,' said he, 'I have repeated those prayers night and morning, it is now fifty-five years.' And then he said he would go to sleep. He bent me down over him and kissed me; and he said, 'Look in my Bible, Danforth, when I am gone.' And I went away.

"But I had no thought it was the end. I thought he was tired and would sleep. I knew he was happy, and I wanted him to be alone.

"But in an hour, when the doctor went in gently, he found Nolan had breathed his life away with a smile. He had something pressed close to his lips. It was his father's badge of the Order of Cincinnati.

"We looked in his Bible, and there was a slip of paper, at the place where he had marked the text,—

"They desire a country, even a heavenly: wherefore God is not ashamed to be called their God: for he hath prepared for them a city.'

"On this slip of paper he had written,—

"'Bury me in the sea; it has been my home, and I love it. But will not some one set up a stone for my memory at Fort Adams or at Orleans, that my disgrace may not be more than I ought to bear? Say on it,—

"'*In Memory of*

"'PHILIP NOLAN,

"'*Lieutenant in the Army of the United States.*

"'He loved this country as no other man has loved her; but no man deserved less at her hands.'"

* The phrase is General Taylor's. When Santa Aña brought up his immense army at Buena Vista, he sent a flag of truce to invite Taylor to surrender. "Tell him to go to hell," said old Rough-and-Ready. "Bliss, put that into Spanish." "Perfect Bliss," as this accomplished officer, too early lost, was called, interpreted liberally, replying to the flag, in exquisite Castilian, "Say to General Santa. Aña, that, if he wants us, he must come and take us." And this is the answer which has gone into history.

Suggested Readings

Hale, Edward Everett. *The Life and Letters of Edward Everett Hale*. Boston: Little, Brown, and Company, 1917.

Hale, Edward Everett. *The Man Without a Country*. Boston: Little, Brown, and Company, 1905.

19

Foresaken by the Republic: Toussaint L'Ouverture's Memoir

Dr. Robert D. Madison

Toussaint L'Ouverture (1743?–1803) died a prisoner in the Chateau de Joux in the Jura Mountains in France after leading the most successful slave revolt in history. The French colony of St. Domingue, or Haiti (*land of mountains*), was the richest in the New World. In the chaos of the French Revolution, the slaves of Haiti rose and asserted their own freedom while seeking a place in the new French republic.

Toussaint lived nearly fifty years in slavery before the Haitian revolution gave him the opportunity to rise to the leadership of the free Blacks. As general, he consolidated his influence throughout the island. But as dreams of republican government faded with the ascendancy of Napoleon, it became clear that Haitians would be welcomed only as slaves. During the Peace of Amiens Napoleon sent his own brother-in-law, General Leclerc, to subdue Toussaint and his followers. But Leclerc could not beat the Haitians in their own mountains, and while he negotiated for peace his army on the coasts began to starve and die of fever. Leclerc resumed control of the island, but the Blacks remained free with Toussaint as their *de facto* leader.

By treachery, Toussaint fell into the hands of the French. In the middle of the night he was ushered aboard a waiting French frigate and carried to France. As he left the shores of Haiti forever, he is reputed to have said, "They have only felled the trunk of the tree; branches will sprout, for the roots are numerous and deep." While a prisoner in France, Toussaint wrote the following memoir and defense of his service in behalf of Haitian freedom.

Memoir of General Toussaint L'Ouverture Written by Himself.

It is my duty to render to the French Government an exact account of my conduct. I shall relate the facts with all the simplicity and frankness of an old soldier, adding to them the reflections that naturally suggest themselves. In short, I shall tell the truth, though it be against myself.

The colony of Saint Domingo, of which I was commander, enjoyed the greatest tranquillity; agriculture and commerce flourished there. The island had attained a degree of splendor which it had never before seen. And all this—I dare to say it—was my work.

Nevertheless, as we were upon a war footing, the Commission had published a decree ordering me to take all necessary measures to prevent the enemies of the Republic from penetrating into the island. Accordingly, I ordered all the commanders of the sea-ports not to permit any ships of war to enter into the roadstead, except they were known and had obtained permission from me. If it should be a squadron, no matter from what nation, it was absolutely prohibited from entering the port, or even the roadstead, unless I should myself know where it came from, and the port from which it sailed.

This order was in force, when, on the 26th of January, 1802, a squadron appeared before the Cape. At that time I had left this town to visit the Spanish part, Santo Domingo, for the purpose of inspecting the agriculture. On setting out from Maguâna, I had despatched one of my aides-de-camp to Gen. Dessalinos, Commander-in-chief of the departments of the West and South, who was then at St. Mare, to order him to join me at Gonaïves, or at St. Michel, to accompany me on my journey.

At the time of the squadron's appearance, I was at Santo Domingo, from which place I set out, three days after, to go to Hinche. Passing by Banique, arriving at Papayes, I met my aide-do-camp Couppé and an officer sent by Gen. Christophe, who brought me a letter from the general, by which he informed me of the arrival of the French squadron before the Cape, and assured me that the General-in-chief commanding this squadron had not done him the honor to write to him, but had only sent an officer to order him to prepare accommodations for his forces; that Gen. Christophe having demanded

of this officer whether he was the bearer of letters to him or of dispatches for the General-in-chief, Toussaint L'Ouverture, requesting him to send them to him, that they might reach him at once, this officer replied to him, that he was not charged with any, and that it was not, in fact, a question concerning Gen. Toussaint. "Surrender the town," he continued; "you will be well recompensed; the French Government sends you presents." To which Gen. Christophe replied, "Since you have no letters for the General-in-chief nor for me, you may return and tell your general that he does not know his duty; that it is not thus that people present themselves in a country belonging to France."

Gen. Leclerc having received this answer, summoned Gen. Christophe to deliver the place to him, and, in case of refusal, warned him that on the morning of the next day he should land fifteen thousand men. In response to this, Gen. Christophe begged him to wait for Gen. Toussaint L'Ouverture, to whom he had already sent the intelligence, and would do so the second time, with the greatest celerity. In fact, I received a second letter, and hastened to reach the Cape, in spite of the overflowing of the IIinche, hoping to have the pleasure of embracing my brothers-in-arms from Europe, and to receive at the same time the orders of the French Government; and in order to march with greater speed, I left all my escorts. Between St. Michel and St. Raphael, I met Gen. Dessalines and said to him, "I have sent for you to accompany me on my tour to Port-de-Paix, and to Môle; but that is useless now. I have just received two letters from Gen. Christophe, announcing the arrival of the French squadron before the Cape."

I communicated to him these letters, whereupon he told me that he had seen from St. Marc six large vessels making sail for the coast of Port Républicain; but he was ignorant of what nation they were. I ordered him then to repair promptly to this port, since it was possible that Gen. Christophe having refused the entrance of the Cape to the general commanding the squadron, the latter might have proceeded to

Port Républicain in the hope of finding me there; should this prove true, I ordered him, in advance, to request the general to wait for me, and to assure him that I would go first to the Cape in the hope of meeting him there, and in case I should not find him there, I would repair at once to Port Républicain to confer with him. I set out for the Cape, passing by Vases, the shortest road. On arriving upon the heights of the Grand Boucan, in the place called the Porte-Saint-Jacques, I perceived a fire in the town on the Cape. I urged my horse at full speed to reach this town, to find there the general commanding the squadron, and to ascertain who had caused the conflagration. But, on approaching, I found the roads filled with the inhabitants who had fled from this unfortunate town, and I was unable to penetrate farther because all the passages were cannonaded by the artillery of the vessels which were in the roadstead. I then resolved to go up to the Fort of Bel-Air, but I found this fort evacuated likewise, and all the pieces of cannon spiked.

I was, consequently, obliged to retrace my steps. After passing the hospital, I met Gen. Christophe, and asked him who had ordered the town to be fired. He replied that it was he. I reprimanded him severely for having employed such rigorous measures. "Why," said I to him, "did you not rather make some military arrangements to defend the town until my arrival?" He answered, "What do you wish, general? My duty, necessity, the circumstances, the reiterated threats of the general commanding the squadron, forced me to it. I showed the general the orders of which I was the bearer, but without avail." He added, "that the proclamations spread secretly in the town to seduce the people, and instigate an uprising, were not sanctioned by military usage; that if the commander of the squadron had truly pacific intentions, he would have waited for me; that he would not have employed the means which he used to gain the commander of the Fort of Boque, who is a drunkard; that he would not in consequence have seized this fort; that he would not have put

to death half of the garrison of Fort Liberty; that he would not have made a descent upon Acul, and that, in a word, he would not have committed at first all the hostilities of which he was guilty.

Gen. Christophe joined me, and we continued the route together. On arriving at Haut-du-Cap, we passed through the habitations of Breda as far as the barrier of Boulard, passing by the gardens. There I ordered him to rally his troops, and go into camp on the Bonnet until further orders, and to keep me informed of all the movements he made. I told him that I was going to Hericourt; that there, perhaps, I should receive news from the commander of the squadron; that he would doubtless deliver to me the orders of the Government; that I might even meet him there; that I should then ascertain the reasons which had induced him to come in this manner; and, that, in case he was the bearer of orders from the government, I should request him to communicate them to me, and should in consequence make arrangements with him.

Gen. Christophe left me then to repair to the post which I had assigned to him; but he met a body of troops who fired upon him, forced him to dismount from his horse, plunge into the river, and cross it by swimming.

After separating from Gen. Christophe, I had at my side Adjutant-General Fontaine, two other officers, and my aide-decamp, Couppé, who went in advance; he warned me of the troops on the road. I ordered, him to go forward. He told me that this force was commanded by a general. I then demanded a conference with him. But Couppé had not time to execute my orders; they fired upon us at twenty-five steps from the barrier. My horse was pierced with a ball; another ball carried away the hat of one of my officers. This unexpected circumstance forced me to abandon the open road, to cross the savanna and the forests to reach Héricourt, where I remained three days to wait for news of the commander of the squadron, again without avail.

But, the next day, I received a letter from Gen. Rochambeau, announcing "that the column which he commanded had seized upon Fort Liberty, taken and put to the sword a part of the garrison, which had resisted; that he had not believed the garrison would steep its bayonets in the blood of Frenchmen; on the contrary, he had expected to find it disposed in his favor." I replied to this letter, and, manifesting my indignation to the general, asked to know, "Why he had ordered the massacre of those brave soldiers who had only followed the orders given them; who had, besides, contributed so much to the happiness of the colony and to the triumph of the Republic. Was this the recompense that the French Government had promised them?"

I concluded by saying to Gen. Rochambeau, that "I would fight to the last to avenge the death of these brave soldiers, for my own liberty, and to reestablish tranquillity and order in the colony."

This was, in fact, the resolution I had taken after having reflected deliberately upon the report Gen. Christophe had brought me, upon the danger I had just run, upon the letter of Gen. Rochambeau, and finally upon the conduct of the commander of the squadron.

Having formed my resolution, I went to Gonaives. There I communicated my intentions to Gen. Maurepas, and ordered him to make the most vigorous resistance to all vessels which should appear before Port-de-Paix, where he commanded; and, in case he should not be strong enough,—having only half of a brigade,—to imitate the example of Gen. Christophe and afterward withdraw to the Mountain, taking with him ammunition of all kinds; there to defend himself to the death.

I then went to St. Marc to visit the fortifications. I found that the news of the shameful events which had just taken place had reached this town, and the inhabitants had already fled. I gave orders for all the resistance to be made that the fortifications and munitions would allow of.

As I was on the point of setting out from this town to go to Port-au-Prince and the southern part to give my orders, Captains Jean-Philippe Dupin and Isaac brought me dispatches from Paul L'Ouverture, who commanded at Santo Domingo. Both informed me that a descent had just been made upon Oyarsaval, and that the French and Spaniards who inhabited this place had risen and cut off the roads from Santo Domingo. I acquainted myself with these dispatches. In running over the letter of Gen. Paul and the copy of Gen. Kerverseau's to the commander of the place of Santo Domingo, which was enclosed in it, I saw that this general had made the overture to the commander of the place, and not to Gen. Paul, as he should have done, to make preparations for the landing of his force. I saw also the refusal given by Gen. Paul to this invitation, until he should receive orders from me. I replied to Gen. Paul that I approved his conduct, and ordered him to make all possible effort to defend himself in case of attack; and even to make prisoners of Gen. Kerversoau and his force, if he could. I returned my reply by the captains just mentioned. But foreseeing, on account of the interception of the roads, that they might be arrested and their dispatches demanded, I gave them in charge a second letter, in which I ordered Gen. Paul to use all possible means of conciliation with Gen. Kerverseau. I charged the captains, in case they should be arrested, to conceal the first letter and show only the second.

My reply not arriving as soon as he expected, Gen. Paul sent another black officer with the same dispatches in duplicate. I gave only a receipt to this officer, and sent him back. Of these three messengers two were black and the other white. They were arrested, as I had anticipated; the two blacks were assassinated in violation of all justice and right, contrary to the customs of war; their dispatches were sent to Gen. Kerverseau, who concealed the first letter, and showed to Gen. Paul only the second, in which I had ordered him to enter into negotiations with Gen. Kerverseau. It was in consequence of this letter that Santo Domingo was surrendered.

Having sent off these dispatches, I resumed my route toward the South. I had hardly set forward when I was overtaken by an orderly, coming up at full speed, who brought me a package from Gen. Vernet and a letter from my wife, both announcing to me the arrival from Paris of my two children and their preceptor, of which I was not before aware. I learned also that they were bearers of orders for me from the First Consul. I retraced my steps and flew to Ennery, where I found my two children and the excellent tutor whom the First Consul had had the goodness to give them. I embraced them with the greatest satisfaction and ardor. I then inquired if they were bearers of letters from the First Consul for me. The tutor replied in the affirmative, and handed me a letter which I opened and read about half through; then I folded it, saying that I would reserve the reading of it for a more quiet moment. I begged him then to impart to me the intentions of the Government, and to tell me the name of the commander of the squadron, which I had not yet been able to ascertain. He answered, that his name was Leclerc; that the intention of the Government toward me was very favorable, which was confirmed by my children, and of which I afterwards assured myself by finishing the letter of the First Consul. I observed to them, nevertheless, that if the intentions of the Government were pacific and good regarding me and those who had contributed to the happiness which the colony enjoyed, Gen. Leclerc surely had not followed nor executed the orders he had received, since he had landed on the island like an enemy, and done evil merely for the pleasure of doing it, without addressing himself to the commander or making known to him his powers. I then asked Citizen Coisnon, my children's tutor, if Gen. Leclerc had not given him a dispatch for me or charged him with something to tell me. He replied in the negative, advising me, however, to go to the Cape to confer with the general; my children added their solicitations to persuade me to do so. I represented to them, "that, after the conduct of this general, I could have no confidence in him; that he had landed like an enemy; that, in spite of that, I had believed it my duty to go to meet him in order to prevent the progress of the evil; that he had fired

upon me, and I had run the greatest dangers; that, in short, if his intentions were as pure as those of the Government which sent him, he should have taken the trouble to write to me to inform me of his mission; that, before arriving in the roadstead, he should have sent me an advice-boat with you, sir, and my children,—that being the ordinary practice,—to announce their arrival, and to impart to me his powers; that, since he had observed none of these formalities, the evil was done, and therefore I should refuse decidedly to go in search of him; that, nevertheless, to prove my attachment and submission to the French Government, I would consent to write a letter to Gen. Leclerc. I shall send to him," I continued, "by Mr. Granville, a worthy man, accompanied by my two children and their tutor, whom I shall charge to say to Gen. Leclerc, that it is absolutely dependent upon himself whether this colony is entirely lost, or preserved to France; that I will enter into all possible arrangements with him; that I am ready to submit to the orders of the French Government; but that Gen. Leclerc shall show me orders of which he is bearer, and shall, above all, cease from every species of hostility."

In fact, I wrote the letter, and the deputation set out. In the hope that after the desire I had just manifested to render my submission, order would again be restored, I remained at Gonaïves till the next day. There I learned that two vessels had attacked St. Marc; I proceeded there and learned that they had been repulsed. I returned then to Gonaïves to wait for Gen. Leclerc's reply. Finally, two days after, my two children arrived with the response so much desired, by which the general commanded me to report in person to him, at the Cape, and announced that he had furthermore ordered his generals to advance upon all points; that his orders being given, he could not revoke them. He promised, however, that Gen. Boudet should be stopped at Artibonite; I concluded then, that he did not know the country perfectly, or had been deceived; for, in order to reach Artibonite, it was necessary to have a free passage by St. Marc, which was impossible now, since the two vessels which had attacked this place had been repulsed. He added, further, that they should not attack Môle, only blockade it, since this place had already surrendered. I replied then plainly to the general, "that I should not report to him at the Cape; that his conduct did not inspire me with sufficient confidence; that I was ready to deliver the command to him in conformity with the orders of the First Consul, but that I would not be his lieutenant-general." I besought him again to let me know his intentions, assuring him that I would contribute everything in my power to the reestablishment of order and tranquillity. I added, in conclusion, that if he persisted in his invasion, he would force me to defend myself, although I had but few troops. I sent him this letter with the utmost despatch, by an orderly, who brought me back word, "that he had no reply to make and had taken the field."

The inhabitants of Gonaïves then asked my permission to send a deputation to Gen. Leclerc, which I accorded to them, but he retained the deputation.

The next day I learned that he had taken, without striking a blow and without firing a gun, Dondon, St. Raphael, St. Michel and Marmelade, and that he was prepared to march against Ennery and Gonaïves.

These new hostilities gave rise to new reflections. I thought that the conduct of Gen. Leclerc was entirely contrary to the intentions of the Government, since the First Consul, in his letter, promised peace, while the general made war. I saw that, instead of seeking to arrest this evil, he only increased it. "Does he not fear," I said to myself, "in pursuing such conduct, to be blamed by his Government? Can he hope to be approved by the First Consul, that great man whose equity and impartiality are so well known, while I shall be disapproved?" I resolved then to defend myself, in case of attack; and in spite of my few troops, I made my dispositions accordingly.

Gonaïves not being defensible, I ordered it to be burned, in case retreat was necessary. I placed

Gen. Christophe, who had been obliged to fall back, in the Eribourg road, which leads to Bayonnet, and withdrew myself to Ennery, where a part of my guard of honor had repaired to join and defend me. There I learned that Gros-Morne had just surrendered, and that the army was to march against Gonaïves with three columns; one of these, commanded by Gen. Rochambeau, purposing to pass by Couleuvre and come down upon La Croix, to cut off the road from the town and the passage of the bridge of the Ester.

I ordered Gonaïves to be burned, and, ignorant of Gen. Rochambeau's strength, marched to meet the column, which was making for the bridge of the Ester, at the head of 300 grenadiers of my guard, commanded by their chief, and of sixty mounted guards. We met in a gorge. The attack commenced at six o'clock in the morning with a continuous fire which lasted until noon. Gen. Rochambeau began the attack. I learned from the prisoners I took that the column numbered more than 4,000 men. While I was engaged with Gen. Rochambeau, the column commanded by Gen. Leclerc reached Gonaïves. After the engagement at La Croix, I proceeded to the bridge of the Ester, with artillery, to defend the place, intending to go thence to St. Marc, where I expected to make a desperate resistance. But, on setting out, I learned that Gen. Dessalines, having arrived at this place before me, was obliged to evacuate it and retire to Petite Riviere. I was obliged, after this manœuvre, to slacken my march in order to send in advance the prisoners taken at La Croix, and the wounded to Petite Rivière; and I determined to proceed there myself. When we reached Couriotte, in the plain, I left my troops there, and went in advance alone. I found all the country abandoned.

I received a letter from Gen. Dessalines, informing me that, having learned that the Cahos was to be attacked, he had gone to defend it. I sent an order to him to join me at once. I caused the ammunition and provisions which I had with me to be put in Fort L'Ouverture at the Crête-à-

Pierrot. I ordered Gen. Vernet to procure vessels which would contain water enough to last the garrison during a siege. On the arrival of Gen. Dessalines, I ordered him to take command of the fort and defend it to the last extremity.

For this purpose I left him half of my guards with the chief-of-brigade, Magny, and my two squadrons. I charged him not to allow Gen. Vernet to be exposed to fire, but to let him remain in a safe place to superintend the making of cartridges. Finally, I told Gen. Dessalines that while Gen. Leclerc was attacking this place, I should go into the Northern part, make a diversion, and retake the different places which had been seized; by this manœuvre, I should force the general to retrace his steps and make arrangements with me to preserve this beautiful colony to the Government.

Having given these orders, I took six companies of grenadiers commanded by Gabart, chief of the fourth demi-brigade, and Pourcely, the chief-of-battalion, and marched upon Ennery. I found there a proclamation of Gen. Leclerc, pronouncing me an outlaw. Confident that I had done no wrong with which to reproach myself, that all the disorder which prevailed in the country had been occasioned by Gen. Leclerc; believing myself, besides, the legitimate commander of the island,—I refuted his proclamation and declared him to be outlawed. Without loss of time I resumed my march and recaptured, without violence, St. Michel, St. Raphaël, Dondon, and Marmelade. In this last place I received a letter from Gen. Dessalines, announcing that Gen. Leclerc had marched against Petito Riviere with three columns; that one of these columns, passing by the Cahos and the Grand-Fonds, had captured all the treasures of the Republic coming from Gonaïves, and some silver which the inhabitants had deposited; that it was so heavily loaded with booty it was unable to reach its destination, and had been obliged to turn back to deposit its riches at Port-Republicain; that the two other columns, which had attacked the fort, had been repulsed by the chief-of-brigade, Magny; that Gen. Leclerc, having united his

forces, had ordered a second attack, which had likewise been repelled by himself, Dessalines, who had then arrived. Apprised of these facts, I moved upon Plaisance and captured the camp of Bidouret, who held this place. This camp was occupied by troops of the line. I assaulted all the advanced posts at the same time. Just as I was going to fall upon Plaisance, I received a letter from the commander of Marmelade, which gave me notice that a strong column from the Spanish part was advancing upon this latter place.

I then moved promptly upon this column, which, instead of advancing upon Marmelade, had marched upon Hinche, where I pursued, but was unable to overtake it. I returned to Gonaïves, made myself master of the plain surrounding the town, ready to march upon the Gros-Morne to succor Gen. Maurepas, whom I supposed must be at Port-de-Paix, or else retired to the mountains where I ordered him to encamp, not knowing that he had already capitulated and submitted to Gen. Leclerc.

I received a third letter from Gen. Dessalines, who reported that Gen. Leclerc, having ordered a general assault and been repulsed, had determined to surround the place and bombard it. As soon as I learned the danger with which he was threatened, I hastened to move my troops there to deliver him. Arrived before the camp, I made a reconnoissance, procured the necessary information and prepared to attack it. I could, without fail, have entered the camp by a weak side which I had discovered, and seized the person of Gen. Leclerc and all his staff, but at the moment of execution, I received information that the garrison, failing of water, had been obliged to evacuate the fort. If the project had succeeded, my intention was to send Gen. Leclerc back to the First Consul, rendering to him an exact account of his conduct, and praying him to send me another person worthy of his confidence, to whom I could deliver up the command.

I retired to Grand Fonds to wait for the garrison of Crête-à-Pierrot and to unite my forces. As soon as the garrison arrived, I inquired of Gen. Dessalines where the prisoners were whom he had previously told me were at the Cahos. He replied that a part had been taken by Gen. Rochambeau's column, that another part had been killed in the different attacks that he had endured, and that the rest had escaped in the various marches which he had been obliged to make. This reply evinces the injustice of imputing to me the assassinations which were committed, because, it is said, as chief, I could have prevented them; but am I responsible for the evil which was done in my absence and without my knowledge?

While at Gonaïves (at the commencement of hostilities), I sent my aide-de-camp, Couppé, to Gen. Dessalines, to bid him order the commander of Leogane to take all the inhabitants, men and women, and send them to Port Republicain; to muster all the armed men he could in that place, and prepare himself for a most vigorous resistance in case of attack. My aide-de-camp, Couppé, bearer of my orders, returned and told me that he had not found Gen. Dessalines, but had learned that Leogane had been burned, and that the inhabitants had escaped to Port Republicain.

All these disasters happened just at the time that Gen. Leclerc came. Why did he not inform me of his powers before landing? Why did he land without my order and in defiance of the order of the Commission? Did he not commit the first hostilities? Did he not seek to gain over the generals and other officers under my command by every possible means?

Did he not try to instigate the laborers to rise, by persuading them that I treated them like slaves, and that he had come to break their chains? Ought he to have employed such means in a country where peace and tranquillity reigned?—in a country which was in the power of the Republic?

If I did oblige my fellow-countrymen to work, it was to teach them the value of true liberty without license; it was to prevent corruption of morals; it was for the general happiness of the island, for the interest of the Republic. And I had effectually succeeded in my undertaking, since there could not be found in all the colony a single man unemployed, and the number of beggars had diminished to such a degree that, apart from a few in the towns, not a single one was to be found in the country.

If Gen. Leclerc's intentions had been good, would he have received Golart into his army, and given to him the command of the 9th demi-brigade,—a corps that he had raised at the time that he was chief of battalion? Would he have employed this dangerous rebel, who caused proprietors to be assassinated in their own dwelling-places; who invaded the town of Môle-Saint-Nicolas; who fired upon Gen. Clerveaux, who commanded there; upon Gen. Maurepas and his brigade commander; who made war upon the laborers of Jean-Rabel, from the *Moustiques* and the heights of Port-de-Paix; who carried his audacity so far as to oppose me when I marched against him to force him to submit to his chief, and to retake the territory and the town which he had invaded! The day that he dared to fire upon me, a ball cut the plume from my hat; Bondere, a physician, who accompanied me, was killed at my side, my aides-de-camp were unhorsed. In short, this brigand, after being steeped in every crime, concealed himself in a forest; he only came out of it upon the arrival of the French squadron. Ought Gen. Leclerc to have raised likewise to the rank of brigade commander another rebel, called L'Amour Desrances, who had caused all the inhabitants of the Plain of Cul-de-Sac to be assassinated; who urged the laborers to revolt; who pillaged all this part of the island; against whom, only two months, before the arrival of the squadron, I had been obliged to march, and whom I forced to hide in the forests? Why were rebels and others amicably received, while my subordinates and myself, who remained steadfastly faithful to the French Government, and who had maintained order and tranquillity, were warred upon? Why was it made a crime to have executed the orders of the Government? Why was all the evil which had been done and the disorders which had existed imputed to me? All these facts are known by every inhabitant of St. Domingo. Why, on arriving, did they not go to the root of the evil? Had the troops which gave themselves up to Gen. Leclerc received the order from me? Did they consult me? No. Well! those who committed the wrong did not consult me. It is not right to attribute to me more wrong than I deserve.

I shared these reflections with some prisoners which I had. They replied that it was my influence upon the people which was feared, and that these violent means were employed to destroy it. This caused me new reflections. Considering all the misfortunes which the colony had already suffered, the dwellings destroyed, assassinations committed, the violence exercised even upon women, I forgot all the wrongs which had been done me, to think only of the happiness of the island and the interest of the Government. I determined to obey the order of the First Consul, since Gen. Leclerc had just withdrawn from the Cape with all his forces, after the affair of Crête-a-Pierrot.

Let it be observed that up to this time I had not been able to find an instant in which to reply to the First Consul. I seized with eagerness this momentary quiet to do so. I assured the First Consul of my submission and entire devotion to his orders, but represented to him "that if he did not send another older general to take command, the resistance which I must continue to oppose to Gen. Leclerc would tend to increase the prevalent disorder."

I remembered then that Gen. Dessalines had reported to me that two officers of the squadron—one an aide-de-camp of Gen. Boudet, the other a naval officer, accompanied by two dragoons, sent to stir up a rebellion among the troops—had been made prisoners at the time of the evacuation of Port-au-Prince. I ordered them to be brought before me, and, after conversing with them, sent them back to Gen. Boudet, sending by them a letter with the one which I had written to the First Consul. Just as I was sending off these two officers, I learned that Gen. Hardy had passed Coupe-à-l'Inde with his

army, that he had attacked my possessions, devastated them, and taken away all my animals, among them a horse named Bel-Argent, which I valued very highly. Without losing time, I marched against him with the force I had. I overtook him near Dondon. A fierce engagement took place, which lasted from eleven in the morning till six in the evening.

Before setting out, I had ordered Gen. Dessalines to join the troops which had evacuated Crête-à-Pierrot, and go into camp at Camp-Marchand, informing him that after the battle I should proceed to Marmelade.

Upon my arrival in that place, I received the reply of Gen. Boudet, which he sent me by my nephew Chaney, whom he had previously made prisoner.

That General assured me that my letter would easily reach the First Consul, that, to effect this, he had already sent it to Gen. Leclerc, who had promised him to forward it. Upon the report of my nephew, and after reading the letter of Gen. Boudet, I thought I recognized in him a character of honesty and frankness worthy of a French officer qualified to command. Therefore I addressed myself to him with confidence, begging him to persuade Gen. Leclerc to enter upon terms of conciliation with me. I assured him that ambition had never been my guide, but only honor; that I was ready to give up the command in obedience to the orders of the First Consul, and to make all necessary sacrifices to arrest the progress of the evil. I sent him this letter by my nephew Chancy, whom he kept with him. Two days after, I received a letter sent in haste by an orderly, announcing to me that he had made known my intentions to Gen. Leclerc, and assuring me that the latter was ready to make terms with me, and that I could depend upon the good intentions of the Government with regard to me.

The same day, Gen. Christophe communicated to me a letter which he had just received from a citizen named Vilton, living at the Petite-Anse, and another from Gen. Hardy, both asking him for an interview. I gave permission to Gen.

Christophe to hold these interviews, recommending him to be very circumspect.

Gen. Christophe did not meet this appointment with Gen. Hardy, for he received a letter from Gen. Leclerc, proposing to him another rendezvous. He sent me a copy of this letter and of his reply, and asked my permission to report himself at the place indicated; which I granted, and he went.

Gen. Christophe, on his return, brought me a letter from Gen. Leclerc, saying that he should feel highly satisfied if he could induce me to concert with him, and submit to the orders of the Republic. I replied immediately that I had always been submissive to the French Government, as I had invariably borne arms for it; that if from the beginning I had been treated as I should have been, not a single shot would have been fired; that peace would not have been even disturbed in the island, and that the intention of the Government would have been fulfilled. In short, I showed to Gen. Leclerc, as well as to Gen. Christophe, all my indignation at the course which the latter had pursued, without orders from me.

The next day, I sent to Gen. Leclerc my Adjutant-General Fontaine, bearer of a second letter, in which I asked for an interview at Héricourt, which he refused. Fontaine assured me however, that he had been well received. I was not discouraged. I sent the third time my aide-de-camp, Couppé and my secretary Nathand, assuring him that I was ready to give up the command to him, conformably to the intentions of the First Consul. He replied, that an hour of conversation would be worth more than ten letters, giving me his word of honor that he would act with all the frankness and loyalty that could be expected of a French general. At the same time a proclamation from him was brought me, bidding all citizens to regard as null and void that article of the proclamation of Feb. 10, 1802, which made me an outlaw. "Do not fear," he said in this proclamation, "you and your generals, and the people who are with you, that I shall search out the past conduct of any one; I will

draw the veil of oblivion over the events which have taken place at Saint Domingo; I imitate, in so doing, the example which the First Consul gave to France on the 11th of November. In future, I wish to see in the island only good citizens. You ask repose; after having borne the burden of government so long, repose is due you; but I hope that in your retirement you will use your wisdom, in your moments of leisure, for the prosperity of Saint Domingo."

After this proclamation and the word of honor of the general, I proceeded to the Cape. I submitted myself to Gen. Leclerc in accordance with the wish of the First Consul; I afterward talked with him with all the frankness and cordiality of a soldier who loves and esteems his comrade. He promised me forgetfulness of the past and the protection of the French Government. He agreed with me that we had both been wrong. "You can, General," he said to me, "retire to your home in perfect security. But tell me if Gen. Dessalines will obey my orders, and if I can rely upon him?" I replied that he could; that Gen. Dessalines might have faults, like every man, but that he understood military subordination. I suggested to him, however, that for the public good and to reëstablish the laborers in their occupations, as they were at the time of his arrival in the island, it was necessary that Gen. Dessalines should be recalled to his command at Saint Marc, and Gen. Charles Belair to L'Arcahaye, which he promised me should be done. At eleven in the evening, I took leave of him and withdrew to Héricourt, where I passed the night with Gen. Fressinet, and set out the next morning for Marmelade.

The third day after, I received a letter from Gen. Leclerc, bidding me discharge my footguards and horse-guards. He addressed to me also an order for Gen. Dessalines; I acquainted myself with it and sent it to Gen. Dessalines, telling him to comply with it. And that I might the better fulfil the promises that I had made Gen. Leclerc, I requested Gen. Dessalines to meet me half-way between his house and mine. I urged him to submit, as I had done; I told him that the public interest required me to make great sacrifices, and that I was willing to make them; but as for him, he might keep his command. I said as much to Gen. Charles, also to all the officers with them; finally, I persuaded them, in spite of all the reluctance and regret they evinced, to leave me and go away. They even shed tears. After this interview, all returned to their own homes. Adjutant-General Perrin, whom Gen. Leclerc had sent to Dessalines with his orders, found him very ready to comply with them, since I had previously engaged him to do so in our interview. As we have seen, a promise was made to place Gen. Charles at L'Arcahaye; however, it was not done.

It was unnecessary for me to order the inhabitants of Dondon, St. Michel, St. Raphaël and Marmelade to return to their homes, since they had done so as soon as I had taken possession of these communities; I only advised them to resume their usual occupations. I ordered also the inhabitants of Plaisance and the neighboring places, to return home and begin their labor, too. They expressed fears that they might be disturbed. Therefore I wrote to Gen. Leclerc, reminding him of his promise, and begging him to attend to their execution. He replied, that his orders were already given upon that subject. Meanwhile, the commander of this place had divided his forces and sent detachments into all the districts, which had alarmed the laborers and compelled them to flee to the mountains. I proceeded to Ennory and acquainted Gen. Leclerc with these things, as I had promised him. In this town I found a great many laborers from Gonaïves, whom I persuaded to return home. Before I left Marmelade, I ordered the commander of that place to restore the artillery and ammunition to the commander of Plaisance, in conformity to the desire of Gen. Leclerc. I also ordered the commander at Ennery to return the only piece of artillery there, and also the ammunition, to the commander of Gonaïves.

I then employed myself in rebuilding my houses which had been burned. In a house in the mountains, which had escaped the flames, I had to prepare a comfortable lodging for my wife, who was still in the woods where she had been obliged to take refuge.

While engaged in these occupations, I learned that 500 troops had arrived, to be stationed at Ennery, a little town, which, until then, could not have had more than 50 armed men as a police force; and that a very large detachment had also been sent to St. Michel. I hastened to the town. I saw that all my houses had been pillaged and even the coffers of my laborers carried off. At the very moment when I was entering my complaint to the commander, I pointed out to him the soldiers loaded with fruit of all kinds, even unripe fruit; I also showed him the laborers who, seeing these robberies, were fleeing to other houses in the mountains. I gave an account to Gen. Leclerc of what was going on, and observed to him that the measures which were being taken, far from inspiring confidence, only increased distrust; that the number of troops which he had sent was very considerable, and could only be an injury to agriculture and the inhabitants. I then returned to my house in the mountains.

The next day I received, in this house, a visit from the commander at Ennery, and I saw very clearly that this soldier, instead of making me a visit of politeness, had come to my house merely to reconnoitre my dwelling and the avenues about it, that he might seize me the more easily when he received the order to do so. While talking with him, I was informed that several soldiers had gone with horses and other beasts of burden to one of my residences near the town, where a god-daughter of mine was residing, and had taken away the coffee and other provisions found there. I made complaint to him; Le promised me to put a stop to these robberies and to punish severely those who had been guilty of them. Fearing that my house in the mountains inspired only distrust, I determined to remove to that very house which had just been pillaged, and almost totally destroyed, but two hundred paces from the town. I left my wife in the house which I had prepared for her. I was now occupied in laying out new plantations to replace those which had been destroyed, and in preparing necessary materials for reconstructing my buildings. But every day I experienced new robberies and new vexations. The soldiers came to my house in such large numbers that I dared not have them arrested. In vain I bore my complaints to the commander. I received no satisfaction. Finally, I determined, though Gen. Leclerc had not done me the honor to answer my two former letters upon this subject, to write him a third, which I sent to him at the Cape by my son Placide, for greater security. This, like the others, elicited no reply. But the chief of the staff told me that he would make his report. Some time after, the commander, having come to see me again, one afternoon, found me at the head of my laborers, employed in directing the work of reconstruction. He himself saw my son Isaac drive away several soldiers who had just come to the gate to cut down the bananas and figs. I repeated to him the most earnest complaints. He still promised to stop these disorders. During three weeks that I stayed in this place, I witnessed daily new ravages; every day I received visits from people who came as spies, but they were all witnesses that I was engaged solely in domestic labors. Gen. Brunet himself came, and found me occupied in the same manner. Notwithstanding my conduct, I received a letter from Gen. Leclerc, which, in place of giving me satisfaction in regard to the complaints which I had made to him, accused me of keeping armed men within the borders of Ennery, and ordered me to send them away. Persuaded of my innocence, and that evil-disposed people had deceived him, I replied that I had too much honor to break promises which I had made, and that when I gave up the command to him, it was not without reflection; that, moreover, I had no intention of trying to take it back. I assured him, besides, that I had no knowledge of armed men in the environs of Ennery, and that for three weeks I had been constantly at work on my own place. I sent my son Isaac to give him an account of all the vexations I suffered, and to warn him

that if he did not put an end to them, I should be obliged to leave the place where I was living, and go to my ranche in the Spanish part.

One day, before I received any answer from Gen. Leclerc, I was informed that one of his aides-de-camp, passing by Ennery, had told the commander that he was the bearer of an order for my arrest, addressed to Gen. Brunet. Gen. Leclerc having given his word of honor and promised the protection of the French Government, I refused to believe the report; I even said to some one who advised me to leave my residence, that I had promised to stay there quietly, working to repair the have that had been made; that I had not given up the command and sent away my troops to act so foolishly now; that I did not wish to leave home, and if they came to arrest me, they would find me there; that, besides, I would not give credence to the calumny.

The next day I received a second letter from Gen. Leclerc, by my son whom I sent to him, which read thus:—

"ARMY OF ST. DOMINCO,

"HEADQUARTERS AT CAP FRANÇAIS, June 5, 1802.

"THE GEN.-IN-CHIEF TO GEN. TOUSSAINT:—

"Since you persist, Citizen-General, in thinking that the great number of troops stationed at Plaisance (the Secretary probably wrote Plaisance by mistake, meaning Ennery) frightens the laborers of that district, I have commissioned Gen. Brunet to act in concert with you, and to place a part of these troops in the rear of Gonaïves and one detachment at Plaisance. Let the laborers understand, that, having taken this measure, I shall punish those who leave their dwellings to go to the mountains. Let me know, as soon as this order has been executed, the results which it produces, because, if the means of persuasion which you employ do not succeed, I shall use military measures. I salute you."

The same day I received a letter from Gen. Brunet, of which the following is an extract:—

"ARMY OF SAINT DOMINGO,

"HEADQUARTERS AT GEORGES, June 7, 1802.

"Brunet, Gen. of Division, to the Gen. of Division, Toussaint L'Ouverture:

"Now is the time, Citizen-General, to make known unquestionably to the General-in-chief that those who wish to deceive him in regard to your fidelity are base calumniators, and that your sentiments tend to restore order and tranquillity in your neighborhood. You must assist me in securing free communication to the Cape, which has been interrupted since yesterday, three persons having been murdered by fifty brigands between Ennery and Coupe-à-Pintade. Send in pursuit of these murderers men worthy of confidence, whom you are to pay well; I will keep account of your expenses.

"We have arrangements to make together, my dear General, which it is impossible to do by letter, but which an hour's conference would complete. If I were not worn out by labor and petty cares, I should have been the bearer of my own letter today; but not being able to leave at this time, will you not come to me? If you have recovered from your indisposition, let it be tomorrow; when a good work is to be done, there should be no delay. You will not find in my country-house all the comforts which I could desire before receiving you, but you will find the sincerity of an honest man who desires only the prosperity of the colony and your own happiness. If Madame Toussaint, whom I greatly desire to know, wishes to take the journey, it will give me pleasure. If she needs horses, I will send her mine. I repeat, General, you will never find a sincerer friend than myself.

"With confidence in the Captain-General, with friendship for all who are under him, and hoping that you may enjoy peace, I cordially salute you.

(Signed)
"Brunet.

"P. S. Your servant who has gone to Port-au-Prince passed here this morning; he left with his passport made out in due form."

That very servant, instead of receiving his passport, was arrested, and is now in prison with me.

After reading these two letters, although not very well, I yielded to the solicitations of my sons and others, and set out the same night to see Gen. Brunet, accompanied by two officers only. At eight in the evening I arrived at the General's house. When he met me, I told him that I had received his letter, and also that of the General-in-chief, requesting me to act with him, and that I had come for that purpose; that I had not brought my wife, as he requested, because she never left home, being much occupied with domestic duties, but if sometime, when he was travelling, he would do her the honor of visiting her, she would receive him with pleasure. I said to him that, being ill, my stay must be short asking him, therefore, to finish our business as soon as possible, that I might return.

I handed him the letter of Gen. Leclerc. After reading it, he told me that he had not yet received any order to act in concert with me upon the subject of the letter; he then excused himself for a moment, and went out, after calling an officer to keep me company. He had hardly left the room when an aide-de-camp of Gen. Leclerc entered, accompanied by a large number of soldiers, who surrounded me, seized me, bound me as a criminal, and conducted me on board the frigate Créole.

I claimed the protection which Gen. Brunet, on his word of honor, had promised me, but without avail. I saw him no more. He had probably concealed himself to escape my well-merited reproaches. I afterward learned that he treated my family with great cruelty; that, immediately after my arrest, he sent a detachment of troops to the house where I had been living with a part of my family, mostly women, children, and laborers, and ordered them to set it on fire, compelling the unhappy victims to fly half-naked to the woods that everything had been pillaged and sacked; that the aide-de-camp of Gen. Brunet had even taken from my house fifty-five ounces of gold belonging to me, and thirty-three ounces belonging to one of my nieces, together with all the linen of the family.

Having committed these outrages upon my

dwelling, the commander at Ennery went, at the head of one hundred men, to the house occupied by my wife and nieces, and arrested them, without giving them time to collect any of their effects. They were conducted like criminals to Gonaïves and put on board the frigate Guerrière.

When I was arrested, I had no extra clothing with me. I wrote to my wife, asking her to send me such things as I should need most to the Cape, hoping I should be taken there. This note I sent by an aide-de-camp of Gen. Leclerc, begging that it might be allowed to pass; it did not reach its destination, and I received nothing.

As soon as I was taken on board the Créole, we set sail, and, four leagues from the Cape, found the Héros, to which they transferred me. The next day, my wife and my children, who had been arrested with her, arrived there also. We immediately set sail for France. After a voyage of thirty-two days, during which I endured not only great fatigue, but also every species of hardship, while my wife and children received treatment from which their sex and rank should have preserved them, instead of allowing us to land, they retained us on board sixty-seven days.

After such treatment, could I not justly ask where were the promises of Gen. Leclerc? where was the protection of the French Government? If they no longer needed my services and wished to replace me, should they not have treated me as white French generals are always treated? They are warned when they are to be relieved of their command; a messenger is sent to notify them to resign the command to such and such persons; and in case they refuse to obey, measures are taken to compel them; they can then justly be treated as rebels and sent to France.

I have, in fact, known some generals guilty of criminally neglecting their duties, but who, in consideration of their character, have escaped punishment until they could be brought before superior authority.

Should not Gen. Leclerc have informed me that various charges had been brought against me? Should he not have said to me, "I gave you my word of honor and promised you the protection of the Government; to-day, as you have been found guilty, I am going to send you to that government to give an account of your conduct"? Or, "Government orders you to submit; I convey that order to you"? I have not been so treated; on the other hand, means have been employed against me which are only used against the greatest criminals. Doubtless, I owe this treatment to my color; but my color,—my color,—has it hindered me from serving my country with zeal and fradity? Does the color of my skin impair my honor and my bravery?

But even supposing that I was a criminal, and that Government had ordered my arrest, was it necessary to employ a hundred riflemen to arrest my wife and children in their own home, without regard to their sex, age, and rank; without humanity and without charity? Was it necessary to burn my houses, and to pillage and sack my possessions? No. My wife, my children, my family had no responsibility in the matter; they were not accountable to the Government; it was not lawful to arrest them.

Gen. Leclerc's authority was undisputed; did he fear me as a rival? I can but compare him to the Roman Senate, pursuing Hannibal to the very depths of his retreat.

Upon the arrival of the squadron in the colony, they took advantage of my absence to seize a part of my correspondence, which was at Port-Républicain; another portion, which was in one of my houses, has also been seized since my arrest. Why have they not sent me with this correspondence to give an account of my movements? They have taken forcible possession of my papers in order to charge me with crimes which I have never committed; but I have nothing to fear; this correspondence is sufficient to justify me. They have sent me to France destitute of everything; they have seized my property and my papers, and have spread atrocious calumnies concerning me. Is it not like cutting off a man's legs and telling him to walk? Is it not like cutting out a man's tongue and telling him to talk? Is it not burying a man alive?

In regard to the Constitution, the subject of one charge against me: Having driven from the colony the enemies of the Republic, calmed the factions and united all parties; perceiving, after I had taken possession of St. Domingo, that the Government made no laws for the colony, and feeling the necessity of police regulations for the security and tranquillity of the people, I called an assembly of wise and learned men, composed of deputies from all the communities, to conduct this business. When this assembly met, I represented to its members that they had an arduous and responsible task before them; that they were to make laws adapted to the country, advantageous to the Government, and beneficial to all,—laws suited to the localities, to the character and customs of the inhabitants. The Constitution must be submitted for the sanction of the Government, which alone had the right to adopt or reject it. Therefore, as soon as the Constitution was decided upon and its laws fixed, I sent the whole, by a member of the assembly, to the Government, to obtain its sanction. The errors or faults which this Constitution may contain cannot therefore be imputed to me. At the time of Leclerc's arrival, I had heard nothing from the Government upon this subject. Why to-day do they seek to make a crime of that which is no crime? Why put truth for falsehood, and falsehood for truth? Why put darkness for light and light for darkness?

In a conversation which I had at the Cape with Gen. Leclerc, he told me that while at Samana he had sent a spy to Santo Domingo to learn if I was there, who brought back word that I was. Why did he not go there to find me and give me the orders of the First Consul, before commencing hostilities? He knew my readiness to obey orders. Instead of this, he took advantage of my absence at St. Domingo to proceed to the Cape and send troops to all parts of the colony. This conduct proves that he had no intention of communicating anything to me.

If Gen. Leclerc went to the colony to do evil, it should not be charged upon me. It is true that only one of us can be blamed; but however little one may wish to do me justice, it is clear that he is the author of all the evils which the island has suffered, since, without warning me, he entered the colony, which he found in a state of prosperity, fell upon the inhabitants, who were at their work, contributing to the welfare of the community, and shed their blood upon their native soil. That is the true source of the evil.

If two children were quarrelling together, should not their father or mother see them, find out which was the aggressor, and punish him, or punish them, if they were both wrong? Gen. Leclerc had no right to arrest me; Government alone could arrest us both, hear us, and judge us. Yet Gen. Leclerc enjoys liberty, and I am in a dungeon.

Having given an account of my conduct since the arrival of the fleet at St. Domingo, I will enter into some details of previous events.

Since I entered the service of the Republic, I have not claimed a penny of my salary; Gen. Laveaux, Government agents, all responsible persons connected with the public treasury, can do me this justice, that no one has been more prudent, more disinterested than I. I have only now and then received the extra pay allowed me; very often I have not asked even this. Whenever I have taken money from the treasury, it has been for some public use; the governor (*l'ordonnateur*) has used it as the service required. I remember that once only, when far from home, I borrowed six thousand francs from Citizen Smith, who was governor of the Department of the South.

I will sum up, in a few words, my conduct and the results of my administration. At the time of the evacuation of the English, there was not a penny in the public treasury; money had to be borrowed to pay the troops and the officers of the Republic. When Gen. Leclerc arrived, he found three millions, five hundred thousand francs in the public funds. When I returned to Cayes, after the departure of Gen. Rigaud, the treasury was empty; Gen. Leclerc found three millions there; he found proportionate sums in all the private depositories on the island. Thus it is seen that I did not serve my country from interested motives; but, on the contrary, I served it with honor, fidelity, and integrity, sustained by the hope of receiving, at some future day, flattering acknowledgments from the Government; all who know me will do me this justice.

I have been a slave; I am willing to own it; but I have never received reproaches from my masters.

I have neglected nothing at Saint Domingo for the welfare of the island; I have robbed myself of rest to contribute to it; I have sacrificed everything for it. I have made it my duty and pleasure to develop the resources of this beautiful colony. Zeal, activity, courage,—I have employed them all.

The island was invaded by the enemies of the Republic; I had then but a thousand men, armed with pikes. I sent them back to labor in the field, and organized several regiments, by the authority of Gen. Laveaux.

The Spanish portion had joined the English to make war upon the French. Gen. Desfourneaux was sent to attack Saint-Michel with well-disciplined troops of the line; he could not take it. General Laveaux ordered me to the attack; I carried it. It is to be remarked that, at the time of the attack by Gen. Desfourneaux, the place was not fortified, and that when I took it, it was fortified by bastions in every corner. I also, took Saint-Raphaël and Hinche, and rendered an account to Gen. Laveaux. The English were intrenched at Pont-de-l'Ester; I drove them from the place. They were in possession of Petite Rivière. My ammunition consisted of one case of cartridges which had fallen into the water on my way to the attack; this did not discourage me. I carried the place by assault before day, with my dragoons, and made all the garrison prisoners. I sent them to Gen. Laveaux. I had but one piece of cannon; I took nine at Petite Rivière. Among the posts gained at Petite Rivière, was a fortification defended by seven pieces of cannon, which I attacked, and carried by assault. I also conquered the Spaniards intrenched in the camps of Miraut and Dubourg at Verrettes. I

gained a famous victory over the English in a battle which lasted from six in the morning until nearly night. This battle was so fierce that the roads were filled with the dead, and rivers of blood were seen on every side. I took all the baggage and ammunition of the enemy, and a large number of prisoners. I sent the whole to Gen. Laveaux, giving him an account of the engagement. All the posts of the English upon the heights of Saint Marc were taken in me; the walled fortifications in the mountains of Fond-Baptisto and Délices, the camp of Drouët in the Mathoux mountains, which the English regarded as impregnable, the citadels of Mirebalais, called the Gibraltar of the island, occupied by eleven hundred men, the celebrated camp of l'Acul-du-Saut, the stone fortifications of Trou-d'Eau, three stories high, those of the camp of Décayette and of Beau-Bien,—in short, all the fortifications of the English in this quarter were unable to withstand me, as were those of Neybe, of Saint Jean de la Maguâna, of Las Mathas, of Banique and other places occupied by the Spaniards; all were brought by me under the power of the Republic. I was also exposed to the greatest dangers; several times I narrowly escaped being made prisoner; I shed my blood for my country; I received a ball in the right hip which remains there still; I received a violent blow on the head from a cannon-ball, which knocked out the greater part of my teeth, and loosened the rest. In short, I received upon different occasions seventeen wounds, whose honorable scars still remain. Gen. Laveaux witnessed many of my engagements; he is too honorable not to do me justice: ask him if I ever hesitated to endanger my life, when the good of my country and the triumph of the Republic required it.

If I were to record the various services which I have rendered the Government, I should need many volumes, and even then should not finish them; and, as a reward for all these services, I have been arbitrarily arrested at St. Domingo, bound, and put on board ship like a criminal, without regard for my rank, without the least consideration. Is this the recompense due my labors? Should my conduct lead me to expect such treatment?

I was once rich. At the time of the revolution, I was worth six hundred and forty-eight thousand francs. I spent it in the service of my country. I purchased but one small estate upon which to establish my wife and family. To-day, notwithstanding my disinterestedness, they seek to cover me with opprobrium and infamy; I am made the most unhappy of men; my liberty is taken from me; I am separated from all that I hold dearest in the world,—from a venerable father, a hundred and five years old, who needs my assistance, from a dearly-loved wife, who, I fear, separated from me, cannot endure the afflictions which overwhelm her, and from a cherished family, who made the happiness of my life.

On my arrival in France I wrote to the First Consul and to the Minister of Marine, giving them an account of my situation, and asking their assistance for my family and myself. Undoubtedly, they felt the justice of my request, and gave orders that what I asked should be furnished me. But, instead of this, I have received the old half-worn dress of a soldier, and shoes in the same condition. Did I need this humiliation added to my misfortune?

When I left the ship, I was put into a carriage. I hoped then that I was to be taken before a tribunal to give an account of my conduct, and to be judged. Far from it; without a moment's rest I was taken to a fort on the frontiers of the Republic, and confined in a frightful dungeon.

It is from the depths of this dreary prison that I appeal to the justice and magnanimity of the First Consul. He is too noble and too good a general to turn away from an old soldier, covered with wounds in the service of his country, without giving him the opportunity to justify himself, and to have judgment pronounced upon him.

I ask, then, to be brought before a tribunal or council of war, before which, also, Gen. Leclerc may appear, and that we may both be judged after we have both been heard; equity, reason,

law, all assure me that this justice cannot be refused me.

In passing through France, I have seen in the newspapers an article concerning myself. I am accused in this article of being a rebel and a traitor, and, to justify the accusation, a letter is said to have been intercepted in which I encouraged the laborers of St. Domingo to revolt. I never wrote such a letter, and I defy any one to produce it, to tell me to whom it was addressed, and to bring forward the person. As to the rest of the calumny, it falls of itself; if I had intended to make war, would I have laid down my arms and submitted? No reasonable man, much less a soldier, can believe such an absurdity.

ADDITION TO THE MEMOIRS.

If the Government had sent a wiser man, there would have been no trouble; not a single shot would have been fired.

Why did fear occasion so much injustice on the part of Gen. Leclerc? Why did he violate his word of honor? Upon the arrival of the frigate Guerrière, which brought my wife, why did I see on board a number of people who had been arrested with her? Many of these persons had not fired a shot. They were innocent men, fathers of families, who had been torn from the arms of their wives and children. All these persons had shed their blood to preserve the colony to France; they were officers of my staff, my secretaries, who had done nothing but by my orders; all, therefore, were arrested without cause.

Upon landing at Brest, my wife and children were sent to different destinations, of both of which I am ignorant. Government should do me more justice: my wife and children have done nothing and have nothing to answer for; they should be sent home to watch over our interests. Gen. Leclerc has occasioned all this evil; but I am at the bottom of a dungeon, unable to justify myself. Government is too just to keep my hands tied, and allow Gen. Leclerc to abuse me thus, without listening to me.

Everybody has told me that this Government was just; should I not, then, share its justice and its benefits?

Gen. Leclerc has said in the letter to the minister, which I have seen in the newspaper, that I was waiting for his troops to grow sick, in order to make war and take back the command. This is an atrocious and abominable lie: it is a cowardly act on his part. Although I may not have much knowledge or much education, I have enough good sense to hinder me from contending against the will of my Government; I never thought of it. The French Government is too strong, too powerful, for Gen. Leclerc to think me opposed to it, who am its servant. It it is true, that when Gen. Leclerc marched against me, I said several times that I should make no attack, that I should only defend myself, until July or August; that then I would commence in my turn. But, afterward, I reflected upon the misfortunes of the colony and upon the letter of the First Consul; I then submitted.

I repeat it again: I demand that Gen. Leclerc and myself be judged before a tribunal; that Government should order all my correspondence to be brought; by this means my innocence, and all that I have done for the Republic will be seen, although I know that several letters have been intercepted.

First Consul, father of all soldiers, upright judge, defender of innocence, pronounce my destiny. My wounds are deep; apply to them the healing remedy which will prevent them from opening anew; you are the physician; I rely entirely upon your justice and wisdom!

Suggested Readings

James, C. L. R. *The Black Jacobins; Toussaint L'Ouverture and the San Domingo Revolution.* New York: The Dial Press, 1938.

Moran, Charles B. *Black Triumvirate; A Study of L'Ouverture, Dessalines, Christophe.* New York: Exposition Press, 1957.

Tyson, George F. *Toussaint L'Ouverture.* Englewood Cliffs: Prentice-Hall, 1973.

20

Justice and Responsibility: Herman Melville's Billy Budd

Dr. George Lucas

Nothing seems of greater importance to individuals in society at large, or within a specific organization, than the assurance that opportunities for admission or employment, promotion or advancement in rank, and for rewards (as well as punishments) associated with their individual performance be undertaken—*fairly and impartially*. To seem to do otherwise—that is, to show unjustifiable preference for, or prejudice against, certain individuals on the basis of characteristics or criteria that are wholly irrelevant to the benefit or burden that is being distributed–constitutes *injustice*. To differentiate in a wholly arbitrary fashion between the degree of punishment administered, for example, to two different individuals for what is essentially the same offense will quickly cause anger, resentment, low morale, and general organizational disaffection, perhaps even rebellion, among the members of the group in which this injustice occurs. In particular, wise leaders know that they must uphold the law and administer its sanctions (including punishment) swiftly, impartially, and without regard to personal circumstance, lest their uncertainty or ambiguity be taken as a sign of weakness, ineffectiveness, or even corruption in the administration of the law itself.

Justice, Aristotle observed, is largely a matter of treating equals with equality and giving to each what he or she is due. What is often called *retributive justice* pertains specifically to the problem of infractions of rules or laws and to the nature and degree of the punishment meted out for each such infraction. On Aristotle's principle, we would demand *equality* and an appropriate degree of *proportionality* in the administration of the law, and, in particular, in *assigning punishment* to those who disobey it. Military officers, in particular, as a central feature of their responsibilities for command are charged with this special responsibility for the fair, consistent, and impartial administration of a reasonable code of professional conduct and for enforcing that code through swift, strict, impartial, and appropriate forms of punishment.

The difficulties involved in attempting to live up to this particular responsibility are dramatically portrayed in a distinctly military setting in Herman Melville's famous novel, *Billy Budd*. The story is set in 1797 aboard the British Man o'War *Bellipotent* shortly after the occurrence of two violent shipboard mutinies elsewhere in the British navy. The ship's commander, Captain Vere, and his entire staff of senior and junior naval officers, are thus keenly aware of the sensitivities of the crew concerning conduct and punishment, especially since many of the crew have been "pressed" unwillingly into a tour of sea duty in the first place. The *Bellipotent's* officers view it as their overarching responsibility to maintain good order, discipline, and a decent level of morale through their efficient and impartial enforcement of that code, hoping thereby to stave off any tendencies of the crew toward disaffection and mutiny.

The novel's dilemma arises, however, when a gentle and trusting sailor, much beloved by the ship's crew, stands accused of a capital crime. Billy Budd is a simple lad, uneducated, and possessed of a slight speech impediment. He is harassed mercilessly by a vicious senior noncommissioned officer, John Claggart, who resents Billy's popularity with his men. Claggart brings Billy Budd before Captain Vere and falsely accuses the young seaman of fomenting mutiny among the crew. Astonished, outraged, unable to speak or defend himself otherwise against these malicious charges, Billy instinctively lashes out at Claggart. The blow knocks the senior officer to the deck where he strikes his head against a bulkhead and is instantly killed.

Billy is promptly arrested, thrown in the brig, and a court martial is convened. The ship's officers are aware of Claggart's treachery and are sympathetic to Billy's plight. Although the official punishment for striking an officer (let alone for killing him) is death by hanging, they are inclined to recommend a more lenient punishment in this case, since Claggart's own cruel and unjust antagonism was the cause of the conflict. Captain Vere, however, surprises his officers by arguing against Billy and in favor of enforcing the stern letter of the law. His argument about law, justice, punishment, and moral consistency have intrigued and provoked generations of readers ever since Melville first published this brief but brilliant sketch, which many critics hold to be his finest writing.

Melville's novel was itself inspired by, and partially based upon, an actual occurrence in the American (rather than the British) navy. In the historical case in the early 1840s, a young midshipmen (whose character was considerably less admirable and pure than Billy Budd's) was accused by his ship's captain of fomenting mutiny at sea. The captain convened a court martial, convicted the midshipmen, and had him immediately executed at high sea. The accused in this instance happened to be the son of the sitting Secretary of War, who was not altogether pleased with the charges, let alone with the swift and perfunctory nature of the legal proceedings at sea. Public debate over the ensuing investigation, and the scandal it caused, led directly to the founding of the United States Naval Academy in 1845, in large part to provide a suitable setting for the education and moral development of young officers for the new Republic's navy.

Who in the rainbow can draw the line where the violet tint ends and the orange tint begins? Distinctly we see the difference of the colors, but where exactly does the one first blendingly enter into the other? So with sanity and insanity. In pronounced cases there is no question about them. But in some supposed cases, in various degrees supposedly less pronounced, to draw the exact line of demarcation few will undertake, though for a fee becoming considerate some professional experts will. There is nothing namable but that some men will, or undertake to, do it for pay.

Whether Captain Vere, as the surgeon professionally and privately surmised, was really the sudden victim of any degree of aberration, everyone must determine for himself by such light as this narrative may afford.

That the unhappy event which has been narrated could not have happened at a worse juncture was but too true. For it was close on the heel of the suppressed insurrections, an aftertime very critical to naval authority, demanding from every English sea commander two qualities not readily interfusable—prudence and rigor. Moreover, there was something crucial in the case.

In the jugglery of circumstances preceding and attending the event on board the *Bellipotent*, and in the light of that martial code whereby it was formally to be judged, innocence and guilt personified in Claggart and Budd in effect changed places. In a legal view the apparent victim of the tragedy was he who had sought to victimize a man blameless; and the indisputable deed of the latter, navally regarded, constituted the most heinous of military crimes. Yet more. The essential right and wrong involved in the matter, the clearer that might be, so much the worse for the responsibility of a loyal sea commander, inasmuch as he was not authorized to determine the matter on that primitive basis.

Small wonder then that the *Bellipotent's* captain, though in general a man of rapid decision, felt that circumspectness not less than promptitude was necessary. Until he could decide upon his course, and in each detail; and not only so, but until the concluding measure was upon the point of being enacted, he deemed it advisable, in view of all the circumstances, to guard as much as possible against publicity. Here he mayor may not have erred. Certain it is, however, that subsequently in the confidential talk of more than one or two gun rooms and cabins he was not a little criticized by some officers, a fact imputed by his friends and vehemently by his cousin Jack Denton to professional jealousy of Starry Vere. Some imaginative ground for invidious comment there was. The maintenance of secrecy in the matter, the confining all knowledge of it for a time to the place where the homicide occurred, the quarterdeck cabin; in these particulars lurked some resemblance to the policy adopted in those tragedies of the palace which have occurred more than once in the capital founded by Peter the Barbarian.

The case indeed was such that fain would the *Bellipotent's* captain have deferred taking any action whatever respecting it further than to keep the foretopman a close prisoner till the ship rejoined the squadron and then submitting the matter to the judgment of his admiral.

But a true military officer is in one particular like a true monk. Not with more of self-abnegation will the latter keep his vows of monastic obedience than the former his vows of allegiance to martial duty.

Feeling that unless quick action was taken on it, the deed of the foretopman, so soon as it should be known on the gun decks, would tend to awaken any slumbering embers of the *Nore* among the crew, a sense of the urgency of the case overruled in Captain Vere every other consideration. But though a conscientious disciplinarian, he was no lover of authority for mere authority's sake. Very far was he from embracing opportunities for monopolizing to himself the perils of moral responsibility, none at least that could properly be referred to an official superior or shared with him by his official equals or even subordinates. So thinking, he was glad it would not be at variance with usage to turn the matter over to a summary court of his own officers, reserving to himself, as the one on whom the ultimate accountability would rest, the right of maintaining a supervision of it, or formally or informally interposing at need. Accordingly a drumhead court was summarily convened, he electing the individuals composing it: the first lieutenant, the captain of marines and the sailing master.

In associating an officer of marines with the sea lieutenant and the sailing master in a case having to do with a sailor, the commander perhaps deviated from general custom. He was prompted thereto by the circumstance that he took that soldier to be a judicious person, thoughtful, and not altogether incapable of grappling with a difficult case unprecedented in his prior experience. Yet even as to him he was not without some latent misgiving, for withal he was an extremely good-natured man, an enjoyer of his dinner, a sound sleeper, and inclined to obesity-a man who though he would always maintain his manhood in battle might not prove altogether reliable in a moral dilemma involving aught of the tragic. As to the first lieutenant and the sailing master, Captain Vere could not but be aware that though honest natures, of approved gallantry upon occasion, their intelligence was mostly confined to the matter of active seamanship and the fighting demands of their profession.

The court was held in the same cabin where the unfortunate affair had taken place. This cabin, the commander's, embraced the entire area under the poop deck. Aft, and on either side, was a small stateroom, the one now temporarily a jail and the other a dead-house, and a yet smaller compartment, leaving a space between expanding forward into a goodly oblong of length coinciding with the ship's beam. A skylight of moderate dimension was overhead, and at each cut of the oblong space were two sashed porthole windows easily convertible back into embrasures for short carronades.

All being quickly in readiness, Billy Budd was arraigned, Captain Vere necessarily appearing as the sole witness in the case, and as such temporarily sinking his rank, though singularly maintaining it in a matter apparently trivial, namely that he testified from the ship's weather side, with that object having caused the court to sit on the lee side. Concisely he narrated all that had led up to the catastrophe, omitting nothing in Claggart's accusation and deposing as to the manner in which the prisoner had received it. At this testimony the three officers glanced with no little surprise at Billy Budd, the last man they would have suspected either of the mutinous design alleged by Claggart or the undeniable deed he himself had done. The first lieutenant, taking judicial primacy and turning toward the pris-

oner, said, "Captain Vere has spoken. Is it or is it not as Captain Vere says?"

In response came syllables not so much impeded in the utterance as might have been anticipated. They were these: "Captain Vere tells the truth. It is just as Captain Vere says, but it is not as the master at-arms said. I have eaten the King's bread and I am true to the King."

"I believe you, my man," said the witness, his voice indicating a suppressed emotion not other wise betrayed.

"God will bless you for that, your honor!" not without stammering said Billy, and all but broke down. But immediately he was recalled to self-control by another question, to which with the same emotional difficulty of utterance he said, "No, there was no malice between us. I never bore malice against the master-at-arms. I am sorry that he is dead. I did not mean to kill him. Could I have used my tongue I would not have struck him. But he foully lied to my face and in presence of my captain, and I had to say something, and I could only say it with a blow, God help me!"

In the impulsive aboveboard manner of the frank one the court saw confirmed all that was implied in words that just previously had perplexed them, coming as they did from the testifier to the tragedy and promptly following Billy's impassioned disclaimer of mutinous intent-Captain Vere's words, "I believe you, my man."

Next it was asked of him whether he knew of or suspected aught savoring of incipient trouble (meaning mutiny, though the explicit term was avoided) going on in any section of the ship's company.

The reply lingered. This was naturally imputed by the court to the same vocal embarrassment which had retarded or obstructed previous answers. But in main it was otherwise here, the question immediately recalling to Billy's mind the interview with the afterguardsman in the forechains. But an innate repugnance to playing a part at all approaching that of an informer against one's own shipmates-the same erring sense of uninstructed honor which had stood in the way of his reporting the matter at the time, though as a loyal man-of-war's man it was incumbent on him, and failure so to do, if charged against him and proven, would have subjected him to the heaviest of penalties; this, with the blind feeling now his that nothing really was being hatched, prevailed with him. When the answer came it was a negative.

"One question more," said the officer of marines, now first speaking and with a troubled earnestness. "You tell us that what the master-at-arms said against you was a lie. Now why should he have so lied, so maliciously lied, since you declare there was no malice between you?"

At that question, unintentionally touching on a spiritual sphere wholly obscure to Billy's thoughts, he was nonplused, evincing a confusion indeed that some observers, such as can readily be imagined, would have construed into involuntary evidence of hidden guilt. Nevertheless, he strove some way to answer, but all at once relinquished the vain endeavor, at the same time turning an appealing glance toward Captain Vere as deeming him his best helper and friend. Captain Vere, who had been seated for a time, rose to his feet, addressing the interrogator. "The question you put to him comes naturally enough. But how can he rightly answer it?-or anybody else, unless indeed it be he who lies within there," designating the compartment where lay the corpse. "But the prone one there will not rise to our summons. In effect though, as it seems to me, the point you make is hardly material. Quite aside from any conceivable motive actuating the master-at-arms, and irrespective of the provocation to the blow, a martial court must needs in the present case confine its attention to the blow's consequence, which consequence justly is to be deemed not otherwise than as the striker's deed."

This utterance, the full significance of which it was not at all likely that Billy took in, nevertheless caused him to turn a wistful interrogative look toward the speaker, a look in its dumb expressiveness not unlike that which a dog of generous breed might turn upon his master, seeking in his face some elucidation of a previous gesture ambiguous to the canine intelligence. Nor was the same utterance without marked effect upon the three officers, more especially the soldier. Couched in it seemed to them a meaning unanticipated, involving a prejudgment on the speaker's part. It served to augment a mental disturbance previously evident enough.

The soldier once more spoke, in a tone of suggestive dubiety addressing at once his associates and Captain Vere: "Nobody is present-none of the ship's company, I mean-who might shed lateral light, if any is to be had, upon what remains mysterious in this matter."

"That is thoughtfully put," said Captain Vere; "1 see your drift. Ay, there is a mystery; but, to use a scriptural phrase, it is a 'mystery of iniquity,' a matter for psychologic theologians to discuss. But what has a military court to do with it? Not to add that for us any possible investigation of it is cut off by the lasting tongue-tie of him-in-yonder," again designating the mortuary stateroom. "The prisoner's deed-with that alone we have to do."

To this, and particularly the closing reiteration, the marine soldier, knowing not how aptly to reply, sadly abstained from saying aught. The first lieutenant, who at the outset had not unnaturally assumed primacy in the court, now overrulingly instructed by a glance from Captain Vere, a glance more effective than words, resumed that primacy. Turning to the prisoner "Budd," he said, and scarce in equable tones, "Budd, if you have aught further to say for yourself, say it now."

Upon this the young sailor turned another quick glance toward Captain Vere; then, as taking a hint from that aspect, a hint confirming his own instinct that silence was now best, replied to the lieutenant, "I have said all, sir."

The marine-the same who had been the sentinel without the cabin door at the time that the foretopman, followed by the master-at-arms, entered it-he, standing by the sailor throughout these judicial proceedings, was now directed to take him back to the after compartment originally assigned to the prisoner and his custodian. As the twain disappeared from view, the three officers, as partially liberated from some inward constraint associated with Billy's mere presence, simultaneously stirred in their seats. They exchanged looks of troubled indecision, yet feeling that decide they must and without long delay. For Captain Vere, he for the time stood-unconsciously with his back toward them, apparently in one of his absent fits-gazing out from a sashed porthole to windward upon the monotonous blank of the twilight sea. But the court's silence continuing broken only at moments by brief consultations, in low earnest tones this served to arouse him and energize him. Turning, he to-and-fro paced the cabin athwart; in the returning ascent to windward climbing the slant deck in the ship's lee roll, without knowing it symbolizing thus in his action a mind resolute to surmount difficulties even if against primitive instincts strong as the wind and the sea. Presently he came to a stand before the three. After scanning their faces he stood less as mustering his thoughts for expression than as one only deliberating how best to put them to well-meaning men not intellectually mature, men with whom it was necessary to demonstrate certain principles that were axioms to himself. Similar impatience as to talking is perhaps one reason that deters some minds from addressing any popular assemblies.

When speak he did, something, both in the substance of what he said and his manner of saying it, showed the influence of unshared studies modifying and tempering the practical training of an active career. This, along with his phraseology, now and then was suggestive of the grounds whereon rested that imputation of a certain pedantry socially alleged against him by certain naval men of wholly practical cast, captains who nevertheless would frankly concede that His Majesty's navy mustered no more efficient officer of their grade than Starry Vere.

What he said was to this effect: "Hitherto I have been but the witness, little more; and I should hardly think now to take another tone, that of your coadjutor for the time, did I not perceive in you at the crisis too-a troubled hesitancy, proceeding, I doubt not, from the clash of military duty with moral scruple—scruple vitalized by compassion. For the compassion, how can I otherwise than share it? But, mindful of paramount obligations, I strive against scruples that may tend to enervate decision. Not, gentlemen, that I hide from myself that the case is an exceptional one. Speculatively regarded, it well might be referred to a jury of casuists. But for us here, acting not as casuists or moralists, it is a case practical, and under martial law practically to be dealt with.

"But your scruples: do they move as in a dusk? Challenge them. Make them advance and declare themselves. Come now; do they import something like this: If, mindless of palliating circumstances, we are bound to regard the death of the master-at-arms as the prisoner's deed, shell does that deed constitute a capital crime whereof the penalty is a mortal one. But in natural justice is nothing but the prisoner's overt act to be considered? How can we adjudge to summary and shameful death a fellow creature innocent before God, and whom we feel to be so?-Does that state it aright? You sign sad assent. Well, I too feel that, the full force of that. It is Nature. But do these buttons that we wear attest that our allegiance is to Nature? No, to the King. Though the ocean, which is inviolate Nature primeval, though this be the element where we move and have our being as sailors, yet as the King's officers lies our duty in a sphere correspondingly natural? So little is that true, that in receiving our commissions we in the most important regards ceased to be natural free agents. When war is declared are we the commissioned fighters previously consulted? We fight at command. If our judgments approve the war, that is but coincidence. So in other particulars. So now. For suppose condemnation to follow these present proceedings. Would it be so much we ourselves that would condemn as it would be martial law operating through us? For that law and the rigor of it, we are not responsible. Our vowed responsibility is in this: That however pitilessly that law may operate in any instances, we nevertheless adhere to it and administer it.

"But the exceptional in the matter moves the hearts within you. Even so too is mine moved. But let not warm hearts betray heads that should be cool. Ashore in a criminal case, will an upright judge allow himself off the bench to be waylaid by some tender kinswoman of the accused seeking to touch him with her tearful plea? Well, the heart here, sometimes the feminine in man, is as that piteous woman, and hard though it be, she must here be ruled out."

He paused, earnestly studying them for a moment; then resumed.

"But something in your aspect seems to urge that it is not solely the heart that moves in you, but also the conscience, the private conscience. But tell me whether or not, occupying the position we do, private conscience should not yield to that imperial one formulated in the mode under which alone we officially proceed?"

Here the three men moved in their seats, less convinced than agitated by the course of an argument troubling but the more the spontaneous conflict within.

Perceiving which, the speaker paused for a moment; then abruptly changing his tone, went on.

"To steady us a bit let us recur to the facts.-In wartime at sea a man-of-war's man strikes his superior in grade, and the blow kills. Apart from its effect the blow itself is, according to the Articles of War, a capital crime, Furthermore-"

"Ay, sir," emotionally broke in the officer of marines, "in one sense it was. But surely Budd purposed neither mutiny nor homicide."

"Surely not, my good man. And before a court less arbitrary and more merciful than a martial one, that plea would largely extenuate. At the Last Assizes it shall acquit. But how here? We proceed under the law of the Mutiny Act. In feature no child can resemble his father more than that Act resembles in spirit the thing from which it derives-War. In His Majesty's service-in this ship, indeed-there are Englishmen forced to fight for the King against their will. Against their conscience, for aught we know. Though as their fellow creatures some of us may appreciate their position, yet as navy officers what reck we of it? Still less recks the enemy. Our impressed men he would fain cut down in the same swath with our volunteers. As regards the enemy's naval conscripts, some of whom may even share our own abhorrence of the regicidal French Directory, it is the same on our side. War looks but to the frontage, the appearance. And the Mutiny Act War's child, takes after the father. Budd's intent or non-intent is nothing to the purpose.

"But while, put to it by those anxieties in you which I cannot but respect, I only repeat myself while thus strangely we prolong proceedings that should be summary-the enemy may be sighted and an engagement result. We must do; and one of two things must we do—condemn or let go."

"Can we not convict and yet mitigate the penalty?" asked the sailing master, here speaking, and falteringly, for the first.

"Gentlemen, were that clearly lawful for us under the circumstances, consider the consequences of such clemency. The people" (meaning the ship's company) "have native sense; most of them are familiar with our naval usage and tradition; and how would they take it? Even could you explain to them-which our official position forbids-they, long molded by arbitrary discipline, have not that kind of intelligent responsiveness that might qualify them to comprehend and discriminate. No, to the people the foretopman's deed, however it be worded in the announcement will be plain homicide committed in a flagrant act of mutiny. What penalty for that should follow, they know. But it does not follow. *Why?* they will ruminate. You know what sailors are. Will they not revert to the recent outbreak at the *Nore?* Ay. They know the wellfounded alarm-the panic it struck throughout England. Your clement sentence they would account pusillanimous. They would think that we flinch, that we are afraid of them-afraid of practicing a lawful rigor singularly demanded at this juncture, lest it should provoke new troubles. What shame to us such a conjecture on their part, and how deadly to discipline. You see then, whither, prompted by duty and the law, I steadfastly drive. But I beseech you, my friends, do not take me amiss. I feel as you do for this unfortunate boy. But did he know our hearts, I take him to be of that generous nature that he would feel even for us on whom this military necessity so heavy a compulsion is laid."

With that, crossing the deck he resumed his place by the sashed porthole, tacitly leaving the three to come to a decision. On the cabin's opposite side the troubled court sat silent. Loyal lieges, plain and practical, though at bottom they dissented from some points Captain Vere had put to them, they were without the faculty, hardly had the inclination, to gainsay one whom they felt to be an earnest man, one too not less their superior in mind than in naval rank. But it is not improbable that even such of his words as were not without influence over them, less came home to them than his closing appeal to their instinct as sea officers: in the forethought he threw out as to the practical consequences to discipline, considering the unconfirmed tone of the fleet at the time, should a mall-of-war's mall's violent killing at sea of a superior in grade be allowed to pass for aught else than a capital crime demanding prompt infliction of the penalty.

Not unlikely they were brought to something more or less akin to that harassed frame of mind which in the year 1842 actuated the commander of the U.S. brig-of-war *Somers* to resolve, under the so-called Articles of War, Articles modeled upon the English Mutiny Act, to resolve upon the execution at sea of a midshipman and two sailors as mutineers designing the seizure of the brig. Which resolution was carried out though in a time of peace and within not many days' sail of home. An act vindicated by a naval court of inquiry subsequently convened ashore. History, and here cited without comment. True, the circumstances on board the *Somers* were different from those on board the *Bellipotent*. But the urgency felt, well-warranted or otherwise, was much the same.

Says a writer whom few know, "Forty years after a battle it is easy for a noncombatant to reason about how it ought to

have been fought. It is another thing personally and under fire to have to direct the fighting while involved in the obscuring smoke of it. Much so with respect to other

emergencies involving considerations both practical and moral, and when it is imperative promptly to act. The greater the fog the more it imperils the steamer, and speed is put on

though at the hazard of running somebody down. Little ween the snug card players in the

cabin of the responsibilities of the sleepless man on the bridge."

In brief, Billy Budd was formally convicted and sentenced to be hung at the yardarm in the early morning watch, it being now night. Otherwise, as is customary in such cases, the sentence would have been carried out. In wartime on the field or in the fleet, a mortal punishment decreed by a drumhead court–on the field sometimes decreed by but a nod from the general–follows without delay on the heel of conviction, without appeal.

About the Author

George Lucas is Professor of Philosophy and Associate Chair in the Department of Leadership, Ethics & Law at the U.S. Naval Academy (Annapolis). With Captain Rick Rubel, USN (retired) he is the co-editor of the two-volume series, *Ethics and the Military Profession*, and *Case Studies in Military Ethics* (Pearson/Longman, 2005), used at the Naval and Air Force Academies, as well as in Naval ROTC programs throughout the country.

21

Small Unit and Self-Leadership: C. S. Forester's Rifleman Dodd

Dr. Joseph J. Thomas

If there is a single work of fiction most often recommended and discussed by Marines, it would probably be C.S. Forester's *Rifleman Dodd*. Past Commandants of the Marine Corps Generals Krulak and Mundy thought the book so important they made it mandatory reading for Marines of all ranks. Most Marines who served in the 1990s read and discussed this simple book and marveled at how it captured the virtues of faithfulness to the mission and perseverance in the face of great adversity—essential ingredients for success in Marines and Sailors. The story is also one of human loss and carrying on in spite of tragedy. Both the protagonist and antagonist lose virtually every friend and companion along the way in this brutal guerilla campaign. Both unflinchingly soldier on.

Rifleman Dodd was not always the classic it is now considered to be. In fact, it had been an obscure little book that was long considered a quick read for teenage boys seeking adventure and tales of unwavering character. Upon further scrutiny, however, Forester's work provides a window into the essential elements of honor, courage, and commitment. While *Rifleman Dodd* has always been considered a lesson in the personal qualities of resourcefulness and self-reliance, it has only recently been considered a book packed with leadership lessons. "Self-Leadership" is the initial lesson in the first leadership textbook provided to midshipmen during plebe year at the Naval Academy. It is a concept embedded in psychological theories such as social cognitive theory, intrinsic motivation theory, and cognitive evaluation theory. More importantly, it is self-evident that great leaders must first master the intellect, character, and physical ability that they will demand of subordinates. *Rifleman Dodd* is a primer for those seeking to lead by example.

Rifleman Matthew Dodd of the British Ninety-Fifth Foot, separated from his regiment behind enemy lines as Napoleon's army drives down the Iberian Peninsula, offers a tactical view of early 19th Century insurgency. What we know today of the Peninsular War (1808–1814) is generally limited to Lord Wellington's recovery of Portugal from French domination and his eventual liberation of Spain. The tale of Dodd's attempt to rejoin his unit, all the while exacting as much punishment on the enemy as possible, is a timeless essay on soldiering. Dodd's collaboration with Portuguese villagers evolved into his leadership of the partisans. He inflicted great damage on the French with a rag-tag group of untrained insurgents in spite of a language barrier and cultural differences. The following excerpt from Chapter 13 of *Rifleman Dodd* typifies the small unit and self-leadership lessons contained in the book. Dodd finds himself in a hostile, barren land with women, children and livestock for their sustenance in tow. He faces a unit drawn from the most battle tested army in Europe. He knows and cares little for the political machinations that brought him and his newfound companions to this fight. Dodd simply recognizes his mission to fight the enemy by any means possible.

* * *

Life among the outcasts in the rocky mountain by the river settled down extraordinarily quickly into routine. The Portuguese peasants had been accustomed all their lives to unremitting hard work, and gladly took up what labour there was to be done—it irked them to be idle. So that it was quite willingly that they did sentry-go along the brow of the hill, and slaved to enlarge the cave by the river so that ther might be shelter in it for all. It was the women's task to look after the cattle on the hill and move them from point to point so they might find herbage, but enough to keep them just alive. The constant fear of attack by the French kept every one from quarrelling.

It was all very matter-of-fact and obvious. When shots from the brow of the hill told that an attack was developing there, every one knew what he had to do. The little flock of sheep was driven down to the river's brink and carried one by one on the backs of men and women over the secret ford to the little beach outside the cave. The women drove the large cattle into hidden gullies and left them there, perforce, while they came down for shelter to the cave as well. The men took their muskets and went out to the hillside to skirmish with the enemy. There was ample time for everything to be done, because on the precipitous goat tracks through the rocks and the undergrowth the French soldiers moved so slowly that an interval hours long occurred between the firing of the first warning shots and the arrival of the French anywhere where they might be dangerous.

The very first attack, made only a few days after the arrival of the French, was perhaps the most successful. It was only a short while after daybreak that a musket shot told of the danger, and Dodd had seized his rifle, and, with Bernardino at his side, had hurried to the broad flat rock on the summit which the peasants called "the table" to see what was developing.

It was the usual sort of attack—four columns of men pushing up the hill by perilous goat tracks through the bush. Dodd could catch glimpses of each in turn making the slow ascent whenever the conformation of the ground brought them into view. Each column consisted of a company; even at that distance he could see in the clear air that one column wore the bearskins of the grenadiers of the battalion and another the plumes of the voltigeurs—"light bobs" Dodd called them mentally—the remaining two companies of the battalion had been left behind of course, to act as headquarters guard. The progress of the attackers was inordinately slow. They had continually to halt to enable the rear to catch up with the head. The three sentries who had given the alarm were able to slip round by other paths and take long shots into the caterpillars of men crawling up the slope. Dodd and trhe other half-dozen men who gathered round him had ample time to choose their course of action and glide along the crest away to the flank and by heavy firing there bring one of the columns to a complete stop.

Yet it was a very damaging day. The other columns had broken into smaller parties, which had ranged very thoroughly over the top of the mountain—as thoroughly, that is to say, as twelve small parties could range over an immense hill-top seamed and broken with gullies. One such party must have found the cattle, the four draught bullocks who had drawn the village plough in the days before the French came. And perhaps another party had found Miguel. However it was, Miguel was missing. He might be dead, and his body might be lying somewhere out on the hillside. No one knew what had become of old Miguel, and the women in the cave that night wept for him—more bitterly, perhaps, than the men bewailed the loss of the draught oxen. They sought him the next day over the hill without finding him, but later in the day one of the watchers on the brow of the hill came in with news of him.

He had seen Miguel brought out of the village and buried by the fields; he was sure it was Miguel, even at that distance. The French must have dragged him into the village and murdered him. There was more wailing among the women. Miguel had led a solitary life lately; his wife was dead and his sons had been conscripted into the Army, bet every one in that village was related to everyone else; they had intermarried for generations, even (as was not unusual in those lost villages) within the prohibited degrees. Miguel was mourned by cousins and nieces and daughters-in-law.

The other information which the watchers on the hill brought, to the effect that the French had discovered the hidden stores of food in Miguel's silo, went almost unnoticed in the general dismay.

Nevertheless, Miguel's death was not long unavenged. There came a morning when Bernardino, flushed with excitement, came hurriedly to Dodd and the others and led them to "the table," where they gathered with infinite caution. Bernardino pointed down the hill, and every one followed his gesture. Far down the slope they could see half a dozen men crawling along a path. They were bent double, and moving with such ludicrous care that Bernardino could not help giggling as he pointed to them: it was so amusing to see them picking their way with so much caution and ignorant that they had been observed.

It was Dodd who laid the ambush. He guessed the future route of the little party, and brought his men hurriedly across the slope to where they could await their arrival unseen. He had lain on his stomach with his rifle pushed out in front of him ready for action, and the others had imitated him. And, when one point of their course the Frenchmen had shown up clearly and just within range, he had turned his head and had glowered at his men with such intensity that they had restrained their natural instincts and had not fired, but had waited instead for the better opportunity which Dodd had foreseen.

The volley at ten yards and the instant charge which Dodd had headed had been effective enough. There were three men dead and another one wounded, whose throat Pedro had cut the instant Dodd's back was turned, and the survivors had fled down the path as though the devil were behind them. Dodd would have been glad if they had all been killed, but to kill seven men with a volley from seven muskets even at ten yards was much more than could be expected—a pity, all the same, for Dodd could guess at the moral effect it would have had on the battalion if a whole detachment had been cut off without a trace.

He had forbidden pursuit, calling back Bernardino who had begun to run down the path after the fugitives. There was no sense in running madly about the hill where other enemies were to be found; there might indeed be danger.

Instead, Dodd made the best move possible in taking his men back to "the table" and scanning the hill for further parties of the enemy, and when he saw none he pushed out scouts here and there to seek for them. Two other little groups were located during the day, and Dodd brought up his men to attack them, creeping cautiously through the undergrowth. But meither attack was successful as the first—the first burst of firing had sent them on the alert and it had not been possible to approach them closely. They could only follow them back to the village in a long, straggling fight in which much powder was expended and very few people hurt—several of the Portuguese received flesh wounds.

All the same, it had been a glorious day. The new French plan of pushing small parties up the hill under cover of darkness had been heavily defeated. And every man on the hill now had a good French musket and bayonet and ammunition, taken from the corpses of the slain.

* * *

Cecil Smith, under the pen name C.S. Forester, is the author of two plays, five biographies and 35 novels. He is most noted for the 11 Horatio Hornblower novels detailing the exploits of the great fictional sailor's career from midshipmen to admiral. The books include (US titles), *Beat to Quarters*, *A Ship of the Line*, *Flying Colours*, *Commodore Hornblower*, *Lord Hornblower*, *Mr Midshipman Hornblower*, *Hornblower and the* Atropos, *Lieutenant Hornblower*, *Admiral Hornblower in* the *West Indies*, *Hornblower and the* Hotspur, and *Hornblower in the* Crisis.

Suggested Reading

Forester, C.S. *Rifleman Dodd*. Baltimore: The Nautical & Aviation Publishing Company of America, 1989.

Forester, C. S. *The Captain from Connecticut (Great War Stories)*. The Nautical & Aviation Publishing Company of America, Inc. 1997.

Marshall, S. L. *The Soldier's Load and the Mobility of a Nation*. Quantico, Virginia: The Marine Corps Association, 1965.

Webb, James. *Fields of Fire*. Annapolis: Naval Institute Press, 2000.

22

On Imagination and Critical Thinking: C.S. Forester's The General

Maj Stuart R. Lockhart, USMC

"Men without imagination like Curzon were necessary to execute a military policy devoid of imagination."[1]
—C.S. Forester

Lieutenant-General Sir Herbert Curzon, K.C.M.G., C.B., D.S.O., was a man whose abilities should never have allowed him to graduate to senior command. Abrupt in manner, not prone to expressions of warmth with his men (or his wife!), rigid in thought, and deeply ambitious, his personal skills of leadership exuded a pure devotion to duty and obedience. While these qualities are not necessarily bad in military leaders, when fused with a strict adherence to orthodoxy . . . the results can be catastrophic. And so it was with LtGen Sir Herbert Curzon.

This man never lived. He did, however, in the mind of British author and novelist C.S. Forester, and he is brought to life in *The General*. Perhaps best known for his series of stories detailing the adventures of one of the most famous characters in naval literature, Horatio Hornblower, Forester also penned a work best remembered for its cinematic adaptation, *The African Queen*. On topics relating to land warfare, he did not leave us with a volume of literature of the magnitude of the Hornblower series. After *The General*, *Rifleman Dodd* entertains us with the tale of an individual British soldier, cut off behind French lines during the Peninsular War in Spain in the early 1800s, and his attempts to return to his unit. Dodd's reliance on personal initiative, discipline, and field craft inspired the Marine Corps make it required reading for all recruits during Boot Camp in the mid-1990s. Interestingly, Adolph Hitler made *The General* required reading for officers in the *Wehrmacht* soon after it appeared in print in the late 1930s.

Certainly, *The General* is a novel in the style for which Forester was best known—an ever-

---

[1] C.S. Forester, *The General*. 1936. (Charleston, SC: The Nautical & Aviation Publishing Co., 1999), x.

changing plot as the protagonist maneuvers his way through challenges and ironies, ranging between success and failure. This, along with a highly readable and descriptive writing style, makes *The General* a thoroughly engaging read. It is a book that can be consumed easily in a single sitting.

When Forester first published *The General* in 1936, he hardly intended it to be read for pure enjoyment. Throughout the story, there is a sense that the author was keenly aware of the direction of European affairs at the time, and that the lessons of the Great War, less than twenty years past, must not be repeated. Specifically, unless the British government and military could overcome hidebound conservatism, the military mindset that had produced such tragedies as the Somme Offensive in 1916, with its 60,000 British casualties on the battle's first day, would doom England and its future generations to senseless slaughter.

Forester's creation of Herbert Curzon is the personification of World War I's "brass hat," the pejorative term for senior officers in the British Army who directed its actions and a reference to the gold braiding adorning the visors of their caps. In general, these were officers who derived their experiences from the colonial conflicts of the Victorian period and, for some, romantic yet obsolete branches of service such as the cavalry. Unfortunately, they were unable to grasp the realities of the twentieth century battlefield dominated by the machine gun, quick-firing artillery, and barbed wire. Or at least come to grips with it very quickly with either tactical innovations or technology.

Based on their overarching sense of duty, pride in their regiments, and personal hubris, these officers, when confronted by the realities of trench warfare, derived solutions based on throwing more men and more artillery shells at enemy defenses in order to break the impasse. The fact that this method failed time after time with greater magnitude seemingly did little to deter them. Forester captured the essence of

their thinking by describing the workings of a division's staff officers prior to the Somme:

> . . . it was like the debate of a group of savages as to how to extract a screw from a piece of wood. Accustomed only to nails, they had made one effort to pull out the screw by main force, and now that it had failed they were devising methods of applying more force still, of obtaining more efficient pincers, of using levers and fulcrums so that more men could bring their strength to bear. They could hardly be blamed for not guessing that by rotating the screw it would come out after the exertion of far less effort; it would be a notion so different from anything they had ever encountered that they would laugh at the man who suggested it.

Forester apparently based his character of Herbert Curzon on two men who are still treated with scorn in ordering the deaths of so many young Englishmen: Field Marshals Sir John French and Sir Douglas Haig, the wartime leaders of the British Expeditionary Force (BEF) in France. More than likely, Curzon's qualities, both personally and professionally, are the compilation of several figures. As with most officers of the day, he begins his career on a battlefield far from the muddy, shell-pocked trenches of France.

The Boer War of 1899-1902 in South Africa was a sharply fought guerrilla war that pitted the British Empire and her armies against the fewer, but highly resourceful Boer *commandos*. It was here that many senior British officers who featured so prominently in World War I received their first taste of combat. Like the junior officers of so many armies throughout history, it would be a profound experience for Herbert Curzon as well, testing his leadership through a combination of excitement, confusion, fear, and desperation. It would provide him the foundation of a career that would see his ascent to generalship and command of thousands nearly twenty years later. Lastly, it offered the spring-board to what mattered to an officer of his social standing—knighthood, public honors, and the euphemistic "Bath chair on the Bournemouth promenade"—all gained through the sacrifices of thousands of his soldiers. All of this emerges in Forester's story regarding Curzon, which begins with a brief episode of personal (yet accidental) heroism, at a fictitious battle named Volkslaagte.

The day on which Curzon first stepped over the threshold of history, the day which was to start him towards the command of a hundred thousand men, towards knighthood—and toward the Bath chair on the Bournemouth promenade—found him a worried subaltern in an early South African battle. The landscape around him was of a dull reddish brown; even the scanty grass and the scrubby bushes were brown. The arid plain was seamed with a tangle of ravines and gullies, but its monotony was relieved by the elevation in the distance of half a dozen flat-topped rocky hills, each of them like the others, and all of them like nearly every other *kopje* in South Africa.

Curzon was in command of his squadron of the Twenty-Second Lancers, the Duke of Suffolk's Own, an eminence to which he had been raised by the chances of war.* Three officers senior to him were sick, left behind at various points on the lines of communication, and Captain the Honorable Charles Manningtree-Field, who had been in command when the squadron went into action, was lying dead at Curzon's feet with a Mauser bullet through his head. Curzon was not thinking about Manningtree-Field. His anxiety was such that immediately after the shock of his death, and of the realization that men really can be killed by bullets, his first thought had been that now he could use the Captain's Zeiss binoculars and try and find out what was happening. He stood on the lip of the shallow depression wherein lay Manningtree-Field's body, the two squadron trumpeters, and two or three wounded men, and he stared around him across the featureless landscape.

In a long straggling line to his right and left lay the troopers of the squadron, their forage caps fastened under their chins, firing away industriously at nothing at all, as far as Curzon could see. In a gully to the rear, he knew, were the horses and the horseholders, but beyond that Curzon began to realize that he knew extraordinarily little about the battle which was going on. The squadron was supposed to be out on the right flank of an advancing British firing line, but when they had come galloping up to this position Curzon had not been in command, and he had been so preoccupied with keeping his troop properly closed up that he had not paid sufficient attention to what Manningtree-Field had been doing.

Probably Manningtree-Field had not been too sure himself, because the battle had begun in a muddle amid the cascade of vague orders from the staff, and since then no orders had reached them—and certainly no orders had envisaged their coming under heavy fire at this particular point. As and accompaniment to the sharp rattle of musketry about him, Curzon could hear the deeper sound of artillery in the distance, echoing over the plain with a peculiar discordant quality, and against the intense blue of the sky he could see white puffs of the shrapnel bursts far out to the left, but it was impossible to judge the position of the target at that distance, and there was just enough fold in the flat surface of the plain to conceal from him any sight of troops on the ground.

Meanwhile an invisible enemy was scourging them with a vicious and well-directed fire. The air was full of the sound of rifle bullets spitting and crackling past Curzon's ears as he stood staring through the binoculars. Curzon had an uneasy feeling that they were coming from the

---

* Cavalry units traditionally have different designations from their infantry counterparts. A "squadron" is the equivalent of a "battalion" in the infantry; a "troop" to a "company."

flank as well as from the front, and in the absence of certain knowledge he was rapidly falling prey to the fear that the wily Boers were creeping round to encircle him. A fortnight ago a whole squadron of Lancers—not of his regiment, thank God—had been cut off in that way and forced to surrender, with the result that that regiment was now known throughout South Africa was "Kruger's Own."[13] Curzon sweated with fear at the thought of such a fate overtaking him. He would die rather than surrender, but—would his men? He looked anxiously along the straggling skirmish line.

Troop Sergeant-Major Brown came crawling to him on his hands and knees. Brown was a man of full body, and his face was normally brick red, but this unwonton exertion under the scorching sun colored his cheeks like a beetroot.

"Ain't no orders come for us, sir?" asked Brown, peering up at him.

"No," said Curzon sharply. "And stand up if you want to speak to me."

Brown stood up reluctantly amid the crackle of bullets. After twenty years' service, without having had a shot fired at him, and with his pension in sight, it went against his grain to make a target of himself for a lot of farmers whose idea of war was the lay ambushes behind rocks.

"Come down 'ere, sir, please sir," pleaded Brown in a fever of distress. "We don't want to lose *you*, sir, too, sir."

The loss of the only officer the squadron had left would place Sergeant-Major Brown in command, and Brown was not at all desirous of such responsibility. It was that consideration which caused Curzon to yield to his solicitations, and to step down into the comparative safety of the depression.

"D'you fink we're cut orf, sir?" asked Brown, dropping his voice so as to be unheard by the trumpeters squatting on the rocks at the bottom of the dip.

"No, of course not," said Curzon. "The infantry will be up in line with us soon."

"Ain't no sign of them, is there, sir?" complained Brown. "Expect the beggars are 'eld up somewhere, or lorst their way, or something."

"Nonsense," said Curzon. All his training, both military and social, had been directed against his showing any loss of composure before his inferiors in rank, even if those inferiors should actually be voicing his own fears. He stepped once more to the side of the hollow and stared our over the rolling plain. There was nothing to be seen except the white shrapnel bursts.

"Our orders was to find their flank," said Brown, fidgeting with his sword hilt. "Looks to me more like as if they've found ours."

"Nonsense," repeated Curzon. But just exactly where the Boer firing line was to be found was more than he could say. Those infernal *kopjes* all looked alike to him. He looked once more along the line of skimishers crouching among the rocks, and as he looked he saw, here and there, faces turned towards him. That was a bad sign, for men to be looking over their shoulders in the heat of action. The men must be getting anxious. He could hardly blame them, seeing that they had been trained for years to look upon a battle as a series of charges knee to knee and lance in hand against a serried enemy. This lying down to be shot at by hidden enemies a mile off was foreign to their nature. It was his duty to steady them.

"Stay here, Sergeant-Major," he said. "You will take command if I'm hit."

He stepped out from the hollow, his sword at his side, his uniform spick and span, and walked in leisurely fashion along the firing line. He spoke to the men by name, steadily and unemotionally as he reached each in turn. He felt vaguely as he walked that a joke or two, something to raise a laugh, would be the most effective method of address, but he never was able to joke, and, as it was, his mere presence and unruffled demeanor acted as a tonic on the men. Twice he spoke harshly. Once when he found

[3] A reference of Boer Leader, Paul "Ohm" Kruger.

Trooper Haynes cowering behind rocks without making any attempt to return the fire, and once was when he found Trooper Macguire drinking from his water bottle. Water out here in the veldt was a most precious possession, to be hoarded like a miser's gold, for when there was no more water there would be no fight left in the men.

He walked down the line to one end; he walked back to the other. Sergeant-Major Brown, peeping out from his hollow, watched his officer's fearless passage, and, with the contrariness of human nature, found himself wishing he was with him. Then when Curzon was nearly back in safety again, Brown saw him suddenly swing right round. But next instant, he was walking steadily down the hollow, and only when he was out of sight of the men did he sit down sharply.

"Are you hit sir?" asked Brown, all anxiety.

"Yes. Don't let the men know. I'm still in command."

Brown hastily called the squadron first aid corporal with his haversack of dressings. They ripped open Curzon's coat and bound up the entrance and exit wounds. The destiny which directs the course of bullets had sent this one clean through the fleshy part of the shoulder without touching bone or artery or nerve.

"I'm alright," said Curzon manfully, getting to his feet and pulling his torn coat about him. The arrival of a crawling trooper interrupted Sergeant-Major Brown's protests.

"Message from Sergeant Hancock, sir," said the trooper. "Ammunition's running short."

"Um," said Curzon thoughtfully, and a pause ensued while he digested the information.

"There ain't fifty rounds left in our troop, sir," supplemented the trooper, with the insistence of his class upon harrowing detail.

"All right," blazed Curzon irritably. "All right. Get back to the line."

" 'Ave to do something now, sir," said Sergeant-Major Brown as the trooper crawled away.

"Shut up and be quiet," snapped Curzon.

He was perfectly well aware that he must do something as long as his men had cartridges to fire they would remain in good heart, but once ammunition failed he might expect any ugly incident to occur. There might be a panic, or someone might show a white flag.

"Trumpeter," called Curzon, and the trumpeter leapt up to attention to receive his orders.

The squadron came trailing back to the gully where the horses were waiting. The wounded were being assisted by their friends, but they were all depressed and ominously quiet. A few were swearing, using words of meaningless filth, under their breath.

"What about the dead, sir?" asked Sergeant Hancock, saluting. "The Captain, sir?"

The regiment was still so unversed in war as to feel anxiety in the heat of action about the disposal of the dead—a reminiscence of the warfare against savage enemies which constituted the British Army's sole recent experience. This new worry on top of all the others nearly broke Curzon down. He was on the point of blazing out with "Blast the dead!" but he managed to check himself. Such a violation of the army's recent etiquette would mean trouble with the men.

"I'll see about that later. Get back into your place," he said. "Prepare to mount!"

The squadron followed him down the ravine, the useless lances cocked up at each man's elbow, amid a squeaking of leather and a clashing of iron hooves on the rocks. Curzon's head was beginning to swim, what with the loss of blood, and the pain of the wound, and the strain he had undergone, and the heat of this gully. He had small enough idea of what he wanted to do—or at least he would not admit to himself that what he wanted was to make his way back to some area where the squadron would not be under fire and he might receive orders. The sense of isolation in the presence of an enemy of diabolical cunning and strength was overwhelming. He knew that he must not expose the squadron to fire while in retreat. The men would begin to quicken their horses' pace in that event—the walk would become a trot, the trot a gallop, and his professional reputation would be blasted. The gully they were in constituted at least a shelter from the deadly hail of bullets.

The gully changed direction more than once. Soon Curzon had no idea where he was, nor whither he was going, but he was too tired and in too much pain to think clearly. The distant gunfire seemed to roll about inside his skull; he drooped in his saddle and with difficulty straightened himself up. The fortunate gully continued a long way instead of coming to a rapid indefinite end as most gullies did in that parched plain, and the men—and Sergeant-Major Brown—were content to follow him without question. The sun was by now well down towards the horizon, and they were in the shade.

It was in fact the sight of the blaze of light which was reflected from the level plain in front which roused Curzon to the realization that the gully was about to end beyond the tangle of rocks just in front. He turned in his saddle and held up his hand to the column of men behind; they came sleepily to a halt, the horses cannoning into the hindquarters of the horses in front, and then Curzon urged his horse cautiously forward, his trumpeter close behind.

Peering from the shelter of the rocks Curzon beheld the finest spectacle which could gladden the eyes of a cavalry officer. The gully had led him, all unaware, actually behind the flank of the Boer position. Half a mile in front of him, sited with Boer cunningly on the reverse slope of a fold in the ground, was a battery of field guns sunk into shallow pits, the guns' crews clearly visible round them. There were groups of tethered ponies. There was a hint of rifle trenches far in front of the guns, and behind the guns were wagons and mounted staffs. There was all the vulnerable exposed confusion always to be found behind a firing line and he and his squadron were within easy charging distance of it all, their presence unsuspected.

Curzon fought down the nightmare feeling of unreality which was stealing over him. He filed the squadron out of the gully and brought it up

into line before any Boer had noticed them. Then, forgetting to draw his sword, he set his spurs into his horse and rode steadily, three lengths in front of his charging line, straight at the guns. The trumpeters pealed the charge as the pace quickened.

No undisciplined militia force could withstand the shock of an unexpected attack from the flank, however small the force which delivered it. The Boer defense which had all day held up the English attack collapsed like a pricked balloon. The whole space was black with men running for their ponies. Out on the open plain where the English infantry had barely been maintaining their firing lines the officers sensed what was happening. Some noticed the slackening of the Boer fire. Some saw the Boers rise out of their invisible trenches and run. One officer heard the cavalry trumpets, faint and sweet through the heated air. He yelled to his bugle to sound the charge. The skirmishing line rose up from flank to flank as bugler after bugler took up the call. Curzon had brought them the last necessary impetus for the attack. They poured over the Boer lines to where Curzon, his sword still in its sheath, was sitting dazed upon his horse amid the captured guns.

The battle of Volkslaagte—a very great battle in the eyes of the British public in 1899, wherein nearly 5,000 men a side had been engaged—was won, and Curzon was marked for his Captaincy and the DSO. He was not a man of dreams, but even if he had been, his wildest dreams would not have envisioned the future command of a hundred thousand British soldiers—nor the Bath chair on Bournemouth promenade."

Suggested Reading

For additional reading on the First World War, there is a wealth of material from which to choose. For general works on the war, Hew Strachan's edited history, *World War I: A History* is a scholarly reference with essays on various aspects of the war presented by the prominent historians of the period. John Keegan's *The First*

World War is also a superb account written by one of Britain's most prominent military historians. Many of his other works are considered classics, including *The Face of Battle: A Study of Agincourt, Waterloo, and the Somme*, which compares prominent British battles.

Histories dealing with specific British battles include Lyn Macdonald's works *The Somme* and *They Called it Passchendaele: Story of the Third Battle of Ypres and the Men Who Fought in It*, both of which incorporate many first hand accounts by the participants. Tim Travers has written extensively on the battle tactics of the British Army during the war and his books *The Killing Ground* and *How the War Was Won: Command and Technology in the British Army on the Western Front, 1917-1918* cover this area in great detail. Likewise, the experience of the common soldier is well covered in Denis Winter's *Death's Men: Soldiers of the Great War*.

This war was also noted for the abundance of literature that came out during and after the conflict. The works of such authors as William Butler Yates, Robert Graves, Siegfried Sassoon, Wilfred Owen and others constitute an entire genre of English literature dealing with the impact of the war on society, man's inhumanity to man, and his ways of dealing with the experience of war. One work that delves more deeply into this topic and that of societal remembrance is Paul Fussell's *The Great War in Modern Memory*.

About the Author

Major Stuart R. Lockhart, USMC is an infantry officer and a 1991 graduate of the U.S. Naval Academy. After completing tours with the 1st and 2nd Marine Divisions, and the Marine Corps Recruit Depot in San Diego, he earned his Masters Degree in Military History from Temple University in 2002. He was assigned as an instructor in the History Department at U.S.N.A. when this piece was written. With a primary interest in twentieth century military and naval history, Major Lockhart taught courses in American Naval History, the History of the Marine Corps, and the History of U.S. Military Air Power. He resides in Annapolis, MD with his wife.

23

A Knight for a Castle: Captain Frederick Marryat, RN, and The King's Own

Joel Ira Holwitt, LTJG, USN

Unlike the celebrated novelists C.S. Forester and Patrick O'Brian, Frederick Marryat actually experienced many of the naval incidents in the Napoleonic Wars that he wrote about. In 1806, at the age of 14, Marryat joined the Royal Navy as a midshipman. He first served under the command of Captain Thomas Cochrane, one of the Royal Navy's greatest frigate commanders. At the time, life as a midshipman was a hands-on education at sea, which offered numerous opportunities to risk life and limb in battle, shipwreck, and imprisonment.[1]

Marryat proved himself to be both a competent and brave officer, earning praise and distinction as he rose through the ranks to command numerous Royal Navy ships. While in command of the 28-gun sloop *Ariadne*, he published his first novel, *The Naval Officer, or Scenes and Adventures in the Life of Frank Mildmay* (1829). After his second novel, *The King's Own* (1830), Marryat resigned from the service and transitioned entirely into literature. He became known for writing such classic works as *Peter Simple* (1832-33) and *Mr. Midshipman Easy* (1836). Arguably, he remains the greatest author of nautical fiction in the Age of Fighting Sail.[2]

The following passage is taken from *The King's Own*, when the British frigate *Aspasia* encounters a partially dismasted French ship-of-the-line in a fierce gale off the coast of west Ireland. Although the French ship-of-the-line carries more than twice *Aspasia*'s armament, the terrible weather conditions even the odds, and the British begin a dogged pursuit that will push the sailors of *Aspasia* to the limits of their bravery and dedication.

The action centers on *Aspasia*'s commander,

---

[1] Louis J. Parascandola, introduction to Frederick Marryat, *Peter Simple*, Heart of Oak Sea Classics, ed. Dean King (New York: Henry Holt and Company, 1998), xxii-xiv. See also: Louis J. Parascandola, introduction to Frederick Marryat, *Mr. Midshipman Easy*, Heart of Oak Sea Classics, ed. Dean King (New York: Henry Holt and Company, 1998), xii.

[2] Parascandola, introduction to Marryat, *Peter Simple*, xiv.

Captain M—, who refuses to give up despite increasingly desperate odds. Probably a composite of Marryat, Cochrane, and Edward Pellew, a frigate commander who fought a similar battle against a ship-of-the-line, Captain M—personifies the ideals of utmost commitment, courage, professionalism, and leadership.

The captain's total commitment to his duty is clear from his dogged persistence in maintaining the chase, even after his most experienced subordinate argues that because of the weather and the proximity of the coast, there would be no dishonor in breaking off the pursuit to ensure the safety of *Aspasia*. Captain M—, however, maintains that his duty as a British naval officer requires he and his crew to be willing to risk everything for their country and their mission.

Captain M—also illustrates extreme professionalism and leadership under the most trying of circumstances. It is due in no small measure to his skill as a naval officer that *Aspasia* maintains the uneven battle in gale-force conditions. He also exhibits the iron will necessary to maintain discipline as the situation becomes almost hopeless. A brave warrior who is willing to make the ultimate sacrifice to achieve an important mission, Frederick Marryat's Captain M—is an extraordinary example of solid leadership, bearing, and professionalism under the most intense of conditions, a reflection of the Royal Navy officers with whom Marryat served for over 20 years.

The gale increased rapidly during the first watch. Large drops of rain mingled with the spray, distant thunder rolled to windward, and occasional gleams of lightning pierced through the intense darkness of the night. The officers and men of the watches below, with sealed eyes and thoughtless hearts, were in their hammocks, trusting to those on deck for security. But the night was terrific, and the captain, first lieutenant [Lieutenant Hardy], and master [Sailing Master Pearce][3], from the responsibility of their situations, continued on deck, as did many of the officers termed idlers, such as the surgeon and purser, who, although their presence was not required, felt no inclination to sleep. By four o'clock in the morning the gale was at its height. The lightning darted through the sky in every direction, and the thunder-claps for the time overpowered the noise of the wind as it roared through the shrouds. The sea, striking on the fore-channels, was thrown aft with violence over the quarter-deck and waist of the ship, as she laboured through the agitated sea.

"If this lasts much longer we must take the foresail off of her, and give her the main-staysail," said Hardy to the master.

"We must, indeed," replied the captain, who was standing by them; "but the day is breaking. Let us wait a little—ease her, quartermaster."

"Ease her it is, sir."

At daylight, the gale having rather increased than shown any symptoms of abating, the captain was giving directions for the foresail to be taken off, when the seaman who was stationed to look out on the lee-gangway cried out, "A sail on the lee-beam!"

"A sail on the lee-beam, sir!" reported the officer of the watch to the captain, as he held on by a rope with one hand, and touched his hat with the other.

"Here, youngster, tell the sentry at the cabin door to give you my deck glass," said Captain M—to Merrick, who was one of the midshipmen of the morning watch.

"She's a large ship, sir—main and mizen [sic]

---

[3] In the early 19th century, the first lieutenant and the sailing master were the two right-hand men of a Royal Navy warship's captain. The first lieutenant was the senior lieutenant on board and served as the executive officer of the ship. The sailing master was technically a warrant officer, but he drew higher pay than most senior lieutenants and he generally was the most experienced sailor and navigator on board the ship, excepting the captain. See N.A.M. Rodger, *The Command of the Ocean: A Naval History of Britain*, 1649–1815 (New York: W.W. Norton & Company, 2004), 394. See also: Brian Lavery, *Jack Aubrey Commands: An Historical Companion to the Naval World of Patrick O'Brian* (Annapolis: Naval Institute Press, 2003), 67, 72–73.

masts both gone," reported Hardy, who had mounted up three or four ratlines of the main-rigging.

The midshipman brought up the glass; and the captain, first passing his arm round the fore-brace to secure himself from falling to leeward with the lurching of the ship, as soon as he could bring the strange vessel into the field of the glass exclaimed, "A line-of-battle ship, by Heavens! And if I am any judge of a hull, or the painting of a ship, she is no Englishman." Other glasses were now produced, and the opinion of the captain was corroborated by that of the officers on deck.

"Keep fast the foresail, Mr. Hardy. We'll edge down to her. Quartermaster, see the signal halyards all clear."

The captain went down to his cabin, while the frigate was kept away as he directed, the master standing at the conn. He soon came up again: "Hoist No. 3 at the fore, and No. 8 at the main. We'll see if she can answer the private signal."

It was done, and the frigate, rolling heavily in the trough of the sea, and impelled by the furious elements, rapidly closed with the stranger. In less than an hour they were within half a mile of her; but the private signal remained unanswered.

"Now then, bring her to the wind, Mr. Pearce," said Captain M—, who had his glass upon the vessel.

The frigate was luffed handsomely to the wind, not however without shipping a heavy sea. The gale, which during the time that she was kept away before the wind had the appearance, which it always has, of having decreased in force, now that she presented her broadside to it roared again in all its fury.

"Call the gunner—clear away the long gun forward—try with the rammer whether the shot has started from the cartridge, and then fire across the bows of that vessel."

The men cast loose the gun, and the gunner, taking out the bed and coin to obtain the greatest elevation to counteract the heel of the frigate, watched the lurch, and pitched the shot close to the forefoot of the disabled vessel, who immediately showed French colours over her weather-quarter.

"French colours, sir!" cried two or three at a breath.

"Beat to quarters, Mr. Hardy," said Captain M—.

"Shall we cast loose the main-deck guns?"

"No, no—that will be useless; we shall not be able to fire them, and we may have them through the sides. We'll try her with the carronades."[4]

It was easy to perceive, without the assistance of a glass, that the men on board the French line-of-battle ship were attempting, in no very scientific manner, to get a jury-mast up abaft, that by putting after-sail on her they might keep their vessel to the wind. The foresail they dared not take off, as without any sail to keep her steady, the remaining mast would in all probability have rolled over the side; but without after-sail the ship would not keep to the wind, and the consequence was, that she was two points off the wind, forging fast through the water, notwithstanding that the helm was hard a-lee.

"Where are we now, Mr. Pearce?" interrogated the captain–"about eight or nine leagues from the land?"

"Say seven leagues, sir, if you please," replied the master, "until I can give you an exact answer," and he descended the companion-ladder to work up his reckoning.

"She's leaving us, Mr. Hardy; keep more away, and run abreast of her. Now, my lads, watch the weather roll—round and grape—don't throw a shot away—aim at the quarter-deck

---

[4] A carronade is a relatively lightweight cannon used to hurl heavy shot at short range. Because of their light weight, they would normally be placed on the top deck of a sailing warship, and hence would be the logical choice to use in a gale such as this one. See Dean King, with John B. Hattendorf, and J. Worth Estes, *A Sea of Words: A Lexcon and Companion for Patrick O'Brian's Seafaring Tales* (New York: Henry Holy and Company, 1995), 117.

ports. If we can prevent her from getting up her jury-masts, she is done for."

"As for the matter of that," said the quartermaster, who was captain of one of the quarter-deck guns, "we might save our shot. They haven't *nous* enough to get them up if left all to themselves—however, here's a slap at her."

The frigate had now closed within three cables' length of the line-of-battle ship, and considering the extreme difficulty of hitting any mark under such disadvantages, a well-directed fire was thrown in by her disciplined seamen. The enemy attempted to return the fire from the weather main-deck guns, but it was a service of such difficulty and danger, that he more than once abandoned it. Two or three guns disappearing from the ports, proved that they had either rolled to leeward, or had been precipitated down the hatchways. This was indeed the case, and the French sailors were so much alarmed from the serious disasters that had already ensued, that they either quitted their quarters, or, afraid to stand behind the guns when they were fired, no aim was taken, and the shots were thrown away. Had the two ships been equally manned, the disadvantage, under all the misfortunes of the Frenchman, would have been on the side of the frigate; but the gale itself was more than sufficient employment for the undisciplined crew of the line-of-battle ship. The fire from the frigate was kept up with vigour, although the vessel lurched so heavily, as often to throw the men who were stationed at the guns into the lee scuppers, rolling one over the other in the water with which the decks were floated; but this was only a subject of merriment, and they resumed their task with the careless spirit of British seamen. The fire, difficult as it was to take any precise aim, had the effect intended, that of preventing the French vessel from rigging anything like a jury-mast. Occasionally the line-of-battle ship kept more away, to avoid the grape, by increasing her distance; but the frigate's course was reg-

ulated by that of her opponent, and she continued her galling pursuit.*

It was no time for man to war against man. The powers of Heaven were loose, and in all their fury. The wind howled, the sea raged, the thunder stunned, and the lightning blinded. The Eternal was present in all His majesty; yet pigmy mortals were contending, But Captain M— was unmoved, unawed, unchecked; and the men, stimulated by his example, and careless of everything, heeded not the warring of the elements.

"Sit on your powder-box and keep it dry, you young monkey," said the quartermaster, who was captain of the gun, to the lad who had the cartridge ready for reloading it. The fire upon the French vessel was warmly kept up, when the master again came on deck, and stated to the captain that they could not be more than four leagues from a dead lee-shore, which, by keeping away after the French vessel, they must be nearing fast.

"She cannot stand this long, sir. Look to windward—the gale increases—there is a fresh hand at the 'bellows.' "

The wind now redoubled its fury, and the rain, that took a horizontal instead of a perpendicular direction from the force of the wind, fed the gale instead of lulling it. The thunder rolled; and the frigate was so drenched with water, that the guns were primed and reprimed, without the fire communicating to the powder, which in a few seconds was saturated with the rain and spray. This was but of little consequence, as the squall and torrents of rain had now hid the enemy from their sight. "Look out for her, my men, as soon as the squall passes over," cried Captain M—.

A flash of lightning, that blinded them for a time, was followed by a peal of thunder, so close that the timbers of the ship trembled with the vibration of the air. A second hostile meeting of electricity took place, and the fluid darted down

---

[5] In the interest of saving room and not breaking the flow of action, the chapter headings, including the heading's classical quotation, have been omitted.

the side of the frigate's mainmast, passing through the quarter-deck in the direction of the powder magazine. Captain M—, the first lieutenant, master, and fifty or sixty of the men were struck down by the violence of the shock. Many were killed, more wounded, and the rest, blinded and stunned, staggered and fell to leeward with the lurching of the vessel. Gradually those who were only stunned recovered their legs, and amongst the first was the captain of the frigate. As soon as he could recall his scattered senses, with his usual presence of mind he desired the "fire-roll" to be beat by the drummer, and sent down to ascertain the extent of the mischief. A strong sulphureous [sic] smell pervaded the ship, and flew up the hatchways; and such was the confusion, that some minutes elapsed before any report could be made. It appeared that the electric fluid had passed close to the spirit-room and after-magazine, and escaped through the bottom of the vessel. Before the report had been made, the captain had given directions for taking the wounded down to the surgeon, and the bodies of the dead under the half-deck. The electric matter had divided at the foot of the mainmast, to which it had done no injury; one part, as before mentioned, having gone below, while the other, striking the iron bolt that connected the lower part of the main-bitts, had thence passed to the two foremast quarter-deck carronades, firing them both off at the same moment that it killed and wounded the men who were stationed at them. The effects of the lightning were various. The men who were close to the foot of the main-mast, holding on by the ropes belayed to the main-bitts, were burnt to a cinder, and their blackened corpses lay smoking in the remnants of their clothes; emitting an overpowering ammoniacal stench. Some were only wounded in the arm or leg; but the scathed member was shrivelled [sic] up, and they were borne down the hatchway, howling with intolerable pain. The most awful effects were at the guns. The captains of the two carronades, and several men that were near them, were dead; but had not the equipoise of the bodies been lost by the violent

motion of the ship; their dreadful fate would not have been immediately perceived. Not an injury appeared—every muscle was fixed to the same position as when the fluid entered—the same expression of countenance, the eye like life as it watched the sight on the gun, the body bent forward, the arm extended, the fingers still holding the lanyard attached to the lock. Nothing but palpable evidence could convince one that they were dead.

The boy attending with his powder-box, upon which he had sat by the directions of the captain of the gun, was desired by Captain M-to jump up and assist the men in carrying down the wounded. He sat still on his box, supported between the capstan and the stanchions of the companion hatchway, his eyes apparently fixed upon the captain, but not moving in obedience to the order, although repeated in an angry tone. He was dead!

During the confusion attending this catastrophe, the guns had been deserted. As soon as the wounded men had been taken below, the captain desired the boatswain to pipe to quarters, for the drummer when called to beat the "fire-roll" had been summoned to his last account. The guns were again manned, and the firing recommenced; but a want of energy, and the melancholy silence which prevailed, evidently showed that the men, although they obeyed, did not obey cheerfully.

"Another pull of the fore-staysail, Mr. Hardsett," cried Captain M–through his speaking-trumpet.

"Ay, ay, sir—clap on him, my lads," replied the boatswain, holding his call between his teeth, as he lent the assistance of his powerful frame to the exertions of the men. The sheet was aft, and belayed, and the boatswain indulged in muttered quotations from the Scriptures: "He bringeth forth the clouds from the ends of the world, and sendeth forth lightnings, with rain; bringing the winds out of His treasuries. He smote the first-born of Egypt."

The first lieutenant and master were in close consultation to windward. The captain stood at the lee-gangway, occasionally desiring the quartermaster at the conn to alter the course, regulating his own by that of his disabled enemy.

"I'll speak to him, then," exclaimed Pearce, as the conference broke up, and he went over to leeward to the captain. "Captain M—, I have had the honour to serve under your command some time, and I trust you will allow that I have never shown any want of zeal in the discharge of my duty?"

"No, Mr. Pearce," replied the captain, with a grave smile; "without compliment, you never have."

"Then, sir, you will not be affronted at, or ascribe to unworthy motives, a remark which I wish to make?"

"Most certainly not; as I am persuaded that you will never make any observation inconsistent with your duty, or infringing upon the rules of the service."

"Then, sir, with all due submission to you, I do think, and it is the opinion of the other officers as well, that our present employment, under existing circumstances, is tempting, if not insulting, the Almighty. Look at the sky, look at the raging sea, hear the wind, and call to mind the effects of the lightning not one half-hour since. When the Almighty appears in all His wrath, in all His tremendous majesty, is it a time for us poor mortals to be at strife? What is our feeble artillery, what is the roar of our cannon, compared to the withering and consuming artillery of Heaven? Has He not told us so? And do not the ship's company, by their dispirited conduct since the vessel was struck, acknowledge it? The officers all feel it, sir. Is it not presumptuous—with all due submission, sir, is it not wicked?"

"I respect your feelings as a Christian and as a man," replied Captain M—; "but I must differ with you. That the Almighty power appears, I grant; and I feel, as you do, that God is great, and man weak and impotent. But that this storm

has been raised—that this thunder rolls—that this lightning has blasted us as a warning, I deny. The causes emanate from the Almighty; but He leaves the effects to the arrangements of Nature, which is governed by immutable laws. Had there been no other vessel in sight, this lightning would still have struck us; and this storm will not cease, even if we were to neglect what I consider a duty to our country."

The master touched his hat and made no answer. It was now about one o'clock, and the horizon to leeward, clearing up a little, showed the land upon the lee-beam.

"Land ho!" cried one of the men.

"Indeed," observed the captain to the master; "we are nearer than you thought."

"Something, sir, perhaps; but recollect how many hours you have kept away after this vessel."

"Very true," rejoined the captain; "and the indraught into the bargain. I am not surprised at it."

"Shall we haul our wind, sir? We are on a dead lee-shore."[6]

"No, Mr. Pearce, not until the fate of that vessel is decided."

"Land on the weather-bow!" reported the boatswain.

"Indeed!" said the captain; "then the affair will soon be decided."

The vessels still continued their course in a slanting direction towards the land, pursuer and pursued running on to destruction; but although various indirect hints were given by the first lieutenant and others, Captain M—turned a deaf ear. He surveyed the dangers which presented themselves, and frowned upon them, as if in defiance.

However we may be inclined to extend our admiration to the feelings of self-devotion which governed the conduct of Captain M—, it cannot be a matter of surprise that the officers of the frigate did not coincide with his total indiffer-

---

[6] A lee shore means that land is to leeward of a ship, which is consequently being inexorably blown towards shore..Because sailing ships were at the mercy of the wind, being on a lee shore could be extremely dangerous. See King, *A Sea of Words*, 230.

ence to self in the discharge of his duty. Murmur they did not; but they looked at each other, at the captain, and at the perilous situation of the vessel in silence, and with a restless change of position that indicated their anxiety. Macallan [the ship's surgeon] was below attending to the wounded men, or he would probably have been deputed by the others to have remonstrated with the captain. A few minutes more had elapsed, when the master again addressed him.

"I am afraid, sir, if we continue to stand on, that we shall lose the frigate," said he, respectfully touching his hat.

"Be it so," replied Captain M—; "the enemy will lose a line-of-battle ship; our country will be the gainer when the account is balanced."

"I must be permitted to doubt that, sir; the value of the enemy's ship is certainly greater; but there are other considerations."

"What are they?"

"The value of the respective officers and ships' companies, which must inevitably share the fate of the two vessels. The captain of that ship is not worth his salt. It would be politic to let him live, and continue to command. His ship will always be ours, when we want it; and in the event of a general action, he would make a gap in the enemy's line which might prove of the greatest importance. Now, sir, without drawing the parallel any further—without taking into consideration the value of the respective officers and men—I must take the liberty of observing that, on your account alone, England will be no gainer by the loss of both vessels and crews."

"Thank you for the compliment, which, as it is only feather-weight, I will allow to be thrown into the scale. But I do not agree with you. I consider war but as a game of chess, and will never hesitate to sacrifice a knight for a castle. Provided that castle is lost, Mr. Pearce," continued the captain, pointing to the French vessel, "this little frigate, if necessary, shall be knight-errant enough to bear her company."

"Very good, sir," replied Pearce, again touching his hat; "as master of this ship, I considered it my duty to state my opinion."

"You have done your duty, Mr. Pearce, and I thank you for it; but I have also my duties to perform. One of them is, not to allow the lives of one ship's company, however brave and well-disciplined (and such I must allow to be the one I have the honour to command), to interfere with the general interests of the country we contend for. When a man enters his Majesty's service, his life is no longer to be considered his own; it belongs to his king and country, and is at their disposal. If we are lost, there will be no great difficulty in collecting another ship's company in old England as brave and as good as this. Officers as experienced are anxiously waiting for employment; and the Admiralty will have no trouble in selecting and appointing as good, if not a better captain."

The contending ships were now about two cables' length from each other, with a high rocky coast, lashed with a tremendous surf, about three-quarters of a mile to leeward. The promontory extended about two points on the weather-bow of the frigate, and a low sandy tongue of land spread itself far out on her weather-quarter, so that both vessels were completely embayed. The line-of-battle ship again made a attempt to get up some after-sail; but the well-directed fire of the frigate, whenever she rose on the tops of the mountainous waves, which at intervals hid the hulls of both vessels from each other, drove the Frenchmen from their task of safety, and it was now evident that all command of her was lost. She rolled gunwale under, and her remaining mast went by the board.

"Nothing can save her now, sir," replied the master.

"No," replied the captain; "we have done our work, and must now try to save ourselves."

"Secure the guns—be smart, my lads, you work for your lives. We must put the mainsail on her, Mr. Pearce, and claw off if we can."

The master shook his head. "Hands by the clue-garnets and buntlines—man the mainsheet—let go those leech-lines, youngster—haul aboard."

"It's a pity, too, by G-d," said the captain, looking over the hammock-rails at the French vessel, which was now running before the wind right on to the shore–"eight or nine hundred poor devils will be called to their last account in the course of a few minutes. I wish we could save them."

"You should have thought of that before, sir," said the master, with a grave smile at this reaction of feeling on the part of the captain. "Nothing can save them, and I am afraid that nothing but a slant of wind or a miracle can help ourselves."

"She has struck, sir, and is over on her broadside," said the quartermaster, who was standing on the carronade slide.

"Mind your conn, sir; keep your eyes on the weather-leech of the sail, and not upon that ship," answered the captain, with asperity.

In the meantime the mainsail had been set by the first lieutenant, and the crew, unoccupied, had their eyes directed, for a little while upon the French vessel, which lay on her beam-ends, enveloped in spray; but they also perceived what, during the occupation and anxiety of action, they had not had leisure to attend to, namely, the desperate situation of their own ship. The promontory was now broad on the weather bow, and a reef of rocks, partly above water, extended from it to leeward of the frigate. Such was the anxiety of the ship's company for their own safety, that the eyes of the men were turned away from the stranded vessel, and fixed upon the rocks. The frigate did all that a gallant vessel could do, rising from the trough of the sea, and shaking the water from her, as she was occasionally buried forecastle under, from the great pressure of the sail, cleaving the huge masses of the element with her sharp stem, and trembling fore and aft with the violence of her own exertions. But the mountainous waves took her with irresistible force from her chesstree, retarding her velocity, and forcing her each moment nearer to the reef.

"Wear ship, Mr. Hardy," said the captain, who had not spoken one word since he rebuked the quartermaster; "we have but just room."

The master directed the man at the wheel to put helm up in a firm but subdued tone, for he was at that moment thinking of his wife and children. The ship had just paid off and gathered fresh way, when she struck upon a sunken rock. A loud and piercing cry from the ship's company was followed by an enormous sea striking the frigate on the counter, at once heeling her over and forcing her ahead, so that she slipped off from the rock again into deep water.

"She's off again, sir," said the master.

"It's God's mercy, Mr. Pearce! Bring her to the wind as soon as you can," replied the captain, with composure. But the carpenter now ran up the hatchway, and with a pallid face and hurried tone, declared that the ship was filling fast, and could not be kept afloat more than a few minutes.

"Going down!—going down!" was spread with dreadful rapidity throughout the ship, and all discipline and subordination appeared to be at an end.

Some of the men flew to the boats hoisted up on the quarters, and were casting loose the ropes which secured them, with hands that were tremulous with anxiety and fear.

"Silence there, fore and aft!" roared the captain, in the full compass of his powerful voice. "Every man to his station. Come out of those boats directly."

All obeyed except one man, who still continued to cast loose the gripes.

"Come out, sir," repeated the captain.

"Not I, by G-d!" replied the sailor coolly.

The boarding-pikes, which had been lashed round the spanker-boom, had been detached, either from the shot of the enemy or some other means, and were lying on the deck close to the cabin skylight. The captain seizing one, and poising it brandished over his head, a third time ordered the sailor to leave the boat.

"Every man for himself, and God for us all!" was the cool answer of the refractory seaman.

The pike flew, and entered the man's bowels

up to the hilt. The poor wretch staggered, made a snatch at the davit, missed it, and fell backwards over the gunwale of the boat into the sea.

"My lads," said Captain M-, emphatically addressing the men, who beheld the scene with dismay, "as long as one plank, ay, one toothpick, of this vessel swims, I command, and will be obeyed. Quartermaster, put the helm up. I have but few words to say to you, my men. The vessel is sinking, and we must put her on the reef—boats are useless. If she hangs together, do you hang to her as your only chance. And now farewell, my brave fellows, for we are not all likely to meet again. Look out for a soft place for her, Mr. Pearce, if you can."

"I see but one spot where there is the least chance of her being thrown up, sir. Starboard a little—steady!—so," were the cool directions of the master, as the ship flew with increased velocity to her doom. The captain stood on the carronade slide, from which he had addressed the men. His mien was firm and erect—not a muscle of his countenance was observed to change or move, as the sailors watched it as the barometer of their fate. Awed by the dreadful punishment of the mutineer, and restrained by their long habits of discipline, they awaited their doom in a state of intense anxiety, but in silence.

All this latter description, however, was but the event of about two minutes—which had barely expired, when the frigate dashed upon the reef!

The shock threw the men off their feet as they raised an appealing cry to Heaven, which was mocked by the howling of the wind and the roar of the waters. The masts, which were thrown out from their steps, waved once, twice, and then fell over the sides with a crash, as an enormous sea broke over the vessel, forcing her further on the rocks, and causing every timber and knee in her to start from its place. The

masts, as they fell, and the sea, that at the same moment poured over like an impetuous cataract, swept away thirty or forty of the seamen into the boiling element under the lee. Another and another shock from the resistless and furious waves decided the fate of the resolute captain and master. The frigate parted amidships. The fore-part of her, which was firmly wedged on the rocks, remained. The quarter-deck and after-part turned over to the deep water, and disappeared. An enormous surge curled over it as it went down, and as if disappointed at not being able to wreak its fury upon that part of the vessel which, by sinking, had evaded it, it drove in revenge upon the remainder, forcing it several yards higher upon the reef.

Two-thirds of the ship's company were now gone—the captain, the master, and the major part of the officers and men being on the quarter-deck when the ship divided. The cry of the drowning was not heard amidst the roaring of the elements. The behaviour of the captain and the officers at this dreadful crisis has not been handed down; but if we may judge from what has already been narrated, they met their fate like British seamen.

This excerpt is taken from Chapters 51 through 54 of the 1896 combined edition of some of Marryat's works, excluding chapter headings and the classical quotes at the beginning of the chapters:

Marryat, Captain Frederick. *The King's Own*. In *The King's Own, The Pirate, The Three Cutters*. Illustrated Sterling Edition, with an introduction by W.L. Courtney. Boston: Dana Estes & Company, 1896.[7]

---

[7] McBooks Press has recently reprinted *The King's Own* as part of the Classics of Nautical Fiction Series. See Captain Frederick Marryat, *The King's Own*, Classics of Nautical Fiction Series (Ithaca: McBooks Press, 1999). For the relevant pages in both editions, see pages 347 through 360.

Suggested Readings

Hannay, David. *Life of Frederick Marryat*. New York: M. S. G. Haskell House, 1889.

Lloyd, Christopher. *Captain Marryat and the Old Navy*. London, Longmans, Green and Company, 1939.

Marryat, Frederick. *The King's Own*. Boston: D. Estes & Company, 1896.

Marryat, Florence. *The Life and Letters of Captain Marryat*. New York: D. Appleton, 1872.

Parascandola, Louis J. *Puzzled Which to Choose: Conflicting Socio-Political Views in the Works of Captain Frederick Marryat*. New York: Peter Lang Publishing, 1997.

Pocock, Tom. *Captain Marryat: Seaman, Writer and Adventurer*. Mechanicsburg: Stackpole Books, 2001.

Warner, Oliver. *Captain Marryat: A Rediscovery*. New York: Hyperion Press, 1979.

About the author

Lieutenant (junior grade) Joel Ira Holwitt graduated from the U.S. Naval Academy in 2003. He subsequently earned both a Master of Arts degree and a PhD in military history from The Ohio State University in 2005. A 2006 graduate of the U.S. Navy's Nuclear Power School, he is presently in the nuclear submarine officer training pipeline.

24

Consolation for Loss: President Lincoln's Letter to Mrs. Bixby

Dr. Joseph J. Thomas

The Tom Hanks movie *Saving Private Ryan* brought to the public's consciousness a simple letter from Abraham Lincoln to a grieving widow and mother of five sons lost in battle. The letter was penned at the White House on November 21, 1864. Its stark simplicity and compassion serve as a model for others tasked with the tragic duty of notifying next of kin. Fortunately for Mrs. Bixby, it was later determined that, in fact, "only" two of her sons had been killed. Two had deserted from their units and one was taken prisoner by the Confederates. Regardless of the exact number killed, her grief was addressed by an obviously sympathetic President Lincoln.

* * *

To Mrs Bixby, Boston, Mass.
Dear Madam,

I have been shown in the files of the War Department a statement of the Adjutant General of Massachusetts that you are the mother of five sons who have died glorious on the field of battle. I feel how weak and fruitless must be any word of mine which I should attempt to beguile you from the grief of a loss so overwhelming. But I cannot refrain from tendering you the consolation that may be found in the thanks of the Republic they died to save. I pray that our Heavenly Father may assuage the anguish of your bereavement, and leave you only the cherished memory of the loved and lost, and the solemn pride that must be yours to have laid so costly a sacrifice upon the altar of freedom.

Yours very sincerely and respectfully,
A. Lincoln

Suggested Readings

Basler, Roy P, ed., *Abraham Lincoln: His Speeches and Writings*. Cleveland: The World Publishing Co., 1946.

Hertz, Emanuel. *Abraham Lincoln, a New Portrait*. New York, H. Liveright, Inc., 1931.

25

Eulogy of a Fallen Leader: Walt Whitman's "O Captain! My Captain!"

Dr. Joseph J. Thomas

Walt Whitman was, in many ways the "father of American poetry." His collection *Leaves of Grass* was first published in 1855 and he continued to add poems to it as it was re-published throughout his life. He served as a nurse during the Civil War and many of his works are a reflection of that experience. His most famous poem, "O Captain! My Captain!" is a eulogy to Abraham Lincoln and was memorized by generations of American schoolchildren. It remains one of the most beloved American works of poetry.

> O Captain! my Captain! our fearful trip is
>   done,
> The ship has weather'd every rack, the prize
>   we sought is won,
> The port is near, the bells I hear, the people
>   all exulting,
> While follow eyes the steady keel, the vessel
>   grim and daring:
>   But O heart! heart! heart!
>   O the bleeding drops of red,
>   Where on the deck my Captain lies,
>   Fallen cold and dead.
>
> O Captain! my Captain! rise up and hear the
>   bells;
> Rise up—for you the flag is flung—for you
>   the bugle trills,
> For you the bouquets and ribbon'd
>   wreaths—for you the shores
> a-crowding,
> For you they call, the swaying mass, their
>   eager faces turning;
>   Hear Captain! dear father!
>   This arm beneath your head!
>   It is some dream that on the deck,
>   You've fallen cold and dead.
>
> My Captain does not answer, his lips are pale
>   and still,
> My father does not feel my arm, he has no
>   pulse nor will,

The ship is anchor'd safe and sound, its voy-
    age closed and done,
From fearful trip the victor ship comes in
    with object won;
        Exult, O shores, and ring, O bells!
        But I with mournful tread,
            Walk the deck my Captain lies,
                Fallen cold and dead.

Suggested Readings

Whitman, Walt. *The Civil War Poems*, New
York: Barnes and Noble, 1994.

26

Leadership Defuses Further Insurrection: General Robert E. Lee's Farewell to the Army of Northern Virginia

Dr. Joseph J. Thomas

Unlike his antagonist U.S. Grant, General Robert Edward Lee never wrote his memoirs, published accounts of the Civil War, or commissioned historians to capture his great speeches. Lee, called "the greatest soldier ever produced by the English-speaking peoples," by Winston Churchill, is primarily remembered as a man of action and unimpeachable character. More important to his legacy perhaps is his humble, effective means of encouraging rapprochement with his former enemy. Through simple word and deed, Lee helped repair the social and political fabric rent by the Great War of Rebellion. His brief farewell to his beloved Army of Northern Virginia on April 10, 1865 (issued as General Order No. 9) is a model of elegance and economy of words. This farewell was originally drafted by Colonel Charles Marshall but appeared "calculated to keep alive ill-feeling." Lee changed the language and tone of his farewell to promote good will among his loyal troops.

After four years of arduous service marked by unsurpassed courage and fortitude, the Army of Northern Virginia has been compelled to yield to overwhelming numbers and resources.

I need not tell the brave survivors of so many hard fought battles, who have remained steadfast to the last, that I have consented to this result from no distrust of them; but feeling that valor and devotion could accomplish nothing that could compensate for the loss that must have attended the continuance of the contest, I determined to avoid the useless sacrifice of those whose past services have endeared them to their countrymen.

By the terms of the agreement, officers and men can return to their homes and remain until exchanged. You will take with you the satisfaction that proceeds from the consciousness of duty faithfully performed; and I earnestly pray that a Merciful God will extend to you his blessing and protection.

With an unceasing admiration of your constancy and devotion to your Country, and a grateful remembrance of your kind and generous consideration for myself, I bid you all an affectionate farewell.

R.E. Lee

General

Suggested Reading

Freeman, Douglas S. *Lee's Lieutenants: A Study in Command*, New York: Charles Scribner and Sons, 1935.

Freeman, Douglas S. *R.E. Lee*. New York: Charles Scribner and Sons, 1935.

27

Lesson in Humility: Mark Twain's The Man That Corrupted Hadleyburg

Dr. Robert D. Madison

During his lifetime, Samuel Langhorne Clemens, alias Mark Twain (1835–1910), was America's favorite storyteller. His masterpiece, *Adventures of Huckleberry Finn*, reaches its moral climax when Huck decides to do the "wrong" thing and free Miss Watson's Jim: "All right, then, I'll *go* to hell!" Huck exclaims as he resists the temptation to tell Miss Watson the whereabouts of her "property":

It was awful thoughts, and awful words, but they was said. And I let them stay said; and never more thought about reforming. I shoved the whole thing out of my head; and said I would take up wickedness again, which was in my line, being brung up to it, and the other warn't. And for a starter, I would go to work and steal Jim out of slavery again; and if I could think up anything worse, I would do that, too; because as long as I was in, and in for good, I might as well go the whole hog.

Twain certainly didn't limit his irony to naive narrators like Huck. The title character of "The Man that Corrupted Hadleyburg" comes from a long tradition of tricksters who for good or ill impose their pernicious whims on unsuspecting communities. As in many other cases, it is the corruption itself that both exposes hypocrisy and teaches humility.

* * *

The Man That Corrupted Hadleyburg

It was many years ago. Hadleyburg was the most honest and upright town in all the region around about. It had kept that reputation unsmirched during three generations, and was prouder of it than of any other of its possessions. It was to proud of it, and so anxious to insure its perpetuation, that it began to teach the principles of honest dealing to its babies in the cradle, and made the like teachings the staple of their culture thenceforward through all the years de-

173

voted to their education. Also, throughout the formative years temptations were kept out of the way of the young people, so that their honesty could have every chance to harden and solidify, and become a part of their very bone. The neighboring towns were jealous of this honorable supremacy, and affected to sneer at Hadleyburg's pride in it and call it vanity; but all the same they were obliged to acknowledge that Hadleyburg was in reality an incorruptible town; and if pressed they would also acknowledge that the mere fact that a young man hailed from Hadleyburg was all the recommendation he needed when he went forth from his natal town to seek for responsible employment.

But at last, in the drift of time, Hadleyburg had the ill luck to offend a passing stranger—possibly without knowing it, certainly without caring, for Hadleyburg was sufficient unto itself, and cared not a rap for strangers or their opinions. Still, it would have been well to make an exception in this one's case, for he was a bitter man and revengeful. All through his wanderings during a whole year he kept his injury in mind, and gave all his leisure moments to trying to invent a compensating satisfaction for it. He contrived many plans, and all of them were good, but none of them was quite sweeping enough; the poorest of them would hurt a great many individuals, but what he wanted was a plan which would comprehend the entire town, and not let so much as one person escape unhurt. At last he had a fortunate idea, and when it fell into his brain it lit up his whole head with an evil joy. He began to form a plan at once, saying to himself, "That is the thing to do—I will corrupt the town."

Six months later he went to Hadleyburg, and arrived in a buggy at the house of the old cashier of the bank about ten at night. He got a sack out of the buggy, shouldered it, and staggered with it through the cottage yard, and knocked at the door. A woman's voice said "Come in," and he entered, and set his sack behind the stove in the parlor, saying politely to the old lady who sat reading the *Missionary Herald* by the lamp:

"Pray keep your seat, madam, I will not disturb you. There—now it is pretty well concealed; one would hardly know it was there. Can I see your husband a moment, madam?"

No, he was gone to Brixton, and might not return before morning.

"Very well, madam, it is no matter. I merely wanted to leave that sack in his care, to be delivered to the rightful owner when he shall be found. I am a stranger; he does not know me; I am merely passing through the town to-night to discharge a matter which has been long in my mind. My errand is now completed, and I go pleased and a little proud, and you will never see me again. There is a paper attached to the sack which will explain everything. Good night, madam."

The old lady was afraid of the mysterious big stranger, and was glad to see him go. But her curiosity was roused, and she went straight to the sack and brought away the paper. It began as follows:

TO BE PUBLISHED; *or, the right man sought out by private inquiry—either will answer. This sack contains gold coin weighing a hundred and sixty pounds four ounces—*

"Mercy on us, and the door not locked!"

Mrs. Richards flew to it all in a tremble and locked it, then pulled down the window-shades and stood frightened, worried, and wondering if there was anything else she could do toward making herself and the money more safe. She listened awhile for burglars, then surrendered to curiosity and went back to the lamp and finished reading the paper:

I am a foreigner, and am presently going back to my own country, to remain there permanently. I am grateful to America for what I have received at her hands during my long stay under her flag; and to one of her citizens—a citizen of Hadleyburg—I am especially grateful for a great kindness done me a year or two ago. Two great kindnesses, in fact. I will explain. I was a gambler. I say I WAS. I was a ruined gambler. I arrived in this village at night, hungry and without a penny. I asked for help—in the dark; I was ashamed to beg in the light. I begged of the right man. He gave me twenty dollars—that is to say, he gave me life, as I considered it. He also gave me fortune; for out of that money I have made myself rich at the gaming-table. And finally, a remark which he made to me has remained with me to this day, and has at last conquered me; and in conquering has saved the remnant of my morals; I shall gamble no more. Now I have no idea who that man was, but I want him found, and I want him to have this money, to give away, throw away, or keep, as he pleases. It is merely my way of testifying my gratitude to him. If I could stay, I would find him myself; but no matter, he will be found. This is an honest town, an incorruptible town, and I know I can trust it without fear. This man can be identified by the remark which he made to me; I feel persuaded that he will remember it.

And now my plan is this: If you prefer to conduct the inquiry privately, do so. Tell the contents of this present writing to any one who is likely to be the right man. If he shall answer, 'I am the man; the remark I made was so-and-so,' apply the test—to wit: open the sack, and in it you will find a sealed envelope containing that remark. If the remark mentioned by the candidate tallies with it, give him the money, and ask no further questions, for he is certainly the right man.

But if you shall prefer a public inquiry, then publish this present writing in the local paper—with these instructions added, to wit: Thirty days from now, let the candidate appear at the town-hall at eight in the evening (Friday), and hand his remark, in a sealed envelope, to the Rev. Mr. Burgess (if he will be kind enough to act); and let Mr. Burgess there and then destroy the seals of the sack, open it, and see if the remark is correct; if correct, let the money be delivered with my sincere gratitude, to my benefactor thus identified.

Mrs. Richards sat down, gently quivering with excitement, and was soon lost in thinkings—after this pattern: "What a strange thing it is! . . . And what a fortune for that kind man who set his bread afloat upon the waters! . . . If it had only been my husband that did it!—for we are so poor, so old and poor! . . ." Then, with a sigh—"But it was not my Edward; no, it was not he that

gave a stranger twenty dollars. It is pity, too; I see it now. . . ." Then, with a shudder—"But it is *gambler's* money! the wages of sin: we couldn't take it; we couldn't touch it. I don't like to be near it; it seems a defilement." She moved to a farther chair. . . . "I wish Edward would come and take it to the bank; a burglar might come at any moment; it is dreadful to be here all alone with it."

At eleven Mr. Richards arrived, and while his wife was saying, "I am *so* glad you've come!" he was saying, "I'm so tired—tired clear out; it is dreadful to be poor, and have to make these dismal journeys at my time of life. Always at the grind, grind, grind, on a salary—another man's slave, and he sitting at home in his slippers, rich and comfortable."

"I am so sorry for you, Edward, you know that; but be comforted: we have our livelihood; we have our good name—"

"Yes, Mary, and that is everything. Don't mind my talk—it's just a moment's irritation and doesn't mean anything. Kiss me—there, it's all gone now, and I am not complaining any more. What have you been getting? What's in the sack?"

Then his wife told him the great secret. It dazed him for a moment; then he said:

"It weighs a hundred and sixty pounds? Why, Mary, it's for-ty thousand dollars—think of it—a whole fortune! Not ten men in this village are worth that much. Give me the paper."

He skimmed through it and said:

"Isn't it an adventure! Why, it's a romance; it's like the impossible things one reads about in books, and never sees in life." He was well stirred up now; cheerful, even gleeful. He tapped his old wife on the cheek, and said, humorously, "Why, we're rich; Mary, rich; all we've got to do is to bury the money and burn the papers. If the gambler ever comes to inquire, we'll merely look coldly upon him and say: 'What is this nonsense you are talking! We have never heard of you and your sack of gold before'; and then he would look foolish, and—"

"And in the mean time, while you are running

on with your jokes, the money is still here, and it is fast getting along toward burglar-time."

"True. Very well, what shall we do—make the inquiry private? No, not that; it would spoil the romance. The public method is better. Think what a noise it will make! And it will make all the other towns jealous; for no stranger would trust such a thing to any town but Hadleyburg, and they know it. It's a great card for us. I must get to the printing-office now, or I shall be too late."

"But stop—stop—don't leave me here alone with it, Edward!"

But he was gone. For only a little while, however. Not far from his own house he met the editor-proprietor of the paper, and gave him the document, and said, "Here is a good thing for you, Cox—put it in."

"It may be too late, Mr. Richards, but I'll see."

At home again he and his wife sat down to talk the charming mystery over; they were in no condition for sleep. The first question was, Who could the citizen have been who gave the stranger the twenty dollars? It seemed a simple one; both answered it in the same breath:

"Barclay Goodson."

"Yes," said Richards, "he could have done it, and it would have been like him, but there's not another in the town."

"Everybody will grant that, Edward—grant it privately, anyway. For six months, now, the village has been its own proper self once more—honest, narrow, self-righteous, and stingy."

"It is what he always called it, to the day of his death—said it right out publicly, too."

"Yes, and he was hated for it."

"Oh, of course; but he didn't care. I reckon he was the best-hated man among us, except the Reverend Burgess."

"Well, Burgess deserves it—he will never get another congregation here. Mean as the town is, it knows how to estimate *him*. Edward, doesn't it seem odd that the stranger should appoint Burgess to deliver the money?"

"Well, yes—it does. That is—that is—"

"Why so much that-*is*-ing? Would *you* select him?"

"Mary, maybe the stranger knows him better than this village does."

"Much *that* would help Burgess!"

The husband seemed perplexed for an answer; the wife kept a steady eye upon him, and waited. Finally Richards said, with the hesitancy of one who is making a statement which is likely to encounter doubt:

"Mary, Burgess is not a bad man."

His wife was certainly surprised.

"Nonsense!" she exclaimed.

"He is not a bad man. I know. The whole of his unpopularity had its foundation in that one thing—the thing that made so much noise."

"That 'one thing,' indeed! As if that 'one thing' wasn't enough, all by itself."

"Plenty. Plenty. Only he wasn't guilty of it."

"How you talk! Not guilty of it! Everybody knows he *was* guilty."

"Mary, I give you my word—he was innocent."

"I can't believe it, and I don't. How do you know?"

"It is a confession. I am ashamed, but I will make it. I was the only man who knew he was innocent. I could have saved him, and—and—well, you know how the town was wrought up—I hadn't the pluck to do it. It would have turned everybody against me. I felt mean, ever so mean; but I didn't dare; I hadn't the manliness to face that."

Mary looked troubled, and for a while was silent. Then she said, stammeringly:

"I—I don't think it would have done for you to—to—One mustn't—er—public opinion—one has to be so careful—so—" It was a difficult road, and she got mired; but after a little she got started again. "It was a great pity, but—Why, we couldn't afford it, Edward—we couldn't indeed. Oh, I wouldn't have had you do it for anything!"

"It would have lost us the good will of so many people, Mary; and then—and then—"

"What troubles me now is, what *he* thinks of us, Edward."

"He? *He* doesn't suspect that I could have saved him."

"Oh," exclaimed the wife, in a tone of relief, "I am glad of that! As long as he doesn't know that you could have saved him, he—he—well, that makes it a great deal better. Why, I might have known he didn't know, because he is always trying to be friendly with us, as little encouragement as we give him. More than once people have twitted me with it. There's the Wilsons, and the Wilcoxes, and the Harknesses, they take a mean pleasure in saying, '*Your friend* Burgess,' because they know it pesters me. I wish he wouldn't persist in liking us so; I can't think why he keeps it up."

"I can explain it. It's another confession. When the thing was new and hot, and the town made a plan to ride him on a rail, my conscience hurt me so that I couldn't stand it, and I went privately and gave him notice, and he got out of the town and staid out till it was safe to come back."

"Edward! If the town had found it out—"

"*Don't!* It scares me yet, to think of it. I repented of it the minute it was done; and I was even afraid to tell you, lest your face might betray it to somebody. I didn't sleep any that night, for worrying. But after a few days I saw that no one was going to suspect me, and after that I got to feeling glad I did it. And I feel glad yet, Mary—glad through and through."

"So do I, now, for it would have been a dreadful way to treat him. Yes, I'm glad; for really you did owe him that, you know. But, Edward, suppose it should come out yet, some day!"

"It won't."

"Why?"

"Because everybody thinks it was Goodson."

"Of course they would!"

"Certainly. And of course *he* didn't care. They persuaded poor old Sawlsberry to go and charge it on him, and he went blustering over there and did it. Goodson looked him over, like as if he was hunting for a place on him that he could despise the most, then he says, 'So you are the Committee of Inquiry, are you?' Sawlsberry said that was about what he was. 'Hm. Do they require particulars, or do you reckon a kind of a *general* answer

will do?' 'If they require particulars, I will come back, Mr. Goodson; I will take the general answer first.' 'Very well, then, tell them to go to hell—I reckon that's general enough. And I'll give you some advice, Sawlsberry; when you come back for the particulars, fetch a basket to carry the relics of yourself home in.'"

"Just like Goodson; it's got all the marks. He had only one vanity: he thought he could give advice better than any other person."

"It settled the business, and saved us, Mary. The subject was dropped."

"Bless you, I'm not doubting *that*."

Then they took up the gold-sack mystery again, with strong interest. Soon the conversation began to suffer breaks—interruptions caused by absorbed thinkings. The breaks grew more and more frequent. At last Richards lost himself wholly in thought. He sat long, gazing vacantly at the floor, and by and by he began to punctuate his thoughts with little nervous movements of his hands that seemed to indicate vexation. Meantime his wife too had relapsed into a thoughtful silence, and her movements were beginning to show a troubled discomfort. Finally Richards got up and strode aimlessly about the room, plowing his hands through his hair, much as a somnambulist might do who was having a bad dream. Then he seemed to arrive at a definite purpose; and without a word he put on his hat and passed quickly out of the house. His wife sat brooding, with a drawn face, and did not seem to be aware that she was alone. Now and then she murmured, "Lead us not into t—. . . but—but—we are so poor, so poor! . . . Lead us not into . . . Ah, who would be hurt by it?—and no one would ever know. . . . Lead us . . ." The voice died out in mumblings. After a little she glanced up and muttered in a half-frightened, half-glad way:

"He is gone! But, oh dear, he may be too late—too late. . . . Maybe not—maybe there is still time." She rose and stood thinking, nervously clasping and unclasping her hands. A slight shudder shook her frame, and she said, out of a dry throat, "God forgive me—it's awful to think such things—but ... Lord, how we are made—how strangely we are made!"

She turned the light low, and slipped stealthily over and kneeled down by the sack and felt of its ridgy sides with her hands, and fondled them lovingly; and there was a gloating light in her poor old eyes. She fell into fits of absence; and came half out of them at times to mutter, "If we had only waited!—oh, if we had only waited a little, and not been in such a hurry!"

Meantime Cox had gone home from his office and told his wife all about the strange thing that had happened, and they had talked it over eagerly, and guessed that the late Goodson was the only man in the town who could have helped a suffering stranger with so noble a sum as twenty dollars. Then there was a pause, and the two became thoughtful and silent. And by and by nervous and fidgety. At last the wife said, as if to herself:

"Nobody knows this secret but the Richardses ... and us ... nobody."

The husband came out of his thinkings with a slight start, and gazed wistfully at his wife, whose face was become very pale; then he hesitatingly rose, and glanced furtively at his hat, then at his wife—a sort of mute inquiry. Mrs. Cox swallowed once or twice, with her hand at her throat, then in place of speech she nodded her head. In a moment she was alone, and mumbling to herself.

And now Richards and Cox were hurrying through the deserted streets, from opposite directions. They met, panting, at the foot of the printing-office stairs; by the night light there they read each other's face. Cox whispered:

"Nobody knows about this but us?"

The whispered answer was,

"Not a soul—on honor, not a soul!"

"If it isn't too late to—"

The men were starting up-stairs; at this moment they were overtaken by a boy, and Cox asked:

"Is that you, Johnny?"

"Yes, sir."

"You needn't ship the early mail—nor *any* mail; wait till I tell you."

"It's already gone, sir."

"*Gone?*" It had the sound of an unspeakable disappointment in it.

"Yes, sir. Time-table for Brixton and all the towns beyond changed to-day, sir—had to get the papers in twenty minutes earlier than common. I had to rush; if I had been two minutes later—"

The men turned and walked slowly away, not waiting to hear the rest. Neither of them spoke during ten minutes; then Cox said, in a vexed tone:

"What possessed you to be in such a hurry, *I* can't make out."

The answer was humble enough:

"I see it now, but somehow I never thought, you know, until it was too late. But the next time—"

"Next time be hanged! It won't come in a thousand years."

Then the friends separated without a good night, and dragged themselves home with the gait of mortally stricken men. At their homes their wives sprang up with an eager "Well?"— then saw the answer with their eyes and sank down sorrowing, without waiting for it to come in words. In both houses a discussion followed of a heated sort—a new thing; there had been discussions before, but not heated ones, not ungentle ones. The discussions to-night were a sort of seeming plagiarisms of each other. Mrs. Richards said,

"If you had only waited, Edward—if you had only stopped to think; but no, you must run straight to the printing-office and spread it all over the world."

"It *said* publish it."

"That is nothing; it also said do it privately, if you liked. There, now—is that true, or not?"

"Why, yes—yes, it is true; but when I thought what stir it would make, and what a compliment it was to Hadleyburg that a stranger should trust it so—"

"Oh, certainly, I know all that; but if you had only stopped to think, you would have seen that you *couldn't* find the right man, because he is in his grave, and hasn't left chick nor child nor relation behind him; and as long as the money went to somebody that awfully needed it, and nobody would be hurt by it, and—and—"

She broke down, crying. Her husband tried to think of some comforting thing to say, and presently came out with this:

"But after all, Mary, it must be for the best—it *must* be; we know that. And we must remember that it was so ordered—"

"Ordered! Oh, everything's *ordered*, when a person has to find some way out when he has been stupid. Just the same, it was *ordered* that the money should come to us in this special way, and it was you that must take it on yourself to go meddling with the designs of Providence—and who gave you the right? It was wicked, that is what it was—just blasphemous presumption, and no more becoming to a meek and humble professor of—"

"But, Mary, you know how we have been trained all our lives long, like the whole village, till it is absolutely second nature to us to stop not a single moment to think when there's an honest thing to be done—"

"Oh, I know it, I know it—it's been one everlasting training and training and training in honesty—honesty shielded, from the very cradle, against every possible temptation, and so it's *artificial* honesty, and weak as water when temptation comes, as we have seen this night. God knows I never had shade nor shadow of a doubt of my petrified and indestructible honesty until now—and now, under the very first big and real temptation, I—Edward, it is my belief that this town's honesty is as rotten as mine is; as rotten as yours is. It is a mean town, a hard, stingy town, and hasn't a virtue in the world but this honesty it is so celebrated for and so conceited about; and so help me, I do believe that if ever the day comes that its honesty falls under great temptation, its grand reputation will go to ruin like a

house of cards. There, now, I've made confession, and I feel better; I am a humbug, and I've been one all my life, without knowing it. Let no man call me honest again—I will not have it."

"I—well, Mary, I feel a good deal as you do; I certainly do. It seems strange, too, so strange. I never could have believed it—never."

A long silence followed; both were sunk in thought. At last the wife looked up and said:

"I know what you are thinking, Edward."

Richards had the embarrassed look of a person who is caught.

"I am ashamed to confess it, Mary, but—"

"It's no matter, Edward, I was thinking the same question myself."

"I hope so. State it."

"You were thinking, if a body could only guess out *what the remark was* that Goodson made to the stranger."

"It's perfectly true. I feel guilty and ashamed. And you?"

"I'm past it. Let us make a pallet here; we've got to stand watch till the bank vault opens in the morning and admits the sack. . . . Oh dear, oh dear—if we hadn't made the mistake!"

The pallet was made, and Mary said:

"The open sesame—what could it have been? I do wonder what that remark could have been? But come; we will get to bed now."

"And sleep?"

"No: think."

"Yes, think."

By this time the Coxes too had completed their spat and their reconciliation, and were turning in—to think, to think, and toss, and fret, and worry over what the remark could possibly have been which Goodson made to the stranded derelict; that golden remark; that remark worth forty thousand dollars, cash.

The reason that the village telegraph-office was open later than usual that night was this: The foreman of Cox's paper was the local representative of the Associated Press. One might say its honorary representative, for it wasn't four times a year that he could furnish thirty words that would be accepted. But this time it was different. His despatch stating what he had caught got an instant answer:

Send the whole thing—all the details—twelve hundred words.

A colossal order! The foreman filled the bill; and he was the proudest man in the State. By breakfast-time the next morning the name of Hadleyburg the Incorruptible was on every lip in America, from Montreal to the Gulf, from the glaciers of Alaska to the orange-groves of Florida; and millions and millions of people were discussing the stranger and his money-sack, and wondering if the right man would be found, and hoping some more news about the matter would come soon—right away.

2

Hadleyburg village woke up world-celebrated—astonished—happy—vain. Vain beyond imagination. Its nineteen principal citizens and their wives went about shaking hands with each other, and beaming, and smiling, and congratulating, and saying *this* thing adds a new word to the dictionary—*Hadleyburg,* synonym for *incorruptible*—destined to live in dictionaries forever! And the minor and unimportant citizens and their wives went around acting in much the same way. Everybody ran to the bank to see the gold-sack; and before noon grieved and envious crowds began to flock in from Brixton and all neighboring towns; and that afternoon and next day reporters began to arrive from everywhere to verify the sack and its history and write the whole thing up anew, and make dashing free-hand pictures of the sack, and of Richards's house, and the bank, and the Presbyterian church, and the Baptist church, and the public square, and the town-hall where the test would be applied and the money delivered; and damnable portraits of the Richardses, and Pinkerton the banker, and Cox, and the foreman, and Reverend Burgess, and the postmaster—and even of Jack Halliday, who was the

loafing, good-natured, no-account, irreverent fisherman, hunter, boys' friend, stray-dogs' friend, typical "Sam Lawson" of the town. The little mean, smirking, oily Pinkerton showed the sack to all comers, and rubbed his sleek palms together pleasantly, and enlarged upon the town's fine old reputation for honesty and upon this wonderful indorsement of it, and hoped and believed that the example would now spread far and wide over the American world, and be epoch-making in the matter of moral regeneration. And so on, and so on.

By the end of a week things had quieted down again; the wild intoxication of pride and joy had sobered to a soft, sweet, silent delight—a sort of deep, nameless, unutterable content. All faces bore a look of peaceful, holy happiness.

Then a change came. It was a gradual change: so gradual that its beginnings were hardly noticed; maybe were not noticed at all, except by Jack Halliday, who always noticed everything; and always made fun of it, too, no matter what it was. He began to throw out chaffing remarks about people not looking quite so happy as they did a day or two ago; and next he claimed that the new aspect was deepening to positive sadness; next, that it was taking on a sick look; and finally he said that everybody was become so moody, thoughtful, and absentminded that he could rob the meanest man in town of a cent out of the bottom of his breeches pocket and not disturb his revery.

At this stage—or at about this stage—a saying like this was dropped at bedtime—with a sigh, usually—by the head of each of the nineteen principal households: "Ah, what *could* have been the remark that Goodson made?"

And straightway—with a shudder—came this, from the man's wife:

"Oh, *don't!* What horrible thing are you mulling in your mind? Put it away from you, for God's sake!"

But that question was wrung from those men again the next night—and got the same retort. But weaker.

And the third night the men uttered the question yet again—with anguish, and absently. This time—and the following night—the wives fidgeted feebly, and tried to say something. But didn't.

And the night after that they found their tongues and responded—longingly:

"Oh, if we *could* only guess!"

Halliday's comments grew daily more and more sparklingly disagreeable and disparaging. He went diligently about, laughing at the town, individually and in mass. But his laugh was the only one left in the village: it fell upon a hollow and mournful vacancy and emptiness. Not even a smile was findable anywhere. Halliday carried a cigar-box around on a tripod, playing that it was a camera, and halted all passers and aimed the thing and said, "Ready!—now look pleasant, please," but not even this capital joke could surprise the dreary faces into any softening.

So three weeks passed—one week was left. It was Saturday evening—after supper. Instead of the aforetime Saturday-evening flutter and bustle and shopping and larking, the streets were empty and desolate. Richards and his old wife sat apart in their little parlor—miserable and thinking. This was become their evening habit now: the lifelong habit which had preceded it, of reading, knitting, and contented chat, or receiving or paying neighborly calls, was dead and gone and forgotten, ages ago—two or three weeks ago; nobody talked now, nobody read, nobody visited—the whole village sat at home, sighing, worrying, silent. Trying to guess out that remark.

The postman left a letter. Richards glanced listlessly at the superscription and the postmark—unfamiliar, both—and tossed the letter on the table and resumed his might-have-beens and his hopeless dull miseries where he had left them off. Two or three hours later his wife got wearily up and was going away to bed without a good night—custom now—but she stopped near the letter and eyed it awhile with a dead interest, then broke it open, and began to skim it over.

Richards, sitting there with his chair tilted back against the wall and his chin between his knees, heard something fall. It was his wife. He sprang to her side, but she cried out:

"Leave me alone, I am too happy. Read the letter—read it!"

He did. He devoured it, his brain reeling. The letter was from a distant state, and it said:

I am a stranger to you, but no matter: I have something to tell. I have just arrived home from Mexico, and learned about that episode. Of course you do not know who made that remark, but I know, and I am the only person living who does know. It was GOODSON. *I knew him well, many years ago. I passed through your village that very night, and was his guest till the midnight train came along. I overheard him make that remark to the stranger in the dark—it was in Hale Alley. He and I talked of it the rest of the way home, and while smoking in his house. He mentioned many of your villagers in the course of his talk—most of them in a very uncomplimentary way, but two or three favorably; among these latter yourself. I say "favorably"—nothing stronger. I remember his saying he did not actually* LIKE *any person in the town—not one; but that you—I* THINK *he said you—am almost sure—had done him a very great service once, possibly without knowing the full value of it, and he wished he had a fortune, he would leave it to you when he died, and a curse apiece for the rest of the citizens. Now, then, if it was you that did him that service, you are his legitimate heir, and entitled to the sack of gold. I know that I can trust to your honor and honesty, for in a citizen of Hadleyburg these virtues are an unfailing inheritance, and so I am going to reveal to you the remark, well satisfied that if you are not the right man you will seek and find the right one and see that poor Goodson's debt of gratitude for the service referred to is paid. This is the remark:* "YOU ARE FAR FROM BEING A BAD MAN: GO, AND REFORM."

HOWARD L. STEPHENSON

"Oh, Edward, the money is ours, and I am so grateful, *oh*, so grateful—kiss me, dear, it's forever since we kissed—and we needed it so—the money—and now you are free of Pinkerton and his bank, and nobody's slave any more; it seems to me I could fly for joy."

It was a happy half-hour that the couple spent there on the settee caressing each other; it was the old days come again—days that had begun with their courtship and lasted without a break till the stranger brought the deadly money. By and by the wife said:

"Oh, Edward, how lucky it was you did him that grand service, poor Goodson! I never liked him, but I love him now. And it was fine and beautiful of you never to mention it or brag about it." Then, with a touch of reproach, "But you ought to have told *me*, Edward, you ought to have told your wife, you know."

"Well, I—er—well, Mary, you see—"

"Now stop hemming and hawing, and tell me about it, Edward. I always loved you, and now I'm proud of you. Everybody believes there was only one good generous soul in this village, and now it turns out that you—Edward, why don't you tell me?"

"Well—er—er—Why, Mary, I can't!"

"You *can't? Why* can't you?"

"You see, he—well, he—he made me promise I wouldn't."

The wife looked him over, and said, very slowly:

"Made—you—promise? Edward, what do you tell me that for?"

"Mary, do you think I would lie?"

She was troubled and silent for a moment, then she laid her hand within his and said:

"No . . . no. We have wandered far enough from our bearings—God spare us that! In all your life you have never uttered a lie. But now— now that the foundations of things seem to be crumbling from under us, we—we—"She lost her voice for a moment, then said, brokenly, "Lead us not into temptation. . . . I think you made the promise, Edward. Let it rest so. Let us keep away from that ground. Now—that is all gone by; let us be happy again; it is no time for clouds."

Edward found it something of an effort to comply, for his mind kept wandering—trying to remember what the service was that he had done Goodson.

The couple lay awake the most of the night, Mary happy and busy, Edward busy but not so happy. Mary was planning what she would do with the money. Edward was trying to recall that service. At first his conscience was sore on account of the lie he had told Mary—if it was a lie. After much reflection—suppose it *was* a lie? What then? Was it such a great matter? Aren't we always *acting* lies? Then why not *tell* them? Look at Mary—look what she had done. While he was hurrying off on his honest errand, what was she doing? Lamenting because the papers hadn't been destroyed and the money kept! Is theft better than lying?

That point lost its sting—the lie dropped into the background and left comfort behind it. The next point came to the front: *Had* he rendered that service? Well, here was Goodson's own evidence as reported in Stephenson's letter; there could be no better evidence than that—it was even *proof* that he had rendered it. Of course. So that point was settled. . . .

No, not quite. He recalled with a wince that this unknown Mr. Stephenson was just a trifle unsure as to whether the performer of it was Richards or some other—and, oh dear, he had put Richards on his honor! He must himself decide whither that money must go—and Mr. Stephenson was not doubting that if he was the wrong man he would go honorably and find the right one. Oh, it was odious to put a man in such a situation—ah, why couldn't Stephenson have left out that doubt! What did he want to intrude that for?

Further reflection. How did it happen that *Richards's* name remained in Stephenson's mind as indicating the right man, and not some other man's name? That looked good. Yes, that looked very good. In fact, it went on looking better and better, straight along—until by and by it grew into positive *proof*. And then Richards put the matter at once out of his mind, for he had a private instinct that a proof once established is better left so.

He was feeling reasonably comfortable now, but there was still one other detail that kept pushing itself on his notice: of course he had done that service—that was settled; but what *was* that service? He must recall it—he would not go to sleep till he had recalled it; it would make his peace of mind perfect. And so he thought and thought. He thought of a dozen things—possible services, even probable services—but none of them seemed adequate, none of them seemed large enough, none of them seemed worth the money—worth the fortune Goodson had wished he could leave in his will. And besides, he couldn't remember having done them, anyway. Now, then—now, then—what *kind* of a service would it be that would make a man so inordinately grateful? Ah—the saving of his soul! That must be it. Yes, he could remember, now, how he once set himself the task of converting Goodson, and labored at it as much as—he was going to say three months; but upon closer examination it shrunk to a month, then to a week, then to a day, then to nothing. Yes, he remembered now, and with unwelcome vividness, that Goodson had told him to go to thunder and mind his own business—*he* wasn't hankering to follow Hadleyburg to heaven!

So that solution was a failure—he hadn't saved Goodson's soul. Richards was discouraged. Then after a little came another idea: had he saved Goodson's property? No, that wouldn't do—he hadn't any. His life? That is it! Of course. Why, he might have thought of it before. This time he was on the right track, sure. His imagination-mill was hard at work in a minute, now.

Thereafter during a stretch of two exhausting hours he was busy saving Goodson's life. He saved it in all kinds of difficult and perilous ways. In every case he got it saved satisfactorily up to a certain point; then, just as he was beginning to get well persuaded that it had really happened, a troublesome detail would turn up which made the whole thing impossible. As in the matter of drowning, for instance. In that case he had swum out and tugged Goodson ashore in an unconscious state with a great crowd looking on and applauding, but when he had got it all thought out and was just beginning to remember all about it, a whole swarm of disqualifying details arrived on the ground: the town would have known of the circumstance, Mary would have known of it, it would glare like a limelight in his own memory instead of being an inconspicuous service which he had possibly rendered "without knowing its full value." And at this point he remembered that he couldn't swim, anyway.

Ah—*there* was a point which he had been overlooking from the start: it had to be a service which he had rendered "possibly without knowing the full value of it." Why, really, that ought to be an easy hunt—much easier than those others. And sure enough, by and by he found it. Goodson, years and years ago, came near marrying a very sweet and pretty girl, named Nancy Hewitt, but in some way or other the match had been broken off; the girl died, Goodson remained a bachelor, and by and by became a soured one and a frank despiser of the human species. Soon after the girl's death the village found out, or thought it had found out, that she carried a spoonful of negro blood in her veins. Richards worked at these details a good while, and in the end he thought he remembered things concerning them which must have gotten mislaid in his memory through long neglect. He seemed to dimly remember that it was *he* that found out about the negro blood; that it was he that told the village; that the village told Goodson where they got it; that he thus saved Goodson from marrying the tainted girl; that he had done him this great service "without knowing the full value of it," in fact without knowing that he *was* doing it; but that Goodson knew the value of it, and what a narrow escape he had had, and so went to his grave grateful to his benefactor and wishing he had a fortune to leave him. It was all clear and simple now, and the more he went over it the more luminous and certain it grew; and at last, when he nestled to sleep satisfied and happy, he remembered the whole thing just as if it had been yesterday. In fact, he dimly remembered Goodson's *telling* him his gratitude once. Meantime Mary had spent six thousand dollars on a new house for herself and a pair of slippers for her pastor, and then had fallen peacefully to rest.

That same Saturday evening the postman had delivered a letter to each of the other principal citizens—nineteen letters in all. No two of the envelopes were alike, and no two of the superscriptions were in the same hand, but the letters inside were just like each other in every detail but one. They were exact copies of the letter received by Richards—handwriting and all—and were all signed by Stephenson, but in place of Richard's name each receiver's own name appeared.

All night long eighteen principal citizens did what their caste-brother Richards was doing at the same time—they put in their energies trying to remember what notable service it was that they had unconsciously done Barclay Goodson. In no case was it a holiday job; still they succeeded.

And while they were at this work, which was difficult, their wives put in the night spending the money, which was easy. During that one night the nineteen wives spent an average of seven thousand dollars each out of the forty thousand in the sack—a hundred and thirty-three thousand altogether.

Next day there was a surprise for Jack Halliday. He noticed that the faces of the nineteen chief citizens and their wives bore that expression of peaceful and holy happiness again. He could not understand it, neither was he able to invent any remarks about it that could damage it or disturb it. And so it was his turn to be dissatisfied with life. His private guesses at the reasons for the happiness failed in all instances, upon examination. When he met Mrs. Wilcox and noticed the placid ecstasy in her face, he said to himself, "Her cat has had kittens"—and went and asked the cook: it was not so; the cook had detected the happiness, but did not know the cause. When Halliday found the duplicate ecstasy in the face of "Shadbelly" Billson (village

nickname), he was sure some neighbor of Billson's had broken his leg, but inquiry showed that this had not happened. The subdued ecstasy in Gregory Yates's face could mean but one thing—he was a mother-in-law short: it was another mistake. "And Pinkerton—Pinkerton—he has collected ten cents that he thought he was going to lose." And so on, and so on. In some cases the guesses had to remain in doubt, in the others they proved distinct errors. In the end Halliday said to himself, "Anyway it foots up that there's nineteen Hadleyburg families temporarily in heaven: I don't know how it happened; I only know Providence is off duty to-day."

An architect and builder from the next state had lately ventured to set up a small business in this unpromising village, and his sign had now been hanging out a week. Not a customer yet; he was a discouraged man, and sorry he had come. But his weather changed suddenly now. First one and then another chief citizen's wife said to him privately:

"Come to my house Monday week—but say nothing about it for the present. We think of building."

He got eleven invitations that day. That night he wrote his daughter and broke off her match with her student. He said she could marry a mile higher than that.

Pinkerton the banker and two or three other well-to-do men planned country-seats—but waited. That kind don't count their chickens until they are hatched.

The Wilsons devised a grand new thing—a fancy-dress ball. They made no actual promises, but told all their acquaintanceship in confidence that they were thinking the matter over and thought they should give it—"and if we do, you will be invited, of course." People were surprised, and said, one to another, "Why, they are crazy, those poor Wilsons, they can't afford it." Several among the nineteen said privately to their husbands, "It is a good idea: we will keep still till their cheap thing is over, then *we* will give one that will make it sick."

The days drifted along, and the bill of future

squanderings rose higher and higher, wilder and wilder, more and more foolish and reckless. It began to look as if every member of the nineteen would not only spend his whole forty thousand dollars before receiving-day, but be actually in debt by the time he got the money. In some cases light-headed people did not stop with planning to spend, they really spent—on credit. They bought land, mortgages, farms, speculative stocks, fine clothes, horses, and various other things, paid down the bonus, and made themselves liable for the rest—at ten days. Presently the sober second thought came, and Halliday noticed that a ghastly anxiety was beginning to show up in a good many faces. Again he was puzzled, and didn't know what to make of it. "The Wilcox kittens aren't dead, for they weren't born; nobody's broken a leg; there's no shrinkage in mother-in-laws; *nothing* has happened—it is an unsolvable mystery."

There was another puzzled man, too—the Rev. Mr. Burgess. For days, wherever he went, people seemed to follow him or to be watching out for him; and if he ever found himself in a retired spot, a member of the nineteen would be sure to appear, thrust an envelope privately into his hand, whisper "To be opened at the town-hall Friday evening," then vanish away like a guilty thing. He was expecting that there might be one claimant for the sack—doubtful, however, Goodson being dead—but it never occurred to him that all this crowd might be claimants. When the great Friday came at last, he found that he had nineteen envelopes.

3

The town-hall had never looked finer. The platform at the end of it was backed by a showy draping of flags; at intervals along the walls were festoons of flags; the gallery fronts were clothed in flags; the supporting columns were swathed in flags; all this was to impress the stranger, for he would be there in considerable force, and in a large degree he would be connected with the press. The house was full. The 412 fixed seats were occupied; also the 68 extra chairs which had been packed into the aisles; the steps of the platform were occupied; some distinguished strangers were given seats on the platform; at the horseshoe of tables which fenced the front and sides of the platform sat a strong force of special correspondents who had come from everywhere. It was the best-dressed house the town had ever produced. There were some tolerably expensive toilets there, and in several cases the ladies who wore them had the look of being unfamiliar with that kind of clothes. At least the town thought they had that look, but the notion could have arisen from the town's knowledge of the fact that these ladies had never inhabited such clothes before.

The gold-sack stood on a little table at the front of the platform where all the house could see it. The bulk of the house gazed at it with a burning interest, a mouth-watering interest, a wistful and pathetic interest; a minority of nineteen couples gazed at it tenderly, lovingly, proprietarily, and the male half of this minority kept saying over to themselves the moving little impromptu speeches of thankfulness for the audience's applause and congratulations which they were presently going to get up and deliver. Every now and then one of these got a piece of paper out of his vest pocket and privately glanced at it to refresh his memory.

Of course there was a buzz of conversation going on—there always is; but at last when the Rev. Mr. Burgess rose and laid his hand on the sack he could hear his microbes gnaw, the place was so still. He related the curious history of the sack, then went on to speak in warm terms of Hadleyburg's old and well-earned reputation for spotless honesty, and of the town's just pride in this reputation. He said that this reputation was a treasure of priceless value; that under Providence its value had now become inestimably enhanced, for the recent episode had spread this fame far and wide, and thus had focused the eyes of the American world upon this village, and made its name for all time, as he hoped and believed, a synonym for commercial incorruptibility. [*Applause.*] "And who is to be the guardian of this noble treasure—the community as a whole? No! The responsibility is individual, not communal. From this day forth each and every one of you is in his own person its special guardian, and individually responsible that no harm shall come to it. Do you—does each of you—accept this great trust? [*Tumultuous assent.*] Then all is well. Transmit it to your children and to your children's children. To-day your purity is beyond reproach—see to it that it shall remain so. To-day there is not a person in your community who could be beguiled to touch a penny not his own—see to it that you abide in this grace. ["*We will! we will!*"] This is not the place to make comparisons between ourselves and other communities—some of them ungracious toward us; they have their ways, we have ours; let us be content. [*Applause.*] I am done. Under my hand, my friends, rests a stranger's eloquent recognition of what we are; through him the world will always henceforth know what we are. We do not know who he is, but in your name I utter your gratitude, and ask you to raise your voices in indorsement."

The house rose in a body and made the walls quake with the thunders of its thankfulness for the space of a long minute. Then it sat down, and Mr. Burgess took an envelope out of his pocket. The house held its breath while he slit the envelope open and took from it a slip of paper. He read its contents—slowly and impressively—the audience listening with tranced attention to this magic document, each of whose words stood for an ingot of gold:

"'*The remark which I made to the distressed stranger was this. "You are very far from being a bad man: go, and reform."*'" Then he continued:

"We shall know in a moment now whether the remark here quoted corresponds with the one concealed in the sack; and if that shall prove to be so—and it undoubtedly will—this sack of gold belongs to a fellow-citizen who will henceforth stand before the nation as the symbol of the special virtue which has made our town famous throughout the land—Mr. Billson!"

The house had gotten itself all ready to burst into the proper tornado of applause; but instead of doing it, it seemed stricken with a paralysis; there was a deep hush for a moment or two, then a wave of whispered murmurs swept the place—of about this tenor: "*Billson!* oh, come, this is *too* thin! Twenty dollars to a stranger—or *anybody*—*Billson!* tell it to the marines!" And now at this point the house caught its breath all of a sudden in a new access of astonishment, for it discovered that whereas in one part of the hall Deacon Billson was standing up with his head meekly bowed, in another part of it Lawyer Wilson was doing the same. There was a wondering silence now for a while.

Everybody was puzzled, and nineteen couples were surprised and indignant.

Billson and Wilson turned and stared at each other. Billson asked, bitingly:

"Why do *you* rise, Mr. Wilson?"

"Because I have a right to. Perhaps you will be good enough to explain to the house why *you* rise?"

"With great pleasure. Because I wrote that paper."

"It is an impudent falsity! I wrote it myself."

It was Burgess's turn to be paralyzed. He stood looking vacantly at first one of the men and then the other, and did not seem to know what to do. The house was stupefied. Lawyer Wilson spoke up, now, and said,

"I ask the Chair to read the name signed to that paper." That brought the Chair to itself, and it read out the name:

"'John Wharton *Billson*."

"There!" shouted Billson, "what have you got to say for yourself, now? And what kind of apology are you going to make to me and to this insulted house for the imposture which you have attempted to play here?"

"No apologies are due, sir; and as for the rest of it, I publicly charge you with pilfering my note from Mr. Burgess and substituting a copy of it signed with your own name. There is no other way by which you could have gotten hold of the test-remark; I alone, of living men, possessed the secret of its wording."

There was likely to be a scandalous state of things if this went on; everybody noticed with distress that the shorthand scribes were scribbling like mad; many people were crying "Chair, Chair! Order! order!" Burgess rapped with his gavel, and said:

"Let us not forget the proprieties due. There has evidently been a mistake somewhere, but surely that is all. If Mr. Wilson gave me an envelope—and I remember now that he did—I still have it."

He took one out of his pocket, opened it, glanced at it, looked surprised and worried, and stood silent a few moments. Then he waved his hand in a wandering and mechanical way, and made an effort or two to say something, then gave it up, despondently. Several voices cried out:

"Read it! read it! What is it?"

So he began in a dazed and sleep-walker fashion:

"'*The remark which I made to the unhappy stranger was this: "You are far from being a bad man. [The house gazed at him, marveling.] Go, and reform.*'" [*Murmurs:* "Amazing! what can this mean?"] This one," said the Chair, "is signed Thurlow G. Wilson."

"There!" cried Wilson. "I reckon that settles it! I knew perfectly well my note was purloined."

"Purloined!" retorted Billson. "I'll let you know that neither you nor any man of your kidney must venture to—"

THE CHAIR "Order, gentlemen, order! Take your seats, both of you, please."

They obeyed, shaking their heads and grumbling angrily. The house was profoundly puzzled; it did not know what to do with this curious emergency. Presently Thompson got up. Thompson was the hatter. He would have liked to be a Nineteener; but such was not for him: his stock of hats was not considerable enough for the position. He said:

"Mr. Chairman, if I may be permitted to make a suggestion, can both of these gentlemen be right? I put it to you, sir, can both have happened to say the very same words to the stranger? It seems to me—"

The tanner got up and interrupted him. The tanner was a disgruntled man; he believed himself entitled to be a Nineteener, but he couldn't get recognition. It made him a little unpleasant in his ways and speech. Said he:

"Sho, *that's* not the point! *That* could happen—twice in a hundred years—but not the other thing. *Neither* of them gave the twenty dollars!"

[*A ripple of applause.*]

BILLSON "*I* did!"

WILSON "*I* did!"

Then each accused the other of pilfering.

THE CHAIR "Order! Sit down, if you please—both of you. Neither of the notes has been out of my possession at any moment."

A VOICE "Good—that settles *that!*"

THE TANNER "Mr. Chairman, one thing is now plain: one of these men have been eavesdropping under the other one's bed, and filching family secrets. If it is not unparliamentary to suggest it, I will remark that both are equal to it. [*The Chair.* "Order! order!"] I withdraw the remark, sir, and will confine myself to suggesting that *if* one of them has overheard the other reveal the test-remark to his wife, we shall catch him now."

A VOICE "How?"

THE TANNER "Easily. The two have not quoted the remark in exactly the same words. You would have noticed that, if there hadn't been a considerable stretch of time and an exciting quarrel inserted between the two readings."

A VOICE "Name the difference."

THE TANNER "The word *very* is in Billson's note, and not in the other."

MANY VOICES "That's so—he's right!"

THE TANNER "And so, if the Chair will examine the test-remark in the sack, we shall know which of these two frauds —[*The Chair.* "Order!"]—which of these two adventurers —[*The Chair.* "Order! order!"]—which of these two gentlemen—[*laughter and applause*]—is entitled to wear the belt as being the first dishonest blatherskite ever bred in this town —which he has dishonored, and which will be a sultry place for him from now out!" [*Vigorous applause.*]

MANY VOICES "Open it!—open the sack!"

Mr. Burgess made a slit in the sack, slid his hand in and brought out an envelope. In it were a couple of folded notes. He said:

"One of these is marked, 'Not to be examined until all written communications which have been addressed to the Chair—if any—shall have been read.' The other is marked '*The Test.*' Allow me. It is worded—to wit:

"'I do not require that the first half of the remark which was made to me by my benefactor shall be quoted with exactness, for it was not striking, and could be forgotten; but its closing fifteen words are quite striking, and I think easily rememberable; unless *these* shall be accurately reproduced, let the applicant be regarded as an impostor. My benefactor began by saying he seldom gave advice to any one, but that it always bore the hall-mark of high value when he did give it. Then he said this—and it has never faded from my memory: "*You are far from being a bad man—*"'"

FIFTY VOICES "That settles it—the money's Wilson's! Wilson! Wilson! Speech! Speech!"

People jumped up and crowded around Wilson, wringing his hand and congratulating fervently—meantime the Chair was hammering with the gavel and shouting:

"Order, gentlemen! Order! Order! Let me finish reading, please." When quiet was restored, the reading was resumed— as follows:

"'"*Go, and reform—or, mark my words—some day, for your sins, you will die and go to hell or Hadleyburg—*TRY AND MAKE IT THE FORMER.*"'"

A ghastly silence followed. First an angry cloud began to settle darkly upon the faces of the citizenship; after a pause the cloud began to rise, and a tickled expression tried to take its place; tried so hard that it was only kept under with great and painful difficulty; the reporters, the Brixtonites, and other strangers bent their heads down and shielded their faces with their hands,

and managed to hold in by main strength and heroic courtesy. At this most inopportune time burst upon the stillness the roar of a solitary voice—Jack Halliday's:

"*That's* got the hall-mark on it!"

Then the house let go, strangers and all. Even Mr. Burgess's gravity broke down presently, then the audience considered itself officially absolved from all restraint, and it made the most of its privilege. It was a good long laugh, and a tempestuously whole-hearted one, but it ceased at last— long enough for Mr. Burgess to try to resume, and for the people to get their eyes partially wiped; then it broke out again; and afterward yet again; then at last Burgess was able to get out these serious words:

"It is useless to try to disguise the fact—we find ourselves in the presence of a matter of grave import. It involves the honor of your town, it strikes at the town's good name. The difference of a single word between the test-remarks offered by Mr. Wilson and Mr. Billson was itself a serious thing, since it indicated that one or the other of these gentlemen had committed a theft—"

The two men were sitting limp, nerveless, crushed; but at these words both were electrified into movement, and started to get up—

"Sit down!" said the Chair, sharply, and they obeyed. "That, as I have said, was a serious thing. And it was—but for only one of them. But the matter has become graver; for the honor of *both* is now in formidable peril. Shall I go even further, and say in inextricable peril? *Both* left out the crucial fifteen words." He paused. During several moments he allowed the pervading stillness to gather and deepen its impressive effects, then added: "There would seem to be but one way whereby this could happen. I ask these gentlemen— Was there *collusion?—agreement?*"

A low murmur sifted through the house; its import was, "He's got them both."

Billson was not used to emergencies; he sat in a helpless collapse. But Wilson was a lawyer. He struggled to his feet, pale and worried, and said:

"I ask the indulgence of the house while I explain this most painful matter. I am sorry to say what I am about to say, since it must inflict irreparable injury upon Mr. Billson, whom I have always esteemed and respected until now, and in whose invulnerability to temptation I entirely believed—as did you all. But for the preservation of my own honor I must speak—and with frankness. I confess with shame—and I now beseech your pardon for it—that I said to the ruined stranger all of the words contained in the test-remark, including the disparaging fifteen. [*Sensation.*] When the late publication was made I recalled them, and I resolved to claim the sack of coin, for by every right I was entitled to it. Now I will ask you to consider this point, and weigh it well: that stranger's gratitude to me that night knew no bounds; he said himself that he could find no words for it that were adequate, and that if he should ever be able he would repay me a thousandfold. Now, then, I ask you this: Could I expect— could I believe—could I even remotely imagine—that, feeling as he did, he would do so ungrateful a thing as to add those quite unnecessary fifteen words to his test?—set a trap for me?—expose me as a slanderer of my own town before my own people assembled in a public hall? It was preposterous; it was impossible. His test would contain only the kindly opening clause of my remark. Of that I had no shadow of doubt. You would have thought as I did. You would not have expected a base betrayal from one whom you had befriended and against whom you had committed no offense. And so, with perfect confidence, perfect trust, I wrote on a piece of paper the opening words—ending with 'Go, and reform,'—and signed it. When I was about to put it in an envelope I was called into my back office, and without thinking I left the paper lying open on my desk." He stopped, turned his head slowly toward Billson, waited a moment, then added: "I ask you to note this: when I returned, a little later, Mr. Billson was retiring by my street door." [*Sensation.*]

In a moment Billson was on his feet and shouting:

"It's a lie! It's an infamous lie!"

THE CHAIR "Be seated, sir! Mr. Wilson has the floor."

Billson's friends pulled him into his seat and quieted him, and Wilson went on:

"Those are the simple facts. My note was now lying in a different place on the table from where I had left it. I noticed that, but attached no importance to it, thinking a draught had blown it there. That Mr. Billson would read a private paper was a thing which could not occur to me; he was a honorable man, and he would be above that. If you will allow me to say it, I think his extra word '*very*' stands explained; it is attributable to a defect of memory. I was the only man in the world who could furnish here any detail of the test-remark—by *honorable* means. I have finished."

There is nothing in the world like a persuasive speech to fuddle the mental apparatus and upset the convictions and debauch the emotions of an audience not practised in the tricks and delusions of oratory. Wilson sat down victorious. The house submerged him in tides of approving applause; friends swarmed to him and shook him by the hand and congratulated him, and Billson was shouted down and not allowed to say a word. The Chair hammered and hammered with its gavel, and kept shouting:

"But let us proceed, gentlemen, let us proceed!"

At last there was a measurable degree of quiet, and the hatter said:

"But what is there to proceed with, sir, but to deliver the money?"

VOICES "That's it! That's it! Come forward, Wilson!"

THE HATTER "I move three cheers for Mr. Wilson, Symbol of the special virtue which—"

The cheers burst forth before he could finish; and in the midst of them—and in the midst of the clamor of the gavel also—some enthusiasts mounted Wilson on a big friend's shoulder and were going to fetch him in triumph to the platform. The Chair's voice now rose above the noise—

"Order! To your places! You forget that there

is still a document to be read." When quiet had been restored he took up the document, and was going to read it, but laid it down again, saying, "I forgot; this is not to be read until all written communications received by me have first been read." He took an envelope out of his pocket, removed its inclosure, glanced at it—seemed astonished—held it out and gazed at it—stared at it.

Twenty or thirty voices cried out:

"What is it? Read it! read it!"

And he did—slowly, and wondering:

"*The remark which I made to the stranger—*[Voices. "Hello! how's this?"]—*was this: "You are far from being a bad man." [Voices. "Great Scott!"] "Go, and reform." [Voices. "Oh, saw my leg off!"]* Signed by Mr. Pinkerton, the banker."

The pandemonium of delight which turned itself loose now was of a sort to make the judicious weep. Those whose withers were unwrung laughed till the tears ran down; the reporters, in throes of laughter, set down disordered pothooks which would never in the world be decipherable; and a sleeping dog jumped up, scared out of its wits, and barked itself crazy at the turmoil. All manner of cries were scattered through the din: "We're getting rich—*two* Symbols of Incorruptibility!—without counting Billson!" "*Three!*—count Shadbelly in—we can't have too many!" "All right—Billson's elected!" "Alas, poor Wilson—victim of *two* thieves!"

A POWERFUL VOICE "Silence! The Chair's fishing up something more out of its pocket."

VOICES "Hurrah! Is it something fresh? Read it! read! read!"

THE CHAIR [*reading*] "*The remark which I made,*' etc.: "*You are far from being a bad man. "Go,*" ' etc. Signed, 'Gregory Yates.'"

TORNADO OF VOICES "Four Symbols!" "'Rah for Yates!" "Fish again!"

The house was in a roaring humor now, and ready to get all the fun out of the occasion that might be in it. Several Nineteeners, looking pale and distressed, got up and began to work their way toward the aisles, but a score of shouts went up:

"The doors, the doors—close the doors; no Incorruptible shall leave this place! Sit down, everybody!"

The mandate was obeyed.

"Fish again! Read! read!"

The Chair fished again, and once more the familiar words began to fall from its lips—" '*You are far from being a bad man.*' "

"Name! name! What's his name?"

" 'L. Ingoldsby Sargent.' "

"Five elected! Pile up the Symbols! Go on, go on!"

" '*You are far from being a bad—*' "

"Name! name!"

" 'Nicholas Whitworth.' "

"Hooray! hooray! it's a symbolical day!"

Somebody wailed in, and began to sing this rhyme (leaving out "it's") to the lovely "Mikado" tune of "When a man's afraid, a beautiful maid—"; the audience joined in, with joy; then, just in time, somebody contributed another line—

And don't you this forget—

The house roared it out. A third line was at once furnished—

Corruptibles far from Hadleyburg are—

The house roared that one too. As the last note died, Jack Halliday's voice rose high and clear, freighted with a final line—

But the Symbols are here, you bet!

That was sung, with booming enthusiasm. Then the happy house started in at the beginning and sang the four lines through twice, with immense swing and dash, and finished up with a crashing three-times-three and a tiger for "Hadleyburg the Incorruptible and all Symbols of it which we shall find worthy to receive the hall-mark to-night."

Then the shoutings at the Chair began again, all over the place:

"Go on! go on! Read! read some more! Read all you've got!"

"That's it—go on! We are winning eternal celebrity!"

A dozen men got up now and began to protest. They said that this farce was the work of some abandoned joker, and was an insult to the whole community. Without a doubt these signatures were all forgeries—

"Sit down! sit down! Shut up! You are confessing. We'll find *your* names in the lot."

"Mr. Chairman, how many of those envelopes have you got?"

The Chair counted.

"Together with those that have been already examined, there are nineteen."

A storm of derisive applause broke out.

"Perhaps they all contain the secret. I move that you open them all and read every signature that is attached to a note of that sort—and read also the first eight words of the note."

"Second the motion!"

It was put and carried—uproariously. Then poor old Richards got up, and his wife rose and stood at his side. Her head was bent down, so that none might see that she was crying. Her husband gave her his arm, and so supporting her, he began to speak in a quavering voice:

"My friends, you have known us two—Mary and me—all our lives, and I think you have liked us and respected us—"

The Chair interrupted him:

"Allow me. It is quite true—that which you are saying, Mr. Richards: this town *does* know you two; it *does* like you; it *does* respect you; more—it honors you and *loves* you—"

Halliday's voice rang out:

"That's the hall-marked truth, too! If the Chair is right, let the house speak up and say it. Rise! Now, then—hip! hip! hip!—all together!"

The house rose in mass, faced toward the old couple eagerly, filled the air with a snow-storm of waving handkerchiefs, and delivered the cheers with all its affectionate heart.

The Chair then continued:

"What I was going to say is this: We know your good heart, Mr. Richards, but this is not a time for the exercise of charity toward offenders. [*Shouts of "Right! right!"*] I see your generous purpose in your face, but I cannot allow you to plead for these men—"

"But I was going to—"

"Please take your seat, Mr. Richards. We must examine the rest of these notes—simple fairness to the men who have already been exposed requires this. As soon as that has been done—I give you my word for this—you shall be heard."

MANY VOICES "Right!—the Chair is right—no interruption can be permitted at this stage! Go on!—the names! the names!—according to the terms of the motion!"

The old couple sat reluctantly down, and the husband whispered to the wife, "It is pitifully hard to have to wait; the shame will be greater than ever when they find we were only going to plead for *ourselves*."

Straightway the jollity broke loose again with the reading of the names.

" '*You are far from being a bad man*—' Signature, 'Robert J. Titmarsh.'

" '*You are far from being a bad man*—' Signature, 'Eliphalet Weeks.'

" '*You are far from being a bad man*—' Signature, 'Oscar B. Wilder.'"

At this point the house lit upon the idea of taking the eight words out of the Chairman's hands. He was not unthankful for that. Thenceforward he held up each note in its turn, and waited. The house droned out the eight words in a massed and measured and musical deep volume of sound (with a daringly close resemblance to a well-known church chant)—" '*You are f-a-r from being a b-a-a-a-d man.*' " Then the Chair said, "Signature, 'Archibald Wilcox.' " And so on, and so on, name after name, and everybody had an increasingly and gloriously good time except the wretched Nineteen. Now and then, when a particularly shining name was called, the house made the Chair wait while it chanted the whole of the test-remark from the beginning to the closing words, "And go to hell or Hadleyburg—try and make it the for-or-m-e-r!" and in these special cases they added a grand and agonized and imposing "A-a-a-a-*men!*"

The list dwindled, dwindled, dwindled, poor old Richards keeping tally of the count, wincing when a name resembling his own was pronounced, and waiting in miserable suspense for the time to come when it would be his humiliating privilege to rise with Mary and finish his plea, which he was intending to word thus: ". . . for until now we have never done any wrong thing, but have gone our humble way unreproached. We are very poor, we are old, and have no chick nor child to help us; we were sorely tempted, and we fell. It was my purpose when I got up before to make confession and beg that my name might not be read out in this public place, for it seemed to us that we could not bear it; but I was prevented. It was just; it was our place to suffer with the rest. It has been hard for us. It is the first time we have ever heard our name fall from any one's lips—sullied. Be merciful—for the sake of the better days; make our shame as light to bear as in your charity you can." At this point in his revery Mary nudged him, perceiving that his mind was absent. The house was chanting, "You are f-a-r," etc.

"Be ready," Mary whispered. "Your name comes now; he has read eighteen."

The chant ended.

"Next! next! next!" came volleying from all over the house.

Burgess put his hand into his pocket. The old couple, trembling, began to rise. Burgess fumbled a moment, then said,

"I find I have read them all."

Faint with joy and surprise, the couple sank into their seats, and Mary whispered:

"Oh, bless God, we are saved!—he has lost ours—I wouldn't give this for a hundred of those sacks!"

The house burst out with its "Mikado" travesty, and sang it three times with ever-increasing enthusiasm, rising to its feet when it reached for the third time the closing line—

But there's one Symbol left, you bet!

and finishing up with cheers and a tiger for "Hadleyburg purity and our eighteen immortal representatives of it."

Then Wingate, the saddler, got up and proposed cheers "for the cleanest man in town, the one solitary important citizen in it who didn't try to steal that money—Edward Richards."

They were given with great and moving heartiness; then somebody proposed that Richards be elected sole guardian and Symbol of the now Sacred Hadleyburg Tradition, with power and right to stand up and look the whole sarcastic world in the face.

Passed, by acclamation; then they sang the "Mikado" again, and ended it with:

And there's one Symbol left, you bet!

There was a pause; then—

A VOICE "Now, then, who's to get the sack?"

THE TANNER (*with bitter sarcasm*) "That's easy. The money has to be divided among the eighteen Incorruptibles. They gave the suffering stranger twenty dollars apiece—and that remark—each in his turn—it took twenty-two minutes for the procession to move past. Staked the stranger—total contribution, $360. All they want is just the loan back—and interest—forty thousand dollars altogether."

MANY VOICES [*derisively*] "That's it! Divvy! divvy! Be kind to the poor—don't keep them waiting!"

THE CHAIR "Order! I now offer the stranger's remaining document. It says: 'If no claimant shall appear [*grand chorus of groans*] I desire that you open the sack and count out the money to the principal citizens of your town, they to take it in trust [*cries of "Oh! Oh! Oh!"*], and use it in such ways as to them shall seem best for the propagation and preservation of your community's noble reputation for incorruptible honesty [*more cries*]—a reputation to which their names and their efforts will add a new and far-reaching luster.' [*Enthusiastic outburst of sarcastic applause.*] That seems to be all. No—here is a postscript:

'P. S.—CITIZENS OF HADLEYBURG: *There is no test-remark—nobody made one.* [Great sensation.] *There wasn't any pauper stranger, nor any twenty-dollar contribution, nor any accompanying benediction and compliment—these are all inventions.* [General buzz and hum of astonishment and delight.] *Allow me to tell my story—it will take but a word or two. I passed through your town at a certain time, and received a deep offense which I had not earned. Any other man would have been content to kill one or two of you and call it square, but to me that would have been a trivial revenge, and inadequate; for the dead do not* suffer. *Besides, I could not kill you all—and, anyway, made as I am, even that would not have satisfied me. I wanted to damage every man in the place, and every woman—and not in their bodies or in their estate, but in their vanity—the place where feeble and foolish people are most vulnerable. So I disguised myself and came back and studied you. You were easy game. You had an old and lofty reputation for honesty, and naturally you were proud of it— it was your treasure of treasures, the very apple of your eye. As soon as I found out that you carefully and vigilantly kept yourselves and your children* out of *temptation, I knew how to proceed. Why, you simple creatures, the weakest of all weak things is a virtue which has not been tested in the fire. I laid a plan, and gathered a list of names. My project was to corrupt Hadleyburg the Incorruptible. My idea was to make liars and thieves of nearly half a hundred smirchless men and women who had never in their lives uttered a lie or stolen a penny. I was afraid of Goodson. He was neither born nor reared in Hadleyburg. I was afraid that if I started to operate my scheme by getting my letter laid before you, you would say to yourselves, "Goodson is the only man among us who would give away twenty dollars to a poor devil"—and then you might not bite at my bait. But Heaven took Goodson; then I knew I was safe, and I set my trap and baited it. It may be that I shall not catch all the men to whom I mailed the pretended test secret, but I shall catch the most of them, if I know Hadleyburg nature.* [Voices. *"Right—he got every last one of them."*] *I believe they will even steal ostensible* gamble-money, *rather than miss, poor, tempted, and mistrained fellows. I am hoping to eternally and everlastingly squelch your vanity and give Hadleyburg a new renown—one that will* stick— *and spread far. If I have succeeded, open the sack and summon the Committee on Propagation and Preservation of the Hadleyburg Reputation.*

A CYCLONE OF VOICES "Open it! Open it! The Eighteen to the front! Committee on Propagation of the Tradition! Forward—the Incorruptibles!"

The Chair ripped the sack wide, and gathered up a handful of bright, broad, yellow coins, shook them together, then examined them—

"Friends, they are only gilded disks of lead!"

There was a crashing outbreak of delight over this news, and when the noise had subsided, the tanner called out:

"By right of apparent seniority in this business, Mr. Wilson is Chairman of the Committee on Propagation of the Tradition. I suggest that he step forward on behalf of his pals, and receive in trust the money."

A HUNDRED VOICES "Wilson! Wilson! Wilson! Speech! Speech!"

WILSON [*in a voice trembling with anger*] "You will allow me to say, and without apologies for my language, *damn* the money!"

A VOICE "Oh, and him a Baptist!"

A VOICE "Seventeen Symbols left! Step up, gentlemen, and assume your trust!"

There was a pause—no response.

THE SADDLER "Mr. Chairman, we've got *one* clean man left, anyway, out of the late aristocracy; and he needs money, and deserves it I move that you appoint Jack Halliday to get up there and auction off that sack of gilt twenty-dollar pieces, and give the result to the right man—the man whom Hadleyburg delights to honor—Edward Richards."

This was received with great enthusiasm, the dog taking a hand again; the saddler started the bids at a dollar, the Brixton folk and Barnum's representative fought hard for it, the people cheered every jump that the bids made, the excitement climbed moment by moment higher and higher, the bidders got on their mettle and grew steadily more and more daring, more and more determined, the jumps went from a dollar up to five, then to ten, then to twenty, then fifty, then to a hundred, then—

At the beginning of the auction Richards whispered in distress to his wife: "O Mary, can we allow it? It—it—you see, it is an honor-reward, a testimonial to purity of character, and— and—can we allow it? Hadn't I better get up and—O Mary, what ought we to do?—what do you think we —[*Halliday's voice. "Fifteen I'm bid!—fifteen for the sack!—twenty!—ah, thanks!—thirty—thanks again! Thirty, thirty, thirty!—do I heard forty?—forty it is! Keep the ball rolling, gentlemen, keep it rolling!—fifty! thanks, noble Roman! going at fifty, fifty, fifty!—seventy!—ninety!—splendid!—a hundred!—pile it up, pile it up!—hundred and twenty—forty!—just in time!—hundred and fifty!*—TWO *hundred!—superb! Do I hear two h—thanks!—two hundred and fifty!—"*]

"It is another temptation, Edward—I'm all in a tremble—but, oh, we've escaped *one* temptation, and that ought to warn us to—["*Six did I hear?—thanks!—six-fifty, six-f—*SEVEN *hundred!"*] And yet, Edward, when you think—nobody susp.—["*Eight hundred dollars!—hurrah!—make it nine!—Mr. Parsons, did I hear you say—thanks—nine!—this noble sack of virgin lead going at only nine hundred dollars, gilding and all—come! do I hear—a thousand!—gratefully yours!—did some one say eleven?—a sack which is going to be the most celebrated in the whole Uni—*] O Edward" (beginning to sob), "we are *so* poor!—but—but—do as you think best—do as you think best."

Edward fell—that is, he sat still; sat with a conscience which was not satisfied, but which was overpowered by circumstances.

Meantime a stranger, who looked like an amateur detective gotten up as an impossible English earl, had been watching the evening's proceedings with manifest interest, and with a contented expression in his face; and he had been privately commenting to himself. He was now soliloquizing somewhat like this: "None of the Eighteen are bidding; that is not satisfactory; I must change that—the dramatic unities require it; they must buy the sack they tried to steal; they must pay a heavy price, too—some of them are rich. And another thing, when I make a mistake in Hadleyburg nature the man that puts that error upon me is entitled to a high honorarium, and some one must pay it. This poor old Richards has brought my judgment to shame; he is an honest man:—I don't understand it, but I acknowledge it. Yes, he saw my deuces *and* with a straight flush, and by rights the pot is his. And it

shall be a jack-pot, too, if I can manage it. He disappointed me, but let that pass."

He was watching the bidding. At a thousand, the market broke; the prices tumbled swiftly. He waited—and still watched. One competitor dropped out; then another, and another. He put in a bid or two, now. When the bids had sunk to ten dollars, he added a five; some one raised him a three; he waited a moment, then flung in a fifty-dollar jump, and the sack was his—at $1,282. The house broke out in cheers—then stopped; for he was on his feet, and had lifted his hand. He began to speak.

"I desire to say a word, and ask a favor. I am a speculator in rarities, and I have dealings with persons interested in numismatics all over the world. I can make a profit on this purchase, just as it stands; but there is a way, if I can get your approval, whereby I can make every one of these leaden twenty-dollar pieces worth its face in gold, and perhaps more. Grant me that approval, and I will give part of my gains to your Mr. Richards, whose invulnerable probity you have so justly and so cordially recognized to-night; his share shall be ten thousand dollars, and I will hand him the money to-morrow. [*Great applause from the house.* But the "invulnerable probity" made the Richardses blush prettily; however, it went for modesty, and did no harm.] If you will pass my proposition by a good majority—I would like a two-thirds vote—I will regard that as the town's consent, and that is all I ask. Rarities are always helped by any device which will rouse curiosity and compel remark. Now if I may have your permission to stamp upon the faces of each of these ostensible coins the names of the eighteen gentlemen who—"

Nine-tenths of the audience were on their feet in a moment—dog and all—and the proposition was carried with a whirlwind of approving applause and laughter.

They sat down, and all the Symbols except "Dr." Clay Harkness got up, violently protesting against the proposed outrage, and threatening to—

"I beg you not to threaten me," said the stranger, calmly. "I know my legal rights, and am not accustomed to being frightened at bluster." [*Applause*.] He sat down. "Dr." Harkness saw an opportunity here. He was one of the two very rich men of the place, and Pinkerton was the other. Harkness was proprietor of a mint; that is to say, a popular patent medicine. He was running for the legislature on one ticket, and Pinkerton on the other. It was a close race and a hot one, and getting hotter every day. Both had strong appetites for money; each had bought a great tract of land, with a purpose; there was going to be a new railway, and each wanted to be in the legislature and help locate the route to his own advantage; a single vote might make the decision, and with it two or three fortunes. The stake was large, and Harkness was a daring speculator. He was sitting close to the stranger. He leaned over while one or another of the other Symbols was entertaining the house with protests and appeals, and asked, in a whisper.

"What is your price for the sack?"

"Forty thousand dollars."

"I'll give you twenty."

"No."

"Twenty-five."

"No."

"Say thirty."

"The price is forty thousand dollars; not a penny less."

"All right, I'll give it. I will come to the hotel at ten in the morning. I don't want it known: will see you privately."

"Very good." Then the stranger got up and said to the house:

"I find it late. The speeches of these gentlemen are not without merit, not without interest, not without grace; yet if I may be excused I will take my leave. I thank you for the great favor which you have shown me in granting my petition. I ask the Chair to keep the sack for me until to-morrow, and to hand these three five-hundred-dollar notes to Mr. Richards." They were passed up to the Chair. "At nine I will call for the sack, and at eleven will deliver the rest of the ten thousand to Mr. Richards in person, at his home. Good night."

Then he slipped out, and left the audience making a vast noise which was composed of a mixture of cheers, the "Mikado" song, dog-disapproval, and the chant, "You are f-a-r from being a b-a-a-d man—a-a-a-a-men!"

4

At home the Richardses had to endure congratulations and compliments until midnight. Then they were left to themselves. They looked a little sad, and they sat silent and thinking. Finally Mary sighed and said,

"Do you think we are to blame, Edward—*much* to blame?" and her eyes wandered to the accusing triplet of big bank-notes lying on the table, where the congratulators had been gloating over them and reverently fingering them. Edward did not answer at once; then he brought out a sigh and said, hesitatingly:

"We—we couldn't help it, Mary. It—well, it was ordered. *All* things are."

Mary glanced up and looked at him steadily, but he didn't return the look. Presently she said:

"I thought congratulations and praises always tasted good. But—it seems to me, now—Edward?"

"Well?"

"Are you going to stay in the bank?"

"N-no."

"Resign?"

"In the morning—by note."

"It does seem best."

Richards bowed his head in his hands and muttered:

"Before, I was not afraid to let oceans of people's money pour through my hands, but—Mary, I am so tired, so tired—"

"We will go to bed."

At nine in the morning the stranger called for the sack and took it to the hotel in a cab. At ten Harkness had a talk with him privately. The stranger asked for and got five checks on a metropolitan bank—drawn to "Bearer"—four for $1,500 each, and one for $34,000. He put one of the former in his pocketbook, and the remainder, representing $38,500, he put in an envelope, and with these he added a note, which he wrote after Harkness was gone. At eleven he called at the Richards house and knocked. Mrs. Richards peeped through the shutters, then went and received the envelope, and the stranger disappeared without a word. She came back flushed and a little unsteady on her legs, and gasped out:

"I am sure I recognized him! Last night it seemed to me that maybe I had seen him somewhere before."

"He is the man that brought the sack here?"

"I am almost sure of it."

"Then he is the ostensible Stephenson, too, and sold every important citizen in this town with his bogus secret. Now if he has sent checks instead of money, we are sold, too, after we thought we had escaped. I was beginning to feel fairly comfortable once more, after my night's rest, but the look of that envelope makes me sick. It isn't fat enough; $8,500 in even the largest bank-notes makes more bulk than that."

"Edward, why do you object to checks?"

"Checks signed by Stephenson! I am resigned to take the $8,500 if it could come in bank-notes—for it does seem that it was so ordered, Mary—but I have never had much courage, and I have not the pluck to try to market a check signed with that disastrous name. It would be a trap. That man tried to catch me; we escaped somehow or other; and now he is trying a new way. If it is checks—"

"Oh, Edward, it is *too* bad!" and she held up the checks and began to cry.

"Put them in the fire! quick! we mustn't be tempted. It is a trick to make the world laugh at *us*, along with the rest, and—Give them to *me*, since you can't do it!" He snatched them and tried to hold his grip till he could get to the stove; but he was human, he was a cashier, and he stopped a moment to make sure of the signature. Then he came near to fainting.

"Fan me, Mary, fan me! They are the same as gold!"

"Oh, how lovely, Edward! Why?"

"Signed by Harkness. What can the mystery of that be, Mary?"

"Edward, do you think—"

"Look here—look at this! Fifteen—fifteen—fifteen—thirty-four. Thirty-eight thousand five hundred! Mary, the sack isn't worth twelve dollars, and Harkness—apparently—has paid about par for it."

"And does it all come to us, do you think—instead of the ten thousand?"

"Why, it looks like it. And the checks are made to 'Bearer,' too."

"Is that good, Edward? What is it for?"

"A hint to collect them at some distant bank, I reckon. Perhaps Harkness doesn't want the matter known. What is that—a note?"

"Yes. It was with the checks."

It was in the "Stephenson" handwriting, but there was no signature. It said:

"I am a disappointed man. Your honesty is beyond the reach of temptation. I had a different idea about it, but I wronged you in that, and I beg pardon, and do it sincerely. I honor you—and that is sincere too. This town is not worthy to kiss the hem of your garment. Dear sir, I made a square bet with myself that there were nineteen debauchable men in your self-righteous community. I have lost. Take the whole pot, you are entitled to it."

Richards drew a deep sigh, and said:

"It seems written with fire—it burns so. Mary—I am miserable again."

"I, too. Ah, dear, I wish—"

"To think, Mary—he *believes* in me."

"Oh, don't, Edward—I can't bear it."

"If those beautiful words were deserved, Mary—and God knows I believed I deserved them once—I think I could give the forty thousand dollars for them. And I would put that paper away, as representing more than gold and jewels, and keep it always. But now—We could not live in the shadow of its accusing presence, Mary."

He put it in the fire.

A messenger arrived and delivered an envelope.

Richards took from it a note and read it; it was from Burgess.

"You saved me, in a difficult time. I saved you last night. It was at cost of a lie, but I made the sacrifice freely, and out of a grateful heart. None in this village knows so well as I know how brave and good and noble you are. At bottom you cannot respect me, knowing as you do of that matter of which I am accused, and by the general voice condemned; but I beg that you will at least believe that I am grateful man; it will help me to bear my burden."

[*Signed*]

BURGESS

"Saved, once more. And on such terms!" He put the note in the fire. "I—I wish I were dead, Mary, I wish I were out of it all."

"Oh, these are bitter, bitter days, Edward. The stabs, through their very generosity, are so deep—and they come so fast!"

Three days before the election each of two thousand voters suddenly found himself in possession of a prized memento—one of the renowned bogus double-eagles. Around one of its faces was stamped these words: "THE REMARK I MADE TO THE POOR STRANGER WAS—" Around the other face was stamped these: "GO, AND REFORM. [SIGNED] PINKERTON." Thus the entire remaining refuse of the renowned joke was emptied upon a single head, and with calamitous effect. It revived the recent vast laugh and concentrated it upon Pinkerton; and Harkness's election was a walkover.

Within twenty-four hours after the Richardses had received their checks their consciences were quieting down, discouraged; the old couple were learning to reconcile themselves to the sin which they had committed. But they were to learn, now, that a sin takes on new and real terrors when there seems a chance that it is going to be found out. This gives it a fresh and most substantial and important aspect. At church the morning sermon was of the usual pattern; it was the same old things said in the same old way; they had heard them a thousand times and found

them innocuous, next to meaningless, and easy to sleep under; but now it was different: the sermon seemed to bristle with accusations; it seemed aimed straight and specially at people who were concealing deadly sins. After church they got away from the mob of congratulators as soon as they could, and hurried homeward, chilled to the bone at they did not know what—vague, shadowy, indefinite fears. And by chance they caught a glimpse of Mr. Burgess as he turned a corner. He paid no attention to their nod of recognition! He hadn't seen it; but they did not know that. What could his conduct mean? It might mean—it might mean—oh, a dozen dreadful things. Was it possible that he knew that Richards could have cleared him of guilt in that bygone time, and had been silently waiting for a chance to even up accounts? At home, in their distress they got to imagining that their servant might have been in the next room listening when Richards revealed the secret to his wife that he knew of Burgess's innocence; next, Richards began to imagine that he had heard the swish of a gown in there at that time; next, he was sure he *had* heard it. They would call Sarah in, on a pretext, and watch her face: if she had been betraying them to Mr. Burgess, it would show in her manner. They asked her some questions—questions which were so random and incoherent and seemingly purposeless that the girl felt sure that the old people's minds had been affected by their sudden good fortune; the sharp and watchful gaze which they bent upon her frightened her, and that completed the business. She blushed, she became nervous and confused, and to the old people these were plain signs of guilt—guilt of some fearful sort or other—without doubt she was a spy and a traitor. When they were alone again they began to piece many unrelated things together and get horrible results out of the combination. When things had got about to the worst, Richards was delivered of a sudden gasp, and his wife asked:

"Oh, what is it?—what is it?"

"The note—Burgess's note! Its language was sarcastic, I see it now." He quoted: "'At bottom you cannot respect me, *knowing*, as you do, of *that matter* of which I am accused'—oh, it is perfectly plain, now, God help me! He knows that I know! You see the ingenuity of the phrasing. It was a trap—and like a fool, I walked into it. And Mary—?"

"Oh, it is dreadful—I know what you are going to say—he didn't return your transcript of the pretended test-remark."

"No—kept it to destroy us with. Mary, he has exposed us to some already. I know it—I know it well. I saw it in a dozen faces after church. Ah, he wouldn't answer our nod of recognition—*he* knew what he had been doing!"

In the night the doctor was called. The news went around in the morning that the old couple were rather seriously ill—prostrated by the exhausting excitement growing out of their great windfall, the congratulations, and the late hours, the doctor said. The town was sincerely distressed; for these old people were about all it had left to be proud of, now.

Two days later the news was worse. The old couple were delirious, and were doing strange things. By witness of the nurses, Richards had exhibited checks—for $8,500? No—for an amazing sum—$38,500! What could be the explanation of this gigantic piece of luck?

The following day the nurses had more news—and wonderful. They had concluded to hide the checks, lest harm come to them; but when they searched they were gone from under the patient's pillow—vanished away. The patient said:

"Let the pillow alone; what do you want?"

"We thought it best that the checks—"

"You will never see them again—they are destroyed. They came from Satan. I saw the hell-brand on them, and I knew they were sent to betray me to sin." Then he fell to gabbling strange and dreadful things which were not clearly understandable, and which the doctor admonished them to keep to themselves.

Richards was right; the checks were never seen again.

A nurse must have talked in her sleep, for within two days the forbidden gabblings were the property of the town; and they were of a surprising sort. They seemed to indicate that Richards had been a claimant for the sack himself, and that Burgess had concealed that fact and then maliciously betrayed it.

Burgess was taxed with this and stoutly denied it. And he said it was not fair to attach weight to the chatter of a sick old man who was out of his mind. Still, suspicion was in the air, and there was much talk.

After a day or two it was reported that Mrs. Richards's delirious deliveries were getting to be duplicates of her husband's. Suspicion flamed up into conviction, now, and the town's pride in the purity of its one undiscredited important citizen began to dim down and flicker toward extinction.

Six days passed, then came more news. The old couple were dying. Richards's mind cleared in his latest hour, and sent for Burgess. Burgess said:

"Let the room be cleared. I think he wishes to say something in privacy."

"No!" said Richards: "I want witnesses. I want you all to hear my confession, so that I may die a man, and not a dog. I was clean—artificially—like the rest; and like the rest I fell when temptation came. I signed a lie, and claimed the miserable sack. Mr. Burgess remembered that I had done him a service, and in gratitude (and ignorance) he suppressed my claim and saved me. You know the thing that was charged against Burgess years ago. My testimony, and mine alone, could have cleared him, and I was a coward, and left him to suffer disgrace—"

"No—no—Mr. Richards, you—"

"My servant betrayed my secret to him—"

"No one has betrayed anything to me—"

—"and then he did a natural and justifiable thing, he repented of the saving kindness which he had done me, and he *exposed* me—as I deserved—"

"Never!—I make oath—"

"Out of my heart I forgive him."

Burgess's impassioned protestations fell upon

deaf ears; the dying man passed away without knowing that once more he had done poor Burgess a wrong. The old wife died that night.

The last of the sacred Nineteen had fallen a prey to the fiendish sack; the town was stripped of the last rag of its ancient glory. Its mourning was not showy, but it was deep.

By act of the Legislature—upon prayer and petition—Hadleyburg was allowed to change its name to (never mind what—I will not give it away), and leave one word out of the motto that for many generations had graced the town's official seal.

It is an honest town once more, and the man will have to rise early that catches it napping again.

Suggested Readings

Anderson, Benedict. *Imagined Communities: Reflections on the Origin and Spread of Nationalism*, revised edition, New York: Verso, 1991.

Archer, William. "The Man That Corrupted Hadleyburg-New Parable," *The Critic*, Vol. 37, November, 1900, pp. 413–415.

Briden, Earl F. "Twainian Pedagogy and the No-Account Lessons of Hadleyburg," *Studies in Short Fiction*, Vol. 28, No. 2, 1991, pp. 125–134.

28

Seize The Day: George Eliot's Poem "Count That Day Lost"

Dr. Joseph J. Thomas

British author and poet George Eliot (actually a pseudonymn for Mary Ann Evans) was born in Warwickshire England in 1819. Alternating between skeptic agnostic and devout evangelical, she studied and experimented with several Christian denominations. Her lifelong quest for truth provided her with a simple finding: that virtue is its own reward. Her novels were critical of blind ambition and selfishness. Her poem *Count That Day Lost* summarizes the essential value of positive human interaction.

> If you sit down at set of sun
> And count the acts that you have done,
>   And, counting, find
> One self-denying deed, one word
> That eased the heart of him who heard,
>   One glance most kind
> That fell like sunshine where it went
> Then you may count that day well spent.
>
> But if, through all the livelong day,
> You've cheered no heart, by yea or nay
>   If, through it all
> You've nothing done that you can trace
> That brought the sunshine to one face
>   No act most small
> That helped some soul and nothing cost
> Then count that day as worse than lost.

Suggested Readings

Canfield, Jack L. and Mark Victor Hansen. *Chicken Soup for the Soul*. Deerfield Beach: Health Communications, 2001.

Eliot, George. *George Eliot: Selected Work*. London: Random House, 1995.

Haight, Gordon S., *George Eliot: A Biography*, Oxford: Oxford University Press, 1968.

Haight, Gordon S., ed., *George Eliot: Letters*, New Haven: Connecticut, Yale University Press, 1954.

Uglow, Jennifer, *George Eliot*, London: Virago, 1987.

29

Ingredients of Leadership: Rudyard Kipling's Poem "If—"

Ensign Christopher R. Pisani, USN

Interestingly, Kipling wrote "If" with the British military leader, Sir Leander Starr Jameson, in mind. In 1895, Jameson had led 600 volunteers from the British South African Police in a failed raid against the Boer colony of Transvaal, in southern Africa. What became known as the Jameson Raid was later cited as a major factor in bringing about the Boer War of 1899, which ran until 1902. The war was an attempt to establish South Africa as a British possession, of course to give the British sole ownership of the gold and diamond mines. But the story was spun quite the opposite in Britain. The British defeat was interpreted as a victory, and Jameson was portrayed as a daring hero and was knighted for his heroic, yet failed efforts.

If—

If you can keep your head when all about you
    Are losing theirs and blaming it on you;
If you can trust yourself when all men doubt
    you,
    But make allowance for their doubting
    too;
If you can wait and not be tired by waiting,
    Or, being lied about, don't deal in lies,
Or, being hated, don't give way to hating,
    And yet don't look too good, nor talk too
    wise;

If you can dream-and not make dreams your
    master;
If you can think-and not make thoughts your
    aim;
If you can meet with triumph and disaster
    And treat those two impostors just the
    same;
If you can bear to hear the truth you've spoken
    Twisted by knaves to make a trap for fools,
Or watch the things you gave your life to
    broken,

And stoop and build 'em up with worn-out
    tools;

If you can make one heap of all your
    winnings
    And risk it on one turn of pitch-and-toss,
And lose, and start again at your beginnings
    And never breathe a word about your loss;
If you can force your heart and nerve and
    sinew
    To serve your turn long after they are
    gone,
And so hold on when there is nothing in you
    Except the Will which says to them: "Hold
    on!"

If you can talk with crowds and keep your
    virtue,
    Or walk with kings-nor lose the common
    touch;
If neither foes nor loving friends can hurt
    you;
    If all men count with you, but none too
    much;
If you can fill the unforgiving minute
    With sixty seconds' worth of distance run-
Yours is the Earth and everything that's in it,
    And—which is more—you'll be a Man, my
    son!

Kipling's "If" has sage advice for everyone. It is a collage of postulates for keeping one's life "in-check." It inspires us to strive for success but cautions us to maintain a proper perspective along the way.

Kipling's words have served me well. My Plebe year was a disaster. But for a 4–3 vote by the AC Board in favor of "retention," I would have been "separated" for failing three of five core courses. My company officer and battalion officer, both of whom wholeheartedly supported my retention, remarked that the AC Board's decision was unprecedented. Having been reborn, I repeated the three classes and earned A's in each.

Kipling's words come to mind when I recall my appearance before the AC Board:

If you can trust yourself when all men doubt you,
But make allowance for their doubting too . . . (3–4)

Standing before the AC Board is an almost surreal experience. The room is filled with decision-makers whose faces express skepticism. You speak, hoping to overcome rather than confirm their doubts. If you are lucky, the confidence and trust that you have in yourself prevails. However, from that day forward, you will walk with a gate that has a slight hitch.

I came across this poem while in Bancroft Hall, getting help from a classmate for the third and most difficult class to be repeated. He had offered to tutor me every weekday evening for the entire fall semester of my Youngster year. The poem had been given to him on I-Day by his late grandmother. It was thumbtacked to his corkboard, the only visible personal space permitted in the room. He was a very bright midshipman, having done very well, academically. However, he had had a terrible time trying to pass the semi-annual physical readiness test (PRT). No matter what he did, he could not meet the minimum time of ten minutes and thirty seconds for the mile and one-half run.

Throughout my semesters at Annapolis, I had excelled in the PRT. In exchange for my classmate's tutoring, I had agreed to serve as his personal trainer—a *quid pro quo* that any midshipman could appreciate. Although we would train together, his progress was slow. He was required to attend remedial PT, running in the early mornings and late afternoons. This group became know as the "goon squad," and he became a sustaining member.

My classmate recalled for me the verse from "If" that his grandmother cited when he told her of his embarrassment:

Or watch the things you gave your life to, broken,
  And stoop and build 'em up with worn-out tools;
       (15–16)

My classmate had to fix that which was broken, physically. His body had betrayed him. He had to defeat this traitor and restore his self-confidence.

At the end of the fall semester of our Firstie year, the line in the sand had been drawn. The Superintendent had informed our class that there would be a special PRT after we returned from the Christmas break. Those who did not pass it simply would not graduate and be commissioned. This classmate, who had had an otherwise sterling midshipman career, was now faced with a final, "all or nothing" obstacle.

It was one of those gloomy and cold, zero-dark-thirty mornings, with the Severn being covered by a thin film of ice and the night's freshly fallen snow. Our noses and cheeks felt the sting of the frost, as we shivered in silence. After having crossed the finish line with time to spare, I stood looking for his face amongst the stragglers. At last, around the final turn of Farragut Field he came into sight. Our entire company cheered him on, knowing his predicament. "10:29!" shouted the Physical Education Officer.

Kipling's words echoed out *across* the still Severn that dark, chilly morning:

*If you can force your heart and nerve and
sinew*
  To serve your turn long after they are gone,
And so hold on when there is nothing in you
  *Except the Will which says to them: "Hold
  on!" (21–24)*

Kipling's words of encouragement, though written in 1909, are timeless. Memorialized over the entrance way to Wimbledon's Centre Court for all contestants to read, is the following verse:

*If you can meet with triumph and disaster
  And treat those two impostors just the same
  . . . (11–12)*

My classmate and I faced the imposters of triumph and disaster, head-on. He had triumphed over the seemingly insurmountable PRT, and I had shed the millstone of academic failure. Neither of us will ever forget the agony of self-doubt, nor the ecstasy of self-confidence when confronting our adversaries.

Still, we draw strength from Kipling's final and most moving stanza:

*If you can fill the unforgiving minute
  With sixty seconds' worth of distance run—
  Yours is the Earth and everything that's in it,
  And—which is more—you'll be a Man, my
  son! (29–32)*

Life is filled with battles won and battles lost. With each battle, lessons are learned. We draw from those lessons that which will serve us along Life's path, for better or for worse. Kipling shares his lessons-learned and the balance that must be maintained in order to make our journey purposeful.

Every grandparent ought to present a copy of "If," suitable for thumbtacking, to his or her college-bound grandchild.

Suggested Readings

Bodelsen, C. A. *Aspects of Kipling's Art.* New York: Barnes & Noble, 1964.

Kipling, Rudyard. *Complete Verse.* London. Kyle Cathie Limited, 2002.

Low, Gail Ching-Liang. *White Skins/Black Masks: Representation and Colonialism.* New York: Routledge, 1996.

Manley, Seon. *Rudyard Kipling, Creative Adventurer.* New York: Vanguard Press, 1965.

Tompkins, J. M. S. *The Art of Rudyard Kipling.* Lincoln: University of Nebraska Press, 1965.

About the Author

Ensign Christopher R. Pisani, USN, was graduated and commissioned from the United States Naval Academy in 2005 with a Bachelor of Science Degree in Political Science, with an emphasis in International Relations. He was the first U.S. midshipman to participate in the French Navy's traditional six-month training campaign since the program's inception in 1864. Aboard the legendary helicopter carrier, FS JEANNE D'ARC (R97), and the anti-submarine destroyer, FS GEORGE LEYGUES (D640), the 2005 campaign took him to numerous ports of call in Europe, Africa, and Asia. It included two unexpected humanitarian missions, OPERATION BERYX (France) and OPERATION UNIFIED ASSISTANCE (USA). He worked for thirty-eight days in the Aceh Province of northern Sumatra, Indonesia, to assist in the wake of the world's worst natural disaster, the tsunami of December 26, 2004. Ensign Pisani has chosen Surface Warfare as his service selection, and his first assignment has been to serve in Japan aboard the USS BLUE RIDGE (LLC 19), the command ship for the U.S. Navy's Seventh Fleet (Pacific).

30

Rarity of Loyal Friendship: Rudyard Kipling's Poem "The Thousandth Man"

Dr. Joseph J. Thomas

Rudyard Kipling (1865–1936) is widely considered the unofficial poet laureate of the last stages of the British Empire. Many of his novels and poems celebrate Britain's imperialism and contain more than a touch of jingoism and ethnocentrism. Born in Bombay, India, but educated in English boarding schools, Kipling was well-traveled. He lived in South Africa and the United States for brief periods but his work usually focued on his beloved place of birth, India. Kipling was the first Englishman to receive the Nobel Prize for literature and his autobiography, *Something of Myself*, was published after his death in 1937. Today Kipling rests at Poet's Corner in Westminster Abbey. His poem "The Thousandth Man" is typical of his romantic fascination with the virtues of loyalty, friendship, and honor.

The Thousandth Man

One man in a thousand, Solomon says,
Will stick more close than a brother.
And it's worth while seeking him half your
    days
If you find him before the other.
Nine hundred and ninety-nine depend
On what the world sees in you,
But the Thousandth Man will stand your
    friend
With the whole round world agin you.

'Tis neither promise nor prayer nor show
Will settle the finding for' ee.
Nine hundred and ninety-nine of 'em go
By your looks, or your acts, or your glory,
But if he finds you and you find him,
The rest of the world don't matter;
For the Thousandth Man will sink or swim
With you in any water.

You can use his purse with no more talk
Than he uses yours for his spendings,

And laugh and meet in your daily walk
As though there had been no lendings.
Nine hundred and ninety-nine of' em call
For silver and gold in their dealings;
But the Thousandth Man he's worth 'em all,
Because you can show him your feelings.

His wrong's your wrong, and his right's your
    right,
In season or out of season.
Stand up and back it in all men's sight
With *that* for your only reason!
Nine hundred and ninety-nine can't bide
The shame or mocking or laughter,
But the Thousandth Man will stand by your
    side
To the gallows-foot-and after!

Suggested Readings

Kipling, Rudyard. *Rudyard Kipling: Complete Verse*. London: Kyle Cathie Limited, 2002.

Maurice, Frederick D. *The Friendship of Books, and Other Lectures*. London: Macmillan, 1874.

Kotter, John P. *Leading Change*. Boston, Mass.: Harvard Business School Press, 1996.

Maxwell, John C. *The 21 Indispensable Qualities of a Leader: Becoming the Person that People Will Want to Follow*. Nashville: T. Nelson, 1999.

Watkins, Michael. *The First 90 Days: Critical Success Strategies for New Leaders at All Levels*. Boston: Harvard Business School Press, 2003.

31

We Shall Die Like Gentlemen: Scott's Last Expedition

Dr. Robert D. Madison

Robert Falcon Scott (1868–1912), a captain in the Royal Navy, led two scientific expeditions to the Antarctic continent. Part of the agenda for the second journey was a trek to the South Pole, undertaken to elucidate the geologic history of the continent. With a Norwegian expedition led by Roald Amundsen on the glacier-covered continent at the same time, it was perhaps inevitable that the journey should become to some extent a race.

Leaving New Zealand in late 1910 on the last leg of the ocean journey to Antarctica, Scott in the *Terra Nova* planned to spend nearly a year in preparations for the "overland" part of the journey. On the first of November, 1911, they started out in relays. For nearly three more months they slogged over the polar ice cap. On January 18 they arrived in the vicinity of the Pole—and found a tent with the record of Amundsen's arrival a month before.

"Well, we have turned our back now on the goal of our ambition," Scott wrote in his journal, "and must face our 800 miles of solid dragging—and good-bye to most of the day-dreams." The story of their return comes from the record of Scott's journal, published in 1913 as *Scott's Last Expedition*.

CHAPTER XX

THE LAST MARCH

Sunday, February 18.—R.32. Temp.-5.5°. At Shambles Camp. We gave ourselves 5 hours' sleep at the lower glacier depôt after the horrible night, and came on at about 3 to-day to this camp, coming fairly easily over the divide. Here with plenty of horsemeat we have had a fine supper, to be followed by others such, and so continue a more plentiful era if we can keep good marches up. New life seems to come with greater food almost immediately, but I am anxious about the Barrier surfaces.

Monday, February 19.—Lunch T. -16°. It was late (past noon) before we got away to-day, as I gave nearly 8 hours sleep, and much camp work was done shifting sledges and fitting up new one with mast, &c., packing horsemeat and personal effects. The surface was every bit as bad as I expected, the sun shining brightly on it and its covering of soft loose sandy snow. We have come out about 2' on the old tracks. Perhaps lucky to have a fine day for this and our camp work, but we shall want wind or change of sliding conditions to do anything on such a surface as we have got. I fear there will not be much change for the next 3 or 4 days.

R. 33. Temp. -17°. We have struggled out 4.6 miles in a short day over a really terrible surface—it has been like pulling over desert sand, not the least glide in the world. If this goes on we shall have a bad time, but I sincerely trust it is only the result of this windless area close to the coast and that, as we are making steadily outwards, we shall shortly escape it. It is perhaps premature to be anxious about covering distance. In all other respects things are improving. We have our sleeping-bags spread on the sledge and they are drying, but, above all, we have our full measure of food again. To-night we had a sort of stew fry of pemmican and horseflesh, and voted it the best hoosh we had ever had on a sledge journey. The absence of poor Evans is a help to the commissariat, but if he had been here in a fit state we might have got along faster. I wonder what is in store for us, with some little alarm at the lateness of the season.

Monday, February 20.—R.34. Lunch Temp. -13°; Supper Temp. -15°. Same terrible surface; four hours' hard plodding in morning brought us to our Desolation Camp, where we had the four-day blizzard. We looked for more pony meat, but found none. After lunch we took to ski with some improvement of comfort. Total mileage for day 7—the ski tracks pretty plain and easily followed this afternoon. We have left another cairn behind. Terribly slow progress,

but we hope for better things as we clear the land. There is a tendency to cloud over in the S.E. to-night, which may turn to our advantage. At present our sledge and ski leave deeply ploughed tracks which can be seen winding for miles behind. It is distressing, but as usual trials are forgotten when we camp, and good food is our lot. Pray God we get better travelling as we are not fit as we were, and the season is advancing apace.

Tuesday, February 21.—R.35. Lunch Temp. –9½°; Supper Temp. -11°. Gloomy and overcast when we started; a good deal warmer. The marching almost as bad as yesterday. Heavy toiling all day, inspiring gloomiest thoughts at times. Rays of comfort when we picked up tracks and cairns. At lunch we seemed to have missed the way, but an hour or two after we passed the last pony walls, and since, we struck a tent ring, ending the march actually on our old pony-tracks. There is a critical spot here with a long stretch between cairns. If we can tide that over we get on the regular cairn route, and with luck should stick to it; but everything depends on the weather. We never won a march of 8½ miles with greater difficulty, but we can't go on like this. We are drawing away from the land and perhaps may get better things in a day or two. I devoutly hope so.

Wednesday, February 22.—R.36. Supper Temp. -2°. There is little doubt we are in for a rotten critical time going home, and the lateness of the season may make it really serious. Shortly after starting to-day the wind grew very fresh from the S.E. with strong surface drift. We lost the faint track immediately, though covering ground fairly rapidly. Lunch came without sight of the cairn we had hoped to pass. In the afternoon, Bowers being sure we were too far to the west, steered out. Result, we have passed another pony camp without seeing it. Looking at the map to-night there is no doubt we are too far to the east. With clear weather we ought to be able to correct the mistake, but will the weather get clear? It's a gloomy position, more especially as one sees the same difficulty returning even when we have corrected the error. The wind is dying down to-night and the sky clearing in the south, which is hopeful. Meanwhile it is satisfactory to note that such untoward events fail to damp the spirit of the party. To-night we had a pony hoosh so excellent and filling that one feels really strong and vigorous again.

Thursday, February 23.—R.37. Lunch Temp. -9.8°; Supper Temp. -12°. Started in sunshine, wind almost dropped. Luckily Bowers took a round of angles and with help of the chart we fogged out that we must be inside rather than outside tracks. The data were so meagre that it seemed a great responsibility to march out and we were none of us happy about it. But just as we decided to lunch, Bowers' wonderful sharp eyes detected an old double lunch cairn, the theodolite telescope confirmed it, and our spirits rose accordingly. This afternoon we marched on and picked up another cairn; then on and camped only 2½ miles from the depôt. We cannot see it, but, given fine weather, we cannot miss it. We are, therefore, extraordinarily relieved. Covered 8.2 miles in 7 hours, showing we can do 10 to 12 on this surface. Things are again looking up, as we are on the regular line of cairns, with no gaps right home, I hope.

Friday, February 24.—Lunch. Beautiful day—too beautiful—an hour after starting loose ice crystals spoiling surface. Saw depôt and reached it middle forenoon. Found store in order except shortage oil[26]—shall have to be *very* saving with fuel—otherwise have ten full days' provision from to-night and shall have less than 70 miles to go. Note from Meares who passed through December 15, saying surface bad; from Atkinson, after fine marching (2¼ days from pony depôt), reporting Keohane better after sickness. Short note from Evans, not very cheerful, saying surface bad, temperature high. Think he must have been a little anxious. It is an immense relief to have picked up this depôt and, for the time, anxieties are thrust aside. There is no doubt we have been rising steadily since leaving the Shambles Camp. The coastal Barrier descends except where glaciers press out. Undulation still but

flattening out. Surface soft on top, curiously hard below. Great difference now between night and day temperatures. Quite warm as I write in tent. We are on tracks with half-march cairn ahead; have covered 4½ miles. Poor Wilson has a fearful attack snow-blindness consequent on yesterday's efforts. Wish we had more fuel.

Night camp R. 38. Temp. -17°. A little despondent again. We had a really terrible surface this afternoon and only covered 4 miles. We are on the track just beyond a lunch cairn. It really will be a bad business if we are to have this pulling all through. I don't know what to think, but the rapid closing of the season is ominous. It is great luck having the horsemeat to add to our ration. To-night we have had a real fine 'hoosh.' It is a race between the season and hard conditions and our fitness and good food.

Saturday, February 25.—Lunch Temp. -12°. Managed just 6 miles this morning. Started somewhat despondent; not relieved when pulling seemed to show no improvement. Bit by bit surface grew better, less sastrugi, more glide, slight following wind for a time. Then we began to travel a little faster. But the pulling is still *very* hard; undulations disappearing but inequalities remain.

Twenty-six Camp walls about 2 miles ahead, all tracks in sight—Evans' track very conspicuous. This is something in favour, but the pulling is tiring us, though we are getting into better ski drawing again. Bowers hasn't quite the trick and is a little hurt at my criticisms, but I never doubted his heart. Very much easier—write diary at lunch—excellent meal—now one pannikin very strong tea—four biscuits and butter.

Hope for better things this afternoon, but no improvement apparent. Oh! for a little wind—E. Evans evidently had plenty.

R.39. Temp. -20°. Better march in afternoon. Day yields 11.4 miles—the first double figure of steady dragging for a long time, but it meant and will mean hard work if we can't get a wind to help us. Evans evidently had a strong wind here, S.E. I should think. The temperature goes very low at night now when the sky is clear as at present. As a matter of fact this is wonderfully fair weather—the only drawback the spoiling of the surface and absence of wind. We see all tracks very plain, but the pony-walls have evidently been badly drifted up. Some kind people had substituted a cairn at last camp 27. The old cairns do not seem to have suffered much.

Sunday, February 26.—Lunch Temp. -17°. Sky overcast at start, but able see tracks and cairn distinct at long distance. Did a little better, 6½ miles to date. Bowers and Wilson now in front. Find great relief pulling behind with no necessity to keep attention on track. Very cold nights now and cold feet starting march, as day footgear doesn't dry at all. We are doing well on our food, but we ought to have yet more. I hope the next depôt, now only 50 miles, will find us with enough surplus to open out. The fuel shortage still an anxiety.

R.40. Temp. -21°. Nine hours' solid marching has given us 11½ miles. Only 43 miles from the next depôt. Wonderfully fine weather but cold, very cold. Nothing dries and we get our feet cold too often. We want more food yet and especially more fat. Fuel is woefully short. We can scarcely hope to get a better surface at this season, but I wish we could have some help from the wind, though it might shake us badly if the temp didn't rise.

Monday, February 27.—Desperately cold last night: -33° when we got up, with -37° minimum. Some suffering from cold feet, but all got good rest. We *must* open out on food soon. But we have done 7 miles this morning and hope for some 5 this afternoon. Overcast sky and good surface till now, when sun shows again. It is good to be marching the cairns up, but there is still much to be anxious about. We talk of little but food, except after meals. Land disappearing in satisfactory manner. Pray God we have no further set-backs. We are naturally always discussing possibility of meeting dogs, where and when, &c. It is a critical position. We may find ourselves in safety at next depôt, but there is a horrid element of doubt.

Camp R.41. Temp. -32°. Still fine clear weather but very cold—absolutely calm to-night. We have got off an excellent march for these days (12.2) and are much earlier than usual in our bags. 31 miles to depôt, 3 days' fuel at a pinch, and 6 days' food. Things begin to look a little better; we can open out a little on food from to-morrow night, I think.

Very curious surface—soft recent sastrugi which sink underfoot, and between, a sort of flaky crust with large crystals beneath.

Tuesday, February 28.—Lunch. Thermometer went below -40° last night; it was desperately cold for us, but we had a fair night. I decided to slightly increase food; the effect is undoubtedly good. Started marching in -32° with a slight north-westerly breeze—blighting. Many cold feet this morning; long time over foot gear, but we are earlier. Shall camp earlier and get the chance of a good night, if not the reality. Things must be critical till we reach the depôt, and the more I think of matters, the more I anticipate their remaining so after that event. Only 24½ miles from the depôt. The sun shines brightly, but there is little warmth in it. There is no doubt the middle of the Barrier is a pretty awful locality.

Camp 42. Splendid pony hoosh sent us to bed and sleep happily after a horrid day, wind continuing; did 11½ miles. Temp. not quite so low, but expect we are in for cold night (Temp. -27°).

Wednesday, February 29.—Lunch. Cold night. Minimum Temp. -37.5°; -30° with north-west wind, force 4, when we got up. Frightfully cold starting; luckily Bowers and Oates in their last new finnesko; keeping my old ones for present. Expected awful march and for first hour got it. Then things improved and we camped after 5½ hours marching close to lunch camp—22½. Next camp is our depôt and it is exactly 13 miles. It ought not to take more than 1½ days; we pray for another fine one. The oil will just about spin out in that event, and we arrive 3 clear days' food in hand. The increase of ration has had an enormously beneficial result. Mountains now looking small. Wind still very light from west—cannot understand this wind.

Thursday, March 1.—Lunch. Very cold last night—minimum -41.5°. Cold start to march, too, as usual now. Got away at 8 and have marched within sight of depôt; flag something under 3 miles away. We did 11½ yesterday and marched 6 this morning. Heavy dragging yesterday and *very* heavy this morning. Apart from sledging considerations the weather is wonderful. Cloudless days and nights and the wind trifling. Worse luck, the light airs come from the north and keep us horribly cold. For this lunch hour the exception has come. There is a bright and comparatively warm sun. All our gear is out drying.

Friday, March 2.—Lunch. Misfortunes rarely come singly. We marched to the (Middle Barrier) depôt fairly easily yesterday afternoon, and since that have suffered three distinct blows which have placed us in a bad position. First we found a shortage of oil; with most rigid economy it can scarce carry us to the next depôt on this surface (71 miles away). Second, Titus Oates disclosed his feet, the toes showing very bad indeed, evidently bitten by the late temperatures. The third blow came in the night, when the wind, which we had hailed with some joy, brought dark overcast weather. It fell below -40° in the night, and this morning it took 1½ hours to get our foot gear on, but we got away before eight. We lost cairn and tracks together and made as steady as we could N. by W., but have seen nothing. Worse was to come—the surface is simply awful. In spite of strong wind and full sail we have only done 5½ miles. We are in a *very* queer street since there is no doubt we cannot do the extra marches and feel the cold horribly.

Saturday, March 3.—Lunch. We picked up the track again yesterday, finding ourselves to the eastward. Did close on 10 miles and things looked a trifle better; but this morning the outlook is blacker than ever. Started well and with good breeze; for an hour made good headway; then the surface grew awful beyond words. The wind drew forward; every circumstance was against us. After 4¼ hours things so bad that we camped, having covered 4½ miles. (R.46.) One cannot consider this a fault of our own—certainly we were pulling hard this morning —it was more than three parts surface which held us back— the wind at strongest, powerless to move the sledge. When the light is good it is easy to see the reason. The surface, lately a very good hard one, is coated with a thin layer of woolly crystals, formed by radiation no doubt. These are too firmly fixed to be removed by the wind and cause impossible friction on the runners. God help us, we can't keep up this pulling, that is certain. Amongst ourselves we are unendingly cheerful, but what each man feels in his heart I can only guess. Pulling on foot gear in the morning is getter slower and slower, therefore every day more dangerous.

Sunday, March 4.—Lunch. Things looking *very* black indeed. As usual we forgot our trouble last night, got into our bags, slept splendidly on good hoosh, woke and had another, and started marching. Sun shining brightly, tracks clear, but surface covered with sandy frostrime. All the morning we had to pull with all our strength, and in 4½ hours we covered 3½ miles. Last night it was overcast and thick, surface bad; this morning sun shining and surface as bad as ever. One has little to hope for except perhaps strong dry wind—an unlikely contingency at this time of year. Under the immediate surface crystals is a hard sustrugi surface, which must have been excellent 'for pulling a week or two ago. We are about 42 miles from the next depôt and have a week's food, but only about 3 to 4 days' fuel—we are as economical of the latter as one can possibly be, and we cannot afford to save food and pull as we are pulling. We are in a very tight place indeed, but none of us despondent *yet*, or at least we preserve every semblance of good cheer, but one's heart sinks as the sledge stops dead at some sastrugi behind which the surface sand lies thickly heaped. For the moment the temperature is on the -20°—an improvement which makes us much more comfortable, but a colder snap is bound to come again soon. I fear that Oates at least will weather such an event very poorly. Providence to our aid! We can expect little from man now except the possibility of extra food at the next depôt. It will be real bad if we get there and find the same shortage of oil. Shall we get there? Such a short distance it would have appeared to us on the summit! I don't know what I should do if Wilson and Bowers weren't so determinedly cheerful over things.

Monday, March 5.—Lunch. Regret to say going from bad to worse. We got a slant of wind yesterday afternoon, and going on 5 hours we converted our wretched morning run of 3½ miles into something over 9. We went to bed on a cup of cocoa and pemmican solid with the chill off. (R. 47.) The result is telling on all, but mainly on. Oates, whose feet are in a wretched condition. One swelled up tremendously last night and he is very lame this morning. We started march on tea and pemmican as last night—we pretend to prefer the pemmican this way. Marched for 5 hours this morning over a slightly better surface covered with high moundy sastrugi. Sledge capsized twice; we pulled on foot, covering about 5½ miles. We are two pony marches and 4 miles about from our depôt. Our fuel dreadfully low and the poor Soldier nearly done. It is pathetic enough because we can do nothing for him; more hot food might do a little, but only a little, I fear. We none of us expected these terribly low temperatures, and of the rest of us Wilson is feeling them most; mainly, I fear, from his self-sacrificing devotion in doctoring Oates' feet. We cannot help each other, each has enough to do to take care of himself. We get cold on the march when the trudging is heavy, and the wind pierces our warm garments. The others, all of them, are unendingly cheerful when in the tent. We mean to see the game through with a proper spirit, but it's tough work to be pulling harder than we ever pulled in our lives for long hours, and to feel that the progress is so slow. One can only say 'God help us!' and plod on our weary way, cold and very miserable, though outwardly cheerful. We

talk of all sorts of subjects in the tent, not much of food now, since we decided to take the risk of running a full ration. We simply couldn't go hungry at this time.

Tuesday, March 6.—Lunch. We did a little better with help of wind yesterday afternoon, finishing 9½ miles for the day, and 27 miles from depôt. (R.48.) But this morning things have been awful. It was warm in the night and for the first time during the journey I overslept myself by more than an hour; then we were slow with foot gear; then, pulling with all our might (for our lives) we could scarcely advance at rate of a mile an hour; then it grew thick and three times we had to get out of harness to search for tracks. The result is something less than 3½ miles for the forenoon. The sun is shining now and the wind gone. Poor Oates is unable to pull, sits on the sledge when we are track-searching—he is wonderfully plucky, as his feet must be giving him great pain. He makes no complaint, but his spirits only come up in spurts now, and he grows more silent in the tent. We are making a spirit lamp to try and replace the primus when our oil is exhausted. It will be a very poor substitute and we've not got much spirit. If we could have kept up our 9-mile days we might have got within reasonable distance of the depôt before running out, but nothing but a strong wind and good surface can help us now, and though we had quite a good breeze this morning, the sledge came as heavy as lead. If we were all fit I should have hopes of getting through, but the poor Soldier has become a terrible hindrance, though he does his utmost and suffers much I fear.

Wednesday, March 7.—A little worse I fear. One of Oates' feet *very* bad this morning; he is wonderfully brave. We still talk of what we will do together at home.

We only made 6½ miles yesterday. (R. 49.) This morning in 4½ hours we did just over 4 miles. We are 16 from our depôt. If we only find the correct proportion of food there and this surface continues, we may get to the next depôt [Mt. Hooper, 72 miles farther] but not to One

Ton Camp. We hope against hope that the dogs have been to Mt. Hooper; then we might pull through. If there is a shortage of oil again we can have little hope. One feels that for poor Oates the crisis is near, but none of us are improving, though we are wonderfully fit considering the really excessive work we are doing. We are only kept going by good food. No wind this morning till a chill northerly air came ahead. Sun bright and cairns showing up well. I should like to keep the track to the end.

Thursday, March 8.—Lunch. Worse and worse in morning; poor Oates' left foot can never last out, and time over foot gear something awful. Have to wait in night foot gear for nearly an hour before I start changing, and then am generally first to be ready. Wilson's feet giving trouble now, but this mainly because he gives so much help to others. We did 4½ miles this morning and are now 8½ miles from the depôt— a ridiculously small distance to feel in difficulties, yet on this surface we know we cannot equal half our old marches, and that for that effort we expend nearly double the energy. The great question is, What shall we find at the depôt? If the dogs have visited it we may get along a good distance, but if there is another short allowance of fuel, God help us indeed. We are in a very bad way, I fear, in any case.

Saturday, March 10.—Things steadily downhill. Oates' foot worse. He has rare pluck and must know that he can never get through. He asked Wilson if he had a chance this morning, and of course Bill had to say he didn't know. In point of fact he has none. Apart from him, if he went under now, I doubt whether we could get through. With great care we might have a dog's chance, but no more. The weather conditions are awful, and our gear gets steadily more icy and difficult to manage. At the same time of course poor Titus is the greatest handicap. He keeps us waiting in the morning until we have partly lost the warming effect of our good breakfast, when the only wise policy is to be up and away at once; again at lunch. Poor chap! it is too

pathetic to watch him; one cannot but try to cheer him up.

Yesterday we marched up the depôt, Mt. Hooper. Cold comfort. Shortage on our allowance all round. I don't know that anyone is to blame. The dogs which would have been our salvation have evidently failed. Meares had a bad trip home I suppose.

This morning it was calm when we breakfasted, but the wind came from W.N.W. as we broke camp. It rapidly grew in strength. After travelling for half an hour I saw that none of us could go on facing such conditions. We were forced to camp and are spending the rest of the day in a comfortless blizzard camp, wind quite foul. (R.52.)

Sunday, March 11.—Titus Oates is very near the end, one feels. What we or he will do, God only knows. We discussed the matter after breakfast; he is a brave fine fellow and understands the situation, but he practically asked for advice. Nothing could be said but to urge him to march as long as he could. One satisfactory result to the discussion; I practically ordered Wilson to hand over the means of ending our troubles to us, so that anyone of us may know how to do so. Wilson had no choice between doing so and our ransacking the medicine case. We have 30 opium tabloids apiece and he is left with a tube of morphine. So far the tragical side of our story. (R.53.)

The sky completely overcast when we started this morning. We could see nothing, lost the tracks, and doubtless have been swaying a good deal since—3.1 miles for the forenoon—terribly heavy dragging—expected it. Know that 6 miles is about the limit of our endurance now, if we get no help from wind or surfaces. We have 7 days' food and should be about 55 miles from One Ton Camp to-night, 6 ° 7 ° 42, leaving us 13 miles short of our distance, even if things get no worse. Meanwhile the season rapidly advances.

Monday, March 12.—We did 6.9 miles yesterday, under our necessary average. Things are left much the same, Oates not pulling much, and now with hands as well as feet pretty well useless. We did 4 miles this morning in 4 hours 20 min.—we may hope for 3 this afternoon, 7 ° 6 ° 42. We shall be 47 miles from the depôt. I doubt if we can possibly do it. The surface remains awful, the cold intense, and our physical condition running down. God help us! Not a breath of favourable wind for more than a week, and apparently liable to head winds at any moment.

Wednesday, March 14.—No doubt about the going downhill, but everything going wrong for us. Yesterday we woke to a strong northerly wind with temp. -37°. Could n't face it, so remained in camp (R.54) till 2, then did 5¼ miles. Wanted to march later, but party feeling the cold badly as the breeze (N.) never took off entirely, and as the sun sank the temp. fell. Long time getting supper in dark. (R.55.)

This morning started with southerly breeze, set sail and passed another cairn at good speed; half-way, however, the wind shifted to W. by S. or W.S.W., blew through our wind clothes and into our mits. Poor Wilson horribly cold, could not get off ski for some time. Bowers and I practically made camp, and when we got into the tent at last we were all deadly cold. Then temp. now midday down -43° and the wind strong. We *must* go on, but now the making of every camp must be more difficult and dangerous. It must be near the end, but a pretty merciful end. Poor Oates got it again in the foot. I shudder to think what it will be like to-morrow. It is only with greatest pains rest of us keep off frostbites. No idea there could be temperatures like this at this time of year with such winds. Truly awful outside the tent. Must fight it out to the last biscuit, but can't reduce rations.

Friday, March 16 *or Saturday* 17.—Lost track of dates, but think the last correct. Tragedy all along the line. At lunch, the day before yesterday, poor Titus Oates said he could n't go on; he proposed we should leave him in his sleeping-bag. That we could not do, and induced him to come on, on the afternoon march. In spite of its

awful nature for him he struggled on and we made a few miles. At night he was worse and we knew the end had come.

Should this be found I want these facts recorded. Oates' last thoughts were of his Mother, but immediately before he took pride in thinking that his regiment would be pleased with the bold way in which he met his death. We can testify to his bravery. He has borne intense suffering for weeks without complaint, and to the very last was able and willing to discuss outside subjects. He did not—would not—give up hope to the very end. He was a brave soul. This was the end. He slept through the night before last, hoping not to wake; but he woke in the morning—yesterday. It was blowing a blizzard. He said, 'I am just going outside and may be some time.' He went out into the blizzard and we have not seen him since.

I take this opportunity of saying that we have stuck to our sick companions to the last. In case of Edgar Evans, when absolutely out of food and he lay insensible, the safety of the remainder seemed to demand his abandonment, but Providence mercifully removed him at this critical moment. He died a natural death, and we did not leave him till two hours after his death. We knew that poor Oates was walking to his death, but though we tried to dissuade him, we knew it was the act of a brave man and an English gentleman. We all hope to meet the end with a similar spirit, and assuredly the end is not far.

I can only write at lunch and then only occasionally. The cold is intense, -40° at midday. My companions are unendingly cheerful, but we are all on the verge of serious frostbites, and though we constantly talk of fetching through I don't think anyone of us believes it in his heart.

We are cold on the march now, and at all times except meals. Yesterday we had to lay up for a blizzard and to-day we move dreadfully slowly. We are at No. 14 pony camp, only two pony marches from One Ton Depôt. We leave here our theodolite, a camera, and Oates' sleeping-bags. Diaries, &c., and geological specimens carried at Wilson's special request, will be found with us or on our sledge.

Sunday, March 18.—To-day, lunch, we are 21 miles from the depôt. Ill fortune presses, but better may come. We have had more wind and drift from ahead yesterday; had to stop marching; wind N.W., force 4, temp. -35°. No human being could face it, and we are worn out *nearly*.

My right foot has gone, nearly all the toes—two days ago I was proud possessor of best feet. These are the steps of my downfall. Like an ass I mixed a small spoonful of curry powder with my melted pemmican—it gave me violent indigestion. I lay awake and in pain all night; woke and felt done on the march; foot went and I didn't know it. A very small measure of neglect and have a foot which is not pleasant to contemplate. Bowers takes first place in condition, but there is not much to choose after all. The others are still confident of getting through—or pretend to be—I don't know! We have the last *half* fill of oil in our primus and a very small quantity of spirit—this alone between us and thirst. The wind is fair for the moment, and that is perhaps a fact to help. The mileage would have seemed ridiculously small on our outward journey.

Monday, March 19.—Lunch. We camped with difficulty last night, and were dreadfully cold till after our supper of cold pemmican and biscuit and a half a pannikin of cocoa cooked over the spirit. Then, contrary to expectation, we got warm and all slept well. To-day we started in the usual dragging manner. Sledge dreadfully heavy. We are 15½ miles from the depôt and ought to get there in three days. What progress! We have two days' food but barely a day's fuel. All our feet are getting bad—Wilson's best, my right foot worst, left all right. There is no chance to nurse one's feet till we can get hot food into us. Amputation is the least I can hope for now, but will the trouble spread? That is the serious question. The weather doesn't give us a chance—the wind from N. to N.W. and -40° temp. to-day.

Wednesday, March 21.—Got within 11 miles of depôt Monday night; had to lay up all yester-day in severe blizzard.[27] To-day forlorn hope, Wilson and Bowers going to depôt for fuel.

Thursday, March 22 and 23.—Blizzard bad as ever—Wilson and Bowers unable to start—tomorrow last chance—no fuel and only one or two of food left—must be near the end. Have decided it shall be natural—we shall march for the depôt with or without our effects and die in our tracks.

Thursday, March 29.—Since the 21st we have had a continuous gale from W.S.W. and S.W. We had fuel to make two cups of tea apiece and bare food for two days on the 20th. Every day we have been ready to start for our depôt *11 miles* away, but outside the door of the tent it remains a scene of whirling drift. I do not think we can hope for any better things now. We shall stick it out to the end, but we are getting weaker, of course, and the end cannot be far.

It seems a pity, but I do not think I can write more.

R. SCOTT

For God's sake look after our people.

Wilson and Bowers were found in the attitude of sleep, their sleeping-bags closed over their heads as they would naturally close them.

Scott died later. He had thrown back the flaps of his sleeping-bag and opened his coat. The little wallet containing the three notebooks was under his shoulders and his arm flung across Wilson. So they were found eight months later.

With the diaries in the tent were found the following letters:

To Mrs. E. A. Wilson
MY DEAR MRS. E. A. WILSON

If this letter reaches you Bill and I will have gone out together. We are very near it now and I should like you to know how splendid he was at the end—everlastingly cheerful and ready to sacrifice himself for others, never a word of blame to me for leading him into this mess. He is not suffering, luckily, at least only minor discomforts.

His eyes have a comfortable blue look of hope

and his mind is peaceful with the satisfaction of his faith in regarding himself as part of the great scheme of the Almighty. I can do no more to comfort you than to tell you that he died as he lived, a brave, true man—the best of comrades and staunchest of friends.

My whole heart goes out to you in pity,

Yours,

R. SCOTT

To Mrs. Bowers

MY DEAR MRS. BOWERS,

I am afraid this will reach you after one of the heaviest blows of your life.

I write when we are very near the end of our journey, and I am finishing it in company with two gallant, noble gentlemen. One of these is your son. He had come to be one of my closest and soundest friends, and I appreciate his wonderful upright nature, his ability and energy. As the troubles have thickened his dauntless spirit ever shone brighter and he has remained cheerful, hopeful, and indomitable to the end.

The ways of Providence are inscrutable, but there must be some reason why such a young, vigorous and promising life is taken.

My whole heart goes out in pity for you.

Yours,

R. SCOTT.

To the end he has talked of you and his sisters. One sees what a happy home he must have had and perhaps it is well to look back on nothing but happiness.

He remains unselfish, self-reliant and splendidly hopeful to the end, believing in God's mercy to you.

To Sir J. M. Barrie

MY DEAR BARRIE,

We are pegging out in a very comfortless spot. Hoping this letter may be found and sent to you, I write a word of farewell. . . . More practically I want you to help my widow and my boy—your godson. We are showing that Englishmen can still die with a bold spirit, fighting it

out to the end. It will be known that we have accomplished our object in reaching the Pole, and that we have done everything possible, even to sacrificing ourselves in order to save sick companions. I think this makes an example for Englishmen of the future, and that the country ought to help those who are left behind to mourn us. I leave my poor girl and your godson, Wilson leaves a widow, and Edgar Evans also a widow in humble circumstances. Do what you can to get their claims recognised. Goodbye. I am not at all afraid of the end, but sad to miss many a humble pleasure which I had planned for the future on our long marches. I may not have proved a great explorer, but we have done the greatest march ever made and come very near to great success. Goodbye, my dear friend,

Yours ever,

R. SCOTT.

We are in a desperate state, feet frozen, &c. No fuel and a long way from food, but it would do your heart good to be in our tent, to hear our songs and the cheery conversation as to what we will do when we get to Hut Point.

Later.—We are very near the end, but have not and will not lose our good cheer. We have four days of storm in our tent and nowhere's food or fuel. We did intend to finish ourselves when things proved like this, but we have decided to die naturally in the track.

As a dying man, my dear friend, be good to my wife and child. Give the boy a chance in life if the State won't do it. He ought to have good stuff in him. . . . I never met a man in my life whom I admired and loved more than you, but I never could show you how much your friendship meant to me, for you had much to give and I nothing.

To the Right Hon. Sir Edgar Speyer, Bart.

Dated March 16, 1912. Lat. 79.5°.

MY DEAR SIR EDGAR,

I hope this may reach you. I fear we must go and that it leaves the Expedition in a bad muddle. But we have been to the Pole and we shall die like gentlemen. I regret only for the women we leave behind.

I thank you a thousand times for your help and support and your generous kindness. If this diary is found it will show how we stuck by dying companions and fought the thing out well to the end. I think this will show that the Spirit of pluck and power to endure has not passed out of our race. . . .

Wilson, the best fellow that ever stepped, has sacrificed himself again and again to the sick men of the party. . . .

I write to many friends hoping the letters will reach them some time after we are found next year.

We very nearly came through, and it's a pity to have missed it, but lately I have felt that we have overshot our mark. No one is to blame and I hope no attempt will be made to suggest that we have lacked support.

Good-bye to you and your dear kind wife.
Yours ever sincerely,
R. SCOTT.

To Vice-Admiral Sir Francis Charles Bridgeman, K.C.V.O., K.C.B.

MY DEAR SIR FRANCIS,

I fear we have shipped up; a close shave; I am writing a few letters which I hope will be delivered some day. I want to thank you for the friendship you gave me of late years, and to tell you how extraordinarily pleasant I found it to serve under you. I want to tell you that I was *not* too old for this job. It was the younger men that went under first. . . . After all we are setting a good example to our countrymen, if not by getting into a tight place, by facing it like men when we were there. We could have come through had we neglected the sick.

Good-bye, and good-bye to dear Lady Bridgeman.
Yours ever,
R. SCOTT.

Excuse writing—it is -40°, and has been for nigh a month.

To Vice-Admiral Sir George le Clerc Egerton, K.C.B.

MY DEAR SIR GEORGE,

I fear we have shot our bolt—but we have been to Pole and done the longest journey on record.

I hope these letters may find their destination some day.

Subsidiary reasons of our failure to return are due to the sickness of different members of the party, but the real thing that has stopped us is the awful weather and unexpected cold towards the end of the journey.

This traverse of the Barrier has been quite three times as severe as any experience we had on the summit.

There is no accounting for it, but the result has thrown out my calculations, and here we are little more than 100 miles from the base and petering out.

Good-bye. Please see my widow is looked after as far as Admiralty is concerned.
R. SCOTT.

My kindest regards to Lady Egerton. I can never forget all your kindness.

To Mr. J. J. Kinsey—Christchurch
March 24th, 1912.

MY DEAR KINSEY,

I'm afraid we are pretty well done—four days of blizzard just as we were getting to the last depôt. My thoughts have been with you often. You have been a brick. You will pull the expedition through, I'm sure.

My thoughts are for my wife and boy. Will you do what you can for them if the country won't.

I want the boy to have a good chance in the world, but you know the circumstances well enough.

If I knew the wife and boy were in safe keeping I should have little regret in leaving the world, for I feel that the country need not be ashamed of us—our journey has been the biggest on record, and nothing but the most exceptional hard luck at the end would have caused us to fail to return. We have been to the S. pole as we set out. God bless you and dear Mrs. Kinsey. It is good to remember you and your kindness.

> Your friend,
> R. SCOTT.

Letters to his Mother, his Wife, his Brother-in-law (Sir William Ellison Macartney), Admiral Sir Lewis Beaumont, and Mr. and Mrs. Reginald Smith were also found, from which come the following extracts:

The Great God has called me and I feel it will add a fearful blow to the heavy ones that have fallen on you in life. But take comfort in that I die at peace with the world and myself—not afraid.

Indeed it has been most singularly unfortunate, for the risks I have taken never seemed excessive.

. . . I want to tell you that we have missed getting through by a narrow margin which was justifiably within the risk of such a journey. . . . After all, we have given our lives for our country—we have actually made the longest journey on record, and we have been the first Englishmen at the South Pole.

You must understand that it is too cold to write much. . . . It's a pity the luck doesn't come our way, because every detail of equipment is right.

I shall not have suffered any pain, but leave the world fresh from harness and full of good health and vigour.

Since writing the above we got to within 11 miles of our depôt, with one hot meal and two days' cold food. We should have got through but have been held for *four* days by a frightful storm. I think the best chance has gone. We have decided not to kill ourselves, but to fight to the last for that depôt, but in the fighting there is a painless end.

Make the boy interested in natural history if you can; it is better than games; they encourage it at some schools. I know you will keep him in the open air.

Above all, he must guard and you must guard

him against indolence. Make him a strenuous man. I had to force myself into being strenuous as you know—had always an inclination to be idle.

There is a piece of the Union Jack I put up at the South Pole in my private kit bag, together with Amundsen's black flag and other trifles. Send a small piece of the Union Jack to the King and a small piece to Queen Alexandra.

What lots and lots I could tell you of this journey. How much better has it been than lounging in too great comfort at home. What tales you would have for the boys. But what a price to pay.

Tell Sir Clements I thought much of him and never regretted him putting me in command of the *Discovery*.

MESSAGE TO THE PUBLIC

THE causes of the disaster are not due to faulty organisation, but to misfortune in all risks which had to be undertaken.

1. The loss of pony transport in March 1911 obliged me to start later than I had intended, and obliged the limits of stuff transported to be narrowed.
2. The weather throughout the outward journey, and especially the long gale in 83° S., stopped us.
3. The soft snow in lower reaches of glacier again reduced pace.

We fought these untoward events with a will and conquered, but it cut into our provision reserve.

Every detail of our food supplies, clothing and depôts made on the interior ice-sheet and over that long stretch of 700 miles to the Pole and back, worked out to perfection. The advance party would have returned to the glacier in fine form and with surplus of food, but for the astonishing failure of the man whom we had least expected to fail. Edgar Evans was thought the strongest man of the party.

The Beardmore Glacier is not difficult in fine weather, but on our return we did not get a single completely fine day; this with a sick companion enormously increased our anxieties.

As I have said elsewhere we got into frightfully rough ice and Edgar Evans received a concussion of the brain—he died a natural death, but left us a shaken party with the season unduly advanced.

But all the facts above enumerated were as nothing to the surprise which awaited us on the Barrier. I maintain that our arrangements for returning were quite adequate, and that no one in the world would have expected the temperatures and surfaces which we encountered at this time of the year. On the summit in lat. 85° 86° we had -20°, -30°. On the Barrier in lat. 82°, 10,000 feet lower, we had -30° in the day, -47° at night pretty regularly, with continuous head wind during our day marches. It is clear that these circumstances come on very suddenly, and our wreck is certainly due to this sudden advent of severe weather, which does not seem to have any satisfactory cause. I do not think human beings ever came through such a month as we have come through, and we should have got through in spite of the weather but for the sickening of a second companion, Captain Oates, and a shortage of fuel in our depôts for which I cannot account, and finally, but for the storm which has fallen on us within 11 miles of the depôt at which we hoped to secure our final supplies. Surely misfortune could scarcely have exceeded this last blow. We arrived within 11 miles of our old One Ton Camp with fuel for one last meal and food for two days. For four days we have been unable to leave the tent—the gale howling about us. We are weak, writing is difficult, but for my own sake I do not regret this journey, which has shown that Englishmen can endure hardships, help one another, and meet death with as great a fortitude as ever in the past. We took risks, we knew we took them; things have come out against us, and therefore we have no cause for complaint, but bow to the will of Providence, determined still to do our best to the last.

But if we have been willing to give our lives to this enterprise, which is for the honour of our country, I appeal to our countrymen to see that those who depend on us are properly cared for.

Had we lived, I should have had a tale to tell of the hardihood, endurance, and courage of my companions which would have stirred the heart of every Englishman. These rough notes and our dead bodies must tell the tale, but surely, surely, a great rich country like ours will see that those who are dependent on us are properly provided for.

R. SCOTT.

* Sledges were left at the chief depôts to replace damaged ones.
* It will be remembered that he was already stricken with scurvy.
* For the last six days the dogs had been waiting at One Ton Camp under Cherry-Garrard and Demetri. The supporting party had come out as arranged on the chance of hurrying the Pole travellers back over the last stages of their journey in time to catch the ship. Scott had dated his probable return to Hut Point anywhere between mid-March and early April. Calculating from the speed of the other return parties, Dr. Atkinson looked for him to reach One Ton Camp between March 3 and 10. Here Cherry-Garrard met four days of blizzard; then there remained little more than enough dog food to bring the teams home. He could either push south one more march and back, at imminent risk of missing Scott on the way, or stay two days at the Camp where Scott was bound to come, if he came at all. His wise decision, his hardships and endurance and recounted by Dr. Atkinson in Vol. II., 'The Last Year at Cape Evans.'
* The 60th camp from the Pole.

Suggested Readings

Scott, Robert F. *The Diaries of Captain Robert Scott: a Record of the Second Antarctic Expedition 1910–1912*. High Wycombe: University Microfilms, 1968.

Scott, Robert F. *Scott's Last Expedition: The Journals*. New York: Carroll & Graf, 1996.

Scott, Robert F. *The Voyage of the Discovery*. New York: Dodd, Mead and Company, 1913.

32

No Man Could Wish For More: President Woodrow Wilson's Commencement Address to the US Naval Academy Class of 1916

Dr. Joseph J. Thomas

While there have been numerous inspiring calls to duty at the commencement ceremonies of the U.S Naval Academy, perhaps none have been more direct and brief then President Woodrow Wilson's address to the Naval Academy Class of 1916. Particularly impressive is the fact that he spoke from neither notes nor prepared text. Less than a year later, President Wilson's words would take on greater significance as the US declared war on Germany.

* * *

Mr. Superintendent, young gentlemen, ladies and gentlemen:

It had not been my purpose when I came here to say anything today, but as I sit here and look at you youngsters, I find that my feeling is a very personal feeling indeed. I know some of the things that you have been through, and I admire the way in which you have responded to the new call of duty. I would feel that I had not done either you or myself justice if I did not tell you so.

I have thought that there was one interesting bond that united us. You were at Washington three years ago and saw me get into trouble, and now, I am here to see the beginning of your trouble. Your trouble will last longer than mine, but I doubt if it will be any more interesting. I have had a liberal education in the last three years, with which nothing that I underwent before bears the slightest comparison. But what I want to say to you young gentlemen is this: I can illustrate it in this way. Once and again when youngsters here or at West Point have forgotten themselves and done something that they ought not to do and were about to be disciplined, perhaps severely, for it, I have been appealed to by their friends to excuse them from the penalty. Knowing that I have spent most of my life at a college, they commonly say to me, "You know college boys. You know what they are. They are heedless youngsters very often, and they ought not to be held up to the same standards of responsibility that older men must submit to." And I have always replied, "Yes; I know college boys. But while these youngsters are college boys, they are something more. They are officers of the United States. They are not merely college boys. If they were, I would look at derelictions of duty on their part in another spirit; but any dereliction of duty on the party of a naval officer of the United States may involve the fortunes of a nation and cannot be overlooked." Do you not see the difference? You cannot indulge yourselves in weaknesses, gentlemen. You cannot forget your duty for a moment, because there might come a time when that weak spot in you should affect you in the midst of a great engagement, and then the whole history of the world might be changed by what you did not do or did wrong.

So that the personal feeling I have for you is this: we are all bound together. I for the time being and you permanently, under a special obligation, the most solemn that the mind can conceive. The fortunes of a nation are confided to us. Now, that ought not to depress a man. Sometimes I think that nothing is worthwhile that is not hard. You do not improve your muscle by doing the easy thing; you improve it by doing the hard thing, and you get your zest by doing a thing that is difficult, not a thing that is easy. I would a great deal rather, so far as my sense of enjoyment is concerned, have something strenuous to do than have something that can be done leisurely and without a stimulation of the faculties.

Therefore, I congratulate you that you are going to live your lives under the most stimulating compulsion that any man can feel the sense, not of private duty merely, but of public duty also. And then if you perform that duty, there is a reward awaiting you which is superior to any other reward in the world. That is the affectionate remembrance of your fellow men their honor, their affection. No man could wish for more than that or find anything higher than that to strive for. And, therefore, I want you to know, gentlemen, if it is any satisfaction to you, that I shall personally follow your careers in the days that are ahead of you with real personal interest. I wish you Godspeed, and remind you that yours is the honor of the United States.

Suggested Readings

Brands H. W. and Arthur M. Schlesinger. *Woodrow Wilson 1913–1921: The American Presidents Series*. New York: Henry Holt & Company, 2003.

Clements, Kendrick A. *Woodrow Wilson: World Statesman*. Chicago: Ivan R. Dee Publisher, 1999.

Thompson, J.A. *Woodrow Wilson: Profiles in Power*. Upper Saddle River: Longman, 2002.

33

The Path to Leadership: Theodore Roosevelt Praises the Strenuous Life

Dr. Joseph J. Thomas

Theodore Roosevelt, widely considered among the greatest "natural leaders" of the men elected president of the United States, would not have seemed pre-ordained as such in his youth. Suffering from asthma, poor eyesight, and a variety of physical ailments, young "Teddy" seemed destined for a life of infirmity. His unyielding will (along with the encouragement of his family) led him to develop himself physically, morally, and mentally. His "The Strenuous Life" speech was delivered on April 10, 1899 and delineates how anyone with grit and determination can succeed in America. The speech was delivered a year after he resigned as Assistant Secretary of the Navy to join the "Rough Riders" for expeditionary operations in Cuba.

I wish to preach, not the doctrine of ignoble ease, but the doctrine of the strenuous life, the life of toil and effort, of labor and strife; to preach that highest form of success which comes, not to the man who desires mere easy peace, but to the man who does not shrink from danger, from hardship, or from bitter toil, and who out of these wins the splendid ultimate triumph.

A life of slothful ease, a life of that peace which springs merely from lack either of desire or of power to strive after great things, is as little worthy of a nation as of an individual. I ask only that what every self-respecting American demands from himself and from his sons shall be demanded of the American nation as a whole. Who among you would teach your boys that ease, that peace, is to be the first consideration in their eyes-to be the ultimate goal after which they strive? . . . You work yourselves, and you bring up your sons to work. If you are rich and are worth your salt, you will teach your sons that though they may have leisure, it not to be spent in idleness; for wisely used leisure merely means that those who possess it, being free from the necessity of working for their livelihood, are all the more bound to carry on some kind of nonre-munerative work in science, in letters, in art, in exploration, in historical research work of the type we most need in this country .the successful carrying out of which reflects most honor upon the nation. We do not admire the man of timid peace. We admire the man who embodies victo-rious effort; the man who never wrongs his neighbor, who is prompt to help a friend, but who has those virile qualities necessary to win in the stern strife of actual life. It is hard to fail, but it is worse never to have tried to succeed. . . .

In the last analysis a healthy state can exist only when the men and women who make it up lead clean, vigorous, healthy lives; when the chil-dren are so trained that they shall endeavor, not to shirk difficulties, but to overcome them; not to seek ease, but to know how to wrest triumph from toil and risk. The man must be glad to do a man's work, to dare and endure and to labor; to keep himself, and to keep those dependent upon him. The woman must be the housewife, the helpmeet of the homemaker, the wise and fear-less mother of many healthy children. In one of Daudet's powerful and melancholy books he speaks of' 'the fear of maternity, the haunting terror of the young wife of the present day." When such words can be truthfully written of a nation, that nation is rotten to the heart's core. When men fear work or fear righteous war, when women fear motherhood, they tremble on the brink of doom; and well it is that they should vanish from the earth, where they are fit subjects for the scorn of all men and women who are themselves strong and brave and high-minded.

As it is with the individual, so it is with the na-tion. It is a base untruth to say that happy is the nation that has no history .Thrice happy is the nation that has a glorious history. Far better it is to dare mighty things, to win glorious triumphs, even though checkered by failure, than to take rank with those poor spirits who neither enjoy much nor suffer much, because they live in the gray twilight that knows not victory nor defeat. If in 1861 the men who loved the Union had be-

lieved that peace was the end of all things, and war and strife the worst of all things, and had acted up to their belief, we would have saved hundreds of thousands of lives, we would have saved hundreds of millions of dollars. Moreover, besides saving all the blood and treasure we then lavished. we would have prevented the heart-break of many women, the dissolution of many homes, and we would have spared the country those months of gloom and shame when it seemed as if our armies marched only to defeat. We could have avoided all this suffering simply by shrinking from strife. And if we had thus avoided it, we would have shown that we were weaklings, and that we were unfit to stand among the great nations of the earth. Thank God for the iron in the blood of our fathers, the men who upheld the wisdom of Lincoln, and bore sword or rifle in the armies of Grant! Let us, the children of the men who proved them-selves equal to the mighty days, let us, the chil-dren of the men who carried the great Civil War to a triumphant conclusion, praise the God of our fathers that the ignoble counsels of peace were rejected; that the suffering and loss, the blackness of sorrow and despair, were unflinch-ingly faced, and the years of strife endured; for in the end the slave was freed, the Union re-stored, and the mighty American Republic placed once more as a helmeted queen among nations.

We of this generation do not have to face a task such as that our fathers faced, but we have our tasks, and woe to us if we fail to perform them! . . .

The timid man, the lazy man, the man who distrusts his country, the over-civilized man, who has lost the great fighting, masterful virtues, the ignorant man, and the man of dull mind, whose soul is incapable of feeling the mighty lift that thrills "stem men with empires in their brains"-all these, of course, shrink from seeing the nation undertake its new duties; shrink from seeing us build a navy and an army adequate to our needs; shrink from seeing us do our share of the world's work, by bringing order out of chaos in the great, fair tropic islands from which the valor of our soldiers and sailors has driven the Spanish flag. These are the men who fear the strenuous life, who fear the only national life which is really worth leading. They believe in that cloistered life which saps the hardy virtues in a nation, as it saps them in the individual; or else they are wedded to that base spirit of gain and greed which recognizes in commercialism the be-all and end-all of national life, instead of realizing that, though an indispensable element, it is, after all, but one of the many elements that go to make up true national greatness. No country can long endure if its foundations are not laid deep in the material prosperity which comes from thrift, from business energy and enterprise, from hard, unsparing effort in the fields of industrial activity; but neither was any nation ever yet truly great if it relied upon material prosperity alone. All honor must be paid to the architects of our material prosperity, to the great captains of industry who have built our factories and our railroads, to the strong men who toil for wealth with brain or hand: for great is the debt of the nation to these and their kind. But our debt is yet greater to the men whose highest type is to be found in a statesman like Lincoln, a soldier like Grant. They showed by their lives that they recognized the law of work, the law of strife; they toiled to win a competence for themselves and those dependent upon them; but they recognized that there were yet other and even loftier duties—duties to the nation and duties to the race.

We cannot sit huddled within our own borders and avow ourselves merely an assemblage of well-to-do hucksters who care nothing for what happens beyond. Such a policy would defeat even its own end; for as the nations grow to have ever wider and wider interests, and are brought into closer and closer contact, If we are to hold our own in the struggle for naval and commercial supremacy, we must build up our power without our own borders. We must build the Isthmian canal, and we must grasp the points of vantage which will enable us to have our say in deciding the destiny of the oceans of the East and the West. . . .

The army and the navy are the sword and the shield which this nation must carry if she is to do her duty among the nations of the earth–if she is not to stand merely as the China of the Western Hemisphere. Our proper conduct toward the tropic islands we have wrested from Spain is merely the form which our duty has taken at the moment. Of course, we are bound to handle the affairs of our own household well. We must see that there is civic honesty, civic cleanliness, civic good sense in our home administration of city, state, and nation. We must strive for honesty in office, for honesty toward the creditors of the nation and of the individual; for the widest freedom of individual initiative where possible, and for the wisest control of individual initiative where it is hostile to the welfare of the many. But because we set our own household in order we are not thereby excused from playing our part in the great affairs of the world. A man's first duty is to take his own home, but he is not thereby excused from doing his duty to the state; for if he fails in this second duty it is under the penalty of ceasing to be a freeman. In the same way, while a nation's first duty is within its own borders, it is not thereby absolved from facing its duties in the world as a whole; and if it refuses to do so, it merely forfeits its right to struggle for a place among the peoples that shape the destiny of mankind. . . .

England's rule in India and Egypt has been of great benefit to England, for it has trained up generations of men accustomed to look at the larger and loftier side of public life. It has been of even greater benefit to India and Egypt. And finally, and most of all, it has advanced the cause of civilization. So, if we do our duty aright in the Philippines, we will add to that national renown which is the highest and finest part of national life, will greatly benefit the people of the Philippine Islands, and, above all, we will play our part well in the great work of uplifting mankind. But to do this work, keep ever in mind that we must show in a very high degree the qualities of courage, of honesty, and of good judgment. Resistance must be stamped out. The first and all-important work to be done is to establish the supremacy of our flag. We must put down armed resistance before we can accomplish anything else, and there should be no parleying, no faltering, in dealing with our foe. As for those in our own country who encourage the foe, we can afford contemptuously to disregard them; but it must be remembered that their utterances are not saved from being treasonable merely by the fact that they are despicable.

When once we have put down armed resistance, when once our rule is acknowledged, then an even more difficult task will begin, for then we must see to it that the islands are administered with absolute honesty and with good judgment. If we let the public service of the islands be turned into the prey of the spoils politician, we shall have begun to tread the path which Spain trod to her own destruction. We must send out there only good and able men, chosen for their fitness, and not because of their partisan service, and these men must not only administer impartial justice to the natives and serve their own government with honesty and fidelity, but must show the utmost tact and fineness, remembering that, with such people as those with whom we are to- deal, weakness is the greatest of crimes, and that next to weakness comes lack of consideration for their principles and prejudices.

I preach to you, then, my countrymen, that our country calls not for the life of ease but for the life of strenuous endeavor. The twentieth century looms before us big with the fate of many nations. If, we stand idly by, if we seek merely swollen, slothful ease and ignoble peace, if we shrink from the hard contests where men must win at hazard of their lives and at the risk of all they hold dear, then the bolder and stronger peoples will pass us by, and will win for themselves the domination of the world. Let us therefore boldly face the life of strife, resolute to do our duty well and manfully; resolute to uphold righteousness by deed and by word; resolute to be both honest and brave, to serve high ideals, yet to use practical methods. Above all, let us shrink from no strife, moral or physical, within or without the nation, provided we are certain that the strife is justified, for it is only through strife, through hard and dangerous endeavor, that we shall ultimately win the goal of true national greatness.

Suggested Reading

Roosevelt, Theodore. *American Ideals, and Other Essays, Social and Political*. New York: G. P. Putnam's sons, 1897.

Roosevelt, Theodore. *The Autobiography of Theodore Roosevelt*. New York: Octagon Books, 1975.

Roosevelt, Theodore. *The Man in the Arena: the Selected Writings of Theodore Roosevelt; a Reader*. New York: Forge, 2003.

Roosevelt, Theodore. *The Rough Riders*. New York: C. Scribner's Sons, 1899.

34

Dreaming by Day: T.E. Lawrence's Seven Pillars of Wisdom

Dr. Robert D. Madison

Thomas Edward Lawrence (1888–1935), or "Lawrence of Arabia," was attached to the Hejaz Expeditionary Force in 1917 as part of Britain's World War I effort to stimy the influence of the Turkish empire. Educated at Oxford, he brought to his military duties a profound understanding of history and culture along with a well-exercised imagination (He was trained in the archeology of the Near-East and later translated Homer's *Odyssey* into English.).

He began writing his account of the revolt in the desert immediately after the war, losing much of his manuscript in a railroad station and having to start over from memory. In 1922 he printed a private edition, and published an abridged version for the public in 1926.

"All men dream," Lawrence wrote in his introduction, "but not equally":

Those who dream by night in the dusty recesses of their minds wake in the day to find that it was vanity: but the dreamers of the day are dangerous men, for they may act their dreams with open eyes, to make it possible. This I did.

Lawrence organized the Arab revolt by unifying quarreling factions under the banner of freedom from Turkish rule. But Arab unity was an abstract idea, difficult for Lawrence to present as a goal worth shedding blood for. In the end, there was blood enough, although not English. "I am proudest of my thirty fights in that I did not have any of our own blood shed," Lawrence wrote; "All our subject provinces to me were not worth one dead Englishman."

Several years after the war, Colonel Lawrence changed his name and enlisted in the fledgling Royal Air Force. He died in a motorcycle accident. The "dream" recorded here, from his *Seven Pillars of Wisdom* (1935), recounts Lawrence's physical and mental exhaustion after "hours of the worst imaginable marching." "The illness, however," Lawrence writes, "had stimulated my ordinarily sluggish fancy." It would also change the course of history.

CHAPTER XXXIII

About ten days I lay in that tent, suffering a bodily weakness which made my animal self crawl away and hide till the shame was passed. As usual in such circumstances my mind cleared, my senses became more acute, and I began at last to think consecutively of the Arab Revolt, as an accustomed duty to rest upon against the pain. It should have been thought out long before, but at my first landing in Hejaz there had been a crying need for action, and we had done what seemed to instinct best, not probing into the why, nor formulating what we really wanted at the end of all. Instinct thus abused without a basis of past knowledge and reflection had grown intuitive, feminine, and was now bleaching my confidence; so in this forced inaction I looked for the equation between my book-reading and my movements, and spent the intervals of uneasy sleeps and dreams in plucking at the tangle of our present.

As I have shown, I was unfortunately as much in command of the campaign as I pleased, and was untrained. In military theory I was tolerably read, my Oxford curiosity having taken me past Napoleon to Clausewitz and his school, to Caemmerer and Moltke, and after the recent Frenchmen. They had all seemed to be one-sided; and after looking at Jomini and Willisen, I had found broader principles in Saxe and Guibert and the eighteenth century. However, Clausewitz was intellectually so much the master of them, and his book so logical and fascinating, that unconsciously I accepted his finality, until a comparison of Kuhne and Foch disgusted me with soldiers, wearied me of their officious glory, making me critical of all their light. In any case, my interest had been abstract, concerned with the theory and philosophy of warfare especially from the metaphysical side.

Now, in the field everything had been concrete, particularly the tiresome problem of Medina; and to distract myself from that I began to recall suitable maxims on the conduct of modern, scientific war. But they would not fit, and it worried me. Hitherto, Medina had been an ob-session for us all; but now that I was ill, its image was not clear, whether it was that we were near to it (one seldom liked the attainable), or whether it was that my eyes were misty with too constant staring at the butt. One afternoon I woke from a hot sleep, running with sweat and pricking with flies, and wondered what on earth was the good of Medina to us? Its harmfulness had been patent when we were at Yenbo and the Turks in it were going to Mecca: but we had changed all that by our march to Wejh. To-day we were blockading the railway, and they only defending it. The garrison of Medina, reduced to an inoffensive size, were sitting in trenches destroying their own power of movement by eating the transport they could no longer feed. We had taken away their power to harm us, and yet wanted to take away their town. It was not a base for us like Wejh, nor a threat like Wadi Ais. What on earth did we want it for?

The camp was bestirring itself after the torpor of the midday hours; and noises from the world outside began to filter in to me past the yellow lining of the tent-canvas, whose every hole and tear was stabbed through by a long dagger of sunlight. I heard the stamping and snorting of the horses plagued with flies where they stood in the shadow of the trees, the complaint of camels, the ringing of coffee mortars, distant shots. To their burden I began to drum out the aim in war. The books gave it pat—the destruction of the armed forces of the enemy by the one process—battle. Victory could be purchased only by blood. This was a hard saying for us. As the Arabs had no organized forces, a Turkish Foch would have no aim. The Arabs would not endure casualties. How would our Clausewitz buy his victory? Von der Goltz had seemed to go deeper, saying it was necessary not to annihilate the enemy, but to break his courage. Only we showed no prospect of ever breaking anybody's courage.

However, Goltz was a humbug, and these wise men must be talking metaphors; for we were indubitably winning our war; and as I pondered slowly, it dawned on me that we had won the Hejaz war. Out of every thousand square miles of Hejaz nine hundred and ninety-nine were now free. Did my provoked jape at Vickery, that rebellion was more like peace than like war, hold as much truth as haste? Perhaps in war the absolute did rule, but for peace a majority was good enough. If we held the rest, the Turks were welcome to the tiny fraction on which they stood, till peace or Doomsday showed them the futility of clinging to our window-pane.

I brushed off the same flies once more from my face patiently, content to know that the Hejaz War was won and finished with: won from the day we took Wejh, if we had had wit to see it. Then I broke the thread of my argument again to listen. The distant shots had grown and tied themselves into long, ragged volleys. They ceased. I strained my ears for the other sounds which I knew would follow. Sure enough across the silence came a rustle like the dragging of a skirt over the flints, around the thin walls of my tent. A pause, while the camel-riders drew up: and then the soggy tapping of canes on the thick of the beasts' necks to make them kneel.

They knelt without noise: and I timed it in my memory: first the hesitation, as the camels, looking down, felt the soil with one foot for a soft place; then the muffled thud and the sudden loosening of breath as they dropped on their fore-legs, since this party had come far and were tired; then the shuffle as the hind legs were folded in, and the rocking as they tossed from side to side thrusting outward with their knees to bury them in the cooler subsoil below the burning flints, while the riders, with a quick soft patter of bare feet, like birds over the ground, were led off tacitly either to the coffee hearth or to Abdulla's tent, according to their business. The camels would rest there, uneasily switching their tails across the shingle till their masters were free and looked to their stabling.

I had made a comfortable beginning of doctrine, but was left still to find an alternative end and means of war. Ours seemed unlike the ritual of which Foch was priest; and I recalled him, to see a difference in kind between him and us. In his modern war—absolute war he called it—two nations professing incompatible philosophies put them to the test of force. Philosophically, it was idiotic, for while opinions were arguable, convictions needed shooting to be cured; and the struggle could end only when the supporters of the one immaterial principle had no more means of resistance against the supporters of the other. It sounded like a twentieth-century restatement of the wars of religion, whose logical end was utter destruction of one creed, and whose protagonists believed that God's judgement would prevail. This might do for France and Germany, but would not represent the British attitude. Our Army was not intelligently maintaining a philosophic conception in Flanders or on the Canal. Efforts to make our men hate the enemy usually made them hate the fighting. Indeed Foch had knocked out his own argument by saying that such war depended on levy in mass, and was impossible with professional armies; while the old army was still the British ideal, and its manner the ambition of our ranks and our files. To me the Foch war seemed only an exterminative variety, no more absolute than another. One could as explicably call it 'murder war'. Clausewitz enumerated all sorts of war ... personal wars, joint-proxy duels, for dynastic reasons ... expulsive wars, in party politics ... commercial wars, for trade objects ... two wars seemed seldom alike. Often the parties did not know their aim, and blundered till the march of events took control. Victory in general habit leaned to the clear-sighted, though fortune and superior intelligence could make a sad muddle of nature's 'inexorable' law.

I wondered why Feisal wanted to fight the Turks, and why the Arabs helped him, and saw that their aim was geographical, to extrude the Turk from all Arabic-speaking lands in Asia. Their peace ideal of liberty could exercise itself only so. In pursuit of the ideal conditions we might kill Turks, because we disliked them very much; but the killing was a pure luxury. If they would go quietly the war would end. If not, we would urge them, or try to drive them out. In the last resort, we should be compelled to the desperate course of blood and the maxims of 'murder war', but as cheaply as could be for ourselves, since the Arabs fought for freedom, and that was a pleasure to be tasted only by a man alive. Posterity was a chilly thing to work for, no matter how much a man happened to love his own, or other people's already-produced children.

At this point a slave slapped my tent-door, and asked if the Emir might call. So I struggled into more clothes, and crawled over to his great tent to sound the depth of motive in him. It was a comfortable place, luxuriously shaded and carpeted deep in strident rugs, the aniline-dyed spoils of Hussein Mabeirig's house in Rabegh. Abdulla passed most of his day in it, laughing with his friends, and playing games with Mohammed Hassan, the court jester. I set the ball of conversation rolling between him and Shakir and the chance sheikhs, among whom was the fire-hearted Ferhan el Aida, the son of Doughty's Motlog; and I was rewarded, for Abdullas' words were definite. He contrasted his hearer's present independence with their past servitude to Turkey, and roundly said that talk of Turkish heresy, or the immoral doctrine of *Yeni-Turan*, or the illegitimate Caliphate was beside the point. It was Arab country, and the Turks were in it: that was the one issue. My argument preened itself.

The next day a great complication of boils developed out, to conceal my lessened fever, and to chain me down yet longer in impotence upon my face in this stinking tent. When it grew too hot for dreamless dozing, I picked up my tangle again, and went on ravelling it out, considering now the whole house of war in its structural aspect, which was strategy, in its arrangements, which were tactics, and in the sentiment of its inhabitants, which was psychology; for my personal duty was command, and the commander, like the master architect, was responsible for all.

The first confusion was the false antithesis between strategy, the aim in war, the synoptic regard seeing each part relative to the whole, and tactics, the means towards a strategic end, the

particular steps of its staircase. They seemed only points of view from which to ponder the elements of war, the Algebraical element of things, a Biological element of lives, and the Psychological element of ideas.

The algebraical element looked to me a pure science, subject to mathematical law, inhuman. It dealt with known variables, fixed conditions, space and time, inorganic things like hills and climates and railways, with mankind in type-masses too great for individual variety, with all artificial aids and the extensions given our faculties by mechanical invention. It was essentially formulable.

Here was a pompous, professorial beginning. My wits, hostile to the abstract, took refuge in Arabia again. Translated into Arabic, the algebraic factor would first take practical account of the area we wished to deliver, and I began idly to calculate how many square miles: sixty: eighty: one hundred: perhaps one hundred and forty thousand square miles. And how would the Turks defend all that? No doubt by a trench line across the bottom, if we came like an army with banners; but suppose we were (as we might be) an influence, an idea, a thing intangible, invulnerable, without front or back, drifting about like a gas? Armies were like plants, immobile, firm-rooted, nourished through long stems to the head. We might be a vapour, blowing where we listed. Our kingdoms lay in each man's mind; and as we wanted nothing material to live on, so we might offer nothing material to the killing. It seemed a regular soldier might be helpless without a target, owning only what he sat on, and subjugating only what, by order, he could poke his rifle at.

Then I figured out how many men they would need to sit on all this ground, to save it from our attack-in-depth, sedition putting up her head in every unoccupied one of those hundred thousand square miles. I knew the Turkish Army exactly, and even allowing for their recent extension of faculty by aeroplanes and guns and armoured trains (which made the earth a smaller battlefield) still it seemed they would have need of a fortified post every four square miles, and a post could not be less than twenty men. If so, they would need six hundred thousand men to meet the illwills of all the Arab peoples, combined with the active hostility of a few zealots.

How many zealots could we have? At present we had nearly fifty thousand: sufficient for the day. It seemed the assets in this element of war were ours. If we realized our raw materials and were apt with them, then climate, railway, desert, and technical weapons could also be attached to our interests. The Turks were stupid; the Germans behind them dogmatical. They would believe that rebellion was absolute like war, and deal with it on the analogy of war. Analogy in human things was fudge, anyhow; and war upon rebellion was messy and slow, like eating soup with a knife.

This was enough of the concrete; so I sheered off *episteme*, the mathematical element, and plunged into the nature of the biological factor in command. Its crisis seemed to be the breaking point, life and death, or less finally, wear and tear. The war-philosophers had properly made an art of it, and had elevated one item, 'effusion of blood', to the height of an essential, which became humanity in battle, an act touching every side of our corporal being, and very warm. A line of variability. Man, persisted like leaven through its estimates, making them irregular. The components were sensitive and illogical, and generals guarded themselves by the device of a reserve, the significant medium of their art. Goltz had said that if you knew the enemy's strength, and he was fully deployed, then you could dispense with a reserve: but this was never. The possibility of accident, of some flaw in materials was always in the general's mind, and the reserve unconsciously held to meet it.

The 'felt' element in troops, not expressible in figures, had to be guessed at by the equivalent of Plato's *doxa*, and the greatest commander of men was he whose intuitions most nearly happened. Nine-tenths of tactics were certain enough to be teachable in schools; but the irrational tenth was like the kingfisher flashing across the pool, and in it lay the test of generals. It could be ensued only by instinct (sharpened by thought practising the stroke) until at the crisis it came naturally, a reflex. There had been men whose *doxa* so nearly approached perfection that by its road they reached the certainty of *episteme*. The Greeks might have called such genius for command *noesis* had they bothered to rationalize revolt.

My mind see-sawed back to apply this to ourselves, and at once knew that it was not bounded by mankind, that it applied also to materials. In Turkey things were scarce and precious, men less esteemed than equipment. Our cue was to destroy, not the Turk's army, but his minerals. The death of a Turkish bridge or rail, machine or gun or charge of high explosive, was more profitable to us than the death of a Turk. In the Arab Army at the moment we were chary both of materials and of men. Governments saw men only in mass; but our men, being irregulars, were not formations, but individuals. An individual death, like a pebble dropped in water, might make but a brief hole; yet rings of sorrow widened out therefrom. We could not afford casualties.

Materials were easier to replace. It was our obvious policy to be superior in some one tangible branch; gun-cotton or machine-guns or whatever could be made decisive. Orthodoxy had laid down the maxim, applied to men, of being superior at the critical point and moment of attack. We might be superior in equipment in one dominant moment or respect; and for both things and men we might give the doctrine a twisted negative side, for cheapness' sake, and be weaker than the enemy everywhere except in that one point or matter. The decision of what was critical would always be ours. Most wars were wars of contact, both forces striving into touch to avoid tactical surprise. Ours should be a war of detachment. We were to contain the enemy by the silent threat of a vast unknown desert, not disclosing ourselves till we attacked. The attack might be nominal, directed not against him, but against his stuff; so it would not seek either his strength or his weakness, but his most accessible material. In railway-cutting it would be usually an empty stretch of rail; and the more empty, the greater the tactical success. We might turn our average into a rule (not a law, since war was antinomian) and develop a habit of never engaging the enemy. This would chime with the numerical plea for never affording a target. Many Turks on our front had no chance all the war to fire on us, and we were never on the defensive except by accident and in error.

The corollary of such a rule was perfect 'intelligence', so that we could plan in certainty. The chief agent must be the general's head; and his understanding must be faultless, leaving no room for chance. Morale, if built on knowledge, was broken by ignorance. When we knew all about the enemy we should be comfortable. We must take more pains in the service of news than any regular staff.

I was getting through my subject. The algebraical factor had been translated into terms of Arabia, and fitted like a glove. It promised victory. The biological factor had dictated to us a development of the tactical line most in accord with the genius of our tribesmen. There remained the psychological element to build up an apt shape. I went to Xenophon and stole, to name it, his word *diathetics*, which had been the art of Cyrus before he struck.

Of this our 'propaganda' was the stained and ignoble offspring. It was the pathic, almost the ethical, in war. Some of it concerned the crowd, an adjustment of its spirit to the point where it became useful to exploit in action, and the predirection of this changing spirit to a certain end. Some of it concerned the individual, and then it became a rare art of human kindness, transcending, by purposed emotion, the gradual logical sequence of the mind. It was more subtle than tactics, and better worth doing, because it dealt with uncontrollables, with subjects incapable of direct command. It considered the capacity for mood of our men, their complexities and mutability, and the cultivation of whatever in them promised to profit our intention. We had to

arrange their minds in order of battle just as carefully and as formally as other officers would arrange their bodies. And not only our own men's minds, though naturally they came first. We must also arrange the minds of the enemy, so far as we could reach them; then those other minds of the nation supporting us behind the firing line, since more than half the battle passed there in the back; then the minds of the enemy nation waiting the verdict; and of the neutrals looking on; circle beyond circle.

There were many humiliating material limits, but no moral impossibilities; so that the scope of our diathetical activities was unbounded. On it we should mainly depend for the means of victory on the Arab front: and the novelty of it was our advantage. The printing press, and each newly-discovered method of communication favoured the intellectual above the physical, civilization paying the mind always from the body's funds. We kindergarten soldiers were beginning our art of war in the atmosphere of the twentieth century, receiving our weapons without prejudice. To the regular officer, with the tradition of forty generations of service behind him, the antique arms were the most honoured. As we had seldom to concern ourselves with what our men did, but always with what they thought, the diathetic for us would be more than half the command. In Europe it was set a little aside, and entrusted to men outside the General Staff. In Asia the regular elements were so weak that irregulars could not let the metaphysical weapon rust unused.

Battles in Arabia were a mistake, since we profited in them only by the ammunition the enemy fired off. Napoleon had said it was rare to find generals willing to fight battles; but the curse of this war was that so few would do anything else. Saxe had told us that irrational battles were the refuges of fools: rather they seemed to me impositions on the side which believed itself weaker, hazards made unavoidable either by lack of land room or by the need to defend a material property dearer than the lives of soldiers. We had nothing material to lose, so our best line was to defend nothing and to shoot nothing. Our cards were speed and time, not hitting power. The invention of bully beef had profited us more than the invention of gunpowder, but gave us strategical, rather than tactical strength, since in Arabia range was more than force, space greater than the power of armies.

I had now been eight days lying in this remote tent, keeping my ideas general,* till my brain, sick of unsupported thinking, had to be dragged to its work by an effort of will, and went off into a doze whenever that effort was relaxed. The fever passed: my dysentery ceased; and with restored strength the present again became actual to me. Facts concrete and pertinent thrust themselves into my reveries; and my inconstant wit bore aside towards all these roads of escape. So I hurried into line my shadowy principles, to have them once precise before my power to evoke them faded.

It seemed to me proven that our rebellion had an unassailable base, guarded not only from attack, but from the fear of attack. It had a sophisticated alien enemy, disposed as an army of occupation in an area greater than could be dominated effectively from fortified posts. It had a friendly population, of which some two in the hundred were active, and the rest quietly sympathetic to the point of not betraying the movements of the minority. The active rebels had the virtues of secrecy and self-control, and the qualities of speed, endurance and independence of arteries of supply. They had technical equipment enough to paralyse the enemy's communications. A province would be won when we had taught the civilians in it to die for our ideal of freedom. The presence of the enemy was secondary. Final victory seemed certain, if the war lasted long enough for us to work it out.

CHAPTER XXXIV

Obviously I was well again, and I remembered the reason of my journey to Wadi Ais. The Turks meant to march out of Medina, and Sir Archibald Murray wanted us to attack them in professional form. It was irksome that he should come butting into our show from Egypt, asking from us alien activities. Yet the British were the bigger; and the Arabs lived only by grace of their shadow. We were yoked to Sir Archibald Murray, and must work with him, to the point of sacrificing our non-essential interests for his, if they would not be reconciled. At the same time we could not possibly act alike. Feisal might be a free gas: Sir Archibald's army, probably the most cumbrous in the world, had to be laboriously pushed forward on its belly. It was ridiculous to suppose it could keep pace with ethical conceptions as nimble as the Arab Movement: doubtful even if it would understand them. However, perhaps by hindering the railway we could frighten the Turks off their plan to evacuate Medina, and give them reason to remain in the town on the defensive; a conclusion highly serviceable to both Arabs and English, though possibly neither would see it, yet.

Accordingly, I wandered into Abdulla's tent, announcing my complete recovery and an ambition to do something to the Hejaz railway. Here were men, guns, machine-guns, explosives and automatic mines: enough for a main effort. But Abdulla was apathetic. He wanted to talk about the Royal families of Europe, or the Battle of the Somme: the slow march of his own war bored him. However, Sherif Shakir, his cousin and second in command, was fired to enthusiasm, and secured us licence to do our worst. Shakir loved the Ateiba, and swore they were the best tribe on earth; so we settled to take mostly Ateiba with us. Then we thought we might have a mountain gun, one of the Egyptian Army Krupp veterans, which had been sent by Feisal to Abdulla from Wejh as a present.

Shakir promised to collect the force, and we agreed that I should go in front (gently, as befitted my weakness) and search for a target. The nearest and biggest was Aba el Naam Station. With me went Raho, Algerian officer in the French Army, and member of Bremond's mission, a very hard-working and honest fellow. Our guide was Mohammed el Kadhi, whose old

father, Dakhil-Allah, hereditary lawman of the
Juheina, had guided the Turks down to Yenbo
last December. Mohammed was eighteen, solid
and silent natured. Sherif Fauzan el Harith, the
famous warrior who had captured Eshref at Jan-
bila, escorted us, with about twenty Ateiba and
five or six Juheina adventurers.

We left on March the twenty-sixth, while Sir
Archibald Murray was attacking Gaza; and rode
down Wadi Ais; but after three hours the heat
proved too much for me, and we stopped by a
great sidr tree (lote or ju-jube, but the fruit was
scarce) and rested under it the midday hours.
Sidr trees cast heavy shade: there was a cool east
wind, and few flies. Wadi Ais was luxuriant with
thorn trees and grass, and its air full of white
butterflies and scents of wild flowers; so that we
did not remount till late in the afternoon, and
then did only a short march, leaving Wadi Ais by
the right, after passing in an angle of the valley a
ruined terrace and cistern. Once there had been
villages in this part, with the underground waters carefully employed in their frequent gardens; but now it was waste.

The following morning we had two hours'
rough riding around the spurs of Jebel Serd into
Wadi Turaa, a historic valley, linked by an easy
pass to Wadi Yenbo. We spent this midday also
under a tree, near some Juheina tents, where
Mohammed guested while we slept. Then we
rode on rather crookedly for two more hours,
and camped after dark. By ill luck an early spring
scorpion stung me severely on the left hand
while I lay down to sleep. The place swelled up;
and my arm became stiff and sore.

At five next morning, after a long night, we
restarted, and passed through the last hills, out
into the Jurf, an undulating open space which
ran up southward to Jebel Antar, a crater with a
split and castellated top, making it a landmark.
We turned half-right in the plain, to get under
cover of the low hills which screened it from
Wadi Hamdh, in whose bed the railway lay. Behind these hills we rode southward till opposite
Aba el Naam. There we halted to camp, close to
the enemy but quite in safety. The hill-top com-

manded them; and we climbed it before sunset
for a first view of the station.

The hill was, perhaps, six hundred feet high
and steep, and I made many stages of it, resting
on my way up: but the sight from the top was
good. The railway was some three miles off. The
station had a pair of large, two-storied houses of
basalt, a circular water-tower, and other buildings. There were bell-tents, huts and trenches,
but no sign of guns. We could see about three
hundred men in all.

We heard that the Turks patrolled their
neighbourhood actively at night. A bad habit
this: so we sent off two men to lie by each block-
house, and fire a few shots after dark. The
enemy, thinking it a prelude to attack, stood-to
in their trenches all night, while we were comfortably sleeping; but the cold woke us early with
a restless dawn wind blowing across the Jurf, and
singing in the great trees round our camp. As we
climbed to our observation point the sun conquered the clouds and an hour later it grew very
hot.

We lay like lizards in the long grass round the
stones of the foremost cairn upon the hill-top
and saw the garrison parade. Three hundred and
ninety-nine infantry, little toy men, ran about
when the bugle sounded, and formed up in stiff
lines below the black building till there was
more bugling: then they scattered, and after a
few minutes the smoke of cooking fires went up.
A herd of sheep and goats in charge of a little
ragged boy issued out towards us. Before he
reached the foot of the hills there came a loud
whistling down the valley from the north, and a
tiny, picture-book train rolled slowly into view
across the hollow sounding bridge and halted
just outside the station, panting out white puffs
of steam.

The shepherd lad held on steadily, driving his
goats with shrill cries up our hill for the better
pasture on the western side. We sent two
Juheina down behind a ridge beyond sight of the
enemy, and they ran from each side and caught
him. The lad was of the outcast Heteym, pariahs
of the desert, whose poor children were com-

monly sent on hire as shepherds to the tribes about them. This one cried continually, and made efforts to escape as often as he saw his goats straying uncared-for about the hill. In the end the men lost patience and tied him up roughly, when he screamed for terror that they would kill him. Fauzan had great ado to make him quiet, and then questioned him about his Turkish masters. But all his thoughts were for the flock: his eyes followed them miserably while the tears made edged and crooked tracks down his dirty face.

Shepherds were a class apart. For the ordinary Arab the hearth was a university, about which their world passed and where they heard the best talk, the news of their tribe, its poems, histories, love tales, lawsuits and bargainings. By such constant sharing in the hearth councils they grew up masters of expression, dialecticians, orators, able to sit with dignity in any gathering and never at a loss for moving words. The shepherds missed the whole of this. From infancy they followed their calling, which took them in all seasons and weathers, day and night, into the hills and condemned them to loneliness and brute company. In the wilderness, among the dry bones of nature, they grew up natural, knowing nothing of man and his affairs; hardly sane in ordinary talk; but very wise in plants, wild animals and the habits of their own goats and sheep, whose milk was their chief sustenance. With manhood they became sullen, while a few turned dangerously savage, more animal than man, haunting the flocks, and finding the satisfaction of their adult appetites in them, to the exclusion of more licit affections.

For hours after the shepherd had been suppressed only the sun moved in our view. As it climbed we shifted our cloaks to filter its harshness, and basked in luxurious warmth. The restful hill-top gave me back something of the sense-interests which I had lost since I had been ill. I was able to note once more the typical hill scenery, with its hard stone crests, its sides of bare rock, and lower slopes of loose sliding screes, packed, as the base was approached, solidly with a thin dry soil. The stone itself was glistening, yellow, sunburned stuff; metallic in ring, and brittle; splitting red or green or brown as the case might be. From every soft place sprouted thorn-bushes; and there was frequent grass, usually growing from one root in a dozen stout blades, knee-high and straw-coloured: the heads were empty ears between many-feathered arrows of silvery down. With these, and with a shorter grass, whose bottle-brush heads of pearly grey reached only to the ankle, the hillsides were furred white and bowed themselves lowly towards us with each puff of the casual wind.

Verdure it was not, but excellent pasturage; and in the valleys were bigger tufts of grass, coarse, waist-high and bright green when fresh though they soon faded to the burned yellow of ordinary life. They grew thickly in all the beds of water-ribbed sand and shingle, between the occasional thorn trees, some of which stood forty feet in height. The sidr trees, with their dry, sugary fruit, were rare. But bushes of browned tamarisk, tall broom, other varieties of coarse grass, some flowers, and everything which had thorns, flourished about our camp, and made it a rich sample of the vegetation of the Hejaz highlands. Only one of the plants profited ourselves, and that was the hemeid; a sorrel with fleshy heart-shaped leaves, whose pleasant acidity stayed our thirst.

At dusk we climbed down again with the goat-herd prisoner, and what we could gather of his flock. Our main body would come this night, so that Fauzan and I wandered out across the darkling plain till we found a pleasant gun-position in some low ridges not two thousand yards from the station. On our return, very tired, fires were burning among the trees. Shakir had just arrived, and his men and ours were roasting goat-flesh contentedly. The shepherd was tied up behind my sleeping place, because he had gone frantic when his charges were unlawfully slaughtered. He refused to taste the supper; and we only forced bread and rice into him by the threat of dire punishment if he insulted our hospitality. They tried to convince him that we should take the station next day and kill his masters; but he would not be comforted, and afterwards, for fear lest he escape, had to be lashed to his tree again.

After supper Shakir told me that he had brought only three hundred men instead of the agreed eight or nine hundred. However, it was his war, and therefore his tune, so we hastily modified the plans. We would not take the station; we would frighten it by a frontal artillery attack, while we mined the railway to the north and south, in the hope of trapping that halted train. Accordingly we chose a party of Garland-trained dynamiters who should blow up something north of the bridge at dawn, to seal that direction; while I went off with high explosive and a machine-gun with its crew to lay a mine to the south of the station, the probable direction from which the Turks would seek or send help, in their emergency.

Mohammed el Khadi guided us to a deserted bit of line just before midnight. I dismounted and fingered its thrilling rails for the first time during the war. Then, in an hour's busy work, we laid the mine, which was a trigger action to fire into twenty pounds of blasting gelatine when the weight of the locomotive overhead deflected the metals. Afterwards we posted the machine-gunners in a little bush-screened watercourse, four hundred yards from and fully commanding the spot where we hoped the train would be derailed. They were to hide there; while we went on to cut the telegraph, that isolation might persuade Aba el Naam to send their train for reinforcements, as our main attack developed.

So we rode another half-hour, and then turned in to the line, and again were fortunate to strike an unoccupied place. Unhappily the four remaining Juheina proved unable to climb a telegraph pole, and I had to struggle up it myself. It was all I could do, after my illness; and when the third wire was cut the flimsy pole shook so that I lost grip, and came slipping down the sixteen feet upon the stout shoulders of Mohammed, who ran in to break my fall, and nearly

got broken himself. We took a few minutes to breathe, but afterwards were able to regain our camels. Eventually we arrived in camp just as the others had saddled up to go forward.

Our mine-laying had taken four hours longer than we had planned and the delay put us in the dilemma either of getting no rest, or of letting the main body march without us. Finally by Shakir's will we let them go, and fell down under our trees for an hour's sleep, without which I felt I should collapse utterly. The time was just before daybreak, an hour when the uneasiness of the air affected trees and animals, and made even men-sleepers turn over sighingly. Mohammed, who wanted to see the fight, awoke. To get me up he came over and cried the morning prayer-call in my ear, the raucous voice sounding battle, murder, and sudden death across my dreams. I sat up and rubbed the sand out of red-rimmed aching eyes, as we disputed vehemently of prayer and sleep. He pleaded that there was not a battle every day, and showed the cuts and bruises sustained during the night in helping me. By my blackness and blueness I could feel for him, and we rode off to catch the army, after loosing the still unhappy shepherd boy, with advice to wait for our return.

A band of trodden untidiness in a sweep of gleaming water-rounded sand showed us the way, and we arrived just as the guns opened fire. They did excellently, and crashed in all the top of one building, damaged the second, hit the pump-room, and holed the water-tank. One lucky shell caught the front waggon of the train in the siding, and it took fire furiously. This alarmed the locomotive, which uncoupled and went off southward. We watched her hungrily as she approached our mine, and when she was on it there came a soft cloud of dust and a report and she stood still. The damage was to the front part, as she was reversed and the charge had exploded late; but, while the drivers got out, and jacked up the front wheels and tinkered at them, we waited and waited in vain for the machine-gun to open fire. Later we learned that the gunners, afraid of their loneliness, had packed up and marched to join us when we began shooting. Half an hour after, the repaired engine went away towards Jebel Antar, going at a foot pace and clanking loudly; but going none the less.

Our Arabs worked in towards the station, under cover of the bombardment, while we gnashed our teeth at the machine-gunners. Smoke clouds from the fired trucks screened the Arab advance which wiped out one enemy outpost, and captured another. The Turks withdrew their surviving detachments to the main position, and waited rigorously in their trenches for the assault, which they were in no better spirit to repel than we were to deliver. With our advantages in ground the place would have been a gift to us, if only we had had some of Feisal's men to charge home.

Meanwhile the wood, tents and trucks in the station were burning, and the smoke was too thick for us to shoot, so we broke off the action. We had taken thirty prisoners, a mare, two camels and some more sheep; and had killed and wounded seventy of the garrison, at a cost to ourselves of one man slightly hurt. Traffic was held up for three days of repair and investigation. So we did not wholly fail.

*Not perhaps as successfully as here. I thought out my problems mainly in terms of Hejaz, illustrated by what I knew of its men and its geography. These would have been too long if written down; and the argument has been compressed into an abstract form in which it smells more of the lamp than of the field. All military writing does, worse luck.

CHAPTER XXXV

We left two parties in the neighbourhood to damage the line on the next day and the next, while we rode to Abdullah's camp on April the first. Shakir, splendid in habit, held a grand parade on entry, and had thousands of joy-shots fired in honour of his partial victory. The easy-going camp made carnival.

In the evening I went wandering in the thorn-grove behind the tents, till I began to see through the thick branches a wild light, from bursts of raw flame; and across the flame and smoke came the rhythm of drums, in tune with hand-clapping, and the deep roar of a tribal chorus. I crept up quietly, and saw an immense fire, ringed by hundreds of Ataiba sitting on the ground one by the other, gazing intently on Shakir, who, upright and alone in their midst, performed the dance of their song. He had put off his cloak, and wore only his white head-veil and white robes; the powerful firelight was reflected by these and by his pale, ravaged face. As he sang he threw back his head, and at the close of each phrase raised his hands, to let the full sleeves run back upon his shoulders, while he waved his bare arms weirdly. The tribe around him beat time with their hands, or bayed out the refrains at his nod. The grove of trees where I stood outside the circle of light was thronged with Arabs of stranger tribes, whispering, and watching the Atban.

In the morning we determined on another visit to the line, for fuller trial of the automatic mine-action which had half-failed at Aba el Naam. Old Dakhil-Allah said that he would come with me himself on this trip, the project of looting a train had tempted him. With us went some forty of the Juheina, who seemed to me stouter men than the high-bred Ateiba. However, one of the chiefs of the Ataiba, Sultan el Abbud, a boon friend of Abdulla and Shakir, refused to be left behind. This good-tempered but hare-brained fellow, sheikh of a poor section of the tribe, had had more horses killed under him in battle than any other Ateibi warrior. He was about twenty-six and a great rider; full of quips and fond of practical jokes, very noisy: tall and strong, with a big, square head, wrinkled forehead, and deep-set bright eyes. A young moustache and beard hid his ruthless jaw and the wide, straight mouth, with white teeth gleaming and locked like a wolf's.

We took a machine-gun and its soldier crew of thirteen with us, to settle our train when caught. Shakir, with his grave courtesy to the Emir's guest, set us on our road for the first half-hour. This time we kept to the Wadi Ais almost to its junction with Hamdh, finding it very green and full of grazing, since it had flooded twice already in this winter. At last we bore off to the right over a ditch on to a flat, and there slept in the sand, rather distressed by a shower of rain which sent little rills over the ground about midnight: but the next morning was bright and hot, and we rode into the huge plain where the three great valleys, Tubja, Ais and Jizil, flowed into and became one with Hamdh. The course of the main stream was overgrown by asla wood, just as at Abu Zereibat, with the same leprous bed of hummocky sand-blisters: but the thicket was only two hundred yards broad, and beyond it the plain with its grained intricacy of shallow torrent-beds stretched for yet further miles. At noon we halted by a place like a wilderness garden, waist deep in juicy grass and flowers, upon which our happy camels gorged themselves for an hour and then sat down, full and astonished.

The day seemed to be hotter and hotter: the sun drew close, and scorched us without intervening air. The clean, sandy soil was so baked that my bare feet could not endure it, and I had to walk in sandals, to the amusement of the Juheina, whose thick soles were proof even against slow fire. As the afternoon passed on the light became dim, but the heat steadily increased with an oppression and sultriness which took me by surprise. I kept turning my head to see if some mass was not just behind me, shutting off the air.

There had been long rolls of thunder all morning in the hills, and the two peaks, Serd and Jasim, were wrapped in folds of dark blue and yellow vapour, which looked motionless and substantial. At last I saw that part of the yellow cloud off Serd was coming slowly against the wind in our direction raising scores of dust devils before its feet.

The cloud was nearly as high as the hill. While it approached, two dust-spouts, tight and symmetrical chimneys, advanced, one on the right and one on the left of its front. Dakhil-Allah responsibly looked ahead and to each side

for shelter, but saw none. He warned me that the storm would be heavy.

When it got near, the wind, which had been scorching our faces with its hot breathlessness, changed suddenly; and, after waiting a moment, blew bitter cold and damp upon our backs. It also increased greatly in violence, and at the same time the sun disappeared, blotted out by thick rags of yellow air over our heads. We stood in a horrible light, ochreous and fitful. The brown wall of cloud from the hills was now very near, rushing changelessly upon us with a loud grinding sound. Three minutes later it struck, wrapping about us a blanket of dust and stinging grains of sand, twisting and turning in violent eddies, and yet advancing eastward at the speed of a strong gale.

We had put our camels' backs to the storm, to march before it: but these internal whirling winds tore our tightly-held cloaks from our hands, filled our eyes, and robbed us of all sense of direction by turning our camels right or left from their course. Sometimes they were blown completely round: once we clashed helplessly together in a vortex, while large bushes, tufts of grass, and even a small tree were torn up by the roots in dense waves of soil about them, and driven against us, or blown over our heads with dangerous force. We never were blinded—it was always possible to see for seven or eight feet to each side—but it was risky to look out, as, in addition to the certain sand-blast, we never knew if we should not meet a flying tree, a rush of pebbles, or a spout of grass-laden dust.

This storm lasted for eighteen minutes, and then leaped forward from us as suddenly as it had come. Our party was scattered over a square mile or more, and before we could rally, while we, our clothes and our camels were yet smothered in dust, yellow and heavy with it from head to foot, down burst torrents of thick rain and muddied us to the skin. The valley began to run in plashes of water, and Dakhil-Allah urged us across it quickly. The wind chopped once more, this time to the north, and the rain came driving before it in harsh sheets of spray. It beat through our woollen cloaks in a moment, and moulded them and our shirts to our bodies, and chilled us to the bone.

We reached the hill-barrier in mid-afternoon, but found the valley bare and shelterless, colder than ever. After riding up it for three or four miles we halted, and climbed a great crag to see the railway which, they said, lay just beyond. On the height the wind was so terrible that we could not cling to the wet slippery rocks against the slapping and bellying of our cloaks and skirts. I took mine off, and climbed the rest of the way half-naked, more easily, and hardly colder than before. But the effort proved useless, the air being too thick for observation. So I worked down, cut and bruised, to the others; and dressed numbly. On our way back we suffered the only casualty of this trip. Sultan had insisted on coming with us, and his Ateibi servant, who must follow him though he had no head for heights, slipped in one bad place with a fall of forty feet to the stones, and plunged down headlong.

When we got back my hands and feet were too broken to serve me longer, and I lay down and shivered for an hour or so while the others buried the dead man in a side valley. On their return they met suddenly an unknown rider on a camel, crossing their track. He fired at them. They fired back, snap-shooting through the rain, and the evening swallowed him. This was disquieting, for surprise was our main ally, and we could only hope that he would not return to warn the Turks that there were raiders in the neighbourhood.

After the heavy camels with the explosives caught us, we mounted again to get closer to the line; but we had no more than started when brazenly down the visible wind in the misted valley came the food-call of Turkish bugles. Dakhil-Allah thrust his ear forward in the direction of the sound, and understood that over there lay Madahrij, the small station below which we meant to operate. So we steered on the hateful noise, hateful because it spoke of supper and of tents, whereas we were shelterless, and on such a night could not hope to make ourselves a

fire and bake bread from the flour and water in our saddle-bags, and consequently must go hungry.

We did not reach the railway till after ten o'clock at night, in conditions of invisibility which made it futile to choose a machine-gun position. At random I pitched upon kilometre 1,121 from Damascus for the mine. It was a complicated mine, with a central trigger to fire simultaneously charges thirty yards apart: and we hoped in this way to get the locomotive whether it was going north or south. Burying the mine took four hours, for the rain had caked the surface and rotted it. Our feet made huge tracks on the flat and on the bank, as though a school of elephants had been dancing there. To hide these marks was out of the question, so we did the other thing, trampling about for hundreds of yards, even bringing up our camels to help, until it looked as though half an army had crossed the valley, and the mine-place was no better and no worse than the rest. Then we went back a safe distance behind some miserable mounds, and cowered down in the open, waiting for day. The cold was intense. Our teeth chattered, and we trembled and hissed involuntarily, while our hands drew in like claws.

At dawn the clouds had disappeared, and a red sun promised, over the very fine broken hills beyond the railway. Old Dakhil-Allah, our active guide and leader in the night, now took general charge, and sent us out singly and in pairs to all the approaches of our hiding-place. He himself crawled up the ridge before us to watch events upon the railway through his glasses. I was praying that there might be no events till the sun had gained power and warmed me, for the shivering fit still jerked me about. However, soon the sun was up and unveiled, and things improved. My clothes were drying. By noon it was nearly as hot as the day before, and we were gasping for shade, and thicker clothes, against the sun.

First of all, though, at six in the morning, Dakhil-Allah reported a trolley, which came from the south, and passed over the mine harmlessly—to our satisfaction, for we had not laid a beautiful compound charge for just four men and a sergeant. Then sixty men sallied out from Madahrij. This disturbed us till we saw that they were to replace five telegraph poles blown down by the storm of the afternoon before. Then at seven-thirty a patrol of eleven men went down the line: two inspecting each rail minutely, three marching each side of the bank looking for cross-tracks, and one, presumably the N.C.O., walking grandly along the metals with nothing to do.

However, to-day they did find something, when they crossed our footprints about kilometre 1,121. They concentrated there upon the permanent way, stared at it, stamped, wandered up and down, scratched the ballast; and thought exhaustively. The time of their search passed slowly for us: but the mine was well hidden, so that eventually they wandered on contentedly towards the south, where they met the Hedia patrol, and both parties sat together in the cool shade of a bridge-arch, and rested after their labours. Meanwhile the train, a heavy train, came along from the south. Nine of its laden trucks held women and children from Medina, civil refugees being deported to Syria, with their household stuff. It ran over the charges without explosion. As artist I was furious; as commander deeply relieved: women and children were not proper spoil.

The Juheina raced to the crest where Dakhil-Allah and myself lay hidden, when they heard the train coming, to see it blown in pieces. Our stone headwork had been built for two, so that the hill-top, a bald cone conspicuously opposite the working party, became suddenly and visibly populous. This was too much for the nerves of the Turks, who fled back into Madahrij, and thence, at about five thousand yards, opened a brisk rifle fire. They must also have telephoned to Hedia, which soon came to life: but since the nearest outpost on that side was about six miles off, its garrisons held their fire, and contented themselves with selections on the bugle, played all day. The distance made it grave and beautiful.

Even the rifle shooting did us no harm; but the disclosure of ourselves was unfortunate. At Madahrij were two hundred men, and at Hedia eleven hundred, and our retreat was by the plain of Hamdh on which Hedia stood. Their mounted troops might sally out and cut our rear. The Juheina had good camels, and so were safe; but the machine-gun was a captured German sledge-Maxim: a heavy load for its tiny mule. The servers were on foot, or on other mules: their top speed would be only six miles an hour, and their fighting value, with a single gun, not high. So after a council of war we rode back with them half-way through the hills, and there dismissed them, with fifteen Juheina, towards Wadi Ais.

This made us mobile, and Dakhil-Allah, Sultan, Mohammed and I rode back with the rest of our party for another look at the line. The sunlight was now terrific, with faint gusts of scorching heat blowing up at us out of the south. We took refuge about ten o'clock under some spacious trees, where we baked bread and lunched, in nice view of the line, and shaded from the worst of the sun. About us, over the gravel, circles of pale shadow from the crisping leaves ran to and fro, like grey, indeterminate bugs, as the slender branches dipped reluctantly in the wind. Our picnic annoyed the Turks, who shot or trumpeted at us incessantly through the middle day and till evening, while we slept in turn.

About five they grew quiet, and we mounted and rode slowly across the open valley towards the railway. Madahrij revived in a paroxysm of fire, and all the trumpets of Hedia blared again. The monkey-pleasure of pulling large and impressive legs was upon us. So when we reached the line we made our camels kneel down beside it, and, led by Dakhil-Allah as Imam, performed a sunset prayer quietly between the rails. It was probably the first prayer of the Juheina for a year or so, and I was a novice, but from a distance we passed muster, and the Turks stopped shooting in bewilderment. This was the first and last time I ever prayed in Arabia as a Moslem.

After the prayer it was still much too light to hide our actions: so we sat round on the embankment smoking, till dusk, when I tried to go off by myself and dig up the mine, to learn, for service on the next occasion, why it had failed. However, the Juheina were as interested in that as I. Along they came in a swarm and clustered over the metals during the search. They brought my heart into my throat, for it took me an hour to find just where the mine was hidden. Laying a Garland mine was shaky work, but scrabbling in pitch darkness up and down a hundred yards of railway, feeling for a hair-trigger buried in the ballast, seemed, at the time, an almost uninsurable occupation. The two charges connected with it were so powerful that they would have rooted out seventy yards of track, and I saw visions of suddenly blowing up, not only myself, but my whole force, every moment. To be sure, such a feat would have properly completed the bewilderment of the Turks!

At last I found it, and ascertained by touch that the lock had sunk one sixteenth of an inch, due to bad setting by myself or because the ground had subsided after the rain. I firmed it into its place. Then, to explain ourselves plausibly to the enemy, we began blowing up things to the north of the mine. We found a little four-arched bridge and put it into the air. Afterwards we turned to rails and cut about two hundred: and while the men were laying and lighting charges I taught Mohammed to climb a splintery pole; together we cut the wires, and with their purchase dragged down other poles. All was done at speed, for we feared lest Turks come after us: and when our explosive work was finished we ran back like hares to our camels, mounted them, and trotted without interruption down the windy valley once more to the plain of Hamdh.

There we were in safety, but old Dakhil-Allah was too pleased with the mess we had made of the line to go soberly. When we were on the sandy flat he beat up his camel into a canter, and we pounded madly after him through the colourless moonlight. The going was perfect, and we never drew rein for three hours, till we over-rode our machinegun and its escort camping on the road home. The soldiers heard our rout yelling through the night, thought us enemies of sorts, and let fly at us with their Maxim: but it jammed after half a belt, and they, being tailors from Mecca, were unhandy with it. So no one was hurt, and we captured them mirthfully.

In the morning we slept lazily long, and breakfasted at Rubiaan, the first well in Wadi Ais. Afterwards we were smoking and talking, about to bring in the camels, when suddenly we felt the distant shock of a great explosion behind us on the railway. We wondered if the mine had been discovered or had done its duty. Two scouts had been left to report, and we rode slowly; for them, and because the rain two days ago had brought down Wadi Ais once more in flood, and its bed was all flecked over with shallow pools of soft, grey water, between banks of silvery mud, which the current had rippled into fish-scales. The warmth of the sun made the surface like fine glue, on which our helpless camels sprawled comically, or went down with a force and completeness surprising in such dignified beasts. Their tempers were roughened each time by our fit of mirth.

The sunlight, the easy march and the expectation of the scouts' news made everything gay, and we developed social virtues: but our limbs, stiff from the exertions of yesterday, and our abundant food, determined us to fall short of Abu Markha for the night. So, near sunset, we chose a dry terrace in the valley to sleep upon. I rode up it first and turned and looked at the men reined in below me in a group, upon their bay camels like copper statues in the fierce light of the setting sun: they seemed to be burning with an inward flame.

Before bread was baked the scouts arrived, to tell us that at dawn the Turks had been busy round our damages; and a little later a locomotive with trucks of rails, and a crowded labour gang on top, had come up from Hedia, and had exploded the mine fore and aft of its wheels. This was everything we had hoped, and we rode back to Abdulla's camp on a morning of perfect springtime, in a singing company. We had proved that a well-laid mine would fire; and that a well-laid mine was difficult even for its maker to discover. These points were of importance; for Newcombe, Garland and Hornby were now out upon the railway, harrying it: and mines were the best weapon yet discovered to make the regular working of their trains costly and uncertain for our Turkish enemy.

Suggested Readings

Brown, Malcolm. *The Letters of T.E. Lawrence*. London: J.M. Dent & Sons, 1988.

Lawrence, T.E. *The Odyssey of Homer*. Oxford: Oxford University Press, 1991.

Lawrence, T.E. *Revolt in the Desert*. New York: Black Dog & Leventhal Publishers, 2005.

Lawrence, T. E. *Seven Pillars of Wisdom, a Triumph*. Garden City: Doubleday, Doran & Company, 1935.

Orlans, Harold. *Lawrence of Arabia, Strange Man of Letters; the Literary Criticism and Correspondence of T.E. Lawrence*. Rutherford: Fairleigh Dickinson University Press, 1993.

Wilson, Jeremy. *Lawrence of Arabia: the Authorized Biography of T.E.* New York: Atheneum, 1990.

35

Summiting Self: Edward Whymper's Scrambles Amongst the Alps

Dr. Robert D. Madison

Edward Whymper (1840–1911), a British artist commissioned to sketch Alpine scenery, led the first successful ascent of the Matterhorn. For a hundred years, adventurers had assaulted the Alpine peaks in search of the thrill of the sublime, and when Whymper arrived among the Alps in 1860 the region was about to enter the "golden age" of mountaineering.

In 1865, the Matterhorn remained the last major peak never to feel the bootnails of a climber on its summit. The local guides came to believe that it was unassailable ("*Anything* but Matterhorn," insisted the experienced guide Christian Almer). During several seasons Whymper had carried out a carefully planned series of ascents, but it appeared that the season of 1865 would end before he could mount an assault on this overpowering peak. A chance meeting with several other Englishmen who had engaged guides at Zermatt, however, combined with the knowledge that another attempt was about to be made from Breuil to the south under the leadership of preeminent guide Jean-Antoine Carrel, gave Whymper the spur at the last moment.

Whymper instantly joined forces with Lord Francis Douglas, Rev. Charles Hudson and his excellent guide Michel Croz, and a young protege of Hudson named Hadow who had "done Mont Blanc in less time than most men." Together with the two Taugwalders, father and son, as porters, the company was complete.

The account that follows is drawn from Whymper's *Scrambles Amongst the Alps*, first published in 1871.

CHAPTER XX

THE FIRST ASCENT OF
THE MATTERHORN

*"Had we succeeded well, We had been reckoned
'mongst the wise: our minds Are so disposed to judge
from the event."*
  EURIPIDES.

*"It is a thoroughly unfair, but an ordinary custom,
to praise or blame designs (which in themselves may
be good or bad) just as they turn out well or ill.
Hence the same actions are at one time attributed to
earnestness and at another to vanity."*
  PLINY MIN.

We started from Zermatt on the 13th of July 1865, at half-past five, on a brilliant and perfectly cloudless morning. We were eight in number—Croz, old Peter and his two sons, Lord F. Douglas, Hadow, Hudson, and I. To ensure steady motion, one tourist and one native walked together. The youngest Taugwalder fell to my share, and the lad marched well, proud to be on the expedition, and happy to show his powers. The wine-bags also fell to my lot to carry, and throughout the day, after each drink, I replenished them secretly with water, so that at the next halt they were found fuller than before! This was considered a good omen, and little short of miraculous.

On the first day we did not intend to ascend to any great height, and we mounted, accordingly, very leisurely; picked up the things which were left in the chapel at the Schwarzsee at 8.20, and proceeded thence along the ridge connecting the Hörnli with the Matterhorn. At half-past eleven we arrived at the base of the actual peak; then quitted the ridge, and clambered round some ledges, on to the eastern face. We were now fairly upon the mountain, and were astonished to find that places which from the Riffel, or even from the Furggen Glacier, looked en-

tirely impracticable, were so easy that we could *run about.*

Before twelve o'clock we had found a good position for the tent, at a height of 11,000 feet. Croz and young Peter went on to see what was above, in order to save time on the following morning. They cut across the heads of the snow-slopes which descended towards the Furggen Glacier, and disappeared round a corner; but shortly afterwards we saw them high up on the face, moving quickly. We others made a solid platform for the tent in a well-protected spot, and then watched eagerly for the return of the men. The stones which they upset told us that they were very high, and we supposed that the way must be easy. At length, just before 3 p.m., we saw them coming down, evidently much excited. "What are they saying, Peter?" "Gentlemen, they say it is no good." But when they came near we heard a different story. "Nothing but what was good; not a difficulty, not a single difficulty! We could have gone to the summit and returned to-day easily!"

We passed the remaining hours of daylight—some basking in the sunshine, some sketching or collecting; and when the sun went down, giving, as it departed, a glorious promise for the morrow, we returned to the tent to arrange for the night. Hudson made tea, I coffee, and we then retired each one to his blanket bag; the Taugwalders, Lord Francis Douglas, and myself, occupying the tent, the others remaining, by preference, outside. Long after dusk the cliffs above echoed with our laughter and with the songs of the guides, for we were happy that night in camp, and feared no evil.

We assembled together outside the tent before dawn on the morning of the 14th, and started directly it was light enough to move. Young Peter came on with us as a guide, and his brother returned to Zermatt. We followed the route which had been taken on the previous day, and in a few minutes turned the rib which had intercepted the view of the eastern face from our tent platform. The whole of this great slope was now revealed, rising for 3,000 feet like a huge natural staircase. Some parts were more, and others were less, easy; but we were not once brought to a halt by any serious impediment, for when an obstruction was met in front it could always be turned to the right or to the left. For the greater part of the way there was, indeed, no occasion for the rope, and sometimes Hudson led, sometimes myself. At 6.20 we had attained a height of 12,800 feet, and halted for half an hour; we then continued the ascent without a break until 9.55, when we stopped for fifty minutes, at a height of 14,000 feet. Twice we struck the north-east ridge and followed it for some little distance,—to no advantage, for it was usually more rotten and steep, and always more difficult than the face. Still, we kept near to it, lest stones perchance might fall.

We had now arrived at the foot of that part which, from the Riffelberg or from Zermatt, seems perpendicular or overhanging, and could no longer continue upon the eastern side. For a little distance we ascended by snow upon the arête—that is, the ridge—descending towards Zermatt, and then, by common consent, turned over to the right, or to the northern side. Before doing so, we made a change in the order of ascent. Croz went first, I followed, Hudson came third; Hadow and old Peter were last. "Now," said Croz, as he led off, "now for something altogether different." The work became difficult and required caution. In some places there was little to hold, and it was desirable that those should be in front who were least likely to slip. The general slope of the mountain at this part was *less* than 40°, and snow had accumulated in, and had filled up, the interstices of the rock-face, leaving only occasional fragments projecting here and there. These were at times covered with a thin film of ice, produced from the melting and refreezing of the snow. It was the counterpart, on a small scale, of the upper 700 feet of the Pointe des Ecrins,—only there was this material difference; the face of the Ecrins was about, or exceeded, an angle of 50°, and the Mat-

terhorn face was less than 40°. It was a place over which any fair mountaineer might pass in safety, and Mr. Hudson ascended this part, and, as far as I know, the entire mountain, without having the slightest assistance rendered to him upon any occasion. Sometimes, after I had taken a hand from Croz, or received a pull, I turned to offer the same to Hudson; but he invariably declined, saying it was not necessary. Mr. Hadow, however, was not accustomed to this kind of work, and required continual assistance. It is only fair to say that the difficulty which he found at this part arose simply and entirely from want of experience.

This solitary difficult part was of no great extent. We bore away over it at first, nearly horizontally, for a distance of about 400 feet; then ascended directly towards the summit for about 60 feet; and then doubled back to the ridge which descends towards Zermatt. A long stride round a rather awkward corner brought us to snow once more. The last doubt vanished! The Matterhorn was ours! Nothing but 200 feet of easy snow remained to be surmounted!

You must now carry your thoughts back to the seven Italians who started from Breuil on the 11th of July. Four days had passed since their departure, and we were tormented with anxiety lest they should arrive on the top before us. All the way up we had talked of them, and many false alarms of "men on the summit" had been raised. The higher we rose, the more intense became the excitement. What if we should be beaten at the last moment? The slope eased off, at length we could be detached, and Croz and I, dashing away, ran a neck-and-neck race, which ended in a dead heat. At 1.40 p.m. the world was at our feet, and the Matterhorn was conquered. Hurrah! Not a footstep could be seen. . . .

We remained on the summit for one hour— "One crowded hour of glorious life."

It passed away too quickly, and we began to prepare for the descent.

CHAPTER XXI

DESCENT OF THE MATTERHORN

Hudson and I again consulted as to the best and safest arrangement of the party. We agreed that it would be best for Croz to go first, and Hadow second; Hudson, who was almost equal to a born mountaineer in sureness of foot, wished to be third; Lord Francis Douglas was placed next, and old Peter, the strongest of the remainder, after him. I suggested to Hudson that we should attach a rope to the rocks on our arrival at the difficult bit, and hold it as we descended, as an additional protection. He approved the idea, but it was not definitely settled that it should be done. The party was being arranged in the above order whilst I was sketching the summit, and they had finished, and were waiting for me to be tied in line, when someone remembered that our names had not been left in a bottle. They requested me to write them down, and moved off while it was being done.

A few minutes afterwards I tied myself to young Peter, ran down after the others, and caught them just as they were commencing the descent of the difficult part. Great care was being taken. Only one man was moving at a time; when he was firmly planted the next advanced, and so on. They had not, however, attached the additional rope to rocks, and nothing was said about it. The suggestion was not made for my own sake, and I am not sure that it even occurred to me again. For some little distance we two followed the others, detached from them, and should have continued so had not Lord Francis Douglas asked me, about 3 p.m., to tie on to old Peter, as he feared, he said, that Taugwalder would not be able to hold his ground if a slip occurred.

A few minutes later, a sharp-eyed lad ran into the Monte Rosa Hotel, to Seiler, saying that he had seen an avalanche fall from the summit of the Matterhorn on to the Matterhorn Glacier. The boy was reproved for telling idle stories; he was right, nevertheless, and this was what he saw.

Michel Croz had laid aside his axe, and in order to give Mr. Hadow greater security, was absolutely taking hold of his legs, and putting his feet, one by one, into their proper positions. So far as I know, no one was actually descending. I cannot speak with certainty, because the two leading men were partially hidden from my sight by an intervening mass of rock, but it is my belief, from the movements of their shoulders, that Croz, having done as I have said, was in the act of turning round, to go down a step or two himself; at this moment Mr. Hadow slipped, fell against him, and knocked him over. I heard one startled exclamation from Croz, then saw him and Mr. Hadow flying downwards; in another moment Hudson was dragged from his steps, and Lord Francis Douglas immediately after him. All this was the work of a moment. Immediately we heard Croz's exclamation, old Peter and I planted ourselves as firmly as the rocks would permit: the rope was taut between us, and the jerk came on us both as on one man. We held; but the rope broke midway between Taugwalder and Lord Francis Douglas. For a few seconds we saw our unfortunate companions sliding downwards on their backs, and spreading out their hands, endeavouring to save themselves. They passed from our sight uninjured, disappeared one by one, and fell from precipice to precipice on the Matterhorn Glacier below, a distance of nearly 4,000 feet in height. From the moment the rope broke it was impossible to help them.

So perished our comrades! For the space of half an hour we remained on the spot without moving a single step. The two men, paralysed by terror, cried like infants, and trembled in such a manner as to threaten us with the fate of the others. Old Peter rent the air with exclamations of "Chamonix! Oh, what will Chamonix say?" He meant, Who would believe that Croz could fall? The young man did nothing but scream or sob, "We are lost! we are lost!" Fixed between the two, I could neither move up nor down. I begged young Peter to descend, but he dared not. Unless he did, we could not advance. Old Peter became alive to the danger, and swelled the cry, "We are lost! we are lost!" The father's fear was natural—he trembled for his son; the young man's fear was cowardly—he thought of self alone. At last old Peter summoned up courage, and changed his position to a rock to which he could fix the rope; the young man then descended, and we all stood together. Immediately we did so, I asked for the rope which had given way, and found, to my surprise—indeed, to my horror—that it was the weakest of the three ropes. It was not brought, and should not have been employed, for the purpose for which it was used. It was old rope, and, compared with the others, was feeble. It was intended as a reserve, in case we had to leave much rope behind, attached to rocks. I saw at once that a serious question was involved, and made him give me the end. It had broken in midair, and it did not appear to have sustained previous injury.

For more than two hours afterwards I thought almost every moment that the next would be my last; for the Taugwalders, utterly unnerved, were not only incapable of giving assistance, but were in such a state that a slip might have been expected from them at any moment. After a time, we were able to do that which should have been done at first, and fixed rope to firm rocks, in addition to being tied together. These ropes were cut from time to time, and were left behind.[1] Even with their assurance the men were afraid to proceed, and several times old Peter turned with ashy face and faltering limbs, and said, with terrible emphasis *"I cannot!"*

About 6 p.m. we arrived at the snow upon the ridge descending towards Zermatt, and all peril was over. We frequently looked, but in vain, for traces of our unfortunate companions; we bent over the ridge and cried to them, but no sound returned. Convinced at last that they were neither within sight nor hearing, we ceased from our useless efforts; and, too cast down for speech, silently gathered up our things, and the

little effects of those who were lost, preparatory to continuing the descent. When, lo! a mighty arch appeared, rising above the Lyskamm, high into the sky. Pale, colourless, and noiseless, but perfectly sharp and defined, except where it was lost in the clouds, this unearthly apparition seemed like a vision from another world; and, almost appalled, we watched with amazement the gradual development of two vast crosses, one on either side. If the Taugwalders had not been the first to perceive it, I should have doubted my senses. They thought it had some connection with the accident, and I, after a while, that it might bear some relation to ourselves. But our movements had no effect upon it. The spectral forms remained motionless. It was a fearful and wonderful sight; unique in my experience, and impressive beyond description, coming at such a moment.

I was ready to leave, and waiting for the others. They had recovered their appetites and the use of their tongues. They spoke in patois, which I did not understand. At length the son said in French, "Monsieur." "Yes." "We are poor men; we have lost our Herr; we shall not get paid; we can ill afford this." "Stop!" I said, interrupting him, "that is nonsense; I shall pay you, of course, just as if your Herr were here." They talked together in their patois for a short time, and then the son spoke again. "We don't wish you to pay us. We wish you to write in the hotel-book at Zermatt, and to your journals, that we have not been paid." "What nonsense are you talking? I don't understand you. What do you mean?" He proceeded—"Why, next year there will be many travellers at Zermatt, and we shall get more *voyageurs*."

Who would answer such a proposition? I made them no reply in words, but they knew very well the indignation that I felt. They filled the cup of bitterness to overflowing, and I tore down the cliff, madly and recklessly, in a way that caused them, more than once, to inquire if I wished to kill them. Night fell; and for an hour the descent was continued in the darkness. At half-past nine a resting-place was found, and upon a wretched slab, barely large enough to hold the three, we passed six miserable hours. At daybreak the descent was resumed, and from the Hörnli ridge we ran down to the chalets of Buhl, and on to Zermatt. Seiler met me at his door, and followed in silence to my room. "What is the matter?" "The Taugwalders and I have returned." He did not need more, and burst into tears; but lost no time in useless lamentations, and set to work to arouse the village. Ere long a score of men had started to ascend the Hohlicht heights, above Kalbermatt and Z'Mutt, which commanded the plateau of the Matterhorn Glacier. They returned after six hours, and reported that they had seen the bodies lying motionless on the snow. This was on Saturday; and they proposed that we should leave on Sunday evening, so as to arrive upon the plateau at daybreak on Monday. Unwilling to lose the slightest chance, the Rev. J. M'Cormick and I resolved to start on Sunday morning. The Zermatt men, threatened with excommunication by their priests if they failed to attend the early mass, were unable to accompany us. To several of them, at least, this was a severe trial. Peter Perren declared with tears that nothing else would have prevented him from joining in the search for his old comrades. Englishmen came to our aid. The Rev. J. Robertson and Mr. J. Phillpotts offered themselves, and their guide Franz Andermatten; another Englishman lent us Joseph Marie and Alexandre Lochmatter. Frédéric Payot, and Jean Tairraz, of Chamonix, also volunteered.

We started at 2 a.m. on Sunday the 16th, and followed the route that we had taken on the previous Thursday as far as the Hörnli. Thence we went down to the right of the ridge, and mounted through the *séracs* of the Matterhorn Glacier. By 8.30 we had got to the plateau at the top of the glacier, and within sight of the corner in which we knew my companions must be. As we saw one weather-beaten man after another raise the telescope, turn deadly pale, and pass it on without a word to the next, we knew that all hope was gone. We approached. They had fallen below as they had fallen above— Croz a little in advance, Hadow near him, and Hudson some distance behind; but of Lord Francis Douglas we could see nothing. We left them where they fell; buried in snow at the base of the grandest cliff of the most majestic mountain of the Alps.

All those who had fallen had been tied with the Manilla, or with the second and equally strong rope, and, consequently, there had been only one link—that between old Peter and Lord Francis Douglas—where the weaker rope had been used. This had a very ugly look for Taugwalder, for it was not possible to suppose that the others would have sanctioned the employment of a rope so greatly inferior in strength when there were more than two hundred and fifty feet of the better qualities still remaining out of use. For the sake of the old guide (who bore a good reputation), and upon all other accounts, it was desirable that this matter should be cleared up; and after my examination before the court of inquiry which was instituted by the Government was over, I handed in a number of questions which were framed so as to afford old Peter an opportunity of exculpating himself from the grave suspicions which at once fell upon him. The questions, I was told, were put and answered; but the answers, although promised, have never reached me.

Meanwhile, the administration sent strict injunctions to recover the bodies, and upon the 19th of July, twenty-one men of Zermatt accomplished that sad and dangerous task. Of the body of Lord Francis Douglas they, too, saw nothing; it was probably still arrested on the rocks above. The remains of Hudson and Hadow were interred upon the north side of the Zermatt Church, in the presence of a reverent crowd of sympathizing friends. The body of Michel Croz lies upon the other side, under a simpler tomb; whose inscription bears honourable testimony to his rectitude, to his courage, and to his devotion.

So the traditional inaccessibility of the Matterhorn was vanquished, and was replaced by legends of a more real character. Others will essay to scale its proud cliffs, but to none will it be the mountain that it was to its early explorers. Others may tread its summit-snows, but none will ever know the feelings of those who first gazed upon its marvellous panorama; and none, I trust, will ever be compelled to tell of joy turned into grief, and of laughter into mourning. It proved to be a stubborn foe; it resisted long, and gave many a hard blow; it was defeated at last with an ease that none could have anticipated, but, like a relentless enemy—conquered but not crushed—it took terrible vengeance. The time may come when the Matterhorn shall have passed away, and nothing, save a heap of shapeless fragments, will mark the spot where the great mountain stood; for, atom by atom, inch by inch, and yard by yard, it yields to forces which nothing can withstand. That time is far distant; and, ages hence, generations unborn will gaze upon its awful precipices, and wonder at its unique form. However exalted may be their ideas, and however exaggerated their expectations, none will come to return disappointed!

The play is over, and the curtain is about to fall. Before we part, a word upon the graver teachings of the mountains. See yonder height! 'Tis far away—unbidden comes the word "Impossible!" "Not so," says the mountaineer. "The way is long, I know; it's difficult—it may be—dangerous. It's possible, I'm sure; I'll seek the way; take counsel of my brother mountaineers, and find how they have gained similar heights, and learned to avoid the dangers." He starts (all slumbering down below); the path is slippery—may be laborious, too. Caution and perseverance gain the day—the height is reached! and those beneath cry, "Incredible; 'tis superhuman!"

We who go mountain-scrambling have constantly set before us the superiority of fixed purpose or perseverance to brute-force. We know that each height, each step, must be gained by patient, laborious toil, and that wishing cannot take the place of working; we know the benefits of mutual aid; that many a difficulty must be encountered, and many an obstacle must be grappled with or turned, but we know that where

there's a will there's a way; and we come back to our daily occupations better fitted to fight the battle of life, and to overcome the impediments which obstruct our paths, strengthened and cheered by the recollection of past labours, and by the memories of victories gained in other fields.

I have not made myself either an advocate or an apologist for mountaineering, nor do I now intend to usurp the functions of a moralist; but my task would have been ill performed if it had been concluded without one reference to the more serious lessons of the mountaineer. We glory in the physical regeneration which is the product of our exertions; we exult over the grandeur of the scenes that are brought before our eyes, the splendours of sunrise and sunset, and the beauties of hill, dale, lake, wood, and waterfall; but we value more highly the development of manliness, and the evolution, under combat with difficulties, of those noble qualities of human nature—courage, patience, endurance, and fortitude.

Some hold these virtues in less estimation, and assign base and contemptible motives to those who indulge in our innocent sport.

Others, again, who are not detractors, find mountaineering, as a sport, to be wholly unintelligible. It is not greatly to be wondered at—we are not all constituted alike. Mountaineering is a pursuit essentially adapted to the young or vigorous, and not to the old or feeble. To the latter, toil may be no pleasure; and it is often said by such persons, "This man is making a toil of pleasure." Let the motto on the title-page be an answer, if an answer be required. Toil he must who goes mountaineering; but out of the toil comes strength (not merely muscular energy— more than that), an awakening of all the faculties; and from the strength arises pleasure. Then, again, it is often asked, in tones which seem to imply that the answer must, at least, be doubtful, "But does it repay you?" Well, we cannot estimate our enjoyment as you measure your wine, or weigh your lead,—it is real, nevertheless. If I could blot out every reminiscence, or erase every memory, still I should say that my scrambles amongst the Alps have repaid me, for they have given me two of the best things a man can possess—health and friends.

The recollections of past pleasures cannot be effaced. Even now as I write they crowd up before me. First comes an endless series of pictures, magnificent in form, effect, and colour. I see the great peaks, with clouded tops, seeming to mount up for ever and ever; I hear the music of the distant herds, the peasant's *jodel*, and the solemn church-bells; and I scent the fragrant breath of the pines: and after these have passed away, another train of thoughts succeeds—of those who have been upright, brave, and true; of kind hearts and bold deeds; and of courtesies received at stranger hands, trifles in themselves, but expressive of that good will towards men which is the essence of charity.

Still, the last, sad memory hovers round, and sometimes drifts across like floating mist, cutting off sunshine, and chilling the remembrance of happier times. There have been joys too great to be described in words, and there have been griefs upon which I have not dared to dwell; and with these in mind I say, Climb if you will, but remember that courage and strength are nought without prudence, and that a momentary negligence may destroy the happiness of a lifetime. Do nothing in haste; look well to each step; and from the beginning think what may be the end.

Suggested Readings

Reynolds, Kev. *Tour of Mont Blanc: Complete Trekking Guide*. Cumbria: Cicerone Press, 2003.

Whymper, Edward. *Scrambles Amongst the Alps in the Years 1860-69*. London: J. Murray, 1871.

36

Persevere at All Costs: Robert Service's Poem "Carry On"

Dr. Joseph J. Thomas

Robert W. Service (1874–1958) was known as a "people's poet." He wrote poems that sold well but were scorned by the literary establishment. Service was fascinated by "the rough and tough—and the tougher the better." His most famous works dealt with the great Yukon gold rush and include "The Cremation of Sam McGee," "The Men That Don't Fit In," and "The Spell of the Yukon." The poem "Carry On" is typical of the spirit of Rob Service and captures an invaluable trait of leaders—perseverence.

* * *

It's easy to fight when everything's right,
And you're mad with the thrill and the glory;
It's easy to cheer when victory's near,
And wallow in fields that are gory.
It's a different song when everything's wrong,
When you're feeling infernally mortal;
When it's ten against one, and hope there is
    none, Buck up,
little soldier, and chortle:

Carry on! Carry on!
There isn't much punch in your blow.
You're glaring and staring and hitting out
    blind;
You're muddy and bloody, but never you
    mind. Carry on! Carry on!
You haven't the ghost of a show.
It's looking like death, but while you've a
    breath,
Carry on, my son! Carry on!

And so in the strife of the battle of life
It's easy to fight when you're winning;
It's easy to slave, and starve and be brave,
When the dawn of success is beginning.
But the man who can meet despair and de-
    feat
With a cheer, there's the man of God's
    choosing;

The man who can fight to Heaven's own
    height
Is the man who can fight when he's losing.
Carry on! Carry on!
Things never were looming so black.
But show that you haven't a cowardly streak,
And though you're unlucky you never are
    weak.
Carry on! Carry on!
Brace up for another attack.
It's looking like hell, but-you never can tell:
Carry on, old man! Carry on!

There are some who drift out in the deserts
    of doubt,
And some who in brutishness wallow;
There are others, I know, who in piety go
Because of a Heaven to follow.
But to labor with zest, and to give of your
    best,
For the sweetness and joy of the giving;
To help folks along with a hand and a song;
Why, there's the real sunshine of living.

Carry on! Carry on!
Fight the good fight and true;
Believe in your mission, greet life with a
    cheer;
There's big work to do, and that's why you
    are here.
Carry on! Carry on!
Let the world be the better for you;
And at last when you die, let this be your cry:
Carry on my soul! Carry on!

Suggested Readings

Epictetus. *The Enchiridion*. Indianapolis: Bobbs-
Merrill, 1955.

Service, Robert W. *Best of Robert Service*. New
York: Penguin, 1978.

Stockdale, James B. *Thoughts of a Philosophical
Fighter Pilot*. Stanford: Hoover Institution
Press, 1995.

37

Luckiest Man on the Face of the Earth: Lou Gehrig's Farewell to Yankee Stadium

Dr. Joseph J. Thomas

One doesn't need to be a Yankee fan, or even a sports fan, to appreciate the stoic courage of baseball great Lou Gehrig as he bid farewell to teammates, fans, and friends on July 4, 1939.

Called by New York columnist Jim Murray a "symbol of indestructibility—a Gibraltar in cleats," Gehrig was widely considered the very embodiment of leadership-by-example by generations of American sports fans. His final address at Yankee Stadium provides an indication of why he was so known. The speech's simple humility and appreciation for the support, love, and friendship of others is a testimonial to the human spirit. The 1942 movie *Pride of the Yankees* based on Gehrig's story served as a "buttress against self pity and defeatism" for the American home front during WWII. Lou Gehrig died of Amyotrophic Lateral Sclerosis on June 2, 1941. His ashes were buried in Valhalla, New York.

"Fans, for the past two weeks you have been reading about the bad break I got. Yet today I consider myself the luckiest man on the face of this earth. I have been in ballparks for seventeen years and have never received anything but kindness and encouragement from you fans.

Look at these grand men. Which of you wouldn't consider it the highlight of his career just to associate with them for even one day? Sure, I'm lucky. Who wouldn't consider it an honor to have known Jacob Ruppert? Also, the builder of baseball's greatest empire, Ed Barrow? To have spent six years with that wonderful little fellow, Miller Huggins? Then to have spent the next nine years with that outstanding leader, that smart student of psychology, the best manager in baseball today, Joe McCarthy? Sure, I'm lucky.

When the New York Giants, a team you would give your right arm to beat, and vice versa, sends you a gift—that's something. When everybody down to the groundskeepers and those boys in white coats remember you with trophies—that's something. When you have a wonderful mother-in-law who takes sides with you in squabbles with her own daughter—that's something. When you have a father and a mother who work all their lives so you can have an education and build your body—it's a blessing. When you have a wife who has been a tower of strength and shown more courage than you dreamed existed—that's the finest I know.

So I close in saying that I may have had a tough break, but I have an awful lot to live for.

Suggested Readings

Eig, Jonathan. *Luckiest Man: The Life and Death of Lou Gehrig*. New York: Simon & Schuster, 2005.

Pride of the Yankees. Dir. Sam Wood, Perf. Gary Cooper, 1942.

38

Victory at All Costs: Winston Churchill's Address to Parliament

Dr. Joseph J. Thomas

Winston Churchill's "Blood, Toil, Tears, and Sweat" speech was made to the House of Commons on May 13, 1940 and still stands among the pre-eminent exhortations to "bear the burdens of war" ever delivered. Churchill had been prime minister a mere three days before he delivered this address and the attention of his nation was squarely upon him. Britain responded immediately and the message became a turning point in the stand against the rise of European facism. The treasury of Churchill's speeches, quotes, and witisisms is vast; this particular speech announced his position as a world leader and, as such, is perhaps his most important.

* * *

On Friday evening last I received from His Majesty the mission to form a new administration.

It was the evident will of Parliament and the nation that this should be conceived on the broadest possible basis and that it should include all parties.

I have already completed the most important part of this task. A war cabinet has been formed of five members, representing, with the Labour, Opposition, and Liberals, the unity of the nation.

It was necessary that this should be done in one single day on account of the extreme urgency and rigor of events. Other key positions were filled yesterday. I am submitting a further list to the king tonight. I hope to complete the appointment of principal ministers during tomorrow.

The appointment of other ministers usually takes a little longer. I trust when Parliament meets again this part of my task will be completed and that the administration will be complete in all respects.

I considered it in the public interest to suggest to the Speaker that the House should be summoned today. At the end of today's proceedings, the adjournment of the House will be proposed until May 21 with provision for earlier meeting if need be. Business for that will be notified to MPs at the earliest opportunity.

I now invite the House by a resolution to record its approval of the steps taken and declare its confidence in the new government. The resolution:

"That this House welcomes the formation of a government representing the united and inflexible resolve of the nation to prosecute the war with Germany to a victorious conclusion."

To form an administration of this scale and complexity is a serious undertaking in itself. But we are in the preliminary phase of one of the greatest battles in history .We are in action at many other points-in Norway and in Holland-and we have to be prepared in the Mediterranean. The air battle is continuing, and many preparations have to be made here at home.

In this crisis I think I may be pardoned if I do not address the House at any length today, and I hope that any of my friends and colleagues or former colleagues who are affected by the political reconstruction will make all allowances for any lack of ceremony with which it has been necessary to act.

I say to the House as I said to ministers who have joined this government, I have nothing to offer but blood, toil, tears, and sweat. We have before us an ordeal of the most grievous kind. We have before us many, many months of struggle and suffering.

You ask, what is our policy? I say it is to wage war by land, sea, and air. War with all our might and with all the strength God has given us, and to wage war against a monstrous tyranny never surpassed in the dark and lamentable catalogue of human crime. That is our policy.

You ask, what is our aim? I can answer in one word. It is victory.

Victory at all costs-victory in spite of all terrors-victory, however long and hard the road may be, for without victory there is no survival.

Let that be realized. No survival for the British Empire, no survival for all that the British Empire has stood for, no survival for the urge, the impulse of the ages, that mankind shall move forward toward his goal.

I take up my task in buoyancy and hope. I feel sure that our cause will not be suffered to fail among men.

I feel entitled at this juncture, at this time, to claim the aid of all and to say, "Come then, let us go forward together with our united strength."

Suggested Readings

Churchill, Winston, Sir. *Churchill in His Own Words; Years of Greatness, Memorable Speeches of the Man of the Century*. New York: Capricorn Books, 1966.

Churchill, Winston, Sir. *Blood, Toil, Tears, and Sweat: the Speeches of Winston Churchill*. Boston: Houghton Mifflin, 1989.

39

War as the Ultimate Moral Test: E.B. Sledge's With the Old Breed At Peleliu and Okinawa

Maj Shawn P. Callahan, USMC

Eugene Sledge was a 21-year old Private First Class when he joined the First Marine Division, the "Old Breed," in the summer of 1944. He served as a mortarman in Kilo Company of the 3rd Battalion, 5th Marines through two of the most brutal campaigns of World War II: Peleliu and Okinawa. Each of these campaigns was characterized by sustained combat in bitter battles of attrition. The Japanese ultimately lost, but only after inflicting horrible casualties on the attacking Marines. Entire units were chewed up by the Japanese defenses, so that one battalion after the next had to be fed into the meat grinders. Although he was one of the few men who escaped the campaign physically unharmed, Sledge had experienced war at its worst. *With the Old Breed* is one of the seminal works of both World War II and Marine Corps history, recounting his experiences with such brutal honesty that the reader cannot help but share Sledge's physical revulsion to the horrors of war.

In this particular passage, Sledge finds himself a transformed man from the untested new replacement he had been before the landing on Peleliu just two weeks earlier. Without realizing it, he has become inured to the death and brutality that surrounds him. Acts which he had previously abhorred, like the collecting of gold teeth from enemy corpses, now seem natural and rational to him. By participating in this grim act we see Sledge morally broken by war—his ethical foundation appears to have been washed completely away, leaving him the shell of a man he once was. Fortunately for him, the quick thinking of a friend who had more successfully resisted the inhumanity of war saved him from an act he would have regretted for the rest of his life.

This passage also demonstrates war as a moral test in another sense. While in limited wars and counterinsurgencies ethical conduct can certainly contribute toward victory, in total war, by definition a purely pragmatic contest (where actions, not principles, determine victory), the moral element of war more clearly assumes its other meaning. Here "moral" refers to the emotive, or spiritual element of war: the internal belief that victory is still possible which every man must have in order to keep fighting. Clausewitz developed this as a key element in his theory of war, observing that forces which are better equipped, led, and trained can be beaten if they can be convinced that victory is unattainable. Essentially, war is a contest of wills, with victory going to the side that holds on to hope, and the will to fight, for the longest. Sledge's account reveals the heavy burden placed upon his spirit by the battle for Peleliu. After weeks of combat he has only to witnesses another unit's bloody failure, suffering no injury himself, and he begins to succumb to the thought that all hope is lost. Here again he is saved by some timely kind words from one of his comrades—in this case his lieutenant—which help him find his way. Ultimately, Sledge's work reveals not only the horrors of war, but also the notion that a timely act of kindness and humanity can save men's bodies and souls from the abyss.

We set up our two mortars in a large crater near the now knocked-out pillbox and registered in the guns for the night. The ammo carriers dug into the softer coral around the edge of the crater. An amtrac brought up rations and a unit of fire for the company. The wind began to blow briskly, and it got cloudy and heavily overcast. As darkness settled, heavy clouds scudded across the sky. The scene reminded me of hurricane weather on the Gulf Coast back home.

Not far behind us, the heat of the fire burning in the pillbox exploded Japanese grenades and small-arms ammunition. All night occasional shifts of wind blew the nauseating smell of burning flesh our way. The rain feel in torrents, and the wind blew hard. Ships fired star shells to illuminate the battlefield for our battalion. But as soon as the parachute of a star shell opened, the wind swept it swiftly along like some invisible hand snatching away a candle. In the few hun-

dred yards they still had at the northern end of the island, the enemy was fairly quiet.

The next morning, again with the help of tanks and amtracs, our battalion took most of the remainder of Ngesebus. Our casualties were remarkably low for the number of Japanese we killed. In midafternoon we learned that an army unit would relieve us shortly and complete the job on the northern end of Ngesebus.

Our mortar section halted to await orders and dispersed among some open bushes. In our midst was the wreckage of a Japanese heavy machine gun and the remains of the squad that had been wiped out by Company K. The squad members had been killed in the exact positions to be occupied by such a squad "according to the book."

At first glace the dead gunner appeared about to fire his deadly weapon. He still sat bolt upright in the proper firing position behind the breech of his machine gun. Even in death his eyes stared widely along the gun sights. Despite the vacant look of his dilated pupils, I couldn't believe he was dead. Cold chills ran along my spine. Gooseflesh tickled my back. It seemed as though he was looking through me into all eternity, that at any instant he would raise his hands—which rested in a relaxed manner on his thighs—grip the handles on the breech, and press the thumb trigger. The bright shiny brass slugs in the strip clip appeared as ready as the gunner, anxious to speed out, to kill, to maim more of the "American devils." But he would rot, and they would corrode. Neither he nor his ammo could do any more for the emperor.

The crown of the gunner's skull had been blasted off, probably by one of our automatic weapons. His riddled steel helmet lay on the deck like a punctured tin can. The assistant gunner lay beside the gun. Apparently, he had just opened a small green wooden chest filled with strip clips of machine-gun cartridges when he was killed. Several other Japanese soldiers, ammo carriers, lay strung out at intervals behind the gun.

A Company K rifleman who had been in the

fight that knocked out the machine-gun crew sat on his helmet nearby and told us the story. The action had taken place the day before while the mortar section was fighting at the pillbox. The rifleman said, "The thing that I just couldn't believe was the way those Nip ammo carriers could chop chop around here on the double with those heavy boxes of ammo on their backs."

Each ammo box had two leather straps, and each ammo carrier had a heavy box on his back with the straps around his shoulders. I lifted one of the ammo chests. It weighed more than our mortar. What the Japanese lacked in height, the certainly compensated for in muscle.

"I'd sure hate to hafta lug that thing around, wouldn't you?" asked the Marine. "When they got hit," he continued, "they fell to the deck like a brick because of all that weight."

As we talked, I noticed a fellow mortarman sitting next to me. He held a handful of coral pebbles in his left hand. With his right hand he idly tossed them into the open skull of the Japanese machine gunner. Each time his pitch was true I heard a little splash of rainwater in the ghastly receptacle. My buddy tossed the coral chunks as casually as a boy casting pebbles into a puddle on some muddy road back home; there was nothing malicious in his action. The war had so brutalized us it was beyond belief.

I noticed gold teeth glistening brightly between the lips of several of the dead Japanese lying around us. Harvesting gold teeth was one facet of stripping enemy dead that I hadn't practiced so far. But stopping beside a corpse with a particularly tempting number of shining crown, I took out my kabar and bent over to make the extractions.

A hand grasped me on the shoulder, and I straightened to see who it was. "What are you going to do, Sledgehammer?" asked Doc Caswell. His expression was a mix of sadness and reproach as he looked intently at me.

"Just though I'd collect some gold teeth," I replied.

"Don't do it."

"Why not, Doc?"

"You don't want to do that sort of thing. What would your folks think if they knew?"

"Well, my dad's a doctor, and I bet he'd think it was kinda interesting," I replied, bending down to resume my task.

"No! The germs, Sledgehammer! You might get germs from them."

I stopped and looked inquiringly at Doc and said, "Germs? Gosh, I never thought of that."

"Yeah, you got to be careful about germs around all these dead Nips, you know," he said vehemently.

"Well, then, I guess I'd better just cut off the insignia on his collar and leave his nasty teeth alone. You think that's safe, Doc?"

"I guess so," he replied with an approving nod.

Reflecting on the episode after the war, I realized that Doc Caswell didn't really have germs in mind. He was a good friend and a fine, genuine person whose sensitivity hadn't been crushed out by the war. He was merely trying to help me retain some of mine and not become completely callous and harsh.

There was little firing going on now because 3/5 [3rd Battalion, 5th Marines] was preparing to pull back as it was relieved by an army battalion. Our tanks, two of which had been parked near us, started toward the beach. As the rattled and clanked away, I hoped they weren't leaving prematurely.

Suddenly we were jolted by the terrific blast of a Japanese 75mm artillery piece slightly to our right. We flung ourselves flat on the deck. The shriek and explosion of the shell followed instantly. Fragments tore through the air. The gun fired again rapidly.

"Jesus, what's that?" gasped a man near me.

"It's a Nip 75, and God is he close," another said.

Each time the gun fired I felt the shock and pressure waves from the muzzle blast. I was terror stricken. We began to hear shouts of "Corpsman" on our right.

"For chrissake, get them tanks back up here," someone yelled. I looked toward the tanks just in time to see several wheel around and come speeding back to help the pinned-down infantrymen.

"Mortar section, stand by," someone yelled. We might be called to fire on the enemy gun, but as yet we didn't know its location.

The tanks went into action and almost immediately knocked out the weapon. Calls came from our right for corpsmen and stretcher bearers. Several of our ammo carriers went with the corpsmen to act as stretcher bearers. Word filtered along to us that quite a number of casualties had been caused by the terrible point-blank fire of the enemy cannon. Most of those hit were members of the company that was tied in with us on our right.

Our ammo carriers and corpsmen returned shortly with a distressing account of the men next to us caught directly in front of the Japanese gun when it opened fire from a camouflaged position. When I saw one of our men's face, I knew how bad it had been. He appeared absolutely stricken with horror. I often had seen him laugh and curse the Japanese when we were under heavy shelling or scrambling out of the way of a machine-gun or sniper fire. Never during the entire Peleliu campaign, or later during the bloody fighting on Okinawa, did I see such an expression on his face.

He grimaced as he described how he and the man with him put one of the casualties, someone we all knew, on a stretcher. "We knew he was hit bad, and he had passed out. I tried to lift the poor guy under his shoulders, and he (pointing to the other mortarman) lifted his knees. Just as we almost got him on the stretcher, the poor guy's body came apart. God! It was awful!"

He and the man with him looked away as everyone groaned and slowly shook their heads. We had been terrified by the enemy gun firing point-blank like that. It was an awful experience. It had been bad enough on us, but it was unbearable for those unfortunates who were in the direct line of fire.

Our company had been off to one side and had suffered no casualties during the ordeal, but it was one of the more shocking experiences I endured during the war. As I have said earlier, to be shelled was terrifying, and to be shelled in the open on your feet was horrible; but to be shelled point-blank was so shocking that it almost drove the most resilient and toughest among us to panic. Words can't convey the awesome sensation of actually feeling the muzzle blasts that accompanied the shrieks and concussions of those artillery shells fired from a gun so close by. We felt profound pity for our fellow Marines who had caught its full destructive force.

During mid-afternoon as we waited for the army infantry, we sat numbly looking at nothing with the "bulkhead stare." The shock, horror, fear, and fatigue of fifteen days of combat were wearing us down physically and emotionally. I could see it in the dirty, bearded faces of my remaining comrades: they had a hollow-eyed vacant look peculiar to men under extreme stress for days and nights on end.

"Short but rough. Three days, maybe four," the division CG [Commanding General] had said before Peleliu. Now we had been at it for fifteen terrible days with no end in sight.

I felt myself choking up. I slowly turned my back to the men facing me, as I sat on my helmet, and put my face in my hands to try to shut out reality. I began sobbing. The harder I tried to stop the worse it got. My body shuddered and shook. Tears flowed out of my scratchy eyes. I was sickened and revolted to see healthy young men get hurt and killed day after day. I felt I couldn't take it any more. I was so terribly tired and so emotionally wrung out from being afraid for days on end that I seemed to have no reserve strength left.

The dead were safe. Those who had gotten a million-dollar wound were lucky. None of us left had any idea that we were just midway through what was to be a month-long ordeal for the 5th Marines and the 7th Marines.

I felt a hand on my shoulder and looked up at the tired, bloodshot eyes of Duke, our lieutenant. "What's the matter, Sledgehammer?" he asked in a sympathetic voice. After I told him how I felt, he said, "I know what you mean. I feel the same way. But take it easy. We've got to keep going. It'll be over soon, and we'll be back on Pavuvu." His understanding gave me the strength I needed, enough strength to endure fifteen more terrible days and nights.

When long files of soldiers accompanied by amtracs loaded with barbed wire and other supplies came by, we received orders to move out. We were glad to see those army men. As we shouldered our weapons and loads, a buddy said to me, "Sure wish we could dig in behind barbed wire at night. Makes a fella' feel more secure." I agreed as we walked wearily toward the beach.

After crossing back to northern Peleliu on 29 September, 3/5 bivouacked east of Umurbrogol Mountain in the Ngardololok area. We were familiar with this area from the first week of the campaign. It was fairly quiet and had been the bivouac area of the shattered 1st Marines for about a week after they came off the line and awaited ships to take them to Pavuvu.

We were able to rest, but we were uneasy. As usual we asked about the fate of friends in other units, more often than not with depressing results. Rumor had the 5th Marines slated to join the 7th Marines already fighting on those dreaded coral ridges that had been the near destruction of the 1st Marines. The men tried not to think about it as they sat around in the muggy shade, brewed hot coffee in their canteen cups, and swapped souvenirs and small talk. From the north came the constant rattle of machine guns and the rumble of shells.

Suggested Reading

Sledge, E.B. *With the Old Breed At Peleliu and Okinawa*. Annapolis: Naval Institute Press, 1981.

Caputo, Philip. *A Rumor of War*. New York: Henry Holt and Company, 1977.

Leckie, Robert. *Helmet for My Pillow*. New York: Random House, 1957.

About the Author

Major Shawn P. Callahan is a 1992 graduate of the U.S. Naval Academy. He is an F-18D Weapons and Sensors Officer and a Marine historian who teaches American and naval history at the U.S. Naval Academy.

---

[8] E.B. Sledge, With the Old Breed at peleliu and Okinawa (Annapolis: Naval Institute Press, 1981), 121–126.

40

Dare to Try: Edgar A. Guest's Poem "The Things That Haven't Been Done Before"

Dr. Joseph J. Thomas

Edgar Albert Guest (1881-1959), like George Eliot (see "Count That Day Lost"), was born in Warwickshire, England, but moved with his family to the US at age eleven. He gained a national following while serving as a reporter for the *Detroit Free Press* by publishing a poem a day to supplement the daily news. His poems were read by millions of Americans and were syndicated in over 250 papers nationwide. Guest's poetry inspired a generation and he was named the "Poet Laureate of Michigan" in 1952. "The Things That Haven't Been Done Before" is typical of his simple and accessible style and is sage advice for leaders striking out on uncharted paths.

* * *

The things that haven't been done before,
   Those are the things to try;
Columbus dreamed of an unknown shore
   At the rim of the far-flung sky,
And his heart was bold and his faith was
     strong
   As he ventured in dangers new,
And he paid no heed to the jeering throng
   Or the fears of the doubting crew.

The many will follow the beaten track
   With guideposts on the way.
They live and have lived for ages back
   With a chart for every day.
Someone has told them it's safe to go
   On the road he has traveled o'er,
And all that they ever strive to know
   Are the things that were known before.
A few strike out, without map or chart,
   Where never a man has been,
From the beaten paths they draw apart
   To see what no man has seen.
There are deeds they hunger alone to do;
   Though battered and bruised and sore,
They blaze the path for the many, who
   Do nothing not done before.

The things that haven't been done before
  Are the tasks worthwhile today; Are you
  one of the flock that follows, or Are you
    one
  that shall lead the way? Are you one of the
timid souls that quail
  At the jeers of a doubting crew,
Or dare you, whether you win or fail,
  Strike out for a goal that's new?

Suggested Readings

Guest, Edgar. *All in a Life-Time*. Chicago: Reilly and Lee, 1938.

Guest, Edgar. *All That Matters*. Chicago: Reilly and Lee, 1922.

Guest, Edgar. *Collected Verse*. Chicago: Reilly and Lee, 1934.

Guest, Edgar. *Life's Highway*. Chicago: Reilly and Lee, 1933.

41

Flawed Fellowship and Uncompromised Integrity: Bolt's A Man For All Seasons

Dr. Anne Marie Drew and Captain Gary D. Noble, USN

Leadership has many aspects: among them, confidence, persuasion, audacity, competence. But at its core, leadership must contain integrity, which is the strength to do what you believe to be right, even when no one is following.

In the following scene, we meet a man who refuses to compromise his integrity, even though that refusal will cost him his life.

The hour is 0100. The place, the Tower of London. The year, 1535. Thomas More, the former Lord Chancellor, has been hauled from his prison cell yet again to answer for his silence. The immediate crisis of conscience arises because Henry VIII, the King and a friend to Thomas, has issued the Act of Succession. Concurrently, all English subjects must swear to the Oath of Supremacy, which proclaims the lawfulness of the Act; the legality of Henry's divorcing Queen Catherine; and the legitimacy of a subsequent marriage to Anne Boleyn. All subjects, including Thomas, unwilling to take the oath are threatened with the charge of high treason.

* * *

CROMWELL *Sir Thomas, have you seen this document before?*

MORE *Many times.*

CROMWELL *It is the Act of Succession. These are the names of those who have sworn to it.*

MORE *I have, as you say, seen it before.*

CROMWELL *Will you swear to it?*

MORE *No.*

NORFOLK *Thomas, we must know plainly—*

CROMWELL *(Throws down document) Your Grace, please!*

NORFOLK *Master Cromwell!(They regard each other in hatred.)*

CROMWELL *I beg Your Grace's pardon. (Sighing, rests his head in his hands)*

NORFOLK *Thomas, we must know plainly whether you recognize the offspring of Queen Anne as heirs to His Majesty.*

MORE *The King in Parliament tells me they are. Of course I recognize them.*

NORFOLK   *Will you swear that you do?*

MORE   *Yes.*

NORFOLK   *Then why won't you swear to the Act?*

CROMWELL   *(Impatiently) Because there is more than that in the Act.*

NORFOLK   *Is that it?*

MORE   *(After a pause) Yes.*

NORFOLK   *Then we must find out what it is in the Act that he objects to!*

CROMWELL   *Brilliant (Norfolk rounds on him) God's wounds.*

CRANMER   *(Hastily) Your Grace—May I try?*

NORFOLK   *Certainly. I've no pretension to be an expert in police work.*

(During the next speech Cromwell straightens up and folds arms resignedly)

CRANMER   *(Clears his throat fussily) Sir Thomas, it states in the preamble that The King's former marriage to the Lady Catherine, was unlawful, she being previously married to his brother's wife and the—er—"Pope" having no authority to sanction it. (Gently) Is that what you deny? (No reply) Is that what you dispute? (No reply) Is that what you are not sure of? (No reply)*

NORFOLK   *Thomas, you insult the King and His council in the person of the Lord Archbishop!*

MORE   *I insult no one. I will not take the oath. I will not tell you why I will not.*

NORFOLK   *Then your reasons must be treasonable!*

MORE   *Not "must be"; may be.*

NORFOLK   *It's a fair assumption*

MORE   *The law requires more than an assumption: the law requires a fact. (Cromwell looks at him and away again)*

CRANMER   *I cannot judge your legal standing in the case; but until I know the ground of your objections, I can only guess your spiritual standing too.*

MORE   *(For second furiously affronted; then humor overtakes him) If you're willing to guess at that, Your Grace, it should be a small matter to guess my objections.*

CROMWELL   *(Quickly) You do have objections to the Act?*

NORFOLK   *(Happily) Well, we know that, Cromwell!*

MORE   *You don't, my Lord. You may suppose I have objections. All you know is that I will not swear to it. From sheer delight to give you trouble it might be.*

NORFOLK   *Is it material why you won't?*

MORE   *It's most material. For refusing to swear, my goods are forfeit and I am condemned to life imprisonment. You cannot lawfully harm me further. But if you were right in supposing I had reasons for refusing and right again in supposing my reasons to be treasonable, the law would let you cut my head off.*

NORFOLK   *(He has followed with some difficulty) Oh yes.*

CROMWELL   *(An admiring murmur) Oh, well done, Sir Thomas. I've been trying to make that clear to His Grace for some time.*

NORFOLK   *(Hardly responds to the insult; his face is gloomy and disgusted) Oh confound all this . . . (With real dignity) I'm not a scholar, as Master Cromwell never tires of pointing out, and frankly I don't know whether the marriage was lawful or not. But damn it, Thomas, look at those names . . . You know those men! Can't you do what I did and come with us for fellowship?*

MORE   *(Moved) And when we stand before God, and you are sent to Paradise for doing according to your conscience, and I am damned for not doing according to mine, will you come with me, for fellowship? (102–105)*

Sir Thomas More and the Duke of Norfolk have been fast friends for many years. Norfolk doesn't understand Thomas' persistence in refusing to swear to the oath and implores him to "come with us for fellowship" (105). It is natural to want to preserve that which we have labored to create; be it a career, a lifestyle, or an image. By his continued silence, Thomas is threatening Norfolk's lifestyle. Thomas understands and regrets the pain his refusal costs those who love him. Even for the fellowship of the family he loves and the friends he cherishes, he cannot come along because he believes the King's actions are antithetical to divine law. Further, he believes that Henry's policies have set England on a chaotic course, where even the laws of the land will not be able to protect the citizens.

FELLOWSHIP GONE AWRY

In many ways the Duke of Norfolk's invoking of fellowship, of friendship is not far removed from the Naval Academy's insistence that the ship and shipmates must come before self. Norfolk reminds More that an individual's sense of self must be subsumed into the greater good of the state. Norfolk knows that Thomas believes that Henry's actions are wrong. Still, he wants his friend to ignore his own beliefs and go along with what everyone else is doing. What Norfolk fails to acknowledge or perhaps understand is that on some issues, an individual's integrity must be placed above all else.

The year 1992 brought just such an issue to front and center at The Naval Academy. When the Electrical Engineering (EE) examination was compromised in the Fall Semester of that year, hundreds of midshipmen fell victim to a misguided sense of the "ship-shipmate-self" concept. Believing that their own integrity could be temporarily put on hold, these midshipmen chose to remain silent, as the reality of the compromised exam became clear. More than one midshipmen, in testifying before the Inspector General's staff, admitted being suspicious when the "good gouge" of the night before the exam, turned out to be the actual test questions. Further, they explained that rather than bilge on their shipmates who'd provided them with stolen questions, they remained silent. These students failed to understand that Ship-Shipmate-Self represents the priority of military loyalties, a priority that guides the ethical actions of leaders. However, the underlying conviction of any such prioritization is the absolute integrity of those involved. Loyalty to shipmates does not

and cannot require that people violate their own integrity.

If we allow a bit of an anachronism here, we can suggest that Thomas applied Ship-Shipmate-Self to his circumstance. According to what he believed was right, he put the needs of the ship [of state] above his personal needs. He could not go along, out of loyalty or fellowship, with his friends. The former Lord Chancellor knew that to help his country, he needed to keep his integrity in tact.

HISTORICAL BACKGROUND

The road that leads to Thomas' imprisonment and ultimate execution is a convoluted one. In 1485, King Henry's father had ended England's War of the Roses by defeating Richard III on Bosworth Field. Before that time England had been embroiled in civil butcheries and mayhem. The very real threat of a return to that anarchy loomed large, should Henry VIII die without a male heir.

Shortly after becoming King in 1509, it was sensible for Henry to take his brother's widow as his bride; however, the choice required a Papal dispensation because church law forbid such a marriage. Henry married the petite, pretty, and deeply spiritual Catherine. For several years, Henry and Catherine were very happy together. But when each of Catherine's pregnancies ended in miscarriage or stillbirth, Henry grew worried. The live birth of their daughter Mary, in 1516, gave Henry temporary hope that a male heir would be born. The stillbirth of yet another son in 1518 convinced Henry that God was displeased at his breaking spiritual law as cited in Leviticus 18:16: "Thou shalt not uncover the nakedness of thy brother's wife."

King Henry decided his marriage to Catherine was sinful. Desperate for a male heir, King Henry asked the Pope to grant dispensation from the original dispensation so he would be free to marry his mistress, Anne Boleyn. The Pope steadfastly refused every petition to annul the marriage. Henry , determined to have his own way, severed all ties with the Church of Rome; established himself as Supreme Head of the Church of England; granted himself a divorce from Catherine; and promptly married his, by-now pregnant mistress, Anne Boleyn.

THE POPULAR APPEAL OF HENRY'S PLAN

To guarantee the loyalty of his subjects, Henry demanded that everyone in England take the Oath of Supremacy, an Oath stating that Henry was the legitimate head of the Church of England.

For many subjects, the oath struck a welcome chord. Martin Luther's Ninety-five Theses had been nailed to the Wittenberg Cathedral in 1517. Thousands of people, including many in England, believed that Martin Luther's charges against the Catholic Church were valid ones. Consequently, the King's break with Rome was welcome relief from the Papacy's religious arrogance and political strong-arming. For other subjects, taking the oath fit comfortably into the rationalization that the Pope was corrupt and the Church was rife with wicked clergy. In addition, Henry's grief over the lack of a legitimate male heir resonated with many of his subjects. Taking the Oath of Supremacy, then, was not difficult for such citizens.

Furthermore, King Henry's brutality proved compelling enough motivation to convince most fence-sitters that they, too, should take the Oath. Their concern for their own safety and the safety of their families overcame any compulsion to question the morality of the King's wishes. Swearing to the Oath was almost perfunctory: The King ordered it and, as loyal subjects, the masses swore to it.

While Thomas More acknowledged the Church of Rome's flaws, he believed in the Apostolic Succession of the Pope as "our only link with Christ" (73). Despite the threat of the King's wrath, Thomas does not believe severing ties with Rome is a God-given solution and he openly refuses to join the "war on the Pope" (73)

by quietly refusing to take the oath. It is a refusal that will cost him his mortal life.

WHO IS THOMAS MORE?

As *A Man For All Seasons* makes clear, Thomas More was, by every measure, a success. Well-educated, he was an accomplished lawyer, who served, as a young man, in the household of the influential Cardinal Morton. A prolific and popular author, Thomas later became a judge. In that capacity, he was universally acknowledged to be fair-minded and incorruptible, at a time when bribery was common.

The Common Man, who narrates Robert Bolt's play, tells us that Thomas was a "scholar and by popular repute, a saint. His scholarship is supported by his writings; saintliness is a quality less easy to establish. But from his willful indifference to realities which were obvious to quite ordinary contemporaries, it seems all too probable that he had it" (33). Thomas' sainthood, although a fascinating and inspirational topic, is not of primary concern here. His flesh and blood, his very mortal self matters to us. For in those areas, his life intersects our own.

Thomas was self-aware. His love of women, especially in his youth, was well-known. That love of women made Thomas abandon his thoughts of the priesthood because he knew a celibate life was not for him. He'd rather be a faithful husband than a bad priest.

Certainly, Thomas had his detractors and his contradictions. Humorous and warm-hearted, he was also capable of melancholy and anger. A man of great faith, he says of God, "I find him rather too subtle. I don't know where he is nor want he wants" (57). He could be vindictive and petty and downright cruel in his pursuit of heretics. Nonetheless, Thomas was deeply loved by a wide circle of friends and family. His house in Chelsea often reverberated with the sounds of laughter and children and good friends gathered round the hearth and table. He loved the life of the mind. He loved God. He cherished his family.

One has to wonder what compelled such a man to give up such a life.

Like so many of Thomas' contemporaries, we might see Thomas' unyielding refusal to take the oath as an unrealistic adherence to the truth, like the kind of slavish absolutism sometimes attributed to Emmanuel Kant. But Thomas was skilled at navigating the murky waters of the Court. His career would never have blossomed without a measure of pragmatism, nor extended so far without a functioning sense of compromise.

We might be tempted to see his actions as purely willful. Living an enviable existence, having risen to a position of authority and leadership, how silly, we might think, that Thomas balked at swearing to a simple oath. An oath that did not trouble most of the English citizenry. Still, this man who well understood the utility, even the necessity, of compromise found himself unwilling to compromise his integrity.

MORE'S UNCOMPROMSIED INTEGRITY

Thomas More's integrity is assaulted by a barrage of insults, second-guessing, and bribery. This very integrity, this sense of self that helped elevate him to his position of leadership within Henry's court, becomes the very characteristic that family, friends, and colleagues question.

For example, when Thomas learns that King Henry has severed all ties to the Church of Rome, Thomas resigns as Lord Chancellor. His wife, Alice, immediately reminds him of his obligations as a provider and chides him for jeopardizing the life they have built together. "Master More," she asks him, "you're taken for a wise man. Is this wisdom-to betray your ability, abandon practice, forget your station and your duty to your kin and behave like a printed book?" (73). She continues to press home this point when she subsequently snaps at him ". . . if I'm to lose my rank and fall to housekeeping, I want to know the reason" (76).

The Duke of Norfolk, similarly bewildered by Thomas' resignation, accuses his friend of cowardice. As the Great Seal of Office is removed from around Thomas' shoulders, Norfolk asks Thomas to explain himself . "Well, Thomas, why?" Norfolk demands. "Make me understand because I'll tell you from where I stand this looks like cowardice" (73). When Thomas subsequently tries to make Norfolk understand, the Duke is incredulous. He exclaims and states, "You'll forfeit all you've got–which includes the respect of your country–for a theory?" (74)

Henry VIII, of course, presses hard on Thomas' reluctance to go along with everyone else. Henry explains that everyone else concedes to the moral righteousness of his divorcing Queen Catherine. Then he asks More, "How is it that you cannot see? Everyone else does" (48). More, thinking he sees a way out, eagerly asks in return, "Then why does Your Grace need my poor support?" (48) The King's answer cuts right to the core of the importance of integrity in leadership. The King answers Thomas with these words:

"Because you are honest. What's more to the purpose, you're known to be honest."

There are those like Norfolk who follow me because I wear the crown, and there are those like Master Cromwell who follow me because they are like jackals with sharp teeth and I am their lion, and there is a mass that follows me because follows anything that moves—and there is you. (48)

So even as Henry has come to rely on More's integrity, he needs Thomas to bend that integrity just enough to help him negotiate the putting away of Queen Catherine. Thomas, however, cannot bend, even to the point of death. At the very end of More's trial, when the guilty verdict is clear, Cromwell gives the former Lord Chancellor one last chance to save himself. Cromwell states: "Now I must ask the court's indulgence. I have a message for the prisoner from the King. Sir Thomas, I am empowered to tell you that even now . . ." More cuts Cromwell off by interrupting, "No, no. It cannot be . . ." (125)

Thomas knows he can save his life by accepting the King's conditions. He will not save his life by imperiling his soul. As he faces his sentencing, More tells the assembled court:

To avoid this I have taken every path my winding wits could find. . . . I am the King's true subject and pray for him and all the realm. I do none harm, I say none harm, I think none harm. And if this be not enough to keep a man alive, in good faith, I long not to live. (126)

Thomas believes that some things are worth dying for. Defending tangibles like family, home and country are natural reflexes for most of us. But sacrificing to preserve intangibles like liberty, justice, and freedom requires a courage that sometimes runs counter to our natural impulses. That is what makes Thomas More's life a great example of leadership. He had unshakeable beliefs about right and wrong; the strength of his convictions; and the courage to lead when no one followed.

His example of sacrifice is doubly impressive because there were ways out of the morass that Henry's actions created. Any number of people, from Norfolk to Cromwell to the King himself, tried to offer Thomas a path to freedom. Thomas refused those offers because to accept any of them meant compromising his own integrity.

Suggested Readings

Ackroyd, Peter. *The Life of Thomas More*. London: Chatto and Windus, 1998.

Bolt, Robert. *A Man For All Seasons*. New York: Samuel French, 2004.

Marius, Richard. *Thomas More*. New York: Alfred Knopf, 1984.

Rupp, Gordon. *Thomas More: The King's Good Servant*. London, Collins, 1978.

About the Authors

Anne Marie Drew is an English Professor at USNA, where she has served as Department Chair and Director of Masqueraders. Among her publication credits is *Letters From Annapolis: The Midshipmen Write Home* (Naval Institute Press, 1998). Her latest book is *Praying Thieves* (Morehouse, 2006).

Gary D. Noble is a former instructor at the US Naval Academy. At USNA, he taught core courses in Ethics and Leadership, Weapons Systems Engineering, and frequently facilitated the First Class Capstone Leadership Seminar. Captain Noble has deployed twice in support of the Global War On Terror: first ordered to Ras Al Qulayah, Kuwait for OPERATION Enduring Freedom and later ordered to Baghdad, Iraq for OPERATION Iraqi Freedom. Captain Noble is currently the Director of the Navy Element at the US Army's Command & General Staff College.

42

The Race is Almost Won: Jill Wolf's "Don't Quit"

ENS Benjamin Pittard, USN

My parents gave me Jill Wolf's poem "Don't Quit" when I graduated from the Naval Academy. It is printed on a piece of plastic the size of a credit card, and I carry it in my wallet. Despite its simple diction and rhyme scheme, this poem offers a message to any junior officer faced with unfamiliar challenges. We may stumble in front of our first division, or fail land navigation at TBS, or a test at Flight or Nuclear Power School, but, fortunately, we are measured less by these mistakes and more by how we persevere through these missteps. We will undoubtedly make mistakes in the upcoming years, but to fail due to a lack of effort or to quit entirely would be unacceptable. Wherever you find yourself, I hope you are able to draw strength from this poem. I look forward to reciting it, in cadence, as I run up and down the beaches of Coronado.

> Don't quit when the tide is lowest,
>   For it's just about to turn;
> Don't quit over doubts and questions,
> For there's something you may learn.
>
> Don't quit when the night is darkest,
>   For it's just a while 'til dawn;
> Don't quit when you've run the farthest,
>   For the race is almost won.
>
> Don't quit when the hill is steepest,
>   For your goal is almost nigh;
> Don't quit, for you're not a failure
> Until you fail to try.

About the Author

ENS Benjamin Pittard graduated from the US Naval Academy in 2005 and has service-selected Naval Special Warfare (SEAL). He is temporarily assigned to the Officer Development Section at USNA while awaiting language and basic underwater demolition training at Coronado, CA.

43

Farewell to Arms: Douglas MacArthur's "Duty, Honor, Country" *Speech*

Dr. Joseph J. Thomas

In what may be the finest, most colorful and evocative farewell address ever delivered by an American military figure, General of the Army Douglas MacArthur's "Duty, Honor, Country" captures the lessons of nearly six decades of brilliant (if controversial) military service. The speech was delivered at West Point on May 12, 1962 to the Corps of Cadets at the United States Military Academy. MacArthur seeks to distill the lessons of character and responsibility in a poetic tribute to the profession of arms. In doing so, he reminds his listeners of his own place in American military history.

* * *

No human being could fail to be deeply moved by such a tribute as this, coming from a profession I have served so long and a people I have loved so well. It fills me with an emotion I cannot express. But this award is not intended primarily for a personality, but to symbolize a great moral code-the code of conduct and chivalry of those who guard1his beloved land of culture and ancient descent.

"Duty," "honor," "country" those three hallowed words reverently dictate what you want to be, what you can be, what you will be. They are your rallying point to build courage when courage seems to fail, to regain faith when there seems to be little cause for faith, to create hope when hope becomes forlorn.

Unhappily, I possess neither that eloquence of diction, that poetry of imagination, nor that brilliance of metaphor to tell you all that they mean.

The unbelievers will say they are but words, but a slogan, but a flamboyant phrase. Every pedant, every demagogue, every cynic, every hypocrite, every troublemaker, and, I am sorry to say, some others of an entirely different character, will try to downgrade them even, to the extent of mockery and ridicule.

But these are some of the things they build. They build your basic character. They mold you for your future roles as the custodians of the nation's defense. They make you strong enough to know when you are weak, and brave enough to face yourself when you are afraid.

They teach you to be proud and unbending in honest failure, but humble and gentle in success; not to substitute words for action; not to seek the path of comfort, but to face the stress and spur of difficulty and challenge; to learn to stand up in the storm, but to have compassion on those who fall; to master yourself before you seek to master others; to have a heart that is clean, a goal that is high; to learn to laugh, yet never forget how to weep; to reach into the future, yet never neglect the past; to be serious, yet never take yourself too seriously; to be modest so that you will remember the simplicity of true greatness; the open mind of true wisdom, the meekness of true strength.

They give you a temperate will, a quality of imagination, a vigor of the emotions, a freshness of the deep springs of life, a temperamental predominance of courage over timidity, an appetite for adventure over love of ease.

They create in your heart the sense of wonder, the unfailing hope of what next, and the joy and inspiration of life. They teach you in this way to be an officer and a gentleman.

And what sort of soldiers are those you are to lead? Are they reliable?

Are they brave? Are they capable of victory?

Their story is known to all of you. It is the story of the American man-at-arms. My estimate of him was formed on the battlefields many, many years ago, and has never changed. I regarded him then, as I regard him now, as one of the world's noblest figures-not only as one of the finest military characters, but also as one of the most stainless.

His name and fame are the birthright of every American citizen. In his youth and strength, his love and loyalty, he gave all that mortality can give. He needs no eulogy from me, or from any other man. He has written his own history and written it in red on his enemy's breast.

In twenty campaigns, on a hundred battle-fields, around a thousand campfires, I have witnessed that enduring fortitude, that patriotic self-abnegation, and that invincible determination which have carved his statue in the hearts of his people.

From one end of the world to the other, he has drained deep the chalice of courage. As I listened to those songs in memory's eye, I could see those staggering columns of the First World War, bending under soggy packs on many a weary march, from dripping dusk to drizzling dawn, slogging ankle deep through mire of shell-pocked roads; to form grimly for the attack, blue-lipped, covered with sludge and mud, chilled by the wind and rain, driving home to their objective, and for many, to the judgment seat of God.

I do not know the dignity of their birth, but I do know the glory of their death. They died unquestioning, uncomplaining, with faith in their hearts, and on their lips the hope that we would go on to victory.

Always for them: duty, honor, country. Always their blood, and sweat, and tears, as they saw the way and the light. And twenty years after, on the other side of the globe, against the filth of dirty foxholes, the stench of ghostly trenches, the slime of dripping dugouts, those boiling suns of the relentless heat, those torrential rains of devastating storms, the loneliness and utter desolation of jungle trails, the bitterness of long separation of those they loved and cherished, the deadly pestilence of tropic disease, the horror of stricken areas of war:

Their resolute and determined defense, their swift and sure attack, their indomitable purpose, their complete and decisive victory-always victory, always through the bloody haze of their last reverberating shot, the vision of gaunt, ghastly men, reverently following your password of duty, honor, country.

You now face a new world, a world of change. The thrust into the outer space of the satellite spheres missiles marks a beginning of another epoch in the long story of mankind. In the five or more billions of years the scientists tell us it has taken to form the earth in the three or more billion years of development of the human race, there has never been a more abrupt or staggering evolution.

We deal now, not with things of this world alone, but with the illimitable distances and yet unfathomed mysteries of the universe. We are reaching out for a new and boundless frontier. We speak in strange terms of harnessing the cosmic energy, of making winds and tides work for us…of the primary target in war, no longer limited to the armed forces of an enemy, but instead to include his civil population; of ultimate conflict between a united human race and the sinister forces of some other planetary galaxy; such dreams and fantasies as to make life the most exciting of all times.

And through all this welter of change and development your mission remains fixed, determined, inviolable. It is to win our wars. Everything else in your professional career is but corollary to this vital dedication. All other public purpose, all other public projects, all other public needs, great and small, will find others for their accomplishments; but you are the ones who are trained to fight.

Yours is the profession of arms, the will to win, the sure knowledge that in war there is no substitute for victory, that if you lose, the nation will be destroyed, that the very obsession of your public service must be duty, honor, country.

Others will debate the controversial issues, national and international, which divide men's minds. But serene, calm, aloof, you stand as the nation's war guardians, as its lifeguards from the raging tides of international conflict, as its gladiators in the arena of battle. For a century and a half you have defended, guarded, and protected it hallowed traditions of liberty and freedom, of right and justice.

Let civilian voiced argue the merits or demerits of our processes of government: whether our strength is being sapped by deficit financing indulged in too long, be federal paternalism grown too might, by power groups grown too arrogant, by politics grown too corrupt, by crime grown to rampant, by morals grown too low, by taxes grown too high, by extremists grown too violent; whether our personal liberties are as firm and complete as they should be.

These great national problems aren't for your professional participation or military solution. Your guidepost stands out like a tenfold beacon in the night: duty, honor, country.

You are the lever which binds together the entire fabric of our national system of defense. From your ranks come the great captains who hold the nation's destiny in their hands the moment the war tocsin sounds.

The long gray line has never failed us. Were you to do so, a million ghosts in olive drab, in brown khaki, in blue and gray, would rise from their white crosses, thundering those magic words: duty, honor, country.

This does not mean that you are warmongers. On the contrary, the soldier above all other people prays for peace, for he must suffer and bear the deepest wounds and scars of war. But always in our ears ring the ominous words of Plato, that wisest of all philosophers: "Only the dead have seen the end of war."

The shadows are lengthening for me. The twilight is here. My days of old have vanished-tone and tints. They have gone glimmering through the dreams of things that were. Their memory is one of wondrous beauty, watered by tears and coaxed and caressed by the smiles of yesterday. I listen, then, but with thirsty ear, for the witching melody of faint bugles blowing reveille, of far drums beating the long roll.

In my dreams I hear again the crash of guns, the rattle of musketry, the strange, mournful mutter of the battlefield. But in the evening of my memory I come back to West Point. Always there echoes and re-echoes: duty, honor, country.

Today marks my final roll call with you. But I want you to know that when I cross the river, my last conscious thoughts will be of the corps, and the corps, and the corps.

I bid you farewell.

Suggested Readings

Gunther, John. *The Riddle of MacArthur*. Green-wood Press: 1975.

Leary, William M. *MacArthur and the American Century: A Reader*. University of Nebraska Press: 2001.

MacArthur, Douglas. *Reminiscences*. United States Naval Institute: 2001.

Manchester, William. *American Caesar: Douglas MacArthur 1880–1964*. Laurel: 1983.

Perret, Geoffrey. *Old Soldiers Never Die: The Life and Legend of Douglas MacArthur*. Random House: 1996.

Rovere, Richard H. and Arthur Schlesinger. *General MacArthur and President Truman: The Struggle for Control of American Foreign Policy*. Transaction Publishers: 1992.

Schaller, Michael. *Douglas MacArthur: The Far Eastern General*. Replica Books: 2001.

44

Commitment and Sacrifice: Anton Myrer's Once an Eagle

LtCol Michael J. Gough, USMC

Anyone who ever goes in harm's way should read this book. It is a gut-wrenching, soul-searching drama of a warrior of conscience in an age of crisis. Its action is crisp, and its characters create life-long memories. I first read *Once an Eagle* about 25 years ago as a teenager, and I still vividly remember reading this extraordinary work. I remember plucking this book off of my father's bookcase and idly leafing through it without much interest. I remember reading the first few pages with no intention of reading the entire voluminous work. Three pages later, however, and I was hooked.

Once an Eagle draws the reader into the tactical action of combat. The author's own personal experiences as an enlisted Marine in World War II and his extensive research on warfare seed this novel with credible and thought-provoking action. The main character, Sam Damon, embodies strength of character and commitment to duty. His keen understanding of warfare and his dedication to his subordinates are in constant tension with mission accomplishment and the sacrifices and wastes of war. This tension on the battlefield and at home makes the reader struggle alongside Sam, attempting to find the moral balance between the needs of the country and the stark reality and vagaries of warfare.

The following excerpt from Chapter 2 of *Once an Eagle* exemplifies the novel's gritty pace and the main character's ability to focus on the mission despite seemingly insurmountable odds. The action takes place in World War I after Sam's unit gets thrown into a disastrous night battle with the Germans. Sam's platoon is shattered by a German offensive, and Sam and a group of survivors have to fight their way back to friendly lines. When Sam sees an opportunity to seize some strategically important terrain, he convinces this reluctant group to forego an easy route to repatriation and leads them through a series of demanding combat actions.

He moved with infinite patience, his rifle held easily in the crooks of his elbows. The wheat was high, and darker than the wheat back home; their molasses-colored tassels bobbed gently above his head, bending down to him. He reached the ditch, waited for Raebyrne and Henderson, and then moved more rapidly, pausing every ten feet or so and listening. He encountered a German knapsack with broken straps, abandoned or blown from the back of some attacker, and a holed canteen. Insects hummed overhead, and far off, over the edge of the woods, an observation balloon hung like a fat silvery earthworm. He felt no fear at all. There was only the ditch and the blunt, dark tower of the farmhouse gliding along above the wheat halms. Twice he stopped and studied the tower, but could see nothing moving behind the louvers. Behind him he could hear Raebyrne crawling, a faint, slithering rustle.

He reached the edge of the wheat and raised his head cautiously. The view from the woods had foreshortened the distance; it was a good forty feet to the wall. A cart lay on its side, shattered, one wheel high in the air, its steel rim glinting in the sun. The apple trees, laden with small golden fruit, drooped in the still heat. He felt a tremendous thirst, and swallowed noisily. His watch said 11:48. Nine and a half minutes since they'd started. A lark danced high overhead, threw out a liquid burst of melody and fell away downwind, and with the sight of the bird he felt all at once immeasurably tired, assailed by fears. What if Devlin couldn't make it to that hummock-like ledge? What if a German was watching him right now through those slanted shutters? If there were a gun or a few riflemen down on that vast ground floor of the barn they would all be dead in minutes—

Don't think of that. The thing was to get in there, get over behind the wall. Eleven minutes. Time enough. He rose to one knee, lifted himself soundlessly and ran to the overturned cart and crouched there, breathing through his open mouth. He crept to the break in the wall, one

hand on the dusty yellow mortar. So far so good. He turned back to signal Raebyrne—froze as he heard a short burst of machine gun fire. *Tak-atak-atak-a.* Maxim gun. They were up there. A rifle cracked, then another; he thought he heard a cry.

He put his head around the broken edge of wall, withdrew it. There was the cavernous opening. A wagon stood inside, a caisson—he could see the square green chest in the gloom. Nothing had moved.

It was at that moment that he heard the second machine gun, its clamor riding in over the first—and now beyond all doubt a series of high, yelping cries. Hit. Someone was hit. Oh, the bastards! He ducked through the break in the wall. A strand of barbed wire almost tore his helmet off, another snagged his right leg, crazy looping strands; he wrenched free in a series of frantic, tottering hops, hurdled over more wire and raced across the little courtyard under the clattering noise of the guns. The stone well with its little iron windlass, a scythe lying on the packed dirt with its broad scimitar blade and wooden cradle, half a dozen sacks full of grain, or dirt—his eyes found them all with a singular clarity, riveted on them; left them behind. He leaped over a high stone lintel, half-blinded by the sudden gloom, tripped on something and sprawled into a crate, banging his helmet against the wood, his breath singing in his lungs. He raised his head and looked right into a young, wild face, a shock of bright blond hair. A German, sitting propped up on a little platform. His tunic was open and his chest was heavily bandaged, and his right arm. Near him a body lay facedown, half-covered by a tarpaulin. Immediately above his head Damon heard the Maxim firing in long, even runs, muffled through the heavily timbered ceiling. For a brief, terrible moment he and the wounded German stared at each other. Then the machine gun stopped, the German opened his mouth to cry out in warning, and Damon bayoneted him through the throat. The boy fell over on his side. Blood spurted in swift dark jets over the white gauze.

No one. There was no one else. The caisson was loaded with some packs and boxes and that was all. He glanced back toward the doorway. He was alone. Ahead of him was a stairway of heavy timbers that turned twice on itself as it rose to the tower room. There might be a man on guard posted on the stairs, at one of the turns. No. There would be no one. Hurry. He had to hurry. If he only had grenades! He searched the two dead Germans in furious haste, found none on them, and straightened.

All right, then.

He snapped his rifle off safety, drew his pistol and ran a round into the chamber, hooked his little finger through the trigger guard. He crossed the room, went up ten steps and peered around the corner, swiftly ducking his head back in. No one. Good. The Maxim paused and started again, a long, yammering burst, and he went up the next flight two at a time, around the next turn, the next, and there they were—a vivid, quick tableau in the dim light coming in through the slits of the louvers: the gunner, bareheaded, hunched forward over his spade grips; his belt feeder easing the glittering belt of cartridges into the guides; the helper on his knees prying the cover from a box of belts; behind them an officer standing immaculate and erect, his field glasses to his eyes, on his face a squinting half-smile, like some count inspecting a rare and beautiful collection of lepidoptera—and on the far side of the gun, staring straight at him, a grenadier sitting on his hams with his back against the wall. But this man was unwounded and he had a Mauser rifle lying across his thighs.

Then everything happened at once. The grenadier raised his rifle, the helper too saw Damon and cried out, reaching for his Mauser. Damon, his knee on the third step from the top of the flight, fired; the grenadier doubled over himself without a sound; he shifted to the helper, who leaped up and then flopped out and down, slapping his hand against the floor. The officer swung toward Damon—in one motion flung the glasses at him an clutched at his pistol holster; the glasses struck Damon's helmet, drove it down over his eyes. He flipped it back with his left hand, his head ringing, in time to see the belt feeder drop the belt and duck behind the gun while the gunner wrenched at the mount, trying desperately to swing the gun around—a frantic series of actions that seemed to contain whole eternities of dreamy nightmare possibility as Damon, still without shifting position, fired at the belt feeder and missed, then at the officer, whose pistol flew back out of his hand and hit the far wall with a sharp crack as he fell, than at the bareheaded gunner, who had realized his error and let go the gun, was grappling for his pistol: he gave a brief, choked cry and slumped over the barrel of the Maxim. Damon snapped the Colt into his hand. The belt feeder rose up suddenly, his arm shot up over his shoulder and a black truncheon floated over Damon's head, struck the wall and clattered on down the stairs. Damon fired the Colt and the belt feeder slammed back into the wall, his helmet bouncing away; he snatched at another grenade and Damon hit him again and he went down. The first grenade burst beyond the bend in the stairs, a roar that shook the building. Then there was silence in the little room, broken only by the sound of the belt feeder's helmet rolling around on the timbered floor.

Never taking his eyes off the five figures Damon clawed a fresh clip out of his belt, tapped the steel noses once against the stock of his rifle, and thumbed it into the Springfield's magazine by feel. Not one of them had moved. He came up the last three steps cautiously, conscious of the other Maxim still firing. He glanced behind him down the stairway, where dust rose in a blinding white cloud. Crouching he checked the bodies; he had hit every man squarely between the eyes except the belt feeder, who was shot over the heart and in the belly, and who was plainly dying. He rolled the man over again, picked up his Springfield and moved to the louvers on the west side. One of them had been re-moved, and through the enlarged aperture he could look down on the other gun crew on the roof of the adjoining building, about fifty yards away. The roof had been hit by shellfire, and they were lying flat under the rough timber frame, protected by a few dozen sandbags. A grenadier was firing his rifle below Damon's right, behind the building. They had spotted Raebyrne or Henderson, then. For a second or two he studied the prone group, then, keeping his rifle barrel inside the louvers, fired from right to left: first the sergeant, then the grenadier, then the helper; moving toward the gun. The belt feeder, who saw the helper fall and must have realized what had happened leaped to his feet with astonishing speed, did a funny little dance in the center of the roof, catlike, bewil-dered—all at once threw his hands and shouted something.

"All right," Damon called back. "You—stay—there! *Stay!*" He reloaded his rifle and looked around. The silence was suddenly almost over-powering. He was breathing heavily and his mouth was dry; aside from that he felt perfectly calm. He went over and picked up the German officer's field glasses and found to his surprise they weren't even scratched. He flipped the strap over his neck and swept the fields to the east and north, along the edge of the trees. He could see no movement anywhere. He might have been in a tower on the Gobi desert.

He heard the clump of boots on the stairs and then, swung his rifle around. Raebyrne's face popped into sight and out again.

"Come on, Reb," he said.

They came up in a rush: Raebyrne, followed closely by Henderson and Devlin; then Brewster and Schilz. Once inside the room they stopped and stared at him and then at the dead Germans, the pools of blood seeping into the rough planks at their feet. Someone whistled softly.

"—You shot 'em all up, Sarge," Raebyrne ex-claimed, "—like a hawk in an old hen coop!"

Devlin said, "You all right, Sam?"

"Sure I'm all right. How'd you make out?"

"Not bad. We made it about twenty yards or so down that draw before they spotted us."

"You got you a bleeding high orficer," Rae-byrne crowed, bending over. "Look at his shiny go-to-a-meeting boots!"

Devlin went on: "Poletti got up and ran at the first burst."

"Jesus Christ."

"I know. I couldn't hold him. He was pretty jumpy, Sam. And it looked an awful long way to that wall. I didn't think myself we'd—" He broke off, said: "That Lujak stopped one in the arm."

Damon scowled. Down to six effectives now. "Where is he?"

"Lying behind the wall," Brewster volun-teered. "He's not feeling too well."

Raebyrne cackled. "I imagine he's feeling right dauncy, is Mister Lujak." He wagged his head in wonder. "Old Sarge! He said he'd do it and he did it. The whole Peeroossian army! Hot deggerty damn . . ."

Devlin was saying: "Sam there's another gun—"

"I know. I took care of it."

They all fell silent again. Devlin blinked at him. "You mean you got *them* all, too?"

"All but one. They didn't know I was up here. Now, look . . ." He took Devlin's arm and drew him over to the east louvers. "You see those sand—"

Except for the four dead, the roof was empty. "Son of a bitch! He's decided to run for it—we can't let that happen. He mustn't get back. Dev, take two men—"

He stopped with a grunt; there he was, under the apple trees, running hard toward the distant patch of woods. He fired almost without aiming: the gunner staggered, stumbled and fell into a little pile of hay beside a tree. Damon put an-other round into him to make sure, heard De-vlin's rifle right beside him; the body jerked with the impact and was still.

"God damn fool," he muttered. That was bad, a real lapse. He should have kept his eyes on him until they had him tied up—the whole plan could have been jeopardized . . . He shook his head as if to clear it, turned around again. They were all staring at him; they looked like drunks in the early stages—all eagerness and confusion. Get them going, the inner monitor said crisply. All of them. You're wasting time. You may not have much of it.

"All right," he said, "now let's get going. We're in here, and we're going to stay here. Dev, go on over and check out that Maxim gun. Set it up facing the other way. Toward the embankment."

"The other way?"

"Yes. Pile your sandbags at that end and pull out some planks at the gable. I'm going to turn this one around, too."

"Why, Sam?"

"Just a hunch. I think they're going to run up some reserves. I'll send you Henderson and Schilz as soon as I can. On the double, now."

"Check."

"One more thing. Don't fire until I do, no matter what."

"Right, Sam."

It was as if someone else were issuing orders—someone with a marvelously clear head, an eye for all contingencies. He sent Raebyrne with Henderson to get Jason and Burgess, he sent Brewster to fill all their canteens from the well in the courtyard, he had Schilz bring up a couple of the louvered slats on the north face, and dragged the gun around so it commanded the long field behind them. Raebyrne found some black bread and sausage and a bucket of cold coffee that tasted like burned chestnuts; they bandaged Lujak, who had what appeared to be a flesh wound just above the elbow and who was by now thoroughly cowed; they carried the dead Germans downstairs and covered them all with the tarpaulin. Within twenty minutes Damon was sitting calmly in the tower room with Raebyrne and Brewster, chewing the dense black bread and sweeping the horizon with his new-found field glasses.

"High on the hog." Raebyrne proclaimed. He had stuck the dead Lieutenant's Luger into the waistband of his trousers and was pouring from hand to hand some of the button's he'd cut from the officer's tunic. "You know what they say, Sarge."

"What's that?"

"When times cain't get worse, they got to get better." He squinted shrewdly at the ceiling. "I knew all along you were making the correct move."

"You didn't sound very much like it back there in the woods," Brewster rejoined.

"Well, that's because I need time to come to a decision. I was just weighing the prodes and the corns."

"The what?"

"The prodes and the corns. I knew we could do it all the while."

"Did you," Damon said. "What took you so long getting up here, by the way?"

Raebyrne made a quick, woeful grimace. "Little bit of bad luck, Sarge. I made it over to the wall in fine form, and saw you duck inside. So I took off through the wall like a catamount in rut—and got myself hung up on that bantangled wire and down I went, ass over appetite. And when I got up I was like a puppy on a leash, pulling and hauling and not getting anywhere. And finally, just as I was about to give it all up as a bad job, I come loose and went helling on in. Trouble is, it was plumb mass dark after all that direct sunshine, and I couldn't make out thing-one. By the time I found the stairs that grand old fusillade broke out up above. I said, 'That's old Sarge up there, doing battle,' and away I went. *And boom!*—off went that hand bomb, and smoke and steel shavings all over creation, and back down I went again." He grinned happily, licked his lips. "So you can see, Sarge, it was bad luck that turned good. Because if I'd have been just a touch earlier, you'd have had to scratch old Reb. And there'd go your war . . ." He went off into his high-pitched cackle. "You get the two downstairs on the way by?"

Bent over the Maxim, studying it, Damon shook his head. "No."

Raebyrne blinked. "But Sarge, one of 'em was bayoneted in the—"

"Shut up, Raebyrne," the Sergeant said crossly. He had forgotten about the wounded man on the platform. Pumping the cocking handle he felt himself begin to tremble. The other two were silent, and he knew they were watching him. What the hell, he told himself fiercely, I had no choice. One yip out of him and we'd all be dead. But the tremor remained, and he rocked the gun up and down on its elevation bar. There is a price for everything, the thought came to him; a bleak solace. There are no free tickets to any land, and it doesn't matter if—

"Sarge!" Raebyrne hissed from the slits. "Two of 'em coming this way . . ."

Two soldiers were coming directly toward them across the field; slender, awkward figures wearing the little round gray fatigue caps with the red piping around the band. Each was carrying two rectangular green metal boxes, just like the boxes on the floor by this foot. They had their rifles slung over their shoulders.

"Ammunition," he said briefly. "We can use it. Reb, you and Brewster go downstairs and keep out of sight. Let them come in and then cover them. Let them come in. No shooting, now."

They left. Damon kept moving form side to side, studying the woods, the distant skyline with his glasses. It was hard to say. Maybe he'd guessed wrong. If he had, they were done for, and he had sacrificed ten men to not much purpose. Why was it so quiet? Only a distant muttering, like summer thunder; no rifle fire anywhere. Where had everybody gone? And yet the Germans apparently intended to support these guns.

They came up the stairs, after a few minutes—two rawboned kids, looking ludicrous in the heavy square-toed boots. They were surly with fear. Brewster said something to them in German, and the taller one smiled a quick, frightened smile and bowed.

"What'd you tell him?" Damon demanded.

Brewster looked at him steadily out of his blackened, swollen eyes. "Sarge, I told them that they were prisoners of war and would not be harmed."

He nodded. "Ask them if they are sending reinforcements to these buildings."

Brewster questioned them for a while without much success. They were Army Service Corps kids, they had just had the surprise of their young lives, and they obviously knew nothing beyond the specific orders they'd been given.

"Tie them up," he said.

"With what, Sarge?" Raebyrne asked.

"I don't know—find some rope, use your belts—just tie them up," he said irritably. He felt all at once unutterably tired; there seemed to be no end to this day of stealth and worry and decisions. He watched Raebyrne and Brewster fussing with the prisoners, glanced over at the roof of the other building, where Devlin and Henderson were shifting sandbags. He was weary from carrying the weight of their apathy, their fear, their unfocused resentment.

"Sergeant," Lujak's voice said behind him, tentative and querulous. "Sergeant, we don't have to stay now."

"What?"

"Now that the machine guns—now the German's aren't here anymore. We could go back across the field to our lines. You remember, you said—"

He whirled around. "*Will* you shut your mouth!" he said with such vehemence that the wounded man gasped in fright. "I'm running this outfit, and until I'm wounded or killed, what I say goes . . ." The thought had been in his own mind, and Lujak's giving voice to it had enraged him. "What the hell's the matter with you—you're acting like a bunch of old women!" Brewster was watching him curiously and he turned away—saw Devlin was crouched behind his gun, signaling him frantically with his hands and pointing toward the north. He raised the glasses.

In the woods out of which they had come an hour before, shadows moved back and forth against the light; he had an impression of animation, a stirring, like a snake's coils in deep foliage. And then all at once there they were—a column of men, marching in perfect order diagonally across their field of vision toward the western patch of forest; their rifles slung, their free arms swinging ponderously. An officer was moving beside them, waving a crumpled piece of paper in one hand. He heard Brewster give a muffled exclamation.

"All right," he said between his teeth. He felt perfectly calm again, completely in control. "All right."

"Je-sus, Sarge," Raebyrne whispered, "there's a hundred crawling thousand of them . . . !"

"No, there isn't," he answered calmly, passing his glasses over the nicely aligned ranks, the blank broad faces. "They're in company strength. That's all." He went back and crouched behind the Maxim. "All right. Brewster, you're going to be belt feeder. Take it like this, see?—run it up out of the box."

"Right."

"Reb, take Brewster's rifle and stand there—right there. Lujak, here's my Springfield. You will load for Raebyrne."

"Sergeant, my arm—"

"You've got two of them, haven't you? I said: *you will load for him.*" He settled himself, adjusted the sight slotted in its vertical guides. "All right now, not till I give you the word," he said to Raebyrne. "You will not fire until I give the word."

They were three hundred and fifty yards away, coming with surprising speed. The ditch that he had used for cover on the east flank of the farm took a sharp turn about a hundred yards or so from where they were sitting, deepened, and ran off toward the northwest. They would have to cross it if they kept on.

"Range three hundred," Raebyrne said, and released his safety.

"Easy, now." They were nearer. Their present course, if they held to it, would take them about fifty yards from Devlin's building. Going up to support Brigny-le-Thiep, then. They came on confidently, in silence; some NCO was counting cadence—and gazing at the column, so smart and fresh and vulnerable, Damon felt a sharp twinge of regret. In a few seconds, he was going to kill, or try to kill, all of them. Damn fools. They should have sent out a patrol or two. No—someone had reported in: *We hold Brigny farm,* and so of course they'd never thought to question it. Thank God they had incompetence on their side, too."

"Hell's fire, Sarge, they're going to be eating out of our mess kits . . ."

"Relax," he said. "The nearer the better." Up to a point. He rose and glanced at the roof across the yard. They were crouched behind their sandbag barricade; Devlin was behind the gun, Schilz at the belt, Henderson holding his rifle. While he watched, Devlin slowly turned his head up at the tower; his eyes were shining with tension.

"Range one fifty," Raebyrne said.

"Sarge—"

"Hang on now." The officer had paused, was consulting a paper, obviously a map. The sergeant's cadence came sharply across the wheat now. Oh, the God damned fools! A rage mounted in the back of his head, but cold. He threw one last glance back toward the south. Nothing. Where in Christ's name were they all—had the whole lousy AEF vanished off the face of the earth?

They had reached the ditch. The first ranks dipped into it and clambered up the near side, slowly and in poor formation. It was deep, then, and fairly wide. Good. All the better.

Range a *hundred,*" Raebyrne breathed.

He knew they were all gazing at him now, even Raebyrne. The blood was driving against his temples and throat; his knuckles were white on the grips.

"—Sarge," Brewster was whispering hoarsely, "Sarge, I can see that fellow's mustache, that fellow—"

As the second detachment went into the ditch he called: "Open fire!" and thumbed the gun.

Suggested Reading

Card, Orson Scott. *Ender's Game*. New York: Tor Books, 1991.

Myrer, Anton. *Once an Eagle*. New York: Harper Torch, 1996.

West Jr., F.J. *The Village*. New York: Pocket Books, 2003.

About the Author

Lieutenant Colonel Michael J. Gough is a Marine Corps Harrier pilot and is currently assigned to the Division of Professional Development at the U.S. Naval Academy.

45

Duty, Leadership and Moral Dilemmas: Frank O'Connor's Guests of the Nation

Kevin A. Brooks, Maj, USMC

The concept of duty is a fundamental cornerstone to military service. Along with honor, integrity, and accountability, duty becomes ingrained in the mindset of all military personnel. Leadership and duty are intrinsically linked, since good leadership encompasses a duty to one's subordinates, just as good followership encompasses a duty to one's leaders. The professional mantra of the Naval Academy—"Ship, shipmate, self"—evokes a sense of duty and priority. Naval, and all military, personnel learn to place the welfare of the unit and other unit members above their own interests, which implies a sense of duty to the greater common good. Good leaders learn to place the welfare of their men and women above their own needs. In other words, the military sense of duty implies the traditional "Golden Rule."

Yet history is rife with examples of military people using a corrupted sense of duty to explain or justify their misguided actions. Think of the Nuremburg trials or the My Lai massacre or the Abu Ghraib incidents—all examples of questionable, even criminal, conduct which participants attempted to justify using the concept of "duty." Duty, loyalty and accountability may become cloudy and confused in the heat of battle or the heat of enthusiasm.

Frank O'Connor explores the dark side of duty in his short story "Guests of the Nation." The fictional story portrays the imprisonment of two British soldiers by Irish soldiers during Ireland's war for independence from Britain. In addition to the two British prisoners, the central characters are two Irish soldiers acting as guards and one Irish non-com in charge of the party. The issue at hand involves the execution of the British soldiers, which takes place at the conclusion of the story. The Irish guards, Bonaparte and Noble, oppose the killing, but their leader, Donovan, insists that the prisoners must be executed. Duty—to peers, to seniors, to the enemy, to the law—is the central theme of the story. Yet, equally important to the notion of duty is the notion of leadership. Good leadership should rarely, if ever, place one in conflict with proper duty. It's only when priorities become skewed, when loyalties become misaligned, when expediency trumps accountability, that leaders place followers on the horns of a dilemma, using "duty" to justify their actions.

The story begins with a murky, confusing setting. Technically, the Irishmen should be guarding the Englishmen; yet, the author depicts everyone sitting around a campfire, playing cards. The "guards" and "prisoners" refer to each other as "chums." The men engage in friendly banter, lively political and religious debates and good-natured humor. The setting and description lull the reader into a false sense of security and peace; it is easy to forget that two peoples are at war and the men are on opposing sides. The interaction between the Irishmen and the Englishmen brings the issue of duty and leadership into question. Why would guards call their prisoners "chums?" Should enemies play cards together? Obviously, the notion of duty, not to mention security and protocol, appears somewhat lax in this setting.

The situation deteriorates further with Donovan's announcement to the Englishman that "there were four of our fellows shot in Cork this morning and now you're to be shot as a reprisal." The narrator, Bonaparte, goes on to say that Donovan continues with "the usual rigmarole about duty and how unpleasant it is," to which Bonaparte replies, "I never noticed that people who talk a lot about duty find it much of a trouble to them." These passages contain the critical essence of this story—the concept of proper duty and the associated aspect of proper leadership. Donovan considers a "reprisal" killing to be an acceptable duty, regardless of the connotations of the word "reprisal." Bonaparte reveals his troubled attitude with his retort. Donovan seems to see the situation in black and white, while Bonaparte sees only grey. However, neither man acts with decisive leadership to make a more enlightened decision.

At several points in the story, O'Connor describes Donovan as "excited" about the impending reprisal. Certainly, there are many connotations for this word, but the author shows clearly that Donovan's excitement stems from his belief in reprisal or revenge. He has no problem killing the Englishmen. He tells them, "I never said I had anything against you. But why did your people take out four of our prisoners and shoot them in cold blood?" Ironically, Donovan is willing and eager to kill the Englishmen in cold blood. One might use several terms to describe the intended action against the prisoners—execution, killing, murder, revenge, reprisal—but a conscientious military person would not use the word "duty." Just before the killing, Donovan says again, "You understand that we're only doing our duty?" Even if ordered to execute the Englishmen, Donovan might realize the order could be unlawful, requiring an act of moral leadership to stop the bloodshed.

For their part, Noble and Bonaparte fail to execute any leadership in this situation. They allow Donovan to bully them into complicity. Although both men believe the killing is wrong, neither one stands up to Donovan. They don't believe the excuse of "duty," yet they don't have the courage to exercise proper moral leadership to prevent the killing. In the end, despite their personal feelings, they bear as much guilt as Donovan for their behavior.

While this story focuses on the concept of duty, the connection with leadership should not be overlooked. Donovan, Noble and Bonaparte have chances to exercise sound leadership by questioning this misguided notion of duty, but each man fails to do so. The execution of an unlawful or illegal order is a corruption of proper duty, and the application of a corrupt sense of duty is a failure of proper leadership. Donovan is the senior person with authority, and thus he must bear the brunt of the blame; however, the complicit behavior of Noble and Bonaparte can not be ignored. The failure of sound leadership and the corruption of duty leads to the chilling execution of two men.

I

At dusk the big Englishman, Belcher, would shift his long legs out of the ashes and say "Well, chums, what about it?" and Noble or me would say "All right, chum" (for we had picked up some of their curious expressions), and the little Englishman, Hawkins, would light the lamp and bring out the cards. Sometimes Jeremiah Donovan would come up and supervise the game and get excited over Hawkins's cards, which he always played badly, and shout at him as if he was one of our own "Ah, you divil, you, why didn't you play the tray?"

But ordinarily Jeremiah was a sober and contented poor devil like the big Englishman, Belcher, and was looked up to only because he was a fair hand at documents, though he was slow enough even with them. He wore a small cloth hat and big gaiters over his long pants, and you seldom saw him with his hands out of his pockets. He reddened when you talked to him, tilting from toe to heel and back, and looking down all the time at his big farmer's feet. Noble and me used to make fun of his broad accent, because we were from the town.

I couldn't at the time see the point of me and Noble guarding Belcher and Hawkins at all, for it was my belief that you could have planted that pair down anywhere from this to Claregalway and they'd have taken root there like a native weed. I never in my short experience seen two men to take to the country as they did.

They were handed on to us by the Second Battalion when the search for them became too hot, and Noble and myself, being young, took over with a natural feeling of responsibility, but Hawkins made us look like fools when he showed that he knew the country better than we did.

"You're the bloke they calls Bonaparte," he says to me. "Mary Brigid O'Connell told me to ask you what you done with the pair of her brother's socks you borrowed."

For it seemed, as they explained it, that the Second used to have little evenings, and some of the girls of the neighbourhood turned in, and, seeing they were such decent chaps, our fellows couldn't leave the two Englishmen out of them. Hawkins learned to dance "The Walls of Limerick," "The Siege of Ennis," and "The Waves of Tory" as well as any of them, though naturally, he couldn't return the compliment, because our lads at that time did not dance foreign dances on principle.

So whatever privileges Belcher and Hawkins had with the Second they just naturally took with us, and after the first day or two we gave up all pretence of keeping a close eye on them. Not that they could have got far, for they had accents you could cut with a knife and wore khaki tunics and overcoats with civilian pants and boots. But it's my belief that they never had any idea of escaping and were quite content to be where they were.

It was a treat to see how Belcher got off with the old woman of the house where we were staying. She was a great warrant to scold, and cranky even with us, but before ever she had a chance of giving our guests, as I may call them, a lick of her tongue, Belcher had made her his friend for life. She was breaking sticks, and Belcher, who hadn't been more than ten minutes in the house, jumped up from his seat and went over to her.

"Allow me, madam," he says, smiling his queer little smile, "please allow me"; and he takes the bloody hatchet. She was struck too paralytic to speak, and after that, Belcher would be at her heels, carrying a bucket, a basket, or a load of turf, as the case might be. As Noble said, he got into looking before she leapt, and hot water, or any little thing she wanted, Belcher would have it ready for her. For such a huge man (and though I am five foot ten myself I had to look up at him) he had an uncommon shortness—or should I say lack?—of speech. It took us some time to get used to him, walking in and out, like a ghost, without a word. Especially because Hawkins talked enough for a platoon, it was strange to hear big Belcher with his toes in the ashes come out with a solitary "Excuse me, chum," or "That's right, chum." His one and only passion was cards, and I will say for him that he was a good card-player. He could have fleeced myself and Noble, but whatever we lost to him Hawkins lost to us, and Hawkins played with the money Belcher gave him.

Hawkins lost to us because he had too much old gab, and we probably lost to Belcher for the same reason. Hawkins and Noble would spit at one another about religion into the early hours of the morning, and Hawkins worried the soul out of Noble, whose brother was a priest, with a string of questions that would puzzle a cardinal. To make it worse even in treating of holy subjects, Hawkins had a deplorable tongue. I never in all my career met a man who could mix such a variety of cursing and bad language into an argument. He was a terrible man, and a fright to argue. He never did a stroke of work, and when he had no one else to talk to, he got stuck in the old woman.

He met his match in her, for one day when he tried to get her to complain profanely of the drought, she gave him a great comedown by blaming it entirely on Jupiter Pluvius (a deity neither Hawkins nor I had ever heard of, though Noble said that among the pagans it was believed that he had something to do with the rain). Another day he was swearing at the capitalists for starting the German war when the old lady laid down her iron, puckered up her little crab's mouth, and said: "Mr. Hawkins, you can say what you like about the war, and think you'll deceive me because I'm only a simple poor countrywoman, but I know what started the war. It was the Italian Count that stole the heathen divinity out of the temple in Japan. Believe me, Mr. Hawkins, nothing but sorrow and want can follow the people that disturb the hidden powers." A queer old girl, all right.

II

We had our tea one evening, and Hawkins lit the lamp and we all sat into cards. Jeremiah Donovan came in too, and sat down and watched us for a while, and it suddenly struck me that he had no great love for the two English-

men. It came as a great surprise to me, because I hadn't noticed anything about him before.

Late in the evening a really terrible argument blew up between Hawkins and Noble, about capitalists and priests and love of your country.

"The capitalists," says Hawkins with an angry gulp, "pays the priests to tell you about the next world so as you won't notice what the bastards are up to in this."

"Nonsense, man!" says Noble, losing his temper. "Before ever a capitalist was thought of, people believed in the next world."

Hawkins stood up as though he was preaching a sermon. "Oh, they did, did they?" he says with a sneer. "They believed all the things you believe, isn't that what you mean? And you believe that God created Adam, and Adam created Shem, and Shem created Jehoshophat. You believe all that silly old fairytale about Eve and Eden and the apple. Well, listen to me, chum. If you're entitled to hold a silly belief like that, I'm entitled to hold my silly belief—which is that the first thing your God created was a bleeding capitalist with morality and Rolls-Royce complete. Am I right, chum?" he says to Belcher.

"You're right, chum," says Belcher with his amused smile, and got up from the table to stretch his long legs into the fire and stroke his moustache. So, seeing that Jeremiah Donovan was going, and that there was no knowing when the argument about religion would be over, I went out with him. We strolled down to the village together, and then he stopped and started blushing and mumbling and saying I ought to be behind, keeping guard on the prisoners. I didn't like the tone he took with me, and anyway I was bored with life in the cottage, so I replied by asking him what the hell we wanted guarding them at all for. I told him I'd talked it over with Noble, and that we'd both rather be out with a fighting column.

"What use are those fellows to us?" says I.

He looked at me in surprise and said: "I thought you knew we were keeping them as hostages."

"Hostages?" I said.

"The enemy have prisoners belonging to us," he says, "and now they're talking of shooting them. If they shoot our prisoners, we'll shoot theirs."

"Shoot them?" I said.

"What else did you think we were keeping them for?" he says.

"Wasn't it very unforeseen of you not to warn Noble and myself of that in the beginning?" I said.

"How was it?" says he. "You might have known it."

"We couldn't know it, Jeremiah Donovan," says I. "How could we when they were on our hands so long?"

"The enemy have our prisoners as long and longer," says he.

"That's not the same thing at all," says I.

"What difference is there?" says he.

I couldn't tell him, because I knew he wouldn't understand. If it was only an old dog that was going to the vet's, you'd try and not get too fond of him, but Jeremiah Donovan wasn't a man that would ever be in danger of that. "And when is this thing going to be decided?" says I.

"We might hear tonight," he says. "Or tomorrow or the next day at latest. So if it's only hanging round here that's a trouble to you, you'll be free soon enough."

It wasn't the hanging round that was a trouble to me at all by this time. I had worse things to worry about. When I got back to the cottage the argument was still on. Hawkins was holding forth in his best style, maintaining that there was no next world, and Noble was maintaining that there was; but I could see that Hawkins had had the best of it.

"Do you know what, chum?" he was saying with a saucy smile. "I think you're just as big a bleeding unbeliever as I am. You say you believe in the next world, and you know just as much about the next world as I do, which is sweet damn-all. What's heaven? You don't know. Where's heaven? You don't know. You know sweet damn-all! I ask you again, do they wear wings?"

"Very well, then," says Noble, "they do. Is that enough for you? They do wear wings."

"Where do they get them, then? Who makes them? Have they a factory for wings? Have they a sort of store where you hands in your chit and takes your bleeding wings?"

"You're an impossible man to argue with," says Noble. "Now, listen to me—" And they were off again.

It was long after midnight when we locked up and went to bed. As I blew out the candle I told Noble what Jeremiah Donovan was after telling me. Noble took it very quietly. When we'd been in bed about an hour he asked me did I think we ought to tell the Englishmen. I didn't think we should, because it was more than likely that the English wouldn't shoot our men, and even if they did, the brigade officers, who were always up and down with the Second Battalion and knew the Englishmen well, wouldn't be likely to want them plugged. "I think so too," says Noble. "It would be great cruelty to put the wind to them now."

"It was very unforeseen of Jeremiah Donovan anyhow," says I.

It was next morning that we found it so hard to face Belcher and Hawkins. We went about the house all day scarcely saying a word. Belcher didn't seem to notice; he was stretched into the ashes as usual, with his look unusual of waiting in quietness for something unforeseen to happen, but Hawkins noticed and put it down to Noble's being beaten in the argument of the night before.

"Why can't you take a discussion in the proper spirit?" he says severely. "You and your Adam and Eve! I'm a Communist, that's what I am. Communist or anarchist, it all comes to much the same thing." And for hours he went round the house, muttering when the fit took him. "Adam and Eve! Adam and Eve! Nothing better to do with their time than picking bleeding apples!"

III

I don't know how we got through that day, but I was very glad when it was over, the tea things were cleared away, and Belcher said in his peaceable way: "Well, chums, what about it?" We sat round the table and Hawkins took out the cards, and just then I heard Jeremiah Donovan's footstep on the path and a dark presentiment crossed my mind. I rose from the table and caught him before he reached the door.

"What do you want?" I asked.

"I want those two soldier friends of yours," he says, getting red.

"Is that the way, Jeremiah Donovan?" I asked.

"That's the way. There were four of our lads shot this morning, one of them a boy of sixteen."

"That's bad," I said.

At that moment Noble followed me out, and the three of us walked down the path together, talking in whispers. Feeney, the local intelligence officer, was standing by the gate.

"What are you going to do about it?" I asked Jeremiah Donovan.

"I want you and Noble to get them out; tell them they're being shifted again; that'll be the quietest way."

"Leave me out of that," says Noble under his breath.

Jeremiah Donovan looks at him hard. "All right," he says. "You and Feeney get a few tools from the shed and dig a hole by the far end of the bog. Bonaparte and myself will be after you. Don't let anyone see you with the tools. I wouldn't like it to go beyond ourselves."

We saw Feeney and Noble go round to the shed and went in ourselves. I left Jeremiah Donovan to do the explanations. He told them that he had orders to send them back to the Second Battalion. Hawkins let out a mouthful of curses, and you could see that though Belcher didn't say anything, he was a bit upset too. The old woman was for having them stay in spite of us, and she didn't stop advising them until Jeremiah Donovan lost his temper and turned on her. He had a nasty temper, I noticed. It was pitch-dark in the cottage by this time, but no one thought of lighting the lamp, and in the darkness the two Englishmen fetched their top-coats and said good-bye to the old woman.

"Just as a man makes a home of a bleeding place, some bastard at headquarters thinks you're too cushy and shunts you out" says Hawkins, shaking her hand.

"A thousand thanks, madam," says Belcher. "A thousand thanks for everything"—as though he'd made it up.

We went round to the back of the house and down towards the bog. It was only then that Jeremiah Donovan told them. He was shaking with excitement.

"There were four of our fellows shot in Cork this morning and now you're to be shot as a reprisal."

"What are you talking about?" snaps Hawkins. "It's bad enough being mucked about as we are without having to put up with your funny jokes."

"It isn't a joke," says Donovan. "I'm sorry, Hawkins, but it's true," and begins on the usual rigmarole about duty and how unpleasant it is.

I never noticed that people who talk a lot about duty find it much of a trouble to them.

"Oh, cut it out!" says Hawkins.

"Ask Bonaparte," says Donovan, seeing that Hawkins isn't taking him seriously. "Isn't it true, Bonaparte?"

"It is," I say, and Hawkins stops.

"Ah, for Christ's sake, chum!"

"You don't sound as if you meant it."

"If he doesn't mean it, I do," says Donovan, working himself up.

"What have you against me, Jeremiah Donovan?"

"I never said I had anything against you. But why did your people take out four of our prisoners and shoot them in cold blood?"

He took Hawkins by the arm and dragged him on, but it was impossible to make him understand that we were in earnest. I had the Smith and Wesson in my pocket and I kept fingering it and wondering what I'd do if they put up a fight for it or ran, and wishing to God they'd do one or the other. I knew if I they did run for it, that I'd never fire on them. Hawkins wanted to know was Noble in it, and when we said yes, he asked us why Noble wanted to plug him. Why did any of us want to plug him? What had he done to us? Weren't we all chums? Didn't we understand him and didn't he understand us? Did we imagine for an instant that he'd shoot us for all the so-and-so officers in the so-and so British Army?

By this time we'd reached the bog, and I was so sick I couldn't even answer him. We walked along the edge of it in the darkness, and every now and then Hawkins would call a halt and begin all over again, as if lie was wound up, about our being chums, and 1 knew that nothing but the sight of the grave would convince him that we had to do it. And all the time I was hoping that something would happen; that they'd run for it or that Noble would take over the responsibility from me. I had the feeling that it was worse on Noble than on me.

IV

At last we saw the lantern in the distance and made towards it. Noble was carrying it, and Feeney was standing somewhere in the darkness behind him, and the picture of them so still and silent in the bogland brought it home to me that we were in earnest, and banished the last bit of hope I had.

Belcher, on recognizing Noble, said: "Hallo, chum," in his quiet way, but Hawkins flew at him at once, and the argument began all over again, only this time Noble had nothing to say for himself and stood with his head down, holding the lantern between his legs.

It was Jeremiah Donovan who did the answering. For the twentieth time, as though it was haunting his mind, Hawkins asked if anybody thought he'd shoot Noble.

"Yes, you would," says Jeremiah Donovan.

"No, I wouldn't, damn you!"

"You would, because you'd know you'd be shot for not doing it."

"I wouldn't, not if I was to be shot twenty times over. I wouldn't shoot a pal. And Belcher wouldn't—isn't that right, Belcher?"

"That's right, chum," Belcher said, but more by way of answering the question than of joining in the argument. Belcher sounded as though whatever unforeseen thing he'd always been waiting for had come at last.

"Anyway, who says Noble would be shot if I wasn't? What do you think I'd do if I was in his place, out in the middle of a blasted bog?"

"What would you do?" asks Donovan.

"I'd go with him wherever he was going, of course. Share my last bob with him and stick by him through thick and thin. No one can ever say of me that I let down a pal."

"We had enough of this," says Jeremiah Donovan, cocking his revolver. "Is there any message you want to send?"

"No, there isn't."

"Do you want to say your prayers?"

Hawkins came out with a cold-blooded remark that even shocked me and turned on Noble again. "Listen to me, Noble," he says. "You and me are chums. You can't come over to my side, so I'll come over to your side. That show you I mean what I say? Give me a rifle and I'll go along with you and the other lads."

Nobody answered him. We knew that was no way out.

"Hear what I'm saying?" he says. "I'm through with it. I'm a deserter or anything else you like. I don't believe in your stuff, but it's no worse than mine. That satisfy you?"

Noble raised his head, but Donovan began to speak and he lowered it again without replying. "For the last time, have you any messages to send?" says Donovan in a cold excited sort of voice.

"Shut up, Donovan! You don't understand me, but these lads do. They're not the sort to make a pal and kill a pal. They're not the tools of any capitalist."

I alone of the crowd saw Donovan raise his Webley to the back of Hawkins's neck, and as he did so I shut my eyes and tried to pray. Hawkins had begun to say something else when Donovan fired, and as I opened my eyes at the bang, I saw Hawkins stagger at the knees and lie out flat at Noble's feet, slowly and as quiet as a kid falling asleep, with the lantern-light on his lean legs and bright farmer's boots. We all stood very still, watching him settle out in the last agony.

Then Belcher took out a handkerchief and began to tie it about his own eyes (in our excitement we'd forgotten to do the same for Hawkins), and, seeing it wasn't big enough, turned and asked for the loan of mine. I gave it to him and he knotted the two together and pointed with his foot at Hawkins.

"He's not quite dead," he says. "Better give him another."

Sure enough, Hawkins's left knee is beginning to rise. I bend down and put my gun to his head; then, recollecting myself, I get up again. Belcher understands what's in my mind.

"Give him his first," he says. "I don't mind. Poor bastard, we don't know what's happening to him now."

I knelt and fired. By this time I didn't seem to know what I was doing. Belcher, who was fumbling a bit awkwardly with the handkerchiefs, came out with a laugh as he heard the shot. It was the first time I heard him laugh and it sent a shudder down my back; it sounded so unnatural.

"Poor hugger!" he said quietly. "And last night he was so curious about it all. It's very queer, chums, I always think. Now he knows as much about it as they'll ever let him know, and last night he was all in the dark."

Donovan helped him to tie the handkerchiefs about his eyes. "Thanks, chum," he said. Donovan asked if there were any messages he wanted sent.

"No, chum," he says. "Not for me. If any of you would like to write to Hawkins's mother, you'll find a letter from her in his pocket. He and his mother were great chums. But my missus left me eight years ago. Went away with another fellow and took the kid with her. I like the feeling of a home, as you may have noticed, but I couldn't start again after that."

It was an extraordinary thing, but in those few minutes Belcher said more than in all the weeks before. It was just as if the sound of the shot had started a flood of talk in him and he could go on the whole night like that, quite happily, talking about himself. We stood round like fools now that he couldn't see us any longer. Donovan looked at Noble, and Noble shook his head. Then Donovan raised his Webley, and at that moment Belcher gives his queer laugh again. He may have thought we were talking about him, or perhaps he noticed the same thing I'd noticed and couldn't understand it.

"Excuse me, chums," he says. "I feel I'm talking the hell of a lot, and so silly, about my being so handy about a house and things like that. But this thing came on me suddenly. You'll forgive me, I'm sure."

"You don't want to say a prayer?" asks Donovan.

"No, chum," he says. "I don't think it would help. I'm ready, and you boys want to get it over."

"You understand that we're only doing our duty?" says Donovan.

Belcher's head was raised like a blind man's so that you could only see his chin and the tip of his nose in the lantern-light. "I never could make out what duty was myself," he said. "I think you're all good lads, if that's what you mean. I'm not complaining."

Noble, just as if he couldn't bear any more of it, raised his fist at Donovan, and in a flash Donovan raised his gun and fired. The big man went over like a sack of meal, and this time there was no need for a second shot.

I don't remember much about the burying, but that it was worse than all the rest because we had to carry them to the grave. It was all mad lonely with nothing but a patch of lantern-light between ourselves and the dark, and birds hooting and screeching all round, disturbed by the guns. Noble went through Hawkins's belongings to find the letter from his mother, and then joined his hands together. He did the same with Belcher. Then, when we'd filled in the grave, we separated from Jeremiah Donovan and Feeney and took our tools back to the shed. All the way we didn't speak a word. The kitchen was dark and cold as we'd left it, and the old woman was sitting over the hearth, saying her beads. We walked past her into the room, and Noble struck a match to light the lamp. She rose quietly and came to the doorway with all her cantankerousness gone.

"What did ye do with them?" she asked in a whisper, and Noble started so that the match went out in his hand.

"What's that?" he asked without turning round.

"I heard ye," she said.

"What did you hear?" asked Noble.

"I heard ye. Do ye think I didn't hear ye, putting the spade back in the houseen?"

Noble struck another match and this time the lamp lit for him. "Was that what ye did to them?" she asked.

Then, by God, in the very doorway, she fell on her knees and began praying, and after looking at her for a minute or two Noble did the same by the fireplace. I pushed my way out past her and left them at it. I stood at the door, watching the stars and listening to the shrieking of the birds dying out over the bogs. It is so strange what you feel at times like that that you can't describe it. Noble says he saw everything ten times the size, as though there were nothing in the whole world but that little patch of bog with the two Englishmen stiffening into it, but with me it was as if the patch of bog where the Englishmen were was a million miles away, and even Noble and the old woman, mumbling behind me, and the birds and the bloody stars were all far away, and I was somehow very small and very lost and lonely like a child astray in the snow. And anything that happened to me afterwards, I never felt the same about again.

Suggested Reading

O'Connor, Frank. *Collected Stories*. New York: Vintage, 1984.

Crane, Stephen. *The Red Badge of Courage*. New York: Norton, 1994.

Bierce, Ambrose. "An Occurrence at Owl Creek Bridge." *Tales of Soldiers and Civilians and Other Stories*. New York: Penguin, 2000.

Tolstoy, Leo. "The Death of Ivan Ilych." *The Death of Ivan Ilych and Other Stories*. New York: Penguin, 1989.

About the Author

Major Kevin Brooks, USMC has a B.S. in English from the United States Naval Academy and an M.A. in English Literature from the University of Maryland. He is a career F/A-18 pilot with numerous deployments and combat service in Operation Iraqi Freedom. Currently, he is a Senior Instructor in the English Department at the Naval Academy. His previous work includes a contribution on Joe Foss for *Leadership Embodied*.

46

Lessons in Combat Leadership: Tim O'Brien's The Things They Carried

Maj Kevin Brooks, USMC

A close examination of Tim O'Brien's arguably "anti-war" story, "The Things They Carried," reveals some interesting and compelling commentary on combat leadership. Set in the jungles of South Vietnam during the Vietnam War, the story evokes a tone consistent with many Vietnam War stories, namely one of disillusionment with the war's circumstances and progress. The principal characters, a platoon of soldiers led by Lieutenant Jimmy Cross, display varying attitudes of complacency, boredom, depression and distraction. However, the gradual change in attitude, demeanor and action demonstrated by Lt Cross speaks directly to the nature of combat leadership and two of its fundamental elements—mission accomplishment and troop welfare. Lt Cross begins as a daydreaming romantic longing for home, but matures into a focused, seasoned combat leader who realizes finally that the best chance for success and survival requires his complete attention to duty and dedication to his men. His growth as a leader reveals important lessons on leadership, lessons of value for any generation of military leaders.

Newly commissioned young officers can easily relate to Jimmy Cross. His thoughts revolve around his girlfriend, his family, his homesickness—all typical preoccupations of youth. He spends much of his time reading and re-reading letters from his girlfriend, Martha, and gazing at her picture, while reminiscing about college memories. Such behavior is typical, natural and not inherently harmful, unless one is presently situated in a combat zone and responsible for the safety and leadership of several young soldiers. Lt Cross chooses, consciously or not, a particularly poor time for distraction and daydreaming. While his men are attempting to patrol the jungle and search the Viet Cong tunnels, young Jimmy finds himself preoccupied with his relationship with Martha and his longing for home. To make matters worse, Jimmy reveals that

Martha isn't really his "girlfriend" per se, but actually just a college friend. Unfortunately, Jimmy has fallen in love with Martha and his preoccupation borders on an obsession, creating an even more precarious situation for a combat leader and for his men.

The author portrays Lt Cross's attitude and actions as an apparent analogy for the entire war; one sees the parallels of forced involvement, lack of commitment to success, a desire to withdraw, and the naive wish that the whole situation would just go away. The attitude of Lt Cross and his soldiers about the war gives the story its "anti-war" tone. Everyone seems preoccupied with things other than tactics, mission effectiveness, military discipline and the overall goal of winning the war. The story's title illustrates this problem. The soldiers carry their physical load of personal and professional gear, but, perhaps more importantly, they carry the intangible weight of numerous mental and emotional loads: the fear of embarrassment and cowardice, the struggle for survival and subsequent fear of death, the longing for home, and the psychological terror of combat. All of these factors create a situation rife with distraction and disillusionment. In addition, the soldiers carry out a series of seemingly pointless and increasingly mundane missions, leading to an increase in complacency and a lack of military discipline. The platoon's situation, like the entire war, seems to be an endless repetition of risk without reward.

In the presence of such factors, the requirement for firm, practical, alert leadership is paramount. The survival of these men is critically dependent upon strong leadership, due to their distractions and complacency. Unfortunately, Lt Cross is arguably the worst offender in the platoon. His excessive daydreaming and melancholy attitude place his platoon in grave danger. Rather than focusing on military tactics, Cross focuses on nostalgic memories. Rather than worrying about the safety of his men, he worries about the future of his relationship with Martha. His misguided priorities and misplaced attention

prevent him from being an effective platoon leader. The eventual result is deadly.

In the middle of the story, one of Lt Cross's men, Ted Lavender, is killed by sniper fire. Immediately, Lt Cross places responsibility and blame for the death upon himself. One might argue that, in combat, an officer can not protect all of his men all of the time. However, when Ted Lavender is shot, Lt Cross is daydreaming about Martha, rather than leading his men. Lt Cross realizes that his behavior may not have caused Lavender's death but it was certainly a casual factor. This realization is the pivotal moment in the story. Tragically, it takes the avoidable death of a soldier to snap Lt Cross out of his melancholic malaise. Yet, from this point forward, Lt Cross changes in several positive ways.

Cross realizes finally that leadership is more than simply being in charge; it is more than telling people what to do or looking at a map and telling people where to go or deciding who goes into the tunnel today. After Lavender's death, Cross realizes that true leadership involves total commitment to your people and your mission. It requires keen observation of your people and aggressive attention to detail, especially in combat. Leadership requires knowing your people—their strengths and weaknesses, their problems, their habits, their mannerisms, and their fears. An effective leader isn't just in charge; he/she must be a mentor, a teacher, a counselor, a disciplinarian, a mediator and a positive role model. Lt Cross understands finally, and with shame, that his behavior has been a poor example for his men and, more importantly, it put everyone's life at greater risk. Combat intensifies everything about leadership. There is less margin for error, less time for indecision, greater risk of injury and death. Thus, leadership in combat requires more effort, more energy, more commitment than any other situation.

Near the conclusion of the story, Lt Cross decides to change his leadership style and his daily actions. He vows to embrace a greater sense of commitment to his men and his mission. As O'Brien states, Cross "reminded himself that his obligation was not to be loved but to lead." Cross has finally come to terms with his environment and his responsibilities. He accepts his previous failures and moves forward, imbued with a new sense of purpose and positive energy. The story leaves the reader with an optimistic feeling about Lt Cross and his men. One believes that the past struggles led to a positive reform and a greater chance for survival and success. Ultimately, leadership plays a crucial role in this transformation and the final message of the story. The ability of Cross to embrace and embody a style of strong, effective leadership will likely be the difference between success and failure, possibly between life and death, for these men. The overall lesson for the reader is that effective combat leadership is the cornerstone for success and survival.

First Lieutenant Jimmy Cross carried letters from a girl named Martha, a junior at Mount Sebastian College in New Jersey. They were not love letters, but Lieutenant Cross was hoping, so he kept them folded in plastic at the bottom of his rucksack. In the late afternoon, after a day's march, he would dig his foxhole, wash his hands under a canteen, unwrap the letters, hold them with the tips of his fingers, and spend the last hour of light pretending. He would imagine romantic camping trips into the White Mountains in New Hampshire. He would sometimes taste the envelope flaps, knowing her tongue had been there. More than anything, he wanted Martha to love him as he loved her, but the letters were mostly chatty, elusive on the matter of love. She was a virgin, he was almost sure. She was an English major at Mount Sebastian, and she wrote beautifully about her professors and roommates and midterm exams, about her respect for Chaucer and her great affection for Virginia Woolf. She often quoted lines of poetry; she never mentioned the war, except to say, Jimmy, take care of yourself. The letters

weighed 10 ounces. They were signed Love, Martha, but Lieutenant Cross understood that Love was only a way of signing and did not mean what he sometimes pretended it meant. At dusk, he would carefully return the letters to his rucksack. Slowly, a bit distracted, he would get up and move among his men, checking the perimeter, then at full dark he would return to his hole and watch the night and wonder if Martha was a virgin.

The things they carried were largely determined by necessity. Among the necessities or near-necessities were P-38 can openers, pocket knives, heat tabs, wristwatches, dog tags, mosquito repellent, chewing gum, candy, cigarettes, salt tablets, packets of Kool-Aid, lighters, matches, sewing kits, Military Payment Certificates, C rations, and two or three canteens of water. Together, these items weighed between 15 and 20 pounds, depending upon a man's habits or rate of metabolism. Henry Dobbins, who was a big man, carried extra rations; he was especially fond of canned peaches in heavy syrup over pound cake. Dave Jensen, who practiced field hygiene, carried a toothbrush, dental floss, and several hotel-sized bars of soap he'd stolen on R&R in Sydney, Australia. Ted Lavender, who was scared, carried tranquilizers until he was shot in the head outside the village of Than Khe in mid-April. By necessity, and because it was SOP, they all carried steel helmets that weighed 5 pounds including the liner and camouflage cover. They carried the standard fatigue jackets and trousers. Very few carried underwear. On their feet they carried jungle boots—2.1 pounds—and Dave Jensen carried three pairs of socks and a can of Dr. Scholl's foot powder as a precaution against trench *foot*. Until he was shot, Ted Lavender carried 6 or 7 ounces of premium dope, which for him was a necessity. Mitchell Sanders, the RTO, carried condoms. Norman Bowker carried a diary. Rat Kiley carried comic books. Kiowa, a devout Baptist, carried an illustrated New Testament that had been presented to him by his father, who taught Sunday school in Oklahoma City, Oklahoma. As a hedge against bad times, however, Kiowa also carried his grandmother's distrust of the white man, his grandfather's old hunting hatchet. Necessity dictated. Because the land was mined and booby-trapped, it was SOP for each man to carry a steel-centered, nylon- covered flak jacket, which weighed 6.7 pounds, but which on hot days seemed much heavier. Because you could die so quickly, each man carried at least one large compress bandage, usually in the helmet band for easy access. Because the nights were cold, and because the monsoons were wet, each carried a green plastic poncho that could be used as a raincoat or groundsheet or makeshift tent. With its quilted liner, the poncho weighed almost 2 pounds, but it was worth every ounce. In April, for instance, when Ted Lavender was shot, they used his poncho to wrap him up, then to carry him across the paddy, then to lift him into the chopper that took him away.

They were called legs or grunts. To carry something was to hump it, as when Lieutenant Jimmy Cross humped his love for Martha up the hills and through the swamps. In its intransitive form, to hump meant to walk, or to march, but it implied burdens far beyond the intransitive. Almost everyone humped photographs. In his wallet, Lieutenant Cross carried two photographs of Martha. The first was a Kodacolor snapshot signed Love, though he knew better. She stood against a brick wall. Her eyes were gray and neutral, her lips slightly open as she stared straight-on at the camera. At night, sometimes, Lieutenant Cross wondered who had taken the picture, because he knew she had boyfriends, because he loved her so much, and because he could see the shadow of the picture-taker spreading out against the brick wall. The second photograph had been clipped from the 1968 Mount Sebastian yearbook. It was an action shot—women's volleyball—and Martha was bent horizontal to the floor, reaching, the palms of her hands in sharp focus, the tongue taut, the expression frank and competitive. There was no

visible sweat. She wore white gym shorts. Her legs, he thought, were almost certainly the legs of a virgin, dry and without hair, the left knee cocked and carrying her entire weight, which was just over 100 pounds. Lieutenant Cross remembered touching that left knee. A dark theater, he remembered, and the movie was *Bonnie and Clyde*, and Martha wore a tweed skirt, and during the final scene, when he touched her knee, she turned and looked at him in a sad, sober way that made him pull his hand back, but he would always remember the feel of the tweed skirt and the knee beneath it and the sound of the gunfire that killed Bonnie and Clyde, how embarrassing it was, how slow and oppressive. He remembered kissing her good night at the dorm door. Right then, he thought, he should've done something brave. He should've carried her up the stairs to her room and tied her to the bed and touched that left knee all night long. He should've risked it. Whenever he looked at the photographs, he thought of new things he should've done.

What they carried was partly a function of rank, partly of field specialty. As a first lieutenant and platoon leader, Jimmy Cross carried a compass, maps, code books, binoculars, and a .45-caliber pistol that weighed 2.9 pounds fully loaded. He carried a strobe light and the responsibility for the lives of his men. As an RTO, Mitchell Sanders carried the PRC-25 radio, a killer, 26 pounds with its battery. As a medic, Rat Kiley carried a canvas satchel filled with morphine and plasma and malaria tablets and surgical tape and comic books and all the things a medic must carry, including M&M's for especially bad wounds, for a total weight of nearly 20 pounds. As a big man, therefore a machine gunner, Henry Dobbins carried the M-60, which weighed 23 pounds unloaded, but which was almost always loaded. In addition, Dobbins carried between 10 and 15 pounds of ammunition draped in belts across his chest and shoulders. As PFCs or Spec 4s, most of them were common grunts and carried the standard M-1 6 gas-operated assault rifle. The weapon weighed 7.5 pounds unloaded, 8.2 pounds with its full 20-round magazine. Depending on numerous factors, such as topography and psychology, the riflemen carried anywhere from 12 to 20 magazines, usually in cloth bandoliers, adding on another 8.4 pounds at minimum, 14 pounds at maximum. When it was available, they also carried M-1 6 maintenance gear—rods and steel brushes and swabs and tubes of LSA oil—all of which weighed about a pound. Among the grunts, some carried the M-79 grenade launcher, 5.9 pounds unloaded, a reasonably light weapon except for the ammunition, which was heavy. A single round weighed 10 ounces. The typical load was 25 rounds. But Ted Lavender, who was scared, carried 34 rounds when he was shot and killed outside Than Khe, and he went down under an exceptional burden, more than 20 pounds of ammunition, plus the flak jacket and helmet and rations and water and toilet paper and tranquilizers and all the rest, plus the unweighed fear. He was dead weight. There was no twitching or flopping. Kiowa, who saw **it** happen, said it was like watching a rock fall, or a big sandbag or something—just boom, then down—not like the movies where the dead guy rolls around and does fancy spins and goes ass over teakettle— not like that, Kiowa said, the poor bastard just flat-fuck fell. Boom. Down. Nothing else. It was a bright morning in mid-April. Lieutenant Cross felt the pain. He blamed himself. They stripped off Lavender's canteens and ammo, all the heavy things, and Rat Kiley said the obvious, the guy's dead, and Mitchell Sanders used his radio to report one U.S. KIA and to request a chopper. Then they wrapped Lavender in his poncho. They carried him out to a dry paddy, established security, and sat smoking the dead man's dope until the chopper came. Lieutenant Cross kept to himself. He pictured Martha's smooth young face, thinking he loved her more than anything, more than his men, and now Ted Lavender was dead because he loved her so much and could not stop thinking about her. When the dustoff arrived, they carried

Lavender aboard. Afterward they burned Than Khe. They marched until dusk, then dug their holes, and that night Kiowa kept explaining how you had to be there, how fast it was, how the poor guy just dropped like so much concrete. Boom-down, he said. Like cement.

In addition to the three standard weapons— the M-60, M-16, and M-79—they carried whatever presented itself, or whatever seemed appropriate as a means of killing or staying alive. They carried catch-as-catch-can. At various times, in various situations, they carried M-14s and CAR15s and Swedish Ks and grease guns and captured AK-47s and Chi-Coms and RPGs and Simonov carbines and black market Uzis and .38-caliber Smith & Wesson handguns and 66 mm LAWs and shotguns and silencers and blackjacks and bayonets and C-4 plastic explosives. Lee Strunk carried a slingshot; a weapon of last resort, he called it. Mitchell Sanders carried brass knuckles. Kiowa carried his grandfather's feathered hatchet. Every third or fourth man carried a Claymore antipersonnel mine—3 .5 pounds with its firing device. They all carried fragmentation grenades— 14 ounces each. They all carried at least one M- 18 colored smoke grenade—24 ounces. Some carried CS or tear gas grenades. Some carried white phosphorus grenades. They carried all they could bear, and then some, including a silent awe for the terrible power of the things they carried.

In the first week of April, before Lavender died, Lieutenant Jimmy Cross received a good-luck charm from Martha. It was a simple pebble, an ounce at most. Smooth to the touch, it was a milky white color with flecks of orange and violet, oval-shaped, like a miniature egg. In the accompanying letter, Martha wrote that she had found the pebble on the Jersey shoreline, precisely where the land touched water at high tide, where things came together but also separated. It was this separate-but-together quality, she wrote, that had inspired her to pick up the pebble and to carry it in her breast pocket for several days, where it seemed weightless, and then to send it through the mail, by air, as a token of her truest feelings for him. Lieutenant Cross found this romantic. But he wondered what her truest feelings were, exactly, and what she meant by separate- but-together. He wondered how the tides and waves had come into play on that afternoon along the Jersey shoreline when Martha saw the pebble and bent down to rescue it from geology. He imagined bare feet. Martha was a poet, with the poet's sensibilities, and her feet would be brown and bare, the toenails unpainted, the eyes chilly and somber like the ocean in March, and though it was painful, he wondered who had been with her that afternoon. He imagined a pair of shadows moving along the strip of sand where things came together but also separated. It was phantom jealousy, he knew, but he couldn't help himself. He loved her so much. On the march, through the hot days of early April, he carried the pebble in his mouth, turning it with his tongue, tasting sea salt and moisture. His mind wandered. He had difficulty keeping his attention on the war. On occasion he would yell at his men to spread out the column, to keep their eyes open, but then he would slip away into daydreams, just pretending, walking barefoot along the Jersey shore, with Martha, carrying nothing. He would feel himself rising. Sun and waves and gentle *winds*, all love and lightness.

What they carried varied by mission. When a mission took them to the mountains, they carried mosquito netting, machetes, canvas tarps, and extra bug juice. If a mission seemed especially hazardous, or if it involved a place they knew to be bad, they carried everything they could. In certain heavily mined AOs, where the land was dense with Toe Poppers and Bouncing Betties, they took turns humping a 28-pound mine detector. With its headphones and big sensing plate, the equipment was a stress on the lower back and shoulders, awkward to handle, often useless because of the shrapnel in the earth, but they carried it anyway, partly for safety, partly for the illusion of safety. On ambush, or other night missions, they carried peculiar little odds and ends. Kiowa always took

along his New Testament and a pair of moccasins for silence. Dave Jensen carried nightsight vitamins high in carotene. Lee Strunk carried his slingshot; ammo, he claimed, would never be a problem. Rat Kiley carried brandy and M&M's candy. Until he was shot, Ted Lavender carried the starlight scope, which weighed 6.3 pounds with its aluminum carrying case. Henry Dobbins carried his girlfriend's pantyhose wrapped around his neck as a comforter. They all carried ghosts. When dark came, they would move out single file across the meadows and paddies to their ambush coordinates, where they would quietly set up the Clay- mores and lie down and spend the night waiting.

Other missions were more complicated and required special equipment. In mid-April, it was their mission to search out and destroy the elaborate tunnel complexes in the Than Khe area south of Chu Lai. To blow the tunnels, they carried one-pound blocks of pentrite high explosives, four blocks to a man, 68 pounds in all. They carried wiring, detonators, and battery-powered clackers. Dave Jensen carried earplugs. Most often, before blowing the tunnels, they were ordered by higher command to search them, which was considered bad news, but by and large they just shrugged and carried out orders. Because he was a big man, Henry Dobbins was excused from tunnel duty. The others would draw numbers. Before Lavender died there were 17 men in the platoon, and whoever drew the number 17 would strip off his gear and crawl in headfirst with a flashlight and Lieutenant Cross's .45-caliber pistol. The rest of them would fan out as security. They would sit down or kneel, not facing the hole, listening to the ground beneath them, imagining cobwebs and ghosts, whatever was down there—the tunnel walls squeezing in—how the flashlight seemed impossibly heavy in the hand and how it was tunnel vision in the very strictest sense, compression in all ways, even time, and how you had to wiggle in—ass and elbows—a swallowed-up feeling— and how you found yourself worrying about odd things: Will your flashlight go dead? Do rats carry rabies? If you screamed, how far would the sound carry? Would your buddies hear it? Would they have the courage to drag you out? In some respects, though not many, the waiting was worse than the tunnel itself. Imagination was a killer.

On April 16, when Lee Strunk drew the number 17, he laughed and muttered something and went down quickly. The morning was hot and very still. Not good, Kiowa said. He looked at the tunnel opening, then out across a dry paddy toward the village of Than Khe. Nothing moved. No clouds or birds or people. As they waited, the men smoked and drank Kool-Aid, not talking much, feeling sympathy for Lee Strunk but also feeling the luck of the draw. You win some, you lose some, said Mitchell Sanders, and sometimes you settle for a rain check. It was a tired line and no one laughed. Henry Dobbins ate a tropical chocolate bar. Ted Lavender popped a tranquilizer and went off to pee.

After five minutes, Lieutenant Jimmy Cross moved to the tunnel, leaned down, and examined the darkness. Trouble, he thought—a cave-in maybe. And then suddenly, without willing it, he was thinking about Martha. The stresses and fractures, the quick collapse, the two of them buried alive under all that weight. Dense, crushing love. Kneeling, watching the hole, he tried to concentrate on Lee Strunk and the war, all the dangers, but his love was too much for him, he felt paralyzed, he wanted to sleep *inside* her lungs *and* breathe her blood and be smothered. He wanted her to be a virgin and not a virgin, all at once. He wanted to know her, intimate secrets: Why poetry? Why so sad? Why that grayness in her eyes? Why so alone? Not lonely, just alone— riding her bike across campus or sitting off by herself in the cafeteria—even dancing, she danced alone—and it was the aloneness that filled him with love, He remembered telling her that one evening. How she nodded and looked away. And how) later, when he kissed her, she received the kiss without returning it, her eyes

wide open, not afraid, not a virgin's eyes, just flat and uninvolved.

Lieutenant Cross gazed at the tunnel. But he was not there. He was buried with Martha under the white sand at the Jersey shore. They were pressed together, and the pebble in his mouth was her tongue. He was smiling. Vaguely, he was aware of how quiet the day was, the sullen paddies, yet he could not bring himself to worry about matters of security. He was beyond that. He was just a kid at war, in love. He was twenty-four years old. He couldn't help it. A few moments later Lee Strunk crawled out of the tunnel. He came up grinning, filthy but alive. Lieutenant Cross nodded and closed his eyes while the others clapped Strunk on the back and made jokes about rising from the dead. Worms, Rat Kiley said. Right out of the grave. Fuckin' zombie. The men laughed. They all felt great relief. Spook city, said Mitchell Sanders. Lee Strunk made a funny ghost sound, a kind of moaning, yet very happy, and right then, when Strunk made that high happy moaning sound, when he went *Ahhooooo*, right then Ted Lavender was shot in the head on his way back from peeing. He lay with his mouth open. The teeth were broken. There was a swollen black bruise under his left eye. The cheekbone was gone. Oh shit, Rat Kiley said, the guy's dead. The guy's dead, he kept saying, which seemed profound—the guy's dead. I mean really.

The things they carried were determined to some extent by superstition. Lieutenant Cross carried his good- luck pebble. Dave Jensen carried a rabbit's foot. Norman Bowker, otherwise a very gentle person, carried a thumb that had been presented to him as a gift by Mitchell Sanders. The thumb was dark brown, rubbery to the touch, and weighed 4 ounces at most. It had been cut from a VC corpse, a boy of fifteen or sixteen. They'd found him at the bottom of an irrigation ditch, badly burned, flies in his mouth and eyes. The boy wore black shorts and sandals. At the time of his death he had been carrying a pouch of rice, a rifle, and three magazines of ammunition. You want my opinion, Mitchell Sanders said, there's a definite moral here. He put his hand on the dead boy's wrist. He was quiet for a time, as if counting a pulse, then he patted the stomach, almost affectionately, and used Kiowa's hunting hatchet to remove the thumb. Henry Dobbins asked what the moral was. Moral? You know. *Moral.* Sanders wrapped the thumb in toilet paper and handed it across to Norman Bowker. There was no blood. Smiling, he kicked the boy's head, watched the flies scatter, and said, It's like with that old TV show— Paladin. Have gun, will travel. Henry Dobbins thought about it. Yeah, well, he finally said. I don't see no moral. There it *is*, man. Fuck off.

They carried USO stationery and pencils and pens. They carried Sterno, safety pins, trip flares, signal flares, spools of wire, razor blades, chewing tobacco, liberated joss sticks and statuettes of the smiling Buddha, candles, grease pencils, *The Stars and Stripes*, fingernail clippers, Psy Ops leaflets, bush hats, bolos, and much more. Twice a week, when the resupply choppers came in, they carried hot chow in green mermite cans and large canvas bags filled with iced beer and soda pop. They carried plastic water containers, each with a 2-gallon capacity. Mitchell Sanders carried a set of starched tiger fatigues for special occasions. Henry Dobbins carried Black Flag insecticide. Dave Jensen carried empty sandbags that could be filled at night for added protection. Lee Strunk carried tanning lotion. Some things they carried in common. Taking turns, they carried the big PRC-77 scrambler radio, which weighed 30 pounds with its battery. They shared the weight of memory. They took up what others could no longer bear. Often, they carried each other, the wounded or weak. They carried infections. They carried chess sets, basketballs, Vietnamese- English dictionaries, insignia of rank, Bronze Stars and Purple Hearts, plastic cards imprinted with the Code of Conduct. They carried diseases, among them malaria and dysentery. They carried lice and ringworm and leeches and paddy algae and

various rots and molds. They carried the land itself—Vietnam' the place, the soil—a powdery orange-red dust that covered their boots and fatigues and faces. They carried the sky. The whole atmosphere, they carried it, the humidity, the monsoons, the stink of fungus and decay, all of it, they carried gravity. They moved like mules. By daylight they took sniper fire, at night they were mortared, but it was not battle, it was just the endless march, village to village, without purpose, nothing won or lost. They marched for the sake of the march. They plodded along slowly, dumbly, leaning forward against the heat, unthinking, all blood and bone, simple grunts, soldiering with their legs, toiling up the hills and down into the paddies and across the rivers and up again and down, just humping, one step and then the next and then another, but no volition, no will, because it was automatic, it was anatomy, and the war was entirely a matter of posture and carriage, the hump was everything, a kind of inertia, a kind of emptiness, a dullness of desire and intellect and conscience and hope and human sensibility. Their principles were in their feet. Their calculations were biological. They had no sense of strategy or mission. They searched the villages without knowing what to look for, not caring, kicking over jars of rice, frisking children and old men, blowing tunnels, sometimes setting fires and sometimes not, then forming up and moving on to the next village, then other villages, where it would always be the same. They carried their own lives. The pressures were enormous. In the heat of early afternoon, they would remove their helmets and flak jackets, walking bare, which was dangerous but which helped ease the strain. They would often discard things along the route of march. Purely for comfort, they would throw away rations, blow their Claymores and grenades, no matter, because by nightfall the resupply choppers would arrive with more of the same, then a day or two later still more, fresh watermelons and crates of ammunition and sunglasses and woolen sweaters—the resources were stunning-.——

sparklers for the Fourth of July, colored eggs for Easter—it was the great American war chest—the fruits of science, the smokestacks, the canneries, the arsenals at Hartford, the Minnesota forests, the machine shops, the vast fields of corn and wheat—they carried like freight trains; they carried it on their backs and shoulders—and for all the ambiguities of Vietnam, all the mysteries and unknowns, there was at least the single abiding certainty that they would never be at a loss for things to carry.

After the chopper took Lavender away, Lieutenant Jimmy Cross led his men into the village of Than Khe. They burned everything. They shot chickens and dogs, they trashed the village well, they called in artillery and watched the wreckage, then they marched for several hours through the hot afternoon, and then at dusk, while Kiowa explained how Lavender died, Lieutenant Cross found himself trembling. He tried not to cry. With his entrenching tool, which weighed 5 pounds, he began digging a hole in the earth. He felt shame. He hated himself. He had loved Martha more than his men, and as a consequence Lavender was now dead, and this was something he would have to carry like a stone in his stomach for the rest of the war. All he could do was dig. He used his entrenching tool like an ax, slashing, feeling both love and hate, and then later, when it was full dark, he sat at the bottom of his foxhole and wept. It went on for a long while. In part, he was grieving for Ted Lavender, but mostly it was for Martha, and for himself, because she belonged to another world, which was not quite real, and because she was a junior at Mount Sebastian College in New Jersey, a poet and a virgin and uninvolved, and because he realized she did not love him and never would.

Like cement, Kiowa whispered in the dark. I swear to God—boom, down. Not a word. I've heard this, said Norman Bowker. A pisser, you know? Still Zipping himself up. Zapped while Zipping. All right, fine. That's enough. Yeah, but you had to see it, the guy just— *I heard*, man. Cement. So why not shut the fuck *up?* Kiowa

shook his head sadly and glanced over at the hole where Lieutenant Jimmy Cross sat watching the night. The air was thick and wet. A warm dense fog had settled over the paddies and there was the stillness that precedes rain. After a time Kiowa sighed. One thing for sure, he said. The lieutenant's in some deep hurt. I mean that crying jag—the way he was carrying On—it wasn't fake or anything, it was real heavy-duty hurt. The man cares. Sure, Norman Bowker said. Say what you want, the man does care. We all got problems. Not Lavender. No, I guess not, Bowker said. Do me a *favor*, though. Shut up? That's a smart Indian. Shut up.

Shrugging, Kiowa pulled off his boots, He wanted to say more, just to lighten up his sleep, but instead he opened his New Testament and arranged it beneath his head as a pillow. The fog made things seem hollow and unattached. He tried not to think about Ted Lavender, but then he was thinking how fast it was, no drama, down and dead, and how it was hard to feel anything except surprise. It seemed unchristian. He wished he could find some great sadness, or even anger, but the emotion wasn't there and he couldn't make it happen. Mostly he felt pleased to be alive. He liked the smell of the New Testament under his cheek, the leather and ink and paper and glue, whatever the chemicals were. He liked hearing the sounds of night. Even his fatigue, it felt fine, the stiff muscles and the prickly awareness of his own body, a floating feeling. He enjoyed not being dead. Lying there, Kiowa admired Lieutenant Jimmy Cross's capacity for grief. He wanted to share the man's pain, he wanted to care as Jimmy Cross cared. And yet when he closed his eyes, all he could think was Boom-down, and all he could feel was the pleasure of having his boots off and the fog curling in around him and the damp soil and the Bible smells and the plush comfort of night. After a moment Norman Bowker sat up in the dark. What the hell, he said. You want to talk, *talk*. Tell it Forget it. No, man, go on. One thing I hate, it's a silent Indian.

For the most part they carried themselves with poise, a kind of dignity. Now and then, however, there were times of panic, when they squealed or wanted to squeal but couldn't, when they twitched and made moaning sounds and covered their heads and said Dear Jesus and flopped around on the earth and fired their weapons blindly and cringed and sobbed and begged for the noise to stop and went wild and made stupid promises to themselves and to God and to their mothers and fathers, hoping not to die. In different ways, it happened to all of them. Afterward, when the firing ended, they would blink and peek up. They would touch their bodies, feeling shame, then quickly hiding it. They would force themselves to stand. As if in slow motion, frame by frame, the world would take on the old logic—absolute silence, then the wind, then sunlight, then voices. It was the burden of being alive. Awkwardly, the men would reassemble themselves, first in private, then in groups, becoming soldiers again. They would repair the leaks in their eyes. They would check for casualties, call in dustoffs, light cigarettes, try to smile) clear their throats and spit and begin cleaning their weapons. After a time someone would shake his head and say, No lie, I almost shit my pants, and someone else would laugh, which meant it was bad, yes, but the guy had obviously not shit his pants, it wasn't that bad, and in any case nobody would ever do such a thing and then go ahead and talk about it. They would squint into the dense, oppressive sunlight. For a few moments, perhaps, they would fall silent, lighting a joint and tracking its passage from man to man, inhaling, holding in the humiliation. Scary stuff, one of them might say. But then someone else would grin or flick his eyebrows and say, Roger-dodger, almost cut me a new asshole, *almost*.

There were numerous such poses. Some carried themselves with a sort of wistful resignation, others with pride or stiff soldierly discipline or good humor or macho zeal. They were afraid of dying but they were even more afraid to show it.

They found jokes to tell. They used a hard vocabulary to contain the terrible softness. *Greased* they'd say. *Offed, lit up, zapped while zipping.* It wasn't cruelty, just stage presence. They were actors. When someone died, it wasn't quite dying, because in a curious way it seemed scripted, and because they had their lines mostly memorized, irony mixed with tragedy, and because they called it by other names, as if to encyst and destroy the reality of death itself. They kicked corpses. They cut off thumbs. They talked grunt lingo. They told stories about Ted Lavender's supply of tranquilizers, how the poor guy didn't feel a thing how incredibly tranquil he was. There's a moral here, said Mitchell Sanders. They were waiting for Lavender's chopper, smoking the dead man's dope. The moral's pretty obvious, Sanders said, and winked. Stay away from drugs. No joke, they'll ruin your day every time. Cute, said Henry Dobbins. Mind blower, get it? Talk about wiggy. Nothing left, just blood and brains.

They made themselves laugh. There it is, they'd say. Over and over—there it is, my friend, there it is—as if the repetition itself were an act of poise, a balance between crazy and almost crazy, knowing without going, there it is, which meant be cool, let it ride, because Oh yeah, man, you can't change what can't be changed, there it is, there it absolutely and positively and fucking well *is*.

They were tough. They carried all the emotional baggage of men who might die. Grief, terror, love, longing—these were intangibles, but the intangibles had their own mass and specific gravity, they had tangible weight. They carried shameful memories. They carried the common secret of cowardice barely restrained, the instinct to run or freeze or hide, and in many respects this was the heaviest burden of all, for it could never be put down, it required perfect balance and perfect posture. They carried their reputations. They carried the soldier's greatest fear, which was the fear of blushing. Men killed, and died, because they were embarrassed not to. It was what had brought them to the war in the first place, nothing positive, no dreams of glory or honor, just to avoid the blush of dishonor. They died so as not to die of embarrassment. They crawled into tunnels and walked point and advanced under fire. Each morning, despite the unknowns, they made their legs move. They endured. They kept humping. They did not submit to the obvious alternative, which was simply to close the eyes and fall. So easy, really. Go limp and tumble to the ground and let the muscles unwind and not speak and not budge until your buddies picked you up and lifted you into the chopper that would roar and dip its nose and carry you off to the world. A mere matter of falling, yet no one ever fell. It was not courage, exactly; the object was not valor. Rather, they were too frightened to be cowards.

By and large they carried these things inside, maintaining the masks of composure. They sneered at sick call. They spoke bitterly about guys who had found release by shooting off their own toes or fingers. Pussies, they'd say. Candy-asses. It was fierce, mocking talk, with only a trace of envy or awe, but even so the image played itself out behind their eyes. They imagined the muzzle against flesh. So easy: squeeze the trigger and blow away a toe. They imagined it. They imagined the quick, sweet pain, then the evacuation to Japan, then a hospital with warm beds and cute geisha nurses. And they dreamed of freedom birds. At night, on guard, staring into the dark, they were carried away by jumbo jets. They felt the rush of takeoff. *Gone!* they yelled. And then velocity—wings and engines—a smiling stewardess—but it was more than a plane, it was a real bird, a big sleek silver bird with feathers and talons and high screeching. They were flying. The weights fell off; there was nothing to bear. They laughed and held on tight, feeling the cold slap of wind and altitude, soaring, thinking *It's over, I'm gone!*—they were naked, they were light and free—it was all lightness, bright and fast and buoyant, light as light, a helium buzz in the brain, a giddy bubbling in the lungs as they

were taken up over the clouds and the war, beyond duty, beyond gravity and mortification and global entanglements—*Sin loi* they yelled. *I'm sorry, motherfuckers, but I'm out of it, I'm goofed, i'm on a space cruise, I'm gone!*—and it was a restful, unencumbered sensation, just riding the light waves, sailing that big silver freedom bird over the mountains and oceans, over America, over the farms and great sleeping cities and cemeteries and highways and the golden arches of McDonald's, it was flight a kind of fleeing, a kind of falling, falling higher and higher, spinning off the edge of the earth and beyond the sun and through the vast, silent vacuum where there were no burdens and where everything weighed exactly nothing—*Gone!* they screamed. *I'm sorry but I'm gone!*—and so at night, not quite dreaming, they gave themselves over to lightness, they were carried, they were purely borne.

On the morning after Ted Lavender died, First Lieutenant Jimmy Cross crouched at the bottom of his foxhole and burned Martha's letters, Then he burned the two photographs. There was a steady rain falling, which made it difficult, but he used heat tabs and Sterno to build a small fire, screening it with his body, holding the photographs over the tight blue flame with the tips of his fingers. He realized it was only a gesture. Stupid, he thought. Sentimental, too, but mostly just stupid. Lavender was dead. You couldn't burn the blame. Besides, the letters were in his head. And even now, without photographs, Lieutenant Cross could see Martha playing volleyball in her white gym shorts and yellow T-shirt. He could see her moving in the rain, When the fire died out, Lieutenant Cross pulled his poncho over his shoulders and ate breakfast from a can. There was no great mystery, he decided.

In those burned letters Martha had never mentioned the war, except to say, Jimmy, take care of yourself. She wasn't involved. She signed the letters Love, but it wasn't love, and all the fine lines and technicalities did not matter. Virginity was no longer an issue. He hated her. Yes, he did. He hated her. Love, too, but it was a hard, hating kind of love. The morning came up wet and blurry. Everything seemed part of everything else, the fog and Martha and the deepening rain. He was a soldier, after all. Half smiling, Lieutenant Jimmy Cross took out his maps. He shook his head hard, as if to clear it, then bent forward and began planning the day's march. In ten minutes, or maybe twenty, he would rouse the men and they would pack up and head west, where the maps showed the country to be green and inviting. They would do what they had always done. The rain might add some weight, but otherwise it would be one more day layered upon all the other days. He was realistic about it. There was that new hardness in his stomach. He loved her but he hated her. No more fantasies, he told himself.

Henceforth, when he thought about Martha, it would be only to think that she belonged elsewhere. He would shut down the daydreams. This was not Mount Sebastian, it was another world, where there were no pretty poems or midterm exams, a place where men died because of carelessness and gross stupidity. Kiowa was right. Boom-down, and you were dead, never partly dead. Briefly, in the rain, Lieutenant Cross saw Martha's gray eyes gazing back at him. He understood. It was very sad, he thought. The things men carried inside. The things men did or felt they had to do. He almost nodded at her, but didn't.

Instead he went back to his maps. He was now determined to perform his duties firmly and without negligence. It wouldn't help Lavender, he knew that, but from this point on he would comport himself as an officer. He would dispose of his good-luck pebble. Swallow it, maybe, or use Lee Strunk's slingshot, or just drop it along the trail. On the march he would impose strict field discipline. He would be careful to send out flank security, to prevent straggling or bunching up, to keep his troops moving at the proper pace and at the proper interval. He would insist on clean weapons. He would confiscate the remainder of Lavender's dope. Later in the day, perhaps, he would call the men together and speak to them plainly. He would accept the blame for what had happened to Ted Lavender. He would be a man about it. He would look them in the eyes, keeping his chin level, and he would issue the new SOPs in a calm, impersonal tone of voice, a lieutenant's voice, leaving no room for argument or discussion. Commencing immediately, he'd tell them, they would no longer abandon equipment along the route of march. They would police up their acts. They would get their shit together, and keep it together, and maintain it neatly and in good working order.

He would not tolerate laxity. He would show strength, distancing himself. Among the men there would be grumbling, of course, and maybe worse, because their days would seem longer and their loads heavier, but Lieutenant Jimmy Cross reminded himself that his obligation was not to be loved but to lead. He would dispense with love; it was not now a factor. And if anyone quarreled or complained, he would simply tighten his lips and arrange his shoulders in the correct command posture. He might give a curt little nod. Or he might not. He might just shrug and say, Carry on, then they would saddle up and form into a column and move out toward the villages west of Than Khe.

Suggested Reading

Bonn, Maria S., "Can Stories Save Us? Tim O'Brien and the Efficacy of the Text," *Critique: Studies in Contemporary Fiction*, Vol. 36, No. 1, Fall, 1994, pp. 2–14.

Caputo, Philip. *A Rumor of War*. New York: Holt, 1996.

Coffey, Michael, "*An Interview with Tim O'Brien.*" *Publishers Weekly*, 16 February 1990.

Harris, Robert R., "Too Embarrassed Not to Kill: A Review of *The Things They Carried*," *New York Times Book Review*, March 11, 1990, p. 8.

Karnow, Stanley. *Vietnam: A History*. New York: Viking Press, 1983.

Moore, Hal. *We Were Soldiers Once . . . and Young*. New York: Random House, 1992.

O'Brien, Tim. *Going After Cacciato*. New York: Broadway, 1999.

O'Brien, Tim. *If I Die in a Combat Zone*. New York: Broadway, 1999.

O'Brien, Tim. *The Things they Carried*. New York: Broadway Books, 1998.

47

Leadership is About Building Relationships: Jeffrey Marx's Season of Life

Donald H. Horner, Jr., USNA Class of 1961 Distinguished Professor of Leadership Education

If you could speak to every boy in the world . . . how would you explain your own definition of what it means to be a man? 'It's about relationships and a cause,' Joe said. 'Simple as that. What's a man created to do? He's created to be a son, a father, a husband, a brother, and so on. And all a man does is, he lives in those relationships . . . If I blow it there . . . nothing else really matters.'

Background and Introduction

I was introduced to *Season of Life* in the Spring of 2005 when a friend of mine, Josh Martinelli, gave me a copy of the book as a belated and unexpected Christmas present. A "man's man" and former Marine who commanded an artillery battery in Vietnam, Josh presented the book to me in my Luce Hall office at the Naval Academy during one of his "I'm just here to check on you" visits. He said simply: "Let me know what you think of it." A true gentleman equally dedicated to his God and to serving Midshipmen through various volunteer activities—he's the public address announcer for the Navy ice hockey team and is involved in a host of spiritual outreach programs for Mids of all denominations—Josh offered only that, "You might be able to use the book in some of your classes."

Talk about the understatement of the year.

I found the book so compelling, revealing, and inspirational that to-date I've made the text mandatory reading in an Advanced Leadership Course, a course on Race, Gender, and Ethnicity, and a graduate course called "Models of Leadership in Complex Organizations." Students typically give the book rave reviews, and even the most critical opine that the book was worth the read.

My initial reaction to *Season of Life* was not as favorable. As I read the acknowledgments, book jacket, and first few chapters, I found myself saying: "Oh, no. Here we go again. Another thinly veiled, bible-thumping attempt to proselytize the unconverted and make us all God-loving wimpy men." Even the book's subtitle—"*A Football Star, a Boy, a Journey to Manhood*"—turned me off as being oxymoronic and melodramatic. I could hear violins playing in the background, as religiously motivated psychobabble somehow made its way onto what remains for me the most sacred of athletic venues: the American football field—the ultimate field of friendly strife.

Despite these sentiments, I ploughed ahead, determined to read the book if for no other reason than to be able to answer my friend's rhetorical question: "What'd ya think?" And, the more I read, the more uncomfortable I became. The educator in me responded to the discomfort in an analytical way. I thought: "Hmm. We know that *real* learning occurs when we're moved *out* of our comfort zone, when we are *forced* to confront information and data that are not necessarily *compatible* with our life experiences in or out of the classroom. Hmm. Maybe I'm onto something here. Hmm, well, yup. *Real* learning occurs when we're faced with *dissonant* information that has to processed and somehow integrated into our frames of reference, so that these frames—these paradigms we use to live life—are *altered*." I thus convinced myself that reading *Season of Life* was, despite the pain, probably good for me. And, sports-nut that I am, it didn't hurt that the book's backdrop was a high school football team making its way through a challenging season. I decided to play through the pain in the hope that the book would provide some intellectual gain, however marginal.

My initial pain and uneasiness were mitigated by the realities and simple truths upon which the book is based. The book appealed to me on two primary levels: as a man and as a teacher. I quickly came to realize that *Season of Life* was uniquely inspirational and applicable not only to my life but also to a host of academic genres—particularly leadership. After about thirty pages I was convinced that the value of *Season of Life* lies in its recognition that leadership—the process of an organizational leader motivating followers to

pursue and achieve organizational goals in a manner consistent with core values—is all about building positive, meaningful relationships. Somehow, here was a book that was able to distill the thousands of studies[2] on leadership into one simple, poignant truth: Leadership is about building relationships.

Excerpts from *Season of Life*

A bit of table setting is necessary before presenting an excerpt from the book. The author, Jeffrey Marx, never intended to write *Season of Life*. By that I mean that Marx, Pulitzer Prize winning author that he is, didn't plan or envision a book of this sort. He didn't choose a topic, research it, investigate it, and then write about it. Imitating life itself, the book just sort of happened.

In January 2001, Marx left his office in Washington, D.C. seeking to renew a friendship with a childhood hero, former Baltimore Colt defensive lineman Joe Ehrmann. Marx was a ball boy for the Colts, a Baltimore franchise in the National Football League (NFL), from 1974 to 1983. Ehrmann had been an All-American at Syracuse University, and was a Co-Captain and an NFL All-Pro with the Colts during that same period. *Season of Life* chronicles the renewal of the Marx -Ehrmann relationship, and a season spent with the Gilman Prep Greyhounds, a high school football team in Baltimore that Ehrmann helped coach. The story told and the lessons learned, however, are not about football Xs and Os. The book is about what it means to live life the right way. It's about building relationships, making maximum use of one's talents and abilities, and engaging in leadership by serving others. Marx narrates throughout. Below are two excerpts that provide a glimpse into the essence of this wonderful book.

Leadership as a Sense of Community

The 2001 Gilman football team came together for its first practice at eight in the morning on a warm and overcast Monday. It was August 13. After driving from Capitol Hill to the leafy Roland Park neighborhood of Baltimore—a forty-eight mile trip I would repeat many times during the next three months—I was greeted by the familiar sound of cleats on concrete. It was the same sound that used to fill that tunnel at Memorial Stadium, only now it was the click-clacking of boys pounding a paved path en route to a secluded practice field tucked away in the woods behind their school. For the boys, the short walk through the woods opened up to a rectangular plot of land—striped with fresh white sidelines and yard markings—on which they would transform themselves from classmates into teammates, from friends into family. For me, the walk yielded an introduction to an unmistakably unique high school sports program—and to a season that captured both my mind and my heart in ways that I never could have anticipated.

When I arrived, Joe was standing near the corner of the field, welcoming everyone back from summer vacation, sharing hugs and handshakes as if he were running for mayor.

"Hey, Coach Ehrmann."

"Great to see you, Coach Ehrmann."

It was strange to hear the boys addressing him that way. I was still working on the transition from thinking of Joe as an "ex-Colt" to viewing him as a minister, "the Reverend Joe." Now he was "Coach Ehrmann" as well. Joe was the defensive coordinator. He was encircled by a few of the boys, introducing me around, when the shrill sound of a whistle violated the serenity of the morning.

"Bring it up, boys." The booming voice prompted immediate scurrying toward the center of the nearby end zone. "Let's go. Everyone up."

The shouted instruction emanated from an oversized teddy bear of a man, a big, thick guy with a buzz cut of brown hair, wearing baggy, nylon mesh shorts and a Gilman T-shirt with the sleeves cut away to free his massive upper arms. He was the head coach, Francis "Biff" Poggi, a former Gilman football player (class of 1979) and now a wealthy business owner who devoted much of his time to philanthropy. Financial management was his business—his local investment company, Samuel James Limited, had been quite successful in a wide range of public and private equity deals—but working with children was his passion. Biff was Joe's best friend and the man with whom he had started Building Men for Others. Their roles varied depending on the setting and context in which they were implementing their program for boys and men, but at Gilman they generally stuck with a single formula. Joe was the ecclesiastic authority who often stood in the shadows but always provided wisdom and guidance. Biff was the program's public face and its animated voice. And now it was time for his opening remarks to the team.

In a sense, the same scene was unfolding that very day, or perhaps it would happen in the next week or so, on high school fields throughout the nation. Tough guys of all shapes and sizes were strapping on helmets with the boundless excitement of youth and the anticipation that comes with the clean slate of a new year. On another level, though, what happened that first day at Gilman was entirely unlike anything normally associated with high school football. It started with the signature exchange of the Gilman football program—this time between Biff and the gathered throng of eighty boys, freshmen through seniors, who would spend the next week practicing together before being split into varsity and junior varsity teams.

"What is our job?" Biff asked on behalf of himself, Joe, and the eight other assistant coaches.

"To love us," most of the boys yelled back. The older boys had already been through this routine more than enough times to know the proper answer. The younger boys, new to Gilman football, would soon catch on.

"And what is *your* job?" Biff shot back.

"To love each other," the boys responded.

I would quickly come to realize that this standard exchange—always initiated by Biff or Joe—

was just as much a part of Gilman football as running or tackling.

"I don't care if you're big or small, huge muscles or no muscles, never even played football or star of the team—I don't care about any of that stuff," Biff went on to tell the boys, who sat in the grass while he spoke. "If you're here, then you're one of us, and we love you. Simple as that."

Biff paused.

"Look at me, boys," he started again. Most of them were already staring up in at least the general direction of his six-foot-three, 300-pound frame. Thanks to the combination of his physical stature and his never-ending passion for both football and the overall well-being of his players—"my boys," he always called them—Biff never had much of a problem holding their attention. But he often used that "look at me" phrase with a rhetorical device to signal when something really important was coming.

"Look at me, boys," Biff said. "We're gonna go through this whole thing as a team. We are the Gilman football community. A *community*. This is the only place probably in your whole life where you're gonna be together and work together with a group as diverse as this—racially, socially, economically, you name it. It's a beautiful thing to be together like this. You'll never find anything else like it in the world—simply won't happen. So enjoy it. Make the most of this. It's yours."

Biff asked the boys to take a few moments and look around at one another. With heads swiveling, what they saw was indeed a melting pot of black and white, rich and poor, city and suburb. Though an elite private school for boys only, Gilman had long prided itself on diversity, and thanks to the effect of recruiting and a powerful equalizer known as financial aid, the football team offered an even better cross section of society than the overall student population.

Heads were still turning when Biff broke the silence with slowly spoken words strung together into chunks for emphasis: "The relation-

ships that you make here . . . you will always have them . . . for the rest of your life . . . the rest of your life."

Biff was speaking just above a whisper now. There was something magical about the spell of such a big, powerful man turning down the volume like that. His players were totally locked in.

"Cherish this, boys," Biff said. "Cherish this."

So what if The Associated Press had recently anointed Gilman as the top-ranked team in Maryland and USA *Today* had picked the Greyhounds for the pre-season Top Ten of the entire East? Gilman football did not exist for anyone on the outside looking in. It was not about public accolades. It was about living in community. It was about fostering relationships. It was about learning the importance of serving others. Oh, sure, Biff allowed that he was definitely in favor of beating archrival McDonogh—the same McDonogh at which I had spent that fateful summer of 1974 with the Colts. In fact, winning that one game and successfully defending the league championship (Conference A of the Maryland Interscholastic Athletic Association) were the only performance-related goals he announced to the boys. But such accomplishments would only be by-products of a much broader agenda. The only thing that really mattered to Biff and Joe was offering a solid foundation on which the boys could later construct lives of meaning and value.

I watched a variety of football drills and conditioning exercises during that first day on the field in the woods. I also listened in on offensive and defensive strategy sessions in the team meeting room on the second floor of the school's field house. At one point, I even heard the Reverend Joe Ehrmann temporarily abandon the soft language of his day job when he introduced the three P's expected of anyone who wanted to play defense for him. Penetrate. Pursue. Punish. "All eleven men flying to the ball," Joe said. "All eleven men. Every single play."

Still, no matter how much football I saw and heard during those initial hours of the season, I drove away thinking only about the philosophi-

cal overview Biff had shared with the boys during those first few minutes of the morning. If a
Martian had just happened to land on Earth and
somehow found himself witnessing only that in-
troductory talk, a perfectly logical communiqué
home might have included a summary such as
this: "Learned about some sort of group gathering called football. It teaches boys to love."[3]

Leadership as Building Relationships

I went to see Joe in his office . . . the last Friday in September. It was a cool, crisp morning.
Our topic was relationships . . .

"What breeds terrorism?" he said. "It's rela-
tionally driven. It's hatred. It's prejudice. It's religious intolerance. It's racism. We live in a world
that *breeds* this stuff. And I think each of us has
got to get back to some sense of the world we
live in, in *my* sphere of influence, how am I alle-
viating some of it? What am I doing to make a
difference? Because we have the same kind of
hatred throughout our own society, and all it
does is spell death, man, whether it's death of
dreams, death of hopes, or physical death."

Ultimately, Joe said, the building of relationships is really no different for an average guy
striving to be a good man than it is for a world
leader struggling with the causes and effects of
terrorism. In both cases, strategic goals and consistent effort are required, and relationships
work best when lubricated with affirmation and
empathy. No matter what direction our conversation about relationships took, Joe somehow
brought it back to the importance of empathy.

"Paula [Joe's wife] and I spend a lot of time
teaching our kids empathy," Joe told me.

"How do you do that?" I asked.

"Oh, I think it's about constantly asking questions," Joe said. "You know, somebody called so-
and-so fat. 'How d you think that made that
person feel? How's it feel when somebody calls
you something you don't like? How's it feel when
people aren't nice to *you*? How's it *feel*? Well,
would you ever want to be responsible for doing
that to somebody?"

Joe called empathy "the single greatest trait of
humanity that separates us from other animals."

I already had a solid understanding of what
Joe called "false" masculinity—the societal-
based, age-related progression from athletic
ability to sexual conquest to economic success.
Now asked him to explain his notion of "strategic" masculinity—how he had come up with the
term and what it meant to him. Joe started by
talking about the influence a father has on a son.

"I think there are three kinds of dads in this
world," Joe said. "There are dads that are totally
absent . . . no presence whatsoever. They're just
gone. And the percentage of them in this country is staggering. The second kind is a da that has
presence, he's in the kid's life, he's in the home or
he shows up at the school, but he doesn't deal
with the more profound issues. They're the dads
that invest the time and money, and they care,
but when they die it's kind of, 'Wow, I never really knew who my dad was.' And then the third
kind is a strategic dad. He has a clear and compelling definition of masculinity and a code of
conduct for being a man. He understands the
importance of whatever transcendent cause he
has in his life. It's strategic fatherhood . . . a clear
definition and understanding of what it means to
be a man and how a man lives."

"So it's strategic in the sense that it's something the father—or any man—has to actually
think through," I said. "This is not something
that happens on its own."

"Right," Joe said. "It's intentional."

"Also pretty unusual, though, right?"

"Very unusual," Joe said. "As a dad, if you
want to send a boy into the world with the same
sense of masculinity based on the importance of
relationships, being a man built for others rather
than a man living only for himself, then you really need to be there for him as a model and a
teacher. But most men have no concept about
any of this. They've never really thought it
through."

"Which is sad," I said.

"Well, what we end up with is a cycle that
keeps going," Joe said. "The father has no clue

what it means to be a man, no strategic definition whatsoever. The son gets whatever the dad gives him. And so the whole thing keeps getting repeated. Without a definition, most of us don't even know whether we're good men or not. But most of us feel that whatever the criteria are, we're just below whatever that definition is."

I asked a hypothetical question: "If you could speak to every boy in the world—let's pretend you could wipe out anything they've already seen or heard from their fathers or anybody else—how would you explain your own definition of what it means to be a man?

"It's about relationships and a cause,' Joe said. 'Simple as that. What's a man created to do? He's created to be a son, a father, a husband, a brother, and so on. And all a man does is, he lives in those relationships. So I'm going to measure my masculinity—and it's really about my humanity—based on how successful I am as a husband. If I blow it there, or I blow it as a dad, nothing else really matters. All the power and prestige and possessions in the world never make up for failed relationships."[4]

Leadership Takeaways

From these excerpts one derives some sense of the true value of the book. Jeffrey Marx combines a compelling story with great lessons about life, including uncommon reflections on masculinity, teamwork, community, and relationships. If read with an eye towards leadership or leader development, abundant takeaways are readily apparent.

Rather than sharing my personal reflections about the leadership takeaways—leadership "teaching points" or "lessons," if you will—it is perhaps of more value to share my students' reflections about the book. As mentioned earlier, I've used *Season of Life* in several courses at the Naval Academy, including an advanced undergraduate leadership course. Here, in the students' own words, are three examples of leadership lessons found in *Season of Life*.

Lesson 1: Leadership and Masculinity Demystified

MIDN 2/C Mikaela Rodkin, USNA '07

The demystification of the traditional measures of masculinity is a significant leadership lesson. Joe Ehrmann, the powerhouse behind the new movement of male leadership development, abandons judging any sort of masculine worth based on money, physical prowess, or sexual dominance. Instead, through experience and observation, he accurately places relationships with loved ones, relationships with others, a good heart ready to aid those in need, and to be selfless in the face of any adversary as the new totem-pole of leadership masculinity. Leadership development occurs by placing others before yourself, working for the team as a unit rather than for individual glory. Peer leadership within the team is constantly being encouraged and monitored by the coaches. Decisions are made with the senior members of the team, and the captains of the teams lead the players as much as the coaches. Qualities normally associated with letting down your guard or appearing weak, in Ehrmann's style, is actually what makes a man powerful in his own security within himself and those around him.

Lesson 2: Leadership and the Art of Problem Solving

MIDN 2/C Joseph Fitzgerald, USNA '07

Season of Life points out another crucial element of good leadership: the art of problem solving. A number of times in the story, a player will go to one of the coaches with a personal problem they are experiencing at the time. As Colin Powell explains, the day your people stop coming to you with their problems is the day you've stopped leading them. This situation is never the case for Biff or Joe, coaches of the Gilman football team. They fully devote themselves to working out the problems with their people and giving them the special attention they need. Doing this is what good leadership is all about. Leadership relies not only on the leader knowing and understanding the led, but also caring about them. Acting on behalf of others out of a genuine sense of love and concern for their well-being is an indispensable component of good leadership.

Lesson 3: Leadership by Affirmation

MIDN 2/C Matthew Bridge, USNA '07

Biff and Joe's high school football team is built upon love. They let the players know that they love them and that they will need to love each other. They lead by affirmation rather than shame. They are positive towards their team and do not shame anyone on the team. This makes the boys feel good about themselves, which in turn enhances team performance. They stress that trying your hardest *is* more important than winning a victory. Both coaches believe that maximum use of available talent is the great equalizer—that the person who has two talents and brings both to the playing field of life is more valued than the person with ten talents and uses only five.

The love—the affirmation—that the players have towards one another is more important than anything else because it teaches them personal lessons that will eventually make them, their team, and the world, better. *Season of Life* demonstrates that leaders who ask "What can I do for you?" achieve better results in the end. By being centered on others and using affirmation as a leadership technique, a tighter bond is formed within the team. The resulting cohesion—cohesion through affirmation—is ultimately what produces high performing teams.

Concluding Thoughts

I'm delighted to report that I no longer find myself uncomfortable reading *Season of Life*. Of course, by now I've read the book at least five times. In retrospect and in all candor, my initial reaction is probably better described as *fear* rather than discomfort. I was *fearful* that the content and subject matter somehow didn't *fit* with my view of masculinity, football, life, and leadership.

You may recall, though, that I decided to continue with that initial reading "if for no other reason than to be able to answer my friend's rhetorical question: "What'd ya think?"" In essence, I read the book because of the relationship with my friend, Josh Martinelli. I didn't want to let him down, didn't wish to answer his "What'd ya think?" with a short "I never read it." Interesting, isn't it? I read the book that first time because of my *relationship* with Josh. He led me to read the book. And that's the inspiration for the book and for this paper: leadership—and life—is based on relationships.

I commend *Season of Life* to you at your earliest opportunity. After you've read it, give a copy to someone you love—or someone you don't. Start building better relationships. Lead!

Endnotes

[1] Jeffrey Marx, *Season of Life* (2003), New York: Simon & Schuster, p. 99.
[2] The word "thousands" is used here with precision. The field of leadership has been *over studied* to the point of fragmentation. In short, the field lacks synthesis and integration, and no overarching, all encompassing theory of leadership yet exists. As of 1989, over 10,000 articles and books had been published about leadership. See Horner (1996), "A Different Twist: Nonrational Views of Leadership," *Military Review* (December), p. 45–50.
[3] Marx, p. 41–45.
[4] Marx, p. 96–99.

About the Author

Dr. Donnie Horner is the USNA Class of 1961 Distinguished Professor of Leadership Education in the Department of Leadership, Ethics, and Law. Previously he was the Director of the Leadership Development Program at The Pennsylvania State University, University Park, PA. A West Point graduate, Horner also received an M.S. in Transportation Systems from MIT and an M.A. and Ph.D. in Sociology from Stanford University. As a career Army officer, Horner commanded units at the Platoon, Company, and Battalion levels. While a troop commander, Horner served in many overseas locations, including duty during conflict in Panama and Bosnia.

48

The Norm of Reciprocity: James Norman Hall's "Sing: A Song of Sixpence"

Dr. Donald W. Chisholm

There is no duty more indispensable than that of returning a kindness . . . all men distrust one forgetful of a benefit.
— Cicero

Every organization, including the military, must find ways to connect the personal motivations of its members with its objectives. It must do this in order to attract and retain members with the skills and abilities it requires and to secure their essential contributions to the organization. In the military, this may and often does translate into asking individuals to place themselves in arduous conditions, hazardous circumstances, and to be willing to make the ultimate sacrifice in support of the mission.

In consequence, militaries develop, elaborate, and maintain formal economies of incentives, both objective and subjective. Objective incentives include pay, allowances, retirement and health benefits, promotion, and assignment to duty. But no organization ever has sufficient resources to secure individual contributions solely through objective incentives. They must inevitably resort to subjective incentives, which include the intentional inculcation of attachment to key values such as national symbols, obedience to superior officers, traditions of service, valor, selflessness, and sacrifice, and standards of professionalism. Subjective incentives in the military also include formal recognition of individual and unit contributions and achievements through a well-articulated system of citations, medals, and ribbons, among other symbolic rewards.

Effective military leaders also recognize that securing individual contributions to the organization requires extending well beyond the formal objective and subjective economies of incentives. Military professionals and students of the military have long realized that soldiers do not lay down their lives for abstract ideals and symbols; rather they do so for their fellow soldiers. At root, this constitutes the recognition that militaries, like other organizations, despite their instrumental purposes and complicated technologies, are also, perhaps most fundamentally, social structures.

Social structures are founded in social exchange between and among individuals. Social exchange is predicated upon the norm of reciprocity, which has been called the basis for all human society: one should help those who have helped you; one should not hurt those who have helped you. Because social exchanges are not readily quantifiable individuals are able only to calculate roughly the balance of favors owed. It has been said that the first kindness can never be fully repaid. Adherence to the norm of reciprocity dampens conflict and creates social integration. Iterations of kindness and repayment produce mutual trust, which constitutes, as Kenneth Arrow has observed, an "important lubricant of organizations."

Effective leaders, whether division officers or fleet commanders, understand and use the norm of reciprocity to facilitate individual and unit morale, unit cohesion, and to secure individual contributions toward the organization's objectives. They promote the development of both horizontal and vertical systems of mutual obligation among their unit's members. Simple and unexpected acts of kindness by leaders toward their subordinates generate considerable goodwill and typically repay themselves many times over in important ways not often foreseeable in specific terms at the time of the act—a reservoir of goodwill that can be drawn upon as future events dictate.

It is in this vein that James Norman Hall's unlikely story about his days as a starving writer in the Tahiti of the 1920s is offered here. Notwithstanding his then dire circumstances, Hall performed a simple act of kindness toward a neighbor, which act ultimately brought him more benefits in return than he could easily sum. Therein lies a profound lesson for anyone who will lead those who go in harm's way.

Although best known for his authorship (with

Charles Nordhoff) of the epic *Mutiny on the Bounty* trilogy, and many other books, stories, and essays, Hall was no stranger to the military. Born in 1887, raised in Iowa, educated at Grinnell College, in 1914 while on a bicycle trip in Great Britain, he enlisted in "Kitchener's Mob," the British Expeditionary Force, serving as a machine gunner in France until discharged at the end of 1915. In October 1916 he enlisted in the Lafayette Escadrille and in June 1917 began flying in combat. He crashed and was injured twice, each time returning to his flying duties. Already highly decorated (Medaille Militaire and Croix de Guerre) and well-known, in early 1918, Hall transferred to the famous 94th Pursuit "Hat in the Ring" Squadron as a captain, where Eddie Rickenbacker flew with him and he gained more recognition and glory (Distinguished Service Cross). In early May he was shot down behind German lines, captured and imprisoned until mid-November 1917, when he was allowed to escape.

Hall met Charles Nordhoff (also an aviator) when they were both commissioned to write the official history of the Lafayette Escadrille. After completing their history, despairing of the excesses of industrial civilization, they made their way in 1920 to Tahiti, where both lived and wrote for the rest of their lives.

In those days, while living at the Aina Pare, a hotel on the Papeete waterfront, I had so little success at writing that my funds dwindled to the vanishing point. It seemed the part of wisdom to retire for time to one of the remote country districts until I could repair my fortunes. On the southern side of the island, thirty-five miles from the town, I found a piece of land, an acre in extent, with a one-room house on it precisely suited to my needs. The veranda overlooked the sea, unbroken by any land as far as the Antarctic Circle, and a mountain stream flowed through my small domain so that I had both fresh water and sea-water bathing. But a more important feature was the cheapness of the rental—three dollars per month.

The land thereabout was so fertile that I decided to make a vegetable garden. In the tropics gardening would be a delightful occupation, I thought, and it might prove so profitable that I would not need to attempt earning my living at my old trade of authorship. So I set to work hopefully enough, glad to the necessity which had brought me to this decision.

The experience was disillusioning. Millions of ants carried away most of my seed, and if any happened to be overlooked by the ants, the moment they set forth green shoots these were sheared off by the land crabs. After months of patient effort, all that I had to show for my toil were a few ears of sweet corn—or, better, sweet corn cobs, for rats had eaten off the kernels—three small tomatoes, and one squash. Having estimated my time as worth, at a modest figure, twenty cents an hour, and adding expenditures for seed, garden tools, and so on, I found that these vegetables cost me $15.50 each.

Nevertheless, I resolved to try once more and ordered—from America, this time—a small quantity of fresh seed, for my funds were low indeed, and furthermore, because of my innumerable enemies I meant to garden on a reduced front. But when I had cleared away the weeds—how marvelously they had flourished meanwhile, without care!—and saw the hosts of ants drawn up in waiting battalions, and the ground perforated like a sieve with the holes of land crabs, with a crab at the entrance of each hole waving his keen-edge nippers in the air, I lost heart. "It is useless," I thought. "I'd better make another attempt at writing." I should be able to earn at least twenty cents an hour. Therefore, I put away my tools and let Nature plant whatever she would in my garden plot. She shoes, as before, lantana and a vicious weed called "false tobacco."

That afternoon as I was oiling and cleaning my typewriter, which had long been rusting in disuse, a Chinese named Hop Sing drove past my door in his dilapidated spring wagon. He lived a quarter of a mile down the lagoon beach from my place, in a house he had build himself

from the boards of old packing cases. I knew that he had a vegetable garden of sorts, although he raised only sweet potatoes and a very tough variety of field corn; so I hailed him, thinking he might have use for my dollar's worth of seed. He stopped willingly enough, and I brought out to him a small packet each of beans, sweet corn (Golden bantam), squash, pumpkin, lettuce, and tomato seed, all the best varieties. Sing grunted expressions of mild interest while I explained what the various packets contained, and when I had finished, asked "How much?" "Oh, nothing at all," I said. "It's a little present for you." He grasped the back of his seat to steady himself, perhaps, from the shock of receiving a present from a stranger, and his black eyes glittered a trifle more brightly, but these were the only evidence of emotion, if it may be called emotion, that he displayed.

I forgot Hop Sing forthwith. There were other things to think of, chiefly the precarious state of my finances. Having counted upon my garden to furnish food, I had spent my little capital all too freely. I had received in the meantime one check for twelve dollars and another for ten dollars in payment for some newspaper articles I had written earlier. Luckily my rent was paid several months in advance, but I had left only one hundred and twenty-eight francs—a little more than five dollars, American, at the current rate of exchange—and not another penny to be expected until I had written something: story, sketch, whatnot. The manuscript would have to be sent to America, my only market, and even though it should be accepted at once—a remote possibility—I could not hope to receive a check from such a distance for at least three months. How was I to live in the meantime? There were plenty of bananas on my place and about fifty coconut palms; but my landlord, a native, reserved the right to both the fruit and the nuts, which was no more than fair considering the modest rental he asked for house and grounds. He gathered the nuts as they fell and the bananas were picked green to be sent to the Papeete market. I thought of fishing, but remembering past experiences I knew it would be foolish to count on that. I had no better luck at fishing than I had at gardening. No, I would have to live, somehow, on my one hundred and twenty-eight francs. That, of course, was impossible, so I resolved not even to try. I kept twenty-eight francs for native tobacco, and invested the remainder of my cash in sweet potatoes and tinned beef. When the food was gone—well, I would worry about that when the time came.

Three days later I was on page two of a sketch which I planned to call "Settling Down in Polynesia," a story of some experiences I had had the summer before. It was Sunday, but necessity knows no holy days, and I was doing my utmost to work. But the mere fact of having to work seemed to make accomplishment impossible. I had written and rewritten the two pages of my story, trying with each new draft to blacken page three. I was aroused from a mood of profound dejection by a knock at the door.

It was Hop Sing, and with him were his wife, their three small children, and a wizened little man shaped like an interrogation point. Hop was dressed in a clean cotton undershirt and a pair of dungaree trousers. His wife wore a pajama suit of black silk, and her hair was elaborately dressed. She carried one child on her arm, led another by the hand, and the third, a baby, rode comfortably in a sling on here back. The children were beautifully dressed, and each of them wore a little skull-cap of blue silk, with flowers and butterflies embroidered on them with gold thread. The ancient wore a robe like a dressing gown. He was very feeble and got down from the wagon with difficulty. It was pathetic to see the effort it cost him to walk. He would advance his staff a few inches and, grasping it with both hands, make a shuffling hop up to it. Then he would rest for a moment while gathering strength for a new movement. We helped him up the steps, and at length were seated on my back veranda, Mrs. Sing sitting sidewise in her chair because of the baby in the sling. My unwashed breakfast dishes were on the table, and several slices of fried sweet potatoes on a greasy

plate looked anything but appetizing. I was ashamed of the disorder of the place, the more so because this was the first visit I'd ever had from the Sing family. Hop Sing and his wife looked around them in appraising fashion, but I could not judge from their faces what they thought of my housekeeping.

"My fadda-law,: said Sing, indicating the old man.

I smiled and nodded.

A rather long silence followed. I felt embarrassed and could think of nothing to say.

"What name, you?" he then asked.

I told him. Another interval of silence. I gave my forefinger to the child on Mrs. Sing's lap. It clasped it gravely and held on. Mrs. Sing smiled. Her father, too, smiled; at least, his face wrinkled suddenly, like a pool into which several pebbles have been thrown. The baby in the sling was asleep, its chubby arms sticking straight out. It looked like a doll rather than a baby. The oldest child, a boy of six or seven, had the curious mature look and the air of precocious wisdom one often sees on the faces of Chinese children.

Sing took from his pocket one of the packets of seeds I had given him.

"What name, this?" he asked.

"In English? . . . Corn, sweet corn. Golden Bantam," I replied. "Very good. Tahiti corn no good—too tough. This corn fine."

"You get from Melica?"

I nodded. He brought forth the other packets. "All this Melican seed?"

It was, I said, and of the best varieties.

He was silent for a moment; then he said: "Make fine garden, now. Make plenty big tomato, plenty corn, plenty squash. Bimeby you see."

Thinking of my three tomatoes about the size of pigeon's eggs I was not sanguine about Hop Sing's being plenty big. However, I expressed the hope that they might be. I brought out a seed catalogue and showed him illustrations in color of various kinds of vegetables. The pictures, of course, showed products in their highest imaginative perfection. He was much interested and exchanged remarks with his father-in-law. Meanwhile, one of those heavy showers common at Tahiti in the rainy season broke with violence. The thunder of water on my tin roof was deafening. Soon the cloud melted into pure sunlight, the last of it descending in a fine mist shot through with rainbow lights. Sing went out to his wagon and returned with three fine watermelons. He made a second excursion, bringing this time a live fowl, a bottle of Dubonnet (*vin aperitif*), and a basket containing seventeen eggs. All of these articles he placed on my kitchen table.

"Littly plesent, you," he said, with a deprecatory gesture. Mrs. Sing and her father then rose and all three shook my hand, bidding me goodby with smiles and nods. A moment later they drive off, leaving me astonished and genuinely moved at this expression of Chinese friendliness.

It would be difficult to exaggerate the value, to me, of their generous gift. Tinned beef is a nourishing food, but I had lost all relish for it during the First Great War. As for sweet potatoes, I had eaten so many while knocking about the Pacific on trading schooners that I could scarcely endure the sight of them. How welcome, then, was this more palatable food! I thought of having a chicken dinner at once, but on second thought decided to preserve my fowl. Perhaps she would lay, and if I could somehow procure a rooster I might from this small beginning raise enough chickens to provide for all my needs. So I staked the hen out in the dooryard with a string tied to her leg, and having found several coconuts partly eaten by rats, I broke these open and gave her a good meal. Then, having dined on a six-egg omelet with half a watermelon for dessert, I resumed my work with interest and enthusiasm. All the afternoon the bell of my typewriter rang with the steady persistence of an alarm gong at a railroad crossing, and pages of manuscript fell on the floor around me like autumn leaves after a heavy frost. By six o'clock that evening I had reached the end of my "Settling Down" story.

I had no time to lose if I was to get it into the northbound mail. The monthly steamer from New Zealand to San Francisco was due at Papeete on Monday. I decided to go into town to post the manuscript myself, not being willing to trust the native mail with so precious a document. A motor bus ran daily between Papeete and Taravao, a village just beyond my place, but the fare for the round trip was twenty-four francs. I would need at least ten francs to for stamps and expenses in town, so I decided to walk to Papeete, and if I had enough money left, to ride back. Having fortified myself with another six-egg omelet and a small glass of Dubonnet, I set out.

It was a beautiful night, dewy and still and fresh, with a full moon rising above the palm trees on the Taravao isthmus. The road wound around the shoulders of the hills, now skirting the sea, now crossing the mouths of broad valleys where the land breeze from the mountains blew cool and refreshing. I had glimpses through the trees of lofty precipices festooned with the silvery smoke of waterfalls, and, on the left hand, of the lagoon bordered by the reef, where great combers caught the moonlight in lines of white fire. From native houses along the road came snatches of song, a strange mixture of airs, part French, part Tahitian, to the accompaniment of guitars, accordions, and mouth organs. On verandas here and there women were busy with their ironing, sitting cross-legged on the floor with a lamp beside them, and far out on the lagoon the lights of the fishermen were beginning to appear.

I walked briskly along the road, feeling at peace with the world and with myself. How pleasant, how wise it would be, I thought, really to settle down on this remote island paradise and remain here for the rest of my life. Where else could I find kindlier people, or a life more suited to one of my indolent habits? If it were true that man's wealth may be estimated in terms of tings he can do without, then in that sense I might soon hope to achieve affluence. Material possession added little to the sum of one's happiness, and I could always earn enough at writing to provide for the simple necessities of life. Whenever the mild-eyed, melancholy tropical wolves came sniffing apologetically at my door, I could write a story of one sort or another, and live on the proceeds of the sale of it until it became necessary to write another.

Musing thus hopefully I proceeded on my way, but toward midnight, when I had covered about half the distance to Papeete, I found myself again thinking of food. The nourishment stored in my second six-egg omelet had already been absorbed and its energy expended. I had a drink of water from a mountain stream and tightened my belt a notch or two. "I'll have a good breakfast when I reach town," I thought. For four francs I could buy a large portion of chop suey at one of the Chinese restaurants. That would suffice until I had returned to the country, which I meant to do as soon as I had posted my manuscript.

At a place where the road followed a lonely strip of beach I came to a thatched hut, and sitting near it by a driftwood fire were an old native man and woman. I halted to enjoy the beauty of the scene. The stems of the coconut palms were black against the firelight, which flickered over the faces of the old couple and cast huge shadows behind them. They saw me and called out, "*Haere mai ta maa!*" ("Come and eat!") This is merely a friendly greeting, and I replied in the customary way, "*Paia vau*" ("I'm not hungry"), but if my empty stomach could have spoken it would have made indignant denial of the statement. Evidently they really meant that I should partake of their midnight supper. They were roasting over the coals what appeared to be shellfish and some kind of native vegetable, and an appetizing fragrance filled the air.

"Come," said the old woman; "try this. It is very good." And putting several generous portions in a coconut shell, she held it up to me.

Good? I should think it was! The meat of the shellfish was delicately flavored and the vegetable had real substance and a nutlike taste. My hosts were delighted to see the relish with which I ate and urged more food upon me.

"Eat, eat!" said the old man. "We have plenty, enough for a dozen," And he pointed to several buckets filled with uncooked food. So, being hungry, I ate with a will.

"What kind of shellfish are these?" I asked. "Did you catch them on the reef?"

"These are not shellfish. They're *tupas*," the old man said.

"What!" I exclaimed.

Tupas are land crabs, and those I had been eating with such relish were members of the pestiferous family, countless in numbers, which had assisted the ants in ruining my garden. I hadn't known that they were edible but my hosts told me that Tahitians thought them a great delicacy, which they are, in truth, if one is really *hungry*. *As for the vegetable, it was not a vegetable at all, but a nut, the fruit of the mape*, the Pacific chestnut tree. These trees flourish on Tahiti. They are found along the banks of streams, and in other moist or swampy places. There was a grove of them on my place and the ground beneath was littered with nuts, which my landlord never disturbed, and which I had not bothered to examine, not knowing they were good to eat.

I was appalled at the thought of the time I had wasted trying to make a garden, when all the while there was an inexhaustible supply of food at hand, to be enjoyed without labor, to be had for the mere taking. But no, the taking of land crabs could not be such a simple matter. I remembered the wariness of those that infested my garden. They did all their damage in my absence. The moment they saw me they scurried to their holes and, if I made so much as a move in their direction, dodged down to safety. I had once caught one by digging him out, but that cost me half an hour of hard work.

I asked the old man how he caught them, and he showed me a method so simple and easy that I wondered I had not thought of it. He had a fishpole and a line, but instead of a hook at the end of the line, he tied there a bunch of green leaves from the hibiscus tree. These leaves and the blossoms of the hibiscus are the principal food of land crabs when there is no garden stuff at hand. We went a little way from the hut to a spot in full moonlight where there were many crab holes. "Now stand very still," he said. In a moment the crabs, which had vanished at our approach, came warily up again. He then cast his bait much as one does in fly-fishing. The crabs fastened their nippers in the leaves, each of them trying to drag the bundle to his hole. The old man gave the line a deft jerk, and the crabs, not being able to disengage their nippers quickly enough, were dragged to his feet. He pounced upon them and threw them into the bucket with the others.

I then tried my hand, with success that I was tempted to return home at once and begin fishing in my garden. But more prudent counsels prevailed. One's appetite for food so plentiful and so easily procured might become jaded in time. Furthermore I would need a certain amount of money for paper, typewriter ribbons, shaving materials, and such. So I bade farewell to my friendly hosts and proceeded on my way, reaching Papeete at dawn, just as the steamer which was to carry my manuscript to America was entering the harbor. Stamps for the parcel cost three francs. I breathed over it a silent prayer and slipped it into the letter chute.

I have heard travelers call Papeete a tropical slum, and it must be admitted that it does leave something to be desired in the way of cleanliness and sanitation. Nevertheless it is a colorful town, particularly in the early morning, when the people are going to and from the market place. Everyone is abroad at that hour, and the French and Chinese restaurants are filled with folk exchanging gossip over their morning coffee. I had a good breakfast at the cost of four francs, then strolled along the waterfront, doubly enjoying the gaiety of the scene after my long sojourn in the country. I was walking along the Quai de Commerce looking at the shipping when someone touched my shoulder. It was a bald, fat little Chinese who had evidently been running after me. He was so out of breath that he could not speak for a moment. Then he began speaking in Chinese-Tahitian, a sort of *biche-la-mer* I don't

understand. I shook my head. He renewed his efforts, speaking earnestly and rapidly, and I caught the name Hop Sing.

"Hop Sing?" I said.

"*E! E!*" (Yes! Yes!) he replied, and of a sudden found some English words.

"You know Hop Sing? Hop Sing flen, you?"

Yes, I said, I knew him. "Hop Sing live close me, Papeari."

Papeari was the name of the district where I was living.

The face of the Chinese glowed with pleasure.

"*Maitai, maitai!*" ("Good!") Hop Sing send me letta. I know name, you! You give seed, put in gloun, make garden. Maitai! Maitai! Hop Sing glad. Me glad. Hop Sing brudda-law, me."

"What name, you?" I asked.

"Lee Fat. Keep store, over there." And he pointed down the street. "When you go back Papeari?"

"Go this morning, on motor bus," I said.

"Goo-by," said the Chinese, and rushed away without another word. I was surprised at the abrupt leave-taking and stood looking after him, touched at the thought of this odd little man chasing me down the street to thank me for the trifling favor I had done his brother-in-law.

I sat on the bench near the post office to wait for the motor bus. "The beachcombers' bench," it was called, for it was usually occupied on steamer day with waifs and strays from various parts of the world who sit there waiting for the distribution of the monthly mail, always expecting letters containing money and nearly always disappointed. "I'm in the same boat now," I thought. "Three months hence I'll be sitting here nursing the same forlorn hope." It was possible, of course, that my manuscript would sell at once, but repeated past experience warned me that it would be foolish to count on it. Well, I still had twenty-one francs and would have none left after paying my bus fare. Certainly, I would not starve, with land crabs and mape nuts to eat. Meanwhile I would work as never before, sending out manuscripts as long as I could find money for postage. Having made this resolve I put my worries aside.

It was nearly midday when I arrived at Papeari. While paying the driver my fare, the boy who attended to the distribution to parcels put a box down beside me.

"You've made a mistake," I said. "That isn't mine."

"Yes it is," he replied.

"No, no. I didn't have a box and I've ordered nothing from town."

He insisted, however, that it was mine. A Chinese had brought it just before the bus left the market, he said, and had paid for its carriage to my place. I still thought there was some mistake, but upon prying off the lid I found a card with "Lee Fat. NO. 118" printed on it. Every Chinese on Tahiti has a number, for identification purposes. Under the name was written, in pencil: "Mr. Hall, for you."

The parcel contained the following articles: a two-pound box of New Zealand chocolates, a paper bag of litchi nuts, one quart of champagne (Louis Roederer), and a Chinese lacquered box with a gold dragon on the lid. In the box were two silk handkerchiefs and a silk pajama suit.

I was tempted to open the champagne at once that I might drink long life and abundant health to Hop Sing and his brother-in-law, Lee Fat, No. 118: but I had no ice, and I knew that I could not drink a quart of champagne without have a headache afterward. So I tied a string to the bottle and lowered it into the cistern to cool. Then I went out to attend to my hen.

She was gone. The string was still tied to the stake, but she had worked her foot out of the noose and vanished. After a long search I found her under the back steps. She had laid an egg and was sitting on it. Evidently she was ready to set when Hop Sing brought her to me. The egg under her was probably unfertilized so I took that out. Then I made her a nest of the excelsior which had been packed around the articles in Lee Fat's gift box, and placed in it the five eggs remaining from Hop Sing's gift. The hen settled down on them with contented cluckings, and

when comfortable closed her eyes as much to say: "Now then, all I ask is to be left alone, and twenty-one days hence we shall see what we shall see."

It seems to me now that the definite upward trend in the graph of my fortunes began that afternoon when I started land-crab fishing. I could not eat a tenth of the crabs I caught, so I made a pen of stakes set closely together and driven deeply into the ground, and turned the surplus loose inside it. They immediately dug new holes for themselves, but this did not disturb me, for I knew that I cold easily catch them again. It occurred to me that by feeding them regularly on hibiscus leaves and blossoms I might add to their size and increase the delicacy of their flavor. The experiment was highly successful. The crabs throve on regular and abundant food, and I throve upon them. At the time of Hop Sing's visit, what with worry and an uncongenial diet, I was very thin, but within six weeks I had gained fourteen pounds.

Meanwhile, promptly upon the appointed day, my hen stepped out of her nest followed by four chicks. I was quite as proud of them as she was and doubtless took more credit to myself on the occasion than the facts warranted. I fed the hen and her brood a mixture of roasted land crabs and mape nuts, and never have I seen baby chicks grow more rapidly.

It may seem incredible that my bottle of champagne should have remained unbroached during this time, but such is the case. In my interest in crab-and-chicken farming I had quite forgotten it; but one day when my landlord was gathering coconuts in a nearby grove I invited him in to share it with me. He was more than willing, and his somewhat reserved attitude toward me altered with the first glass. I then learned the reason for his coolness. He told me that his last tenant had not only eaten bananas and coconuts to which he had no right, but had gone away without paying his rent, three months in arrears at the time. Gathering, from the simplicity of my way of life, that I too had little money, he feared that I might play him the same trick. I reassured him on this point and we drank confusion to his former tenant, wherever he might be. Several of my landlord's children had accompanied him to the house and shared among them the box of chocolates. It was a merry little party, and after much pleasant talk my landlord left me with repeated expressions of good will.

The next morning I found on my back veranda a bunch of bananas and a copra sack half filled with mangoes and oranges, gifts from my landlord and his family. Not infrequently, thereafter, Mata, his wife, would send me baked fish, breadfruit, and mountain plantain fresh from her native oven, and I remembered with deep gratitude that I really owed these benefits to Hop Sing.

Meanwhile, I worked steadily at writing, and Hop Sing's garden was flourishing. All the seeds I had given him had sprouted and gave promise of a rich harvest under his patient, ceaseless care. He was always at work, and so too was Mrs. Sing, despite the demands on her time made by three small children. Sometimes of a late afternoon I walked down to their place. They always greeted me in the most friendly way, but never for a moment did they leave off working. "Surely," I would think, "the Chinese deserve to inherit the earth, and doubtless will inherit it if industry and patience count for anything." Even the ancient, not Mrs. Sing's father but her grandfather, as I was to learn, was far from being useless, despite his little strength; and the oldest hild, although only a baby himself, took care of his smaller brother. Mrs. Sing was usually to be found in a little back shed sorting and cleaning vegetables for the Papeete market. All of her members were busy at once. She rocked the smallest baby, which lay in a cradle hanging from a rafter, by means of a cord attached to her foot. Now and then she pulled another cord which hung just over her head. This one ran by a system of pulleys to the garden where there was a sort of jumping-jack scarecrow to frighten away those robbers, the mynah birds. Meanwhile the vegetable got themselves cleaned and deftly packed in little baskets.

The ancient was a baker, and twice a week, after his long day's toil in the garden, Hop Sing made the rounds of the district in his spring wagon, selling crisp loaves of bread and pineapple tarts to the native population. During these excursions he often left something at my gate, either a tart or a loaf of bread. No protest on my part served to dry up his fountain of generosity for my wretched little gift of seed.

Under these circumstances the weeks passed so pleasantly that steamer day—the third since the posting of my manuscript—was at hand before I realized it. I walked into town once more and waited on the familiar bench til the mail should be distributed. I waited through the latter part of the afternoon until everyone in Papeete and its environs had called for their letters. I waited until the sun was sinking behind the mountains of Moorea and the post office was about to close. Then, summing all my resolution, I mounted the steps and walked to the delivery window, saying inwardly: "It's useless to ask. I'm quite certain to be disappointed." The girl who presided there went hastily through a small number of letters from the "H" box.

"No, there's nothing for you," she said, with a smile so typical of post-office clerks who preside at General Delivery windows.

I made a ghastly attempt to smile in return and was going toward the door when she called after me:

"Oh! Just a moment! What name did you say?"

I repeated it, enunciating the words with the utmost care.

"Yes, there is one letter," she said. "Fifty centimes postage due."

Having paid this I had left only a twenty-five centime piece, the smallest coin used in French Oceania. But little that mattered. The letter contained a gracious note accepting my manuscript, and a check for five hundred dollars.

To those living luxurious lives in the high latitudes, five hundred dollars may seem a trifling sum, but it was a fortune to me. I had never be-fore received even half that amount for anything I had written. With the half of it, plus two dol-lars, I could pay the rental for my house and grounds for a period of seven years, and the two hundred and fifty remaining would suffice for other expenses for a time nearly as long, pro-vided that I lived as modestly in the future as I had in the immediate past. But now, with bright vistas of ease and plenty and peace of mind opening out before me, I found myself per-versely considering the idea of leaving Tahiti. The northbound steamer to San Francisco would be due shortly, and I fell to considering the varied experience I might now have by virtue of movement and my five hundred dollars. Re-membering past fortunes in authorship, I knew that it was the part of wisdom to remain on Tahiti, where living was, for the first time, within my means. And yet, if I did not go now, I might have to wait long before I should again have enough money for a steamboat ticket. I walked the streets of Papeete until a late hour, anxiously considering this matter. The clock in the cathe-dral was striking two before the decision—to go—was made.

Hop Sing was in town on the day of my de-parture. He had come with garden produce, and both he and Lee Fat came to see me off. Fat in-sisted on my accepting a pair of Russian-leather bedroom slippers and a Chinese fan of blue silk embellished with gold butterflies hovering over a fantasy of flowers. Sing's parting gift was a bas-ket of tomatoes as large as oranges, and a dozen ears of sweet corn (Golden Bantam). They smiled good-bys as the steamer backed away from the wharf and headed for the passage to the open sea. I then went to my cabin, in order that departure from that most beautiful of islands might be a little less poignant. While I was un-packing my bag, a steward looked in.

"You've been assigned to the doctor's table, sir," he said. "It's a table for four, but this trip there's only one other gentleman there beside yourself. Is that satisfactory?"

"Quite," I replied. "By the way, will you please have this corn prepared and served at lun-cheon? Take a couple of ears for yourself if you care to."

"Thank you, sir. I hope the other gentleman at your table likes sweet corn He's done nothing but complain about the food ever since we left Wellington, and to tell you the truth, it's not what it might be."

The doctor did not come down for luncheon. I had just seated myself when the other passen-ger at his table came in. He was a tall, spare man with a drooping moustache and a bilious com-plexion. He was dressed in a baggy linen coat and knickerbockers and low white shoes. He sat down without even a nod in my direction and adjusted a pair of nose glasses, picking up the menu card, puffing out his cheeks as he exam-ined it, letting the air escape dejectedly through his lips. He struck me as being a man who would be extremely hard to please in the matter of food or anything else. He was partaking gloomily of a dish of creamed tinned salmon when the steward brought in a platter with eight splendid ears of Golden Bantam corn steaming on it. He gazed at it in astonishment.

"Take this away," he said to the steward, pushing the dish of salmon to one side, "and bring me another dinner plate."

Never before had I seen a man give himself up to the enjoyment of food with such purely physical abandon. On would have thought that he had not eaten for days. When he had finished his second ear, he said: "Steward, where does this corn come from? It's not on the card."

"No sir, it's not on the regular bill. It's a gift to the table from the gentleman sitting opposite you."

He gave me a grudging glance as though he had just become aware of my presence.

"Consider yourself thanked, sir," he said, brusquely.

I nodded.

"Is this corn of your own growing?"

"Well, yes, in a sense," I replied.

He plowed a hasty furrow along his third ear before speaking again. Then he said: "What do you mean by 'in a sense'? You either raised it or you didn't, I should think."

He had a waspish, peppery way of speaking as though he had been long accustomed to asking whomever whatever he chose, with the certainty of a deferential reply. In view of the fact that he was eating my—or rather, Hops Sing's—corn, I felt that he might have made an effort, at least, to be gracious. Therefore I merely said, as coldly as possible, "Oh, you'd have to live on Tahiti to understand that." Having finished my luncheon I rose and left him there, still eating corn.

Half an hour later I was standing at the rail, aft, watching the peak of Orohena, the highest mountain on Tahiti, slowly sinking into the sea. A hand was laid on my arm, and, turning, I found my table companion.

"Well, sir," he said, "one would think that you were about to jump overboard."

"I have been considering it," I replied, "but it's too far to swim back, now."

"You like Tahiti as much as that? Well, I don't wonder. An island where they grow such delicious corn must be a good place to live. I ate six of those ears—finished the lot, in fact."

"I'm glad you enjoyed it," I replied.

"See here! You mustn't mind my grumpiness. I'm afraid I was a little brusque at lunch. I've got dyspepsia, and a wayward liver and an enlarged spleen—Lord knows what all else is the matter with me. Gives me a sort of jaundiced outlook on life. But I want you to know that I'm grateful. Sweet corn is one of the few things I can eat without suffering afterward. Now, then, tell me something about your island. I didn't go ashore. Useless to try seeing even a small island in six hours. It's only an aggravation."

I scarcely knew how it came about, but within a few minutes I was talking as freely as though to an old friend. I told him of the beauty of the islands in the eastern Pacific, of the changing life, of the mingling races; of the strange outcroppings of savage beliefs and customs through the shale of what in those parts is called civilization. Presently I halted, thinking he might be bored.

"Not at all," he said. "Well, you've had an interesting time, evidently, and you seem to have made good use of your eyes and ears. You're an American, aren't you? What do you do for a living—besides raising sweet corn 'in a sense'?" he added, with a smile.

I told him that I was an itinerant journalist.

"Is that so?" he said, looking interested. "Got any of your stuff with you?"

"A few sketches of various sorts," I replied.

"Would you mind letting me see them?"

"Not in the least." And so, at his suggestion, I brought out a small sheaf of manuscript, six slight papers on various island subjects, each of them about two thousand words long. He settled himself in his deck chair and adjusted his glasses.

"Come back in an hour from now," he said, "and I'll tell you what I think of them."

He thought two of them worthless, and, strangely enough, these were the ones I thought best.

"But these four are not bad. What do you want for them?"

"You—you mean you would like to buy them?" I asked.

"Yes, of course. But I forgot to tell you: I'm a director of a newspaper syndicate in the U.S.A. We can use these sketches. Tropical island stuff is always popular. Interest in the South Seas never wanes, and it never will as long as life is what it is in America. . . . Well, what do you want for them?"

"Oh, I don't know. . . ." I said. I was about to add: "Would one hundred dollars be too much?" meaning one hundred for the four. He interrupted me.

"Give you one hundred and fifty each for them. Is that agreeable?"

I admitted that it was.

That evening I set down on paper, for my own amusement, a list as complete as I could make it of all the benefits, direct and indirect, accruing to me from my trifling gift to Hop Sing. With this before me I came to the conclusion that Adam himself, the first husbandman, even under the exceptionally favorable conditions prevailing in the Garden of Eden before the Fall, could not have reaped such a rich and varied harvest as I did from my garden at Tahiti. And it all came from a dollar's worth of seed.

Suggested Reading

Barnard, Chester I. *The Functions of the Executive*. Cambridge: Harvard University Press, 1971 [first published 1938].

Blau, Peter M. *Exchange and Power in Social Life*. Chicago: University of Chicago Press, 1964.

Briand, Paul L. *In Search of Paradise: The Nordhoff-Hall Story*. New York: Duell, Sloan, and Pearce, 1966.

Gouldner, Alvin. "The Norm of Reciprocity: A Preliminary Statement." *American Sociological Review* 25(1960): 161–178.

Hall, James Norman. *Kitchener's Mob*. London: Constable, 1916.

Nordhoff, Charles and James Norman Hall. *Mutiny on the Bounty*. Boston: Little, Brown and Co., 1932.

———. *Men Against the Sea*. Boston: Little, Brown and Co., 1934.

———. *Pitcairn's Island*. Boston: Little, Brown and Co., 1934.

About the Author

Dr. Donald W. Chisholm joined the Naval War College in 2000. Before coming to the Naval War College, he taught at several universities, including the University of Illinois at Chicago and the University of California, Los Angeles, where he was founding member of the School of Public Policy and Social Research. Professor Chisholm earned his AB, MA, and PhD in political science at the University of California, Berkeley. His chief fields of interest include military history, organization theory, administrative behavior, policy analysis, and American political institutions. His research has examined the planning and execution of joint military operations; cognitive and organizational limits on rationality; organizational adaptation and innovation; organizational failure and reliability, particularly in high-risk technologies; and privatization of public activities. He is author of *Coordination Without Hierarchy: Informal Structures in Multi-Organizational Systems* (University of California Press, 1989) and *Waiting for Dead Men's Shoes: Origins and Development of the U.S. Navy's Officer Personnel System, 1793-1941* (Stanford University Press, 2001), for which he received the 2001 Rear Admiral Samuel Eliot Morison Award for Distinguished Contribution to Naval Literature. He has also published a number of articles in professional journals, including *Joint Forces Quarterly*, *Parameters*, and the *Naval War College Review*.

49

Perfect Sustained Fury: Mark Helprin's North Light

Dr. Mark McWilliams

Written with the immediacy of the present tense, Mark Helprin's "North Light" explores the challenges faced by an Israeli mechanized unit as they wait to be sent into action. This small group of reserves includes both veterans and young soldiers who have not faced combat. Because they has just been called up to respond to a surprise attack, many have come straight from their families. Helprin, who served in the Israeli Defense Forces and the British Merchant Navy, considers the difficulties of motivating such a diverse group of soldiers on the verge of engagement.

Helprin's narrator, a member of the unit, distinguishes between kinds of courage. The young men, the men "responsible only to themselves," need only overcome the fear of the unknown. For these men who have not yet faced combat, fear is like that faced by "members of a sports team before an important match."

The narrator seems dismissive—or envious—of "that kind of fear" that can be summed up by comparisons to sports teams. He knows such analogies hopelessly understate the radically unpredictable terrors of combat. As one of the older soldiers, the "married men" who are veterans of the Six Day War and other conflicts, the narrator cannot rely on the courage of the young, on courage based on a desire to be tested in battle. The veterans need a different kind of courage, a courage that "is the forced step of going into battle when you want anything in the world but that, when there is every reason to stay out, when you have been through all the tests, and passed them, and think that it's all over." All too aware of the dangers they face, these older soldiers struggle to find the motivation to act.

The "married men" struggle because of their keen awareness of how much they have to lose. The sudden transition from civilian to soldier makes it difficult to adapt. Called up with "the taste of your wife's mouth in your mouth" and "the smell of her perfume on your wrists," these soldiers have kissed their children in the morning and must go into action in the afternoon. Desperate not to die, they risk succumbing to "the slow self-made fear which demands constant hesitation" which, in combat, becomes "the most efficient of all killers."

In the end, though, Helprin suggests that unit effectiveness depends on such differences melting away in the "energy and fury" that allows a soldier to sense the "flow" of "hard combat." Here, as elsewhere in his work, Helprin compares combat soldiers to ballet dancers or mountain climbers or musicians: battle requires "the smooth, courageous, trancelike movements that will keep them out of trouble." For these reservists, anger—at delay, at incompetence, at the enemy—offers an escape from fear into this flow. In the "perfect sustained fury" necessary for combat, soldiers can pay attention to the "thousand signals and signs" that will help them survive.

Implicitly, Helprin's story raises questions about who should bear the burden of a country's defense. The narrator believes that the old veterans have more to lose, but young readers of the story often challenge that assumption. In addition to the young who have always formed a substantial portion of its combat forces, today's U.S. military has the highest ratio of married soldiers in its history. The diverse experience of soldiers in the ranks is increased as well through an unprecedented reliance on the reserves, on those who cycle between military and civilian life, often with little warning. Helprin's story, then, while based in the realities of the Israeli Army, now more than ever captures the challenges faced by our own armed forces. Leading such diverse units requires recognizing differing backgrounds and needs, just as Helprin's sergeant does in timing his request to go into action to the moment the readiness of his men— both the young soldiers and the old veterans—peaks.

Mark Helprin is widely known as the author of *A Soldier of the Great War*, *Memoir from* *Antproof Case*, *Refiner's Fire*, *Winter's Tale*, and other novels along with his three short story collections; he has also worked as a speechwriter for the first President Bush and, recently, as a columnist for the *Wall Street Journal*.

North Light

—A Recollection in the Present Tense

We are being held back. We are poised at a curve in the road on the southern ridge of a small valley. The sun shines from behind, illuminating with flawless light the moves and countermoves of several score tanks below us. For a long time, we have been absorbed in the mystery of matching the puffs of white smoke from tank cannon with the sounds that follow. The columns themselves move silently: only the great roar rising from the battle proves it not to be a dream.

A man next to me is deeply absorbed in sniffing his wrist. "What are you doing?" I ask.

"My wife," he says. "I can still smell her perfume on my wrist, and I can taste the taste of her mouth. It's sweet."

We were called up this morning. The war is two days old. Now it is afternoon, and we are being held back—even though our forces below are greatly outnumbered. We are being held back until nightfall, when we will have a better chance on the plain; for it is packed with tanks, and we have only two old half-tracks. They are loaded with guns—it is true—but they are lightly armored, they are slow, and they present high targets. We expect to move at dusk or just before. Then we will descend into the valley and fight amid the shadows. No one wants this: we are all terrified.

The young ones are frightened because, for most of them, this is the first battle. But their fear is not as strong as the blood which is rising and fills their chests with anger and strength. They have little to lose, being, as they are, only eighteen. They look no more frightened than members of a sports team before an important match: it is that kind of fear, for they are responsible only to themselves.

Married men, on the other hand, are given away by their eyes and faces. They are saying to themselves, "I must not die; I *must not die.*" They are remembering how they used to feel when they were younger; and they know that they have to fight. They may be killed, but if they don't fight they will surely be killed, because the slow self-made fear which demands constant hesitation is the most efficient of all killers. It is not the cautious who die, but the overcautious. The married men are trying to strike an exact balance between their responsibility as soldiers, their fervent desire to stay alive, and their only hope—which is to go into battle with the smooth, courageous, tracelike movements that will keep them out of trouble. Soldiers who do not know how (like dancers or mountain climbers) to let their bodies think for them are very likely to be killed. There is a flow to hard combat; it is not (as it has often been depicted) entirely chance or entirely skill. A thousand signals and signs speak to you, much as in music. And what a sad moment it is when you must, for one reason or another, ignore them. The married men fear this moment. We should have begun hours ago. Being held back is bad luck.

"What time is it?" asks one of the young soldiers. Someone answers him.

"Fourteen hundred." No one in the Israeli Army except high-ranking officers (colonels, generals—and we have no colonels or generals) tells time in this fashion.

"What are you, a general?" asks the young soldier. Everyone laughs, as if this were funny, because we are scared. We should not be held back like this.

Another man, a man who is close to fifty and is worrying about his two sons who are in the Sinai, keeps on looking at his watch. It is expensive and Japanese, with a black dial. He looks at it every minute to see what time it is, because he has actually forgotten. If he were asked what the time was, he would not be able to respond without checking the watch, even though he has

done so fifty times within the last hour. He too is very afraid. The sun glints off the crystal and explodes in our eyes.

As younger men who badly wanted to fight, we thought we knew what courage was. Now we know that courage is the forced step of going into battle when you want anything in the world but that, when there is every reason to stay out, when you have been through all the tests, and passed them, and think that it's all over. Then the war hits like an artillery shell and you are forced to be eighteen again, but you can't be eighteen again; not with the taste of your wife's mouth in your mouth, not with the smell of her perfume on your wrists. The world turns upside down in minutes.

How hard we struggle in trying to remember the easy courage we once had. But we can't. We must either be brave in a different way, or not at all. What is that way? How can we fight like seasoned soldiers when this morning we kissed our children? There is a way, hidden in the history of war. There must be, for we can see them fighting in the valley; and, high in the air, silver specks are dueling in a dream of blue silence.

Why are we merely watching? To be restrained this way is simply not fair. A quick entrance would get the fear over with, and that would help. But, then again, in the Six Day War, we waited for weeks while the Egyptian Army built up against us. And then, after that torture, we burst out and we leapt across the desert, sprinting, full of energy and fury that kept us like dancers—nimble and absorbed—and kept us alive. That is the secret: You have to be angry. When we arrived at the ridge this morning, we were anything but angry. Now we are beginning to get angry. It is our only salvation. We are angry because we are being held back.

We swear, and kick the sides of the half-tracks. We hate the voice on our radio which keeps telling us to hold to our position. We hate that man more than we hate the enemy, for now we want engagement with the enemy. We are beginning to crave battle, and we are getting angrier, and angrier, because we know that by five o'clock we will be worn out. They should let us go now.

A young soldier who has been following the battle, through binoculars, screams. "God!" he says. "Look! Look!"

The Syrians are moving up two columns of armor that will overwhelm our men on the plain below. The sergeant gets on the radio, but from it we hear a sudden waterfall of talk. Holding the microphone in one hand, he listens with us as we discover that they know. They are demanding more air support.

"What air support?" we ask. There is no air-to-ground fighting that we can see. As we watch the Syrians approach, our hearts are full of fear for those of us below. How did our soldiers know? There must be spotters or a patrol deep in, high on a hill, like us. What air support? There are planes all over the place, but not here.

Then we feel our lungs shaking like drums. The hair on our arms and on the back of our necks stands up and we shake as flights of fighters roar over the hill. They are no more than fifty feet above us. We can feel the heat from the tailpipes, and the orange flames are blinding. The noise is superb. They come three at a time; one wave, two three, four, five, and six. These are our pilots. The mass of the machinery flying through the air is so great and graceful that we are stunned beyond the noise. We cheer in anger and in satisfaction. It seems the best thing in the world when, as they pass the ridge (How they hug the ground; what superb pilots!) they dip their wings for our sake. They are descending into a thicket of anti-aircraft missiles and radar-directed guns—and they dip their wings for us.

Now we are hot. The married men feel as if rivers are rushing through them, crossing and crashing, for they are angry and full of energy. The sergeant depresses the lever on the microphone. He identifies himself and says, "In the name of God, we want to go in *now*. Damn you if you don't let us go in."

There is hesitation and silence on the other end. "Who is this?" they ask.

"This is Shimon."

More silence, then, "Okay, Shimon. Move! Move!"

The engines start. Now we have our own thunder. It is not even three o'clock. It is the right time; they've caught us at the right time. The soldiers are not slow in mounting the half-tracks. They sound of our roaring engines has magnified them and they *jump* in. The young drivers race the engines, as they always do.

For a magnificent half minute, we stare into the north light, smiling. The man who tasted the sweet taste of his wife kisses his wrist. The young soldiers are no longer afraid, and the married men are in a perfect sustained fury. Because they love their wives and children, they will not think of them until the battle is over. Now we are soldiers again. The engines are deafening. No longer are we held back. We are shaking; we are crying. Now we stare into the north light, and listen to the explosions below. Now we hear the levers of the gearshifts. Now our drivers exhale and begin to drive. Now we are moving.

Source

"North Light" appears in Helprin's *Ellis Island and Other Stories* (New York: Harvest, 1981): 63–67.

Suggestions for Further Reading

In addition to his many commentaries published in *The Wall Street Journal*, *The New York Times*, and many other publications, Mark Helprin's work includes the following:

Novels

A Soldier of the Great War. New York: Harcourt Brace, Jovanovich, 1991.
Freddy and Fredericka. New York: Penguin, 2005.
Refiner's Fire. New York: Alfred A. Knopf, 1977.

Winter's Tale. New York: Harcourt Brace, Jovanovich, 1983.

Short Story Collections

A Dove of the East and Other Stories. New York: Alfred A. Knopf, 1975.

Ellis Island and Other Stories., New York: Delacorte Press/Seymour Lawrence, 1981.

The Pacific and Other Stories. New York: Penguin Press, 2004.

Illustrated Tales

A City in Winter. New York: Viking, 1996.

Swan Lake. Boston: Houghton Mifflin, 1989.

The Veil of Snows. New York: Viking, 1997.

About the Author

Mark McWilliams, Associate Professor of English at the United States Navel Academy, earned his doctorate from the University of Virginia and specializes in the literature and culture of nineteenth-century America. He lives with his wife and two children in Severna Park, Maryland.

50

Tonight we make a Difference: CAPT Ron Howard's Address to the Crew of the John F. Kennedy (CV 67)

Dr. Joseph J. Thomas

Perhaps the most important words a commander will ever utter are the words spoken to subordinates about to go into harm's way. In addresses of this nature, simple, poignant statements are typically the most remembered and beloved. CAPT Ron Howard, Commanding Officer of the carrier *USS John F. Kennedy*, captured the thoughts of a nation in his compelling message kicking off offensive operations into Afghanistan on March 10, 2002.

* * *

Good evening onboard John F Kennedy, Carrier Air Wing SEVEN, and Carrier Air Wing SEVEN, and Carrier Group Six. We are currently proceeding at best speed to our launch point for tonight's strikes, off the coast of Pakistan, nearly 700 miles south of our targets in Afghanistan.

At midnight, CVW 7 will launch into the dark night, and strike their first blows of Operation Enduring Freedom, the war on terrorism. For us this is a culminating point in space, a culminating point in time, and a culminating point in history.

Our enemy is a group of religious fanatics, who pervert the peace of Islam and twist its meaning to justify the murder of thousands of innocents at the Twin Towers of New York, at the Pentagon, and in a field in Pennsylvania. They hate us and attack us because they oppose all that is good about America. They hate us because we are prosperous. They hate us because we are tolerant. They hate us because we are happy. Mostly, they hate us because we are free and because we will "pay any price, bear any burden, meet any hardship, support any friend or oppose any foe to assure the survival and success of liberty." Make no mistake—this is fight for Western Civilization. If these monsters are not destroyed they will destroy us, and our children and children's children will live in fear forever.

America is the only nation that can stop them and destroy them. Only America has the strength of character and the vast resources to hunt these fanatics down anywhere in the world. We have friends and Allies but we are the leaders of the world our forefathers made and died for. Our Naval power has been the principal weapon of our resolve. Great ships and great crews have gone before us—ENTERPRISE, CARL VINSON, KITTY HAWK, TEDDY ROOSEVELT, JOHN STENNIS. Tonight, our enemies will feel the power of USS JOHN F KENNEDY.

It is now our turn to strike for justice and we will strike hard. Millions of Americans wish they could be here tonight with us. They saw the Twin Towers fall, and watched helplessly, wanting to do something to defend America and our way of life. For us tonight, that wait and that helplessness are over. We have reached the point where we are all part of something so much greater than ourselves. For the rest of our lives, no matter whether we stay in the Navy or move on to civilian life, no matter what we do or where we go, we will remember that on 10 March 2002, we came together and struck a blow for freedom.

All of us are volunteers. Most of us joined the Navy to serve our country and better ourselves. Tonight and in the nights to come we are given the opportunity of a lifetime, a chance to truly make a difference in the world. Our namesake John F. Kennedy wrote that "a single person can make a difference, and every person should try." Tonight, WE make a difference! We represent America in all its power and diversity. We are men and women, rich and poor, black and white, and all colors of the human rainbow. We are Christian, Jew, and yes, Muslim. WE ARE AMERICA.

This war will not be short, pleasant, or easy. It has already required the sacrifice of our firefighters, our policemen, our soldiers, our Sailors, our airmen, and our Marines. More sacrifices will be made. In the end we will win, precisely because we are those things that the terrorists hate—prosperous, happy, tolerant, and most of all, free.

Those Americans who wish they could be here with us are, in fact, here with us in spirit. Never before in American history has our nation been so completely unified and resolute in purpose. Every one of them is cheering us on, praying for our safety and our success. Our families are behind us 100%.

We will not let them down. We are, and will be, men and women of honor, courage, and commitment. I believe, as Abraham Lincoln said, that "America is the last, best hope for the world". Tonight we hold a shining beacon of that hope. We shall keep it burning brightly.

Stay sharp. Stay focused. Stay safe. Use the training that has made you the best Sailors in the world, the best Sailors in the history of the world.

Trust in your faith, and in your shipmates. God bless us all, and God bless America.

Suggested Readings

Benjamin, Daniel, ed. *America and the World in theAge of Terror: a New Landscape in International Relations.* Washington, D.C.: CSIS Press, Center for Strategic and International Studies, 2005.

Davis, John, ed. *The Global War on Terrorism: Assessing the American Response.* New York: Nova Science Publishers, 2005.

51

We Go to Liberate: LtCol Tim Collins' Address to the Royal Irish Guards

Dr. Joseph J. Thomas

Those of us who have worked with the British have often envied their command of the language. British military leaders seem to "turn a phrase" more elegantly, more effectively than we Americans seem often able to do. LtCol Collins of the Irish Guards sends his forces off on March 22, 2003 with Shakespearean grace, while keeping the message clear and concise. Of all the political rhetoric and lofty speechmaking surrounding Operation Iraqi Freedom, it is of interest that a cigar smoking field grade officer with "the air of a Rambo but the literary touch of Rimbaud" gives us the most lasting imagery of the very purpose of the war. Collins' speech was reprinted in the *London Times* along with a photo of its author, cigar clenched in teeth. His words drew comparisons to Lincoln's *Gettysburg Address* and Churchill's towering war speeches.

* * *

We go to liberate not to conquer. We will not fly our flags in their country . . .

We are entering Iraq to free a people and the only flag which will be flown in that ancient land is their own. Show respect for them . . .

There are some who are alive at this moment who will not be alive shortly. Those who do not wish to go on that journey, we will not send.

As for the others I expect you to rock their world. Wipe them out if that is what they choose. But if you are ferocious in battle remember to be magnanimous in victory.

Iraq is steeped in history. It is the site of the Garden of Eden, of the Great Flood and the birthplace of Abraham. Tread lightly there.

You will see things that no man could pay to see and you will have to go a long way to find a more decent, generous and upright people than the Iraqis.

You will be embarrassed by their hospitality even though they have nothing.

Don't treat them as refugees for they are in their own country. Their children will be poor, in years to come they will know that the light of liberation in their lives was brought by you.

If there are casualties of war then remember that when they woke up and got dressed in the morning they did not plan to die this day.

Allow them dignity in death. Bury them properly and mark their graves.

We will put them in their sleeping bags and send them back. There will be no time for sorrow.

The enemy should be in no doubt that we are his nemesis and that we are bringing about his rightful destruction.

There are many regional commanders who have stains on their souls and they are stoking the fires of hell for Saddam.

He and his forces will be destroyed by this coalition for what they have done. As they die they will know their deeds have brought them to this place. Show them no pity.

It is a big step to take another human life. It is not to be done lightly.

I know of men who have taken life needlessly in other conflicts, I can assure you they live with the mark of Cain upon them.

If someone surrenders to you then remember they have that right in international law and ensure that one day they go home to their family.

The ones who wish to fight, well, we aim to please.

If you harm the regiment or its history by over enthusiasm in killing or in cowardice, know it is your family who will suffer.

You will be shunned unless your conduct is of the highest for your deeds will follow you down through history. We will bring shame on neither our uniform or our nation.

It is not a question of if, it's a question of when. We know he has already devolved the decision to lower commanders, and that means he has already taken the decision himself. If we survive the first strike we will survive the attack.

As for ourselves, let's bring everyone home and leave Iraq a better place for us having been there. Our business now is north.

Suggested Readings

Keegan, John. *The Iraq War.* New York: A.A. Knopf, 2004.

Walker, Martin. *The Iraq War as Witnessed by the Correspondents and Photographers of United Press International.* Washington, D.C.: Brassey's, 2004.

52

Bear any Burden, Pay any Price, to Preserve our Freedoms: Judge William Young's Sentencing of "Shoe Bomber" Richard Reid

Dr. Joseph J. Thomas

U.S. District Court Judge William Young captured the spirit of much of America in "facing down terrorism" when he sentenced British citizen and recent convert to radical Islamic fundamentalism Richard Reid. Judge Young's obvious resolve struck a chord with the American people. His sentencing of Reid bears all the great marks of effective speechmaking: it is emotional, simple, evocative language; it contains tough words for tough times; it reflects the resolute nature of the American people in time of war.

Mr. Richard C. Reid, hearken now to the sentence the Court imposes upon you.

On counts 1, 5 and 6 the Court sentences you to life in prison in the custody of the United States Attorney General.

On counts 2, 3, 4 and 7, the Court sentences you to 20 years in prison on each count, the sentence on each count to run consecutive with the other.

That's 80 years.

On count 8 the Court sentences you to the mandatory 30 years consecutive to the 80 years just imposed.

The Court imposes upon you each of the eight counts a fine of $250,000 for the aggregate fine of $2 million.

The Court accepts the government's recommendation with respect to restitution and orders restitution in the amount of $298.17 to Andre Bousquet and $5,784 to American Airlines.

The Court imposes upon you the $800 special assessment.

The Court imposes upon you five years supervised release simply because the law requires it.

But the life sentences are real life sentences so I need go no further.

This is the sentence that is provided for by our statutes. It is a fair and just sentence. It is a righteous sentence. Let me explain this to you.

We are not afraid of you or any of your terrorist co-conspirators, Mr. Reid. We are Americans. We have been through the fire before. There is all too much war talk here. And I say that to everyone with the utmost respect.

Here in this court, where we deal with individuals as individuals, and care for individuals as individuals, as human beings, we reach out for justice.

You are not an enemy combatant. You are a terrorist. You are not a soldier in any war. You are a terrorist. To give you that reference, to call you a soldier, gives you far too much stature.

Whether it is the officers of government who do it or your attorney who does it, or that happens to be your view, you are a terrorist.

And we do not negotiate with terrorists. We do not treat with terrorists.

We do not sign documents with terrorists. We hunt them down one by one and bring them to justice.

So war talk is way out of line in this court. You are a big fellow. But you are not that big. You're no warrior. I know warriors. You are a terrorist. A species of criminal guilty of multiple attempted murders.

In a very real sense, State Trooper Santiago had it right when you first were taken off that plane and into custody and you wondered where the press and where the TV crews were, and he said you're no big deal.

You're no big deal.

What your counsel, what your able counsel, and what the equally able United States attorneys have grappled with and what I have as honestly as I know how tried to grapple with, is why you did something so horrific.

What was it that led you here to this courtroom today? I have listened respectfully to what you have to say. And I ask you to search your heart and ask yourself what sort of unfathomable hate led you to do what you are guilty and admit you are guilty of doing. And I have an answer for you. It may not satisfy you. But as I search this entire record, it comes as close to understanding as I know.

It seems to me you hate the one thing that is most precious. You hate our freedom. Our individual freedom. Our individual freedom to live as we choose, to come and go as we choose, to believe or not believe as we individually choose.

Here, in this society, the very winds carry freedom. They carry it everywhere from sea to shining sea.

It is because we prize individual freedom so much that you are here in this beautiful courtroom. So that everyone can see, truly see that justice is administered fairly, individually, and discretely.

It is for freedom's sake that your lawyers are striving so vigorously on your behalf and have filed appeals, will go on in their, their representation of you before other judges. We are about it. Because we all know that the way we treat you, Mr. Reid, is the measure of our own liberties. Make no mistake though. It is yet true that we will bear any burden, pay any price, to preserve our freedoms.

Look around this courtroom. Mark it well. The world is not going to long remember what you or I say here. Day after tomorrow it will be forgotten. But this, however, will long endure. Here in this courtroom and courtrooms all across America, the American people will gather to see that justice, individual justice, justice, not war, individual justice is in fact being done.

The very President of the United States through his officers will have to come into courtrooms and lay out evidence on which specific matters can be judged, and juries of citizens will gather to sit and judge that evidence democratically, to mold and shape and refine our sense of justice.

See that flag, Mr. Reid? That's the flag of the United States of America. That flag will fly there long after this is all forgotten. That flag stands for freedom. You know it always will.

Custody Officer, stand him down.

Suggested Readings

Benjamin, Daniel, ed. *America and the World in the Age of Terror: a New Landscape in International Relations*. Washington, D.C.: CSIS Press, Center for Strategic and International Studies, 2005.

Davis, John, ed. *The Global War on Terrorism: Assessing the American Response*. New York: Nova Science Publishers, 2005.

53

Mission Orders: Col John Allen's Commandant's Intent

BGen John R. Allen, USMC

Commandant's Intent
COL John R. Allen, USMC
Commandant of Midshipmen

Enduring Intent Commander's intent creates a common vision for an organization and binds it with a unity of purpose. Intent defines the essence of the leadership of the commander and provides scope and direction to those bound by its provisions. Intent is the fastest; most secure, and most immediate means of communication, for it does not rely on electronic transfer or some other mechanism of transmission. Intent, properly and completely expressed, provides subordinate commanders the general guidance necessary for the exercise of their leadership and discretion, but does not stifle initiative. My intent, as expressed in this document, relies for its success on a common vision among the midshipmen, faculty and staff of the Naval Academy. It rests upon an explicit understanding of the mission of the Academy and an implicit acceptance of the high principles which define the officer corps of the naval service. In this way, my intent is enduring, for it rests on a foundation of commitment.

Faithfulness to higher . . . the substance of lower *For a commander's intent to be successful, it must derive from and be faithful to the intent of senior commanders and institutional objectives and values. My intent represents my leadership principles and values, but derives from the mission of the United States Naval Academy:*

To develop midshipmen morally, mentally and physically and to imbue them with the highest ideals of duty, honor and loyalty in order to provide graduates who are dedicated to a career of naval service and have potential for future development in mind and character to assume the highest responsibilities of command, citizenship and government.

My intent also closely reflects the vision of the Superintendent as expressed in the Strategic Plan:

Provide leaders of great character, competence, vision and drive to transform the Navy and Marine Corps and serve the nation in a century of promise and uncertainty

These twin pillars provide the framework and context within which we will move forward in the development of the midshipmen of the Brigade. My intent also borrows from the vision and operating concepts of both the Dean of Academics and the Director of Athletics, bringing a unity of purpose to our efforts.

Subordinate intent within the Brigade should flow from and reflect this statement, and while it embodies the essence of the individual leadership of subordinates, it remains faithful to the precepts of my intent expressed herein.

The Commission There is no greater demonstration of the trust of the Republic than in its expression and bestowal of an officer's commission. The commission itself is sworn to before God in a manner exactly as our forbears swore to place their blades in the service of high moral principle. Today, the oath of office, the essence of the commission, elicits from each officer a solemn promise of commitment to uphold a set of principles enshrined in the Constitution of the United States of America. It is a total commitment.

"I do solemnly swear that I will support and defend the Constitution of the United States against all enemies foreign and domestic and I will bear true faith and allegiance to the same. That I take this obligation freely, without any mental reservation or purpose of evasion and I will well and faithfully discharge the duties of the office upon which I am about to enter so help me God."

Only a very few are selected for the privilege of a commission and its conferment takes on great personal and institutional commitment—commitment that runs the spectrum from daily execution of orders to, if necessary, the supreme

sacrifice. In 1950, there emerged a book still found today in our libraries, the *Armed Forces Officer*. In this first edition, the author, S. L. A. Marshall, attempted to convey the profound deference of the nation that attends the award of a commission:

"Other than the officer corps, there is no group within our society toward which the obligation of the nation is more fully expressed. Even so, other Americans regard this fact with pride, rather than with envy. They accept the principle that some unusual advantage should attend exceptional and unremitting responsibility. Whatever path an American officer may walk, the officer enjoys prestige. Though little is known of the officer's intrinsic merit, the officer will be given the respect of fellow citizens, unless that officer proves to be utterly undeserving."

The phrase "exceptional and unremitting responsibility" captures the essence of the prestige accorded the officer. No other position in American life carries with it so immediate a rendering of personal commitment and the potential for sacrifice. The expected demands on an officer are truly *exceptional*, not only in terms of individual commitment, but also in the reality that in no other walk of life . . . in no other profession . . . will the immediate consequences of one's orders have mortal effect on those who are the led. The officers of the naval service give orders that may send Sailors or Marines to their deaths or may demand Sailors or Marines take the life of another human being. This is the essence of the "exceptional" nature of the commission, and is the profound extension and unique province of the duties of an officer. But demands of and on an officer are also great; the weight of this kind of responsibility is constant, and it compounds with rank and responsibility. The weight of the commission is, then, *unremitting*, and demands a moral and spiritual endurance uncommonly found among the citizenry of the nation. The demands of leadership in war, the ultimate role of an officer of the naval service, will exact a high price from officers as they discharge their exceptional and unremitting responsibilities. Here is found our obligation to develop midshipmen morally.

Orientation on combat Simply put, our orientation at the Naval Academy should focus on creating an officer capable of operating in and withstanding the demands of leading Sailors and Marines in combat. It is far easier . . . and far better . . . for us to visualize the nature and the complexities of combat and work backward from there to Bancroft Hall, the playing field, and the classroom. If combat is our polestar in all we say and do in the preparation of the midshipmen, then so much else is immediately revealed about what we stand for and how we will operate within the Brigade of Midshipmen. The midshipmen must understand and embrace the concept that the culture of the Brigade flows from this orientation alone. This, then, places much of the culture of the Brigade into immediate and sharp focus, and the imperative will immediately become obvious for the proper treatment of fellow midshipmen, and to demonstrate, at a cultural level, loyalty, respect, dignity, and proper human relations. The truth of battle, the relentless demands on the human soul in combat, provide clear context and ample evidence for defining the culture of the Brigade. Here we will provide constant emphasis.

The Midshipman as a public figure Every midshipman is a public figure in the fullest sense of the term. In accepting an appointment as a midshipman in the United States Navy, these young men and women have assumed the mantle of and obligation for the highest professional and moral conduct. The Brigade, and the midshipmen who populate its ranks, stand a breed apart . . . they are special. The American people have simply come to expect more from the midshipmen of the Brigade. They have an implicit trust and explicit expectation midshipmen stand for something admirable, something worthy of emulation. The father of our Navy, John Paul Jones gave voice to this expectation in his expression of the qualifications of a naval officer. These words, though two centuries old, have never rung more true, and provide a roadmap for our own efforts in creating officers of the Naval Service:

It is by no means enough that an officer of the Navy should be a capable mariner. He must be that of course, but also a great deal more. He should be as well a gentleman of refined manners, punctilious courtesy, and the nicest sense of personal honor.

He should be the soul of tact, patience, firmness and charity. No meritorious act of a subordinate should escape his attention or be left to pass with its reward, even if the reward is only a word of approval. Conversely he should not be blind to a single fault in any subordinate, though at the same time he should be quick to distinguish error from malice, thoughtlessness from incompetency, and well-meant short coming for heedless or stupid blunder. In one word, every commander should keep constantly before him the great truth, that to be well obeyed, he must be perfectly esteemed.

These higher qualities are our bond with the American people—the mothers and fathers of America—who go to their rest each night content their precious children are being led and served by officers, graduates of the Naval Academy, who stand for something as ladies and gentlemen. There is no disconnect between the calling of the profession of arms and a lifetime of dedicated service and selflessness as a lady or a gentleman. Indeed, the very term "officer and a gentleman" is a most perfect union and illustration of the reality of war and the necessity that it be prosecuted by men and women of the highest morale principle. For war, unconstrained by honor and high moral principle, is quickly reduced to murder, mayhem, and all the basest tendencies of mankind.

Shakespeare's magnificent play *Henry V* is a remarkable distillation of the highest qualities of officership, and is remembered today among the officers of the naval service primarily for Harry's "band of brothers" soliloquy on the morning of the Battle of Agincourt. There is, however, an earlier testament by Harry during the siege of Harflew where Harry the King (Henry the V) truly lays out the uniqueness of the officer. As the initial English assault on the breach of the French battlement of Harflew fails; Harry exhorts his countrymen with these lines:

Once more into the breach dear friends,
    once more;
    Or close the wall up with our English
    dead.
In peace there's nothing so becomes a man
    As modest stillness and humility;
But when the blast of war blows in our ears,
    Then imitate the action of the tiger;
Stiffen the sinews, conjure up the blood,
Disguise fair nature with hard-favor'd rage;
    Then lend the eye a terrible aspect. . . .

Shakespeare's intent here is obvious. The nature of the officer in peace is enduring, it survives intact the ravages and dynamics of battle. "*Modest stillness* and *humility*," the wonderful, traditional defining characteristics of an officer of the naval service do not change during emergency, they still closely govern the soul of the warrior. But, there will assuredly come the time when our leadership will be tested in crisis or war. Here, we will not . . . we will never . . . discard the higher qualities of what defines the officer corps, and what defines us as ladies and gentlemen. *Imitate* the action of the tiger . . . *disguise* fair nature with hard favor'd rage" . . . *lend* the eye a terrible aspect. The horror of battle and the base, primordial nature of combat can quickly overwhelm the civilized sensibilities of its participants. Here, the officer corps, leading

from the front, masters at arms in the traditional sense, never departs the gentle nature of who we are. And here, the future of the officer corps, our precious midshipmen, learns from our own lifestyles in Bancroft Hall, and in the classrooms, and on the playing fields of the Naval Academy. Here, through our own precept and example, we provide the midshipmen the certainty of the counterbalance and the restraining influence they must become and they must master to effectively lead their Sailors and Marines through the many ugly realities of war.

Character as a function of combat leadership The great force multiplier in combat is character . . . not technology . . . not numbers . . . but character. Character is the foundation of decision making in combat. Character underlies courage in its most profound sense. While there may be some debate on the exact definition of character there can be no doubt what we must do. A man or woman of character is one whose existence rests upon a solid moral foundation. This foundation sustains the officer during the greatest trials and crises and will provide the crucial moral orientation for decision making at the moment of greatest need. In World War One, a British surgeon on the Western Front, Lord Moran, closely observed the prosecution of the war. He was profoundly moved by the willingness and readiness of the soldiers to sacrifice their all on behalf of the officers who led them. He would conclude these soldiers endured so much because of their certainty in the moral authority of their young officers to lead them, a certainty flowing from their perceptions of the character of the officers. In his landmark book *Anatomy of Courage*, Lord Moran would say of character:

Courage can be judged apart from danger only if the social significance and meaning of courage is known to us, namely that a man of character in peace becomes a man of courage in war. He cannot be selfish in peace and yet be unselfish in war. Character as Aristotle taught is a habit, the daily choice of right instead of wrong; it is a moral quality which grows to maturity in peace and is not suddenly developed on the outbreak of war. For war, in spite of much that we have heard to the contrary, has no power to transform, it merely exaggerates the good and evil that are in us, till it is plain for all to read; it cannot change it exposes. Man's fate in battle is worked out before war begins. For his acts in war are dictated not by courage, nor by fear, but by conscience, of which war is the final test. The man whose quick conscience is the secret of his success in battle has the same clear cut feelings about right and wrong before war makes them obvious to all. If you know a man in peace, you know him in war.

A great combat leader of World War Two was once asked his view on the meaning of character. Without hesitation, he said character was the determining factor in an officer's ability to make a decision. The stronger the character, the greater the proclivity to decide . . . to act . . . to do the right thing, regardless of the potential consequences. Importantly, we know a large part of character is integrity. Deriving from the Latin *integritas*, integrity . . . *integritas* . . . symbolized the soundness of the armor plate covering the breasts of the Legionnaires of the Roman Empire. With integrity, all was possible in battle and all was whole. Absent integrity, there was vulnerability; indeed, there would be a "disintegrity" or disintegration. Integrity, then, is that unfailing trait that above all others, the Sailors and Marines of our Naval service demand of their officers. These young Sailors and Marines will never give voice to this absolute demand, they will simply and innocently expect it of us. Absent integrity, an officer has no moral authority to lead.

The reality of war . . . human factors *Human factors dominate war and have most frequently been decisive in determining success or failure in battle. Fear, fatigue, and other emotional and physical crises will be central to our study of and preparation for the prospect of war. As well, death, dying, and killing are the common wages of combat, and have a dramatic impact on both unit cohesion and the individual officer. These effects we know to be substantial; they are often immediate and remorseless, and they cannot be discounted or dismissed. We must do everything in our capacity to equip the midshipmen with a clear understanding of the peculiar nature of human factors and their centrality to battle outcomes. There will not be a single action or battle which we will study or in which we will serve during our careers where the outcome was or is not, to some extent, decided by human factors. The strengths and the limitations on humanity in war are felt by both sides, as opponents will both feel fear . . . both endure mind numbing fatigue . . . both deal with limitations and the frailties of physical conditions. Thus, the seeds of victory or defeat are carried within us at all times. We can exploit them, or be subject to them. The officer who understands the human factors inherent in combat operations will reduce the vulnerabilities of his or her own Sailors or Marines, while exploiting the same limitations within the opponent.*

Combat Conditioning. War exacts great personal sacrifice from the officers of the naval service. Preparing for this sacrifice requires that we learn to live to be ready at all times to lead at the point of impact. If we are ready for this moment of truth, we will be ready for all else. Combat conditioning is consistent with our orientation on combat and our focus on human factors in war. Combat conditioning brings home the reality of combat in our own personal preparation for the moment of truth and spans comprehensive, inextricably linked moral, intellectual, and physical preparations. The midshipmen must understand their moral obligation . . . their duty . . . their personal commitment to combat conditioning.

At the moral level, the midshipmen must understand the centrality of the role of character, integrity, and ethics in the demands of leading Sailors and Marines at the point of impact. I am not interested in teaching any of these concepts to the midshipmen in order to make them good midshipmen; I am interested in our preparing them to be ready for commissioned service and their leadership responsibilities for war. If we do this properly, they'll become exceptional midshipmen as they confront the reality and the enormity of their duty.

Intellectual conditioning provides a clear and

abiding understanding of the human factors of war, but it also, more importantly, lights a flame of lifelong and habitual *fascination* with the study of the profession of arms oriented on the penetrating and abiding reading and analysis of military history. Once oriented on an unambiguous commitment to personal professional development, midshipmen will be more ready for that moment of truth at the point of impact.

Finally, at a physical level, combat conditioning links the mind, the soul, and the body in complete readiness for the ravages of war. Where the mind ends and body begins is a point we do not fully understand. But the fact they are interrelated is well known, and the conditioning of the body enhances the ability of the mind to resist the psychological toll and mental burden of leadership. We know from personal experience and from our study of history, most of the decision making imperative for young officers in crisis and in combat comes on the verge of physical exhaustion. The ability to withstand these effects is a direct function of conditioning both at an individual and team level. We know fatigue and sleep deprivation are the harbingers of fear. We also know well-conditioned warriors are inherently better able to resist the onset of fear or the psychological dislocation that accompanies the friction and unknowns of a battlefield. War exposes weakness in all its forms. It exposes the fault lines in our preparations. We must paint the picture of the totality of combat conditioning and the duty of midshipmen to think in these terms and their obligations . . . indeed their sacred and inherent duty . . . to understand and grasp this concept.

The Brigade and its spirit The word *inspiration* derives from theology and implies the act of inspiring someone has the effect of filling that person with the Holy Spirit. Today the word is used differently, but no less importantly, to connote a person or an organization seized with and animated by an inner motivation. For far too long, the spirit of the Brigade has implicitly been a function of one or more sports teams. This is too narrow a definition of the spirit of the Brigade of Midshipmen. We must elevate the spirit of the Brigade to the level of the institution and the naval service and create leverage and synergy from the legacy of the Naval Academy and the naval service. Here, I ask we exploit of the "silent messages" within the Yard to illustrate and give voice and form to the idea of the higher spirit for the Brigade. "Don't give up the ship." "Take her down!" "Non Sibi Sed Patriae," Memorial Hall, the John Paul Jones Crypt, etc., etc. Here there is high moral principle. Here there is sacrifice. Here there is unity of purpose. And here there can be agreement and unanimity by all midshipmen on what this institution stands for and its central role in the naval service and the defense of America. The spirit of the Brigade should be oriented here . . . should flow from here . . . and not be permitted to slip or to be concentrated on lesser, narrower issues, except insofar as we consciously elect to focus our spirit for specific events. That said, we must also be part of the spirit of the Brigade; we must also by word and deed, inspire . . . *to fill with the spirit* . . . the midshipmen. Our own acts, in consonance with the silent messages mentioned above, provide verification of the spirit we seek to imbue in the midshipmen. If we are able to create a spirit based upon high moral principle and grounded on the realities of our naval heritage, virtually every other dimension of the growth and development of the Brigade will follow.

Duty and accountability One of the greatest contributions we can make to the development of the midshipmen is imbuing them with the concept of duty. It is at once a function and a privilege. Never will we assign duty as punishment, for the accomplishment of duty is a statement of trust. Those who stand duty have been tested, evaluated, been observed, and have been found worthy to be accorded the privilege of standing and receiving the responsibilities inherent in this function. Duty in the functional connotation, is an achievement, and thus is never punitive. Duty as a concept is one of the highest pinnacles of commitment we can hope to convey to the midshipmen. Of all our American military figures, the man for whom duty took on nearly spiritual meaning was General Robert E. Lee. Of duty, he wrote his son:

> "Duty then is the sublimest word in our language. Do your duty in all things.... You cannot do more, you should never wish to do less."

I use the term "spiritual" intentionally because I want to convey the idea of sacred commitment in the concept of *duty*. The ship's captain who, though wounded, will not quit the bridge. The pilot who drives on inexorably on the target, though the ground fire is thick and almost certainly deadly. The Marine lieutenant who presses the attack at the cost of his life. The submarine skipper on the bridge, wounded and dying, whose final order to the crew is "take her down!" These are manifestations of officers doing their duty. Few experiences can be more poignant in gaining this understanding than a visit to Memorial Hall, which enshrines the names of our honored dead—graduates who did their duty as they were given the light to see their cause, and who perished in the endeavor. From the Bible, we know the passage "From everyone who has been given much, much will be required; and to whom they entrusted much, of him they will ask all the more" (Luke 12:48). There can be almost no more perfect manner of teaching duty than by emphasizing that the traits selflessness, sacrifice, servitude, and humility contribute most to doing one's duty. Beyond living these qualities ourselves every day—and very visibly—in front of our midshipmen, we must teach them duty; this runs the gamut from personal uniform preparations, to academic steadfastness, to making hard moral decisions, to a willingness to sacrifice.

The mentor and the protégé *There can be no more personal relationship . . . no more valuable relationship . . . at the Naval Academy than that of the mentor and the protégé. American military history is punctuated with examples of great mentor relationships: Fox Connor with young Dwight Eisenhower,* *and George Marshall with Albert C. Wedemeyer are but two. Connor and Marshall both took young officers under their wings and produced two of the most influential officers of World War II. I strongly encourage the mentor/protégé relationship. We know it cannot be forced. The relationship grows from personal admiration and is based both on a desire to teach and instruct by the mentor, and a desire to grow and learn by the protégé. I encourage the development of this relationship whenever and wherever possible.*

Upon the fields of friendly strife . . . *Sports and sporting competition are two of the most important endeavors carried on at the Naval Academy. Indeed, the importance of sports in the preparation of officers for war once prompted Douglas MacArthur to observe:*

> "Upon the fields of friendly strife are sown the seeds that on other days and on other fields will reap the fruits of victory."

Here, at Annapolis, on the fields of friendly strife, midshipmen will observe and learn leadership in adversity, the power of cohesion in small units, and the imperative of continuing on under conditions of duress, pain, and loss. Here too will be the opportunity to learn the high moral principle of sportsmanship, and this must be a one of our points of greatest emphasis and instruction in all our sports endeavors. The midshipmen must be taught the lessons of humility and graciousness in victory, and courage, forbearance, and endurance in defeat. There is no room for arrogance in the personality of a serving officer, but arrogance can sometimes be the stepchild of victory. Arrogance blinds the officer to failing, and often results in complacency or in overlooking weakness. Wherever possible we must seek to eradicate, or at least diminish, the negative effects arrogance, for over time, arrogance almost certainly results in defeat.

The Officer Representatives (O-Reps) are vital to the process and success of athletics at the Naval Academy. The O-Rep is my direct representative to the team, and in this sense represents and advocates the standards of the Naval

Academy to the team. These standards include, but are not limited to, academic performance and study, personal appearance and uniform wear, and conduct and honor. As well, sports teams tend to have their own cultures deriving in large part from the popular cultures that surround so many of the sports in the civilian sector. The O-Rep is directly responsible for managing the culture of his or her sport to ensure its congruence with the paramount and preeminent culture at USNA: that of the naval service. The O-Rep will be vigilant in this role, and will act carefully to ensure it remains so.

The Four Class System Wherever possible, we must seek to enhance, strengthen, and reinforce the four class system. The publication "Waypoints" best describes the various echelons of responsibility and achievement we seek in the class distinctions. In general, this is my guidance for the implementation of the four class system: The fourth class year is one of transition where Plebes emerge from the state of imposed discipline to the essentials and reality of self discipline. In this metamorphosis is the secret of success for the remaining three years as a midshipman and for the future as an officer. The strongest character is grounded in self discipline and the maturation of the fourth class midshipmen in this area must receive great emphasis. Third class midshipmen are gaining strength and initiative. During this year, and in the aftermath of fourth class year, they are seeking to establish equilibrium with their grades and professional development. The third class are the mentors of the Plebes. In the aggregate, the second class are the holders and keepers of the standards of the Brigade and are the engine for the development of the fourth class. Finally, the first class are in their final throes of preparation for a commission. We must place their continued development as the number one priority. Serving as officers, the first class lead the Brigade.

The distinctions between and among the classes are a matter of degree, and should be grounded at all times in the attainment of re-

sponsibility, increased duty, and the final, professional preparations for departure from the Naval Academy, to assume leadership positions in the naval service. While greater seniority carries increased privilege, we should do all we can to minimize the natural pursuit of privilege and emphasize the attainment of responsibility. Our clear message to the Brigade should be that increased seniority carries with it increased servitude, increased humility, and increased self-sacrifice. We MUST teach the midshipmen privilege is an irrelevant side benefit to greater responsibility.

Personal Professional Development *In his record of the Peloponnesian Wars, Thucydides is reputed to have observed:*

"That [state] which separates its scholars from its warriors will have its thinking done by cowards, and its fighting done by fools"

Our country cannot afford to separate its thinkers from it warriors, and thus we will study and grow together as a group of warrior scholars. The two principal directions we will pursue in our professional development will be in the areas of education and training theory, intended to assist in the continued development of the midshipmen, and professional military education geared to prepare the members of the staff for future and long term duty in the naval service. I seek to create in the members of the staff a fascination for learning the profession of arms . . . to acquire a 5000 year old mind . . . through a dedicated and abiding reading of military history. What do I mean by the 5000 year old mind? Some years ago, I was fortunate to know one of the great living American historians, Professor Jay Luvaas, a scholar of the American Civil War. In our discussions about professional reading he observed the entire march and evolution of military history written over the last 5000 years of the recorded history of Western Civilization is laid bare at the feet of the warrior scholar. War and its many component factors . . . in particular the human factors of war and the challenges of command in combat . . . are recorded through the eyes of enumerable participants and historians. When consumed by the student of the profession, each book read contributes in some manner . . . large or small . . . to the memories of the student. These second hand memories compound and build until the student finds it difficult to distinguish between actual personal experience and the memories created vicariously through reading. In essence, Professor Luvaas contended, while it is impossible to do anything about the age of one's body, there is no reason why a student of the profession of arms cannot have a 5000 year old mind. In the course of our program of learning, each battalion team will be assigned the responsibility for one topic a month. I will do the first topic . . . a battle study of the Battle of Antietam. Following that, we will alternate between discussions of educational and training theory and the military history or doctrine discussions.

Endstate The endstate of our efforts will be a midshipman transformed over the four year journey of the Naval Academy. All the above comes now to bear on our labors to shape and prepare the young student of the profession of arms to serve as a commissioned officer in the naval service. All of the above will bring us to the ideal product of the Naval Academy depicted as follows:

> The midshipman . . . a man or woman of character, imbued with unimpeachable integrity, *honor*, and an understanding of the power of spiritual development. A man or woman of profound *moral and physical courage* for whom the Academy experience is a deep personal *commitment* to preparing for a career as a commissioned officer with the exceptional and unremitting responsibility of leading Sailors or Marines in war, peace, and in crisis. A midshipman for whom the term *duty* carries sacred meaning, and for which the midshipman is willing to endure sacrifice, personal hardship and adversity. A midshipman who is committed to lifelong learning about the profession of arms.

Suggested Readings

Dyer, Frederick H. *A Compendium of the War of the Rebellion.* New York: T. Yoseloff, 1959.

Fox, William F. *Regimental Losses in the American Civil War, 1861–1865.* Albany: Albany Publishing Co, 1889.

Simpkin, Richard E. *Race to the Swift: Thoughts on Twenty-First Century Warfare.* Washington, D.C.: Brassey's Defence, 1985.

Shakespeare, William. *Henry V.* New York: Penguin, 1968.

Thucydides. *History of the Peloponnesian War.* New York: W.W. Norton & Co., 1998.

United States Dept. of Defense. *The Armed Forces Officer.* Washington D.C.: U.S. Govt. Printing Office, 1950.

United States Marine Corps. *A Book on Books.* Washington, D.C.: U.S. Marine Corps, 1992.

United States War Dept. *The war of the Rebellion: a Compilation of the Official Records of the Union and Confederate Armies.* Washington D.C.: Govt. Printing Office, 1880-1901.

About the Author

Brigadier General Allen became the 79th Commandant of Midshipmen in January 2002, the first Marine Corps officer to serve in this position in the history of the Naval Academy. Brigadier General Allen graduated from the Naval Academy with the Class of 1976 and received a Bachelor of Science degree in Operations Analysis. He is a 1998 Distinguished Graduate of the National War College. He holds a Master of Arts degree in Government from Georgetown University, a Master of Science degree in Strategic Intelligence from the Defense Intelligence College, and a Master of Science degree in National Security Strategy from the National War College.

54

Stirring the Hearts of the Always Faithful: Col Brian "Irish" Egan's Marine Birthday Ball Address to Expeditionary Warfare Training Group (Pacific)

Dr. Joseph J. Thomas

Of all the celebratory speeches that a Marine may be called upon to deliver, there is none more important, none more sacred than the keynote speech delivered at a Marine Corps Birthday Ball. Seasoned speakers take months to prepare their notes, sweat the details, and rehearse their lines and gestures. When one is delivered effectively, it combines homage to the institution, the individuals present, those who have gone before, and guests of the celebration. To be considered a success it must be funny, irreverent, and heart-felt. To be remembered, it must contain an appeal to the inexplicable bond that characterizes and distinguishes Marines. It should contain a little cheerleading, well-meaning barbs for sister services, and a helping of abuse on our foes (past, present, or future).

There have been countless overwhelmingly successful addresses delivered in honor of the Marine Corps birthday. However, few mix all the pre-requisite ingredients for success better than Col Brian "Irish" Egan's address to the Expeditionary Warfare Training Group (Pacific) on 10 November 2002. A remarkable officer in many ways, Egan is perhaps best known for his wit and wisdoms, gregarious nature, and ability to make mundane occasions exciting. Few can match his ability to entertain Marines celebrating their collective birthday. Fewer match his unbridled love of Marines and the Marine Corps. He remains a legend deeply connected to the Corps.

*   *   *

Ladies, gentlemen, honored guests, Marines; first of all, I must tell you that I am deeply moved and honored to have been asked to speak to the Marines and sailors of Expeditionary Warfare Training Group Pacific tonight. It is also fitting that we celebrate with our Navy brethren; after all, we are the boat people. The steel of the Navy-Marine Corps team has been honed in countless fights in every clime and place. In a world of unprecedented political instability, the potential for employment of the Navy and Marine Corps team is ever present. Wherever salt water can reach, in any ocean of the world—Marines and Sailors are on-watch and ready. There will be no question that they are ready to do whatever needs to be done to protect our national interests, wherever they are threatened. I also really envy this outfit working for the likes of himself: Col Rick West and Col Jeff Powers : two men abandoned by wolves and raised by their parents...I know that he's the type of leader who I would follow into hell itself just to watch him make the devil dance!!! You know, it makes no difference where we celebrate our birthday. In a grand ballroom with a close companion by our side or in a dark, muddy foxhole in some 3rd world shithole with a match stuck in an MRE chocolate death cake, the sentiment is the same. Of course, you will agree it's always a nicer event with appropriate libations. Our gathering this evening represents that elite fraternity of citizens who has put our nation first. You have each given up your most precious commodity—your time. No one can ever give that back. [24 hours in a day, and 24 beers to a case—coincidence? I think not!] you each realize that our nation may perish because too few of our people know what freedom really costs. It doesn't come without sacrifice, often on the field of battle. In our history as a nation only 4 million Americans have earned the right to be called "Marine." In each generation the Marines have found the few, the proud, the brave. It is this brotherhood of Marines that has stood together not only in the pride of our nation's and corps's great victories, but also in the pain of death. the marine corps has been betting its honor, its mission and the collective and individual hides of its members for more than two centuries on the premise that teenaged marine privates who are as green as their field uniforms can be trusted absolutely to rise to the demands of their duty. at the cost, if necessary, of their lives. Think for a minute about the Iwo Jima Memorial in Washington DC, the most famous monument of the 20th century. The words inscribed in stone are 'un-common valor was a common virtue." it doesn't say, "it was easy. . . ."

As I look back I think of how lucky we all are to be here tonight. Many of our contemporaries are not. They never got a chance to fulfill their dreams, and it is in their memory and that of countless other Marines that we honor this evening. Despite a lot of Hollywood hoorah and hype to the contrary, the Marine Corps does not recruit rocket scientists or in monesteries, so why are we surprised that a young Marine likes to fight, raise hell and chase members of the opposite sex?

Our secret is that we can take ordinary young Americans and teach them that if they will work together and depend upon each other totally, they can work miracles. That trust, that confidence in others dependability, that sure knowledge that down in the crunch, is the individual Marines' sword and shield.

Marine drill instructors have always been masters of an unfailing alchemy which converts disoriented youths into proud, lean, self-reliant citizens—into whose hands our nation's most sensitive and critical affairs can be entrusted. Every one of us shed the vestiges of civilian life and stood bewildered on the yellow footprints and wondered what the hell we were doing, while some maniac berated our family lineage—unless you went to boot camp in San Diego, of course, where they never raise their voice. You know, at Parris Island, when we memorized the general orders, ya had to say 'em before a match burned down, but i hear tell that in San Diego they use a flashlight and wait for the batteries to run out!!!

Each generation of Marines since 1775 has faced challenges. Your generation is no exception. We Marines know when we take the oath of enlistment that the task that awaits us will not be easy. This is indeed a difficult time for our nation and our corps. Make no mistake; we are at war with an elusive and determined enemy. I spent my entire career fighting the evil empire, aka communism, and was very proud to do so.

America won that fight against a very tough opponent. It took great effort and many years of sustained vigilence and sacrifice by so many whose names we will never know. Your nation needs your skills now more than ever. This campaign will be long and arduous, and I know you will more than rise to the challenge. Old Osama, Saddam and their pecker-head running mates are gonna be in a world of hurt, that's for sure.

Believe it or not, you are all joined together on an extraordinary journey, the memory of which will last forever. There will be as many wonderful moments and great sea stories of who you were and what you did, the rules you broke, and the scams you pulled, as there are Marines on the morning report. Hell, lets admit it, some of us are just incident reports waiting for a date-time-group.

Remember:

- telling mom and dad and family that you are enlisting and seeing dad's eyes well up with unabashed pride and the look of worry come over moms face because she knows what Marines do and where her baby will be going
- the initial silence and uneasy jokes as the bus enters the MCRD gate in the middle of the night
- the first shattering look at what used to be
- open squad-bays, lined up rows of locker boxes and double-deck steel cots, and side-byside crappers because modesty is a thing of the past
- the quick flicker of time between taps and that awful sound of a metal shitcan rolling down the center of the squadbay accompanied by that awful braying of "get up, get up and lock your body!"
- feet aching from hours on the grinder, lickin and stickin and maggies drawers
- countless pushups and a strange new sound as real bullets pass close overhead
- the downright haunting beauty of cadence sung by unseen voices
- corfams on liberty in a strange new town ("how didja know I was a Marine?")

- long weary hours of field days, formations, and waiting for the word that always changes
- the smell of the inside of a GP tent on a hot afternoon
- lister bags and chow lines, and, "spread out, goddamnit!!"
- long humps at night and sleeping on cold, rocky ground, foot powder, moleskin, aching blistered feet,the soft grey light of dawn mixed with cleared throats, loud farts and wry commentary: "come on you scroungy rat bastards, time to rise and shine and behold the beauty of another grand and glorious day in our beloved Corps!"
- boot lieutenents who ain't even shaving yet and company gunnies older than dirt and harder than woodpecker lips
- the whine of rotor blades and overpowering smell of jp5; door gunners and .50 cals ready to rock and roll
- MREs, tabasco, and chocolate death cake
- the old slit trench and the joys of indoor plumbing
- understanding the pucker factor: where the more hairy the situation, the tighter your sphincter gets, the formula is: s=suction + h=hairy situation + i=interest in staying alive + t=tracers coming your way [best expressed as shit!!!]
- curious blends of monotony, tension, physical exertion and a special sort of discipline that other services can only envy.

And if all these things which we all shared, can—by some mindless logic of a witless pissant who is completely ignorant of what it's all about—be called just another job, then I don't know shit from apple butter.

In all honesty, I will not tell you that every day in the Corps is great. There are certainly peaks and valleys...not being selected for a school or promotion; seeing someone else get the command that you worked so hard for; standing at attention listening to the mournful sound of taps being played at the funeral of a close friend or brother Marine; but the peaks more than make up for any disappointment.

- being entrusted with the mantle of command
- knowing that what you are doing does affect the future of our nation, our corps and your family
- getting a Marine back on track after they step on their sword, then seeing that young Marine years later as a SNCO and knowing that you made the right call when everyone else wanted them to burn.

I am not naive, and also know the wives go through some gut wrenching feelings; mine surely has . . . when you dislike the corps for what it does to us and to you . . .

The trips that were cancelled at the 11th hour for what at the time seemed like such a bogus reason, missed birthdays, holidays and late nights just waiting for us to be secured. But that all fades into insignificance at an event such as this, when you look at the ceremony or formation and know that's your marine out there, who represents all that is right and good with America , or the pride you feel when someone actually thanks them for being a Marine and defending our way of life, or even better when someone tells you how much your Marine has meant to their spouse!!!

We all know that our corps is steeped in tradition. NCOs only need to feel the rough cloth of the "blood stripe" on their dress blue trousers which distinguishes officers and NCOs from non-rated Marines. I must also comment that Marine officers and NCOs carry a sword for what it implies rather than its use. You may not know that Marine NCOs are the only NCOs in any branch of the regular us armed forces who still have the privilege of carrying a sword. Our shared duty is to lead, and the sword best symbolizes the warrior image.

To the NCOs here this evening, you and I share a special bond enjoyed by very few. As you can see from my bio, I once held the distinguished title as a Sergeant of Marines. For that

and many other reasons, NCOs will always have a special place in my heart.

Tonight, then, we celebrate the "holy grail"—the birthday of our Corps. and the least that I can do is fill the grail with good Irish whiskey—so come on up later and see me, lads, for a bit o' Bushmills' finest.

To the Staff NCOs, I gotta tell you that you have always been my heroes. For it was a SNCO who taught me and everyone here how to be a Marine. Not an easy task. But I guess it worked! We all remember the SNCO I'm talking about—probably was our Senior DI. Hell, after all these years I still remember GySgt R.P. Hunt, who I swear at MCRD PISC in July/August, never broke a sweat and could make milk curdle just by looking at it. If he walked in right now, I'd just start bending and thrusting, because I owed him at least 1 million . . . SNCOs also carry the extremely critical responsibility of serving as the vital link between the young (or old fart) officer and the enlisted Marines in their charge. It is this unspoken relationship which is the main fabric around which our Corps is woven.

To the officers, I urge you to seek command at every opportunity. There is nothing finer that a man can do than to lead Marines. Never forget, that a commander exists only for his Marines. Take care of them and together there is nothing you cannot do.

Uniforms may change, nicknames change, budget and popular sentiment changes, but through it all, there is one abiding constant—the basic issue, raggedy-ass, do-or-die Marine. He will do damn near anything asked of him, under terrible conditions, with better results and fewer complaints than any civilized non-Marine should have reason to expect. And we, who have been privileged to lead them, make plans and execute missions based more on that one abiding constant than anything else. My god, its a presumption so grandiose and absurd that it appears almost foolhardy, except that for 227 years it has kept the wolf away from America's door.

Let me also direct some remarks to those of you on the check-to-wife program. We each owe much of who and what we are as marines to our biggest fan—our spouse, whose love, devotion and support is so important. Many Marines leave our Corps because of an unhappy spouse. I completely understand that spouses put up with a lot of crap, and frequently must endure uncertainty, hardships, and loneliness. You are the silent heroes, and should be honored this evening. We all laugh sometimes, and say that the only thing harder than being a Marine is being married to one—you all know it's true. As many of you know, USMC also means "Uncle Sam's Misguided Children!" We're hard to live with, and the Corps is a hard task master and fickle mistress who sooner or later will break your heart. So to all spouses, I say—thanks for sharing your Marine with our Corps. To the rest of the beautiful ladies here this evening, I salute your good judgment in spending some time with America's finest: a United States Marine!!

To my fellow retired and Marines who are no longer on active duty, we too have an important job ahead. I have it on good authority that we have been permanently assigned to recruiting duty. Yep, we are authorized by the CMC to interact with the youth of America so that the best and brightest continue to follow our colors. Guess that means that sea stories are authorized and, of course, they are all true!! The only difference between a fairy tale and a sea story, as we all know, is one begins with "once upon a time," and the other with "this is a no-shitter!!!"

You know that being a Marine is serious business. We're not a social club or a fraternal organization. We don't sell cookies or magazines. We're an assemblage of "warriors"—nothing more. We're in the ass-kicking business, and we do it the old fashioned way, up close and personal with a rifle and bayonet. The mere association of the word "Marine" with a crisis is an automatic source of confidence to America, and encouragement to all. We marines know that we must not only be better than everyone else, but different as well. . . . and we are!!! Marines walk down the street with that salty, audacious swagger that tells the world we are a roguishly handsome, cocky, conceited, self-centered, overbearing, mean, amphibious, sob whose sole purpose in life is to perpetrate hellacious, romping, stomping, death and destruction upon the festering sores of America's enemies around the globe . . . we now own this side of the street, and just maybe we'll come over to the other side, kick your ass, and take over that one too! Are ya listening Bin Laden!!!! !!!! And you too Sadaam Insane. We are coming, and we are very pissed, and we intend to permanently close out your health record!! Oooorah!!!

We each fought long and hard to gain the coveted title—U.S. Marine. On the day when we finally became Marines, in our hearts, a flame of devotion and fierce pride burned brightly. We should never do anything to extinguish that flame in our or any other Marine's heart. I urge you to keep that flame burning brightly. That flame will keep you warm when times are hard, and your motivation might falter. It will provide light in the darkest of nights. Use it, draw strength from it, keep it shining on your marines. Keep the feeling of being a Marine alive: the feeling of your first command; the sound of a unit humping along to the eternal rhythm that only those boots can make; the feeling of rebirth as the sun creeps up over the horizon and you await the order to move out. It's waiting in the darkness and solitude of night before jumping off in the attack; being packed in the throbbing belly of a helicopter or AMTRAC not knowing where you are going or if it will fly or float; or gazing from the deck of a gator at night on an empty sea. It's the beauty of a crimson dawn on a lonely hilltop at the far flung reaches of the empire; the loneliness of a long deployment and the joy of homecoming. It's the feeling you have when a Marine tells you that you have made a difference in his or her life. I may no longer be on active duty, but by God, I still feel that way. And if you don't, turn in your ID card to SgtMaj Jones and go on home.

I'd like to share some things i know, for what they're worth. they're just statements that need no explanation:

- focus on what's important, always try to do the right thing and do the thing right!
- don't pole vault over mouse turds.
- trust your instincts.
- if you say you will deliver . . . you had better be the world's best mailman.
- what scares me—a major who says, "I've been thinking"
  —a second lieutenant who says, "in my experience"
  —a sergeant who says; "hey sir, watch this shit"
- learn how to listen.
- accept that some days you are the pigeon; some days you are the statue.
- be for things, not against them.
- remember, the mind of the average Lance Corporal is not only crazy; it is crazier than we can imagine.
- and, finally, every day we make deposits in our subordinates' memory banks. Would your check clear, or would it be returned for insufficient funds?

Through it all, I urge you—never forget how to laugh and enjoy life. I don't trust anyone who can't laugh. That's one of my basic rules. After all, being a Marine is about as much fun as you can have with your clothes on!! See? Laughter is good for the soul!!!

While my journey through life as an active duty Marine, is over—for many of you, it's just beginning. I am not sure that I could survive as a young Marine today. My page 12 certainly wouldn't support re-enlistment, that's for damn sure, I'd have been 6105ed and gone. And for some of the stunts I have pulled and lived to tell the tale, will now get you a general court martial

and duck dinner!! Guess that's why I never got a good conduct medal!!

When I was young, not that I am old, all I worried about was staying alive to see one more sunrise. You have a lot tougher challenges: a smaller Marine Corps, its tougher to stay, slower promotions. Hell, in my day, if you could fog a mirror and hadn't murdered anyone, say, in the last week, you could re-enlist. There ain't nothing like being on the varsity. In the parade of years, surely adjutants call sounded only yesterday. And yet, seemingly at the double-time, an entire generation of Marines have passed in review. I, like you, once sat out in the audience and listened to an old fart colonel like myself philosophize on what being a Marine is all about (of course, now that I are one, colonels are a lot younger and better looking). But the message is the same: no matter where you are assigned or what MOS you carry—datadink, sparkchaser, stewburner, wiredog, buttplate, remington raider, grunt, gunbunny, rotorhead, brig rat, legal beagle, ,skivvie stacker, MP, boxkicker— what you do and how well you do it is important. Always remember that the destiny of our corps depends on each of you. For each and every one of you, are the corps. Let us then reaffirm our commitment to those values and virtues which distinguish us as Marines.

I am very angry that there are people in this nation who feel it is inappropriate to wear a flag on their lapel because they are on the news, or in a public job or public school, and don't want to offend foreign students. What a crock of crap. I pity the person who tries to remove the flag from my lapel or that of anyone else here tonight!! The stars and stripes is a symbol of all that we hold dear as Americans. If you have never been abroad, or in harm's way, and seen that flag flying upon your return, then you will never know the deep pride and honor one feels to see it wave.

History will judge us. Our enemies do not really understand who we are. We are the nation of

Mickey Mouse, Mickey Mantle, Microsoft, Monday night football and the Marines. The steel of our resolve has been forged in the heat of countless battles in every clime and place. make no mistake, we are coming . . . and we will destroy you and all that you stand for.

In closing, I would like to share with you a quote from Major Gene Duncan that best expresses what I have been trying to say:

I have grown to look upon marines as
    something sacred;
I have laughed with them and cried with
    them;
cursed them and prayed for them;
shivered and sweltered with them;
suffered with them;
fought with them, bled with them, and held
    them in my arms while they died.
I have buried them.
and all the time, I have loved them.

Thank you, and God Bless America, Semper Fi, and Happy Birthday, Marines!

Suggested Reading

Moore, William T. *The Raggedy Ass Marines*. Boonville: Gene Duncan, 1985.

Duncan, H. G. *The Birth of Clint McQuade*. Boonville: Gene Duncan, 1988.

Duncan, H. G. *Brown Side Out: More Marine Corps Sea Stories*. Lake Worth: DUBE Distributors, 1981.

Duncan, H. G. *Clint McQuade, USMC: the New Beginning*. Boonville: Gene Duncan, 1990.

Duncan, H. G. *Green Side Out: Marine Corps Sea Stories*. Blountstown: Gene Duncan Books, 1980.

Duncan, H. G. *Run in Circles*. Boonville: Gene Duncan, 1982.

Duncan, H. G. *The Second Wind: a Study in Retirement Non-Adjustment*. Blountstown: Gayle Publishers, 1987.

55

Strategic Vision: General Michael Hagee's Seabasing Speech to the US Naval Academy

Dr. Joseph J. Thomas

Great Leaders have the ability to express complex matters in simple-to-understand terms. They are able to lay out sweeping imperatives in compact sentences. In this way, effective leaders communicate messages to subordinates and drive the direction of the organizations they lead. Commandant of the Marine Corps General Mike Hagee captured the very essence of the Navy-Marine future operational concept of seabasing while at the US Naval Academy May 04, 2003.

* * *

Thank you very much.

I can tell you in June of 1968, I never thought I'd be standing here. In fact, the Superintendent and I are classmates, and we were reminiscing just a little over a year ago in Southern California at another classmate's house- who has done very well incidentally. We were sitting on top of a hill drinking a beer and watching the sun go down, in shorts, talking about what we were going to do when we out next summer. This was not in his plan, and it was not in my plan; but it is really exciting for me to be here, and I'm really happy to see all the midshipmen. I served three tours here and that is usually the kiss of death, but obviously it worked out OK. So its all right to come back here, and this is a great place to come back to.

Sometimes when I give a talk, especially in the evening, I'm reminded of a story that Lt. General Pagonis tells in his book Building Mountains. After the first Gulf War, he went to talk to a class of fifth graders, and he said at the beginning of his speech, "My job is to tell you what I do. You're job is to listen." Immediately a little girl's hand went up and he said 'Yes?' She said, "General, if we finish our job before you do, can we go home?" I had dinner here tonight with a couple of firsties and they say that you all have something to do tonight—that you have to study, so I'll try to make my remarks short. I really look forward to the questions and answers.

I'm also reminded of a Marine who graduated from boot camp some time ago. He came from a small town in the Midwest. In fact he was the first individual to come into the Marine Corps from this small town. They were so proud of him that they all saw him off to boot camp at the railroad station. He did very well at boot camp; he was number one in his class and he went home in a set of dress blues. He was very proud. He knew that the town was going to be waiting to see him when he came into the train station, but when he arrived there was no one there. So he checked with the stationmaster and as luck would have it the town drunk had died that day. This particular town drunk is not the individual that you see on the late movie—the friendly, fatherly type of drunk. This was a bad guy. Anyway, the entire town was out at the cemetery, so this young Marine went out to join his fellow townspeople there. As he arrived, the chaplain was having trouble finding words to say about this individual. There was a long pause and finally the preacher said, "Does anyone else have anything to say about our dearly departed?" Silence. This Marine stepped forward, came to attention, looked out and said, "Well, if no one has anything to say about our dearly departed, I have a few words to say about the Marine Corps." WellI want to say a few words about the Marine Corps, but I'm really going to talk about the Navy/Marine Corps team tonight. I would like to say just a little bit about what the Navy/Marine Corps team has done, or is doing, over in Iraq right now.

Today 67% of the operating forces of the Marine Corps are fully deployed. Almost 80% are either forward deployed, forward stationed, or forward based. We have almost 70,000 Marines in Iraq right now. You see what they are doing on television, and they are performing absolutely magnificently. I visited 21 of those Marines this afternoon at Bethesda—some of them missing legs, some of them missing arms, and one individual missing an eye. And they only wanted one thing and that was to go back to their Marines in Iraq. That's the type of young people that we have today.

But let me tell you a couple of things that you don't see on the news. Within almost three weeks notice we launched an amphibious task force from the east coast, seven amphibs (amphibious ships) with 6,000 Marines. We launched seven amphibs from the west coast with almost 7,000 Marines, and 30 days later those 14 ships arrived in Iraq and all those Marines off-loaded. Right now we have close to 80% of the amphibs forward deployed.

We brought in three maritime prepositioning squadrons—11 ships. We off-loaded those 11 ships through one port in 16 days. The equipment readiness on the first squadron was 98.5%. The equipment that came off the second squadron was 99.1%. The equipment that came off of that first squadron can supply and sustain a Marine brigade, 17,000 Marines, for up to 30 days. And the same is the case of the equipment that came off of the second squadron. No other nation in the world, no other armed force in the world can do that, bar none. And that's what I'd like to talk a little bit about tonight and that is seabasing.

From what I understand you had a good day today talking about Seabasing. In fact I understand the last hour of the day was hand grenades at 10 meters. And that's good, because this is a very important subject. To me Seabasing, at least my vision of Seabasing, differs a little bit from what I heard you talked about today. Seabasing, as a national capability, can have a significant effect on our ability to project combat power. I think it maybe the most exciting thing, since we first came up with amphibious warfare. I'm not going to be here to see it to completion, but those of you sitting out there in the cheap seats; you are going to see it.

Seabasing to me is not a thing, or is not a platform; it's an aggregation of capabilities at sea. It's composed of four pillars. There's the command

and control pillar. We call it force net. There is the defensive capability. We call it sea shield. There's the offensive capability—a set of offensive capabilities—and we call it sea strike. And then there's the sea base that provides the logistics—a set of logistics capabilities. And that in my mind is what we're talking about when we talk about Seabasing—the whole package.

Now, there's no surprise that the Navy and Marine Corps have been doing this for years. We did the island hopping campaign in World War II. More recently, we've conducted numerous non-permissive combat evacuations from various embassies and countries. And then, most recently in Afghanistan we projected combat power ashore 400 miles into Rhino, and then we projected combat power up to Kandahar in Afghanistan. It had to be done fast. The Navy and the Marine Corps had the only capability to project combat power from sea into that airfield—to take it down at the time the combatant commander wanted to take it down. We do not have the capability, at least in my mind, to do it the way that I think we should be able to do it in 2015 or 2020. We had to use an intermediate support base in Pakistan, because our helicopters cannot fly far enough or carry enough equipment to project combat power that far. So I don't think that we are there yet. Another example of Seabasing that few people know about happened was when I was the eleventh MEU Commander. We came out of the Gulf, in 1992, and were headed for Singapore when we got a message from the joint staff that said "wrong direction, turn right and go to Somalia." This was in September 1992 before the United States really got involved in Somalia. We went down there to bring in the Pakistani armed forces.

We flew in, met with some of the warlords, and arranged security on the airfield. The Air Force flew in some of their TALCE (Tactical Airlift Control Element). We took them back Out to sea each night and would take them in during the day and take the Pakistani's in, and then go back out to sea. That's the concept of

seabasing. Where you're actually projecting sovereignty. We did not have a footprint ashore or a command and control node or an intel node—everything was at sea.

Another example was East Timor. I happened to be in East Timor and the security situation was not very good. We brought in a large amphib. You have no idea what an LHD looks like in a very small harbor. It is big! That ship came into that harbor and the security situation immediately improved, and then we sent Marines ashore, Medcaps—medical capabilities ashore. They worked with the Timorians there and then every night we would go back out to sea. That's seabasing. You bring what capabilities you need, whether it is combat, whether it is logistics, whether it is command and control. They are stationed out there in the international waters and you project that ashore.

Now I mentioned the future. So what will be different in 2015 or 2020?

Let's use the example of Kuwait. What if we were unable to go into Kuwait? What if we didn't have pre-positioned supplies there? What if we still had to do a regime change in Iraq? With seabasing you go into the Gulf; you do what we call RSO & I—reception, staging, onward movement, and integration. You bring the force together at sea, you assemble it at sea, you rehearse it at sea and then, unlike in World War II where you had to grab a beachhead and build sustainment on the beach before you projected combat power inland, you go directly to the objective. You take down Umm Qasar from the sea. You take down Basra from the sea with Naval surface fires providing your indirect fire support. That's my idea of seabasing.

Why is that important for the future? I would argue for a couple of reasons: Number one is access. Look at what's happening right now with our allies and our inability to get access to put forces ashore at what's called an intermediate support base. My sense is that the access problem is going to become much more difficult in the future. The second point concerns where people are moving. They're moving to these so-called mega cities. And where are these cities located? 75 to 80 percent of them are within 800 miles of the oceans in the littorals.

Well what's important about a city? Look at history; look at what we're doing right now—where are we going? Basra, An Nasiriya, Baghdad, because that is the center of gravity. That is where you have to go if there is a problem, and a lot of these cities sit on major lines of communication which, from a military standpoint, means you need to go in there. And finally the proliferation of weapons, cheap weapons, gives some of these countries the ability to come up with anti-access strategies that would prevent us from coming in. So I argue that we need, this nation needs, the capability to project combat power from the sea.

What advantage is this to the war fighter? Number one: he's got terrific maneuver space—the ocean. He is not restricted. Number two: he has freedom of action. Number three: I believe we have reduced vulnerability to attack. There are individuals here who believe that you can take down those ships at sea. I would argue that it's a whole lot more difficult to take down that ship at sea than it is Kuwait International Airport. I know where that is. And finally, I believe it increases the agility and speed.

Since I'm at the Naval Academy, I can talk about the second derivative force. All of you up there know what the second derivative force is, right? What's the first derivative? Slope or speed right? And what's the second derivative? The second derivative is the rate of change or acceleration, right? So if you're at sea, able to project force quicker than anyone else, you may not need as much. Let me give you an example, a current example. It looked like Saddam Hussein was going to light off the oil fields. So what happened? First, we attacked with very short notice and took down the oil fields, and at the same time with the Brits, we took down the port of Umm Qasar. No one expected it. What did we find in the port? Three barges filled with mines

that they would have laid in the channel if we had given them a chance. What does that mean? We didn't need the minesweepers there. Think about the ramifications that having speed at the right moment could bring. Now, what do we need to do this? One thing is we don't have the platforms to do this. In the Marine Corps we need the Osprey, the MV-22. It gives us the legs and the speed to go far inland, and the capability to lift.

We need the joint strike fighter. We need to ensure that we come up with the right design for the LHA replacement. We need to ensure that we come up with the right design for the maritime pre-positioning force future. We're working on that now, but some of you sitting out there, some of you Midshipman, will work on that too. We need the littoral combat ship. We also need force net, network-centric warfare, and they must be plug-and-play. So when the Army comes in, when the Air Force comes in, they plug into that command and control system. Since this is a national capability it absolutely must have joint application. That's one of the hard ones there. The other hard one is logistics. We have to come up with a new way to provide logistics from the sea to that force. The Navy does this very, very well. They re-supply their ships all the time. We need to take the next step, flow that logistics through the seabase ashore. And finally we need to have long-range fires. I think that will be provided, at least the service fires, by the DDX.

So that's my idea of seabasing. I strongly believe it is a capability that this nation needs. It's not the only capability we need. We cannot be a one-trick-pony; but it is a capability that we need and it must be joint. And I would also argue that the Naval services have to be the executive agent of this particular capability. And I look forward to your questions.

I thank you all very much. Good luck!

Suggested Readings

Clark, Vern Adm. "Sea Power 21— Projecting Decisive Joint Capabilities." *U.S. Naval Proceedings.* Vol. 128/10/1. http://www.usni.org/Proceedings/Articles02/proCNO10.htm.

U.S. Marine Corps. "Maritime Prepositioning Force 2010 and Beyond." *Marine Corps Concept Paper.* U.S. Marine Corps Headquarters, 1997. http://www.fas.org/man/dod-101/sys/ship/docs/mpf-2010.htm.

U.S. Marine Corps. "Seabased Logistics." *Marine Corps Concept Paper.* Marine Corps Combat Development Command. http://www.fas.org/man/dod-101/sys/ship/docs/sbl.htm.

56

Listen, Learn, Lead: ADM Mike Mullen's Assumption of Duties as Chief of Naval Operations

Dr. Joseph J. Thomas

"Assumption of Command" speeches rank among the most difficult to prepare and difficult to deliver. The imperative to thank those who enabled your success, your vision for the organization, and your honoring of the individual you replace vie for space in this normally brief address. ADM Mike Mullen's assumption of Chief of Naval Operations at the U.S. Naval Academy, Annapolis MD on Friday, July 22, 2005 is one such example of this manner of address effectively made.

* * *

Well, good morning. It is a great Navy day.

Secretary Rumsfeld, thank you sir, for being here today. You pay tribute to all of us by your presence. And thank you for the confidence you have expressed in me.

I am most grateful as well for the support of President Bush. You have been, and remain a warrior of indomitable spirit, passion and energy, leading our military with confidence and courage; exactly what we needed to help us deal with the harsh realities to which we awoke on September 11, 2001. I very much look forward to working closely with you in continuing to transform our Navy to conquer those harsh realities.

Secretary England, you know that Deborah and I are ecstatic to still have you and Dottie close at hand. Your leadership, guidance, friendship have become integral to our lives. That our Navy and Marine Corps team has risen to confront the challenges of this new century head on, together and with great success, is testament, sir, to your steady hand. I have learned much from your example and am excited about working for you again.

I would also like to recognize General Mike Hagee, the Commandant of the Marine Corps, a classmate and a friend. Mike, Silke thanks for coming. Who would have dreamt of this in 1964? You and I have spoken about where we are and where we are now, many times, but let me just say again how delighted and proud I am to be joining you as a member of the Navy Department's leadership team. You, General Jim Jones before you, Admiral Clark and Secretary England have all worked, pulled together diligently and with purpose to sharpen the blade that is naval warfare at sea and ashore. And I look forward to working closely with you to keep that blade sharp.

There are, of course, many other people to whom I owe a great deal and without whom I would not be so fortunate as to be standing here today. Mentors like Bob McNitt, Jim Winnefeld, George Sullivan, countless more who coached and taught me. Family—and there are lots of them here—friends and classmates, and there are a lot of classmates here as well, and you supported me. My Mom and Dad, though not here in body, I know are here in spirit, and they believed in me. And of course, my best friend and the love of my life, Deborah, who means the world to me and with whom I've just celebrated our 35th wedding anniversary.

Deborah and I have been blessed as well with two extraordinary sons, Jack and Michael, and are, of course, immensely proud of both of them. My sons have, as good sons will, helped keep my feet planted firmly on the ground even when I was at sea, which was a lot. I want to thank them both for that and for their unfailing love and support.

Secretary Rumsfeld, sir, going back to your comments, I just want to say that I couldn't agree more with your assessment of the Navy that Admiral Clark has led and turned over to me. I believe it is the best it has ever been, manned by the world's finest Sailors. And I want you to know I am going to keep it that way.

I want you to know that I believe in who we are and what we do for the nation; that when the President talks about the "forward defense of freedom," when he talks about taking the fight to the enemy, he can continue to count on the United States Navy.

I believe our families are every bit a factor in our ability to do that as is our technology and

our training and I'm going to work hard to recognize their service. I believe we derive enormous strength from our diversity, that we need leaders for and leaders from all parts of our Navy. And I believe in the power of our past to inspire and instruct.

But I also believe that the only constant in our future is change—that real success in the world in which we live today and the one our grandchildren will inherit will come only as a result of hard work and the willingness to adapt.

Most importantly, I believe strongly in a sense of duty—my duty—to consider first and foremost the good of the country and to take care of the Navy I now lead.

I will keep close the advice of one of my heroes, Admiral Raymond Spruance, that a person's "judgment is best when he can forget himself and any reputation he may have acquired, and concentrate wholly on making the right decisions." I pledge to you, Mr. Secretary, to Secretary England and to everyone in our Navy today my best effort always to try to make the right decisions.

Vern, I don't think quite frankly that I could add anything of substance to what has already been said about your remarkable career and the extraordinary impact you have had on our Navy.

You led us ably in peace and in war and through unprecedented change. You are always telling Sailors to "go write some history," and they have. But you also, by re-making the Navy, have made history yourself.

We are not the same. In almost every conceivable way, we are not the same Navy we were five years ago. We don't think the same, we don't plan the same, we don't operate the same or fight the same. We are more capable, more ready, more effective and more efficient. We are, without question, a stronger Navy because of you. Thank you for your service, your friendship, your counsel; and for letting me be a part of your team. I am truly, deeply in your debt.

And a big part of that team, of course, is Connie. And Connie, I would be remiss if I didn't add my thanks to you as well for everything you have done on behalf of our Navy, especially our Navy families, over the course of Vern's career. You've been at his side every step of the way, supporting him, guiding him—working to improve the quality of life for our Sailors and their families. And I think it's fair to say that you, too, have worn the "cloth of the nation," as Vern likes to say. Though I know we'll stay in touch, Deborah and I will miss you both dearly. And the Navy will miss you dearly.

To the men and women who serve that Navy today, let me just say I stand before you a very humble man. Humble at the prospect of coming behind a visionary like Vern Clark. Humble at the three major challenges that lay before us: to sustain our high level of readiness and our ability to respond, to build a fleet for the future and to develop a workforce for the 21st century. And humble at the opportunity to continue serving alongside all of you, the most talented Sailors this Navy has ever put to sea.

To me, there is no higher honor.

I started my career here at the Naval Academy forty-one years ago. I will never forget that day. No plebe ever forgets that day. I owe an awful lot to the Naval Academy for what it did for me, for the tremendous start it gave me. In my formative years, no other group of people, save my family, and no other institution, had a more profound effect on me. But it was out there in the fleet at sea with Sailors that I fell in love with the Navy. It was there I learned the most valuable lessons of life and leadership. There I learned that with every great opportunity comes an even greater obligation to listen, to learn, and to lead.

Today the Navy grants me yet another great opportunity, and I intend to make good on my obligation in return.

Listen. Learn. Lead.

Those will be my watchwords these next four years, a challenge to both myself and to all of you. Given the world around us, the threats we face, we have no choice.

We must be able to transform ourselves and our thinking quickly in response to an ever-changing, ever-challenging and ever more joint security environment. Our enemies take no rest. Neither can we.

We must look out, not within. We must be able and willing to admit when we don't know something, when we don't have all the answers; and then have the passion and energy to go find them.

We must be able to allow that, though we are clearly more ready today than we have ever been, we have much work yet to do and effort to expend to be ready for tomorrow. Our nation and its citizens are depending on it. Our allies and our sister services are depending on it. The men and women, who are walking point in harm's way, fighting and, yes, dying, to keep freedom's hope alive, are depending on it.

Admiral Clark put us in a position of enormous strength. He took this Navy to a point, reformed us to a point, where we can now make decisions we simply couldn't make before. What we do with that strength, the kind of Navy we build and put to sea in the future, is entirely up to us. The tiller is in our hands.

One hundred years ago to this very day, at the dawn of the 20th century, the body of John Paul Jones was brought here to the Naval Academy. President Theodore Roosevelt, a great supporter of the United States Navy, would later speak at the burial ceremony. Not surprisingly, he talked about the need for a strong Navy and about how a maritime nation such as America couldn't hope to preserve liberty without one. He talked about training and readiness, about how important it was always to be prepared for war—to have ships and Sailors ready to fight at a moment's notice. He told the crowd assembled that they and the Navy's leaders had a responsibility to invest wisely in a fleet and in weapons that could carry the day not only for a day but for decades still to come. And yet, recalling the simple courage Jones displayed under fire, "None of these things," he said, "can avail unless in the moment of crisis the heart rises level with the crisis."

Today, at the dawn of the 21st century, we

find ourselves again in a moment of crisis; at war, defending freedom here at home by defending freedom around the globe. It is no small task, no easy business. It is the work of a generation or more, the struggle of an age.

I look around me today, and I see plainly that our hearts are level with it, and I am glad—I am grateful that I can continue serving as a Sailor in this Navy, at this time, with all of you.

We are strong enough to hold that tiller. We do have the courage. We will succeed. God bless you. God bless our country. And God bless our Navy. Thank you.

Before assuming the position of Chief of Naval Operations ADM Mullen specified his vision and beliefs (excerpts):

As you start to grapple with the issues that will shape my vision and priorities, I thought it would be valuable for to get a sharper sense of who I am and what I believe in.

Here is how I would describe myself: "I am a husband and father, an American, a sailor in the United States Navy, and a naval officer—in that order."

To define the sort of CNO I intend to be, let me spell out my beliefs: the things, both tangible and intangible, that move, motivate and inspire me.

- I believe in the United States Navy—in who we are, where we have come from and where we are going. I have devoted my entire adult life to this service because I fundamentally believe that America, as a maritime nation, needs a strong Navy.
- I believe everyone in our Navy is a sailor. It doesn't matter whether you wear a business suit to work or khakis or dungarees. If you have made the commitment to serve your country by serving your Navy, you are a Sailor. I am a Sailor, and I am proud of it.
- We need leaders from—and leaders for— every part of our Navy. We all—no matter where we stand in the chain of command—

have a responsibility to develop our own leadership potential and the leadership potential of those in our charge.

- I believe in the power of our past to inspire and instruct. We are the inheritors of a proud legacy. We should also recognize that many of the challenges faced in prior conflicts are similar to those we face today: piracy, insurgency, anti-access strategies, etc. We must capture those lessons, study them and apply them to current operations where applicable.

While we certainly learn from the past, we cannot—and should not—try to live in it. So,

- I believe the only constant in our future is change. We are a nation again at war, fighting a new and elusive enemy who thinks, studies and adapts. We must likewise be agile and flexible enough to continuously place him at risk and adapt quickly in a technologically challenging environment.
- I believe in jointness—not because it's trendy, but because it works. Nobody goes it alone.
- I believe in the Navy-Marine Corps team. Ours is a special relationship, born with this great republic and strengthened through war and peace.
- I believe in taking risks. Risk is inherent in everything we do—we should run neither from it nor heedlessly towards it. We would do well to remember that the risks we incur by our actions are far less severe than those we incur by our inaction.
- I believe in the 80 percent solution. I don't need—and frankly I don't always want—a complete and thoroughly greased plan before we march out on something. If it's a good idea we ought to be able to give it a try and modify it as we go along.
- I believe in holding myself and others accountable to high standards.
- I believe in the chain of command. It is time- and battle-tested, the bedrock principle upon which all military organizations are built. I use it, and I expect others to do so as well.

- I believe in substance over style, results over rhetoric. It matters a whole lot less to me how something is packaged than what is actually in that package. The real measure of success in any endeavor is the effect achieved—the end result.

But effective communications are a must in today's information age, so

- I believe in open, honest communications— in saying exactly what I mean as simply as I can. Likewise, when I ask someone what they think about something, I want them to tell me what they think—not what they think I want them to think. These are my beliefs, and I feel strongly about them.

Suggested Readings

Kotter, John P. *Leading Change*. Boston, Mass.: Harvard Business School Press, 1996.

Maxwell, John C. *The 21 Indispensable Qualities of a Leader: Becoming the Person that People Will Want to Follow*. Nashville: T. Nelson, 1999.

Watkins, Michael. *The First 90 Days: Critical Success Strategies for New Leaders at All Levels*. Boston: Harvard Business School Press, 2003.

Afterword

A MEMORANDUM FOR STUDENTS OF THE PROFESSION OF ARMS

on

PERSONAL AND PROFESSIONAL DEVELOPMENT

Brigadier General John R. Allen, USMC

1. The significance of personal professional development

    Learning our profession—the profession of arms—must be a lifelong and abiding pursuit for the professional serving officer. There can be no equal to, and indeed no substitute for, the officer who has spent a career immersed in the study of the art and science of war. An officer will likely spend no more than three and half years in formal, resident professional military education (PME) over a twenty-year career. With the preponderance of our time split between the operating forces, the support establishment, and "B" billets, we must assume the responsibility and provide for our own development. Unfortunately, unit level PME programs wax and wane based on commanders' predilections and experience, and operational commitments or other periodic interruptions. Only the individual officer can be fully in charge of his or her professional development.

2. Where to start

    a. *Non-resident professional military education.* After graduation from USNA, you will find opportunities for Navy—or Marine Corps—sponsored education. Keep an eye out for them and always strive to be a part of a non-resident PME program. This type of study is also known as distance learning or correspondence training. The Marine Corps Institute is an example of a distance learning school and offers myriad courses across many fields and functions in the Marine Corps.

    b. *Professional Reading List.* (Appendix D) is provided for you. It is divided into a core group, a list for each class, and a list for service-selection-specific books. I challenge each of you to read at least one of these books a year to help improve your overall professional base.

c. *The Marine Corps Commandant's Reading List*. In 1989, the Commandant of the Marine Corps, General Al Gray, published the first edition of the Commandant's Reading List, a compilation of books intended to focus the professional reading efforts of the entire Marine Corps. Organized vertically by rank and horizontally by subject matter, the reading list is a "first stop" for Marines seeking to read subject matter on issues critical to their professional development for their particular rank or grade. Today, the Marine Corps University maintains the list. It is constantly under revision, but its contents are presented in a 1997 publication called *A Book on Books*. *A Book on Books* provides excellent overall guidance on professional reading and lists all the books in the Commandant's Reading List by rank and category, providing short synopses of the book for the prospective reader. *A Book on Books* like the reading list itself, is under revision by the University.

d. *The Chief of Naval Operations Reading List*. Available at: http://www.hq.navy.mil/n3n5/Reading.htm

e. *Individual reading and personal professional study … seek your answers in history*. Jay Luvaas, a great American and Civil War historian, once said, "There is no excuse among professional officers for not having a 5000 year old mind." What he meant was that across the sweep of recorded time the literature of war lays at our feet nearly the sum total of man's warfare experience. In these works, there are lessons to be found that provide guideposts for virtually every challenge or dilemma we may encounter on the modern battlefield; new technologies notwithstanding. Additionally, reading provides us vicarious experience about war, experience which, in a very real sense, can serve as personal sense of conflict. One of the great military educators of the 20th

Century, British Major General J.F.C. Fuller counseled the serving officer to read history. He said:

Here history can help us, and in place of being looked upon as a clay pit to dig brick out of it should be considered an inexhaustible quarry of psychological ore. It does not really matter much what a certain general did at a certain date, but what *is* [emphasis his] of importance is *why* [emphasis his] he did it in a certain set of circumstances. The object of education is not so much to discover 'what to think' as to learn 'how to think'.

Adolph Von Schell, a German officer student who attended American Army schools during the inter-war years, said it best when he observed in 1931,

This problem [coping with the mental struggles of battle] will be even more serious in future wars, when machinery rules the battlefield, than it was in the past. In peace maneuvers, such matters cannot be depicted. *We can learn only from experience or by analogy from searching military history.* As leaders, we must constantly seek some means to prepare our soldiers for these grave psychological blows that war strikes at morale and nerves."

The remainder of this paper will address personal professional reading and study. I provide these thoughts as a distillation of my own thinking on the subject and offer some techniques for professional reading assembled from the over thirty years I have dedicated my life to this study. Remember, these are all just the ideas of one student of the art of war. Many times over the years I have said to myself "If I'd just known this," or "Had I just done that," I would have been so much better prepared, not just as a serving officer, but also as a lifelong student of the art of war. In many cases these lessons would have been immediately obvious to me had I been more thoroughly engaged a program of personal professional reading.

3. Individual Reading

a. *Choose a strategic direction.* Seek a general or strategic direction for your reading, something of interest—something of value from the profession of arms. I choose my reading across three general areas, all of them related to my strategic direction: *decision making in combat.* The three areas that contribute most to my strategic direction are maneuver warfare studies, readings in character in decision making, and human factors in combat. My purpose in this paragraph is not to convince you of this, or any particular strategic direction. This one, with its three components, suits me; something else will suit each other officer in his or her reading. I chose this direction early in my career because I thought it would directly impact my professional needs. It has sustained me throughout my professional development, but unfortunately I came at the idea of a strategic direction relatively late in my career. I would simply offer the observation that one's strategic direction should be carefully selected to account for the requirement for long term professional education while supporting short-term technical, tactical, and spiritual needs.

b. *Objective-based reading.* Just as we would do a reconnaissance before crossing the line of departure in the attack, I carefully examine every book before I launch into the reading. Given the limited time I have available, reading is a significant commitment for me and I "choose my battles" carefully. Before descending into the subject matter, ask yourself the following questions:

1. *Does this book constitute part of the body of literature for my strategic direction?*
2. *If it does, when I'm done, what do I seek to get out of this particular book?*

I establish a professional objective, or objectives, for each book I read. Each objective is derived from, or contributes to, the context of my strategic direction. As an example, I once read Simpkin's *Race to the Swift*. Simpkin writes about maneuver warfare in a scientific manner, explaining aspects of the tactics in physical terms. I found the book very useful for me, as I had been educated at the undergraduate level as an operations analyst, and tended to view the world in quantitative terms. I established an objective for this book to aid me in bridging the inherently qualitative discussion of maneuver warfare with the quantitative nature of my education. In the end, it was excellent in placing some of the larger principles of maneuver warfare and high mobility operations squarely into a context I understood. Thus, before I began the serious reading of *Race to the Swift* I understood how it would fit into my strategic direction, by helping me to understand and to apply maneuver warfare principles in a tactical and a technical manner.

c. *Choose the author carefully.* A related point to choosing the "right" book is choosing the "right" author. As with books, not all authors are created equal. If I am going to invest the time to read, I will spend no small amount of effort considering the author as well as the title. Pose yourself the questions:

1. *Why is this author writing on this subject? Is there an agenda?*
2. *How much original research is contained herein, or is this simply a regurgitation of past work?*

A great Marine leader and scholar once told me I could not go wrong reading everything written by J. F. C. Fuller and B. H. Liddell-Hart. For years I have collected their works, and I must say that early in my studies of maneuver warfare and human factors in war they shaped my thinking and were instrumental in helping me create a "lens" through which I would there-after always view conflict. The authors who have made a difference for me in my professional reading are many, but some who have had a profound affect upon me are G. F. R. Henderson, Douglas Southall Freeman, S. L. A. Marshall, Steven Ambrose, Russ Weigley, Barbara Tuchman, John Keegan, Michael Howard, Martin Van Creveld, Al Millett, Williamson Murray, and John W. Thomason.

There are so many, and I am reluctant to mention even one for fear of neglecting or injuring another, except to offer to new readers in professional military studies some assurance and hope that they need not consider the relative "worth" of any one of these writers very long before deciding their work might fit their own strategic directions. If my house were on fire and we were all running for our lives, I would first save my family, and then all my volumes by these writers. *Bottomline*: the author is as important as the work itself, and I counsel you to choose the two carefully... *and together*.

Let me make a related point about the author. Every book an officer reads effects a subtle, nearly imperceptible change in our makeup: our vocabulary is enhanced, our knowledge of sentence construction and composition improves, which translates directly into improved communications skills. Simply put, a reader is a scholar. If my own speech and writing seem a bit "heavy" it is because I have been reading the British inter-war authors and Douglas Southall Freeman for years. The echoes of their words and their thought processes can be found—if usually poorly rendered—in my own communications. The author will not only shape a student's lens, the officer will be changed forever, intellectually, by the influence. An officer would be well advised to select that kind of change very carefully.

   d. *Study a campaign*. Without any structure, officers often wander for years over the landscape of military literature. This lack of focus, suffering from a literal "aimlessness," inhibits concentration and serves to dissipate the energy of a useful study of the art of war. Selecting a military campaign offers the student a nearly endless variation and combination of case studies for one's own strategic direction. A serious campaign study affords the student the opportunity to study many different aspects of war: levels of war (strategic, operational, tactical); leadership at every level; the effects of human factors in combat; decision-making under pressure and duress; and such functional issues as logistics, communications, transportation, engineering, medical, casualty replacement, cavalry operations, etc.

Many campaigns will also permit studies in socio-political, civil-military, and political-military issues. For years, I have studied General Robert E. Lee's Southern Maryland Campaign of 1862, culminating in the Battle of Sharpsburg (Antietam). With the exception of the effects of modern weapons, I have found the answers to virtually every question I have asked about the profession of arms and the study of the art of war in the literature surrounding the Southern Maryland Campaign. The advantage of studying a single campaign is the student builds continuity in context—that is, familiarity—with the subject matter at hand, and will come to know the leaders and their personalities, the terrain, the conditions of battle, the units, the successes, and the failures, etc. Having concentrated on one campaign, I have not been forced to relearn all the timeless nuances of battle with each new book or situation I read. In some form or fashion, every author who writes on this campaign will deal with the same issues. This approach offers continuity and reinforcement.

Why did I choose the Southern Maryland Campaign? The body of literature surrounding this war in general, and this battle in particular, is huge and begins with the *Official Records*. I would caution the student with this last consideration, the size of the body of literature surrounding a campaign should be one of the principal determining factors in selecting a cam-

paign. The more the writing, the more and varied are the facets available for study.

    e. *Why study the American Civil War?* It is use-
ful at this point to digress for a moment
and discuss the issue of the study American
Civil War by a serving officer of the 21st
Century. I am partial to Civil War studies
for several reasons. First, as I have already
mentioned, the body of literature surrounding this conflict is great; at this point
the published works number in excess of
70,000 volumes consisting of personal
memoirs, unit histories, battle and campaign studies, etc. Second, the post-war
Federal Government, sensing the need to
preserve records of this enormous American struggle, commissioned an official effort to assemble and organize all of the
available documentation. Commissioners
from both the Union and the former Confederate armies participated in this effort
and the result was a staggering assembly of
documents published in 129 volumes from
1888-1901, known thereafter as *The War of
the Rebellion: A Compilation of the official
records of the Union and Confederate Armies*.
Today, researchers call them the *Official
Records of the Civil War* or simply the "OR."
These resources are a matchless record of
the orders, reports, and evaluations of both
sides. All written in English, these records
represent one of the finest recorded assemblies of the writings of *both* belligerents in
any conflict at any time in history. A re-
searcher need not speak a foreign language,
nor rely on someone else's translation in
order to delve deeply into this conflict.

Unfortunately, few of us can maintain this
kind of library (since each of the volumes of the
OR measures well in excess of 600 pages). However, Guild Press of Indiana has now published
the sum total of these 129 volumes, plus Dyer's
Compendium of the War of the Rebellion plus Fox's
Regimental Losses in the American Civil War all in
one CD for about $65 (http://www.guildpress.

com) [this is not an endorsement of this product
by the Naval Academy or the Navy or Marine
Corps]. A naval version of the OR was also assembled in about sixty volumes and it is also now
available from Guild Press. Finally, as an officer,
I know I will return to Quantico and the Washington, D.C. area on numerous occasions
throughout my career. Near these two locations
are most of the large battlefields of the Eastern
Theater of Operations of the Civil War. To walk
the ground of these battlefields, with the writings and the maps of both sides, offers an incom-
parable opportunity to study the art of war at
nearly the "molecular" level of detail.

    f. *Don't force a book.* Ben Jonson once said:
"Some books are to be chewed and digested . . ." meaning some books will simply not be easy to read. Once a student has
selected those authors with whom he or she
is comfortable, then the reading eventually
becomes easier and more predictable. But
on occasion, a student will select a book
that just "reads hard." My advice when a
student is laboring through a book is simply to put it down. Unless it is part of an
academic assignment, don't force the reading; it may not be time yet for the student
to grasp the material. This subject matter
may yet be too advanced, or the writing
style too difficult to accommodate learning
at this particular moment. Get another
book by a different, credible author on a
similar subject, and try again. I have found,
over the years that "going around" a literary surface often set me up for success at a
later point in the previous book. Time for
professional reading is simply too precious
a commodity to the student engaged in serious personal professional development.
Grinding through a book can be too costly
in terms of time, and the waste of valuable,
irreplaceable enthusiasm.

    g. *Look for the references.* When I choose a
book in the context of my strategic direction, I will frequently spend some time in
the notes (foot or endnotes) and bibliogra-

phy of the book before I commit to reading. With regard to notes, as I proceed through a book I usually use two bookmarks. One keeps my place in the text of the book, while one helps me track my progress through the notes. Most of the great writers were also great researchers, and their books are replete with notes containing research insights and additional information deemed important, but not sufficiently so, to appear in the text proper. Two examples of this achievement are Coddington's, *The Campaign of Gettysburg*, and English's and Gudmundsson's, *On Infantry*. Coddington's book contains over 300 pages of endnotes that paint a brilliant picture of the peripheral aspects of the campaign. The additional information, and the opinions expressed in the "second book within a book" made this work a true treasure for the comprehensive study of this battle.

Similarly, I have read *On Infantry* at every rank since it was first published in 1981. Its endnotes are one of the most useful assemblages of additional information on infantry and small unit cohesion and operations I have found in any book I have ever read. Because of their content, and the way they are arranged, these notes and references have taught me something new from this book each time I read it. Those who read and do not select a book for its notes, or worse read a book and ignore the notes, miss the sometimes-crucial "inner book."

In addition, for the serious student of an event, battle, or leader, the bibliography is pure gold, mined by the author and presented here simply for the cost of the book. The notes and bibliography complete the literature. There is however, one exception to this rule. Many of the greatest historians who have contributed to the body of literature on war have been "narrative historians," men and women who weave the threads of history as a great story. These historians, among them Samuel Eliot Morrison and Shelby Foote, write with wonderful clarity of thought, enthralling the reader in the story line, but provide few notes, or perhaps even bibliographies. For the student this may not matter, for I personally love narrative history, unless I contemplate some additional research.

h. *Marking a book and using marginalia.* For years I have watched officers mark and annotate their books as they have attempted to highlight something important on a page. I have seen pages literally covered with yellow highlighter pen or completely underlined. Let me offer the "vertical bar" technique. As one reads the text, if something important appears, place a single vertical bar in margin spanning the relevant lines of text. Of the text deemed important enough to be set-off with a vertical bar, the single vertical bar is important text; two vertical parallel lines sets-off the next most important text on the page. Finally, the most important text on a page, something perhaps so important one would consider memorizing it or committing it to a note card, is annotated with three parallel vertical bars. This text, set-off with three vertical bars, is "pure gold" and represents the essence of the principal points to be taken from this portion of the book.

Marginalia represent the reference notes one writes in the margins to "hold a thought" on that page or to express an opinion with regard to the text. As the name implies, marginalia can be written in the margin immediately adjacent to the particular passage, or may be written as a "call away," set-off using an asterisk in the text and writing the note on the top or bottom of that page, or can be written at the end of the chapter in white space frequently found there. Marginalia offer a snapshot in time of the student's thinking on the subject at hand, and provides a student a valuable record of his or her impressions of the text for future reference or research. For those who collect books, let me caution that marginalia can cause a significant loss in value in first editions or rare volumes.

That is not to say don't write in these kinds of books. Simply recognize the cost of marginalia in devaluing the monetary worth of certain books.

4. <u>Summary.</u>

We must be lifelong students of the profession of arms. That term carries certain obligations, the most important of which is to be ready for war. That readiness flows from the obligation to study the art of war in a constant, systematic and long-tern manner. Some of our development will occur in the schools we attend. Some will occur in the PME programs of our units. The preponderance, however, must occur as a result of our own volition and initiative to study. A leader is a reader. A reader is a scholar. A scholar is a communicator. The one flows into the other with all these qualities being inter-related. In the end they find their most urgent expression in battle. When we reach the point of impact—on whatever battlefield that may be— the officer who will prevail is one for whom the study of the art of war has been an abiding, personal, and lifelong search. The officer with the 5000-year-old mind will win.

Good hunting and Semper Fidelis.

Suggested Readings

Dyer, Frederick H. *A Compendium of the War of the Rebellion.* New York: T. Yoseloff, 1959.

Fox, William F. *Regimental Losses in the American Civil War, 1861–1865.* Albany: Albany Publishing Co, 1889.

Simpkin, Richard E. *Race to the Swift: Thoughts on Twenty-First Century Warfare.* Washington, D.C.: Brassey's Defence, 1985.

Shakespeare, William. *Henry V.* New York: Penguin, 1968.

Thucydides. *History of the Peloponnesian War.* New York: W.W. Norton & Co., 1998.

United States Dept. of Defense. *The Armed Forces Officer.* Washington D.C.: U.S. Govt. Printing Office, 1950.

United States Marine Corps. *A Book on Books.* Washington, D.C.: U.S. Marine Corps, 1992.

United States War Dept. *The war of the Rebellion: a Compilation of the Official Records of the Union and Confederate Armies.* Washington D.C.: Govt. Printing Office, 1880-1901.

Appendices

Appendix A: Useful Quotes

The following is a compilation of quotations I have collected over the years. I have found the borrowed words of great leaders and thinkers throughout history to be useful for several purposes: I incorporate quotations into my writing in order to add *gravitas* to ideas I am trying to relate to my readers; I sprinkle particularly apt quotations in speeches or lectures I deliver to inform and entertain the audience in more effective ways than I can accomplish without them; and finally, I look to them for inspiration in my thinking when pressed with a challenge or vexed with writers block. For whatever purpose you employ quotations, enjoy.

* * *

"A Nation that insists on drawing a broad line of demarkation between its warriors and its scholars will have its thinking done by cowards and its fighting done by fools."

—LtCol Sir William Butler.

"Many years ago, as a cadet hoping some day to be an officer, I was poring over the 'Principles of War,' listed in the old Field Service Regulations, when the Sergeant-Major came up to me. He surveyed me with kindly amusement. "Don't bother your head about all them things, me lad,' he said. 'There's only one principle of war and that's this. Hit the other fellow, as quick as you can, and as hard as you can, where it hurts him most, when he ain't lookin'!'"

—Sir William Slim

"We train for certainty, and educate for uncertainty."

—Anon.

"If officers are unaccustomed to rigorous training they will be worried and hesitant in battle. If leaders are not thoroughly trained they will inwardly quail when they face the enemy."

—Sun Tzu, *The Art of War*

"We must remember that one man is much the same as another, and that he is best who is trained in the severest school."

—Thucydides.

"Few men are born brave; many become so through training and force of discipline."

—Flavius Vegetius Renatus,

"Body and spirit I surrendered whole
To harsh instructors—and received a soul."

—Kipling, 'Epitaphs,' 1919

"In no other profession are the penalties for employing untrained personnel so appalling or so irrevocable as in the military."

—MacArthur

"A pint of sweat will save a gallon of blood."

—Patton

"We have verified the inevitable—that inadequately trained officers cannot train troops effectively."

—Gen L.J. McNair

"Truly then, it is killing men with kindness not to insist upon physical standards during training which will give them a maximum fitness for the extraordinary stresses of campaigning in war."

—S.L.A Marshall

"All military forces remain relatively undisciplined until physically toughened and mentally conditioned to unusual exertion."

—S.L.A. Marshall

"Old Corps, New Corps—it doesn't make a damn bit of difference as long as it's the Marine Corps."

—BGen "Chesty" Puller, 1953

"The supreme quality for leadership is unquestionably integrity. Without it, no real success is possible, no matter whether it is on a section gang, a football field, in an army, or in an office."

—Dwight D. Eisenhower

"A king does not abide within his tent while his men bleed and die upon the field. A king does not dine while his men go hungry, nor sleep when they stand watch upon the wall. A king does not command his men's loyalty through fear nor purchase it with gold; he earnes their love by the sweat of his own back and the pains he endures for their sake. That which he comprises the harshest burden, a king lifts first and sets down last. A king does not require service of those he leads but provides it to them. He serves them, not they him."

—Stephen Pressfield, *Gates of Fire*

"These are the times that try men's souls. The summer soldier and the sunshine patriot will, in the crisis, shrink from the service of their country; but he that stands it now, deserves the thanks of man and woman. Tyranny, like hell, is not easily conquered; yet we have this consolation with us, that the harder the conflict, the more glorious the triumph. What we obtain too cheap, we esteem too lightly: it is dearness only that gives everything its value."

—Thomas Paine

"Let us have faith that right makes might; and in that faith let us, to the end, dare to do our duty as we understand it."

—Abraham Lincoln

"It is not the critic who counts; not the man who points out how the strong man stumbles, or where the doer of deeds could have done better. The credit belongs to the man who is actually in the arena; whose face is marred by dust and sweat and blood; who strives valiantly; who errs and comes short again and again. Who knows the great enthusiasms, the great devotions, and spends himself in a worthy cause. Who at the best knows in the end the triumph of high achievement; and who at the worst, if he fails, at least fails while daring greatly, so that his place shall never be with those cold and timid souls who know neither victory nor defeat."

—Theodore Roosevelt

"The greatest want of the world is men who will not be bought or sold; men who in their inmost souls are true and honest; men who do not fear to call sin by its right name; men whose conscience is as true to duty as the needle to the pole; men who will stand for the right though the heavens fall."

—E.B. White

"Rather fail with honor than succeed by fraud."

—Sophocles

"Of men who have a sense of honor, more come through alive than are slain, but for those who flee comes neither glory nor any help."

—Homer

"Too often in this war did leaders fight each other while the troops fought the foe."

—B.H. Liddell Hart

"Mine honour is my life; both grow in one; take honour from me and my life is done."

—Shakespeare

"The Marine Corps' style of warfare requires intelligent leaders with a penchant for boldness and initiative down to the lowest levels. Boldness is an essential moral trait in a leader, for it generates combat power beyond the physical means at hand. Initiative, the willingness to act on one's own judgment, is a prerequisite for boldness. These traits carried to excess can lead to rashness, but we must realize that errors from junior leaders stemming from overboldness are a necessary part of learning. We should deal with such errors leniently; there must be no "zero defects" mentality. Not only must we not stifle boldness or initiative, we must continue to encourage both traits *in spite of mistakes*. On the other hand, we should deal severely with errors of inaction or timidity. We will not accept lack of orders as justification for inaction; it is each Marine's *duty* to take initiative as the situation demands."

—FMFM 1 Warfighting

"Marine human material was not one whit better than that of the human society from which it came. But it had been hammered into form in a different forge, hardened with a different fire. The Marines were the closest thing to legions the nation had. They would follow their colors from the shores of home to the seacoast of Bohemia, and fight well at either place . . . A Marine Corps officer was still an officer, and a sergeant behaved the way good sergeants had behaved since the time of Caesar, expecting no nonsense, allowing none. And Marine leaders had never lost sight of their primary—their only—mission, which was to fight."

—T.R. Fehrenbach

"A spirit of comradeship and brotherhood in arms came into being in the training camps and on the battlefields. This spirit is too fine a thing to be allowed to die. It must be fostered and kept alive and made the moving force in all Marine Corps Organizations."

—MajGen John A. Lejeune

"Leaders must have a strong sense of the great responsibility of their office; the resources they will expend in war are human lives."

—FMFM 1 Warfighting

"No folly is more costly than the folly of intolerant idealism."

—Winston Churchill

"Never give in. Never. Never. Never. Never."

—Winston Churchill

"The price of greatness is responsibility."

—Winston Churchill

"I like a man who grins when he fights."

—Winston Churchill

"If you will not fight for the right when you can easily win without bloodshed, if you will not fight when your victory will be sure and not too costly, you may come to the moment when you will have to fight with all the odds against you and only a small chance of survival. There may even be a worse case: you may have to fight when there is no hope of victory, because it is better to perish than to live as slaves."

—Winston Churchill

"Courage is the first of human qualities because it is the quality that guarantees all the others."

—Winston Churchill

"Danger—if you meet it promptly and without flinching—you will reduce the danger by half. Never run away from anything. Never!"

—Winston Churchill

"Many forms of Government have been tried, and will be tried in this world of sin and woe. No one pretends that democracy is perfect or all-wise. Indeed, it has been said that democracy is the 'worst' form of Government except all those others that have been tried from time to time."

—Winston Churchill

". . . You ask, What is our policy? I will say; 'It is to wage war, by sea, land and air, with all our might and with all the strength that God can give us: to wage war against a monstrous tyranny, never surpassed in the dark lamentable catalogue of human crime. That is our policy.' You ask, What is our aim? I can answer with one word: Victory—victory at all costs, victory in spite of all terror, victory however long and hard the road may be; for without victory there is no survival."

—Winston Churchill

"If you have an important point to make, don't try to be subtle or clever. Use a pile driver. Hit the point once. Then come back and hit it again. Then hit it a third time—a tremendous whack."

—Winston Churchill

"We shall not flag or fail. We shall go on to the end. We shall fight in France, we shall fight on the seas and the oceans, we shall fight with growing confidence and growing strength in the air, we shall defend our island, whatever the cost may be. We shall fight on the beaches, we shall fight on the landing grounds, we shall fight in the fields and in the streets, we shall fight in the hills; we shall never surrender."

—Winston Churchill

"He only earns his freedom and his life Who takes them every day by storm."

—Goethe

"The first and last thing required of genius is the love of truth."

—Goethe

"The price of freedom is eternal vigilance."

—Thomas Jefferson

"In matters of style, swim with the current; In matters of principle, stand like a rock."

—Thomas Jefferson

"I would rather be exposed to the inconveniences attending too much liberty than to those attending too small a degree of it."

—Thomas Jefferson

"I have sworn upon the altar of God eternal hostility against every form of tyranny over the mind of man."

—Thomas Jefferson

"I find that the harder I work, the more luck I seem to have."

—Thomas Jefferson

"Rebellion to tyrants is obedience to God."

—Thomas Jefferson

"We hold these truths to be self-evident, that all men are created equal; that they are endowed by their Creator with inherent and inalienable rights; that among these, are life, liberty, and the pursuit of happiness; that to secure these rights, governments are instituted among men, deriving their just powers from the consent of the governed; that whenever any form of government becomes destructive of these ends, it is the right of the people to alter or abolish it, and to institute new government, laying its foundation on such principles, and organizing its powers in such form, as to them shall seem most likely to effect their safety and happiness."

—Thomas Jefferson

"It is well to be up before daybreak, for such habits contribute to health, wealth, and wisdom."

—Aristotle

"Character is that which reveals moral purpose, exposing the class of things a man chooses or avoids."

—Aristotle

". . . you are not engaged so much in acquiring knowledge as in making mental efforts under criticism: A certain amount of knowledge you can indeed with average faculties acquire so as to retain; nor need you regret the hours that you have spent on much that is forgotten, for the shadow of lost knowledge at least protects you from many illusions.
But you go to a great school, not for knowledge so much as for arts and habits; for the habit of attention, for the art of expression, for the art of assuming at a moment's notice a new intellectual posture, for the art of entering quickly into another person's thoughts, for the habit of submitting to censure and refutation, for the art of indicating assent or dissent in graduated terms, for the habit of regarding minute points of accuracy, for the habit of working out what is possible in a given time, for taste, for discrimination, for mental courage and mental soberness:
Above all, you go to a great school for self-knowledge."

— William Johnson Cory

"The ideal man bears the accidents of life with dignity and grace, making the best of circumstances."

—Aristotle

"In the arena of human life the honors and rewards fall to those who show their good qualities in action."

—Aristotle

"The essential thing is action. Action has three stages: the decision born of thought, the order or preparation for execution, and the execution itself. All three stages are governed by the will.

The will is rooted in character, and for the man of action character is of more critical importance than intellect. Intellect without will is worthless, will without intellect is dangerous."

—Hans von Seekt

"Dignity does not consist in possessing honors, but in deserving them."

—Aristotle

"He who has never learned to obey cannot be a good commander."

—Aristotle

"I count him braver who overcomes his desires than him who conquers his enemies; for the hardest victory is over self."

—Aristotle

"We are what we repeatedly do. Excellence, therefore, is not an act but a habit."

—Aristotle

"Wicked men obey from fear; good men, from love."

—Aristotle

"It is the mark of an educated mind to be able to entertain a thought without accepting it."

—Aristotle

"All who have meditated on the art of governing mankind have been convinced that the fate of empires depends on the education of youth."

—Aristotle

"The worst form of inequality is to try to make unequal things equal."

—Aristotle

"Those who educate children well are more to be honored than parents, for these only gave life, those the art of living well."

—Aristotle

"An apt and true reply was given to Alexander the Great by a pirate who had been seized. For when that king had asked the man what he meant by keeping hostile possession of the sea, he answered with bold pride. 'What thou meanest by seizing the whole earth; but because I do it with a petty ship, I am called a robber, whilst thou who dost it with a great fleet art styled emperor.'"

—St. Augustine

"The good Christian should beware of mathematicians, and all those who make empty prophecies. The danger already exists that the mathematicians have made a covenant with the devil to darken the spirit and to confine man in the bonds of Hell."

—St. Augustine

"Bad company is like a nail driven into a post, which, after the first or second blow, may be drawn out with little difficulty; but being once driven up to the head, the pincers cannot take hold to draw it out, but which can only be done by the destruction of the wood."

—St. Augustine

"Be always displeased with what thou art, if your desirest to attain to what thou art not; for where thou hast pleased thyself, there thou abidest. But if thou have enough thou perisheth. Always add, always walk, always proceed. Neither stand still, nor go back, nor deviate."

—St. Augustine

"If it is not right do not do it; if it is not true do not say it."

—Marcus Aurelius

"And thou wilt give thyself relief, if thou doest every act of thy life as if it were the last."

—Marcus Aurelius

"The art of living is more like that of wrestling than of dancing; the main thing is to stand firm and be ready for an unseen attack."

—Marcus Aurelius

"If you are distressed by anything external, the pain is not due to the thing itself but to your own estimate of it; and this you have the power to revoke at any moment."

—Marcus Aurelius

"A wise man will make more opportunities than he finds."

—Francis Bacon

"Knowledge itself is power."

—Francis Bacon

"Whoever is out of patience is out of possession of his soul. Men must not turn into bees, and kill themselves in stinging others."

—Francis Bacon

"Silentium, stultorum virtus: Silence is the virtue of fools."

—Francis Bacon

"In war the chief incalculable is the human will."

—B.H. Liddell Hart

"Positions are seldom lost because they have been destroyed, but almost invariably because the leader has decided in his own mind that the position can not be held."

—A.A. Vandegrift

"Battles are won by slaughter and manoeuvre. The greater the general, the more he contributes in manoeuvre, the less he demands in slaughter."

—Winston Churchill

"Imagination was given to man to compensate him for what he is not; a sense of humor to console him for what he is."

—Francis Bacon

"If money be not thy servant, it will be thy master. The covetous man cannot so properly be said to possess wealth, as that may be said to possess him."

—Francis Bacon

"Some books are to be tasted; others swallowed; and some to be chewed and digested."

—Francis Bacon

"A little philosophy inclineth man's mind to atheism, but depth of philosophy bringeth a man's mind about to religion."

—Francis Bacon

"Reading maketh a full man, conference a ready man, and writing an exact man."

—Francis Bacon

"All rising to a great place is by a winding stair."

—Francis Bacon

"Injustice anywhere is a threat to justice everywhere."

—Martin Luther King

"The quality, not the longevity, of one's life is what is important."

—Martin Luther King

"One who condones evil is just as guilty as the one who perpetrates it."

—Martin Luther King

"Leadership is a choice, not a position."

—Dr. Stephen R. Covey

"Never let them see you sweat. They may see you fail, and accept that failure, but Marines (and Sailors) will quickly lose confidence in you if they see you panic."

—LtCol Joe Thomas, USMC (Ret.)

"The principle on which to manage an army is to set up one standard of courage which all must reach."

—SunTzu

"Perfect courage and utter cowardice are two extremes that rarely occur. No one can answer for his courage when he has never been in danger. Courage, in soldiers, is a dangerous profession they follow to earn their living."

—Rochefoucauld

"The courage of the troops must be reborn daily. . . nothing is so variable . . . the true skill of the general consists in knowing how to guarantee it."

—de Saxe

"As to moral courage, I have rarely met with two o'clock in the morning courage: I mean unprepared courage."

—Napoleon

"War is the realm of danger; therefore courage is the soldier's first requirement. Courage is of two kinds: courage in the face of personal danger, and courage to accept responsibility, either before the tribunal of some outside power or before the court of one's conscience."

—Carl von Clausewitz

"The most essential qualities for a general will always be: first, a high moral courage, capable of great resolution; second, a physical courage which takes no account of danger. His scientific or military acquirements are secondary to these."

—Jomini

"Courage is rightly esteemed the first of human qualities, because . . . it is the quality that guarantees all others."

—Sir Winston S. Churchill

"On the field there is no substitute for courage, no other binding influence toward unity of action. Troops will excuse almost any stupidity; excessive timidity is simply unforgivable."

—S. L. A. Marshall

"An army of deer led by a lion is more to be feared than an army of lions led by a deer."

—Philip II of Macedon

"The leader must himself believe that willing obedience always beats forced obedience, and that he can get this only by really knowing what should be done. Thus he can secure obedience from his men because he can convince them that he knows best, precisely as a good doctor makes his patients obey him. Also he must be ready to suffer more hardships than he asks of his soldiers more fatigue, greater extremes of heat and cold."

—Xenophon

"A leader is a dealer in hope."

—Napoleon

"The more the leader is in the habit of demanding from his men, the surer he will be that his demands will be answered."

—Carl von Clausewitz

"The moral equilibrium of the man is tremendously affected by an outward calmness on the part of the leader. The soldier's nerves, taut from anxiety of what lies ahead, will be soothed and healed if the leader sets an example of coolness. Bewildered by the noise and confusion of battle, the man feels instinctively that the situation cannot be so dangerous as it appears if he sees that his leader remains unaffected, that his orders are given clearly and deliberately, and that his tactics show decision and judgment. However 'jumpy' the man feels, the inspiration of his leader's example shames him into swallowing his own fear. But if the leader reveals himself irresolute and confused, the more even than if he shows personal fear, the infection spreads instantly to his men." (July 1921)

—Basil Liddell Hart

"The quality of leadership needs, above all, spirit, intelligence, and sympathy. Spirit is needed to fire men to self-sacrificing achievements; intelligence, because men will only respect and follow a leader whom they feel knows his profession thoroughly; sympathy, to understand the mentality of each individual in order to draw out the best that is in him. Given these qualities, men will conquer fear to follow a leader." (July 1921)

—Basil Liddell Hart

"The real leader displays his quality in his triumphs over adversity, however great it may be."

—General of the Army George C. Marshall, 18 September 1941, address to 1st Officer Candidate Class, Fort Benning, Georgia

"No man is a leader until his appointment is ratified in the minds and hearts of his men."

—Anon.

"A leader is a man who has the ability to get other people to do what they don't want to do, and like it."

—Harry S. Truman

"Leadership can be taught, but not character. The one arises from the other. A successful leader of men must have character, ability and be prepared to take unlimited responsibility. Responsibility can only be learned by taking responsibility; you cannot learn the piano without playing on one. Leadership is the practical application of character. It implies the ability to command to make obedience proud and free."

—Colonel Richard Meinertzhagen

"I hold that leadership is not a science, but an art. It conceives an ideal, states it as an objective, and than seeks actively and earnestly to attain it, everlastingly preserving, because the records of war are full of successes coming to those leaders who stuck it out just a little longer than their opponents."

—General Mathew B. Ridgway

"One of my cardinal rules of battle leadership— or leadership in any field—is to be yourself, to strive to apply the basic principles of art of war, and to seek to accomplish your assigned missions by your own methods and in your own way."

—General Mathew B. Ridgway

"Leadership must be based on goodwill. Goodwill does not mean posturing and, least of all, pandering to the mob. It means obvious and wholehearted commitment to helping followers. We are tired of leaders we fear, tired of leaders we love, and most tired of leaders who let us take liberties with them. What we need for leaders are men of the heart who are so helpful that they, in effect, do away with the need of their jobs. But leaders like that are never out of a job, never out of followers. Strange as it sounds, great leaders gain authority by giving it away."

—Admiral James B. Stockdale

"One final aspect of leadership is the frequent necessity to be a philosopher, able to understand and to explain the lack of a moral economy in this universe, for many people have a great deal of difficulty with the fact that virtue is not always rewarded nor is evil always punished. To handle tragedy may indeed be the mark of an educated man, for one of the principal goals of education is to prepare us for failure. To say that is not to encourage resignation to the whims of fate, but to acknowledge the need for forethought about how to cope with undeserved reverses. It's important that our leadership steel themselves against the natural reaction of lashing out or withdrawing when it happens. The test of character is not 'hanging in there' when the light at the end of the tunnel is expected but performance of duty and persistence of example when the situation rules out the possibility of the light ever coming."

—Admiral James B. Stockdale

"There are three types of leader: Those who make things happen; those who watch things happen; and those who wonder what happened!"

—Anon.

"The man who spends more sleepless nights with his army and who works harder in drilling his troops runs the fewest risks in fighting the foe."

—The Emperor Maurice

"The soldiers like training provided it is carried out sensibly."

—Field Marshal Prince Aleksandr V. Suvorov

"Make peace a time of training for war, and battle an exhibition of bravery."

—The Emperor Maurice

"My troops are good and well-disciplined, and the most important thing of all is that I have thoroughly habituated them to perform everything that they are required to execute. You will do something more easily, to a higher standard, and more bravely when you know that you will do it well."

—Frederick the Great

"There is no studying the battlefield. It is then simply a case of doing what is possible, to make use of what one knows and, in order to make a little possible, one must know much."

—Marshal of France Ferdinand Foch

"There is a tendency in peace time to conduct training by use of stereotyped situations which are solved by stereotyped solutions. In war, however, we cannot say, 'This situation is so and so according to the rules which I have learned, I must attack or defend'. The situations that confront one in war are generally obscure, highly complicated and never conform to type. They must be met by an alert mind, untrammeled by set forms and fixed ideas. In our peace-time tactical training we should use difficult, highly imaginative situations and require clear, concise and simple orders, The more difficult the situations, the more simple the order must be. Above all let us kill everything stereotyped; otherwise it will kill us."

—Captain Adolf von Schell

"Troops must be toughened mentally so that adverse conditions will not divert them from their mission. Fatigue, loss of sleep, limited rations, adverse weather conditions and other hardships must not weaken the determination to find and destroy the enemy."

—General Lesley J. McNair

"The commander must be at constant pains to keep his troops abreast of all the latest tactical experience and developments, and must insist on their practical application. He must see to it that his subordinates are trained in accordance with the latest requirements. The best form of welfare for the troops is first-class training, for this saves unnecessary casualties."

—Field Marshal Erwin Rommel

"To bring men to a proper degree of Subordination, is not the work of a day, a month, or even a year."

—General George Washington

"Military sway lies not merely in warships and arms, but also in the immaterial power that wields them. If we consider that a gun whose every shot tells can hold its own against a hundred guns which can hit only one shot in a hundred, we seamen must seek military power spiritually. The cause of the recent victory of our navy, though it was in a great degree due to the Imperial virtue, must also be attributed to our training in peaceful times which produced its fruit in war."

—Admiral Marquis Togo Heihachiro

"The definition of military training is success in battle. In my opinion that is the only objective of military training. It wouldn't make any sense to have a military organization on the backs of the American taxpayers with any other definition. I've believed that ever since I've been a Marine."

—Lieutenant General Lewis 'Chesty' Puller

"No speech of admonition can be so fine that it will at once make those who hear it good men if they are not good already; it would surely not make archers good if they had not had previous practice in shooting; neither could it make lancers good, nor horsemen; it cannot even make men able to endure bodily labour, unless they have been trained to do it before."

—Cyrus the Younger

"The greatest difficulty I find is in causing orders and regulations to be obeyed. This arises not from a spirit of disobedience, but from ignorance."

—General Robert E. Lee

"Untutored courage is useless in the face of educated bullets."

—General George S. Patton

"The first day I was at camp I was afraid I was going to die. The next two weeks my sole fear was that I wasn't going to die. And after that I knew I'd never die because I'd become so hard nothing could kill me."

—Anon.

"Battles are fought by platoons and squads. Place emphasis on small unit combat instruction so that it is conducted with the same precision as close-order drill."

—General George S. Patton, Jr.

"Participation in sport may help turn a mild bookkeeper into a warrior if it has conditioned his mind so that he relishes the contest. The act of teaching one man to participate with other men in any training endeavor is frequently the first step in the development of new traits of receptiveness and outward giving in his character. It is from the acquiring of the habit of working with the group and of feeling responsible to the group that his thoughts are apt to turn ultimately to the welfare of the group when tactical disintegration occurs in battle; the more deeply this is impressed into his consciousness, the quicker will he revert under pressure to thinking and acting on behalf of the group."

—S. L. A. Marshall

"More emphasis will be placed on the hardening of men and officers. All soldiers and officers should be able to run a mile with combat pack in ten minutes and march eight miles in two hours. When soldiers are in actual contact with the enemy, it is almost impossible to maintain physical condition, but if the physical condition is high before they gain contact, it will not fall off sufficiently during contact to be detrimental."

—General George S. Patton

"I am a United States Sailor.
I will support and defend the Constitution of the United States of America and I will obey the orders of those appointed over me.
I represent the fighting spirit of the Navy and those who have gone before me to defend freedom and democracy around the world.
I proudly serve my country's Navy combat team with Honor, Courage and Commitment.
I am committed to excellence and the fair treatment of all."

—The Sailor's Creed

"When troops lack the coordinated response which comes of long, varied and rigorous exercises, their combat losses will be excessive, and they will lack cohesion in their action against the enemy, and they will uselessly expend much of their initial velocity."

—Brigadier General S. L. A. Marshall

"The highest form of physical training that an officer can undergo is the physical conditioning of his own men."

—Brigadier General S. L. A. Marshall

"The great man is more difficult to point out than the great artist. In an art or profession the man who has outdistanced his rivals (or who has the reputation of having done so) is called great in his work, with reservations as to his character. But the great man must exhibit different merit. It is easier to say who are not great men than who are. They should have great virtues. It is agreed that Cromwell was a most intrepid general, profound statesman, and the man best qualified to conduct the party, parliament, or army of his day, yet no writer has called him a

great man because, al though he possessed great qualities, he possessed not a single great virtue."

—Francois Marie Arouet de Voltaire

"All ages have said and repeated that one should strive to know one's self. This is a strange demand which no one up to now has measured up to and, strictly considered, no one should. With all his study and effort, man is directed to what is outside, to the world about him, and he is kept busy coming to know this and to master it to the extent that his purposes require. Of himself he has knowledge only when he enjoys or suffers, and thus it is only through pain and pleasure that he finds out what he has to seek and what to avoid. But in general man has to grope his way. He knows not whence he comes nor whither he goes; he knows little of the world and himself least of all."

—Johann Wolfgang von Goethe

"Cease to brag to me of America, and its model institutions and constitutions. To men in their sleep there is nothing granted in this world: nothing or as good as nothing, to men that sit idly caucusing and ballot-boxing on the graves of their heroic ancestors, saying, "It is well, it is well!" Corn and bacon are granted: not a very sublime boon, on such conditions; a boon moreover which, on such conditions, cannot last! No: America too will have to strain its energies, in quite other fashion than this; to crack its sinews, and all but break its heart, as the rest of us have had to do, in thousandfold wrestle with the Pythons and mud-demons, before it can become a habitation for the gods. America's battle is yet to fight; and we, sorrowful though nothing doubting, will wish her strength for it. New spiritual Pythons, plenty of them; enormous megatherians, as ugly as were ever born of mud, loom huge and hideous out of the twilight Future of America; and she will have her own agony, and her own victory, but on other terms than she is yet aware of."

—Thomas Carlyle

"It is very easy in the world to live by the opinion of the world. It is very easy in solitude to be self-centered. But the finished man is he who in the midst of the crowd keeps with perfect sweetness the independence of solitude. I knew a man of simple habits and earnest character who never put out his hand nor opened his lips to court the public, and having survived several rotten reputations of younger men, Honor came at last and sat down with him upon his private bench from which he had never stirred.

—Ralph Waldo Emerson

"The despotism of *custom* is everywhere the standing hindrance to human advancement, being in unceasing antagonism to that disposition to aim at something better than customary, which is called, according to circumstances, the spirit of liberty, or that of progress or improvement. The spirit of improvement is not always a spirit of liberty, for it may aim at forcing improvements on an unwilling people; and the spirit of liberty, in so far as it resists such attempts, may ally itself locally and temporarily with the opponents of improvement; but the only unfailing and permanent source of improvement is liberty, since by it there are as many possible independent centers of improvement as there are individuals."

—John Stuart Mill

"What is all wisdom save a collection of platitudes? Take fifty of our current proverbial sayings—they are so trite, so threadbare, that we can hardly bring our lips to utter them. None the less they embody the concentrated experience of the race, and the man who orders his life according to their teaching cannot go far wrong. How easy that seems! Has anyone ever done so? Never. Has any man ever attained to inner harmony by pondering the experience of others? Not since the world began! He must pass through the fire."

—Norman Douglas

"Human beings differ profoundly in regard to the tendency to regard their lives as a whole. To some men it is natural to do so, and essential to happiness to be able to do so with some satisfaction. To others life is a series of detached incidents without directed movement and without unity. I think the former sort are more likely to achieve happiness than the latter, since they will gradually build up those circumstances from which they can derive contentment and self-respect, whereas the other will be blown about by the winds of circumstance, now this way, now that, without ever arriving at any haven. The habit of viewing life as a whole is an essential part both of wisdom and of true morality, and is one of the things which ought to be encouraged in education."

—Bertrand Russell

"Individuality reigns over the living world, but it is more clearly and powerfully revealed in man. Everything man has accomplished in art, science and industry is due to his inbred individuality. Individuality was the moving force which raised man from the depths of savagery to the civilization of our day. A nation which attempts to suppress man's drive toward great individuality and to standardize thoughts, ideas and behavior, in a word, to reduce man to the status of an automaton, is going *against* the evolutionary process. Such a nation has no future in the civilized sense of that term. A political or social movement which in its ignorance hopes to suppress the individuality of man, as is the case with Russian communism, not only is a reactionary force by itself, but actually is waging a lost battle. For the individualistic drives of the human race cannot be stopped by any force within nature, least of all by the stupid terrorism practiced by a police state."

—Boris Sokoloff

"Sacrifice signifies neither amputation nor repentance. It is, in essence, an act. It is the gift of oneself to the being of which one forms a part.

Only he can understand what a farm is, what a country is, who shall have sacrificed part of himself to his farm or his country, sought to save it, struggled to make it beautiful.

We had, bit by bit, introduced a code for the collectivity which neglected the existence of man. That code explains early why the individual should sacrifice himself for the community. It does not explain clearly and without ambiguity why the community should sacrifice itself for a single member. Why is it equitable that a thousand die to deliver a single man from unjust imprisonment? And yet it is this principle alone which differentiates us from the anthill and which is the source of the grandeur of mankind."

—Antoine de Saint-Exupery

"As soon as you begin to take yourself seriously and imagine that your virtues are important because they are yours, you become the prisoner of your own vanity and even your best works will blind and deceive you. Then, in order to defend yourself, you will begin to see sins and faults everywhere in the actions of other men. And the more unreasonable importance you attach to yourself and to your own works, the more you will tend to build up your own idea of yourself *by* condemning other people. Some of the most virtuous men in the world are also the bitterest and most unhappy, because they have unconsciously come to believe that all their happiness depends on their being more virtuous than other men."

—Thomas Merton

Appendix B: Classics of Naval Literature Series

In the U.S. Naval Institute Press' *Classics of Naval Literature Series* editor James Sweetman writes "This series makes available new editions of classic works of naval history, biography, and fiction. Each volume is complete and unabridged and includes an authoritative introduction written specifically for Classics of Naval Literature." As a single source for some of the finest and most important works on the subject of naval leadership, the series is still unsurpassed. If *Leadership Explored* whets the appetite to read further, *Classics of Naval Literature* is a multi-course meal. Each volume contains timeless wisdom appropriate for the contemporary reader. Best of all, each work is an absolute pleasure to read.

The series includes:

Beach, Edward L. *Run Silent, Run Deep*..

Buell, Thomas B. *The Quiet Warrior: A Biography of Admiral Raymond A. Spruance*.

Buenzle, Fred J. and A. Grove Day. *Bluejacket: An Autobiography*

Clark Charles E. *My Fifty Years in the Navy*.

Dewey, George. *Autobigraphy of George Dewey*.

Forester, C.S. *The Good Shepherd*.

Frederick Marryat. *Mr. Midshipman Easy*.

Goodrich, Marcus. *Delilah*..

Guttridge, Leonard F. and Jay D. Smith. *The Commodores*.

Hendrick, Burton J. and William S. Sims. *The Victory at Sea*.

Hobson, Richard Pearson. *The Sinking of the Merrimac*.

McKenna Richard. *The Sand Pebbles*.

Melville, Herman. *White Jacket*.

Monsarrat, Nicholas. *The Cruel Sea*.

Morison, Samuel Eliot. *John Paul Jones: A Sailor's Biography*.

Nordhoff, Charles. *Sailor Life on Man of War and Merchant Vessel*.

Parker, William Harwar. *Recollections of a Naval Officer, 1841–1865*.

Porter, David. *Journal of a Cruise Made to the Pacific Ocean by David Porter in the United States Figate Essex in the Years 1812, 1813, and 1814.*

Roosevelt, Theodore. *The Naval War of 1812.*

Sinclair, Arthur W. *Two Years on the Alabama.*

Slocum, Joshua. *Sailing Alone Around the World.*

Sprout, Harold and Margaret Sprout. *The Rise of American Seapower, 1775–1918.*

Stafford, Edward P. *The Big E.*

Wouk, Herman. *The Caine Mutiny.*

Young, Filson. *With the Battle Cruisers.*

Appendix C:
The Marine Corps Reading List

FMFRP 0-64 *A Book on Books*

Why We Have the Professional Reading Program and How It Can Work for You

Read and reread the campaigns of Alexander, Hannibal, Caesar, Gustaphus Adolphus, Turenne, Eugene and Frederick; take them as your mode;, that is the only way of becoming a great captain: to obtain the secrets of the art of war.

—Napoleon

Our goal as Marines is to be ready for war. Some of the ways we achieve that goal include combat training, the maintenance of weapons and equipment, and physical fitness. These steps alone, however, do not prepare us adequately for war as we would find ourselves physically ready, but mentally unprepared to fight. Mental readiness is attained partially through training, but primarily it is acquired as a result of professionally oriented education.

The ability to make clear and swift judgments amidst chaos is what sets warriors apart intellectually. Practice in the field and in wargames is important to improving our military judgment, but its development remains anchored to a sound understanding of war. Through education we can equip ourselves to make sound military judgments even in chaotic and uncertain situations. And it is here that professional reading plays a vital role.

Professional reading enriches our knowledge and understanding of war. This by itself, however, is not the primary reason for pursuing a professional reading program. Timely and correct actions taken on the battlefield are. How do we translate written words into sound military decisions? Obviously, the first step is to read. Then, we must relate what we have read to what we actually do in training, field exercises, wargames, leadership, and the like. The means of accomplishing this are many and varied, but some proven methods are discussed below.

Reading in Depth About a Single Battle

The professional reading program is designed to enhance every Marines' understanding of the subject of war. The thorough study of a single battle goes a long way towards attaining that military literacy.

Take the battle of Tarawa, for instance. You might begin with Robert Sherrod's *Tarawa*, and then supplement your reading by looking up Tarawa in the indexes of Isely and Crowl's *The U.S. Marines and Amphibious War*, Moskin's *The Marine Corps Story*, and Spector's *Eagle Against the Sun*. By the time you have studied one battle in this way, you will have learned much about your profession on multiple levels. You will

- Learn how the Japanese defended the island; how they integrated artillery and armor into their defense and how they made extensive use of bunkers and other field fortifications (including coconut logs at the beach to make it difficult for men and machines to traverse).
- Learn what Marines did to penetrate these defenses; how they employed reconnaissance, task-organized rifle squads, and combined arms in the form of artillery, naval gunfire, and aviation.
- Learn how the Japanese Naval Infantry on Tarawa was moved to fight virtually to the last man and reflect on why.
- Realize that American aviation at Tarawa was virtually unopposed—and take that into account.
- See that a static defense, isolated on something such as an island, is defeatable, no matter how strong—and come to grips with the number of casualties it cost to reduce such a defense.

In seeing how this *irresistible force* clashed and grappled with what seemed an *immovable object*,

you will make discoveries about offensive and defensive tactics, reconnaissance, and combined arms. Lessons of intelligence are inescapable, as you view the two sides groping to come to terms with one another.

But there will be much more. Study of this one battle will also take you to the higher levels of war, the operational and strategic.

In setting the stage for the story of Tarawa, each author gives you his or her own version of why we attacked Tarawa and probably something about why the Japanese defended it.

If you trace these concepts back through Admiral Nimitz at Pearl Harbor and on to Washington, or back to Tokyo on the Japanese side, you

- Will learn much about the opposing strategies and the campaigns waged to support them.
- May, in fact, conclude that the Japanese high command in Tokyo never expected to hold Tarawa, or they never would have allowed it to become so isolated.
- Will discover that communications were vital on both sides but did not work as planned, and that the ramifications of this were major, especially for the Japanese. This will teach you lessons about command and control.
- Will see how reserves were employed and how they might have been better employed.
- Will see how technological foresight equipped us with the amphibious vehicles we needed, but that no one actually foresaw how many we would need or why we would need them because of the fog and friction, the ever present uncertainty of war.
- Will learn about the moral dimensions of war and leadership, especially in Sherrod's book:

    What kind of men did it take?
    How frightened were they?
    How did they overcome their fears?
    Where did they get their courage?
    What does it mean to be a Marine, anyway?

So now, studying this single battle has revealed lessons about the operational art, strategy, communications, technology, the friction of war, leadership, and morale. Marines who know one battle well know more about their profession than those who have read a hundred manuals. They may not be able to define what they know, or divide the battle into phases, or tell you where the line of departure was, or who manufactured the aircraft or what kind of alloys were in the metal of the machines. They may still need to read some manuals, but they have gained a sensing of what the battle was about. Robert Sherrod, when he wrote about Tarawa, didn't write to teach people how to fight. He wrote to relate his experience. The serious reader can learn a lot about how to fight by reflecting on the experience that Robert Sherrod has related.

Much—in fact most—of what the reader has learned about Tarawa, can be applied to other battles. Such things as courage, leadership, stratagem, dispersion, and focus have applied in every battle and will apply to future battles. They can be learned equally well from thorough studies of Tarawa, Khe Sanh, Chosin, Iwo Jima, Belleau Wood, Gettysburg, or Cannae.

Reading About Many Battles

We have already discussed how your military literacy improves if you read in-depth about a single battle. It follows that reading about many battles should improve your military literacy that much more. That is why you are encouraged to read several books a year. In so doing, you will discover that some aspects of battle are timeless, never changing from antiquity through the present, in cold climates or hot, in jungle or desert. Other aspects do change and one of the best ways you can gain professional insights into which things stay the same and which things change is to read about many different battles.

Reading About Subjects Other Than Battles

History gives you an appreciation for the realities of your profession. This is essential. But you should read more than history. Read military theory as well, including Sun-tzu, Clausewitz, Bernard Brodie, or Michael Howard.

A word of caution here! The works of theorists often get condensed and simplified. This may be done, for example, on the assumption that the reader does not wish to tackle something as lengthy and profound as Clausewitz, and so his ideas are condensed into simplified principles or even procedures. That is how much of our previous doctrine was written. The reader of such condensed works unwittingly becomes the prisoner of someone else's theories. The only way for us to gain our freedom from this kind of imprisonment is to read about the human experience in war ourselves, then draw our own conclusions. Remember, all these theorists developed their theories by first studying battle. They then developed conclusions about war in general. You may arrive at different conclusions. In order to assert that your ideas are as good or better than someone else's, you have a responsibility to do at least as much study of real war as he did.

Do not restrict yourself to battles alone. Campaigns and wars need to be studied too. They can be studied with or without focusing on the battles.

Read good fiction. *The Red Badge of Courage* is on the list, for instance. It is well known that its author was never in combat. Yet he had a real-life understanding of fear and what fear does to people. Anyone who has been in combat and read *The Red Badge of Courage* recognizes that Stephen Crane did an excellent job of describing fear. Because Marine leaders must work with their Marines to discourage them from taking counsel of their fears, it is important for us to be literate in the subject. Read about subjects such as this through the best commentators our culture has to offer.

Do not restrict yourself to reading only those books that are on the Marine Corps reading list! The requirement is small—two to three books a year—for a reason. It allows you to read the classics, other books not directly related to warfighting, and the kinds of books you enjoy the most.

It is also just as important for you to know what you are fighting for and what you stand for as it is to know how to fight. The *Iliad*, the *Odyssey*, the works of Plato, the Declaration of Independence, and the Constitution of the United States are all works we need to be familiar with if we are to be well-rounded professionals tasked with guarding our nation. You will notice that the Constitution, which we as Marines are sworn to defend, is the only selection assigned to all grades.

How to Read

Some Marines are anxious about this program because they do not read well. Fear not. The best way to learn to read is to read. *Read slowly*. Speed will come in time. Besides, speed is not an important thing. Understanding is. It is not the number of books you read that will help you in combat. It is what you learn from these books. The main thing to remember is that the professional reading program is not an exercise in speed reading. It is an exercise in understanding.

If you have been in love and read a love letter, you already know how to read. Dr. Mortimer Adler's analogy continues:

When people are in love and reading a love letter they read every word three ways: they read between the lines and in the margins; they read the whole in terms of the parts, and each part in terms of the whole; they grow sensitive to context and ambiguity, to insinuation and implication; they perceive the color of words, the odor of phrases, and the weight of sentences. They may even take the punctuation into account. Then, if never before or after, they read.

It is for this reason that reading is so different from watching television. When we are reading,

the mind is active. When we are watching television, it is passive. We grow intellectually, as we do physically, when we are active, not passive.

You may want to read Dr. Adler's *How to Read a Book*, especially if you are in a leadership position. It is a great help in explaining to others why it is important to read, what one gains from reading, and how best to get the most out of it. Because the Corps is depending on leaders in the chain of command to make the professional reading program work, many Marine leaders will want to read Adler's book.

What to Read

We have individual goals and common goals for our professional reading program. Marines should pick their books according to their needs, filling in areas where they are weak and reinforcing where they are strong. A commander may also make choices for the unit, especially when he or she identifies a need for the unit to read a single work or to read on a specific topic. We *do not* want reading contests—attempts to see which unit can read more. This would conflict with the spirit of the program.

The listed books are seed corn to stimulate interests in reading about our profession. Marines should be encouraged to read works that are not on the list, too. Both the individual and the Corps benefit each time a Marine discovers a new work that is relevant and useful. New material is always coming out, more than any centralized official body can ever discover. To that end, chapter 3 of this manual provides both general battle references and recommended periodicals that can help Marines remain current in our changing world.

What Not To Read

Nothing. There is nothing that Marines are discouraged from reading. We are not in the business of book banning or censorship. Marines can and should read whatever they want.

About the Book List

Why are books listed? The list consists of those books that are especially helpful in learning the profession; that is, learning the art of war. The list was compiled by Marines or scholars who have worked closely with Marines. Therefore, each book helped some Marine or a friend of the Marine Corps to learn about the art of war. The same book might help you too.

Why aren't books listed? There are any number of reasons for not listing certain books. Some of the best books in the world are not on the list. But no two persons are likely to agree on what the best books in the world really are. The list serves as a guide to give all Marines a common basis, a foundation for understanding and communication.

Implementation and Impact of the Program

Implementing the program is not complicated. All the information you need is contained in this book. The manner in which the program is implemented is left up to the discretion and initiative of commanders and individuals.

Do not anticipate a reporting process or a centralized requirement for written exams designed to assure that Marines are reading. The Commandant does indeed desire assurance that Marines are reading, but he depends entirely upon his chain of command to see that this is done.

How do leaders know if their Marines are reading? By talking to them. By observing them in the field. And, most importantly, by reading, themselves.

We should not rule out the possibility of a Marine knowing a great deal about the profession of warfare without reading. If that is the case, the Marine certainly deserves to be rated along with those who do read. However. the probability of a Marine being an expert on war without reading is slim. Our Vietnam veterans are becoming fewer and fewer in number, and even they have a limited perspective if they do not read. Most of them have experienced only one war. A corner of Southeast Asia, seven years of time, an oriental culture, a few degrees span of latitude, an issue of communism; these things are far from being representative of war as we are likely to know it in our time. Our reading program purposely covers a vast spectrum of wars including ancient and modern, cold weather and tropical, guerrilla and conventional. Few if any Marines can be as widely knowledgeable as we want them to be without doing, their required reading.

This leads to a question frequently asked: "Will professional reading affect promotion opportunities, fitness reports, assignments. etc.?" Of course it will. Granted, it is knowledge of warfare—more specifically, military judgment derived from that knowledge—that is the determinant, but the connection to professional reading is inescapable.

In evaluating a Marine as a professional warrior, we do not count the number of books read in a year. Instead, we gauge the capacity for sound military judgment. Yes, the Marine Corps certainly expects—in fact requires—the reading of two to three books annually from the list. But the output we desire is the daily display of military judgment that will serve our Marines and the American people in time of war. As a Marine's career progresses, so too should the level of judgment, encompassing higher levels of war and an appreciation for larger and larger units, more equipment, and issues such as sustainability, public opinion, and operational tempo: This progression must come from many ingredients, practice, exercises, and maturity, to name a few. Professional reading speeds that progression and lends a depth of understanding that would otherwise be missing.

Acquiring the Books

The requirement to read breeds an atmosphere that is well known to anyone who has been on a university campus. It has already begun on

Marine bases. Marines will decide which books to buy and which books to borrow based on what they want in their libraries at home for future reference and what they would rather read, ingest, and dispose of. Individual and family budgets and the availability of books in libraries, retail markets, and used book exchanges will also be key factors.

Base libraries have stocked the books on the list. Commands may also establish book exchanges similar to those that exist on university campuses. There are two general concepts for a book exchange:

- First, Marines bring to the exchange listed books they have read and receive in return, at no cost. The Marine may then keep a used book or return it for another.
- In the second concept, used books are bought and sold.

Many people enjoy owning new books, especially editions that are personally meaningful or attractive. Books make wonderful gifts. Some commands have already begun to give a book as a memento where formerly a plaque might have been given.

In Summary

Aristotle recognized education as a necessity for survival in trying conditions, one of which is certainly in war. He called education a "refuge in adversity," while a mere "ornament in prosperity." Napoleon and Alexander the Great were both students and adherents of the idea of self-education.

Often, in times of adversity. there is a call for warriors who know what they are doing. And the American people trust, somewhat blindly, that these warriors will be there when they need them. Whether the warriors will be real or hollow depends on the seriousness with which they prepare. The professional reading program is more than a reading list. It is the cornerstone of a lifelong pursuit of the knowledge won by war-

riors who have gone before us. Having their experience is a great gift that is yours for the taking. It is important for you to draw upon the psdfde. The more you read, the more you will understand, and the richer will be your experience. Most importantly, you will be worthy of the trust that is placed in you as a guardian of our nation.

Private to Lance Corporal

Bowden, Mark. *Black Hawk Down: a Story of Modern War*. New York: Atlantic Monthly Press, 1999.

Forester, C.S. *Rifleman Dodd*. Baltimore: The Nautical & Aviation Publishing Company of America, 1989.

Hubbard, Elbert. *A Message to Garcia*. New York: Peter Pauper Press, 1982.

Marshall, S. L. A. *The Soldier's Load and the Mobility of a Nation*. Quantico: The Marine Corps Association, 1965.

Shaara, Michael. *The Killer Angels: a Novel*. New York: Crown, 1993.

Swinton, Ernest Dunlop. *The Defence of Duffer's Drift*. Wayne: Avery Publisher Group, 1986.

United States of America. *The Constitution of the United States of America*. Washington: U.S. G.P.O. : For sale by the U.S. G.P.O., Supt. of Docs., 1992.

Corporal to Sergeant

Bradley, James. *Flags of our Fathers*. New York: Bantam Books, 2000.

Crane, Stephen. *The Red Badge of Courage*. New York: Macmillan, 1962.

Michaels, G. J. *Tip of the Spear: U.S. Marine Light Armor in the Gulf War*. Annapolis: Naval Institute Press, 1998.

Miller, John G. *The Bridge at Dong Ha*. Annapolis: Naval Institute Press, 1989.

Pressfield, Steven. *Gates of Fire: an Epic Novel of the Battle of Thermopylae*. New York: Doubleday, 1998.

Schell, Adolf Von. *Battle Leadership*. Quantico,

VA: Marine Corps Association, 1999.

Shaara, Jeff. *The Last Full Measure*. New York: Ballantine Books, 1998.

Simmons, Edwin H. *The United States Marines: a History*. Annapolis: Naval Institute Press, 2003.

Sledge, E. B. *With the Old Breed, at Peleliu and Okinawa*. Novato: Presidio Press, 1981.

Webb, James H. *Fields of Fire: a Novel*. Annapolis: Naval Institute Press, 2000.

Staff Sergeant

Ambrose, Stephen. *Pegasus Bridge: June 6, 1944*. New York: Simon and Schuster, 1985.

Fehrenbach, T. R. *This Kind of War: the Classic Korean War History*. Washington: Brassey's, 1994.

Moore, Harold G. *We Were Soldiers Once and Young: Ia Drang, the battle that changed the war in Vietnam*. New York: Random House, 1992.

Patai, Raphael. *The Arab Mind*. New York: Hatherleigh Press, 2002.

Rommel, Erwin. *Infantry Attacks*. Novato: Presidio Press, 1990.

Sajer, Guy. *The Forgotten Soldier*. Washington, D.C.: Brassey's, 2000.

Sun Tzu. *The Art of War*. Boston. Random House, 1988.

Warr, Nicholas. *Phase Line Green: the Battle for Hue*. Annapolis: Naval Institute Press, 1997.

West, Francis J. *The Village*. New York: Harper & Row, 1972.

Gunnery Sergeant

Ambrose, Stephen E. *Citizen Soldiers: the U.S. Army from the Normandy Beaches to the Bulge to the Surrender of Germany, June 7, 1944-May 7, 1945*. New York: Simon & Schuster, 1997.

Boot, Max. *The Savage Wars of Peace: Small Wars and the Rise of American Power*. New York: Basic Books, 2002.

McClain, Sally. *Navajo Weapon: the Navajo Code Talkers*. Tucson: Rio Nuevo Publishers, 2001.

Millett, Allan Reed. *Semper Fidelis: the History of the United States Marine Corps*. New York: Maxwell Macmillan International, 1991.

Powell, Colin L. *My American Journey*. New York: Random House, 1995.

Russ, Martin. *Breakout: the Chosin Reservoir Campaign, Korea 1950*. New York: Fromm International, 1999.

Van Creveld, Martin L. *Command in War*. Cambridge: Harvard University Press, 1985.

Willock, Roger. *Unaccustomed to Fear: a Biography of the Late General Roy S. Geiger*. Quantico: Marine Corps Association, 1983.

Master Sergeant and First Sergeant

Asprey, Robert B. *War in the Shadows: the Guerilla in History*. New York: W. Morrow, 1994.

Chamberlain, Joshua Lawrence. *Bayonet! Forward: My Civil War Reminiscences*. Gettysburg: Stan Clark Military Books, 1994.

Keegan, John. *The Face of Battle*. Harmondsworth: Penguin, 1978.

Keegan, John. *The Mask of Command*. New York: Viking, 1987.

Lawrence, T. E. *Seven Pillars of Wisdom, a Triumph*. Garden City: Doubleday, Doran & Company, 1935.

Leckie, Robert. *Strong Men Armed: the United States Marines Against Japan*. New York: Da Capo Press, 1997.

Phillipson, David. *Band of Brothers*. Annapolis: Naval Institute Press, 1996.

Slim, William Joseph and Viscount Slim. *Defeat into Victory*. New York: D. McKay, 1961.

Master Gunnery Sergeant and Sergeant Major

Krulak, Victor H. *First to Fight: an Inside View of the U.S. Marine Corps*. Annapolis: Naval Institute Press, 1999.

Lejeune, John Archer. *The Reminiscences of a Marine*. Philadelphia, Dorrance and Company, 1930.

Meyers, Bruce F. *Fortune Favors the Brave: the Story of First Force Recon*. Annapolis: Naval Institute Press, 2000.

Twining, Merrill B. *No Bended Knee: the Battle for Guadalcanal: the Memoir of Gen. Merrill B. Twining USMC*. Novato: Presido, 1996.

Warrant Officers

Greene, Graham. *The Quiet American*. New York: Penguin Books, 1996.

Heinl, Robert Debs. *Victory at High Tide: the Inchon-Seoul Campaign*. Annapolis: Nautical & Aviation Pub. Co., 1979.

United States Dept. of Defense. *The Armed Forces Officer*. Washington: U.S. Govt. Print. Off., 1950.

U.S. Marine Corps. *Leading Marines*. Washington, DC: Headquarters, United States Marine Corps, 1995.

U.S. Marine Corps. *Small Wars Manual*. Washington, D.C.: United States Marine Corps, 1997.

Officer Candidate, Cadet or Midshipman

Forester, C. S. *Beat to Quarters*. Boston: Back Bay Books, 1999.

Hoffman, Jon T. *Chesty: the Story of Lieutenant General Lewis B. Puller, USMC*. New York: Random House, 2001.

Hubbard, Elbert. *A Message to Garcia*. New York: Peter Pauper Press, 1982.

Simmons, Edwin H. *The United States Marines: A History*. Annapolis: Naval Institute Press, 2003.

Second Lieutenant

English, John A. *On Infantry*. Westport: Praeger, 1994.

Fehrenbach, T. R. *This Kind of War: The Classic Korean War History*. Washington: Brassey's, 1994.

Forester, C. S. *Rifleman Dodd*. Quantico: Marine Corps University, 1996.

Keegan, John. *The Face of Battle*. Harmondsworth: Penguin, 1978.

Patai, Raphael. *The Arab Mind*. New York: Hatherleigh Press, 2002.

Reasoner, James. *Chancellorsville*. Nashville: Cumberland House, 2000.

Stoffey, Bob. *Cleared Hot!: A Marine Combat Pilot's Vietnam Diary*. New York: St. Martin's Press, 1992.

Turley, G. H. *The Easter Offensive, Vietnam, 1972*. Annapolis: Naval Institute Press, 1995.

Webb, James H. *Fields of Fire: A Novel*. Annapolis: Naval Institute Press, 2000.

First Lieutenant and Chief Warrant Officer 2

Alexander, Joseph H. *Utmost Savagery: the Three Days of Tarawa*. Annapolis: Naval Institute Press, 1995.

Jünger, Ernst. *The Storm of Steel: From the Diary of a German Storm-Troop Officer on the Western Front*. New York: H. Fertig, 1975.

Lederer, William J. *The Ugly American*. New York: Norton, 1958.

Lejeune, John Archer. *The Reminiscences of a Marine*. Philadelphia: Dorrance and Company, 1930.

MacDonald, Charles Brown. *Company Commander*. Washington: Infantry Journal Press, 1947.

Myrer, Anton. *Once an Eagle: a Novel*. New York: HarperCollins, 2000.

Rhodes, Elisha Hunt. *All for the Union: the Civil War Diary and Letters of Elisha Hunt Rhodes*. New York: Orion Books, 1991.

Rommel, Erwin. *Infantry Attacks*. Novato: Presidio Press, 1990.

Sajer, Guy. *The Forgotten Soldier*. Washington, D.C.: Brassey's, c2000.

Shy, John W. *A People Numerous and Armed: Reflections on the Military Struggle for American Independence*. Ann Arbor: University of Michigan Press, 1990.

Captain and Chief Warrant Officer 3

Bailey, J. B. A. *Field Artillery and Firepower*. Annapolis: Naval Institute Press, 2004.

Boot, Max. *The Savage Wars of Peace: Small Wars and the Rise of American Power*. New York: Basic Books, 2002.

Friedman, Thomas L. *From Beirut to Jerusalem*. New York: Farrar, Straus, Giroux, 1991.

Harmon, Christopher C. *Terrorism Today*. Portland: Frank Cass, 2000.

Infantry School. *Infantry in Battle*. Washington, D.C.: Headquarters, U.S. Marine Corps, 1997.

Keegan, John. *Fields of Battle: the Wars for North America*. New York: A.A. Knopf, 1996.

Manchester, William Raymond. *Goodbye, Darkness: a Memoir of the Pacific War*. New York: Dell, 1987.

Spector, Ronald H. *Eagle Against the Sun: the American War with Japan*. New York: Free Press, 1985.

Tanner, Robert G. *Stonewall in the Valley: Thomas J. "Stonewall" Jackson's Shenandoah Valley Campaign, Spring 1862*. Garden City: Doubleday, 1976.

Tzu, Sun. *The Art of War*. New York: Random House, 1988.

Van Creveld, Martin L. *Command in War*. Cambridge: Harvard University Press, 1985.

Willock, Roger. *Unaccustomed to Fear: a Biography of the Late General Roy S. Geiger, U.S.M.C*. Quantico: Marine Corps Association, 1983.

Major and Chief Warrant Officer 4

Anderson, Fred. *The Crucible of War: the Seven Years' War and the Fate of Empire in British North America, 1754–1766*. New York: Alfred A. Knopf, 2000.

Catton, Bruce. *Grant Takes Command*. Boston, Little, Brown, 1969.

Clausewitz, Carl Von. *On War*. New York: Knopf, 1993.

Forester, C. S. *The General*. Baltimore: Nautical & Aviation Pub. Co., 1982.

Keegan, John. *The Mask of Command*. New York: Viking, 1987.

Liddell Hart, Basil Henry, Sir. *Strategy*. New York, Praeger, 1955.

McPherson, James M. *Battle Cry of Freedom: the Civil War Era*. New York: Oxford University Press, 1988.

Middlekauff, Robert. *The Glorious Cause: the American Revolution, 1763–1789*. Oxford: Oxford University Press, 2005.

Millett, Allan Reed. *For the Common Defense: a Military History of the United States of America*. New York: Maxwell Macmillan International, 1994.

Sheehan, Neil. *A Bright Shining Lie: John Paul Vann and America in Vietnam*. New York: Random House, 1988.

Strachan, Hew. *European Armies and the Conduct of War*. Boston: Allen & Unwin, 1983.

Thucydides. *History of the Peloponnesian War*. New York: W.W. Norton & Co., 1998.

Tuchman, Barbara Wertheim. *The Guns of August*. New York, Macmillan, 1962.

Lieutenant Colonel and Chief Warrant Officer 5

Corum, James S. *The Roots of Blitzkrieg: Hans von Seeckt and the German Military Reform*. Lawrence: University Press of Kansas, 1992.

D'Este, Carlo. *Patton: A Genius for War*. New York: HarperPerennial, 1996.

Friedman, Thomas L. *The Lexus and the Olive Tree*. New York: Farrar, Straus, Giroux, 1999.

Handel, Michael I. *Masters of War: Classical Strategic Thought*. Portland: F. Cass, 2001.

Krepinevich, Andrew F. *The Army and Vietnam*. Baltimore: Johns Hopkins University Press, 1986.

Lawrence, T. E. *Seven Pillars of Wisdom; a Triumph*. Garden City: Doubleday, Doran & Co., 1938.

Royster, Charles. *A Revolutionary People at War: the Continental Army and American Character, 1775–1783*. Chapel Hill: University of North Carolina Press, 1979.

Slim, William Joseph Viscount Slim. *Defeat into Victory*. New York: D. McKay, 1961.

Utley, Robert Marshall. *Frontiersmen in Blue: the United States Army and the Indian, 1848–1865*. Lincoln: University of Nebraska Press, 1981.

Van Creveld, Martin L. *Supplying War: Logistics from Wallenstein to Patton*. Cambridge: Cambridge University Press, 1977.

Woodward, Sandy. *One Hundred Days: the Memoirs of the Falklands Battle Group Commander*. Annapolis: Naval Institute Press, 1997.

Colonel to General

Chandler, David G. *The Campaigns of Napoleon*. New York: Macmillan, 1966.

Chang, Iris. *The Rape of Nanking: the Forgotten Holocaust of World War II*. New York: Basic Books, 1997.

Cohen, Eliot A. *Supreme Command: Soldiers, Statesmen, and Leadership in Wartime*. New York: Free Press, 2002.

Eisenhower, Dwight D. *Crusade in Europe*. Garden City: Doubleday, 1948.

Fuller, J. F. C. *The Conduct of War, 1789–1961; a Study of the Impact of the French, Industrial, and Russian Revolutions on War and its Conduct*. New Brunswick, N.J., Rutgers University Press, 1961.

Fuller, J. F. C. *Generalship, its Diseases and their Cure; a Study of the Personal Factor in Command*. Harrisburg: Military Service Publishing Co., 1936.

Hanson, Victor Davis. *Carnage and Culture: Landmark Battles in the Rise of Western Power*. New York: Doubleday, 2001.

Hughes, Wayne P. *Fleet Tactics and Coastal Combat*. Annapolis: Naval Institute Press, 2000.

Kissinger, Henry. *Diplomacy*. New York: Touchstone, 1995.

Lynn, John A.. *Feeding Mars: Logistics in Western Warfare From the Middle Ages to the Present*. Boulder: Westview Press, 1993.

McMaster, H. R. *Dereliction of Duty: Lyndon Johnson, Robert McNamara, the Joint Chiefs of Staff, and the Lies that Led to Vietnam*. New York: HarperCollins, 1997.

McPherson, James M. *Abraham Lincoln and the Second American Revolution*. Oxford: Oxford University Press, 1991.

Millett, Allan R. and Williamson Murray. *Military Innovation in the Interwar Period*. Cambridge: Cambridge University Press, 1996.

Sherman, William T. *Memoirs of General W.T. Sherman*. New York: Library of America, 1990.

Sumida, Jon Tetsuro. *Inventing Grand Strategy and Teaching Command: the Classic Works of Alfred Thayer Mahan Reconsidered*. Baltimore: Johns Hopkins University Press, 1997.

Remarque, Erich Maria. *All Quiet on the Western Front*. New York: Fawcett Columbine, 1996.

Tolstoy, Leo. *War and Peace*. New York: Simon and Schuster, 1942.

Weigley, Russell Frank. *Eisenhower's Lieutenants: the Campaign of France and Germany, 1944–1945*. Bloomington: Indiana University Press, 1990.

Appendix D:The CNO's Professional Reading List

(To include Dr. Mortimer Adler's Response to the Question, "Why Read Books?")

Basic

Beach, Edward Latimer. *Run Silent, Run Deep.* London: Allan Wingate, 1955.

Beach, Edward Latimer. *The United States Navy: 200 years.* New York: H. Holt, 1986.

Clancy, Tom. *Hunt for Red October.* Annapolis: Naval Institute Press, 1984.

Clancy, Tom. *Red Storm Rising.* New York: Putnam, 1986.

Coonts, Stephen. *Flight of the Intruder.* Annapolis: Naval Institute Press, 1986.

Crane, Stephen. *Red Badge of Courage.* New York: D. Appleton and Company, 1925.

Hawking, Stephen W. *Brief History of Time: from the Big Bang to Black Holes.* New York: Bantam Books, 1988.

Lehman, John. *Command of the Seas.* New York: C. Scribner's Sons, 1988.

McKenna, Richard. *The Sand Pebbles: a Novel.* New York: Harper & Row, 1962.

Michener, James Albert. *The Source.* New York: Ballantine, 1965.

Monsarrat, Nicholas. *The Cruel Sea.* New York: A.A. Knopf, 1951.

Morison, Samuel Eliot. *Two Ocean War: a short history of the United States Navy in the Second World War.* Boston: Little, Brown and Co., 1963.

Peters, Thomas J. and Robert H. Waterman, Jr. *In Search of Excellence: Lessons From America's Best-Run Companies.* New York: Harper Business Essentials, 2004.

Remarque, Erich Maria. *All Quiet on the Western Front.* Boston: Little, Brown, and Company, 1929.

Raymond Manchester, William. *American Cae-*

sar: *Douglas MacArthur, 1880–1964.* Boston : Little, Brown, 1978.

Santoli, Al. *Everything We Had: an Oral History of the Vietnam War.* New York: Random House, 1981.

Shaara, Michael. *The Killer Angels.* 1974. New York: Crown, 1993.

Stockdale, James B. *In Love and War: the Story of a Family's Ordeal and Sacrifice During the Vietnam Years.* New York: Harper & Row, 1984.

Smith, Hedrick. *The Russians.* New York: Quadrangle/New York Times Book Co., 1976.

Wolfe, Tom. *The Right Stuff.* New York: Farrar, Straus, and Giroux, 1979.

Wouk, Herman. *The Caine Mutiny, a novel of World War II.* Garden City: Doubleday, 1951.

Wouk Herman. *War and Remembrance.* Boston: Little, Brown, 1978.

Wouk, Herman. *Winds of War: a Novel.* Boston: Little, Brown, 1971.

Zumwalt, Elmo R. *On Watch: a Memoir.* New York: Quadrangle/New York Times Book Co., 1976.

Intermediate

Barron, John. *The KGB Today: the Hidden Hand.* New York: Reader's Digest Press, 1983.

Benedict, Ruth. *Chrysanthemum and the Sword: Patterns of Japanese Culture.* Boston: Houghton Mifflin, 1989.

Blair, Clay. *Silent Victory: the U.S. Submarine War Against Japan.* Annapolis: Naval Institute Press, 2001.

Buell, Thomas B. *Master of Sea Power: a Biography of Fleet Admiral Ernest J. King.* New York: Viking, 1987.

Buell, Thomas B. *The Quiet Warrior: A Biography of Admiral Raymond A. Spruance.* Annapolis: Naval Institute Press, 1987.

Deming, William Edwards. *Out of the Crisis.* Cambridge: Massachusetts Institute of Technology, Center for Advanced Engineering Study, 1986.

Ebenstein, William. *Today's Isms: Communism,* *Fascism, Capitalism, Socialism.* Englewood Cliffs: Prentice-Hall, 1970.

Eisenhower, David. *Eisenhower at War, 1943–1945.* New York: Outlet Book Co., 1991.

Gaddis, John Lewis. *The United States and the Origins of the Cold War, 1941-1947.* New York: Columbia University Press, 2000.

Gann, Ernest Kellogg. *Fate is the Hunter.* New York: Simon and Schuster, 1986.

Gray, Colin S. *The Maritime Strategy, Geopolitics, and the Defense of the West.* New York: National Strategy Information Center, 1986.

Grove, Eric. *The Future of Sea Power.* Annapolis: Naval Institute Press, 1990.

Imai, Masaaki. *Kaizen: the Key to Japan's Competitive Success.* New York: McGraw-Hill, 1986.

Johnson, Paul. *Modern Times: the World From the Twenties to the Eighties.* New York: Harper & Row, 1983.

Karnow, Stanley. *Vietnam: A History.* New York: Penguin Books, 1997.

Keegan, John. *The Face of Battle.* Harmondsworth: Penguin, 1978.

Keegan, John. *The Mask of Command.* New York: Viking, 1987.

Keegan, John. *The Price of Admiralty: the Evolution of Naval Warfare.* New York: Viking, 1989.

Keegan, John. *The Second World War.* New York: Viking, 1990.

Krulak, Victor H.. *First to Fight: an Inside View of the U.S. Marine Corps.* Annapolis: Naval Institute Press, 1999.

Larrabee, Eric. *Commander in Chief: Franklin Delano Roosevelt, his lieutenants and their war.* 1987. Annapolis: Naval Institute Press, 2004.

Littwak, Edward. *The Pentagon and the Art of War: the Question of Military Reform.* New York: Simon and Schuster, 1985.

Lord, Carnes. *Presidency and the Management of National Security.* London: Collier Macmillan, 1988.

Manchester, William. *The Last Lion, Winston Spencer Churchill.* New York: Dell Pub., 1984.

Nitze, Paul. *From Hiroshima to Glastnost: at the*

Center of Decision, a Memoir. New York: Grove Weidenfeld, 1989.

Paret, Peter. *Makers of Modern Strategy: From Machiavelli to the Nuclear Age.* Princeton: Princeton University Press, 1986.

Potter, Elmer Belmont. *Admiral Arleigh Burke.* Annapolis: Naval Institute Press, 2004.

Potter, Elmer Belmont. *Bull Halsey.* Annapolis: Naval Institute Press, 2003.

Potter, Elmer Belmont. *Sea Power: A Naval History.* Annapolis: Naval Institute Press, 1981.

Prange, Gordon William. *At Dawn We Slept: the Untold Story of Pearl Harbor.* New York: Penguin Books, 1982.

Prange, Gordon William. *Miracle at Midway.* New York: Penguin Books, 1983.

Sheehan, Neil. *A Bright Shining Lie: John Paul Vann and America in Vietnam.* New York: Random House, 1988.

Smith, Perry McCoy. *Assignment Pentagon: the insider's guide to the Potomac puzzle palace.* Washington: Brassey's, 1993.

Spector, Ronald H.. *Eagle Against the Sun: the American War with Japan.* New York: Vintage Books, 1985.

Sprout, Harold Hance. *The Rise of American Naval Power, 1776-1918.* Annapolis: Naval Institute Press, 1990.

Tuchman, Barbara Wertheim. *The Guns of August.* New York, Macmillan, 1962.

Ulam, Adam Bruno. *The Rivals: America and Russia Since WWII.* New York: Penguin Books, 1976.

Van der Vat, Dan. *The Atlantic Campaign: World War II's Great Struggle at Sea.* New York: Harper & Row, 1988.

Walder, David. *Nelson: A Biography.* New York: Dial Press/J. Wade, 1978.

Walton, Mary. *The Deming Management Method.* New York: Putnam, 1988.

Weigley, Russell Frank. *The American Way of War: a History of United States Military Strategy and Policy.* New York: Macmillan 1973.

Ziegler, Philip. *Mountbatten.* New York: Knopf, 1985.

Advanced

Barnett, Roger W. and Colin S. Gray. *Seapower and Strategy.* Annapolis: Naval Institute Press, 1989.

Brodie, Bernard. *War and Politics.* New York: Macmillan, 1973.

Clausewitz, Carl von. *On War.* New York: Knopf, 1993.

Corbett, Sir Julian Stafford. *Some Principles of Maritime Strategy.* Annapolis: Naval Institute Press, 1988.

Friedman, Thomas L. *From Beirut to Jerusalem.* New York: Anchor Books, 1990.

George, Alexander L. *Deterrence in American Foreign Policy: Theory and Practice.* New York: Columbia University Press, 1974.

Gray, Colin S. *The Geopolitics of Super Power.* Lexington: University Press of Kentucky, 1988.

George, James L. *The U.S. Navy: the View From the Mid-1980s.* Boulder: Westview Press, 1985.

George, James L. *The U.S. Navy in the 1990s: Alternatives for Action.* Annapolis: Naval Institute Press, 1992.

Hone, Thomas C. *Power and Change: the Administrative History of the Office of the Chief of Naval Operations, 1946–1986.* Washington, D.C.: Naval Historical Center, 1989.

Hughes, Wayne P. *Fleet Tactics: Theory and Practice.* Annapolis: Naval Institute Press, 1986.

Huntington, Samuel P. *The Soldier and the State: the Theory and Politics of Civil-Military Relations.* Cambridge: Belknap Press of Harvard University Press, 1957.

Kissinger, Henry. *The White House Years.* Boston: Little, Brown, 1979.

Luttwak, Edward. *Strategy: the Logic of War and Peace.* Cambridge: Belknap Press of Harvard University Press, 2001.

Mahan, Alfred Thayer. *The Influence of Sea Power upon History, 1660–1783.* Newport, R.I.: Naval War College Press, 1991.

Newhouse, John. *Cold Dawn: the Story of SALT.* Washington: Pergamon-Brassey's, 1989.

Palmer, Michael A. *Origins of Maritime Strategy: American Naval Strategy in the First Postwar Decade.* Washington, D.C.: U.S. G.P.O., 1988.

Pfaltzgraff, Jr., Robert L. and Richard H. Shultz, Jr. *U.S. Defense Policy in an Era of Constrained Resources.* Lexington: Lexington Books, 1990.

Revel, Jean Francois. *How Democracies Perish.* Garden City: Doubleday, 1984.

Schlesinger, James. *America at Century's End.* New York: Columbia University Press, 1989.

Sharp, Ulysses S. Grant. *Strategy for Defeat: Vietnam in Retrospect.* San Rafael: Presidio Press, 1978.

Tzu, Sun. *The Art of War.* Boston: Shambhala, 1988.

Tocqueville, Alexis de. *Democracy in America.* New York: Perennial Classics, 2000.

Waltz, Kenneth Neal. *Man, the State, and War: a Theoretical Analysis.* New York: Columbia University Press, 1959.

Winterbotham, Frederick William. *The Ultra Secret.* New York: Harper & Row, 1974.

Wylie, Joseph Caldwell. *Military Strategy: A General Theory of Power Control.* Annapolis: Naval Institute Press, 1989.

Suggested Books on Leadership and Management

Bossidy, Larry et al. *Execution.* London: Random House Business, 2002.

Bradley, James. Flags of Our Fathers: Heroes of Iwo Jima. New York: Bantam Books, 2000.

Buford, Bob. Halftime. Grand Rapids: Zondervan, 1997.

Depree, Max. Leadership is An Art. New York: Doubleday, 1989.

Collins, Jim. Good to Great. New York: Harper Business, 2001.

Covey, Stephen R. The 7 Habits of Highly Effective People. New York: Simon & Schuster, 1989.

Fass, John Morton. Mustin: A Naval Family of the Twentieth Century. Annapolis: Naval Institute Press, 2003.

Goleman, Daniel. Primal Leadership. Boston: Harvard Business School Press, 2002.

Hammond, Sue Annis. The Thin Book of Appreciative Inquiry. Plano: Thin Book Publishing Co., 1998.

Harkins, Phil. Powerful Conversations. New York: McGraw-Hill, 1999.

Kotter, John P. Leading Change. Boston: Harvard Business School Press, 1996.

Krulak, Victor H. First To Fight: An Inside View of the U. S. Marine Corps. Annapolis: Naval Institute Press, 1984.

Kotter, John P. What Leaders Really Do. Boston: Harvard Business School Press, 1999.

Labovitz, George and Victor Rosansky. The Power of Alignment. New York: Wiley, 1997.

Maxwell, John C. The 21 Indispensable Qualities of a Leader. Nashville: T. Nelson, 1999.

McCain, John. Faith Of My Fathers. New York: Random House, 1999.

Monsarrat, Nicholas. The Cruel Sea. New York: A.A. Knopf, 1951.

Nalbatian, Haig et al. Play To Your Strengths. New York: McGraw-Hill, 2004.

Scales, Robert H. and Williamson Murray. The Iraq War. Cambridge: Belknap Press of Harvard University Press, 2003.

Scales, Robert H. Yellow Smoke. Lanham: Rowman & Littlefield Publishers, 2003.

Waitley, Denis. The Psychology of Winning. New York: Simon and Schuster, 1995.

Watkins, Michael. The First 90 Days: Critical Success Strategies for New Leaders at All Levels. Boston: Harvard Business School Press, 2003.

Why Read Great Books?

I would like to share with you a letter that I recently received and my answer to it:

Dear Dr. Adler, Why should we read great books that deal with the problems and concerns of bygone eras? Our social and political problems are so urgent that they demand practically all the time and energy we can devote to serious contemporary reading. Is there any value, besides mere historical interest, in reading books written in the simple obsolete cultures of former times?

People who question or even scorn the study of the past and its works usually assume that the past is entirely different from the present, and that hence we can learn nothing worthwhile from the past. But it is not true that the past is entirely different from the present. We can learn much of value from its similarity and its difference.

A tremendous change in the conditions of human life and in our knowledge and control of the natural world has taken place since ancient times. The ancients had no prevision of our present-day technical and social environment, and hence have no counsel to offer us about the particular problems we confront. But, although social and economic arrangements vary with time and place, man remains man. We and the ancients share a common human nature and hence certain common human experiences and problems.

The poets bear witness that ancient man, too, saw the sun rise and set, felt the wind on his cheek, was possessed by love and desire, experienced ecstasy and elation as well as frustration and disillusion, and knew good and evil. The ancient poets speak across the centuries to us, sometimes more directly and vividly than our contemporary writers. And the ancient prophets and philosophers, in dealing with the basic problems of men living together in society, still have some thing to say to us.

I have elsewhere pointed out that the ancients did not face our problem of providing fulfillment for a large group of elderly citizens. But the passages from Sophocles and Aristophanes show that the ancients, too, were aware of the woes and disabilities of old age. Also, the ancient view that elderly persons have highly developed capacities for practical judgment and philosophical meditation indicate possibilities that might not occur to us if we just looked at the present-day picture.

No former age has faced the possibility that life on earth might be totally exterminated through atomic warfare. But past ages, too, knew war and the extermination and enslavement of whole peoples. Thinkers of the past meditated on the problems of war and peace and make suggestions that are worth listening to. Cicero and Locke show that the human way to settle disputes is by discussion and law, while Dante and Kant propose world government as the way to world peace.

Former ages did not experience particular forms of dictatorship that we have known in this century. But they had firsthand experience of absolute tyranny and the suppression of political liberty. Aristotle's treatise on politics includes a penetrating and systematic analysis of dictatorships, as well as a recommendation of measures to be taken to avoid the extremes of tyranny and anarchy.

We also learn from the past by considering the respects in which it differs from the present. We can discover where we are today and what we have become by knowing what the people of the past did and thought. And part of the past—our personal past and that of the race—always lives in us.

Exclusive preference for either the past or the present is a foolish and wasteful form of snobbishness and provinciality. We must seek what is most worthy in the works of both the past and the present. When we do that, we find that ancient poets, prophets, and philosophers are as much our contemporaries in the world of the mind as the most discerning of present-day writers. In fact, many of the ancient writings speak more directly to our experience and condition than the latest best sellers.

About the Editor

LtCol Joseph J. Thomas, USMC (Ret.) currently serves as The Class of 1971 Distinguished Military Professor of Leadership within the James B. Stockdale Center for Ethical Leadership at the US Naval Academy. Some of his past assignments include 1st and 2nd Marine Aircraft Wings, 26 Marine Expeditionary Unit (Special Operations Capable), Marine Aviation Weapons and Tactics Squadron One, Marine Corps Training and Education Command, Marine Officer Instructor at the University of Notre Dame, and Battalion Officer at the US Naval Academy. He is a past recipient of the General Merritt Edson Leadership Award, The Marine Corps Association's Research and Writing Award, and the Col Donald G. Cook Distinguished Graduate Award from Command and Control Systems School. His last edited work, *Leadership Embodied*, has been purchased by the Naval Academy Foundation for the midshipmen of the US Naval Academy. LtCol Thomas holds a bachelor's degree from Muhlenberg College, is a graduate of Marine Corps Command and Staff College, and holds masters degrees from Syracuse University and the US Army War College. He also holds a Ph.D. from George Mason University. LtCol Thomas and his wife Jackie have three sons Joseph, Jr., Andrew, and Robert.